Introduction to International Economics

Second Edition

Henk Jager
and
Catrinus Jepma

First edition published 1996 by Longman Group Ltd.
This edition published 2011 by
PALGRAVE MACMILLAN

Palgrave Macmillan in the UK is an imprint of Macmillan Publishers Limited, registered in England, company number 785998, of Houndmills, Basingstoke, Hampshire RG21 6XS.

Palgrave Macmillan in the US is a division of St Martin's Press LLC, 175 Fifth Avenue, New York, NY 10010.

Palgrave Macmillan is the global academic imprint of the above companies and has companies and representatives throughout the world.

Palgrave® and Macmillan® are registered trademarks in the United States, the United Kingdom, Europe and other countries.

ISBN 978–0–230–20241–2

This book is printed on paper suitable for recycling and made from fully managed and sustained forest sources. Logging, pulping and manufacturing processes are expected to conform to the environmental regulations of the country of origin.

A catalogue record for this book is available from the British Library.

A catalog record for this book is available from the Library of Congress.

10 9 8 7 6 5 4 3 2 1
20 19 18 17 16 15 14 13 12 11

Printed and bound in China

Contents

List of Tables — vii
List of Figures — ix
Preface — xi
Acknowledgements — xiii

1 Aspects of International Economics — **1**
1.1 Introduction — 1
1.2 The company and its international environment — 2
1.3 Questions raised by the case study — 6

2 Internationalization and the World Economy — **8**
2.1 Introduction — 8
2.2 International trade flows — 9
2.3 The national significance of international trade — 14
2.4 International capital flows — 18
2.5 Summary — 22

3 International Trade Theory — **23**
3.1 Introduction — 23
3.2 Emerging industrial countries: a case study — 24
3.3 Traditional trade theories — 30
3.4 New trade theories — 39
3.5 Summary — 50

4 International Production Factors, Foreign Direct Investment and the Multinational Enterprise — **52**
4.1 Introduction — 52
4.2 The motor vehicle sector: a case study — 53
4.3 Similarities in international trade and international factor mobility — 55
4.4 International factor mobility and the question of distribution — 58
4.5 Inter-temporal trade — 61
4.6 Foreign direct investment — 64
4.7 The multinational enterprise (MNE) — 68
4.8 The MNE and the international relocation of production activities: some theories — 74
4.9 Summary — 83

5 Trade Policy: A Welfare Theory Analysis — 85
5.1   Introduction — 85
5.2   Protectionism — 86
5.3   The optimum tariff theory and other trade measures — 91
5.4   Export policy — 97
5.5   Volume restrictions on trade — 104
5.6   Trade policy and market failures — 107
5.7   Summary — 109

6 Modern Arguments Relating to Protection — 110
6.1   Introduction — 110
6.2   External economies of scale and the competitive position — 110
6.3   Strategic trade policy — 112
6.4   Summary — 116

7 Trade Policy and Market Forms: A Microeconomic Analysis — 118
7.1   Introduction — 118
7.2   The video recorder market: a case study — 119
7.3   Market forms — 121
7.4   Taking advantage of different national sub-markets — 123
7.5   Behaviour on entering international markets under monopolistic competition — 128
7.6   Oligopoly: analysis based on reaction curves — 130
7.7   Duopoly: competitive behaviour in the international market — 131
7.8   Trade policy and international duopoly — 134
7.9   Escalating protection and transfer mechanisms — 137
7.10 International cartels — 139
7.11 Summary — 142

8 The Practice of Protection — 145
8.1   Introduction — 145
8.2   The effectiveness of protection — 148
8.3   The GATT/WTO — 150
8.4   Non-tariff barriers — 159
8.5   Summary — 166

9 Business, Government and Lobbying — 167
9.1   Introduction — 167
9.2   The practice of lobbying: a case study — 167
9.3   Political economy: demand for and supply of protection — 170
9.4   Competition between lobby groups — 175
9.5   Summary — 176
9.6   Appendix: Competition between lobby groups — 177

10 Economic Integration — 180
10.1 Introduction — 180
10.2 Globalization — 180

10.3 Regional economic integration   185
10.4 European economic integration   187
10.5 Summary   192

11 The Balance of Payments and the Foreign-Exchange Market   193
11.1 Introduction   193
11.2 Balance of payments: the classification system   196
11.3 Balance of payments: the accounting practice   199
11.4 Balance-of-payments analysis   205
11.5 The functioning of foreign-exchange markets   207
11.6 The exchange rate: concepts and presentation   209
11.7 Summary   211

12 International Capital Flows   213
12.1 Introduction   213
12.2 Trade credit   216
12.3 Arbitrage and the forward exchange rate   217
12.4 Speculation   221
12.5 Portfolio diversification   222
12.6 Motives for exchange controls   226
12.7 International capital markets and financial centres   228
12.8 Summary   233

13 Exchange-Rate Explanation and Prediction   236
13.1 Introduction   236
13.2 Exchange-rate theory: the long term   237
13.3 Exchange-rate theory: additional short-term explanation   245
13.4 Exchange-rate predictions   251
13.5 Summary   252

14 Exchange-Rate Systems and Effects   254
14.1 Introduction   254
14.2 Exchange-rate systems and policy   254
14.3 The current account and international trade   261
14.4 Inflation   267
14.5 Growth and unemployment   270
14.6 Monetary policy   270
14.7 Fiscal policy   272
14.8 Summary   273

15 International Risk: Types and Hedges   276
15.1 Introduction   276
15.2 Types of international risk   277
15.3 Hedging country risk   284

15.4 Reducing exchange-rate risk   291
15.5 Summary   297

16 International Monetary Cooperation   299
16.1 Introduction   299
16.2 Types of international economic cooperation   300
16.3 International monetary cooperation prior to 1945   305
16.4 International monetary cooperation between 1945 and 1973   308
16.5 International monetary cooperation after 1973   314
16.6 Summary   321

17 A Financial Obstacle to Economic Development: The World Debt Crisis   323
17.1 Introduction   323
17.2 The causes of the world debt crisis of the 1980s   324
17.3 The IMF and the debt problem   332
17.4 The debt crisis   337
17.5 Summary   340

18 A Financial Obstacle to Economic Development: Currency Crises   342
18.1 Introduction   342
18.2 Currency crises: three generations of theories   343
18.3 The Mexican currency crisis, 1994–95   348
18.4 The Asian crisis   351
18.5 Lessons from the crisis   357
18.6 Summary   362

19 Irrevocably Fixed Exchange Rates: Recent Experiences   364
19.1 Introduction   364
19.2 The theory of optimum currency areas   365
19.3 The Franc Zone   368
19.4 The Argentine currency board   371
19.5 The process of European monetary integration   376
19.6 Summary   386

Bibliography   390
Index   398

List of Tables

2.1a Merchandise trade: intra-regional and inter-regional, 2009 ($ billion)   11
2.1b Merchandise trade: shares of values of intra-regional and inter-regional
       trade flows, 2009 (%)   12
2.2 Share of world exports of industrial products, selected countries and years   15
2.3 International trade in goods and services: key data (2009)   16
2.4 World exports of merchandise and commercial services by product
       category, 2009 ($ billion)   17
2.5 Gross flows of capital (per capita, US$)   19
2.6 Emerging market economies: net capital inflows, 1999–2008 ($ billion)   20

3.1 Annual average growth rates of real gross domestic product, 1980–2009   25
3.2 Leading exporters in world merchandise trade, 2009 ($ million)   27
3.3 Number of hours of labour needed to produce one unit of a product   33
3.4 Number of hours of labour needed to produce one litre of wine   42
3.5 Economies of scale in Japan and Thailand – an example   44

4.1 Per capita income in source relative to host countries (current PPP$, 2008)   57
4.2 Current account balances in major economic blocs, 2000–15 ($ billion)   63
4.3 Net FDI and portfolio flows in the three major economic areas, 2005–9
       ($ billion)   64
4.4 Selected indicators of FDI and international production, 1982–2009
       ($ billion, %)   66
4.5 Cross-border mergers and acquisitions, by region/economy of seller and
       purchaser, 1987–2010   69
4.6 The world's top 25 non-financial transnational corporations, 2006   75
4.7 The product life cycle   79

5.1 Annual domestic costs as a result of government intervention in
       agriculture ($ billion)   102
5.2 Welfare impacts from the elimination of global agricultural tariffs and
       subsidies   103

6.1 Calculators: supply, costs and demand   112
6.2 Profit in the case of competition   114
6.3 Profit in the case of a subsidy to Airbus   114

6.4   Profit in the actual situation   115
6.5   Profit given inaccurate information in the case of a subsidy to Airbus   116

7.1   Effects of trade instruments in a duopoly   138

8.1   GATT trade rounds   154
8.2   Percentages of tariffs bound before and after the Uruguay Round
        (percentages are not weighted according to trade volume or value)   158
8.3   Frequency of core non-tariff barriers for selected countries (as % of tariff
        lines affected)   159
8.4   The number of anti-dumping investigations for the most targeted
        countries, 1995–2009   162

11.1 The balance of payments of the G3, 2005 ($ billion)   202

12.1 Shares of the global forex market (countries with shares over 1% in
        April 2010)   232
12.2 Country distribution of international bank liabilities and international
        bonds and notes (amounts outstanding December 2008; in $ billion)   233

13.1 The hamburger standard   241

15.1 A country risk assessment form   287
15.2 Country-risk rating, March 2011   290

16.1 The composition of the world's international monetary reserves (end of
        year, %)   319
16.2 The composition of foreign currency reserves (end of year, %)   320

17.1 Current account balances, 1973–88 ($ billion)   325
17.2 Debt service ratio of developing countries, 1973–86 (%)   326
17.3 Inflation, 1963–88 (%)   329

18.1 Exchange rates against the US dollar (end of year)   352
18.2 Change in the stock market index (in domestic currency, %, in 1997)   352
18.3 Growth, inflation, and current account deficits (%)   353
18.4 Change in real exchange rates against the USA, 1992–96 (period total, %)   353
18.5 Capital flows and reserves in Asia (in billion $; annual amounts)   354

19.1 Convergence criteria: contents, critical values and fulfilments   384

List of Figures

2.1   World merchandise trade and world output in real terms: annual average growth rates for various sub-periods, 1913–2009 (%)   9

2.2   World trade in principal types of goods: average annual growth from 1950 to 2009 (%)   10

2.3   World output of principal types of goods: average annual growth from 1950 to 2009 (%)   10

2.4a World intra-industry trade, 1962, 1975, 1990 and 2006 (% of total trade value)   12

2.4b Export flows within regional blocs: proportion of total export flows of countries, 1990, 1999 and 2009   13

2.5   World merchandise exports by major product group, 2000, 2005 and 2009 (share based on value)   18

2.6   Global capital flows: sources and destination, 2009   21

3.1   China's merchandise exports, 1980–2009   26
3.2   The makeup of Chinese manufacturing exports, 1992–2005   28
3.3   Illustration of differences in comparative costs   33
3.4   Production, consumption and trade with internal economies of scale   41
3.5   National European Competitiveness Index, 2006–7   46

4.1   Top remittance-receiving and remittance-sending countries, 2009   59
4.2   Possible process of development into a multinational enterprise   71
4.3   Trade patterns over life cycle for product introduced in the USA   80

5.1   The optimum tariff   96
5.2   The optimum export levy   98
5.3   Effects of an export tax on the other country   99
5.4   The welfare effect of an export subsidy   100

7.1   Rent snatching by the government   122
7.2   Price differentiation in the European car market   124
7.3   Price discrimination   125
7.4   Reaction curve for a domestic entrepreneur   130
7.5   Reaction curves in a duopoly   132

7.6   Effect on marginal costs of an export subsidy and a tariff   135
7.7   A duopoly in the case of an import tariff on goods supplied to the
       domestic market by a foreign supplier   136
7.8   A duopoly in the case of an export subsidy by the national government
       (situation on the foreign market)   136
7.9   An international duopoly: equilibrium situations under various forms of
       national government trade policy   138
7.10 An international duopoly: a subsidy or tariff war between two countries   139
7.11 Excess profit for a cartel compared with perfect competition   140
7.12 The OPEC cartel oil revenues ($ billion)   142

8.1   Average tariff reductions through GATT rounds   155
8.2   Initiations of anti-dumping and countervailing investigations, 1995–2009   160
8.3   Initiation of anti-dumping investigations, 1995–2008   161

9.1   Costs and gains of lobbying   172
9.2   Lobbying reaction curves   178

11.1 Japan's basic balance ($ billion)   194
11.2 The relationship between the balance of payments and the
       foreign-exchange market   201

12.1 Correlation coefficient and portfolio opportunities: an example   224

13.1 Exchange-rate overshooting   246

14.1 Supply and demand on the foreign-exchange market   256
14.2 The adjustable peg system over time   257
14.3 The J-curve   265

15.1 High-yen efficiency   282
15.2 Structure of a parallel loan   293

16.1 Major nominal exchange rates (1973–2007)   317
16.2 Major real effective exchange rates (1973–2007)   317

17.1 Annual growth of gross national/domestic product, 1973–88 (%)   325

Preface

The idea of producing a new introductory course on International Economics emerged from an initiative taken at the Open University of the Netherlands in the early 1990s to develop a one-year distance teaching programme in the field of International Business. As one of the introductory elements of the programme, a 100-hour course on International Economics was needed. Such a book, covering the whole area of International Economics, was difficult to find: relevant textbooks were either too long or written from the perspective of Economics rather than Business students. This prompted us to write such a book.

So the book was developed for use by students who are interested in International Economic Relations primarily from a practical, business-oriented point of view. Bearing this target group in mind, the use of mathematics was kept to a minimum, with some equations, but no mathematical derivations. Instead, a wealth of supporting figures was used to clarify the text, particularly in the section on international trade. The subject matter was often cross-disciplinary, exploring the adjacent areas of Industrial Organization and International Finance.

The book was published in 1996, both in Dutch and English. The Dutch edition, *Wereldeconomie in beeld – Inzichten in de internationale economie*, was published by Academic Service and the English edition, *Introduction to International Economics*, was published by Pearson Education. Both books were published in cooperation with the Open University of the Netherlands, in Heerlen. Over the course of the next ten years over 10,000 copies of the two books were sold.

This second edition, published by Palgrave Macmillan, has maintained all the features of the first, but tables, figures and indeed the entire text have been substantially updated and new topics added, such as currency crises, and the introduction of the euro and Euro area in 1999 and their subsequent development. Moreover, we have accepted the preferences of many readers of the previous edition to discuss the balance of payments not before but after the treatment of international trade. Compared with the first edition, the size of the book has somewhat increased, and so, while most of the chapters can be read independently of each other, this edition can be used for 100–150 hour courses.

We gratefully acknowledge the support of several people. While writing the first edition we received valuable suggestions, comments and even preliminary texts from Walter Vanthielen, Wytze van der Gaast, Alexander Mollerus and, above all, Elise Kamphuis, our co-author of that edition. Their input has also contributed to the present, second edition. The current edition has also benefitted from the indispensable work of Marius Popescu, especially in relation to the section on trade.

Finally, we would like to thank the staff of Palgrave Macmillan for their constructive support, in particular the book's editors, Jaime Marshall and Aléta Bezuidenhout, for their effective guidance and patience with us as well as their prolonged trust in this project; and Nick Brock and Elizabeth Stone for all their useful suggestions to improve the language and clarity of the text.

Amsterdam/Groningen
18 July 2011

Henk Jager and Catrinus J. Jepma

Acknowledgements

The authors and publisher wish to thank the following for permission to reproduce their material:

Bank for International Settlements for Table 12.2: Shares of the global forex market, *BIS Quarterly Review*, March 2009; and Table 12.1: Country distribution of international bank liabilities and international bond and notes, Triennial Central Bank Survey of Foreign Exchange and Derivatives Market Activity in April 2010: September 2010.

Centre for International Competitiveness for Figure 3.5: National European Competitiveness Index, 2006–07, *European Competitiveness Index 2006–07*.

De Nederlandsche Bank for Table 19.1: Convergence criteria: contents, critical values, and fulfilments, from *Annual Reports* 1995, p. 105 and 1998, p. 68.

Euromoney Institutional Investor PLC for Table 15.2: Country-risk rating, March 2011, *Euromoney*, http://www.euromoney.com/Article/2773235/Country-risk-March-2011.

Financial Times Limited for Table 15.1: A country risk assessment form, *The Banker*, January 1981, p. 74.

International Monetary Fund for Figure 3.2: The makeup of Chinese manufacturing exports, 1992–2005, from 'China's Export Boom' by Amity, M. and Freund, C., 2007, *IMF Finance and Development* 44(3); Table 4.2: Current account balances in major economic blocs, 2000–15, from *World Economic Outlook 2010*, p. 172; Figure 11.1: Trends in Japan's balance of payments, *International Financial Statistics*; Table 11.1: The balance of payments of the G3, 2005, *Balance of Payment Statistics Yearbook, 2006*; Figure 16.1: Major nominal exchange rates (1973–2007), *International Financial Statistics*, various years; Figure 16.2: Major real effective exchange rates (1973–2007), *International Financial Statistics*, various years; Table 16.1: The composition of the world's international monetary reserves and Table 16.2: The composition of foreign currency reserves, *Annual Report*, various years; and Figure 17.1: Growth of gross national/domestic product, 1973–88, Table 17.1: Current account balances, 1973–88, Table 17.2: Debt service ratio, 1973–86 and Table 17.3: Inflation, 1963–88, from *World Economic Outlook*, various years.

NRC Media for Case study 12.1: Bond market reopened to foreigners, from *NRC Handelsblad*, 31 January 1974.

Pearson Education Inc. for Figure 4.2: Possible process of development into a multinational enterprise, Dicken, P., 1986, *Global Shift, Industrial Change in a Turbulent World*, p. 129.

President and Fellows of Harvard College and the Massachusetts Institute of Technology for Table 2.5: Gross flows of capital, in *The Review of Economics and Statistics* 90(2), May 2008.

The Economist Newspaper Ltd for Table 13.1: The hamburger standard, *The Economist,* 16 July 2009 and Figure 15.1: High-yen efficiency, *The Economist*, 8 April 1995.

United Nations for Table 4.4: Selected indicators of FDI and international production, 1982–2009, *World Investment Report 2010,* United Nations Conference on Trade and Development; and Table 4.6: The world's top 25 non-financial transnational corporations, 2006, *World Investment Report 2008,* United Nations Conference on Trade and Development.

The World Bank for Figure 2.4a: World intra-industry trade, 1962, 1975, 1990 and 2006, *World Development Report* 2009.

World Trade Organization (www.wto.org) for Table 2.1a: Merchandise trade: intra-regional and inter-regional, 2009, and Table 2.4: World export of merchandise and commercial services by product category, 2009, *International Trade Statistics 2010*, World Trade Developments in 2007; Table 8.1: GATT trade rounds, 2011; and Table 8.4: The number of anti-dumping investigations of the most targeted countries, 1995–2009, from the Rules Division Anti-dumping Measures Database, March 2010.

Every effort has been made to trace copyright holders, but if any have been inadvertently overlooked we will be pleased to make the necessary arrangements at the first opportunity.

CHAPTER 1

Aspects of International Economics

Introduction

Almost everyone involved in business needs to study international economics and to be aware of developments in international economic relations. Managers need to appreciate how the internationalization of economic activities can affect their companies, leading to success or failure, and students need to learn how developments on foreign markets, through processes of internationalization, can have a substantial influence on domestic markets.

Despite the impact of internationalization, domestic and international market conditions remain separate. One powerful factor is national economic identity: national governments still have a certain amount of sovereignty to carry out their own economic policies. International economics is thus a battlefield in which the forces of internationalized markets compete with national policies and/or the practice of individual businesses. On the one hand, the increasing integration of world markets tends to make national borders less significant, and this process is strengthened by international policy coordination initiatives that tend to reduce national autonomy, such as the European Union, the General Agreement on Trade in Services (GATS), the Agreement on Trade Related Aspects of Intellectual Property Rights (TRIPS), the Kyoto Protocol, the Association of Southeast Asian Nations (ASEAN), the North American Free Trade Agreement (NAFTA) and the General Agreement on Tariffs and Trade (GATT)/World Trade Organization (WTO). On the other hand, many national governments are still motivated to retain as much control as possible, preferring to direct the economy using the instruments available to them, such as national policy action and the regulation of a national currency. This desire to preserve at least some national autonomy inhibits the development of a truly and completely integrated global economy.

Since the Second World War, economic relationships between regions, countries and companies have grown much closer. Internationalization has occurred in the physical world, for example in international commodity markets, in the international transfer of technology, and via the international mobility of factors of production. It has also occurred in the financial world, on the international money and capital markets. Internationalization is being supported by the progressive elimination of many kinds of barriers to trade between countries: in goods, in services and, most recently, in the international mobility of capital.

One direct result of internationalization is that entrepreneurs are increasingly aware of the opportunities of international trade and are expanding their operations outside their national borders, supported by improving transport links and communication networks. As companies establish foreign subsidiaries, form joint ventures and enter other forms of international cooperation, the level of internationalization continues growing even more.

This introductory chapter presents a detailed case study (Section 1.2) of one company, demonstrating how liberalization and deregulation increase the company's competition in its home market and examining how this company responds to these developments. In the following discussion (Section 1.3), we consider various questions of international economics that arise from the case study and illustrate the issues that are central to this book. Later chapters consider these questions in greater depth.

1.2   The company and its international environment

Globalization affects everyone, not only entrepreneurs involved in international trade who face international competition, whether directly or indirectly. Entrepreneurs who trade only in their domestic markets are undoubtedly also influenced by globalization's competitive consequences. For example, a businessman whose purchases and sales are exclusively concentrated in the home market has to take account of potential foreign competition or domestic competitors in their efforts to try to strengthen their market position by internationalization.

The following real-life case study illustrates how consumers can benefit from the processes of internationalization, while also demonstrating that internationalization and, of course, globalization, poses both threats and opportunities to the enterprise. The case study describes a business that had enjoyed a monopoly position in its home market and had been protected by government regulations, but then it lost its non-competitive position when a new government regime that favoured liberalization and internationalization came to power. Subsequently, the company faced increasing competition from foreign-owned companies. The case discusses some of the aspects of internationalization that a company is likely to encounter, and serves as a practical tool to explain the theory. The discussion here is intended as an outline only: later chapters will tackle the same questions in greater depth. After studying all the material in this book, we advise that you re-read the case study to see how your knowledge and understanding have developed.

This case study looks at the Dutch telecoms company KPN, based in The Hague. In 1995, most western telecommunication companies were still (state-owned) monopolies in their home markets. In several countries, however, governments started to challenge these telecom monopolies. Two distinct approaches were adopted: the creation of a rival to the existing company, or the fostering of competition between several companies. By 1998, very few telecom monopolies still remained in Organisation for Economic Co-operation and Development (OECD) countries, and in most countries telecom companies were facing serious competition from foreign competitors.

The case study shows how KPN, through a subsidiary called KPN Mobile, reacted to these changes, first by reorganizing itself to face increased international competition, and then taking even more aggressive strategic steps to establish itself as a major European player in the market for mobile telecoms.

Case study 1.1   Internationalization of the mobile telephone market

KPN Mobile, a division of KPN, was the traditional national telecoms company in the Netherlands. In March 1999, Peter Leblanc and his project team discussed the pros and cons of introducing short message services (SMS) for the users of pre-pay mobile phones. This service already existed for customers with a mobile phone subscription. Were they ready to be the first company in the Netherlands to make this service available to pre-pay users?

The team felt that vigorously increasing international competition in the mobile telephone market was forcing them to act quickly, and so October 1999 was chosen as the deadline to introduce the SMS service for pre-pay users. The first and most important strategic decision the project team had to take was whether or not to offer the services to pre-pay users at all.

Background

Originally, KPN was a government-controlled monopoly in the Dutch (mobile) telephone market. However, in an effort to increase competition, in 1995 the Dutch government decided to award a licence to a second mobile telephone company. This company, Libertel, was the result of a cooperative venture between the Dutch ING bank (which had a 30 per cent share) and the British telephone operator, Vodafone (which held a 70 per cent share).

This development coincided with a rapid growth in the market for mobile phones. In its first year of operation, the number of Libertel subscribers increased to 212,000; over the same period the number of KPN subscribers doubled. The success of Libertel can be attributed to its strategic policy of offering its clients all kinds of new services, such as pre-paid, voice-guided dialling and a new payment system that charged calls by the second.

KPN's policy was essentially to follow Libertel's innovations. At the end of 1998 some 2.8 million Dutch people owned mobile phones, 1.8 million with KPN and 1 million with Libertel. The introduction of one (mainly British) competitor to the Dutch mobile market coincided with enormous growth in this market, and this in turn spurred innovations that created new options for mobile phone users. Other companies were also keen to enter this promising market.

On 12 February 1998, the Dutch Ministry of Transport, Public Works and Management awarded telecom licences to three further competitors, Telfort, Dutchtone and Ben. These 'new' entrants were in fact subsidiaries of the largest foreign telecommunications companies: Telfort was a joint initiative between British Telecom and the Dutch Railway Company (NS); Dutchtone (currently Orange) was a mobile telecoms company in which France Télécom (owning 80 per cent) cooperated with some Dutch banks; and the third competitor, Ben (100 per cent owned by T-Mobile in 2004), was a joint venture of the Belgian company Belgacom and Danish Tele Danmark.

The entry of these new competitors into the Dutch mobile phone market coincided with a dramatic fall in phone charges. At the time when KPN reduced its tariffs by 50 per cent, for example, consumers could choose from more than 140 different subscription packages. These falls in charges contributed to the rapid increase in the demand for mobile phones. At the same time, KPN managed to keep its position as the market leader, but was unable to avoid losing market share in new mobile connections.

KPN's innovations: SMS services for pre-pay clients

The increased competition that KPN faced led it to change its business strategy: instead of following trends, it became increasingly innovative. In this spirit, the project team's goal was to be the first phone provider in the Netherlands to provide SMS services to its pre-pay clients. To achieve this, the team needed first to analyse the commercial viability of this innovation and to identify, should it prove viable, the target group to whom the service would be offered.

To facilitate these analyses, KPN divided its consumer market into segments, each segment being a group of consumers with related needs and specific characteristics. One of these segments, labelled 'young and fast', was identified as being the most promising. The majority of people in this segment owned a mobile phone and already made use of pre-paid services. The team's intuition was that sending short text messages would be very attractive for this segment, because most members of this young group appeared to be socially active and modern and, above all, familiar with IT and telecom products. Moreover, the sending of short messages by pre-pay users was in line with a known shift in trends from 'ear' to 'eye' and from 'content' to 'data'.

For the project team, these were strong arguments in favour of exploring the new option. A multidisciplinary team was assembled, with participants from various backgrounds, including hardware, networking and processing, product development, marketing and distribution.

To estimate the demand for SMS services in the target group, the team decided first to analyse the market situation in the Scandinavian countries (particularly Finland) and in Japan, countries in which there was already a relatively high penetration rate for mobile phones. In Finland, the world's trendsetter for mobile phones, the penetration rate in 1999 was over 90 per cent, and it was anticipated that this rate was expected to further increase, to more than 100 per cent.

Peter Leblanc and his team discovered that, in the Scandinavian countries, people, and in particular young people, were making extensive use of SMS services. Their research showed that Finnish teenagers were as likely to communicate with short text messages as with phone calls. The project team started to investigate the needs and wishes of pre-pay users for sending short messages. Having analysed the characteristics of the foreign and Dutch domestic mobile markets the team concluded that by the end of 1999 the market share for sending short messages by pre-pay users in the Netherlands could be 1 per cent, but that within five years the figures could come close to those of 1999 in Scandinavia.

KPN's next step was to develop an aggressive strategy for the internationalization of the company. As well as seeking international cooperation, they also mounted takeovers in order to strengthen their position in the mobile telecoms services market. In line with this strategy, in 1998 a joint venture was established with the American company Qwest: this resulted in the establishment of a business unit, KPNQwest, which focused on data transport activities. At the end of August 1999, it was announced that KPNQwest was to be floated on the stock market as an independent company; with the principal objective of raising funds for KPN in order to facilitate a major takeover that would further strengthen KPN's position in the European mobile phone market.

The new company strategy was launched at the end of 1999. The major goal of this strategy was to attempt to transform KPN from its then 15th position in the European mobile phone market into one of the top three companies. On 9 December 1999 KPN announced that it had acquired more than a 75 per cent majority of the stocks of E-plus, the third-largest provider of mobile telecommunications services in Germany, which had around 3.5 million customers at that time. The E-plus deal required a bridging loan of some €13 billion, which was guaranteed by an international banking consortium led by J.P. Morgan and ABN AMRO. This loan was to be refinanced by bringing KPN Mobile to the stock market, accompanied by some new loans, and by selling some of its non-core assets.

The total sum required to finance KPN's takeover of E-plus was €18.7 billion. Measured in terms of subscribers, this takeover raised KPN to seventh position in the European mobile phone market, with some 8 million customers. News of the deal was enthusiastically received by stockholders; between 30 November and 31 December 1999, spurred by the overall optimistic market sentiments at the turn of the millennium, the share price of KPN rose from €57 to €94. However, not all of the news was good: one consequence of this transaction was that two of the world's leading credit rating agencies, Moody's and Standard & Poor's, declared that they would lower KPN's credit rating.

Just a few months later, the 'new economy' bubble burst on global stock markets. Collapsing share prices in the Information and Communications Technology (ICT) sector caused a further downgrading of KPN's credit rating, a trend that was further reinforced by KPN's apparent over-investment in subscribing to the auction of UMTS frequencies (radio spectrum frequencies designated for mobile phones) in 2000. KPN's finances went into a downward spiral. At the beginning of 2002, the stock price plummeted to approximately €4, and some commentators raised serious questions about KPN's capability to deal with its significant debts, which in 2001 peaked at the astonishing amount of €23 billion. Accordingly, the world's leading credit rating institutions lowered KPN's credit rating.

Faced by this critical financial position, KPN had no choice but to take remedial measures. By the end of 2004 the company reduced its debt position to a 'mere' €8.3 billion, much lower than its debts of just a few years earlier. In 2005, as a reaction to this positive development, the stock price increased to around €7.5 and it continued to rise thereafter, reaching a level of around €10.2 at the beginning of 2009.

International strategic issues for KPN

KPN's first experiences with internationalization and globalization had demonstrated that the company needed to expand its focus by crossing borders. The main pillar of this strategy was the acquisition of 100 per cent ownership of the German mobile phone operator E-plus, a purchase that had to be approved by the European Commission, which assessed its legitimacy and analysed the possible anti-competitive consequences. On 7 March 2002, the Commission concluded as follows:

> The European Commission has cleared the proposed acquisition by Dutch telecommunications operator KPN of sole control over Germany's third largest mobile phone operator E-Plus. The Commission has found that the transaction would not raise any competition concerns in either the German or Dutch mobile telephony markets or in any other related markets.

In 2009, KPN Mobile was active principally in Belgium (through BASE and Tele2/ Versatel), Germany (through E-plus) and the Netherlands; it also had a presence in Spain (through Orange España) and France (through Bouygues Télécom). In 2007 KPN decided to cease the development of its I-mode service which was the product of KPN's alliance with Japan's NTT Docomo. Two of KPN's main markets experienced considerable growth rates, with increases in revenue of 12.5 per cent in the Netherlands and 4.3 per cent in Germany. This seems quite remarkable considering the fact that by 2007 the Netherlands and Germany were already experiencing penetration rates of over 110 per cent as many consumers used more than one phone. Somewhat surprisingly, in 2007 the revenues in Belgium, the market with the lowest penetration rate (94 per cent), contracted by nearly 2.3 per cent year. In the same year, KPN took over the Dutch computer service provider Getronics, doubling its size and making clear its intentions of expanding into the IT market.

The future for KPN offers many attractive opportunities, but also threats that will require the company to adapt even more extensively. Although internationalization and globalization are said to increase competition and are regarded as beneficial for the consumer, they also have significant other side-effects. As mentioned above, the European Commission keeps an eye on large-scale mergers and acquisitions and on their possible anti-competitive consequences; nevertheless, substantial responsibility for the regulation of the market still lies with national governments. In most European countries 'market watchdogs' are given the power to monitor and, in some cases, punish companies for abusing their position in the market. The Dutch watchdog for the mobile telecommunications market is OPTA, the Independent Mail and Telecommunications Authority. Perhaps unfortunately for KPN, OPTA is doing its job effectively, for it is regarded as one of the most pro-competition market regulators in Europe. As a result, by 2003 the Dutch mobile telecommunications market had become one of the most competitive in the European Union (EU).

The presence of five mobile service providers in the Dutch market at that time was noteworthy, bearing in mind that the Netherlands is one of the European Union's smaller mobile markets. Nevertheless, consumers evidently benefit from the range of providers and the relatively strong levels of competition within the market. When compared with the German and Belgian mobile markets one might conclude that the number of service providers in the other countries is relatively low, especially in Germany, Europe's largest mobile market. Concerns were voiced that anti-competitive forces were 'shaping' the market and that because providers face lower levels of competition in these markets they were able to gain 'fat' that allowed them to compete in other countries. Such factors implied serious threats for KPN and encouraged the other European 'watchdogs' to reflect on how well they themselves were functioning.

By 2008 the situation had changed significantly. Of the three markets, Germany hosted the most mobile network operators (T-Mobile, Vodafone, E-Plus and O_2). The Belgian market was divided between three operators (Proximus, Mobistar and BASE), while the once excessively contested Dutch market through mergers and acquisitions had only three operators (KPN, Vodafone and T-Mobile).

1.3   Questions raised by the case study

Case study 1.1 shows that the opening up of the Dutch mobile telephone market resulted in increased competition from foreign competitors, which was followed almost immediately by falling prices and increased choice for consumers. KPN Mobile changed its strategy from follower to innovator; and in order that it might fulfil this new role it needed both an analysis of the home market and an assessment of developments in comparable foreign product markets.

The case raises questions in a number of different areas:

o **Internationalization** How does internationalization reveal itself? In what different types of international transactions may a company be involved? (These questions are discussed in Chapter 2.)

o **Competition** How does international competition in the telecoms market affect a company such as KPN? How are other market players, such as consumers or competitors, affected by the same processes? More generally, what is the economic impact on the various players in markets that are experiencing intensified international competition and trade? (This is discussed in Chapter 3.)

o **Motivation** Why do former monopolists like British Telecom or France Télécom begin to operate in foreign markets, such as the Dutch mobile market, instead of simply exporting their services to the Netherlands? (Some answers are given in Chapter 4.)

o **Protection** What protective measures can KPN apply in dealing with foreign competition in its domestic market? Who or what determines the introduction of these measures? Is it possible for companies such as KPN to lobby successfully for the preservation of traditional trade barriers and market segmentation? (These issues are considered in Chapter 5.)

As the case study highlights, KPN and the new market entrants were faced with a very swift internationalization process and a fierce battle for market share. The study also indicates the delicate process of international cooperation and foreign (hostile) takeovers. Such developments raise issues about how such expansionary strategies need to be financed in the international capital market. Internationalization forced the internationally-oriented company to carefully monitor the conditions in the international capital market, to keep track of global financial trends, and to find answers to all kinds of questions related to international finance, such as credit rating, dealing with credit and country risks, and the impact of exchange rate movements. Below are some examples of such questions.

Financing How can international transactions be financed? (See Chapter 12)

Currency To what extent is it important that the substantial financial transactions of a company are executed in different currencies? What different risks do different currencies pose for a company, and how can such risks be minimized or hedged? More generally, what determines the price of one currency relative to another – the exchange rate – and how can such rates be explained? (See Chapters 13 and 15)

Risks What other risks are associated with international transactions? (See Chapter 15)

International arrangements What effect do official international economic arrangements have on all types of businesses? These arrangements include new forms of monetary integration, such as the introduction of the euro in the European Union. (See Chapters 16 and 19)

International institutions Why do national governments with the help of international institutions try to organize and structure the international monetary system and the patterns of international finance? (See Chapters 14 and 16)

Intervention Why might a government or international institution, such as the International Monetary Fund (IMF), consider intervening in the foreign-exchange market, and how successful and effective have such initiatives been in the past? (See Chapter 16)

Country Have developing countries additional risks associated with international transactions? And is there an additional role for the IMF? (See Chapters 17 and 18)

In an effort to seek answers, we can start by asking: 'What can we say, more generally, about the increasing internationalization of the business environment?' Chapter 2 will shed some light on this.

Internationalization and the World Economy

2.1 | Introduction

This chapter introduces the key components of international economic relations, which will be discussed further in later chapters. It outlines the international environment in which businesses operate, discusses the global nature of international economic transactions, and indicates the present scale of the various types of transactions.

Sections 2.2 and 2.3 consider the volume, characteristics and direction of international trade flows, and explore how best to define the 'economic openness' of a country and to measure similarities in the imports and exports of countries. Section 2.4 provides data and figures relating to the characteristics and size of international capital flows. As will become apparent, international financial transactions may arise from a wide range of underlying reasons, which will be discussed in more detail in the second part of this book.

When analysing the international trade flows and financial capital flows that have taken place in recent decades, one phenomenon stands out: the *speed* at which internationalization occurs. This is demonstrated by the substantial growth in virtually all key variables for international economics. Consider the following basic figures:

- o **Domestic earnings** In the period 1980–2007 world real GDP increased by a factor of 1.9. In the preceding period, from 1950 to 1980, it had increased by a factor of 3.8. In 2010, world real GDP is estimated to have fallen by around 1 per cent year on year.
- o **World exports** Over the same periods, the volume of world merchandise exports increased by factors of 2.8 and 8.6, respectively.
- o **Foreign-exchange turnover** The daily turnover of trading on the main foreign-exchange markets across the world, which is often used as an indicator of the overall level of financial activity in terms of cross-border transactions, was estimated at some $45 billion in 1979, and had increased rapidly to around $590 billion by 1989. In the first few years of the new century, the figure rose rapidly to $1,240 billion in 2001, $1,930 billion in 2004 and to a remarkable $3,980 billion in April 2010.
- o **International investment** *Foreign direct investment* (FDI) is an international capital transfer introduced with the aim of acquiring a significant degree of control over a foreign company. The total value of worldwide FDI was about $66 billion per annum

per year for 1981 and 1986 and about $142 billion between 1988 and 1989. In 2006 the developing countries alone received an inflow of FDI of nearly $379 billion.

o **International mergers and acquisitions** The total value of cross-border mergers and acquisitions worldwide totalled some $116 billion in 1991, a figure that also increased significantly, to almost $412 billion in 2003 and $1637 billion in 2007.

2.2 International trade flows

The postwar period witnessed an enormous expansion in the volume of international trade. In almost every year, growth figures for the volume of world trade exceeded those for world production. This was still the case in the early 1970s, when governments introduced a number of new trade restrictions.

Internationalization through trade also affects our daily lives as consumers. Today we consume far more foreign goods and services than was the case only a few decades ago. Enterprises, similarly, process far more foreign goods and services and have many more foreign economic links than in the past.

Figure 2.1 illustrates how international trade has developed in relation to world output over the same time period. International trade expanded significantly in the postwar period. However, due to the postwar recovery, expansion in terms of both trade and output was probably at its strongest during the period 1950–73 rather than during the subsequent periods. Between 1950 and 1973 trade and output expanded by some 8 per cent and 5.5 per cent per annum, respectively, whereas between 1973 and 2007, they grew by some 5 per cent and 2.5 per cent per annum, all in real terms. World trade exports took a major tumble in 2009 when they declined by 12 per cent, while world GDP declined by 2.4 per cent in that year.

The figures also show that the growth rate of trade was lower than the output growth rate during the first half of the twentieth century, a period when many kinds of trade barriers were in place, not least the two world wars. In this period the growth in world output was at a low level (around 2 per cent) and the growth in the volume of international trade was even lower, at about 1 per cent. Figure 2.1 also shows that the growth in world trade, from the first postwar period until 2009, was always significantly above the rates of growth

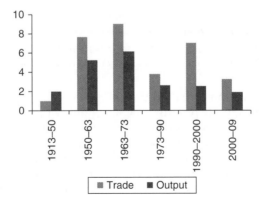

Figure 2.1 World merchandise trade and world output in real terms: annual average growth rates for various sub-periods, 1913–2009 (%)

Sources: For 1913–50: Maddison (1989); for 1950–99: WTO (2000, p. 25); for 2000: UN (2000, p. 4); for 2000–09: WTO (2010) *International Trade Statistics* (own calculations).

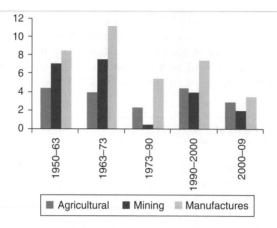

Figure 2.2 World trade in principal types of goods: average annual growth from 1950
to 2009 (%)

Sources: For 1913–50: Maddison (1989); for 1950–99: WTO (2000, p. 25); for 2000: UN (2000, p. 4); for
2000–09: WTO (2010) *International Trade Statistics* (own calculations).

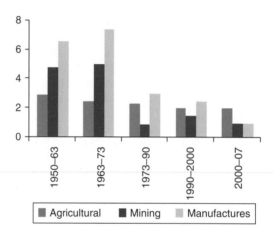

Figure 2.3 World output of principal types of goods: average annual growth from 1950
to 2009 (%)

Sources: For 1913–50: Maddison (1989); for 1950–99: WTO (2000, p. 25); for 2000: UN (2000, p. 4); for
2000–09: WTO (2010) *International Trade Statistics* (own calculations).

of world production. What all this indicates is the continuous integration process in the
world economy, more recently labelled 'globalization'.

Figures 2.2 and 2.3 show the growth rates of, respectively, world trade and world production subdivided into the main product groups: agriculture, mining and manufactures.
The overall picture indicates that both output and trade grew faster during the first half of
the postwar period than during the second half. Additionally, the degree to which there
is a correspondence between the patterns for trade and output is remarkable, suggesting a
clear interrelationship. As in Figure 2.1, the rate of growth in trade almost always exceeds
the rate of growth in output.

Table 2.1a Merchandise trade: intra-regional and inter-regional, 2009 ($ billion)

	Destination							
Origin	North America	SCA	Europe	CIS	Africa	Middle East	Asia	World
North America	**769**	128	292	9	28	49	324	1602
SCA	115	**120**	90	6	13	11	96	459
Europe	366	75	**3620**	147	162	154	426	5016
CIS	23	5	239	**87**	7	14	63	452
Africa	66	9	149	1	**45**	12	85	384
Middle East	60	5	76	4	34	**107**	357	690
Asia	627	95	641	57	102	163	**1846**	3575
World	2026	437	5105	311	391	510	3197	12,178

Note: SCA = South and Central America; CIS = Commonwealth of Independent States.
Source: WTO (2010) *International Trade Statistics* (own calculations).

Finally, the data reveal that the strongest growth rates are in the manufacturing group, in both output and trade, and the lowest rates of growth are for mining and for agricultural products. The percentage increase in demand for a 1 per cent increase in income is called *income elasticity*. These figures tend to confirm that the income elasticity for agricultural products and commodities is generally lower than for manufactures: as world income and output increase, the share of agricultural and mining products falls. However, within the manufacturing category there are many subcategories that have a wide range of growth patterns.

Tables 2.1a and 2.1b show the export flows for the main economic regions of the world, in absolute and relative terms respectively. The tables provide a closer look at the regional patterns of international trade and highlight a number of issues that we will discuss.

First, South–South trade as a share of total world trade is less than 20 per cent and has not grown during 2009. This reflects the underdeveloped trade relationships amongst the developing and transition countries.

Secondly, about half the trade in world merchandise takes place within the various regional (economic) blocs, such as the European Union (EU), the North American Free Trade Agreement (NAFTA) and the Association of South East Asian Nations (ASEAN). This is most evident from the 72.2 per cent share of intraregional trade within Europe alone, which can be attributed to the fact that Europe consists of a large number of countries at relatively short distances: business transactions more easily turn into exports or imports.

Thirdly, there is *intra-industry trade* (IIT), particularly between industrialized countries. This is an important trend in the pattern of international trade and occurs if a country both imports and exports products from a particular product category (see Figure 2.4a). Further evidence for this so-called North–North trade can be found in Figure 2.4b, which illustrates the export flows within the various economic blocs. These figures show that the majority of trade occurs between relatively similar countries. The growth of IIT reflects an increasingly refined pattern of specialization that is now typical for a large number of western companies. In practice, this trade usually concerns alternatives of the same type of product, such as cars: for example, France exports Peugeots and Renaults but imports Toyotas, Opels, Fiats and Volvos.

Table 2.1b Merchandise trade: shares of values of intra-regional and inter-regional trade flows, 2009 (%)

	Destination							
Origin	North America	SCA	Europe	CIS	Africa	Middle East	Asia	World
Share of total								
North America	**48.0**	8.0	18.2	0.6	1.8	3.1	20.2	100.0
SCA	25.0	**26.1**	19.6	1.3	2.8	2.5	20.8	100.0
Europe	7.3	1.5	**72.2**	2.9	3.2	3.1	8.5	100.0
CIS	5.2	1.1	52.9	**19.2**	1.6	3.2	13.9	100.0
Africa	17.1	2.4	38.8	0.3	**11.7**	3.0	22.2	100.0
Middle East	8.7	0.7	11.0	0.5	4.9	**15.5**	51.8	100.0
Asia	17.5	2.7	17.9	1.6	2.8	4.6	**51.6**	100.0
World	16.6	3.6	41.9	2.6	3.2	4.2	26.3	100.0

Note: SCA = South and Central America. CIS = Commonwealth of Independent States.
Source: WTO (2010) *International Trade Statistics* (own calculations).

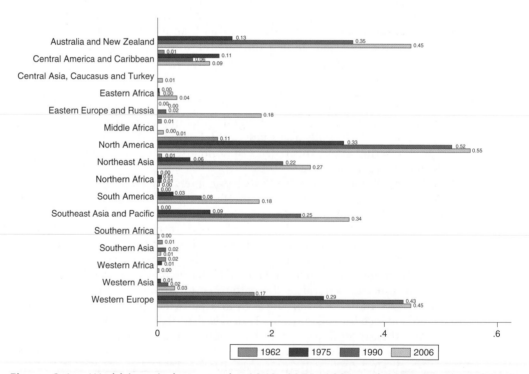

Figure 2.4a World intra-industry trade, 1962, 1975, 1990 and 2006 (% of total trade value)

Notes: Country grouping according to World Bank categorization 'wide coverage' dataset.
Sources: Brulhart (2008); World Bank (2009), *World Development Report 2009*.

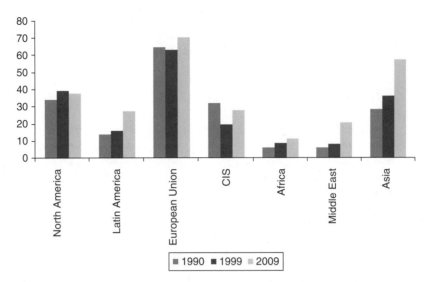

Figure 2.4b   Export flows within regional blocs: proportion of total export flows of countries, 1990, 1999 and 2009

Sources: WTO (2006) *International Trade Statistics*; WTO (2010) *International Trade Statistics*.

The volume of intra-industry trade shown in the statistics depends on the degree of detail of specification of goods and services used by the applicable classification system (SITC and NACE. See Box 2.1). As the degree of detail increases, the recorded volume of IIT tends to fall. Even when trade data meet a highly detailed specification level, a substantial proportion of trade for most countries can still be labelled IIT. Moreover, given a particular IIT classification scheme, the relative size of IIT in overall trade has grown considerably during the postwar period (see Figure 2.4a). The large increase in the volume of IIT over the years is typical of modern trade flows.

Box 2.1   Measuring international trade flows

In international trade statistics, the various flows of goods are classified by a uniform system known as the *Standard International Trade Classification* (SITC) or its European counterpart, NACE (*Nomenclature Générale des Activités Économiques dans les Communautés Européennes*). In this system, goods are classified by a decimal numbering (digit) system, which is refined until the product has been described in the fullest possible detail. The international system extends to nine digits, but the countries themselves can refine their classification even further.

In practice, however, only seven digits are used.

An example:

1 digit SITC 8 'miscellaneous manufactured articles'
3 digits SITC 851 'footwear'
5 digits SITC 851.01 'footwear with outer soles and uppers of rubber or artificial plastic material'

SITC 851.02 'footwear with outer soles of leather or composition leather; footwear (other than footwear falling within heading 851.01) with outer soles of rubber or artificial plastic material'

7 digits SITC 851.02.07 'sand shoes, rubber soled'.

Various indices are used to express the intensity of IIT. One can estimate the overall (*aggregate*) level of trade, taking into account the imports and exports for each category of goods, and if appropriate make an adjustment for any overall difference between them. Using a specific formula, one can calculate the volume of intra-industry trade for each aggregation level.

For a given country, broadly defined categories of goods are more likely to show both imports and exports than more precisely defined categories of products. For example, when Greenaway and Milner (1986) made a calculation of British intra-industry trade for 1982, they found that intra-industry trade measured 97 per cent for SITC 751 (office machines), 41 per cent for SITC 7511 (typewriters) and 10 per cent for SITC 75112 (mechanical typewriters).

It is also worth pointing out that certain countries have managed to make considerable improvements to their position in the international market, while others have experienced a relative decline. This is illustrated by Table 2.2, which shows the shares in exports of industrial products for most of the large trading countries for the period 1965–2009. Countries experiencing strong export growth during this period include the 'NICs' (Newly Industrializing Countries, such as Taiwan, South Korea, Hong Kong and Singapore; later, other countries were also given that title) and, more recently, Spain, China and India in particular. By contrast, the relative importance in world trade of countries such as the UK, Belgium, Switzerland, Sweden and Japan has declined in recent decades. However, the table should not be interpreted as though growth in one country's share of trade automatically reduces another country's scope for trade: trade is not a zero-sum game in which one player's gain is always equal to other players' losses. (Chapter 4 will discuss this in more detail.) As we saw in Figure 2.1, the distribution of percentage shares shown in Table 2.2 came about during a climate of very strong growth in the volume of international trade.

2.3   The national significance of international trade

International trade is important to both industrialized and industrializing countries, as can be seen in Table 2.3. The table shows that countries with relatively small populations tend to import more goods and services per capita than countries with relatively large populations; and, in general, geographically large countries export fewer goods and services per capita than small countries. (For example, in 2009 the USA exported goods and services worth $3374 per capita, compared with $26,063 for the Dutch.) This is because large countries can satisfy most of their own needs whereas small countries, which generally have small economies, need to import relatively large amounts of products and services. Companies in large countries also have a larger domestic sales market than those in small countries, and are under less pressure to sell abroad – or to internationalize.

Table 2.2 Share of world exports of industrial products, selected countries and years

Exporters	Rank							Share						
	1965	1980	1990	1999	2003	2005	2009	1965	1980	1990	1999	2003	2005	2009
Germany	2	1	1	2	1	1	2	13.8	13.9	11.4	9.6	10.0	9.3	9.0
United States	1	2	2	1	2	2	3	15.4	12.2	11.3	12.4	9.6	8.7	8.5
Japan	4	3	3	3	3	4	4	6.8	10.4	8.3	7.5	6.3	5.7	4.6
China	25	24	15	9	4	3	1	0.6	0.8	1.7	3.5	5.8	7.3	9.6
France	5	5	4	4	5	5	6	6.4	7.0	6.2	5.3	5.2	4.4	3.9
United Kingdom	3	4	5	5	6	7	10	9.9	7.2	5.3	4.8	4.1	3.7	2.8
Netherlands	10	8	7	8	7	6	5	3.2	3.2	3.8	3.6	3.9	3.9	4.0
Italy	6	6	4	7	8	8	7	5.0	5.5	6.2	4.1	3.9	3.5	3.2
Canada	9	9	8	6	9	9	12	3.4	2.8	3.8	4.2	3.6	3.4	2.5
Belgium	7	7	9	10	10	10	8	4.6	4.1	3.4	3.1	3.4	3.2	3.0
Hong Kong, China	19	14	11	11	11	11	11	0.9	1.5	2.4	3.1	3.0	2.8	2.6
Korea, Republic of	47	18	13	12	13	12	9	0.1	1.3	1.9	2.6	2.6	2.7	2.9
Spain	30	16	17	16	15	17	16	0.4	1.3	1.6	2.0	2.0	1.8	1.7
Taipei, Chinese (Taiwan)	40	15	12	8	15	16	17	0.1	1.4	1.9	3.6	2.0	1.9	1.6
Singapore	33	22	18	15	16	14	14	0.3	0.9	1.5	2.0	1.9	2.2	2.2
Soviet Union	8	10	10	20*	19*	13*	13	4.4	2.3	3.0	1,3*	1,8*	2,3*	2,4*
Sweden	12	12	16	17	20	21	28	2.4	2.1	1.7	1.5	1.3	1.2	1.1
Switzerland	13	11	14	19	20	20	20	2.3	2.3	1.8	1.4	1.3	1.3	1.4
Brazil	39	28	25	28	25	23	24	0.2	0.7	0.9	0.9	1.0	1.1	1.2
Australia	16	19	20	24	26	27	23	1.1	1.2	1.2	1.1	1.0	1.0	1.2
Denmark	20	26	23	26	28	32	34	0.9	0.8	1.0	0.9	0.9	0.8	0.7
Finland	23	23	27	30	33	35	37	0.7	0.9	0.8	0.7	0.7	0.6	0.5
Chechoslovakia	14	21	11	35**	34**	33**	32	2.1	1.0	2.4	0,5**	0,6**	0,8**	0.9

* Russian Federation
** Czech Republic

Sources: Figures for 1965–86: United States, *Yearbook of Trade Statistics*, various volumes, 1989; figures for 1989: GATT, 1990, vol. 1, p. 30; figures for 1990: GATT, 1991, vol. 2, p. 31; figures for 1999 and 2003: WTO (2004), *International Trade Statistics*, p. 19; figures for 2005: WTO (2006), *International Trade Statistics*, figures for 2007: WTO (2010), *International Trade Statistics*, p. 13.

Table 2.3 International trade in goods and services: key data (2009)

Country	Population (m)	GDP ($ bn)	Imports ($ bn)	Exports ($ bn)	Imports/ capita ($)	Exports/ capita ($)	Imports % GDP	Exports % GDP
USA	310	14,260	1563	1046	5042	3374	11	7
Germany	82	3353	966	1159	11,780	14,134	29	35
Japan	127	5068	500	542	3937	4268	10	11
UK	62	2184	486	357	7839	5758	22	16
Netherlands	16	795	370	417	23,125	26,063	47	52
China	1330	4909	954	1204	717	905	19	25
Singapore	4	177	240	274	60,000	68,500	136	155
Brazil	201	1574	128	153	637	761	8	10
South Africa	49	287	66	66	1347	1347	23	23

Sources: UN (2001); IMF (2001a, 2001b); World Bank (2003); CIA (2010) *World Factbook*.

2.3.1 Trade openness of an economy

Export shares (shown in the last column of Table 2.3) are commonly regarded as clear indicators of a country's degree of economic openness. In reality, however, it is not straightforward to evaluate the openness of an economy, and figures may be misleading.

First, the apparent value of imports and exports may hide a substantial contribution value that was generated in another country. This occurs, for instance, when raw materials are imported and then processed. For a medium-sized, open economy such as that of the Netherlands, only about one-third of its export value, on average, is added domestically; the rest is imported. In the bulk-transit trade, the domestic value-added component of exports is particularly small: the exporting country marginally adds value, apart from transhipment and transport activities, and often functions simply as a port for the 'hinterland'. (When goods are simply imported and re-exported without anything being done to them, such transactions are not recorded in the trade statistics of the transit country.) Normally only part of the export value of goods and services originates domestically, so the export share or export ratio (exports/GDP) can actually rise to above 100 per cent, as is shown for Singapore in Table 2.3. Nevertheless, when the value added domestically differs between countries, even countries with similar export shares may still have different levels of openness, and this openness will be subject to foreign influence. This shows that economic openness is a complex phenomenon.

A second factor that may distort the assessment of a country's degree of economic openness is the country's geographical size. This can be illustrated by a comparison of a large and a small neighbouring European country, the Netherlands and Germany. Even if these countried had identical sales patterns, yet if every business in these two countries were to sell its products within a 200-kilometre radius of the production site, the Netherlands would register a much higher export ratio than Germany. (In practice, of course, geographical distance and 'economic' distance, such as trade barriers, do not coincide for these countries, in part because of differences in language, culture, institutions, currency and so on.)

We can take this argument one step further. The difference in country size also has an affect on the geographical distribution of exports. We find that remote exports represent a smaller share of Dutch exports than of German exports. Because of its smaller geographical size, the Netherlands is therefore more likely than Germany to export *within* Europe. By definition, therefore, there is a lower share of non-European exports in total Dutch exports. This can lead to the incorrect assumption that small countries neglect remote markets.

We might prefer to present the openness of a country in terms of the ratio between imports or exports and *gross domestic product* (GDP). Given that they yield inherently different pictures, should we use average or marginal figures? In some countries the import sector is relatively small, but substantial economic growth demands the use of a relatively large volume of foreign goods: in such a case, the *marginal propensity to import* (the change in imports per unit due to an increase in a nation's GDP) is high, yet there is no correspondingly high *average propensity to import* (a country's total imports in relation to its GDP). The opposite can also happen.

Finally, the reliability of export shares as the indicator of economic openness is also affected by a country's imports portfolio – in other words, the types of products that are imported. If imports consist mainly of the raw materials and energy essential to domestic production, the levels of added value will be high, whereas if imports consist mainly of finished products sold in competition with goods produced domestically, added value will be low. Domestic producers may compete more effectively with imported goods by increasing the efficiency of their own production or lobby for protectionist measures to be taken against foreign competitors.

World trade consists primarily of manufactures, as the data in Table 2.4 and Figure 2.5 indicate. Within this broad category, the largest component is trade in machinery and transport equipment.

A country's exports may be concentrated mainly in primary products (*homogeneous*), or spread across a variety of goods and services (*diversified*). Homogeneous exports will make the exporting country extremely vulnerable to any changes in price or quantity on the world market.

To assess the economic openness of different economies, therefore, one must take account of not only the import and export shares themselves, but also of other factors such as the value-added component of trade, the geographical size of the economy, the marginal and average import and export ratios, the degree to which imports compete with domestic products and services, and the degree of diversification of imports as well as exports.

Table 2.4 World exports of merchandise and commercial services by product category, 2009 ($ billion)

Merchandise	11,787	
Agricultural products		1169
Mining products		2263
Manufactures		8355
Commercial services	3350	
Transportation		700
Travel		870
Other commercial services		1780

Source: WTO (2010), *International Trade Statistics*, p. 3.

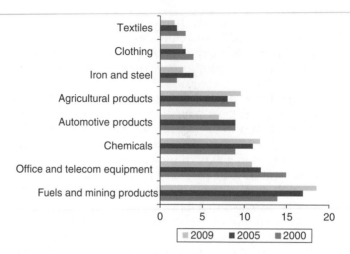

Figure 2.5 World merchandise exports by major product group, 2000, 2005 and 2009 (share based on value)

Source: WTO (2010), *International Trade Statistics*, p. 43.

One final note of caution: unlike *production*, for which the share of services has expanded to levels of about 50–70 per cent in most industrialized countries, the share of services in total *international trade* has remained fairly low: since 2000 it has been ranging between 23 and 25 per cent for industrialized countries' exports, and for the larger developing countries it has ranged between 13 and 18 per cent. This difference reflects two realities: (i) that some services are difficult, if not impossible, to trade internationally; and (ii) that the trade in international services is less liberalized than the trade in commodities. (Unlike services, goods trade has been the subject of multilateral negotiations since the 1950s.)

2.4 International capital flows

From the mid-1970s onwards, the principal barriers to international capital movements were gradually eroded. This led to unprecedented and rapid internationalization of the various financial markets, particularly in the western industrialized countries, starting in the USA and Western Germany. International capital flows now cover a variety of categories: foreign direct investment, international portfolio investment, international bank loans and deposits, and international transfers. Many international transfers occur within a framework of international aid relations.

Table 2.5 shows the increasing levels of financial globalization and internationalization for the period 1970–2000. It presents the flows of capital for the industrial countries, broken down into foreign direct investment flows, portfolio equity flows, debt flows, equity flows, and capital flows. Capital flows are the sum of the absolute value of the corresponding assets (outflows) and liabilities (inflows).

During the 1990s the volume of international capital flows grew, but at the same time became increasingly volatile. When exports exceed imports, there is a *current account deficit*, meaning that foreign capital is necessary to finance the growing trade deficit; and the largest economy in the world, that of the United States, showed widespread and growing current account deficits, which were financed by inflows of capital. By the year 2000, the

Table 2.5 Gross flows of capital (per capita, US$)

	Sample: 122 countries (1970–2000)			
	1970–2000	**1970–1980**	**1981–1990**	**1991–2000**
FDI Flows				
USA, Japan, Western Europe	776.97	206.90	408.01	1495.67
Latin America and Caribbean	108.08	31.17	38.18	208.86
East Asia Pacific	329.21	172.66	289.05	710.41
South Asia	2.76	n.a.	2.10	3.17
Europe and Central Asia	121.73	1.98	4.92	128.31
Sub-Saharan Africa	37.65	41.59	30.82	44.07
Middle East and North Africa	241.08	132.86	118.30	232.50
Portfolio Equity Flows				
USA, Japan, Western Europe	475.35	40.87	181.85	940.42
Latin America and Caribbean	63.18	0.13	0.16	66.81
East Asia Pacific	308.72	71.82	226.69	772.67
South Asia	2.57	n.a.	n.a.	2.57
Europe and Central Asia	37.18	n.a.	3.17	37.25
Sub-Saharan Africa	20.20	0.75	7.01	24.41
Middle East and North Africa	253.24	1177.44	212.90	6.82
Debt Flows				
USA, Japan, Western Europe	2316.13	1606.50	2040.62	3128.11
Latin America and Caribbean	355.52	600.53	438.75	182.55
East Asia Pacific	446.71	326.68	376.99	796.30
South Asia	16.06	12.99	17.33	16.59
Europe and Central Asia	252.45	143.24	130.57	250.70
Sub-Saharan Africa	76.08	94.08	83.52	61.37
Middle East and North Africa	2035.03	2067.75	1134.96	2911.98
Equity Flows				
USA, Japan, Western Europe	1146.60	222.45	532.07	2320.68
Latin America and Caribbean	100.40	31.87	36.36	177.21
East Asia Pacific	469.76	190.82	331.48	1140.52
South Asia	4.90	n.a.	2.71	6.55
Europe and Central Asia	149.02	1.98	6.44	156.41
Sub-Saharan Africa	46.62	41.70	32.67	58.78
Middle East and North Africa	233.08	437.49	116.62	240.53
Capital Flows				
USA, Japan, Western Europe	3473.62	1813.75	2425.07	5118.82
Latin America and Caribbean	368.68	673.65	404.03	236.71
East Asia Pacific	683.29	513.74	473.77	1272.97
South Asia	17.74	14.50	18.69	18.67
Europe and Central Asia	421.64	103.91	133.45	429.59
Sub-Saharan Africa	80.12	104.87	91.79	68.91
Middle East and North Africa	1953.52	2160.63	1270.39	2891.71

Notes: Gross flows represent flows of FDI, portfolio equity investment and debt, divided by population, based on IMF data in dollars and correspond to the sum of the absolute value of increase in assets (outflows) and liabilities (inflows). FDI data are for 72 countries; portfolio for 68 countries and debt data for 122 countries.
Source: Alfaro et al. (2005).

size of the US current account deficit amounted to about two-thirds of the total current accounts of all countries showing a surplus. In that year, net inflows to the USA exceeded $400 billion. Since then, the amount has been growing even more – it reached an annual figure of $1,062 billion in 2006, which is around 8 per cent of US GDP. More impressively, according to the US Treasury Department the net capital inflows into the USA surged to $286.3 billion in October 2008 following a $142.6 billion inflow in September. To a considerable extent this was financed by Asian central banks that accumulated large stocks of dollars in their efforts to maintain the link between the value of their currencies and that of the US dollar.

Another factor that influenced growing volumes and growing volatility in international capital flows was the increased levels of financing (and lending) by developed countries to rapidly expanding developing economies and economies in transition. In particular, during the second half of the 1990s, as a number of international financial crises emerged in these regions, the flows began to fluctuate dramatically. Indicative of these crises were the annual net private worldwide capital flows to emerging market economies (including countries in transition, particularly Central Eastern European Countries), which increased from about $100 billion to almost $225 billion in the period between 1992 and 1996. It declined swiftly to less than $60 billion, on average, in the period 1998–2000, before rising again to a yearly average of $215 billion per year between 2000 and 2007. The annual amounts for 1999–2000 are presented in the first row of Table 2.6.

However, the patterns of the underlying flows were quite different; looking at Table 2.6 one can say that, in general, FDI showed a definite rising trend but that there was a strong private capital outflow over and above the expected FDI and portfolio investment. This private outflow was chiefly the result of high levels of country and currency risk: because of insecurity about interest payments and hyperinflation, money was withdrawn from bank accounts in those countries and instead invested 'safely' in the western world.

It is important to note that Table 2.5 shows the levels of *gross* capital flows per capita and Table 2.6 *net* capital flows. The difference between gross and net can be explained by the fact that in any given year international capital can flow in and out of a country on several separate occasions. Movements of this kind are especially common in times of financial turmoil, and under such circumstances gross capital flows will be considerably greater than net flows. Data from the IMF indicate that between 1985 and 1995, gross global capital flows were two–four times the size of the corresponding net flows; during 1995–99

Table 2.6 Emerging market economies: net capital inflows, 1999–2008 ($ billion)

	1999	2000	2001	2002	2003	2004	2005	2006	2007	2008
Total capital flows	89.7	14.7	95.4	104.0	143.2	193.6	165.3	126.7	176.5	181.8
Net official flows	40.5	−26.1	18.3	6.5	−30.0	−43.5	−111.8	−130.9	−77.7	−96.4
Net private flows	51.7	42.7	79.7	100.7	175.3	238.8	279.3	281.5	263.4	279.7
Direct investment	157.6	151.3	172.0	158.0	151.5	193.4	252.3	255.8	275.1	280.7
Portfolio investment	−1.2	−18.3	−46.7	−39.0	8.4	54.5	63.6	−7.1	−23.8	−13.7
Other private flows	−104.7	−90.3	−45.6	−18.3	15.5	−9.1	−36.6	32.8	12.1	12.6

Source: IMF (2007), *International Trade Statistics*, p. 262, IMF (2008), *International Trade Statistics*, p. 282.

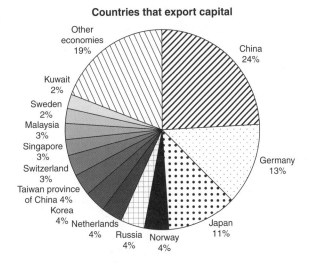

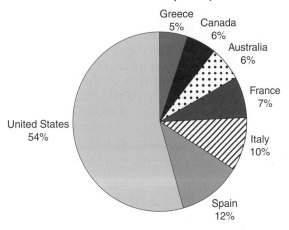

Figure 2.6 Global capital flows: sources and destination, 2009

Source: IMF (2010) *Global Financial Stability Report*, October 2010, p. 169.

this ratio increased to a factor of 4–6. This again shows the increased financial integration since the second half of the 1990s.

Figure 2.6 provides a more specific picture of net global capital flows. It illustrates that in 2009 Japan and the Euro Zone acted as net lenders to the USA and the emerging markets, and in consequence those who received the loans were net borrowers.

The internationalization of financial markets cannot be separated from the internationalization of trade and industry. Companies increasingly look to international markets for their sales, purchases and production, and if there is an increase in the number of international mergers and acquisitions, it should come as no surprise that the corresponding financial activities and transactions should also become more international. The internationalization of business has thus contributed to the tremendous rise in the scale and scope of activities on international financial markets. The underlying fundamental processes and functioning of these markets are discussed in Chapters 12–15.

This chapter has focused on the internationalization – or globalization – of economies. Chapters 3 and 4 will consider why countries are opening up their borders and allowing many businesses to operate on an increasingly international basis. Chapter 11 will discuss recording and defining the various types of international transaction.

2.5 Summary

1. The business environment is continuing to experience increasing **internationalization** and globalization, as indicated by a range of statistical measures. As a result, the international commodity, services and capital markets have all become increasingly important factors in the world economy, for companies as well as for entrepreneurs.
2. In the postwar period, the volume of **world trade** grew faster than world GNP. The growth of world trade in goods, increasingly dominated by intra-industry trade, is lagging behind the expansion of direct investment, and is less significant than growth in the volume of financial business on foreign-exchange markets. Trade patterns show that the majority of trade still occurs between the industrialized countries and within economic blocs.
3. Several diverse trends in **capital flows** can be identified. The first is the strong growth of capital flows, caused in part by the liberalization and deregulation tendencies in the area of international capital transactions. There was an explosive increase in both international portfolio investments and foreign direct investments from the beginning of the 1980s. In the second half of the 1990s, the volatility of international capital flows caused substantial economic disturbances and international financial crises. This volatility may have been exacerbated by the continuously growing US current account deficit, which was financed by an increasing inflow of foreign funds. Another factor contributing to this volatility was the financial turmoil that resulted from various international financial crises over lending, many of which started in the emerging economies.

Questions

1. What do you think will be the effect on the future expansion of international trade and foreign direct investment, of on the one hand, various worldwide ICT developments and, on the other hand, the increased concern about the environment and climate?
2. Imagine that, in future, as a result of concerns about climate change there will be substantial increase in tariffs on physical transport. What effect do you believe this would have on the volume and direction of international trade in goods? In such a scenario, which countries do you think would become the top international traders?
3. What effect do you think a further integration of the European Single Market would have on EU export and import volumes with countries outside the EU?
4. Do you believe that the international credit crisis will prove to be a lasting setback for international financial flows?

CHAPTER 3

International Trade Theory

3.1 | Introduction

In the modern world, businesses in different countries are increasingly linked through a network of trade relations. As we saw in Chapter 2, after the Second World War the growth in global international trade was much faster than the rise in world production. This leads us to ask two key questions:

o Why does international trade take place?
o Who gains or loses from such trade?

In the past, traditional trade theories have attempted to address these questions:

o Why do countries trade with one another?
o What groups in society gain or lose from international trade?
o How can both the regional pattern and the composition of trade flows be explained?

These traditional theories rely on the study of general country characteristics to explain international patterns of competitiveness; they do so by distinguishing between a number of broad categories of economic actors or sectors in the national economies.

By contrast, new trade theory stresses the characteristics of individual industries or companies (factors such as economies of scale, market form and market dominance) rather than national or sectoral characteristics. New trade policy theories address why certain industries are competitive in international markets.

The theories discussed in this chapter attempt to explain why countries trade with one another. It begins with a case study about the economies of China and India, which have experienced rapid economic growth from the 1970s and are generally regarded as emerging economic superpowers.

This introductory case study is followed by a discussion of traditional trade theory based on the concept of comparative costs – that is, the production costs for one commodity expressed in terms of the costs of producing another commodity.

These theories are the foundation of all trade theories and arise from the idea that location factors determine international competitive relationships and the pattern of trade flows. Location factors include:

o a country's level of technological development;
o the availability of factors of production;

    ○ structure of domestic demand; and

    ○ the country's standards, values and culture.

We then consider the possibility that international competitiveness, specialization tendencies and international trade can also be explained by the existence of economies of scale, which occur if larger-scale production reduces the average costs of production. We will show that economies of scale can be used to explain the existence of international trade, even in the absence of comparative cost advantages.

The chapter ends with a discussion of the 'Porter approach', which combines elements of traditional trade theory ('why do countries trade certain goods with one another?') with those of the new trade theory ('why can some industries compete internationally, while others cannot?').

The combination of these various elements probably means that the theory of international trade could best be illustrated through practical examples as it cannot be applied generally to all situations. The multitude of explanatory factors involved imply that each explanation of a real-life situation has to be tailor-made – that is, different trade flows may all require unique clarification. However, for a proper understanding of the main factors influencing international trade, a discussion of the theory will certainly increase your understanding of the underlying mechanisms.

3.2   Emerging industrial countries: a case study

Case study 3.1   The growing role of China and India in the world economy

Over the past few years, safe from the surges in oil prices, the economic rise of China and India has attracted much media coverage. Opinions have been divided; while some predicted China and India would soon assume the reins of the global economy, others, such as Professor Pranab Bardhan of Yale University, argued that despite their great potential, severe structural and institutional problems could hold back these nations for years to come.

Today, however, except for a few who choose to remain sceptical, most specialists predict that China and India will be the new economic superpowers of the twenty-first century. As shown in Table 3.1, with its real GDP expanding at an average of 9.7 per cent annually for nearly three decades now and performing well despite the effects of the world economic crisis, China is the second-largest economy in the world after the USA and trails Germany as the world's second-largest exporter. Over the same period, India's economy has been expanding by around 6 per cent annually, and growth is accelerating even more as investments soar and additional sectors open up to international competition. Although the financial crisis slowed down the economies of both countries, China's strategy to alleviate the effects of the crisis has been very effective, ensuring an annual growth rate of 8.7 per cent at the end of 2009.

Specialists estimate that, with their massive populations, growing labour pools and expanding consumer markets, China and India will be able to sustain annual growth rates of 7–8 per cent throughout the coming decades, even taking into account the many difficulties on the way. According to predictions by Global Insight Inc., by 2015

Table 3.1 Annual average growth rates of real gross domestic product, 1980–2009

Country	1980–90	1995–2005	2006	2007	2009
Canada	3.2	3.5	3.1	2.6	−2.6
China	10.3	8.9	11.1	13.0	8.7
Germany	–	1.4	2.9	2.5	*
India	5.8	6.0	9.2	9.7	5.7
Japan	3.9	0.9	2.4	2.1	−5.2
Netherlands	2.4	2.6	3.0	3.5	−4.0
UK	3.1	2.9	2.8	3.0	−4.9
USA	3.6	3.1	2.9	2.2	−2.4

1995	1996	1997	1998	1999	2000	2001	2002	2003	2004	2005
2.8	1.6	4.2	4.1	5.5	5.2	1.8	2.9	1.8	3.3	2.9
10.9	10.0	9.3	7.8	7.6	8.4	8.3	9.1	10.0	10.1	10.4
1.9	1.0	1.8	2.0	2.0	3.2	1.2	0.0	−0.2	1.2	0.9
7.6	7.4	4.5	6.0	7.1	4.0	5.3	3.6	8.3	8.5	8.8
1.9	2.6	1.4	−1.8	−0.2	2.9	0.2	0.3	1.4	2.7	1.9
3.0	3.4	4.3	3.9	4.7	3.9	1.9	0.1	0.3	2.0	1.5
2.9	2.8	3.0	3.3	3.0	3.8	2.4	2.1	2.7	3.3	1.9
2.5	3.8	4.6	4.2	4.5	3.7	0.8	1.6	2.5	3.6	3.1

Source: UNCTAD *Handbook of Statistics* 2008/2010; http://stats.unctad.org/Handbook/TableViewer/tableView.aspx.

India will have doubled its domestic spending to approximately $700 billion and China could triple its domestic spending to around $2.6 trillion. By the middle of the century, the combined share of global output of the two countries is expected to increase from 8 per cent in 2007 to about 45 per cent. By any estimate, both China and India are expected to dwarf every other economy except that of America and the EU.

Whether as consumers, producers, competitors or financiers, China and India's footprints on the global economy are increasing at an accelerated pace. As shown in Figure 3.1 and 3.2, China's exports have increased more than 670 per cent since 1980 to $1.201 billion in 2009, inspiring *Business Week* to describe China as 'the most competitive manufacturing platform ever'.

India, on the other hand, has become an important actor in the software, design and back-office service markets, with Bangalore now the second most important technology and corporate innovation centre after Silicon Valley.

Not only are China and India formidable powers in low-skilled products, they are rapidly becoming aggressive players in high-skilled services as well, a sector that until now belonged exclusively to developed countries. They are even motivating mainstream economists like Paul Samuelson to rethink consecrated theories on comparative advantage and free trade. The article 'China and India: What You Need to Know' published by

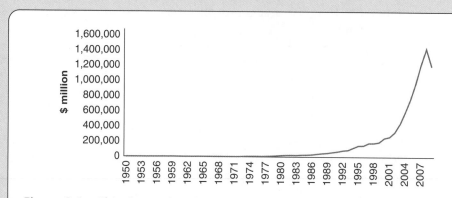

Figure 3.1   China's merchandise exports, 1980–2009

Source: UNCTAD *Handbook of Statistics Online* 2010; http://stats.unctad.org/Handbook/Table Viewer/tableView.aspx.

Business Week on 22 August 2005 discusses the future of America's competitiveness in the face of the rising Asian economies as follows:

> *Rarely has the economic ascent of two still relatively poor nations been watched with such a mixture of awe, opportunism and trepidation. The post war era witnessed economic miracles in Japan and South Korea. But neither was populous enough to power worldwide growth or change the game in a complete spectrum of industries. China and India by contrast, possess the weight and dynamism to transform the 21st century global economy. The closest parallel to their emergence is the saga of the 19th century America... But in a way, even America's rise falls short in comparison to what's happening now. Never has the world seen the simultaneous, sustained takeoffs of two nations that together account for one-third of the planet's population.*

Booming consumer markets

China and India are two of the world's largest consumer markets. China is already the number one customer for mobile phones, with 747 million cellular subscribers at the end of December 2009. This means that 56 per cent of China's total population was subscribed to a mobile communications service. Furthermore, it has the second-largest car market in the world and before long it will inevitably become the largest market for computers, broadband telecoms services, televisions and many other goods. Meanwhile, China's rapidly expanding demand is single-handedly driving up the prices of steel, cement, copper, oil and other materials.

Less attention is being paid to the rise of India's enormous consumer market. For instance, the number of mobile phone subscribers increased from 55 million in 2005 to 374 million by October 2008. India's markets for automobile and consumer electronics are also increasing. Similar to China, India's increasing demand is driven by its fast-growing middle class that is confident about its financial future, independently minded and that regards luxury goods as symbols of status.

Industrial powerhouses

The rate and extent of China's emergence as a manufacturing powerhouse has been breathtaking. As shown in Table 3.2, in 2009 China exported more than $1.2 trillion worth of goods (almost 4.5 times the level of 2002), and in the process overtook Germany to become the world's largest exporter.

Table 3.2 Leading exporters in world merchandise trade, 2009 ($ million)

Rank	Exporters	Value	% of world
1	China	1202.0	9.6
2	Germany	1126.0	9.0
3	USA	1056.0	8.5
4	Japan	581.0	4.6
5	Netherlands	498.0	4.0
6	France	485.0	3.9
7	Italy	406.0	3.2
8	Belgium	370.0	3.0
9	Republic of Korea	364.0	2.9
10	UK	352.0	2.8
21	India	163.0	1.3

Source: WTO (2010) International Trade Statistics, p. 12.

With the system of international textile quotas having ended in 2005, Chinese products account for more than half of all garments imported into the USA. China also produces most of the shoes, handbags, toys and tools that are traded around the world. However, what truly differentiates China from the previous Asian booming export economies is that its share of labour-intensive, low-skilled manufacturing is increasing even as the country is becoming a leader in high-skilled heavy industries and advanced electronics. Figure 3.2 shows the increase in the share of high-tech goods in China's exports compared with 1992. In 2005 China exported high-tech goods worth over $220 billion (28 per cent of total exports). Moreover, according to the China Daily, in the first quarter of 2007 alone the high-tech goods exported by China amounted to over $71.8 billion.

By the end of 2010 China is expected to vigorously increase its passenger vehicle capacity and start exporting cars to Europe and the USA. Furthermore, with the many new silicon wafer plants that started production in 2009, China's semiconductor industry is promising to become a major world player. In addition, at the start of 2011 more than 50 different chemical plants, each involving investments of over $1 billion, were under construction. By contrast, at the time the USA had one similar project.

The belief that China will carry on making low-end products while high-tech manufacturing will remain specific only to advanced nations is dissolving rapidly. But there is more to China's head-spinning manufacturing advantage. The low wages of China's factory workers also apply to managers, bankers, engineers, office staff and directors, which considerably decreases companies' personnel bills. In addition, large capital investments

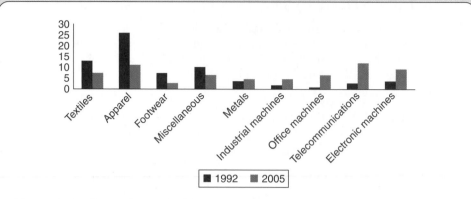

Figure 3.2   The makeup of Chinese manufacturing exports, 1992–2005
Source: Amiti and Freund (2007).

have supplied China with a network of efficient industry-scale infrastructure that is missing in other manufacturing havens such as Mexico or Indonesia.

When compared with China, India's manufacturing sector appears relatively modest. However, the latter is rapidly gaining ground in the areas of software, service and design that could prove to be far more valuable in the long run. India's presence on the world economic stage is more subtle. Products such as Motorola wireless handsets, Linksys network switches and Siemens electronic organizers may have 'Made in China' labels, but most of the software inside (which also carries larger profit margins) was probably developed in the neighbouring country of India. Cities like Bangalore and Hyderabad are rapidly becoming vitally important to high-tech giants such as General Electric, Oracle, Intel, HP, Dell and Texas Instruments. At the turn of the century, India's exports in IT services, call centre work and outsourced research and development (R&D) were negligible. However, according to McKinsey Co., by 2005 exports had reached $22 billion and they are expected to surpass $150 billion by 2012.

As pointed out in a *Business Week* article, 'The Rise of India' (8 December 2003), India is the first developing nation whose launch as a world economic participant has been based on the export of services rather than cheap, low-end manufactured products:

> *This deep source of low cost, high IQ, English speaking brainpower may soon have a more far reaching impact on the U.S. than China. Manufacturing . . . accounts for just 14% of US output and 11% of jobs. India's force is services – which makes up 60% of the US economy and employ two thirds of its workforce. And Indian knowledge workers are making their way up the New Economy food chain, mastering tasks, requiring analysis, marketing acumen, and creativity. This means India is penetrating America's economic core.*

The double-edged sword

China and India's primary advantage, their vast pools of cheap labour, might also prove to be their main weakness. Primarily because of its 'one child' policy, China now has one of the world's most rapidly ageing populations. In a few years the working-age population in China will begin a steep decline, and by 2025 approximately 300 million of its citizens are expected to be over 60 years old. India also has a bumpy road ahead. Managing a population that is expected to reach a mind-boggling 1.7 billion by the middle of the century could prove to be a major challenge. Furthermore, although the number of people living on less than $1 a day dropped from 300 million in 1993 to less than 200 million in 2005, the fact remains that one-fifth of India's population is still living in extreme poverty.

Some other factors could also throw China and India off course. Rampant corruption and heavy pollution accompanying rapid industrialization are vital challenges facing both countries. China has a financial system that is loaded with bad debt and lacks a transparent policy-making system. Meanwhile, India's government is running an unsustainably large budget deficit and, despite its western-style law system, legal issues are resolved at a snail's pace.

However, in spite of the hardships to come, most specialists continue to publish optimistic forecasts about the two economies. Both countries have strong economic fundamentals and, with their enormous labour pools and booming consumer markets, it looks as if they are headed towards healthy economic growth for many years to come.

Should the West be worried?

China and India's recent and spectacular development is one of the most important events in the history of global economics. The last time the world economic order was altered in such a radical way was when the United States made its entrance onto the global stage. In 1820 the collection of British colonies had an economy that was only slightly smaller than that of the leading European countries. However, by 1913, on the eve of the First World War, the United States had become the world's uncontested economic leader with an output twice the size of the second in line. History teaches us that when a new economic superpower enters the scene everyone can benefit. Between 1820 and 1913 the GDP per capita of the USA increased at an average rate of 1.5 per cent – enough to increase real income fourfold. The effects were also felt in Europe, where Germany, Great Britain and France registered 1.1–1.3 per cent average growth – enough to multiply real income threefold. This beneficial evolution was in most part due to the widespread cooperation between the United States and Europe and their ability to profit from each other's technological advancements.

In a similar manner, today's transfer of production to China and India could prove to be in the West's interest, at least under stable market conditions. However, the correlation is known to run both ways; therefore, while economic growth in South East Asia could indeed benefit the West, the increasingly important role China and India will come to play might expose the global economy to an entirely new set of risks. A severe slowdown of the Chinese economy, the collapse of its already shaky banking system or a demographic implosion in India are grim scenarios that would have significant consequences for the world economy as a whole.

This case study raises a number of questions, which will also be discussed in more general terms in the rest of this chapter:

1. How will China's and India's rise affect international production and trade?
2. Why is China so successful in exporting industrial products?

3. What is the connection between the productivity of labour, wages and export performance?
4. How will the rise in real wages affect the two countries' competitiveness?
5. What are the factors that could make future trade between China and India complementary, rather than competitive?
6. Does international trade enhance the level of economic progress?
7. What can be said about the distribution of economic growth generated by international trade?

3.3 Traditional trade theories

The theory about the origins of international trade, and the implications it has for welfare (and its distribution), dates from a period when international trade relations were far less intensive than today.

In the late eighteenth and early nineteenth centuries there was much debate over whether or not governments should regulate international trade, and what effects free international trade would have on the distribution of welfare between countries and between population groups within a country.

As we will show, the central assumption in the development of this theory was concerned with the competitive conditions specified by overall national circumstances. Elements of this assumption are still used in present-day trade theory, even though firm- and market-specific elements have become increasingly important.

3.3.1 Mercantilism

Mercantilist theories were dominant in seventeenth-century Europe. The mercantilists regarded international trade as a *zero-sum game* – in other words, they believed that the gains from international trade of one country resulted in a corresponding loss for another country.

This view surfaced because, at that time (the days of the gold standard), economists focused solely on the international payments generated by international trade transactions when estimating net results. For example, when a country imported more than it exported (deficit), a net payment needed to be made, resulting in a net outflow of gold that was regarded as a net loss for the paying state. This 'loss' of gold was seen as a weakening of national wealth and, hence, national power. The risk of such a welfare loss encouraged the authorities to try to control international trade flows in order to secure their wealth and, preferably, to attain a net inflow of gold from abroad.

By 1800, the theory of mercantilism was being severely criticized by economists such as David Hume, Adam Smith and David Ricardo. They stressed that international trade is a *positive-sum game* (in which there could be benefits for all parties involved) and that the mercantilists were fundamentally wrong in their assumptions. These critics of mercantilism focused on two points:

1. First, the mercantilists highlighted the impact of the accumulation of gold, the money of that time. Hume, in particular, drew attention to the preconceived idea that one could build up a substantial lead in prosperity by accumulating gold. He argued that if real economic activity does not increase, the effect of net gold inflows is mainly inflationary.

   This followed from the general assumption prevailing at the time (the so-called classical dichotomy) that developments in the sphere of money had no serious influence on developments in the sphere of goods (the real economy), despite the fact that flows of goods and money were, in principle, counterparts. This meant that more gold would lead to an increase in prices (due to the increasing quantity of gold, and thus money, available per unit of product) rather than an increased level of economic activity.

The argument was that such an inflationary trend in a gold-accumulating country would weaken its competitive advantage and, implicitly, its ability to export. Moreover, it would become relatively more attractive to buy relatively cheap goods from foreign suppliers than to produce them at home. The combination of these two effects – fewer exports and more imports – contributed to the outflow of the accumulated gold to other countries. This effect was observed in countries such as Spain and Portugal after they had plundered huge quantities of gold and silver from Latin America.

In addition, the mercantilists' conviction was that, when the demand for money remained constant, the extra gold from trade surpluses would lower interest rates and thus stimulate economic activity. But, as was argued by their opponents, inflationary pressures would prevent this from happening. The reason was that not only do investors need interest payments for postponing their consumption, but they also have to be compensated for the negative impact of inflation on their capital. As a result of the inflationary impact of net gold inflows and the upward pressure this has on the interest rate, this Mercantilist argument was also heavily disputed.

2. Secondly, the Mercantilists stressed the need for governments to intervene in international trade. By contrast, Smith and Ricardo both advocated free international trade. Smith, in particular, stressed that free international trade created the opportunity for the optimum international division of labour, which could bring benefits for everyone. In Smith's view, each country ought to specialize in the products in which it has an absolute cost advantage – and therefore a price advantage – over its trading partners.

An absolute cost advantage implies that a country has the lowest production costs worldwide and as a result is also able to supply foreign markets. Let us look at an example of absolute advantage.

Consider a world consisting of only two countries – say Turkey and Greece. Assume they have the same overall wage level. Yet Turkey has higher rates of labour productivity than Greece in producing leather clothing, while Greece's labour productivity is higher in wine production. Another assumption is that the price of a good depends only on labour costs. This means that leather clothing will be produced at a lower cost in Turkey and wine at a lower cost in Greece. If Turkey specializes in the production and export of leather clothing and Greece in the production and export of wine, the total production of both goods in their respective countries will increase. As a result, consumers in both countries will have access to more of both goods under free trade than without free trade.

Smith advanced two additional arguments in favour of international free trade:

1. International trade can help to break down national monopolies, creating healthier competitive relationships.
2. 'Excess' labour resulting from hidden unemployment or other unexploited resources could also be activated by new sales opportunities in the international market.

Although the combination of Smith's and Hume's arguments for free trade appeared fairly convincing, there were still objections to their account.

First, if international trade was left to the free market, some countries would in fact experience a gain, but at the same time other countries would lose out, because countries with high overall levels of productivity would start trading with countries with lower productivity levels. In such a case, the first country could well have an absolute cost advantage over the second in many products, so that the advantaged country would gain, on balance, at the cost of the disadvantaged country. Furthermore, achieving balanced trade would be impossible.

The second objection was that, even if a country as a whole could benefit from the opportunities of trade, this would not necessarily mean that all groups within the country would be better off. There was a well-founded fear that, in practice, free international trade would be beneficial to some groups in a country but detrimental to others.

3.3.2 The comparative cost theory

Ricardo's major contribution to trade theory was to weaken the first of the two objections mentioned above – that international trade would lead to losers as well as winners. In his opinion, every country would benefit from international trade, even if an economy is characterized by low overall levels of productivity. He demonstrated this by using an extremely simple model known as the *comparative cost model* – an analysis that is still applied today.

The comparative cost model links the trend in wages and productivity in order to determine the international competitiveness of a country. It proves that it is not a disadvantage for a country's labour productivity to be lower than that of foreign competitors, as long as its lower productivity is offset by a corresponding lower wage level.

Ricardo's model is based on the following assumptions:

o There are two countries, two products and one production factor: labour.
o Either the technical know-how or the state of technology is different in the two countries.
o There are constant returns to scale (if the input of the production factor increases by x per cent, so will output) and perfect competition.
o Labour moves freely between the two domestic production sectors, searching for the highest remuneration, but does not move abroad.

Let us call the two countries 1 and 2 and say that, in principle, they each produce two products, x and y, using their available quantity of labour. Since we assume that there is perfect competition everywhere and that labour moves freely from one sector to another within a country, in the absence of international trade, domestic demand and supply conditions will determine the price relationship between the two goods. However, if a different demand pattern emerges under conditions of international trade, the economy will adjust accordingly. It is important to realize what combinations of goods a country is technically capable of producing with the given labour potential. In the absence of economies of scale, this can be depicted as a straight line (see Figure 3.3), the *production possibility frontier* (further indicated as the pp curve), which gives the various maximum combinations of goods that a country can produce given its technology and quantity of production factors. In Figure 3.3, lines aa and bb indicate the pp curves of country 1 and country 2, respectively.

Production combinations above (or to the right) of the pp curve are impossible; below (or to the left of) the line are production combinations that are feasible but not optimal. The slope of the pp curve indicates how many units of product y have to be sacrificed to produce an extra unit of product x. We call this the opportunity cost of producing product x. The slope of the pp curve changes if the exchange ratio (which is the reciprocal of the cost ratio, or comparative cost) between x and y changes for some reason (innovation, experience, learning).

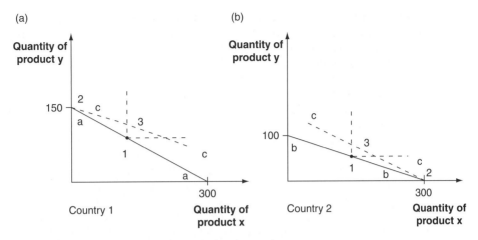

1 = level of consumption and production before free trade
2 = level of production under free trade
section 3 of line cc (bold section) = clearly better consumption under free trade
aa = pp curve of country 1; the slope indicates the opportunity cost of product x in country 1
bb = pp curve of country 2; the slope indicates the opportunity cost of product x in country 2
cc = international exchange ratio; the slope is between the slopes of aa and bb and is the
same for both countries

Figure 3.3 Illustration of differences in comparative costs

It is pure chance if the opportunity costs are the same in both countries, because that
will depend on the available national resources and production conditions (including factors such as the local climate and the available know-how). Those factors determine the
national labour productivity and hence the comparative costs. Since the national production circumstances are very likely to differ between the countries, so will comparative costs.

To illustrate the comparative cost model, let us take two countries, Indonesia and Japan,
and electronics and rice as products x and y (see Table 3.3). Assume that Japan needs two
hours of labour to produce one unit of electronics and six hours to produce one unit of
rice. By comparison it takes Indonesia four labour hours to produce one unit of electronics
and eight hours to produce one unit of rice.

If Japan produces one less unit of electronics, then it can produce one-third of a unit
more of rice; this means that in Japan the opportunity cost of each unit of electronics is
one-third of a unit of rice. In Indonesia the opportunity cost of each unit of electronics is
one-half of a unit of rice.

Since the opportunity costs differ between the two countries, the slopes of their
pp curves are different. This is the case generally if the production costs (in hours of
labour) are lower in both sectors in one country relative to the other country. In our example, the absolute production costs of both rice and electronics are lower in Japan relative

Table 3.3 Number of hours of labour
needed to produce one unit of a product

Country	Electronics	Rice
Japan	2	6
Indonesia	4	8

to Indonesia. However, since the opportunity cost of electronics is lower in Japan than in Indonesia, Japan has a comparative cost advantage in producing electronics and Indonesia has a comparative advantage in producing rice. If countries with different pp curves engaged in free trade, and diverted their production efforts towards the goods for which they have a comparative cost advantage, both countries will stand to benefit from this trade, as we will illustrate with a simple example.

Let us assume that the available quantity of labour in Japan is 600 and in Indonesia 1200. The line aa is now the pp curve for Indonesia; its slope is equal to the opportunity cost of electronics expressed in units of rice (1/2). In the absence of international trade, or in the case of autarky, this is equal to the relative domestic price of electronics or the price of electronics divided by the price of rice. Autarky means that a country is self-sufficient, that it provides for all its own needs and does not trade with other countries. If Indonesia fully specializes in rice, it can produce 1200/8 = 150 units of rice. In Figure 3.3a this is shown by the point of intersection of the pp curve and the y-axis. In an extreme case where Indonesia solely specializes in electronics, it can produce 1200/4 = 300 units. The line bb is the pp curve for Japan. The slope is, again, equal to the opportunity cost of electronics expressed as units of rice. In Japan, the opportunity cost of electronics in units of rice appears to be one-third. In the absence of international trade, this is equal to the relative domestic price of electronics in terms of rice. If Japan specializes in rice alone, it can produce 600/6 = 100 units of rice. If it specializes only in electronics, Japan can produce 600/2 = 300 units of electronics. Like Indonesia, Japan will produce both goods if it is autarkic. Depending on the demand factors, this might, for example, mean 50 units of rice and 150 units of electronics (point 1 in Figure 3.3). Given the domestic price ratio of 1/2, the demand factors can be such that Indonesia produces and consumes 150 units of electronics and 75 units of rice (point 1 in Figure 3.3a).

In the case of absolute autarky, both countries produce a total of 125 units of rice and 300 units of electronics.

Let us assume that a process of international trade is launched and that the existing trade barriers are eradicated. In the case of complete specialization (Indonesia in rice and Japan in electronics), and in accordance with the comparative cost theory, a total of 150 units of rice and 300 units of electronics is produced. As a result, the level of total 'world' production has increased by 25 units of rice.

The quantity of both goods actually imported and exported depends on the demand for the two products in the two countries in this free trade situation. The example clearly illustrates that there is room for both countries to improve their consumption possibilities, and thus to boost real domestic income.

The reason why both countries benefit from free trade is because once borders have been opened a price ratio will be established that depends upon the original cost ratios in the two countries combined with aggregate demand. The international price ratio will lie somewhere between the original two national cost ratios.

In specific cases the demand structure can cause the new price ratio to correspond to the original price ratio in one of the countries, but for reasons of simplicity we will ignore that special case in this instance. So, as we can see from Figure 3.3, specialization combined with the opportunity for exchange of the two goods on the international market (according to the international price ratio) means that both countries can obtain more of both products in various combinations.

Finally, Ricardo's model is used for the following argument. In practice, wages in the various sectors are commonly the same throughout the country. Thus, the ranking of the sectors by labour costs must also roughly imply a ranking in terms of international competitiveness.

If, for some sectors, labour productivity is lower than could be expected on the basis of the country's wage level, a comparative cost disadvantage is likely; either compared to the same sector in other countries, or to other sectors in the same country. When other sectors of the same economy's productivity is higher than the wage level would suggest, then those sectors will exhibit a comparative advantage. The sectors where wages and productivity precisely match represent borderline cases of economic indifference between internationally competitive and non-competitive sectors. Obviously, if, at given productivity levels, the wage level in one of the countries shifts (or vice versa, productivity levels shift at given wage rates), this will cause the borderline to change too, separating internationally competitive from non-competitive sectors. This will affect the countries' import and export pattern.

3.3.3 Criticism

Use of the comparative cost theory allowed Ricardo to demonstrate that trade can actually be beneficial for both countries and that international trade need not be a zero-sum game. This is still the case, even if overall productivity levels are lower in one country, because the only thing that matters for achieving larger consumption combinations of products, available in both countries, is the presence of differing relative production costs.

An objection to his free trade philosophy was that some groups within a country will suffer when introducing international free trade. This point, however, was not really covered in Ricardo's model.

Ricardo apparently believed at the time he was writing (the first decades of the nineteenth century), that a redistribution of income in the UK ought to take place between the landowners and the rising industrialist class. This was because during the Napoleonic Wars food prices in Britain rose as less food was being imported. The British landed gentry benefited from this price increase and tried to safeguard high food prices after the wars by lobbying for protectionism (as a result of the so-called Corn Laws).

This naturally conflicted with the interests of the industrialists, because a protectionist system hinders both imports and exports. Possibly because Ricardo wanted to tone down the internal conflict of interests as much as possible, he conveniently assumed in his writings that those whose prosperity increased by the transition to international free trade (the industrialists) would compensate the losers (the landowners).

However, in the absence of any mechanism to redistribute income, it was far from clear that the latter assumption would be fulfilled. As a result, analysts continued to try to find out what income distribution shifts take place within an economy if it engages in free trade.

3.3.4 The Heckscher–Ohlin–Samuelson (HOS) model

Around a century later, at the beginning of the twentieth century, this quest led to a relatively simple theoretical model developed by the Swedes Eli Heckscher and Bertil Ohlin. Their model was later refined and developed by the American economist Paul Samuelson.

The model was also based on the comparative cost concept and the idea that the competitive position of a location depends on its supply conditions and is, therefore, linked more closely to regions or countries than to individual companies.

An attempt was made to simply describe the principal adjustment processes that occur if two countries decide to open up their borders to one another's products. As in the Ricardian model, this model is based on the idea that a general equilibrium is established in the economies, in which the equilibriums in the various sub-markets are interrelated, in principle.

The HOS model considers two countries, two products, and two factors of production: labour and capital. As in the earlier Ricardian model, the HOS model assumes that there is perfect competition. In contrast to the Ricardian model, for each product the production function is assumed to be the same in both countries. The production function is the technical relationship describing the combination of production factors used to obtain a company's output. An assumed characteristic of the production functions in the HOS model is that if the input of all production factors – in this case labour and capital – increased by x per cent, output will also increase by x per cent. This reflects a similar assumption to that of the Ricardian model on constant returns to scale.

Another assumed characteristic is that if the input of only one production factor increases while the input of the other remains the same the extra output per additional unit of production factor will decline as additional units of that factor are added. This characteristic is usually referred to as the declining marginal productivity of inputs. The marginal productivity of an input factor, say labour, is the increase in the value of output generated by the last unit of labour added as an input in the production process. This is important because production factors are assumed to be rewarded according to their marginal productivity. It is also assumed that consumer preferences are the same in the two countries. However, the available quantities of labour and capital are not the same throughout the world. One country in the HOS model has a relatively large amount of capital, or is capital-abundant, while the other has a relatively large amount of labour, and is thus labour-abundant. For technical reasons, it is usually assumed that, relative to each other, one product is always labour-intensive to make, while the other is capital-intensive.

As the theory assumes that the price (or cost) of a unit of production is determined by its marginal product, the assumption of declining marginal productivity decisively affects the factor prices (wages and interest). It implies, in fact, that wages in the country well endowed with labour will be relatively low so that the country has a comparative cost advantage in the labour-intensive product, while the opposite is true for the other country. Finally, according to the HOS model's assumptions (as well as in the Ricardian model), products can be freely traded internationally, that is, there are no barriers to trade or costs of transportation, but factors of production cannot cross national borders (they are assumed to be internationally immobile).

To illustrate the HOS model, let us again take Japan and Indonesia and assume that both countries are still self-sufficient. Japan again has 600 units of labour and Indonesia 1,200. In addition, the available capital is 400 units in both Japan and Indonesia. The amount of units of labour available in terms of units of capital is 3/2 in Japan and 3 in Indonesia. Thus, Japan is relatively capital-abundant and Indonesia is relatively labour-abundant. Both countries produce both rice and electronics in conditions of economic self-sufficiency.

To simplify, let us assume that at the given levels of wages and interest rates, the production of one unit of electronics requires 4 units of labour and 12 units of capital in both countries. In addition, assume that under the same circumstances the production of one unit of rice costs 20 units of labour and 10 units of capital. The amount of labour relative to capital needed for 1 unit of electronics is 1 : 3 and 2 for a unit of rice. Thus, rice production is labour-intensive and electronics production is capital-intensive.

As labour is relatively scarce in Japan, the marginal productivity of labour will be high, and the wage rate relative to the interest rate will also be high (the latter being the reward per unit of capital, which is the abundant production factor in Japan). In Indonesia the opposite will be true: the wage rate relative to the interest rate is low. This difference in the relative rewards of inputs between the two countries has a vital impact on their comparative costs of producing the two goods. Reasonably assuming that one unit of electronics needs a relatively large amount of capital, and with capital being relatively cheap in Japan, this would imply that Japan can produce electronics at relatively low costs. Again, the opposite is true for Indonesia. Because a relatively large amount of labour input is required to produce rice, Indonesia, with its relatively low wages, will be able to produce rice at relatively low costs. So it follows that Japan has a comparative advantage in producing electronics and Indonesia has a comparative advantage in producing rice.

As in the Ricardian model, unrestricted international trade will establish a single world price ratio between the products that lies somewhere between the original national cost ratios (= price ratios). This generates patterns of specialization in the product in which one country has a comparative advantage. All this establishes the patterns of exports and imports. The export of capital-intensive electronics means that Japan exports capital indirectly, that is, embodied in the exported goods; importing labour-intensive goods (rice) means an indirect importation of labour as a factor of production. This reduces the capital abundance and ameliorates the relative scarcity of labour. Thus, in Japan the price of capital will increase while that of labour will drop. Hence, according to the HOS model, in both countries the price of the abundant factors increases, while the price of the scarce factors declines.

As the production function, and through it access to production technology, is essentially identical in the two countries, it can be shown that the prices of the goods together with the production processes in both countries will show a tendency to converge.

Thus, if a product was originally produced on a more labour-intensive basis in one country than in the other, free trade will cause the gradual disappearance of this difference. Furthermore, the difference in the relative costs of labour and capital between the two countries is also bound to decrease. On top of that, the original differences between the wage levels and interest rates in the two countries will disappear with the process of specialization and trade. This will, at least theoretically, eventually lead to what is called factor price equalization – the same production factor rewards will be enjoyed by both countries.

This can explain why the wage levels of a number of newly industrialized countries (NICs) that have opened up their economies aggressively to international trade and competition seem to have converged with those of their main western trade partners. The factor price equalization phenomenon may explain why wages in the south of the USA increasingly tend to converge with those in the north of Mexico following the creation of the North American Free Trade Agreement (NAFTA). the free trade agreement between the USA, Canada and Mexico that was meant to stimulate trade and investment between those countries.

If factor price equalization has occurred, the comparative cost differences will have disappeared and a new balance (equilibrium) will be established in which the capital intensity of production has adjusted to the new cost ratios (in the labour-rich country, production has become more capital-intensive, and vice versa). Since it is assumed that the available quantities of production factors have remained the same in both countries, the change in the level of wages and interest must have caused a change in the distribution of income between the two production factors.

In the labour-rich country, the welfare of the owners of the labour has risen and that of the owners of the capital has fallen; the reverse is true in the capital-rich country.

Box 3.1 The HOS model in symbols

The HOS model described in the text can be summarized with the aid of symbols. Let us call the two products x and y and their prices p_x and p_y; we indicate Japan and Indonesia by J and I, capital and labour by C and L, and wages and interest as w and i. The starting position for the HOS model, no international trade, is as follows:

$$(L/C)_J < (L/C)_I \qquad\qquad (a)$$

As Japan is abundant in capital and Indonesia in labour:

$$(L/C)_x < (L/C)_y \tag{b}$$

because production of x is capital-intensive and production of y is labour-intensive. (b) applies in both countries (no factor reversal; see following explanation). As illustrated above, it follows from (a) that:

$$(w/i)_J > (w/i)_I \tag{c}$$

And it follows from (b) and (c) that:

$$(p_x/p_y)_J < (p_x/p_y)_I \tag{d}$$

or that Japan has a comparative advantage in producing x and Indonesia in producing y. Under complete free trade, equality eventually arises in:

(d), which is the international terms of trade;
(c), which is factor price equalization.

To summarize, the central mechanism in the HOS model – as in the Ricardian model – is that the transition to international free trade has an influence on the prices of goods. However, if they change, the general equilibrium concept tells us that adjustment processes take place across the entire economy: the competitive sector will expand under free trade, while the other sector contracts under the impact of foreign competition. Further, the simultaneous changes on the markets in the factors of production, labour and capital, lead to a convergence of the wage and interest rates in both countries.

This process will have another important economic implication, namely a change in the domestic distribution of income within the two countries, in terms of the share of total national income that will go to the owners of capital and the share that will go to the workers. From the model we can infer that the owners of the country's abundant factor of production will see their share increase as a result of free trade; however, the owners of the other, scarce, factor of production will be worse off.

In conclusion, the HOS model states that the country as a whole will benefit, but whether that will apply to all owners of factors of production depends upon the willingness of the winners to compensate the losers.

3.3.5 The Leontief paradox

However elegant in its simplicity the HOS model may have been, it did not mark the end of developments in international trade theory.

First, empirical research conducted by Professor Wassily W. Leontief soon after the Second World War showed that the specialization process in the USA did not happen in the way predicted by HOS (a finding replicated in later research).

Where free trade ought to have caused the Americans to concentrate increasingly on producing relatively capital-intensive goods – those goods in which the capital-abundant USA had a comparative advantage – the HOS model's predictions were, however, contradicted by the real-life evidence presented by Leontief, according to which the USA imported capital-intensive goods instead of exporting them.

This finding was labelled the Leontief paradox, and subsequent researchers have attempted to explain the phenomenon. One convincing attempt at solving this paradox was the introduction of a third factor of production – human capital. Human capital is investment in labour via education, which improves the quality of the workforce. The fact that the USA exported relatively labour-intensive goods can be explained by the fact that the USA was abundant in human capital.

It was also stated that part of the reason for international trade is that people otherwise would not have had access to certain goods at all because the goods simply would not have been available domestically (such as oil for Japan, or tropical products and various minerals for Europe or the USA). Since such commodities are often capital-intensive to produce, importing them into the USA adds to the explanation of the capital-intensive character of its imports.

3.3.6 Factor reversal

One fundamental criticism of the HOS model is that it assumes that the sectors can be ranked in order of their capital intensity and that this ranking is the same for all countries.

This does not appear to reflect reality: for example, the agricultural sector in industrialized countries is often characterized by above-average capital intensity, whereas in the developing countries this sector is often relatively labour-intensive. This phenomenon is known as factor reversal and means that it is not always possible to draw a strict dividing line between labour-intensive goods and goods which are relatively capital-intensive. However, the possibility of making such a distinction is a central assumption of the HOS model.

It is clear that if factor reversal is fairly widespread, as some people assume, it will undermine the central idea of traditional trade theory – namely that countries have a comparative cost advantage (national supply conditions) in a range of goods and services which can be universally and objectively specified.

3.4 New trade theories

As the result of increasing doubts about whether or not there are clear systematic patterns observable in the specialization processes of countries, the need arose for the development of new trade theories to address questions such as:

o How can traditional theory explain why Canada (capital abundant) is just as important a net exporter of agricultural products (labour intensive) as Thailand (labour abundant)?
o Why was trade between Japan and the Asian NICs initially complementary but later became competitive, or why is France both an exporter and an importer of cars?

This last issue is known as intra-industry trade (two-sided trade within an industry), as opposed to inter-industry trade (trade between industries), which was the subject of traditional theory. A third question is, how was it possible that, as stated in Chapter 2, the greatest growth in international trade after the Second World War took the form of more intensive mutual trade between countries with fairly similar supply structures (such as in the European Union) and not between countries with very different supply characteristics (such as North = South trade)?

New trade theories have therefore focused increasingly on the following question:

What can we say about the business characteristics of exporting companies as opposed to companies that do not or cannot export?

The intuition is that it is not so much national factors – or, more accurately, location factors – that dictate the goods in which a country can achieve a strong internationally competitive position, but rather other factors relating to specific companies in that country.

By focusing on business characteristics a new and important difference emerged, namely the abandonment of the assumption of constant returns to scale common in traditional trade theories and its replacement with the concept of economies of scale, which means that as a company produces on a larger scale, average costs fall (*internal economies of scale*), but also that costs will decline if numerous other businesses in the same industry are established in the vicinity (*external economies of scale*).

- In the case of *internal* economies of scale, the level of average costs falls because an individual company can produce more efficiently by expanding the scale of its production: the company's earnings increase disproportionately to the increase in use of all factors of production. By a process of continued expansion, the company then gains an ever-increasing advantage over other firms in its sector, thereby ending perfect competition.
- Economies of scale are *external* if an individual company cannot itself influence its average costs by expanding production, but the average costs depend upon the scale and structure of the surrounding industry. This is the case if the industry reaches a size where all kinds of cost-reducing facilities emerge; for instance, education, infrastructure or component suppliers. Thus, internal economies of scale arise at company level, and external economies of scale arise at industry level, often by chance.

As we have argued already, economies of scale also undermine another important assumption of classic trade theories, namely perfect competition. Economies of scale favour scaling up and concentration; if a company, for whatever reason, succeeds in expanding its sales in the (international) market and hence increases its production, it will be able to eliminate its competitors with lower costs.

3.4.1 Internal economies of scale

It should be clear that if internal economies of scale determine international competitiveness in principle, incidental factors or even chance may decide why one country, for example, has a strong aircraft industry and another country has a strong electronics industry. One implication of economies of scale is that even if countries display identical supply conditions (where neither country has a comparative cost advantage, hence, according to traditional theory, there is no reason for specialization), it is still possible for one country to specialize in one product and another country in something else. If they do specialize, production costs can be reduced in both countries by economies of scale, and there are benefits for everyone involved in international trade (see Box 3.2).

Box 3.2 Internal economies of scale and international trade

Let us again take a model involving two countries, two products and two factors of production. There are now internal economies of scale in production in both

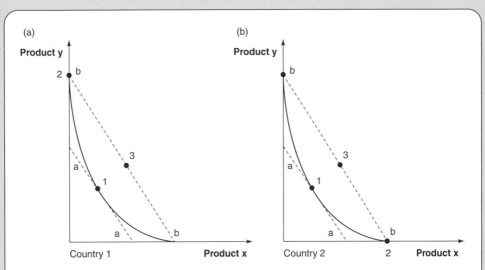

Figure 3.4   Production, consumption and trade with internal economies of scale

sectors. The pp curves of the two countries are identical because we assume that there is no difference between the supply conditions in both countries. This pp curve now has a convex shape (see Figure 3.4). The reason for this is that if we move along a curve to one of the corners, the cost of producing the product that we are making in larger quantities will fall, while for the other product the costs increase, as will be illustrated by the following. In Figure 3.4a at point 2, country 1 specializes in product y only. If country 1 wishes to produce one unit of product x, country 1 will have to sacrifice a relatively large number of units of product y owing to the economies of scale inherent in the production of x and y (check for yourself why the curve is flat in the vicinity of the intersection with the x-axis).

1 = level of production/consumption under self-sufficiency conditions
2 = level of production with international specialization
3 = possible level of consumption with international specialization
slope aa = domestic price ratio under self-sufficiency conditions
slope bb = international price ratio under free trade

Given the pp curve of a country, producers and consumers have to decide on the combination of the two products they want to produce and consume. Obviously an economy will strive to achieve a point situated on the curve since points to the left of the curve are less than optimal (a smaller combination of goods than can be achieved), whereas points to the right of the curve are beyond reach (given the production possibilities restricted by the available production factors and technology).

The preferred product combination is determined by the relative price ratios of the two goods. Assume that at given prices, this relative price is expressed in the figure by the slope of aa. Because that slope also indicates how much of product y needs to be sacrificed at production point 1 to get one extra unit of x (and vice versa) – the resulting ratio obviously reflects the price of x relative to y (check that for yourself) – point 1 is the only equilibrium point of production where the opportunity costs in production and the relative price match. More specifically, if p_x/p_y is 2:1, then only at point 1 is the cost ratio such that 1 unit of x will be exchanged for 2 units of y. At all other points on the pp curve the exchange ratio is different from this.

For producers, the product mix will be optimal at point 1, because at any other point on the pp curve costs will not be in line with prices, which means there is still scope for efficiency gains.

Slopes aa and bb are, again for simplicity, chosen to be identical in both countries, so there are no comparative cost advantages. Secondly, it is also assumed that the emerging international price ratio is equal to the original national price ratio. (In reality, satisfying both assumptions would obviously be pure chance.)

In the case of autarky, production and consumption are at point 1, and both countries' welfare can only increase if each country specializes completely in the production of one of the two products (thus reaching point 2 in both figures). Most of the surplus output is then exchanged for the other product via international trade. The graph shows that in that specific case consumption levels are attainable at point 3 on the bb line, in both countries, so that people in both countries have more of both products than before, even if the international price ratio is exactly the same as the original national price ratio.

As an example, let us identify the two countries in Figure 3.4 as Spain and Portugal. The two countries are identical and both produce wine, using labour as shown in Table 3.4. The table shows that there are internal economies of scale. Assume that both countries have 160 hours of labour available for wine production. In the case of self-sufficiency, both countries can either produce 40 litres of one type of wine or 10 litres of red and 10 litres of white wine. If consumers in both countries wish to drink both red and white wine, the second scenario is applicable.

Table 3.4 Number of hours of labour needed to produce one litre of wine

Litres of wine	Hours of labour	Units of labour per litre of wine
10	80	8
20	120	6
30	150	5
40	160	4
50	200	4

If the two countries trade with one another, wine producers in Portugal can concentrate exclusively on the production of red wine and those in Spain on the production of white wine. Both countries can now produce 40 litres of wine and exchange, say, half of it for another type. Thus, consumers can now have 20 litres of red and 20 litres of white wine instead of only 10 litres of each.

It is reasonable to assume that subsequent developments – which are obviously beyond the scope of this model – may cause producers to diversify their production.

If Portugal is planning to specialize in the production of red wine, for example, dry red wine and sweet red wine (10 litres of each); wine producers in Spain could similarly specialize further in white wine. In this case, free trade means that consumers will have not only more litres of wine, but also four varieties instead of two. Given these economies of scale, international trade increases welfare, not only because more goods are available, but also because there is a greater choice based on greater product differentiation.

Economies of scale need not only be extended to the overall costs of producing a product; they may actually also be important at the pre-production stage, knowing that production consists of a series of sub-activities, ranging from design to assembly and possibly even marketing.

Under certain circumstances, a company can create economies of scale by concentrating on a few sub-activities such as the design and production of certain components or how to assemble them. Other sub-activities then take place elsewhere, perhaps abroad. By doing so, international trade gets an intra-industry trade (IIT) character.

When explaining the location of these sub-activities, people often resort to the familiar concept of comparative costs: labour-intensive assembly takes place where labour is cheap – that is, in developing countries – and the design phase takes place where there is plenty of technological know-how, while the production phase is most likely to be located where the raw materials are readily obtainable. The product life cycle theory presented in Chapter 4 develops this idea further.

3.4.2 External economies of scale

External economies of scale arise if a company gains a cost advantage through the nature and size of its immediate industrial environment; therefore, these advantages have no relation to the volume of its own production.

If a large number of firms in one industry are geographically concentrated in a cluster of businesses, they can generate economies of scale from:

o a good infrastructure,
o a pool of well-trained employees, and
o easy access to suppliers and various services.

It is difficult to predict where situations that cause external economies of scale will occur. For example, why is it that a watch industry is located in Switzerland and why are clusters of semiconductor companies found in Silicon Valley, California? It seems that the country or region where the industry is first established develops an advantage over other countries or regions. External economies of scale cause this advantage to become so significant that it is very difficult for other areas to catch up (see Box 3.3).

Box 3.3   An example of external economies of scale

Both Japan and Thailand can produce calculators. Let us assume that external economies of scale apply to calculator production and that this production takes place under conditions of perfect competition, making the price equal to the average cost (perfect competition assumes the overall absence of any monopoly profit – that is, extra profit beyond the usual margin). The economies of scale cause the aggregate average cost curve to fall.

Japan is the first to set up a calculator industry. Initially, the calculators cost an average of 10,000 units. As demand exceeds supply (see Table 3.5), the supply of calculators will be increased. This may determine each company to produce more in order to benefit from internal economies of scale. It may also encourage other firms to set up factories in the neighbourhood of the company that had begun producing calculators, which will lead to external economies of scale, causing average costs to fall. This process continues as long as there is excess demand from the market and, as is evident from the table, will result in Japan producing 875,000 calculators at an average cost of 250 units each.

Table 3.5 Economies of scale in Japan and Thailand – an example

Japan			Thailand		
Number (× 1000)	Average costs = price	Global demand (× 1000)	Number (× 1000)	Average costs = price	Global demand (× 1000)
1	10,000	1.5	1	6000	3
2	5000	4	2	3000	6
400	1000	700	600	250	875
875	250	875	1000	100	1000

If at that stage another supplier, Thailand, wants to penetrate the market, the only way to do so is by starting production immediately at a massive scale of at least 600,000 units. Because, according to the table, it is only if production exceeds 600,000 units that Thailand can undercut Japan's unit production costs for 875,000 calculators (we assume that the average cost curves for both countries are decreasing). Obviously, such an abrupt expansion could prove far riskier for Thailand than a gradual expansion. Nevertheless, if the industry were to be transferred in this way, then with respect to the size of the market it is clear that Japan will lose its remaining production to Thailand, which produces at a cheaper price and will eventually produce 1,000,000 units at a price of only 100.

3.4.3 Product differentiation

Apart from the criticism of traditional trade theory based on the argument that comparative cost advantages are often less important than economies of scale in determining the patterns of specialization, a second major stream of publications emerged that discuss the characteristics of international trade, which also threatened the basis of traditional trade theory.

These new studies pointed out that a substantial part of production for the international market does not take place in a market with perfect competition, as assumed by traditional trade theory. Attention was drawn to the fact that many sub-markets are controlled by international oligopolies where a small number of companies, often multinationals, operate in the various sub-markets. (As indicated earlier, internal economies of scale are already causing markets to deviate from perfect competition.) These publications also drew attention to factors such as technological advantage, price leadership and market entry barriers. All these factors have led to a complex analysis of how and why international trade exists. We shall discuss this in greater depth in the following chapters.

The literature has also pointed out that even if the number of suppliers on the international market is fairly large (as in, for example, the cosmetics or beer industries), producers still try to convince the consumer that their product is unique. This form of market is known as monopolistic competition: one in which consumers regard products from the different sources as comparable but not the same.

With the recognition of individual consumer preferences, as expressed in demand behaviour, there is more scope for firms to specialize and export varieties of a particular product. Moreover, the producer can choose from a wide range of instruments to try and strengthen its international market position. It was not until the 1970s that economists began to develop models from an industrial organization's point of view. These were based on market forms with imperfect competition as opposed to the classical trade theories which tended to assume that perfect competition was the norm.

3.4.3.1 Monopolistic competition

Monopolistic competition exists if many suppliers have access to the market (competition), but every supplier creates its own sub-market through product variety (monopolistic). In this situation there is a general assumption that internal economies of scale are present, so that the average costs per unit of product will fall and the entrepreneur can make a profit.

As soon as other entrepreneurs discover this profit opportunity, they will enter the market and profits will decline, stabilizing at a certain level. However, the new entrepreneurs will enter the market with slightly differentiated products, which provides every entrepreneur with a certain amount of monopoly power within their own sub-market or segment. The monopolist assumes that there are so many suppliers that his prices do not influence those of his competitors (although the competitors' prices do, of course, influence the price–sales curve of the supplier).

If such a market form exists and if international trade takes place, the resulting expansion in the market will lead to the advantages of larger-scale production and to increasing product differentiation; if the same quantity of production resources is used, consumers will have greater choice while at the same time the average cost per unit of product will have fallen.

3.4.3.2 Oligopoly

In contrast to what was assumed with regard to monopolistic competition, in reality producers who do not have a total monopoly will often take account of their competitors' behaviour. The market form in which the number of suppliers is small enough that they are noticeably influenced by and responsive to one another's actions and reactions is known as *oligopoly*.

The application of oligopoly models in international trade is a complex matter; oligopolists react to one another and we therefore need to know something about the specific competitive behavioural patterns in order to determine pricing and supply behaviour in particular circumstances, together with the possible market outcomes. Those patterns are often hard to predict; sometimes the reactions of competing companies can be so different that almost any price–supply combination is possible. Moreover, oligopolists may or may not cooperate with one another, either formally (for example, through a cartel) or informally (for example, through market information systems, or market division agreements). Although cartels are often prohibited, evidence of informal (tacit) cooperation is very hard to find. Chapter 7, which examines the implications of trade policy, will discuss the oligopolistic market form in more detail.

3.4.4 Importance of national location factors and the Porter analysis

Many analysts still believe that national location factors continue to play a substantial role in determining the level of international competitiveness. This idea continues to form the basis of the *World Competitiveness Report*, published annually by the IMEDE management institute and the World Economic Forum in Geneva. On the basis of approximately 300 indicators (derived partly from business surveys) that are grouped into ten main categories, this report determines the relative competitiveness of more than 30 industrial and industrializing countries.

Another example of international competitiveness analysis is published by the Centre for International Competitiveness (see Figure 3.5). This analysis examines how 27 European countries perform in terms of competitiveness by conducting an analysis of 42 indicators – chief amongst them GDP per capita, labour productivity and activity rate. Each

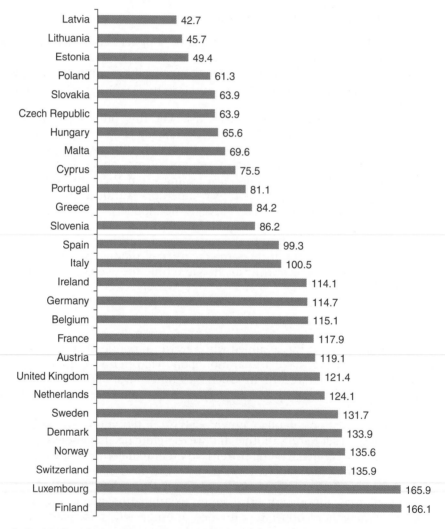

Figure 3.5 National European Competitiveness Index, 2006–7
Source: Centre for International Competitiveness (http://www.cforic.org/downloads.php.)

aspect is scored separately and the most competitive country is the one with the highest (not weighted) overall summation.

3.4.4.1 The Porter analysis

The idea that a combination of production location and business organization factors typically determine whether or not an industry is internationally competitive is also found in the Porter approach, named after its originator, Michael Porter.

Using a large team of researchers, Porter (1990) examined ten industrial countries (Denmark, Germany, Italy, Japan, Korea, Singapore, Sweden, Switzerland, the UK, and the USA) whose industries registered positive results in exports or foreign investment activities during the period 1971 to 1985.

He then examined the circumstances and factors that lay behind these successes. One significant result of this comprehensive study was that country characteristics of the business locations – such as a country's scope for innovation and the continuous modernization of its production facilities – still have a decisive role to play in determining levels of competitiveness. Each country has specific characteristics and structures, making it particularly suited to one type of production rather than another. However, according to Porter, this suitability is based on a much more complex set of determinants than the relative factor costs suggested by traditional trade theory.

In Porter's view, the system of factors determining a country's competitiveness can be represented in the shape of a diamond. The cluster of companies whose production best matches the specific characteristics and structures of the country of location will not only enjoy international success but will also continue to innovate generally, and thus remain strong competitors on the international market.

According to Porter's diamond, the national economic environment for the entrepreneur is determined separately and jointly by four groups of national characteristics:

o the availability and quality of the factors of production;
o the dynamics and quality, and, to a lesser extent, the level of domestic demand;
o the presence of related or supporting industries which are also internationally competitive suppliers and affiliated companies; and
o the circumstances in the country which influence the establishment, organization and management of businesses as well as the nature of domestic conditions of competition business strategy, market structure and competition.

These four types of characteristics were all present, to varying extents, in the theories discussed earlier:

o In both the HOS model and the Ricardian model, the available factors of production played a part in explaining international trade.
o The presence of suppliers and related industries is the most important factor in external economies of scale.
o The nature of demand plays a role in some other theories explaining international patterns of specialization (not discussed in this book).
o The theory regarding market structure and product differentiation is linked to business strategies, the structure of the sector and domestic conditions of competition.

3.4.4.2 The availability and quality of factors of production

Porter divides the factors of production into two groups:

1. The natural or 'inherited' factors such as labour, land, capital, infrastructure, and natural resources.
2. The 'created' factors of production often found in advanced economies: these include human capital, infrastructure and research capacity.

According to Porter, the successful industries are not those that make intensive use of abundant national production factors (as in the HOS model), but those principally using the available 'created' factors of production.

This philosophy also applies to regions or countries: if countries/regions typically benefit from natural factors of production, this is probably favourable from a cost perspective; in the long term, however, the incentives to innovate may be lost, so that the comparative advantage disappears. For this reason it is important to create new factors of production. Indeed, a country's lack of competitiveness can eventually be turned around if it invests more in 'created' factors of production and starts to innovate.

3.4.4.3 Consumer preferences

Consumer preference/demand is important as an incentive for businesses to innovate and to obtain advanced knowledge and competitive advantage. In contrast to traditional trade theories, in this theory the nature of demand is more important than its volume. Demand factors have an important positive influence on competitiveness, particularly if:

o consumer preferences are known to the industry;
o consumers are critical and constantly force entrepreneurs to innovate and make quality adjustments; and
o if national consumers' preferences anticipate global demand.

3.4.4.4 Suppliers and related industries

If an industry has an extensive network of internationally competitive suppliers and a strong domestic business network, it will be able to enjoy significant competitive advantages. Suppliers can give their domestic customers ready access to new information, new ideas, and new understanding and innovations. In short, external economies of scale are apparent. Also of specific importance here is the fact that the suppliers are internationally competitive and make use of short lines of communication.

3.4.4.5 Business strategy, structure and competition

The way in which businesses are established, organized and managed is influenced largely by national habits, standards and values.

Countries also differ in terms of the objectives set by businesses and individuals. These objectives are important in matters such as motivating talented people to make an effort at work, the level and nature of education chosen by employees, the willingness to travel, and so on. The objectives set by employees, coupled with the prestige attached to certain industries at a national level, partly determine the direction of capital flows and of human resources in that country, which, in turn, influence the competitiveness of those industries.

The presence of local competition is the last – and also the most important – factor in the diamond. One important example of this can be found in Switzerland, where competition between pharmaceutical companies such as Hoffmann-La Roche, Ciba-Geigy and Sandoz has resulted in a leading world market position in spite of the relatively small Swiss domestic market. Often it is aggressive domestic competition that causes businesses to turn to foreign markets; this is particularly true of those industries in which large economies of scale are involved.

3.4.4.6 The diamond as a system

The greater the stimulus provided by the various facets of this national environment, including the interaction between companies, the more this will contribute to the success of the clusters of companies located there. Porter identifies two factors as the most important in the integration of all four characteristics into a system which provides a good business climate:

1. the presence of domestic competition
2. the clustering of similar business activities in a particular area

In practice, these two factors seem to act as a strong catalyst for the vitality of businesses.

As far as policy is concerned, one of the consequences of this approach is that there is a role for national government in respect of the national business climate.

Until the 1990s, the partnership between business and government in Japan was often seen as an example of successful government and businesses achieving more effective collaboration than in other industrialized countries. Although significant direct government involvement in the business world is inappropriate according to Porter's approach (except perhaps in the case of countries that are at an early stage of development), total uninvolvement is also undesirable.

The government can perform an important function in stimulating innovation and should create a climate in which entrepreneurs are challenged to improve their performance. This implies a policy of creating and maintaining the right market conditions – in the form of stimulating educational activities, imposing clear and predictable rules and standards, ensuring transparency in regard to competition, stimulating investment in innovation, and promoting flexibility on the labour and capital markets.

3.4.4.7 An application of the Porter approach

The Porter approach can be used to analyse the strengths and weaknesses of a country. In one instance, it was applied to the Netherlands in the second half of the 1980s. Eleven sectors, representing 15 per cent of total exports, were selected on the basis of their international competitiveness. These were further grouped into four clusters:

o agriculture and food: cut flowers, cocoa powder and butter, dairy products and dairy industry machinery;
o chemical: plastics and polymers, industrial textiles;
o electrical engineering: recorded sound media, copying machines; and
o transport: road haulage, lorries, yacht building.

It seemed that the success of these sectors had a lot to do with the presence of the research and knowledge infrastructure and a strong mutual rivalry that did not preclude cooperation in order to achieve certain economies of scale.

It also became apparent that the success of certain sectors could be explained by the combination of:

o small-scale elements (business instinct, improvisational talent and service);
o a traditional approach to business;
o the existence of a national network; and
o a high level of technological development.

Thus, the result was broadly in line with Porter's more general findings.

3.5 | Summary

1. This chapter focused on the origins and nature of trade between countries. Traditional theories have suggested that international trade is based on comparative cost advantages, usually based on the assumption of constant economies of scale and the market form of perfect competition.
2. The foundation for these theories was laid by David Ricardo, and can be illustrated by using a model comprising two countries, two products and one factor of production (labour). If both countries concentrate on exporting the product in which they have a comparative cost advantage (that is, the one with lower production costs, relative to the same product in the other country), both countries will benefit from trade.
3. Later, Heckscher and Ohlin extended the Ricardian model by adding a second factor of production: capital. They also imposed an additional limitation by assuming that for each product the available production technology is the same internationally. They conclude that a country has a comparative advantage in the product that makes intensive use of the production factor that is abundant in that country. The welfare of the owners of these production factors will increase as a result of international trade, while – unless some active income redistribution takes place – the welfare of the owners of the relatively scarce factors of production will decline. Overall, the national welfare of each country still increases in this model through specialization and international trade; but the theoretical basis of the model was undermined, in particular, by the phenomenon of factor reversal (this implies that the same goods are produced in a relatively capital-intensive manner in one country, but in a relatively labour-intensive manner in the other).
4. New trade theories are no longer based on the idea that a country's exports and imports are determined mainly by location circumstances specific to the country. In these theories, characteristics specific to certain sectors or companies are decisive in explaining a country's export structure. Economies of scale, product differentiation and different market forms play a major role in the theory of trade and specialization.
5. The Porter analysis combines various elements of different trade theories, and tries to establish a framework that can describe export successes. It does return in some way to the concept of comparative cost advantage between countries. Although local conditions are combined with the characteristics that a business must satisfy in order to compete internationally, national circumstances are still considered decisive.
6. Finally, the rise of multinational corporations has also necessitated some adjustments to trade theory. It is now suggested that international trade takes place not only via

the export and import of goods, but also via the transfer of factors of production across borders. In the next chapter, the analysis will shift from 'why countries export certain goods' to 'why businesses operate internationally'.

Questions

1. What fundamental concepts can be used to argue that international trade is not a zero-sum game?
2. What main national location factors in the country or region where you live could be utilized to its competitive advantage?
3. Considering the 2008–10 economic crisis and China's relative success in dealing with its effects, what do you think are the main lessons that western economies can learn from the high level of competitiveness of the Chinese economy?

CHAPTER 4

International Production Factors, Foreign Direct Investment and the Multinational Enterprise

4.1 | Introduction

The international trade in goods and services is a form of indirect international transfer of factors of production. One of the essential assumptions of the comparative cost theories discussed in Chapter 3 was that factors of production can move freely between companies and even between sectors within a country, but that they cannot cross national borders.

As the international mobility of goods is shown to promote economic growth and welfare, it is likely that production factors may also become incentivized to move internationally. In fact, as will be shown in Section 4.3, there are numerous similarities between the impact of international trade and international factor mobility on economic welfare, of which the most frequently discussed are the distributive effects of international factor mobility (see Section 4.4).

The statistical material presented in Chapter 2 and in this chapter, show that international economic theories can no longer ignore the mobility of factors of production. This mobility applies not only to labour and entrepreneurship, but also – and increasingly – to capital. As a result of international capital mobility, countries can borrow and lend from each other because of their different time preferences.

Section 4.5 introduces the phenomenon of international capital mobility and discusses international capital flows by considering them as inter-temporal trade. (The import of capital/goods at one point in time versus the promise to export equivalent capital/goods in return at a future time.) One important distinction with regard to long-term international capital flows is between portfolio investment (the prime motive of which is return), and foreign direct investment (FDI, which aims to achieve control over foreign activities; the latter will be discussed in more detail in Section 4.6. As FDI is the key characteristic of multinational enterprises (MNEs), the chapter will end with a discussion of the general characteristics of MNEs (Section 4.7), and some theories that try to account for the existence of MNEs (Section 4.8).

4.2   The motor vehicle sector: a case study

Case study 4.1 focuses on the motor vehicle industry, which is characterized by international business management and fierce levels of competition. The study focuses on the period from the 1980s to the first half of the 1990s, mainly because of the major shifts in international market shares at the time.

The study describes how competition in this sector was first characterized by a rapid increase in the supply of Japanese cars to the American market. Japanese car exports to the USA and Europe were then increasingly replaced by the establishment of Japanese car production facilities in the USA.

Case study 4.1   From car exports to the export of car production facilities

The motor vehicle sector has always experienced fierce international competition. In the 1980s and 1990s the strongly competitive Japanese carmakers saw their share of international markets increasing rapidly. For example, in the USA the market share of Nissan, Honda and Toyota, which stood at 16.5 per cent in 1980, had risen to 23.5 per cent by 1990.

In the first half of the 1980s the American car industry went into decline – something which US manufacturers blamed on unfair competition from Japanese manufacturers. In response, the USA introduced substantial protectionist measures. From 1981 onwards these took the form of 'voluntary' export restraints by Japan under pressure from the USA. These 'voluntary' export restrictions were preceded by an American appeal to the GATT safeguard clause, art. XIX, presumably to exert pressure on Japan to limit exports. As a result, the Japanese share of the American car market fell from 22.6 per cent in 1982 to 18.3 per cent in 1984.

Between 1983 and 1985, there was increased demand for passenger cars in the USA and the financial situation of the US car sector improved. The USA initially planned to end the 'voluntary' export restrictions on Japanese cars in 1985, but later they renounced the idea. The Japanese government retaliated by increasing the number of cars exported. The Japanese share of the US market rose to 20.1 per cent in 1985 and 20.7 per cent in 1986.

Partly in response to the maintenance of the 'voluntary' export restriction on Japanese cars and the fall in the value of the dollar in the first half of the 1980s, Japanese car exports were increasingly replaced by the establishment of Japanese production facilities in the USA, often on a joint-venture basis. The same phenomenon occurred in the EU.

Thus, increasing numbers of Japanese car plants were set up in the USA through FDI. While Ford, Chrysler and General Motors (GM) were closing plants in the USA, Toyota, Nissan and Mitsubishi decided to establish new operations. By 1986, Japanese production facilities already accounted for 5 per cent of US passenger car output. Over the next few years, Japanese production in the American market expanded still further, exceeding 10 per cent per annum (some 1.4 million units) in 1989. By 2000, the share of Japanese car manufacturers in the US market had risen to 25 per cent – the highest ever figure.

In response to the rise of Japanese car sales in the USA, the American industry took a series of initiatives: for example, in the 1980s GM attempted to launch an entirely new car brand. From the early 1990s the USA seemed to regain some of its competitiveness, partly due to a sharp decline in the value of the dollar.

This recovery was also helped by an increase in product quality. GM received 740 complaints per 100 cars in 1981, but the figure had been cut to 168 by 1989. By way of comparison, the number of complaints relating to Japanese cars fell from 188 to 121 over the same period.

In spite of the improvements in the quality of American cars, US producers found it difficult to push their Japanese competitors out of the market. In the period 1989 to 1990, the J.D. Power Customer Satisfaction Survey listed only two American brands in the top ten. In another survey, the three Japanese models manufactured by Toyota – the Camry, Corolla and Cressida – were labelled the best cars in their class. Furthermore, for two successive years, the Honda Accord was the best-selling car in the USA. Moreover, all new Ford and GM models were traditional 'gas-guzzlers', using at least a litre of petrol for every ten kilometres.

In a further development, as the result of close cooperation with the Japanese production facilities, Detroit's Big Three companies (General Motors, Chrysler and Ford) were able to learn a great deal about Japanese production methods and this greatly increased the efficiency of their production.

Although the Americans had been producing cars more efficiently, in the 1990s they were slow to catch up with the Japanese in terms of competitiveness. At the beginning of the 1990s, Japanese plants in the USA took between 13 and 27 man-hours to produce a car, GM between 25 and 30 hours, Ford an average of 20 hours and Chrysler 25.

The market share held by traditional American car manufacturers continued to fall. In July 2007 the sales of foreign brands exceeded those of domestic car brands for the first time. According to the statistical institute Autodata Corporation, in this month the 'Big Three' – the Chrysler Group, General Motors and the Ford Motor Company – held 48.1 per cent of the market while foreign car companies had 51.9 per cent.

In 2008, however, market share was no longer the main concern of American carmakers. The once-mighty US car industry had been contracting for several years, but when the financial crisis hit and loans that had been used to finance the purchase of new cars dried up, the Big Three began to experience severe problems. While Ford and General Motors reported substantial losses of $15.5 billion and $8.7 billion in the second quarter, respectively, Chrysler refused to reveal any information about its financial standing.

Under pressure from a mounting debt of tens of billions of dollars, on 1 June 2009, General Motors was forced to file for Chapter 11 Bankruptcy. The company had to undergo restructuring, its bankruptcy manoeuvre adding an additional cost of $50 billion to the $15 billion already paid by the US Government in bailout relief for 60 per cent ownership.

Case study 4.1 shows that internationalization can also take place through the international mobility of factors of production – in this instance, entrepreneurship and capital. It suggests that the export of Japanese cars is based in part on the comparative advantage achieved through higher labour productivity. There were also differences between carmakers in terms of the quality and speed of innovation of Japanese and American production.

The situation in the motor vehicle sector highlights several aspects of the theories described in earlier chapters:

o comparative advantages and productivity of labour (Ricardo);
o innovation, demand and market structure (Porter); and
o the theory of internal economies of scale.

However, the case study also raises a number of questions, which will be discussed in this chapter as well as in Chapter 5:

o Why were increasing numbers of Japanese carmakers establishing production facilities in the USA and Europe during this period?
o To what extent was the international mobility of Japanese carmakers a unique phenomenon?
o To what extent were the production facilities a substitute for or an extension of car exports?
o Were the Japanese carmakers multinational enterprises?
o Were there incentives, other than seeking an increase in their market share, which prompted companies to invest abroad?
o What were the consequences of the international mobility of the factors of production for the welfare of the countries concerned?

4.3 Similarities in international trade and international factor mobility

First, we will compare the international mobility of production factors with the international trade in goods and services. In practice, the strict distinction between the international transfer of goods and services and that of factors of production is an increasingly artificial one for the following reasons:

(i) A large part of international trade consists of raw materials and semi-manufactured goods; these products can be regarded simultaneously as both outputs (obtained with the help of production factors), and inputs (which contribute to the making of the end product).
(ii) International trade accounts for about one-fifth of the total trade in services. However, it is not always easy to make a distinction between the transfer of human capital and the provision of final services.
(iii) International technology transfer is taking place on a large scale, with know-how being made available by licensing contracts granted to other countries; this cannot be regarded as either international trade or the international transfer of factors of production; however, it does offer a significant advantage to the parties involved.

It is easy to see that as far as the impact on welfare, factor prices and income distribution is concerned there are a number of clear similarities between the effects of international mobility of goods and services (international trade) on the one hand, and the international mobility of factors of production (international factor mobility), on the other hand.

First, both movements contribute to increases in welfare. We discussed the welfare consequences of international trade in Chapter 3. It is clear that the international movement of factors of production can increase the overall levels of welfare if we assume that the two production factors – labour and capital – are rewarded according to their contribution to production.

More specifically, in theory it is often assumed that labour and capital are rewarded according to their marginal productivity – that is, the extra production generated by an extra unit of a production factor, while keeping the amount of the other production factors constant.

This is due to the fact that marginal productivity declines by adding more units of a specific production factor while the other production factor increasingly puts a limit on the additional output. Also assume that the marginal remuneration per unit of production factor is known, that is, the wage that needs to be paid to hire an extra worker for one day's labour input is known.

How much labour will be hired by the producer? Rationally, the producer should continue to extend the labour force until the marginal productivity is equal to the wage rate. This is because as long as the marginal productivity is greater than the wage rate, every extra additional unit of labour input increases overall profits because its marginal productivity is higher than the wage payment.

It is reasonable to assume that production factors will only move abroad if they receive a higher reward for doing so. Imagine, for example, a substantial migration of labour from Poland to Germany. How will this change the marginal productivity of labour in the two countries?

In Poland less labour will be available, therefore – assuming a declining marginal productivity function – the marginal productivity of labour will increase, and so will the wage rates in that country. More generally, labour would have become less abundant, and therefore more expensive.

The opposite will occur in Germany, where there will be a decline in both the marginal productivity of labour and the wage rate. As a result, there will be an increase in the combined overall production in the two countries because the recently migrated labour force makes a higher contribution to overall production in Germany than it used to make in Poland. One simple explanation is that the amount of capital available per labourer is greater in Germany than in Poland, so that their overall production in Germany can be higher.

Economic theory predicts that the international migration of labour has the following consequences:

1. The level of overall production increases, so that there is room for an overall increase in welfare in both countries, provided that the increase in welfare is redistributed properly.
2. The wage rate will increase in Poland, so that the remaining labour can take advantage of their increased relative scarcity.
3. In Germany, the opposite is true: the wage rate declines, so the traditional labour force in Germany is faced with lower wages as a result of the inflow of Polish labourers.
4. The reward for a unit of capital is also affected, since the marginal productivity of capital declines when the amount of labour per unit of capital decreases. This is exactly what happens in Poland because of the emigration of labour, and the owners of capital suffer from the labour outflow.
5. Here again the reverse is true for Germany, where the marginal productivity of capital can benefit from the inflow of additional labour.

These outcomes, predicted by theory, are in line with reality; they might explain why labour unions and employers quite often take different positions in debates on the freedom of international labour migration.

As argued before, international factor mobility is considered to be rooted in the desire of the owners of the production factors to receive a higher reward. As a result, the expected income differential between host and source countries is generally thought of as an important incentive to migrate.

Table 4.1 Per capita income in source relative to host countries (current PPP$, 2008)

Host country	Inflows of foreign population into selected OECD countries	Ratio of source country GDP/capita to host country GDP/capita	Main source country	Host country gdp/capita PPP	Source country gdp/capita PPP$
	Thousands				
United States	1107.1	0.299790356	Mexico	47,700	14,300
Germany	573.8	0.490250696	Poland	35,900	17,600
Japan	344.5	0.177325581	China	34,400	6100
United Kingdom	456	1.089918256	Australia	36,700	40,000
Canada	247.2	0.15443038	China	39,500	6100
Italy	252.4	0.39047619	Romania	31,500	12,300
France	136	0.208333333	Algeria	33,600	7000

*The majority of inmigrants into the UK in 2006 originated from Australia, which in that year had a higher GDP/capita than the UK.
Sources: *International Migration Outlook* (Sopemi, 2009 edn), pp. 44, 295; CIA World Factbook 2009.

Table 4.1 shows that for the major host countries, with the exception of the United Kingdom, average annual per capita income in the source countries in 2008 was less than half of the corresponding level of the host countries. This shows that there can be significant wage incentives to migrate abroad.

Another major implication of the international mobility of labour and capital is that it eventually leads to the international equalization of factor prices. Once again, this result is based on the theory that where there is a decline in the availability of a production factor, its factor price will increase and vice versa.

In theory, if international differences in such rewards stimulate international factor mobility, such mobility will continue up to a point of complete *factor price equalization* (FPE) – that is, when there are identical factor prices in both countries. Here, too, we have an analogy with international trade.

Recall that one of the curious results that were derived from the HOS model in the preceding chapter was that in a general free trade equilibrium situation, factor prices are internationally equal, even if these factors are not internationally mobile. So, according to this model, international trade has the same levelling effect on factor prices than when production factors are internationally mobile and constantly seeking the location with the highest return.

Third, as in the case of international trade, the issue of the impact on income distribution is also crucial in international factor mobility. Which groups will be better off when capital and labour leave or enter a country, and what can we say about the consequences for the distribution of welfare between the countries concerned?

Public debate focuses closely on this type of question, as can be seen from these examples:

o Let us assume that Japanese capital flows to the USA and Japanese firms buy American companies and real estate: is such a development favourable or threatening to the USA?

    ○ Assuming an increase in the flow of immigrant workers and asylum-seekers from Africa and Asia to the EU: is this a threat to the jobs of other people in Europe, and how does it affect the levels of wages and profits?

What are the factors that determine whether or not migration is indeed beneficial and which country stands to gain/lose more from the increased mobility of labour? These distribution aspects will be discussed briefly in the following section.

4.4 International factor mobility and the question of distribution

In the real world, it is difficult to make an unequivocal statement concerning the distribution of international factor mobility.

A first complication is that a production factor such as labour is relatively heterogeneous. If, for example, an untrained Kenyan worker and a Vietnamese software expert both emigrate to France, should they be regarded as equals in economic terms? The answer can only be 'yes' if labour is assumed to be homogeneous. However, in this instance there is a huge difference in terms of human capital.

Let us take a second example: a Canadian investor buys Belgian Treasury bills worth $1 million. At the same time, a Canadian company makes a direct investment in Belgium for the same amount by bringing in a new technology developed in Canada, and applying it very successfully in the Belgian market.

In both cases the financial flow is the same, but there will be very different effects in terms of the transfer of technology. This simple example shows that it is not easy to find a good basis for comparing different types of the same production factor.

A second complication is that changes to one market in a country always have repercussions for other markets because of economic interrelationships. Thus, if the available amount of labour in a country declines suddenly as a result of emigration, there will be an adjustment in the production process. This, in turn, affects the level of production, the prices of goods and services, the prices of other production factors, and so on.

You will recall that this interdependency between product and factor markets was one of the central elements of the HOS model. Thus, we need to understand every relevant economic interrelation within the economy in order to grasp fully the overall impact of the emigration effect. Such a level of understanding is not easy to find.

A third complication is that much of the impact of international factor mobility will depend on how much of the income earned abroad is then remitted to the home countries by migrant workers: the available statistics would suggest that, on average, migrant workers send at least 10 to 15 per cent of their earnings back to their country of origin. To illustrate to what degree remittances vary across receiving countries, Figure 4.1 shows the 2008/9 figures for the top receivers and senders of remittances. According to the World Bank, following several years of significant growth the remittance flows to developing countries began to fall in the third quarter of 2008. Furthermore, this slowdown is expected to intensify in 2009 on account of the global financial crisis. In nominal dollars the remittance flows to developing countries had reached $315 billion in 2009. However, in many corridors, remittance has slowed down since the last quarter of

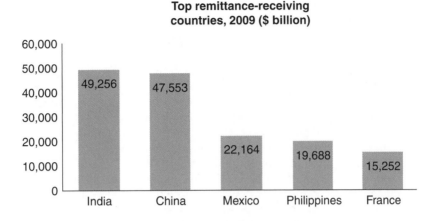

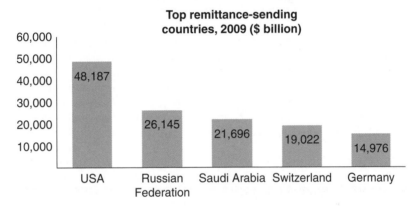

Figure 4.1   Top remittance-receiving and remittance-sending countries, 2009
Source: Development Prospect Groups, World Bank.

2008. (This amount still disregards unregistered transfers, which are also possibly quite significant.)

A fourth, ethical complication concerns the decision to accept the presence of foreign labour in an economy, a decision that is obviously highly dependent on the prevailing economic circumstances at any particular time.

Let us assume that a country is experiencing rapid economic growth, but that future growth is being inhibited by a shortage of labour, which could be solved by an inflow of foreign workers.

However, it could be that some years later the same country faces the opposite economic situation: unemployment and the under-utilization of its production capacity. At this point it would be economically desirable to have immigrant workers leave the country.

The political debate over whether or not such policies are feasible or socially acceptable is inhibiting the development of such policies. Recent structural shifts in OECD economies towards the production of more 'knowledge-intensive' output have raised the demand for skilled labour. This has resulted in a number of OECD countries adapting their legislation in order to facilitate the entry of skilled workers. Such changes often also turn out to be politically sensitive (see Case study 4.2).

Case study 4.2   The impact of Eastern Europeans on the labour market: the case of Poles in Ireland

According to Polish diplomats, several thousand Poles were living in Ireland at the end of 2004, including some 200 immigrants who had been present since the Second World War. According to consular statistics, by 2007 Ireland was playing host to over a quarter of a million Poles – an inflow of labour that has had a considerable impact on the development of the economy. (The number of Polish immigrants has, of course, dropped significantly during the economic crisis of recent years.)

This abrupt change was brought about by two major factors. The first was the economic boom that began in the 1990s. The second factor was Ireland's enlightened decision to open up its labour market to workers from the eight East European countries when they joined the European Union in May 2004. Ireland was one of the few countries from the old EU 15 (the other two being the UK and Sweden) to open its labour market to the new member states from day one. Evidence proves that Ireland's openness was richly rewarded at the time as its 'Celtic Tiger' economy continued to boom.

By 2008 immigrants accounted for just over 15 per cent of Ireland's population. The new foreign workforce played a critical role in restraining wages, even as unemployment rates dropped to historical lows of under 4 per cent. They also stimulated domestic demand, thereby contributing to a considerable housing bubble.

To Ireland's credit, society has accepted these changes quite well with no notable anti-immigration movements. It is also true that, as pointed out by *The Economist*, Poles are fair-skinned, family-loving Roman Catholic north Europeans, who do not test Irish prejudices.

At the start of 2011, Ireland was facing its deepest recession in 20 years. Unemployment rates had risen to more than 12 per cent and it seemed likely that this phenomenon would continue as quarterly figures indicate the first annual dropf in employment since 1991.

Under these tough circumstances a significant number of Poles have already left Ireland to return home where abundant EU regional aid is available for investing and building infrastructure. Furthermore, Poland needs to build football stadiums for the European Football Championship which it will co-host with the Ukraine in 2012.

The ESRI Research Institute forecasted that by April 2010 more than 30,000 immigrants would have left Ireland. If this happens, the unemployment rate will drop by about 1.5 per cent as a direct consequence of emigrating workers. Admittedly, those departing would take their spending power with them but, on balance, this could set a precedent where unemployment is ameliorated by foreigners leaving the country – yet another reward for the open labour market policy.

One example of a potentially unfavourable case of international factor mobility arises when labour and/or capital or even entrepreneurs leave a country en masse and unexpectedly, as might occur during times of war or political insecurity.

Such movements can have substantial economic repercussions, as have occasionally been experienced by various (mainly developing) countries over the years. A lasting and continuous outflow of labour, even on a smaller scale, could also have a seriously disruptive effect on the economy.

For example, the tendency of highly skilled labour in developing countries to leave their home country for better prospects in industrialized countries is frequently referred to as a 'brain drain', reflecting its probable damaging effect. Obviously, the significance of this for a particular country depends mainly on two things: (i) whether or not the emigrants decide to settle permanently in their new country or whether they will eventually return to their country of origin; and (ii) their remittances to family and friends in their home country.

4.5 Inter-temporal trade

When discussing the international mobility of capital, we usually refer to financial capital rather than to physical capital or capital goods.

In itself, financial capital is not a production factor; it only becomes one when it is used to finance an investment and contributes to the creation of physical capital and (additional) production capacity. Clearly financial capital, which is usually transferred electronically, is much easier to transfer internationally than commodities, services or production factors. This explains why international financial capital flows are so enormous, and volatile, especially in the short term. In the long term, the international mobility of financial capital can have a considerable effect on a country's ability to expand its capital stock. Furthermore, in the context of an open international economy, national capital market conditions such as domestic interest rates will be subject to the influence of international financial capital flows.

In the case of net foreign inflows there is no one-to-one correspondence between the availability of that capital and the creation of extra capital goods. Any statistical information about the flows of foreign direct investment and other forms of financial capital (international credit, loans and gifts) can therefore only provide a very rough indication of how it may affect the stock of capital goods in the countries concerned. It is often unclear whether the net inflow of foreign capital causes extra production of capital goods or vice versa.

At the conceptual level, the international mobility of (financial) capital, or international credit, can be interpreted as an exchange between countries in which the possibility of immediate consumption is exchanged for the possibility of greater consumption in the future. This is termed inter-temporal trade and can be explained as follows.

If country A lends money to country B, country B can use that money to buy consumer goods on that day. By contrast, country A has postponed present consumption and will be unable to use this money for consumption until country B repays the loan (with interest).

As far as the inter-temporal aspect is concerned, international credit can be compared with individual borrowing and lending: if a person borrows money from the bank as a loan, that person is able, at least in theory, to speed up his consumption; in return for this favour, the bank will require that person to pay interest on the loan. This interest can be seen as the price that a borrower has to pay for transferring part of his future consumption to the present. Obviously a country that starts borrowing from abroad will face future obligations to pay back the loan and also to pay interest. To be able to do this, borrowing countries have to use the credit productively so that they are indeed able to meet those future obligations. If they are not, they lose creditworthiness, and, if a country's creditworthiness is substantially called into question, situations such as the debt crisis of the early 1980s or the financial crises of the 1990s can arise.

Later in this book we will discuss the balance of payments – a summary of all transactions of a country with the rest of the world during a specific time interval – in greater detail. However, it can be pointed out here that, if a country is a net borrower over a given period, this usually implies that throughout the same period the country's imports will have surpassed its exports by approximately the amount borrowed. In other words, the current account balance for that period is negative. So, the current account balances of countries provide a clear indication of their flows of net borrowing or lending.

Table 4.2 shows global current account balances for the period 2000–15. One clear development that can be observed was that the $65 billion current account surplus recorded for the European Union in 2004 had turned into a deficit of $47.8 billion by 2009. The most striking development, however, was that the already large US deficit recorded in 2002 grew to $788.2 billion by 2006, but then contracted. The USA is clearly a massive net borrower on the international capital market and the rest of the world acts as its net lender. According to IMF estimates, by 2015 the current account deficit of the European Union will have dropped to around $200 million while the deficit of the USA will have again increased – to about $601 billion.

If an economy has a negative balance on its current accounts over a substantial period, the nation can be considered a *debtor country*. Most non-oil-producing developing countries are debtor countries, whereas most industrialized countries show a cumulative current account surplus and are termed *creditor countries*. One clear exception in that regard is the United States which, after having shown significant current account deficits for more than 15 years, has (according to most definitions) become a debtor country.

At this point the question arises of how to explain, in economic terms, why one country can be characterized by a debtor position and another by a creditor position. Or, in other words, why does one country seem to show almost systematic current account deficits and another surpluses?

One way of explaining inter-temporal trade is by considering differences in the *time preferences* of countries. Time preference implies the favouring of immediate expenditure of the available income over postponing the spending. The degree to which one demonstrates such time preference may differ between countries. In the case of a small oil-producing economy faced by rapidly increasing oil prices, the time preference would generally be low. This is the case because there is no point in expending the excess funds at once; in that case the country will display a current account surplus which it can lend abroad.

Most mature industrialized countries are characterized by relatively low time preferences – that is, in these countries there are strong incentives to save for old age, or because the best domestic investment opportunities are considered to have already been exploited.

By contrast, developing countries usually have a relatively high time preference, because they cannot afford the luxury of postponed consumption and, furthermore, they have a young and dynamic population with high demands for consumption. It is clear that a country's high time preference can also be caused either by its government's expansionary/investment policy or by cultural factors. The relatively large-scale use of mortgage-based and consumer credit in the USA can be viewed as an expression of a country's culture of high time preference.

The interest rate represents the return for the postponement of consumption. However, in the absence of international capital flows, countries with a high time preference will tend to have high interest rates, whereas in countries with a low time preference the rates will tend to be low. To sum up:

○ People in a country with a high time preference prefer to spend their income quickly. This means that their demand for consumer goods is high and that they will be prepared to save only if interest rates are high enough. The result is that capital is scarce and only the most profitable investments can be financed.
○ In a country with a low time preference the opposite applies: people are already willing to save at a low interest rate, so it is easier to finance investment projects that have a low prospect of profitability.

Table 4.2 Current account balances in major economic blocs, 2000–15 ($ billion)

	Global current account balances US$ billion										
	2002	2003	2004	2005	2006	2007	2008	2009	2010	2011	2015
Advanced economies	**−217.1**	**−219.3**	**−219.8**	**−409.8**	**−449.9**	**−347.6**	**−528.8**	**−147.3**	**−185.3**	**−220.0**	**−373.7**
United States	−459.1	−521.5	−631.1	−748.7	−803.5	−726.6	−706.1	−418.0	−487.2	−523.9	−638.2
Euro area[1]	47.9	42.9	116.9	45.3	47.6	47.3	−106.0	−43.8	−4.7	13.1	−7.4
Japan	112.6	136.2	172.1	165.7	170.4	211	157.1	141.7	149.7	131.1	113.8
Other advanced economies[2]	81.6	123	122.4	128	135.6	120.7	126.2	172.8	156.9	159.7	158.1
Newly industrialized Asian economies	55.8	80.8	82.9	79.4	89.7	111.7	84.8	142.5	121.3	128.2	152.8
Emerging and developing economies	**80.5**	**149**	**222.3**	**449.7**	**665.6**	**657.9**	**709.2**	**321.7**	**420.1**	**491.1**	**769.1**
Middle East and North Africa*	31.4	63.9	106.2	219.2	286.4	279.2	347.8	34.8	119.1	174	256.7
Central and Estern Europe	−19.3	−32.2	−53.2	−58.5	−87.1	−132.6	−152.1	−37.9	−63.0	−72.4	−99.3
Commonwealth of Independent States[3]	30.3	35.7	63.5	87.5	96.3	71.7	107.5	42.6	78.6	81.4	−4.0
Developing Asia	66.9	85	92.9	167.5	289.2	414.7	424.1	319	349.7	389.9	731.8
Western Hemisphere	−16.2	9.2	21.4	36.7	49.8	14.8	−26.7	−18.6	−47.3	−59.9	−96.2
Sub-Saharan Africa	−12.6	−12.7	−8.5	−2.7	31	10.1	8.6	−18.1	−17.1	−22.0	−20.0
European Union	**18.7**	**17.8**	**65.5**	**−8.3**	**−41.6**	**−69.2**	**−196.1**	**−49.8**	**−34.3**	**−21.1**	**−64.1**

[1] Reflects errors, omissions, and asymmetries in balance of payments statistics on current account, as well as the exclusion of data for international organizations and a

[2] In this table, 'other advanced economies' means advanced economies excluding the United States, Euro area countries, and Japan.

[3] Mongolia, which is not a member of the Commonwealth of Independent States, is included in this group for reasons of geography and similarities in economic structure.

Source: IMF WEO (2010), p. 172.

Table 4.3 Net FDI and portfolio flows in the three major economic areas, 2005–9 ($ billion)

	Curent account balance			Net FDI and portofolio flows			Overall balance		
	2005	2006	2009	2005	2006	2009	2005	2006	2009
USA	−729.0	−788.1	−378.4	−89	−15	−1.2	−818	−803.1	−379.6
EU	46.7	32.9	−77.9	184	140	26.0	230.7	172.9	−51.9
Japan	165.7	170.4	141.8	43	56	61.9	208.7	226.4	203.7

Note: a positive amount is a capital inflow.
Sources: IMF (2010), *World Economic Outlook*, p. 194; UNCTAD (2008) *World Investment Report 2008* and FDISTAT (http://stats. unctad.org/FDI/TableViewer/tableView.aspx). Own calculations.

If we now allow for countries to borrow and lend financial capital internationally, we can approach the international differences in time preference from a different perspective. Under these new conditions, it can be argued that countries with a low interest rate have a comparative advantage in current consumption, and that they will export current consumption by granting loans to (high time preference) countries with a comparative advantage in future consumption (and a higher interest rate). As a consequence, after having introduced the possibility of international credits, financial capital will start flowing from countries where initial interest rates are low to countries where initial interest rates are high. This continuous process will lead to a levelling off of international differences in the scarcity of capital. Thus, the interest rates in different countries will show a tendency to converge, and in the absence of high transaction costs and other obstacles, may ultimately become similar. In other words, if the USA has a high time preference and Japan a low time preference, then – according to this theory – capital will flow systematically from Japan to the USA as long as interest rate differences persist. The data presented in Table 4.3 show the sum of net FDI and long-term portfolio inflows into the main economic blocs for the period 2005–9. They can be interpreted as a reflection of the differences in time preference between the blocs showing the United States' high time preference against the low time preference of Europe and Japan.

4.6 | Foreign direct investment

Through direct investment it is possible for a (national) company to establish overseas production facilities. This will mean that it has production in more than one country and it will have developed itself into a multinational enterprise (MNE). This section will examine what direct investments mean and how this type of capital flow has developed. Section 4.7 specifically discusses the MNE phenomenon, since it is typically MNEs that are responsible for the majority of foreign direct investment activities.

As an example, let us assume that a company with an exclusive selling point – for example, a high-tech device with unique properties developed within the own firm – engages in foreign direct investment. In short, it starts to set up or take over a foreign site in order to start producing its device abroad.

The first question to be asked is: why does the same firm not consider an alternative, such as exporting or licensing agreements, through which it can capitalize on its finding indirectly by exploiting it as an invention?

Various theories focus specifically on the processes that lead to a particular choice between the alternatives just mentioned; the product life cycle theory and the so-called eclectic theory of international entrepreneurial behaviour are just two of those theories, and will be discussed in the final section of this chapter (Section 4.8).

The possibility of transferring capital across borders is not restricted to the portfolio investor or speculator, who is interested solely in return and risk; it also enables businesses to pursue their production goals beyond national frontiers. The latter option may be of interest if a high portion of sales is destined for other countries, or if production abroad is considerably cheaper than it is at home (for example, in the car market as discussed in Case study 4.1).

If the investment capital, instead of goods or services exported, crosses the border, and the investor also gains a certain degree of control over the foreign activities in which it has invested (for example, by acquiring ownership of at least 25 per cent of the business), we call this foreign direct investment (FDI). The control associated with FDI can be established by setting up foreign subsidiaries or branch offices, or by purchasing a substantial proportion of the share capital in the foreign company. The investment activities of multinationals through their foreign subsidiaries are one of the clearest examples of FDI. Initially, it was entrepreneurs in the mining and energy sector who engaged in FDI. Later the majority of foreign direct investments shifted towards the industrial sector, while today there is increasing FDI in the services sector.

The term FDI may cause some confusion because of the tendency to confuse stocks and flows. If we refer to FDI as *flows*, we mean the capital flows satisfying the definition of direct investment, transferred from the home country to the host country in one year. If we consider FDI as a *stock*, we have to add up the total of all annual flows during the preceding periods. It is also very important to state whether we are ultimately referring to gross or net stocks.

In addition to the need for a precise definition of the concept of FDI, it is equally important to be as accurate as possible in valuing FDI. In practice, various complications arise in determining the precise value of FDI, with a lack of reliable statistics being just one of them.

It is often difficult to ascertain how much of the profit reinvested in the subsidiary actually constitutes direct investment. If the profit was first paid out to the parent company and subsequently reinvested in the subsidiary as FDI, the volume of FDI would be relatively transparent. However, if the profit remains with the subsidiary and is used directly to finance new investments, the position is often far less clear. Valuation presents another problem. Let us assume that a French-based parent company invests $20 million in a Brazilian subsidiary; however, the subsidiary has been registering losses for several years. In this case, how should we value the direct investment (stock) if it is clear that this cannot be done by adding up past flows? An investigation of these technical questions is beyond the scope of this discussion; however, it is important to point out that FDI statistics should always be regarded with considerable caution.

Recent figures have shown that FDI is playing an increasing role in internationalization:

o Global FDI outflows reached $1997 billion in 2007, compared with a mere $27 billion in 1982. The global economic crisis meant that the figure decreased to $1114 billion in 2009.
o Despite its importance to the world economy, global FDI outflows experienced a sharp drop in 2001 (Table 4.4), which could indicate that, even for FDI flows, there are some (invisible) boundaries.
o The ratio of world FDI inflows to overall world gross domestic capital formation is now 16.1 per cent, compared with a figure of only 0.9 per cent some 25 years ago.
o Over the same period the ratio of world FDI stock to world GDP increased from 4.7 per cent to 28.5 per cent.

Table 4.4 Selected indicators of FDI and international production, 1982–2009 ($ billion, %)

Item	Value at current prices (billions of dollars)				Annual growth rate (per cent)				
	1990	2005	2008	2009	1991–95	1996–2000	2001–05	2008	2009
FDI inflows	208	986	1771	1114	22.5	40.0	5.2	−15.7	−37.1
FDI outflows	241	893	1929	1101	16.8	36.1	9.2	−14.9	−42.9
FDI inward stock	2082	11525	15491	17743	9.3	18.7	13.3	−13.9	14.5
FDI outward stock	2087	12417	16207	18982	11.9	18.4	14.6	−16.1	17.1
Income on inward FDI	74	791	1113	941	35.1	13.4	31.9	−7.3	−15.5
Income on outward FDI	120	902	1182	1008	20.2	10.3	31.3	−7.7	−14.8
Cross-border M&As	99	462	707	250	49.1	64.0	0.6	−30.9	−64.7
Sales of foreign affiliates	6026	21721	31069[b]	29298[c]	8.8	8.2	18.1	−4.5[b]	−5.7[c]
Gross product of foreign affiliates	1477	4327	6163[d]	5812[e]	6.8	7.0	13.9	−4.3[d]	−5.7[e]
Total assets of foreign affiliates	5938	49252	71694[f]	77057[f]	13.7	19.0	20.9	−4.9[f]	7.5[f]
Exports of foreign affiliates	1498	4319	6663[g]	5186[g]	8.6	3.6	14.8	15.4[g]	−22.2[g]
Employment by foreign affiliates (thousands)	24476	57799	78857[h]	79825[i]	5.5	9.8	6.7	−3.7[h]	1.1[i]
Memorandum									
GDP (in current prices)	22121	45273	60766	55005[j]	5.9	1.3	10.0	10.3	−9.5[j]
Gross fixed capital formation	5099	9833	13822	12404[j]	5.4	1.1	11.0	11.5	−10.3

Royalties and licence fee receipts	29	129	177	..	14.6	8.1	14.6	8.6	..
Exports of goods and services	4414	12,954	19,986	15,716[i]	7.9	3.7	14.8	15.4	−21.4

[a] Data are available only from 1987 onwards.

[b] Data for 2007 and 2008 are based on the following regression result of sales against inward FDI stock (in millions of dollars) for the period 1980–2006: sales = 1471.6211 + 1.9343* inward FDI stock.

[c] Data for 2009 based on the observed year-over change of the sales of 3,659 TNCs' foreign operations between 2008 and 2009.

[d] Data for 2007 and 2008 are based on the following regression result of gross product against inward FDI stock (in millions of dollars) for the period 1982–2006: gross product = 566.7633 + 0.3658* inward FDI stock.

[e] Decline in gross product of foreign affiliates assumed to be the same as the decline in sales.

[f] Data for 2007 and 2008 are based on the following regression result of assets against inward FDI stock (in millions of dollars) for the period 1980–2006: assets = −3387.7138 + 4.9069* inward FDI stock.

[g] Data for 1995–1997 are based on the following regression result of exports of foreign affiliates against inward FDI stock (in millions of dollars) for the period 1982–1994: exports = 139.1489 + 0.6413*FDI inward stock. For 1998–2009, the share of exports of foreign affiliates in world export in 1998 (33.3%) was applied to obtain the values.

[h] Based on the following regression result of employment (in thousands) against inward FDI stock (in millions of dollars) for the period 1980–2006: employment = 17642.5861 + 4.0071*inward FDI stock.

[i] Data for 2009 based on the observed year-over change of the estimated employment of 3,659 TNCs' foreign operations between 2008 and 2009.

[j] Based on data from IMF, World Economic Outlook, April 2010.

Note: Not included in this table are the value of worldwide sales by foreign affiliates associated with their parent firms through non-equity relationships and of the value of sales of the parent firms themselves. Worldwide sales, gross product, total assets, exports, and employment of foreign affiliates are estimated by extrapolating the worldwide data of foreign affiliates of TNCs from Austria, Canada, the Czech Republic, Finland, France, Germany, Italy, Japan, Luxembourg, Portugal, Sweden and the United States for sales; those from the Czech Republic, Portugal, Sweden and the United States for gross product; those from Austria, Germany, Japan and the United States for assets; those from Austria, the Czech Republic, Japan, Portugal, Sweden and the United States for exports; and those from Austria, Germany, Japan, Switzerland and the United States for employment, on the basis of the shares of those countries in worldwide outward FDI stock.

Source: UNCTAD (2010), *World Investment Report 2010: Transnational Corporations and the Infrastructure Challenge.*

If current trends continue, FDI will play an increasingly important position in the future international economy, especially in relation to international trade. In fact, in 2000 the amount of global FDI surpassed the $1 trillion mark, before dropping significantly in the two following years.

One important part of the continuous growth of FDI flows is the increasing number of cross-border mergers and acquisitions. Table 4.5 shows how such cross-border mergers and acquisitions have grown in importance in recent years.

Internationalization through FDI takes place mainly between companies in industrialized countries. In 1999, developed countries attracted $636 billion in FDI flows, almost three-quarters of the world total. In the same year, developing countries received only $208 billion in FDI. The share of developing countries in global FDI inflows fell from about 40 per cent in 1997 to 21 per cent in 1999, then recovered to about 30 per cent in 2003 and dropped slightly in 2007 to 27.3 per cent.

Inward FDI can be particularly important to developing countries. For example, during the 1990s intensive inward FDI, in both the services and manufacturing sectors, played a key role in driving Ireland's economy from its backward state to the booming era of the 'Celtic Tiger'. It helps to provide the necessary capital to achieve economic growth and the transfer of technology and employment. For this reason many developing countries are willing to offer major tax concessions and other favourable arrangements for the establishment of businesses in order both to attract foreign investment and to retain the investment it has already secured. At the same time it is in developing countries that we also find the main opposition to the introduction and presence of FDI:

o First, the opponents claim that there is often no effective transfer of technology.
o They point out further that foreign companies take advantage of the low wages and other favourable production conditions, but that they often channel most of the resulting profit back to their home country.
o Lastly, a common criticism is that national authorities have almost no control or influence over foreign companies because they can easily threaten to leave the country, as a result of the 'footloose' character of their international activities (MNEs don't have their production tied to a particular location, and are therefore able to easily 'move shop' if this course of action is in their best interest.) As a result, foreign companies show little concern for national regulations.

4.7 The multinational enterprise (MNE)

The decisions that lead to international transactions are usually made within companies. It is therefore important to examine the factors that cause individual companies to adopt an increasingly international strategy.

In the initial phase of their development, most companies focus on the home market; this is the predominant form of business organization in most countries. If expansion is restrained by the limitations of the home market, a company may try to sell abroad. Chapter 3 explored the reasons why some companies decide (and are able) to export their products.

In the first instance, the company need not always organize these activities itself. It may be possible, for example, to export through another domestic company (indirect exports) or even by selling licences to other countries for the production technology or any specific characteristics of the product, such as a brand name. However, export activities usually start with the use of foreign sales agents; if exports are successful, businesses often establish

Table 4.5 Cross-border mergers and acquisitions, by region/economy of seller and purchaser, 1987–2010

Country/region	Cross-border M&As, by region/economy of seller, 1987–2008 ($ million)										
	1987	1988	1989	1990	1991	1992	1993	1994	1995	1996	1997
World	97,311	137,630	167,068	200,389	116,642	112,939	123,492	170,575	231,577	264,254	370,987
Developed economies	94,890	135,365	162,761	188,178	108,944	99,080	110,450	154,029	212,556	232,641	302,244
Developing economies	2408	2265	4247	12,211	7159	12,704	12,730	16,407	18,321	29,319	62,874

Country/region	Value of cross-border M&As, by region/economy of purchaser, 1987–2008 (millions of dollars)										
	1987	1988	1989	1990	1991	1992	1993	1994	1995	1996	1997
World	97,311	137,630	167,068	200,389	116,642	112,939	123,492	170,575	231,577	264,254	370,987
Developed economies	84,007	128,920	148,745	175,360	95,982	88,776	83,178	134,629	207,788	235,693	325,120
Developing economies	3554	4700	6621	9975	4687	10,168	12,140	15,376	18,176	22,986	39,977

Cross-border M&As, by region/economy of seller, 1987–2008 ($ million)

1998	1999	2000	2001	2002	2003	2004	2005	2006	2007	2008	2009	2010
692,686	903,868	1,349,777	730,441	483,238	411,302	565,871	929,362	1,118,068	1,637,107	706,543	249,732	125,211
614,232	816,706	1,230,813	650,894	426,036	360,053	469,332	820,358	969,116	1,454,084	581,394	203,530	102,879
78,056	85,444	118,112	76,458	54,595	40,130	48,479	95,738	131,831	152,942	104,812	39,077	21,436

Value of Cross-border M&As, by region/economy of purchaser, 1987–2008 (millions of dollars)

1998	1999	2000	2001	2002	2003	2004	2005	2006	2007	2008	2009	2010
692,686	903,868	1,349,777	730,441	483,238	411,302	565,871	929,362	1,118,068	1,637,107	706,543	249,732	125,211
629,878	847,866	1,209,787	664,422	423,909	344,581	471,033	777,609	930,101	1,410,802	568,041	160,785	94,552
40,106	29,423	120,746	52,976	42,195	36,550	45,894	99,455	156,807	179,969	105,849	73,975	20,721

Note: The data cover only those deals that involve an acquisition of an equity of more than 10%.
Source: UNCTAD (2010) *World Investment Report 2010*, UNCTAD cross-border mergers and acquisitions database www.unctad.org/fdistatistics.

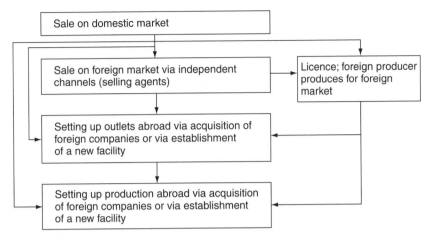

Figure 4.2   Possible process of development into a multinational enterprise
Source: Dicken (1986), p. 129.

or acquire their own foreign sales offices. The final option can be the start of a process towards FDI and the establishment of a multinational enterprise (MNE).

Taking this one step further, the company could consider making an actual foreign investment, for example, in the form of a *joint venture*. In this case, the company participates in some way in a joint foreign subsidiary, together with one or more foreign companies. The joint venture may be set up for the purpose of jointly organizing foreign sales, marketing, distribution, and so on. The legal uncertainties of foreign markets (consider the situation in Eastern Europe or in various developing countries) constitute particularly good reasons for a company to opt for the joint venture option when setting up independent subsidiaries abroad. The host country's policy is often to restrict the influence of foreign companies by requiring a certain national share in the management of those companies. In such circumstances a joint venture is an attractive option.

Continuing the progressive transfer of a company's activities to foreign countries, we arrive automatically at the final stage where the company in question proceeds to relocate a substantial part of its activities abroad. In that case the company develops into a transnational enterprise. If it wants to become a true MNE, then, according to our definition, the management of the business must also adopt an internationally oriented strategy.

Figure 4.2 shows the successive stages that lead to the point where we can refer to an MNE. It illustrates how companies might develop into an MNE by various channels and successive intermediate stages.

4.7.1 Definition of an MNE

If a company owns production facilities in more than one country and the business management embraces an internationally oriented strategy, that company can be labelled an MNE. This classification can cover a very wide range of businesses, ranging from groups with annual sales in excess of the GNP of a medium-sized industrial country, to companies with a turnover of just a few million dollars. It is important to realize that not all MNEs are massive companies.

For this reason, efforts have been made to construct a typology of the MNE so that various sub-categories of MNEs can be distinguished meaningfully. Although any typology contains arbitrary elements, it can be useful to classify MNEs on the basis of criteria such as:

o turnover;

o regional distribution;

o number of countries in which a processing activity takes place;

o share of foreign activities in overall operations; and

o degree to which the organizational structure is internationally oriented.

The typological classification to be constructed on this basis may be important in determining the degree to which the conduct of a particular MNE can be controlled by the local government. The larger the MNE, the wider its international distribution, the greater its dominance of the various markets and the more footloose it is, the weaker the national government's negotiating position in relation to the MNE (see Case study 4.3).

Case study 4.3   Nokia's relocation to Cluj makes sense

At the end of 2008, the Finnish mobile phone manufacturer Nokia decided to transfer its production from Germany to Romania, mainly because workers there had made major concessions regarding their conditions of employment.

This decision caused uproar in Germany, one reason being that following the closure of coal mines in the Nordrhein-Westfalen Land, the Finnish factory had become the second-largest employer in the region, providing more than 2,300 jobs. In contrast to the employees' protests and the politicians' promises to persuade the company to stay, journalists from the *Financial Times Germany* argued that Nokia's decision to relocate to Romania was entirely justified.

In 'Why Nokia is Acting Correctly' Volker Muller of the *Financial Times Germany* salutes Nokia's decision to move its factory from Bochum to Cluj in the face of substantial opposition from politicians and labour organizations. The author argues that the financial aid given in the mid-1990s cannot be expected to guarantee that the factory will remain there forever and that in the Nokia empire Bochum is actually the exception, with most of the other factories being located in lower-cost locations such as Korea, China, Mexico, Brazil, Hungary and now Romania. Furthermore, even if the factory in Germany is still profitable, as was argued by the unions, the falling prices of mobile phones made every cent saved essential for the company's survival in the market.

Olaf Jurgen, in his 'False Debate over Nokia', refers to the scandal around the closing of Nokia's factory in Bochum and raises two essential questions: how free is a company when it decides to close down and move its operations? And what role do state subsidies play in the competition between different locations?

The answer to the first question is straightforward: the decision to build, move or close a factory belongs exclusively to the company and is an essential condition for the proper functioning of a free market economy. It is this flexibility that allows companies to produce in optimal conditions and politicians opposing Nokia's decision to close its factory in Bochum should be consistent in their concerns by also protesting against factories being relocated to Germany from other countries. In respect of government subsidies, it is well known that state subsidies may distort market activity and that politicians will often grant subsidies only where political capital could be gained.

Although it is necessary to distinguish between different categories of MNEs, they share a number of common characteristics:

o companies in the group are legally linked by a common ownership structure;
o member companies have economic links with one another since they have access, in varying degrees, to a common pool of resources, information and control instruments; this concerns not only common access to financial resources, but also joint participation in other aspects, including information and information systems, organizational structures, marketing strategies, patents, and brand names; and
o various companies are all subject to a common overall management philosophy and group strategy, and each one usually has an international orientation.

The above list implies that not only do the subsidiaries of MNEs have financial obligations towards the parent company, as a result of the control and/or shareholding relationship, but that they also have to accept the organizational structure of the parent company.

Financial relations between the parent company and its subsidiaries are complicated substantially by the fact that there is often two-way traffic: the parent company may finance new activities in the subsidiary, while the subsidiary may transfer profits to the parent company. In such circumstances the various international financial dealings offset one another to some extent. In practice, this leads to an increased level of freedom in their accounting, which the business may try to exploit (for example, in order to minimize the group's total tax burden).

This multinational character may be reinforced still further if there is internal trade – such as in components or semi-manufactures – between the parent company and a subsidiary or between the subsidiaries themselves. It has been estimated that the internal trade of MNEs accounts for around a quarter of world trade. In particular, with inter-subsidiary trade there is a certain degree of freedom within the enterprise regarding the valuation of these transactions, so that one can try to transfer the profit internationally to the country with the most favourable tax rules.

The process of valuing transactions within the MNE is also known as *transfer pricing*. The possibility of making use of this is a typical example of the relatively independent position of the MNE in relation to local and/or national government policy. This independence often creates a strong negotiating position with governments, particularly in countries where governments are weak and foreign investors are regarded as key drivers of the economy.

4.7.2 The relative importance of MNEs

The current strong position of MNEs in the world economy is a fairly recent phenomenon, which has developed rapidly over the past few decades. Essentially, this strong growth began in the 1960s, although the volume and quality of the statistical information on FDI does not give a clear picture of the activities of MNEs before the 1970s.

The first thing to note about the increasing importance of the MNE phenomenon in recent decades is the rapid growth in their numbers and in their share of the world economy and world trade, as shown in the following examples:

o United Nations (UN) calculations of the situation at the beginning of the 1990s showed that by that time there were already around 35,000 MNEs, controlling 170,000 subsidiaries.
o By 2000, according to the UNCTAD *World Investment Report*, these numbers had increased to 63,000 parent firms with around 690,000 foreign affiliates and inter-firm arrangements.

o The same source also states that in 1990 the 100 largest MNEs owned $3100 billion of the world's assets, of which $1200 billion related to assets outside the MNE's home country.

o A rough estimate of the total assets of businesses worldwide in 1990 came to approximately $20,000 billion. This would mean that the top 100 MNEs owned roughly one-sixth of the total assets in 1990. At that time the top 300 MNEs held about one-quarter of the world's assets.

o The importance of MNEs for the world economy is even greater if we consider that an estimated 40 to 50 per cent of the international transfer of assets takes place via the same 100 leading MNEs.

More recent data from the UNCTAD *World Investment Report 2008* reinforce the impression of the overriding importance of MNEs in the world economy. Table 4.6 provides some key information relating to the top 25 non-financial MNEs, ranked according to their foreign assets in 2006.

By 2004 the world's top 100 MNEs were based almost exclusively in industrialized countries and concentrated in sectors such as electronics, electrical equipment, automobiles, petroleum, chemicals and pharmaceuticals. In 2007 the production of goods and services by an estimated 79,000 TNCs and their 790,000 foreign affiliates continued to expand, and their FDI stock exceeded $15 trillion. The same foreign affiliates had 84 million employees and their total sales were in the order of $31 trillion – a 21 per cent increase over 2006. At the same time, the sales of all foreign affiliates worldwide amounted to $14 trillion in 1999 (compared with $3 trillion in 1980). The 2007 gross product associated with international production was about 11 per cent of global GDP, whereas in 1982 it had been around 5 per cent.

It is estimated that at least half of all industrial production now takes place in MNEs or similar organizational structures, at least if we exclude those businesses based in the former planned economies. It is striking, however, that FDI, although it is an imperfect indicator of MNE investment, is usually concentrated in only a handful of countries – in 1999 just ten countries received 74 per cent of all global FDI flows. The situation in the developing world is similar where, over the course of the same year, ten countries received about 80 per cent of total FDI flows within these areas. There are no signs that the concentration of international production has been declining over time.

4.8 The MNE and the international relocation of production activities: some theories

In recent decades the enormous growth in the importance, number, and size of MNEs has prompted an increasing interest in the reasons why businesses develop into multinationals.

According to the neoclassical approach, the central idea was that international investment flows came from countries with low capital productivity and should be directed towards countries with high productivity of capital, which allowed businesses to achieve the maximum return on their investment. According to that approach, equilibrium would be reached if this international capital flow equalized the marginal productivity of international capital.

The situation in the early 1960s, which saw an increase in unilateral FDI from the USA to Europe, appeared to support this theory. At that time, the after-tax capital returns achieved by American subsidiaries in Europe were higher than those seen in American industry.

Table 4.6 The world's top 25 non-financial transnational corporations, 2006

($ million and number of employees)

Ranking by:					Assets		Sales		Employment		TNI[b] (Per cent)
Foreign assets	TNI[b]	Corporation	Home economy	Industry[c]	Foreign	Total	Foreign	Total	Foreign[d]	Total	
1	9	Hutchison Whampoa Limited	Hong Kong, China	Diversified	70,762	87,745	25,006	30,236	18,2148	2,20,000	82.0
2	88	CITIC Group	China	Diversified	43,750	2,38,725	5427	22,230	18,305	90,650	21.0
3	11	Cemex S.A.	Mexico	Non-metalic mineral products	40,258	45,084	17,982	21,830	41,586	56,791	81.6
4	41	Samsung Electronics Co., Ltd	Korea, Republic of	Electrical & electronic equipment	28,765	83,738	88,892	1,10,321	77,236	1,61,700	54.2
5	79	Petronas - Petroliam Nasional Bhd	Malaysia	Petroleum expl./ ref./ distr.	28,447	1,06,416	32,477	77,094	7847	39,236	29.6
6	71	Hyundai Motor Company	Korea, Republic of	Motor vehicles	28,359	82,072	33,874	72,523	22,066	78,270	36.5
7	46	China Ocean Shipping (Group) Company	China	Transport and storage	28,066	36,253	18,041	27,431	4581	69,648	49.9
8	61	Lukoil	Russian Federation	Petroleum and natural gas	21,515	71,461	87,637	1,07,680	23,000	1,52,500	42.2

Table 4.6 (Continued)

($ million and number of employees)

Ranking by: Foreign assets	TNI[b]	Corporation	Home economy	Industry[c]	Assets		Sales		Employment		TNI[b] (Per cent)
					Foreign	Total	Foreign	Total	Foreign[d]	Total	
9	67	Vale S.A.	Brazil	Mining & quarrying	19,635	79,931	30,939	37,426	4725	62,490	38.3
10	85	Petróleos De Venezuela	Venezuela, Bolivarian Republic of	Petroleum expl./ ref./ distr.	19,244	1,31,832	52,494	1,26,364	5140	61,909	21.5
11	30	Zain	Kuwait	Telecommunications	18,746	19,761	6034	7452	1151	15,000	61.2
12	22	Jardine Matheson Holdings Ltd	Hong Kong, China	Diversified	17,544	22,098	16,831	22,362	79,276	1,50,000	69.2
13	29	Singtel Ltd	Singapore	Telecommunications	17,326	21,887	6745	10,374	9058	20,000	63.2
14	64	Formosa Plastics Group	Taiwan Province of China	Chemicals	16,937	76,587	17,078	66,259	70,519	94,268	40.9
15	18	Tata Steel Ltd	India	Metal and metal products	16,826	23,868	26,426	32,168	45,864	80,782	69.8
16	91	Petroleo Brasileiro S.A. - Petrobras	Brazil	Petroleum expl./ ref./ distr.	15,075	1,25,695	40,179	1,46,529	6775	74,240	16.2
17	35	Hon Hai Precision Industries	Taiwan Province of China	Electrical & electronic equipment	14,664	26,771	21,727	61,810	5,15,626	61,1000	58.1

18	49	Metalurgica Gerdau S.A.	Brazil	Metal and metal products	13,658	25,750	10,274	23,182	22,315	46,000	48.6
19	21	Abu Dhabi National Energy Company	United Arab Emirates	Utilities (electricity gas and water)	13,519	23,523	3376	4576	1839	2383	69.5
20	82	Oil And Natural Gas Corporation	India	Petroleum expl./ref./distr.	13,477	30,456	4238	27,684	3921	33,035	23.8
21	24	MTN Group, Limited	South Africa	Telecommunications	13,266	18,281	7868	12,403	10,870	16,452	67.4
22	58	LG Corp.	Korea, Republic of	Electrical & electronic equipment	13,256	51,517	44,439	82,060	32,962	64,000	43.8
23	53	Evraz	Russian Federation	Metal and metal products	11,196	19,448	12,805	20,380	29,480	13,4000	47.5
24	20	Qatar Telecom	Qatar	Telecommunications	10,598	20,412	4077	5582	1539	1832	69.7
25	44	América Móvil	Mexico	Telecommunications	10,428	31,481	17,323	31,026	36,353	52,879	52.6

[a] All data are based on the companies' annual reports unless otherwise stated.

[b] TNI, the Transnationality Index, is calculated as the average of the following three ratios: foreign assets to total assets, foreign sales to total sales and foreign employment to total employment.

[c] Industry classification for companies follows the United States Standard Industrial Classification as used by the United States Securities and Exchange Commission (SEC).

[d] In a number of cases foreign employment data were calculated by applying the share of foreign employment in total employment of the previous year to total employment of 2008.

Note: TNCs are MNEs that conduct their activities worldwide without being acknowledged as having a national home base.

Source: UNCTAD (2008), World Investment Report 2008.

In the course of the 1960s the returns achieved by American subsidiaries in Europe generally dropped below the level of returns in the USA; however, the net flow of direct investment from the USA to Europe continued to grow, while FDI flows from Europe to the USA also started to increase. This development contradicted the existing theory, which was already being questioned for three other reasons:

○ First, it was difficult to explain the normal two-way traffic in FDI, and also the fact that FDI takes place predominantly between countries with relatively similar industrial structures.
○ Second, if companies were principally interested in the return on investment, it was not entirely clear why they should want to retain control over their foreign investment.
○ Third, it became increasingly apparent that, due to certain risks and institutional obstacles, companies struggled to estimate the returns on their foreign investments. This initiated the process of searching for new explanations of why the MNE phenomenon was continuing.

Initially, the emphasis was on partial explanations, often based on case studies. For example, in the case of MNEs in the mining and energy sectors, reference was made to factors like securing lines of supply from other countries. In the case of FDI in highly protectionist countries, the emphasis was on evading trade barriers. The exploitation of economies of scale was considered important in the surge in direct investments from the USA, in the 1960s, to the then newly established European Economic Community (EEC; the forerunner of the European Union). Other explanatory factors included risk spreading, tax advantages and market strategy.

Although there was empirical evidence to support the role of all these arguments in the decision process regarding FDI, the offered arguments still fail to offer a systematic explanation for the MNE phenomenon. Two of the most successful attempts to present such a systematic framework are the product life cycle theory and the eclectic approach, which are discussed below.

4.8.1 Product life cycle theory

One of the first attempts to incorporate a number of the above elements into a unified theory was Vernon's product life cycle theory, which was developed in the mid-1960s and was applied principally to the rise of the US MNEs during that period.

Vernon's theory was an attempt to explain the rise and subsequent decline (the so-called life cycle) of US production of goods such as radios, televisions, plastics, transistors and simple electronic products (Vernon, 1966). This theory was particularly popular in the 1960s and 1970s. Vernon's view was that the MNE phenomenon can be attributed to recognizing the existence of various phases in the life cycle of a product. Table 4.7 summarizes the features of the product life cycle theory.

When a new product is introduced, it is difficult for consumers to compare it with those produced by other firms. Total demand for the product, therefore, has low price elasticity in the initial phase, meaning that the volume of demand is relatively insensitive to changes in price.

This means that at this stage in the life cycle the rise in demand is disproportionately small if the producer reduces the price of the product, so that turnover declines. A price reduction of 15 per cent, for example, generates an increase in demand of less than 15 per cent, say 5 per cent. This is called inelastic demand.

While the HOS model was based on stable, identical production functions for a good in different countries, the production functions in the Vernon model depend upon specific

Table 4.7 The product life cycle

Phases	Launch	Growth	Maturity
Demand structure	– low price elasticity of aggregate demand – nature of demand not quite known	– growing price elasticity of demand – start of price competition	– manipulating demand via marketing techniques, product or price differentiation
Production	– short processes – rapid technological changes depending on degree of training – capital intensity low	– mass production methods	– long processing using stable techniques – degree of training irrelevant – capital intensive
Industrial structure	– small number of companies	– large number of companies, associated with losses and mergers	– number of companies declines

phases in the production process. In the initial phase, many alterations and adjustments are made to the design of the product, so that the production process requires non-standard work, the use of specialist skills, and a comparatively short time frame.

In time, the producer should develop a better understanding of the production technology and the customer's wants. As a result the product – and hence the production process – can be standardized. In this *growth* phase, the production process is characterized by internal economies of scale, as the consumer has become more familiar with the product and is also able to compare prices. This causes price elasticity of demand to increase, and the producer will begin to compete on the basis of price advantages. The growing price elasticity of demand means that demand for a given product becomes increasingly sensitive to price changes.

In the *maturity and saturation* phases, the production process is completely standardized and the workers' level of training is no longer an important factor. Now competition takes place via price or product differentiation. Businesses that do not produce efficiently enough will lose out to other competitors who are efficient, for example, because they have better access to particular production factors. It is particularly in this final phase that traditional comparative cost differences regain their importance.

It appears that Vernon assumes that products are subject to predictable technological changes and marketing methods, and that the production processes may vary from country to country. In addition, consumer incomes and their associated preferences may also differ from country to country. Furthermore, in his model Vernon omits the assumption of freely available information made by other models. According to Vernon, this is mainly true within national borders, but even then there are costs associated with the transfer of knowledge between the market and the company. In this regard Vernon remarked that:

(i) if there is strong consumer demand in a given country for product and process innovation, the chance of innovation is greater than in countries where consumer demand is more conservative;

(ii) an entrepreneur generally prefers to invest in innovations for the home market rather than those for the foreign market; and

(iii) the closer the producer is to the market, the lower the costs associated with the transfer of market knowledge.

The Vernon model accounts for the development of MNEs as follows:

o Assuming that information is not freely available, it follows that during the introduction phase it is principally local producers who are aware of the possibilities of introducing a new product to a specific market.
o New products with special characteristics are then developed for the home market. In the case of the USA, for example, high incomes and high labour costs are reflected in strong domestic demand for expensive, high-tech products, and, consequently, a correspondingly high level of domestic supply of such products.
o During the introduction phase (stage 1 in Figure 4.3), the non-standardized character of the production process means that direct communication between consumer and producer is essential in securing further product development. In this phase, production is supposed to take place exclusively on the domestic market, which means that any foreign demand is supplied by exports (see Figure 4.3).
o If the product is so standardized that direct communication between producer and consumer becomes relatively less important than production costs, production will start in other countries. We call this the product's growth phase. The timing depends on economies of scale, tariffs, transport costs, income elasticity of demand and the level of income and market size in other countries.
o According to Vernon, the company initially concentrates on establishing production facilities abroad in order to reduce production and distribution costs or because of the potential threat to its foreign market position.
o The nature of the production cycle indicates that foreign production will take place first in high-income countries. In the beginning, foreign production will also be limited by the fact that foreign production is only sold on the local market in the host country (stage 2).

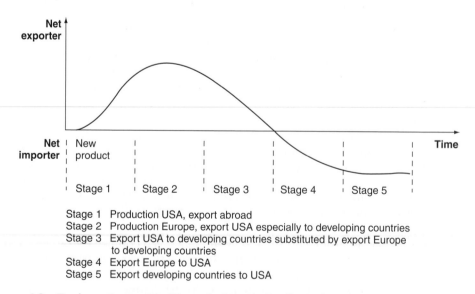

Stage 1   Production USA, export abroad
Stage 2   Production Europe, export USA especially to developing countries
Stage 3   Export USA to developing countries substituted by export Europe
          to developing countries
Stage 4   Export Europe to USA
Stage 5   Export developing countries to USA

Figure 4.3   Trade patterns over life cycle for product introduced in the USA

o As a result of cost advantages, exports (stage 3) from the foreign subsidiaries will gradually increase until, as in our example, the product is imported back into the USA (stage 4); meanwhile, new products are naturally introduced in the USA and go through the same phases.

o In the end, the production process of a product is totally standardized, so that there is scope for economies of scale and mass production. The product can then be produced at low-cost locations in developing countries (stage 5), which is called the product's saturation phase. Thus, as the product life cycle progresses, the optimum production location also changes.

According to this theory, those companies that continue to concentrate on the traditional production of goods in the saturation phase will face stagnant and declining demand, and keen competitors who have established their production facilities in low-wage countries. This causes the 'traditional' businesses to lose their potential for profit. As a result, generally they will be forced to cut back on their own production, diversify or even abandon the product altogether.

Although the product life cycle theory abandons a number of the assumptions of the HOS model, its basis is still the familiar comparative cost concept, albeit in a dynamic context: labour-intensive assembly is located where labour is cheap, for example in developing countries; the design phase takes place where there is plenty of technological know-how; while the production phase may take place where raw materials are readily available.

However, attempts to explain the rise of American MNEs in terms of the product life cycle theory were felt to be increasingly unsatisfactory by the 1970s. It appeared to be increasingly less necessary for a product to be developed on the home market first, before export and FDI could be considered. This was mainly due to the fact that MNEs began acquiring ever-greater knowledge about markets and technological developments outside the USA (in 1979, Vernon himself recognized the ever-increasing 'global scanning capabilities' of the MNEs).

Moreover, the technological and income differential between the USA and other industrial countries has declined in recent years, so that the location characteristics of the USA have become less appropriate in explaining the optimum location for production. As a result, the theory has lost a large part of its attraction. One might argue that the theory is now mainly suited to explaining FDI by small firms, or the FDI of developing countries.

4.8.2 The MNE's eclectic approach

In addition to appearing somewhat outdated, the product life cycle theory also failed to address some fundamental questions about MNEs.

For example, it was not obvious why certain companies within a country become multinationals while others do not. This is surprising because every company in a country can take advantage of the same unique characteristics of the home market. It is also unclear why MNEs wish to retain control over the production process. If a company develops a particular product which can be produced more cheaply abroad, then it can be argued that the company should sell the product either by means of licensing or by exporting. To explain the existence of MNEs, we need a theory that provides a satisfactory answer to this question.

Dunning's *eclectic approach* (so called because it combines elements of various theories) provides us with a satisfying answer. This approach describes the necessary conditions for the emergence of MNEs. These conditions imply the existence of three categories of advantages: ownership, location and internalization.

1. The first condition, *ownership advantage*, means that a given company enjoys unique production conditions/facilities that enable it to generate a future flow of income and profits. These unique production conditions are reserved exclusively for the company in question, but can be used in combination with other production resources, both in the home country and abroad. These unique characteristics may relate to tangible assets, such as exclusive access to certain natural resources, manpower or capital. Equally, they may relate to intangible production assets such as specific technical knowledge, market knowledge, advanced information networks, specific organizational and entrepreneurial qualities or a unique type of market access. If investment is to be successful, the condition concerning ownership advantage will always need to be fulfilled.

2. The second condition, *location advantages*, relates to production in the host country. The production conditions responsible for the additional profitability of the investment are not linked to ownership of a particular business, but rather to a specific production location. These advantages are therefore available to any company investing in production in that location. *Export processing zones (or free trade zones)* are a good example of areas where special measures are being implemented to create exactly such location advantages. These special zones are often situated in emerging economies and usually offer a collection of special facilities to foreign companies. Amongst the amenities offered are: low bureaucracy, tax concessions, a solid infrastructure, a cheap well-trained labour pool and government subsidies.

3. The third condition, *internalization*, means that the company exploits ownership advantages not by contracting out the associated activity, but by deliberately retaining control over it.

   Generally speaking, there are arguments for internalizing economic activities if there is an advantage in the certainty created by incorporating part of the company's economic environment into the business. This is generally the case when a company decides to increase the certainty level of its technology process when it enters the market.

   Not having this type of certainty is known as the *technology transfer* problem. In our example, the technology transfer problem implies that the option of selling a licence to attain an advantage is not appropriate. This can happen for a variety of reasons.

   Let us assume that the ownership advantage is based on the combination of a unique set of workers, their unique organizational structure and their unique use of equipment. It is easy to see that logistical reasons may prevent this advantage from being sold to another company by licensing (unless part of the business is transferred completely).

   In addition, any negotiations regarding the transfer of knowledge through licences can be hampered by either party acting opportunistically. This means that, before reaching a general agreement, a potential licencee could exploit the specific knowledge acquired in the pre-contract phase for its own commercial purposes. However, if for that reason, the potential buyer has to provide incomplete information of the content of the licence, this could lower the licence price to below its true value. This makes the price negotiation process for the licence obscure and results in extra costs. Additionally, the seller is often worried that the costs incurred in creating that specific knowledge would not be covered, especially when other people can make free use of such specific knowledge. This might happen in the case of an information leak and could severely damage the reputation of the original owner.

   Finally, parts of the production process may be internalized – with the aim, for example, of securing reliable supplies or sales. This is termed *vertical integration*. It should be clear that, in this instance, the ownership advantages outweigh the advantages of licensing. Thus, in practice, there are numerous arguments that explain why companies have incentives to maintain control over the exploitation of the exclusive right to use innovations, ideas and organizational characteristics.

The existence of FDI – and thus MNEs – can be explained through the three factors presented above. A company that has an ownership advantage has three options to expand its production. It could:

1. invest internally in the company and export the additional production;
2. invest abroad; or
3. license a third party to handle the additional production.

If there is an additional location advantage in foreign production and an internalization advantage, the first and last options are no longer desirable, leaving only the direct investment option.

4.9 | Summary

1. The theoretical assumption that production factors do not cross borders is not reflected in real-world economic conditions. International differences in income and harsh economic situations have always encouraged the international mobility of labour. Regional economic integration, for example in the European Union, has also promoted the mobility of labour as a factor of production.
2. The liberalization of international capital movements and the corresponding rise of multinational enterprises have greatly increased the international mobility of capital. This raises the question: who stands to gain and who stands to lose from capital mobility?
3. The analysis showed that there are many analogies with the theory of international trade – the international transfer of factors of production is not a zero-sum game. However, an analysis of the distribution problem is complicated for four specific reasons:
   * Factors of production are not homogeneous.
   * All economic markets have to be included in the analysis, since they are strongly interdependent.
   * The final destination of the payments given for the factor of production needs to be known.
   * The effect of factor mobility depends on government control.
4. One distinctive aspect of international capital mobility is that it facilitates international credit transfers between countries. In theory, the credit imbalances/flows between countries can be attributed to the existing inter-country differences in time preferences.
5. Since the 1980s, flows of FDI have increased very rapidly in relation to flows of goods and services. FDI means that an entrepreneur invests in foreign activities and also acquires a certain degree of influence or control over them. If a company has acquired several production facilities in various countries via direct investments, it can be classified as an MNE.

   Vernon's product life cycle theory attempts to explain the MNE phenomenon in terms of the different phases in the life of a product.

   By contrast, Dunning's eclectic approach combines a number of conditions for the existence of MNEs into a single theory. This theory is based on the following elements: location advantages, ownership advantages and markets that function imperfectly. Internalization is identified as the best option.

6. It is clear that the policies of national governments influence all three of these elements in the eclectic theory, explaining the conduct of MNEs. This relationship between companies operating internationally and government policy will be examined in more detail in the chapters that follow.

Questions

1. Considering Case study 4.1, what do you think would be a good strategy for US car manufacturers to adopt in order to expand their share of the domestic market?
2. What do you consider to be the abundant production factor in your country? What could be done to improve its output?
3. Can you think of any positive effects for a country that is experiencing a 'brain drain'?
4. Can you provide arguments why the number of MNEs could steadily decrease over time?

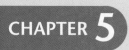

CHAPTER 5

Trade Policy: A Welfare Theory Analysis

5.1 | Introduction

Any discussion of the impact of international free trade on national welfare (see Chapter 3) has a direct bearing on the question of whether or not one should attempt to influence international trade, either directly or indirectly, through government interventions.

Traditional trade theory (see Chapter 3) held that free trade could maximize the level of overall welfare for everyone, even though it was clear that two of the most important assumptions of this theory – namely perfectly competitive/efficient markets and the absence of economies of scale – did not occur in the real world.

Initially, modern trade theories continued to support and reinforce the idea that free trade can eventually produce benefits for all parties, meaning that objections to protectionism have prevailed in the theoretical literature. (A brief note about the terminology used in this chapter: protection means actual trade protection; protectionism means the degree to which a government is generally inclined to grant protection; protectionist measures are measures to protect one's own industry.) This notion of the advantages of free trade and the disadvantages of protectionism was reinforced by the tendency for national economies to become more closely interlinked and for businesses to increase their international operations (as shown in Chapter 2).

Given this background it is perhaps surprising to observe that countries today adopt a wide range of trade policies, from escalating protectionist tendencies to being opened up steadily to international competition. This chapter begins with a case study of India during the early 1990s, a period when the country reversed the direction of its trade policy and switched from a strongly protectionist tradition to a policy in favour of free trade.

India's 'New Economic Policy' was initially a great success. In the early 1990s, India was one of the world's fastest-growing economies: inflation rates were relatively low and the balance of payments could be maintained at comfortable levels. However, the end of the 1990s saw a deterioration in the country's macroeconomic indicators. India responded by adopting a range of measures, including an increase in anti-dumping measures, which might suggest that protectionism was again becoming popular.

In general, the advantages of free trade are clearer at higher levels of economic aggregation. At national and international levels, the advantages of free trade are greater than the disadvantages; but for individual companies or sectors of the economy this might not be the case, since they may suffer from competition as a result of the government's adoption of free trade policies. This can make the discussion of trade policy rather complex.

Trade theory contributes to this discussion by incorporating different starting points. The traditional theory (discussed in Chapter 3) was concerned primarily with national welfare. However, in recent years, it has been increasingly clear that, when describing behaviour with respect to trade policy, it is equally necessary to use models that focus on considerations at the company level (Chapters 6 and 7), the effect of specific interest groups and lobbying, and political influence (Chapters 8 and 9).

This chapter will consider some reasons why governments should adopt protectionist measures. Regarded from the perspective of the welfare implications for a whole country, the arguments condemning protectionism outweigh those that support it.

However, in Chapters 6 to 8 we will tackle protectionism from the point of view of the specific interests of individual companies – and of groups within those companies.

5.2   Protectionism

Case study 5.1 considers present-day India, which, following an era of strict government control of foreign trade, is successfully pursuing a policy oriented towards free trade.

There are some terms that first need explanation here, namely countervailing duties and anti-dumping measures. Both terms refer to an action by a government or firm that aims to influence trade. Although Chapter 8 will consider restrictions in greater detail, we give a brief explanation here for the purpose of Case study 5.1. A dumping complaint is made when a domestic firm accuses a foreign firm of dumping – that is, selling its products on the domestic market at less than the price of the country of origin and/or less than the cost of the products. The accuser's government may then impose levies on the foreign firm's products to make them more expensive. Dumping complaints are often intended to restrict foreign competition. A countervailing duty is an action a country can make to counter the effect of a subsidy: the domestic government can charge a compensating duty on subsidized imports that are found to be destructive for domestic producers.

Case study 5.1   India awakes and discovers the world around it

Protectionism

For many decades India had one of the most complex protectionist regimes in the world, with imports and exports both subject to significant tariff and non-tariff measures.

Before 1991, non-tariff barriers (NTBs) protected 90 per cent of production. Various 'channelling bureaus', a number of import procedures, and an inefficient financial sector delayed goods traffic and provided ample opportunities for corruption.

Instead of making competitiveness the cornerstone of its export policy, the Indian government often opted for a policy of *export subsidies*. In combination with the world's highest import duty (with a weighted average of 112 per cent), these measures formed a barrier behind which domestic businesses were safeguarded from foreign competition.

Although the Indian economy has been liberalizing gradually since the regime of Rajiv Gandhi (1984–91), administrative complexity and bureaucratic delays have limited the benefits of this policy. One study calculated that an exporter needed more than 350 government actions before a large export order could be completed. In 1991 a foreign-exchange crisis forced Prime Minister Narasimha Rao to introduce a radical change in policy.

The foreign-exchange crisis

The Gulf War of 1990–91 led to a rise in oil prices and brought a temporary halt to the remittances to India from expatriate workers in the region. At the same time, non-resident Indians withdrew their Indian deposits rapidly, leaving the country very short of foreign currency.

By the end of 1990, India's foreign debt stood at more than $70 billion. Interest and repayments on that debt were costing India $7 billion – almost 30 per cent of India's export value.

In addition, domestic debt had reached a level where the finance minister could only meet his interest obligations by allowing for a constant increase in the budget deficit. That deficit totalled 8.6 per cent of gross domestic product (GDP) and thus fuelled inflation, which stood at 14 per cent in 1991.

International credit institutions downgraded their rating of India's creditworthiness, some even moving it into the 'credit watch' category, which made it difficult, if not impossible, for the country to borrow money on the international markets. This threatened capital flows to private domestic banks.

In May 1991 the country was forced to sell small quantities of its gold reserves, and if the International Monetary Fund (IMF) had not offered short-term credit, India might well have experienced a financial collapse.

A radical change

Faced by this situation India was forced to introduce comprehensive reform measures. The 'structural adjustment programme' aimed to bring about a drastic reduction in the number of regulations and controls, de-bureaucratization and the introduction of market mechanisms. Soon after Rao took office, there were two devaluations of the rupee and a trade policy plan was put forward, followed by an industry plan. These plans included three common features:

1. First, they acknowledged that India could no longer live in a fantasy world of economic isolation.
2. Secondly, the plans assumed that the country did not have the resources to achieve the required economic growth and must therefore call on the investment potential of the private sector – both at home and abroad.
3. Thirdly, it became clear that India had to reduce its high levels of public expenditure, meaning savings on welfare and poverty alleviation programmes. This had implications for income distribution. A 1992 study identified a rapid downturn in the living standards of the poor and pointed out that the relaxation of export controls on raw materials brought about an increase in the price of cotton yarn, which led directly to the starvation of handloom weavers in Andhra Pradesh.

The new trade policy swept away the complex web of regulations that had been introduced by successive cabinets in an attempt to restrict the level of imports. At a single stroke, Trade Minister Chidambaran abolished the most complicated import rules and some of the export subsidies by introducing a financial instrument called *Exim certificates* which would allow exporters to import goods for an amount equal to the value of their earnings in foreign currency. The objective of this policy was to enable the Indian economy to earn vital foreign currency by its own efforts.

One important element of India's new industry plan was that foreign companies would be allowed to acquire a majority stake in certain branches of industry. These included:

o the manufacture of metalworking machinery;
o energy generation and distribution;
o electrical and electronic machinery;
o telecommunications;
o machine tools;
o agricultural machinery;
o chemicals.

In order to increase their level of international competitiveness, Indian companies were free to conclude agreements relating to the imports of technology, for which they obtained 'automatic licences'. These measures represented substantial strides towards the establishment of a market economy.

Major improvements in macroeconomic performance

The following figures clearly show how the Indian economy has strengthened:

o Between 1995 and 2006 the average annual growth rate of Indian GDP was 6.3 per cent. In 2007 it reached a peak of 9.7 per cent. By comparison, the average annual growth of GDP between 1980 and 1990 had been 5.8 per cent.
o The annual growth rate of export in goods was 12.2 per cent between 1995 and 2006, reaching 23 per cent in 2007. For the services sector the average annual growth was around 18 per cent for the same period.

These advances were achieved despite:

o poor weather that caused negative agricultural growth in the fiscal year 1995–96 and again in the fiscal year 1997–98,
o the Asian financial crisis in 1997 and 1998,
o international sanctions imposed on India and Pakistan following their tests of nuclear devices in 1998,
o the considerable volatility in world oil and commodity prices that occurred in the period 1998–2000.
o the global economic crisis of 2008–09, which brought new challenges to the Indian economy

Tariff barriers down

The improvements in India's economic performance coincided with a policy of trade liberalization. During the period 1991–97 the average level of India's tariffs was reduced from 128 per cent to 34 per cent, and licensing requirements were liberalized for the import of capital goods, raw materials and components. By 2007 the average tariff level had fallen further, to 14.5 per cent (11.5 on non-agricultural products and 34.4 on agricultural products). Export incentives were limited largely to measures that allowed exporters the duty-free importation of intermediate inputs and raw materials.

Since 1997, the Indian authorities have made substantial progress in phasing out the remaining quantitative restrictions on agricultural, textile, and industrial products, and also in respect of investment policies. On 1 April 2001, India removed the quantitative restrictions on imports in respect of the 715 remaining items.

Economic performance deteriorates, anti-dumping measures increase

However, macroeconomic developments during 2000 – including a resurgence of inflation, a slowdown in industrial production, and downward pressure on the rupee and stock prices – underscore the longer-term question of whether or not the basis for achieving sustained and rapid growth has yet been established. This question is raised because:

o Liberalization appears to have been only half-hearted and limited to a small number of sectors. Furthermore, while some regions of India have indeed benefited from foreign goods and influence, most of the country bears little resemblance to a free market.

o Despite gains in the area of poverty reduction since Independence – the poverty rate fell by over 20 per cent after the 1950s and 1960s – roughly 35 per cent of the population remains below the poverty line. Moreover, despite the country's accelerated economic growth, according to the World Bank India is still home to a third of the world's poor. Notably, rural poverty rates have increased and the regional distribution of income has become increasingly stratified. This is due to a combination of a weak fiscal discipline (constraining public development spending) and slowing structural reform (concentrating growth in the less-regulated services sector), which have left little scope for income gains for lower-skilled agricultural and industrial workers.

o In recent years the Indian government has increased its use of anti-dumping duties. At the end of 1998 the country had 43 anti-dumping measures in force. The elimination of quantitative restrictions and a general lowering of tariffs have facilitated increased incidence of other trade remedy instruments such as anti-dumping measures. Thus, between 1995 and the first half of 2008 India's number of anti-dumping measures grew to 520, making India the world's most active user of such instruments. However, as a result there was a significant increase in the number of countervailing duty cases initiated against India's exports. With an absolute number of 133 cases initiated against it in the period between 1995 and the first half of 2008, India was the seventh most targeted country by anti-dumping policies, behind China, South Korea, Taiwan, the USA, Japan and Indonesia.

Sources: IMF (2000, 2001), World Bank (2001), Shurmer-Smith (2000), WTO (2004, 2008), UNCTAD (2008), Indian Ministry of Commerce and Industry (2006), *Annual Report 2006* (http://commerce.nic.in/dgad/annualreport/ANNUAL-REPORT-2005-2006.pdf).

Case study 5.1 raises a number of questions about trade and protectionism:

1. What forms can protectionism take and what are its effects, including the effects on welfare?
2. What arguments were used in favour of self-reliance and protectionist measures?
3. What caused India to change its trade policy?
4. To what extent can specific interest groups influence the outcome of policy changes – and what arguments favouring protection can be expected from those groups that are influenced negatively under free trade?

In connection with trade theory, we have already seen that, within a country, free trade creates 'losers' who fear that they will not be compensated. There are numerous examples of companies or industrial sectors that have lost out – or even disappeared – because they could not withstand international competition. Those groups that are directly affected have a greater interest in lobbying for protection than do consumers who would benefit from free trade, since they fear they have much more to lose. (The subject of protection on the basis of safeguarding the interests of individual entrepreneurs or other specific interest groups is considered in Chapters 7 and 8.)

Before discussing the arguments both in favour and against trade policy intervention, it is important to make a few more general comments:

1. First, protectionism can restrict trade – as happens, for example, in the case of import duties or export levies – but it can also be a stimulus to trade – as, for example, in the case of export subsidies, soft export credit terms or export credit guarantee conditions.

2. Secondly, we can speak of protectionist measures only if the government takes deliberate measures which are intended to exert a direct influence over international trade. If a country tries to stimulate exports and restrict imports by changing its exchange rate or through the adoption of a low-wage policy, this is not usually classed as protectionist behaviour because the influence on trade is indirect. However, Case study 5.2 indicates that, in such a situation, a country is also open to criticism.

3. Thirdly, protectionism usually refers to government policy, but it is clear that the behaviour of businesses can also have an influence on trade. For example, if a number of companies operating internationally conclude a deal that restricts competition, or if they actually form a cartel, this can lead to restrictions on international trade (and can also drive up price levels). However, this is not usually referred to as protectionism because it is not undertaken by national governments.

4. Fourthly, protectionist measures can take many different forms: governments habitually placing their orders exclusively with national companies, development aid being tied only to national tenders, or a tax regime that favours domestic firms. Furthermore, one can speak of protectionism if customs formalities, environmental standards, health regulations or product characteristics are unjustly stricter for imports than for national products.

Case study 5.2   Foreign Sales Corporation Act

The US government allowed American export firms such as Microsoft, Boeing and General Electric to protect their foreign profits by channelling these profits through subsidiaries in tax havens such as Barbados and the Virgin Islands, resulting in an estimated total of $4 billion in tax exemption. During 2004 the EU increasingly criticized this US practice.

In this dispute, the USA argued that some European countries had introduced comparable tax regimes. However, according to EU Trade Commissioner Pascal Lamy, US tax policy distorted international trade because it provided American products with an unfair advantage in other markets. According to Lamy, this phenomenon occurred in an increasing number of sectors, including software and agriculture. As a result, the EU asked the World Trade Organization (WTO) for permission to take compensating trade sanctions (countervailing duties) against the USA.

The granting of the right for the EU to take these sanctions led to a new trade dispute. The $4 billion worth of duties that the EU could impose on imports from the USA was

20 times higher than the trade sanctions the USA had imposed on the EU in previous trade disputes. US Trade Representative Robert Zoellick condemned the disproportionate reaction, remarking that if the EU were actually to exercise these trade sanctions, they would be opting for the 'nuclear' option and escalating the crisis still further.

In May 2006 the United States Senate gave its final approval to a tax-cut bill that includes the repeal of corporate tax breaks that the WTO had classified as illegal export subsidies. The passage of this provision brought to an end the long-standing trade dispute between the USA and the EU. In response, the then EU Trade Commissioner Peter Mandelson announced that pending retaliatory sanctions against the USA worth over €1.8 billion ($2.4 billion) would be suspended immediately.

5.3 | The optimum tariff theory and other trade measures

5.3.1 Protection and welfare

Traditional trade theory concluded that free trade is generally preferable to protection according to the criterion of national welfare. At the same time, however, and from the same point of view, two arguments in favour of protection are traditionally recognized as being theoretically valid.

The first is based on the *optimum tariff* theory. In essence, this argument, developed below, means that one can use import protection to force foreign suppliers to make price concessions, so that a country can maximize its welfare by setting a particular level of tariffs – at least as long as other countries do not retaliate.

The second argument, which will be explained in Section 5.6, is that protectionism can increase a country's welfare if there is a market distortion or *market failure* in that country. Such a failure exists if, for instance, market prices are not an accurate reflection of production costs. The result is that demand and supply react to the wrong process signals so that either too much or too little is produced or consumed. In national terms, this can result in a loss of welfare.

According to this second argument, one can try to limit this loss by introducing trade policy measures. However, this argument holds true only when it is justified to assume that the country confronted with protection does not introduce any retaliatory measures. Thus, both arguments assume a rather asymmetrical situation between trading partners.

In practice, of course, many other arguments are also advanced in defence of protectionism – some of which are concerned with national welfare and some of which are not expressed in economic terms. These non-economic arguments include efforts to achieve independence from other countries in building up basic industries or achieving self-sufficiency in food supplies. (This last argument was actually a central factor in the development of European agricultural policy; see Case study 5.4.)

Other economic arguments for protection can be based on:

o improving a country's economic situation;
o expanding domestic employment;
o increasing the government's revenue; or
o alleviating the national balance of payments position.

In most of these situations, an attempt is made to 'export' national problems to other countries through protection; obviously, this poses a high risk of escalation, because if a number of closely connected economies are all experiencing recession at the same time, as is often the case, and one country decides to restrict imports, this is likely to cause a further deterioration in the economic situation of neighbouring countries. These policies are referred to as 'beggar thy neighbour' policies and, with the deepening of the current crisis, they are considered to pose an increasing threat to the global economy and international trade.

It is a rare and exceptional case when one country is confronted by the under-utilization of its production capacity and, at the same time, another country is overspending; in such an instance, protection methods introduced by the first country do not necessarily conflict with the interests of the second country.

Trade restrictions by the first country can then moderate the overheating of the economy in the second country. Restricting imports from the second country reduces the level of spending in the first country, and exporting more to the second country may alleviate the second country's overstretched use of production capacity.

A protectionist climate often causes people to seek an overseas scapegoat for problems in the domestic economy. If in such cases people look, for instance, at the balance of payments, they may focus not on the overall trends, but on developments in relation to one or more specific trading partners (for example, the US current account deficit in trade with China or the EU; see also Case study 5.3).

Case study 5.3   The USA attempts to block China's entry to the WTO

In September 2001, the USA tried to block the entrance of China to the WTO – something for which China had been pressing over a period of about 15 years. As an additional condition, the US government demanded a privileged position for the US insurance company American International Group (AIG) in the lucrative Chinese insurance market. Washington wanted to secure a privileged position (in comparison with the EU) on the Chinese insurance market, with a particular focus on life insurance. As a justification of this demand, US trade authorities referred to the trade agreement of 1999 between Peking and AIG. According to this agreement, AIG is allowed to set up insurance offices in China, which are wholly owned by AIG.

However, under the new trade agreement between China and the EU, foreign insurance companies were restricted to a maximum of 50 per cent ownership of any new start-ups in China. The other 50 per cent had to be owned by local Chinese businessmen. It was clear that the agreement between China and the EU contradicted the China–USA agreement.

Therefore, the USA, insisted that their bilateral agreement with China would continue in the future without any concessions. The USA referred to the so-called 'grandfather' clause (which implies the application of an old rule to a continuing situation, while a new rule would affect all future situations) or, as the trade representative of the USA, Robert Zoellick, argued: 'China made agreements on the insurance sector as part of a bilateral agreement with the USA. We expect that China will act as agreed.' According to officials of the WTO, the planned entry of China would be threatened if China failed to comply with the request from Washington. A WTO official called the American demand 'absolutely unreasonable'. One consequence would be that the USA would be allowed to retain unfair advantages – which would conflict with both fair and equal market opportunities and also the concept of trade liberalization.

According to a spokesman for the European Commission, China can simply enter the WTO: 'In that case the WTO rules are applicable. If AIG would then stick to its demands, it would be up to the WTO to solve the dispute.'

On 11 December 2001, China became the 143rd member of the WTO. Later, in July 2007, AIG, which was at that time the world's biggest insurer, through its subsidiary AIU Insurance Co., was granted the right to establish a wholly owned subsidiary in China. This new subsidiary was called the AIG General Insurance Company China Limited. Headquartered in Shanghai, with branches in Guangdong and Shenzhen, in 2008 the AIG subsidiary opened a new office in Beijing.

5.3.2 The optimum import tariff

The starting point for the optimum tariff theory is the attempt to maximize a country's welfare. The theory is based on the idea that in certain situations a country can exert so much pressure on the foreign supplier by protectionist measures – for example, through import levies – that the supplier is prepared to cut the price at which he offers the imported goods in order to preserve his market position.

If this is carried out systematically, the importing country *improves its terms of trade*. As mentioned above, the terms of trade indicate the ratio between the export and import prices of a country. An improvement in the terms of trade means that import prices fall relative to export prices, leading to an increase in the level of a country's national income. As we have seen, this applies only if the other country is not able or willing to take protectionist countermeasures. However, it should be made clear that an improvement in the terms of trade means nothing more than an improvement in the terms on which exports are exchanged for imports, thus falling import prices suggest that the same quantity of exports can now buy more imports.

At a given level of national production, this will result in a higher level of goods being available for consumption and investment, which implies a higher national income. Box 5.1 considers two examples that show how an improvement in the terms of trade is reflected in a country's national income.

It is also important to point out that the main argument in support of the optimum tariff (Box 5.2) assumes that economies are able to adapt rapidly to new market conditions. For example, if certain sectors can expand under the influence of trade policy measures while other sectors contract, this will in practice entail adjustment costs for society – for example, in the form of accelerated depreciation or costs in connection with retraining, relocation, and possible unemployment. These costs are disregarded in the analysis given in Box 5.2.

Box 5.1 National income effect of an improvement in the terms of trade

The degree to which a given change in the terms of trade affects a country's welfare depends upon:

o the volume of exports; and
o the extent to which the export sector generates added value.

This can be illustrated by an example. If a country like the Netherlands records a 1 per cent deterioration in the terms of trade in a given year (as was the case in 1991), the implication is that the same quantity of exports can now be exchanged on the international market for 1 per cent less imports than before. The *average export ratio* (the value of exports in relation to GNP) of the Netherlands was about 60 per cent in that year and the value added domestically per unit of exports could be estimated at one-third. In consequence, the total welfare of the Netherlands declined by $-1 \times 0.6 \times 0.33 \approx -0.2$ per cent as a result of the 1 per cent deterioration in the terms of trade. This can be explained through the fact that 1 per cent deterioration only influences Dutch GNP via the export ratio (0.6), and then only in so far as these exports relate to the value added in the Netherlands (one-third of the exports). Although the result in the example means only a slight reduction in GNP, it is a pure loss since it is assumed that the Netherlands still has to maintain a constant level of production.

A somewhat more extreme, but nevertheless realistic, example was the position of the Organization of the Petroleum Exporting Countries (OPEC) at the time of the two oil shocks in the 1970s. For these countries, the sudden spike in the oil prices brought a dramatic improvement in their terms of trade (an increase of around 400 per cent). At the time, the OPEC countries had export ratios of approximately 80 per cent. Assuming that there was a very high domestic value-added component of the oil produced, say 90 per cent, this meant that, for these countries, the terms of trade effects resulted in an increase in GNP of $400 \times 0.8 \times 0.9 = 288$ per cent!

Sometimes the change in a country's terms of trade is not just a mere given, but is influenced by developments in the country's own technological base. For example, let us assume that a 3 per cent improvement in productivity is achieved in the export sector. Let us also assume that, as a result of the situation in the global market, this advantage is reflected in a corresponding reduction in the price of the export product (or a quality improvement) for foreign customers. If the contribution of the export sector to the economy is 25 per cent, the increase in welfare due to a higher sector productivity will be 0.25×3 per cent $= 0.75$ per cent.

However, if this is offset by a 3 per cent deterioration in the terms of trade, the gained welfare drops back by 0.25×3 per cent $= 0.75$ per cent. The result is that there is no net change in welfare – despite the increase in productivity. This example shows that it is easy to see that, when given a slightly different combination of figures, a situation can actually arise in which the negative terms of a trade effect outweigh other, possibly positive, effects. In that case we have a situation in which a technical improvement or economic growth leads to impoverishment. It is easy to deduce that if, in contrast to the above case, the productivity increase had taken place in the sector that was competing with imports and had therefore led to a decline in import prices, the two effects would have had a reinforcing effect on each other.

If protectionism leads to an improvement in the terms of trade, this effect can be seen to have affected the national income of the country that is applying the protectionist measures.

However, other welfare effects will also occur at the same time, and these will have to be offset against the terms of trade effect. Let us assume that protectionism is introduced in the form of an import tariff: in this circumstance the product price is also likely to rise within the country. Unless the price reduction at the border is *greater than* the tariff per unit on the actual product, the price will *rise* in the importing country, where the tariff will, of course, be passed on in the supply price.

If we confine the analysis to the changes in the section of the market where protection applies, we can identify three effects:

(i) Some domestic producers can now produce profitably at this higher price, and for the original producers this higher price may increase the level of profits. This positive effect is reflected in an increase in the producer surplus as a result of protectionism (area a in Figure 5.1, Box 5.2).

(ii) Consumers in the country see that the 'protected' product has now become more expensive, so that some purchasers will drop out – and those that remain will pay more. This negative effect is reflected in a decline in the consumer surplus as a result of protectionism (areas $a + b + c + d$ in Figure 5.1, Box 5.2).

(iii) The government receives tariff revenue on the quantity imported and can then transfer that to its citizens – perhaps by cutting taxes or in other ways. This positive effect is called the tariff effect of protectionism ($c + e$ in Figure 5.1, Box 5.2).

Clearly, it is the balance of these three effects, $e - (b + d)$, that determines whether or not it would be a good idea for a particular country to adopt a protectionist attitude. We can also infer (see Box 5.2, last paragraph) that one tariff is optimal from the country's point of view, because the positive and negative effects do not change to the same extent as a result of a small change in the tariff.

Box 5.2   The optimum tariff

Figure 5.1 illustrates the domestic supply and demand curves of the EU for citrus fruits. The consumer surplus is the positive difference between the selling price of a product and the price which individual consumers are prepared to pay for the same product, aggregated over all consumers. Thus, the consumer surplus under free trade (at P_w) consists of the area above P_w up to the demand curve (line D). The producer surplus is the positive difference between the selling price of the product and the minimum price that the individual domestic entrepreneurs wish to receive on account of their cost structure, aggregated for all producers. Under free trade, this producer surplus is shown by the area below P_w down to the supply curve. The supply curve corresponds with the marginal cost curve.

If the EU introduces a tariff on citrus fruits, this will be reflected in changes in both the producer surplus and the consumer surplus. Say that the tariff causes the price of citrus fruits in the EU to increase to P_t. Consumers now have to pay a higher price than under conditions of free trade, so that the consumer surplus falls by $a + b + c + d$. Domestic producers now receive that higher price for their products, so that the producer's surplus increases by a. As a result of the higher price, the consumption of citrus fruits in the EU falls from Od_2 to Od_1 and EU production increases from Os_1 to Os_2. This means that the government's tariff revenue relates to the volume of imports $Od_1 - Os_2$. Since the difference $P_t - P^*$ shows the level of tariff per unit of product, $c + e$ represents the tariff revenue for the government.

The net welfare effects can now be divided into two components. On the one hand, there is an efficiency loss, shown by triangles $b + d$. This loss will always occur when a tariff is imposed: b and d, in fact, indicate the losses caused to society by the distortion of the price signals for consumers and producers as a result of the imposition of a tariff. On the other hand, there is the gain in welfare based on the terms of trade effect of the imposition of a tariff on citrus fruit imports by the EU, because the tariff led to a fall in EU demand on the world market and, consequently, a fall in the export prices of foreign

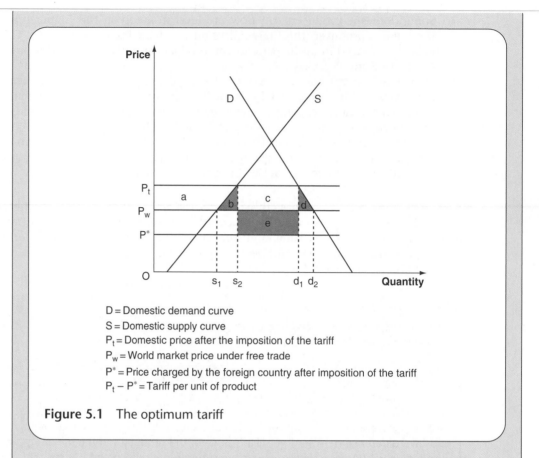

D = Domestic demand curve
S = Domestic supply curve
P_t = Domestic price after the imposition of the tariff
P_w = World market price under free trade
P^* = Price charged by the foreign country after imposition of the tariff
$P_t - P^*$ = Tariff per unit of product

Figure 5.1   The optimum tariff

citrus fruits. This means there will be a positive welfare effect for the EU totalling e. Thus, the ultimate net wealth effect is the balance of the negative effects, b + d, and the positive effect e. Figure 5.1 illustrates graphically that this net effect may be positive.

Since a change in the level of the tariff does not cause areas b and d to change to the same extent as e, it can be intuited that there is a certain tariff level at which the positive net welfare effect is maximized. That level is called the optimum tariff.

Using a similar analysis we can also show that if the country is small, so that it is unable to influence the price on the world market (in Figure 5.1 $P^* = P_w$), there is no possible improvement in the terms of trade. This means that a tariff will always reduce the level of welfare in the protectionist country – that is, the optimum tariff is zero. This is an important finding, first because many smaller countries are unable to influence prices on the international market by means of their protectionist behaviour (thus, it is certainly not always possible to force an improvement in one's terms of trade), and, secondly, because in these cases a country can gain by removing its own protectionist measures even if other countries do not (the country would gain areas b and d in Figure 5.1). It is a common belief that other countries can only be expected to make trade concessions if offered something in return (see also Chapter 9); this philosophy dominated ideas of trade policy during the nineteenth century. However, the theoretical model discussed above shows that unilateral trade concessions can also increase domestic welfare, and this was actually the argument that largely determined the British attitude to trade policy in the latter half of the nineteenth century.

The optimum tariff theory does not apply solely to those imports that represent a threat to an industry in the country in question. It is equally applicable if protectionism is oriented towards exports, in that the government decides to tax exports and not imports. The idea of a government increasing the country's welfare by taxing its own exports may appear paradoxical; after all, one would expect it to have to subsidize its exports for that purpose. But, as will be shown in the section that follows, it is easy to show that, apart from exceptional cases, there are in fact more reasons for the government to tax exports than to subsidize them.

5.4 | Export policy

5.4.1 An export tax

Example: a country exports a large number of units of a product at $10 each and the government imposes a tax of $2 per unit. If all else remains equal, the exporter will receive $10, the foreign customer now has to pay $12, and the government collects $2 per unit sold.

However, at a price of $12 the level of foreign demand can be expected to fall, and this will force domestic suppliers to cut their price until their supply is absorbed by the other country. How the new market equilibrium looks will depend upon how rapidly demand and supply adjust to the change in prices. If the exporter has a substantial influence on the market, then we can anticipate that the eventual situation will be as illustrated in Box 5.3: the price received by the exporter will have fallen, but foreign customers will be forced to pay the export country a higher price overall, because of the export levy.

Box 5.3   The effects of an export levy

Figure 5.2 shows the demand and supply curves for bicycles in the UK. Under conditions of free trade, the quantity $Os_2 - Od_1$ of bicycles is exported at price P. The UK government decides to tax bicycle exports. This will cause bicycle manufacturers in the UK to cut their selling price in order to remain competitive on the world market.

The assumption here is that UK suppliers do not apply any price discrimination on market segments, which means that when they set their prices they make no distinction between export products and products for the domestic market. This means that their price on the UK market also falls to level P, and that the price at which bicycles from the foreign market are offered on the UK market now also falls to level P.

The price at which the bicycles are exported from the UK is now P_t^* – that is, P plus the export tax. The reduction in the price of bicycles on the home market has caused the consumer surplus to increase by the area $a + b$. The producer's surplus has fallen by area $a + b + c + d + e$. At the new price, exports are $Os_1 - Od_2$. When multiplied by the export tax per unit of product, $P_t^* - P$, this yields tax revenue for the government totalling $d + f$. The net welfare effect is the balance of $c + d + e$ (negative) and $d + f$ (positive), or $f - c - e$. The triangles $c + e$ can again be regarded as efficiency losses due to distortions in the consumption and production decisions; f can be attributed to the improvement in the terms of trade resulting from the higher price of export products.

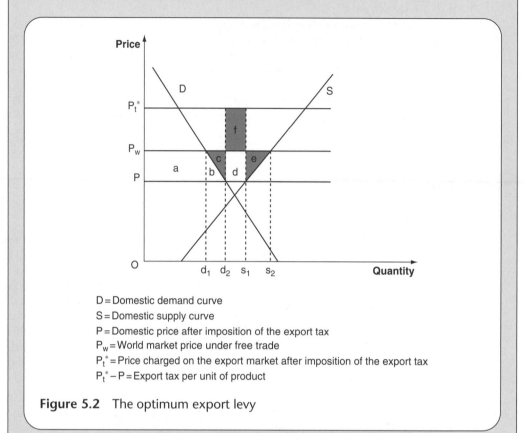

D = Domestic demand curve
S = Domestic supply curve
P = Domestic price after imposition of the export tax
P_w = World market price under free trade
P_t^* = Price charged on the export market after imposition of the export tax
$P_t^* - P$ = Export tax per unit of product

Figure 5.2   The optimum export levy

Whether or not the improvement in the terms of trade (f) will exceed the efficiency loss (c + e) will be determined by three factors: (i) the level of the export tax; (ii) demand and supply elasticities for the product concerned on the home market; and (iii) the elasticity of foreign demand. A smaller and/or more inelastic foreign demand for the product will imply a greater chance of a net positive welfare effect for the country imposing the export tax. This is because, if foreign demand is inelastic, a rise in price will lead to only a small fall in demand.

One final question: what effect does the export tax have upon the combined levels of welfare of the two countries? Figure 5.3 shows a foreign demand curve; for reasons of simplicity, it is assumed that the other country does not actually manufacture any of these products, so that the domestic demand and the demand for imports coincide.

The demand curve in Figure 5.3 indicates the quantity imported by the foreign country at a given price. Before the export tax, the foreign country imports O_{d1}. If the export tax is imposed, the price rise causes foreign demand to fall to O_{d2}. The consumer surplus has now dropped by g + h. g indicates the terms of trade effect and thus reflects the transfer to the UK, but h is the additional loss of welfare for the foreign country caused by the distortion of consumption decisions. The net welfare in both countries together is unaffected by the transfer because that simply means shifting funds from one place

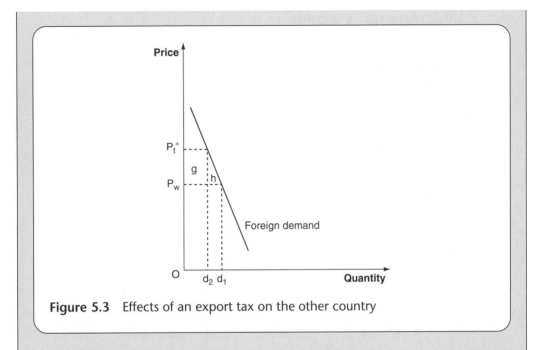

Figure 5.3   Effects of an export tax on the other country

(area g) to another (area f). This leaves only the efficiency losses. In the UK these were c + e in Figure 5.2; we now add h from Figure 5.3. Thus, there has been a net decline in total welfare (by c + e + h): the welfare gained by one country is thus insufficient to compensate for the welfare lost by the other country.

For the country as a whole, this means an improvement in the terms of trade at the expense of the other country, similar to the result of introducing an import levy. This produces two effects which have to be taken together in order to determine the overall welfare effect:

(i) the surpluses of both the producers and the consumers. The former has fallen because some exporters have dropped out at the lower price; in addition, the other exporters receive a lower price than was the case previously. In contrast, the consumer surplus has risen as a result of the price cut on the home market; and

(ii) the government's revenue generated by exports. Some of this can be used, for example, to compensate the producers in one way or another. In this case it is the foreign customers that ultimately support this compensation because they are 'forced' to pay a higher price for the exports (the positive terms of trade effect). This means that there is a good chance that domestic exporters can be compensated in full by using the tariff revenue, and in the end there will still be a net gain in the country's welfare. This appears to be somewhat paradoxical given that, in Figure 5.2, domestic production declines as a result of the export tax and exports fall from $Os_2 - Od_1$ to $Os_1 - Od_2$. Nevertheless, the dominant, positive terms of trade effect ensures that there is a net increase in national welfare. This indicates that the arguments supporting an optimum import tariff are also applicable, in a symmetrical manner, to the optimum export tariff situation. This phenomenon is known as *Lerner's symmetry theorem*.

5.4.2 An export subsidy

Box 5.4 The effects of an export subsidy

In Figure 5.4 we can see that the export subsidy means that other countries are faced by an export curve that has shifted downwards by the amount of the subsidy per unit of exports (Ex'). This shift is logical because the exporter's behaviour is unchanged: if he receives export price x, he still offers the same quantity y as he did before the granting of the subsidy.

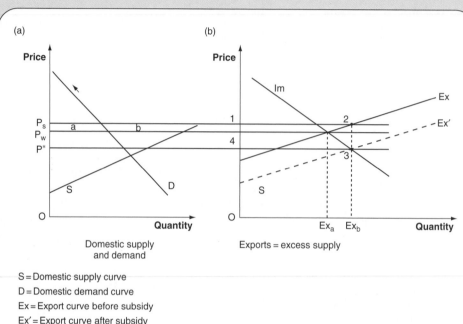

S = Domestic supply curve
D = Domestic demand curve
Ex = Export curve before subsidy
Ex' = Export curve after subsidy
Im = Import curve
P_w = Price before subsidy
P^* = Price on the international market after subsidy
P_s = Price on the home market (= exports) after subsidy
$P_s - P^*$ = Subsidy per unit of product
$Ex_b - Ex_a$ = Increase in exports as a result of the export subsidy

Figure 5.4   The welfare effect of an export subsidy

However, the foreign customer now benefits from the subsidy and sees the export supply as being based on a supply curve that has fallen by the amount of the subsidy per unit. Thus, Ex' is the relevant curve for the foreign customer; Ex is the relevant curve for the exporter. The price on the international market is now P* (demand and supply are equal on the international market), which implies a deterioration in the terms of trade for the exporter.

On the exporter's home market there is now a higher price level – $P^* +$ export subsidy $= P_s$. This is the price that the exporter receives: he receives P^* from the foreign customer and the rest is added by the government. If there is a competing supply in the foreign country, we can assume that its price will settle at the level received for exports, so that the overall domestic price level for this product rises to level P_s.

About the net welfare effect for the exporting country we concluded that it is negative. Initially, the producer's surplus increases by $a + b$; however that is offset by a decline of a in the consumer surplus, leaving a balance b. Furthermore, in order to arrive at this balance – which corresponds roughly to the area above P bounded by 1 and 2 in (b) – an export subsidy is granted totalling 1234. Since $1234 > b$, there is a net loss of welfare. Moreover, as a result of the deterioration in the terms of trade, part of the subsidy is 'lost' to the other country.

For the two countries taken together, the export subsidy in this model also produces a net reduction in welfare. The effect of the change in the terms of trade is again just a transfer of funds, and hence neutral. This leaves the negative effects as a result of efficiency losses through distorted allocation.

Governments will often argue that export subsidies are granted not only in the interests of exporters, but also as a means of promoting employment. We can see from Box 5.4 that, as a result of the subsidy, there is an increase in the level of exports. Domestic consumption declines by only a small amount, so that – all other things being equal – there will be an expansion of both national production and employment.

However, the point is that the subsidies have to come from somewhere – and that therefore the hidden costs of the subsidy must also be taken into account. If this is done, it will often be apparent that there are more cost-effective ways of creating jobs. We shall return to this in Section 5.5.

Research into the actual costs of an export subsidy policy points in the direction suggested by the above theory. The fact that, in practice, export subsidies are far more common than export taxes demonstrates therefore that, in the application of trade policy measures, governments are often persuaded more by specific interests of producers or improper arguments concerning employment, than by arguments based on the total welfare of a country. Case study 5.4 illustrates this by describing the costs of the EU export subsidy policy for agricultural products.

Case study 5.4   Costs of the EU's agricultural policy

One favourite sector for government protection is agriculture. In the EU, for example, this protection is granted partly through measures aimed at the home market – such as production subsidies, guaranteed prices and income supplements – and partly through measures aimed at international trade – including import tariffs and quotas and export subsidies.

These measures form a cohesive package, because the intended higher price level in the EU must not be undermined by cheaper imports from outside the area. That is why internal price guarantees have to be accompanied by import restrictions to correct any price difference between the international and the internal market. One effect of such a policy is that the area's own farmers cannot sell outside the protected market – except at prices which are lower than those guaranteed on the home market. That is why export subsidies are regarded as another logical complement to the guaranteed price system.

The above description gives a broad outline of the EU agricultural policy in relation to several leading products. One of the principal shortcomings of the Common Agricultural Policy (CAP) is that it is excessively expensive. Each year about 46 per cent of the EU's total budget is spent on the CAP. The British Department for Business Innovation and Skills estimates that the artificially high food prices promoted by the CAP add about £9 to the weekly food bill of a family of four and also mean that the income derived from an EU dairy cow is higher than that of half the world's human population.

Another major issue with the CAP is that over time its subsidies encourage overproduction. The EU market is unable to absorb all its agricultural production and therefore the surplus products are sold, cheaply, to developing countries. This causes market distortion by undercutting local farmers who are unable to compete with the heavily subsidized European goods. Of course, the EU is not solely to blame for these developments, since US farmers are also known to dump subsidized agricultural goods on developing markets.

Furthermore, specialists argue that the CAP is encouraging intensive farming, which damages the environment. By guaranteeing minimal prices the CAP makes it economically advantageous for farmers to exploit all the land available, even if this requires the use of heavy chemicals.

According to theory, in order to arrive at an overall assessment of the welfare effects of the support policy described above we must take account of the lower consumer surplus and the higher producer surplus, as well as the costs to the taxpayer. By way of illustration, Table 5.1 shows such calculations for agricultural protection in the leading western blocs – the EU, Japan and the USA.

Finally, we must also consider the terms of trade effects of protection, because, through its system of import restrictions and export subsidies, the EU's agricultural policy influences the situation on world markets. The result is that world market prices are lower than they would have been under a system of free trade. The policy thus also causes the world market to develop increasingly into an unstable market of surpluses. From this point of view, taxpayers are not only supporting their own agricultural sector; they are also subsidizing foreign consumption. On the other hand, in the long term the agricultural

Table 5.1 Annual domestic costs as a result of government intervention in agriculture ($ billion)

Region	Year	Consumer's costs (1)	Taxpayers' costs (2)	Producers' benefits (3)	Total domestic costs (1 + 2−3)
EU	1980	34.6	11.5	30.7	15.4
Japan	1976	7.1	−0.4	2.6	4.1
USA	1985	5.7	10.3	11.6	4.4

Source: Johnsen et al. (1985).

Table 5.2 Welfare impacts from the elimination of global agricultural tariffs and subsidies

Region	Unilateral liberalization industrial countries	Unilateral liberalization developing countries	Global (multilateral) liberalization
Developing countries	−11.8	28.2	18.3
Industrial market economies	48.5	−10.2	45.9
European planned economies	−11.1	−13.1	−23.1
World	25.6	4.9	41.1

Source: Diao and Burfisher (2001).

policy adopted in industrial countries will damage the competitive position of exporters in other countries, including those in the developing world.

Valdés and Zietz (1980) concluded that a tariff reduction in the Organisation for Economic Co-operation and Development (OECD) countries would lead to a general increase in the levels of agricultural prices. This would be beneficial to developing countries that were net exporters of agriculture. In developing countries that were net importers, however, the levels of welfare would decline as a result of the deterioration in their terms of trade.

Research by Diao and Burfisher (2001) suggests that in the event of the elimination of agricultural protection, such as tariffs, domestic support and export subsidies, the world market prices of agricultural products could be expected to rise by an average of 12 per cent. Moreover, the long-term global consequences of consumer purchasing power would amount to around $56 billion annually – around 0.2 per cent of global GDP. Table 5.2 shows the substantial economic gains for the world economy.

With mounting evidence against the protectionist agricultural policies of the developed countries, the WTO is trying to improve the terms of trade for the developing countries, which should be able to gain substantially from a system of free trade. At present, Europe's CAP has undergone significant reforms. Today the EU's CAP policy is demand-driven, with farmers no longer being paid simply to produce. While in the past farmers received more subsidies the more they produced, at present this link has been severed and most of the aid received by farmers is independent of their production volumes. The decoupling of subsidies from production is meant to ensure income stability for farmers while discouraging overproduction. Furthermore, if they are to receive subsidies farmers have to observe strict environmental, food safety, phytosanitary and animal welfare standards.

The WTO views the EU's initiative as a positive development for developing countries, which will now face less unfair competition in the form of dumping prices for agricultural products. The resulting welfare consequences for the less developed world are considered a powerful contribution to the reduction of global poverty.

Even in the case that the developing countries' agricultural products are integrated into western markets, the safety and quality of food needs to be guaranteed. In recent years, western consumers are becoming driven less by price incentives, especially given their increasing concern about food safety following animal epidemics such as BSE and 'bird flu'. Developing countries are increasingly faced by the 'protectionist' effect of western food quality standards.

5.5 | Volume restrictions on trade

The previous section focused on the welfare effect of taxes or subsidies to influence international trade. However, some forms of intervention actually impose restrictions upon the market mechanism itself. These may take the form of an upper limit (or, in some cases, a lower limit) which is set in advance for the volume or value of international trade: for example, no more than a particular quantity or value of a given product may be imported each year, or the customers have to buy a given minimum quantity or value of that product each year.

Developments since the Second World War have shown how, in practice, such 'non-market-conforming' measures are playing an increasing role in trade policy. As we shall see in Chapter 9, specialists argue that the increasing use of 'non-market-conforming' instruments emphasizes the attempt of governments to maintain their influence on international trade and are aimed specifically at countering the GATT's policy of eliminating traditional 'market-conforming' instruments. One very common variant is the voluntary export restraint (VER); that is, the situation in which the exporter decides to restrict the quantity or value of its exports to a particular market (an example of this will be given in Case study 5.5).

Such restraints pose several questions:

○ How does the introduction of a VER influence welfare in the importing country?
○ Do VERs have comparable effects with traditional 'market-conforming' trade policies?

5.5.1 Voluntary export restraint

It should be clear that the application of a VER – as in the case of Japanese cars sold in the EU discussed in Case study 5.5 – will not have a neutral effect on welfare.

First, as a result of the restriction on exports, and therefore the other country's imports of foreign goods, the market price will be higher than if there were no VER. This leads to a transfer of income from the consumers (who pay a higher price for cars) to the domestic and foreign producers (who make higher profits as a result of the higher price). To this extent, the effect is comparable with that of an import tariff.

Secondly, there is a difference: in the case of an import tariff the government of the importing country receives import duties; under the VER, that is not the case (unless we are talking about the theoretical situation in which the government of the importing country is able to auction the right to the VER in some manner).

Thirdly, if the price on the sales market is driven up by the trade restriction while the production costs remain constant, an excess profit is generated. This excess profit normally goes to the foreign producers who manage to secure a position in the limited market. It is also possible, however, for this excess profit to go to the intermediaries who benefit from the higher margins. Thus, in any case it is uncertain whether this excess profit will eventually go to the importing country; it is more likely to end up somewhere abroad. In that case, the welfare effect of the VER for the importing country is less favourable than if imports were restricted by a 'market-conforming' instrument.

5.5.2 Import quota

While the VER limits imports abroad because the exporting country imposes its own restrictions on volume, in the case of an *import quota* the level of imports will be restricted by measures introduced in the importing country. Therefore, an import quota has the same effect as a VER and, at first sight, a similar one to that of an import levy. Here, too, as the result of higher prices a transfer of welfare takes place from domestic consumers to domestic and foreign producers via higher prices.

There is, however, a fundamental difference between an import quota or VER and a tariff: it is not certain that the difference between the international market price and the domestic market price in the importing country will go to the importing country. The result of both an import tariff and a volume restriction is the creation of a scarcity situation of the imported product in the importing country. The result is that the price that people are prepared to pay differs from that at which the exporter would be willing to sell. In the case of an import tariff, this price difference goes to the government of the importing country, which can then pass it on to its own people.

However, if there is any kind of restriction on the volume of imports, then it is not clear which party will succeed in collecting the excess profit:

o The trader who manages to buy the product from the exporter at the export price and sell it at the higher price in the importing country can gain this excess profit.
o If the exporter wants to gain this excess profit, then he has to make certain that he can supply within the quota limits.
o The government of the importing country can only gain the excess profit by auctioning export licences for foreign suppliers or import licences for domestic importers.

A further objection to volume restrictions on the international markets is that they dampen down competition. Thus, foreign firms, possibly offering better terms of supply, have no chance to capitalize on their competitiveness.

Case study 5.5 illustrates the welfare effects of the application of a trade restriction on Japanese cars by the EU.

Case study 5.5   The welfare effects of trade restrictions

A study by Smith and Venables (1991) on the trade restrictions applied by various EU countries to the exports of Japanese cars to the EU includes three estimates of the welfare effects of:

1. the abolition of trade restrictions by the individual EU members;
2. the replacement of the individual trade restrictions of each member by a 'comparable' import tariff for each member; and
3. the replacement of the individual trade restrictions of each member by a common EU trade restriction.

1. The abolition of trade restrictions

As has been stated already, a trade restriction transfers income from consumers to producers. As a result of restrictions on foreign competition, fewer cars will be supplied to the EU market than under conditions of free competition with Japanese producers. This has the effect of increasing car prices, so that part of the consumer surplus is converted into a producer surplus.

According to Smith and Venables, the abolition of the French trade restriction on Japanese cars, for example, will cause the consumer surplus in France to increase by €1.5 billion per annum, while the profit for French car manufacturers will fall by

€940 million per annum, and the French government's tax revenue increase by €168 million per annum. This estimate is based on the assumption that, as a result of abolition of the import restrictions on Japanese cars, a (standard) common EU import tariff of 10.3 per cent is levied; this yields €177 million in import duties. In the study, other welfare effects were not computed.

Italy also records a substantial annual gain in welfare in a comparable situation: an additional €2.7 billion in consumer surplus, while the loss to Italian carmakers is estimated to be some €966 million per annum. Similar welfare effects were also discovered in other countries that applied a trade restriction on Japanese cars (such as the UK, Spain and Portugal).

If all EU member states were to abandon trade restrictions on Japanese cars, this would increase the consumer surplus in the EU by €6.3 billion. In sum, the profits of all EU car manufacturers would fall by €2.7 billion.

2. 'Comparable' import tariffs

France is the only country for which researchers estimated the effects replacing trade restrictions with a 'comparable' tariff would have on national welfare. It must be stated here that, along with Italy, France was, at that time, applying the most strident trade restrictions on Japanese cars in Europe and that the authors assumed the 'comparable' tariff would be set at 34.9 per cent (the tariff at which the production level of EU manufacturers remains constant). In comparison with the above case, the decline in the profits for French producers is smaller ('only' €215 million). In this case the increase in the consumer surplus is €738 million – roughly half the increase found under Advantage 1 above. Finally, the French government obtains additional tariff revenue totalling €354 million.

3. A common trade restriction

In a third exercise, the researchers examined the welfare effects that will occur if each member state replaces its own trade restriction with a common trade restriction that maintains a constant share of the EU market for Japanese producers.

This exercise is of great practical significance because, in the long term, the establishment of the single market in the EU will mean that national import quotas can no longer be applied effectively. The result of the introduction of a common VER is that the welfare effects are much smaller than if the individual trade restrictions were totally abolished (case 1). In this case, the consumer surpluses in France and Italy would increase by €520 million and €1.3 billion, respectively, while the carmakers' profits in these two countries are estimated to fall by €251 million and €481 million, respectively. It is noteworthy in this case that a country such as Germany, which does not impose any trade restrictions on Japanese cars, is confronted by a substantial loss of welfare: here, the consumer surplus falls by €1 billion while the German carmakers' profits increase by only €77 million. For the EU as a whole, replacing the individual trade restrictions of its member states with a common trade restriction yields only a small increase in the consumer surplus (€197 million), while at the same time, producing a decline of €405 million in the profits of the EU motor vehicle sector.

A more recent example of increasing welfare resulting from the abolition of trade restrictions was provided by EU lawmakers. In February 2008 they approved plans to remove the final remaining obstacles to the free flow of goods within the European market. The package of laws was targeted at the 15 per cent of goods traded within the EU that are not covered by EU-wide technical rules. Although the new law bundle refers only to the low volume of trade relating to a limited number of goods – bread, bicycles, furniture, ladders, pasta, it has been estimated that, in the future, it could save European consumers a massive €150 billion each year. This example verifies that it is not only the liberalization of international trade but also that of internal trade that can have a significant effect on the level of general welfare.

Case study 5.5 concludes that the protection of EU producers through the imposition of trade restrictions leads to a loss of welfare for EU member states. This loss is at its greatest if each member imposes its own trade restrictions: the loss of welfare to consumers is considerable as a result of the higher EU market price, while the higher price also transfers part of the welfare to the Japanese producers. In the case of a common trade restriction, there are smaller welfare losses in the EU, but this measure will also lead to a higher car market price in the EU, so that there is again a transfer of welfare to Japan at the expense of European consumers.

5.6 Trade policy and market failures

The objectives of governments and businesses are not always identical. The government can be expected to consider the welfare of the country as a whole, whereas the company considers only its own profit and survival.

Of course, this distinction is not always so clear-cut: driven by political opportunism, governments often allow themselves to be persuaded by lobbies and thus specific interest groups; similarly, in the spirit of corporate governance, companies sometimes feel a social responsibility, which is expressed, for example, in their sponsorship of sporting or cultural events. In principle, however, this difference in objectives can be assumed to be true.

5.6.1 External effects

It may be the case that a government, after weighing up the risk and the expected returns, believes that a certain economic activity, such as the establishment of a multinational subsidiary, must go ahead whereas the company – possibly together with the potential financier – concludes that the investment is unjustified. For example, such a difference of views can occur if the business generates positive spin-offs – for example, improving the conditions for setting up other businesses by creating infrastructure and training facilities. (Here the reader will recognize the elements of the concept of external economies of scale, as explained in Chapter 3.)

Often, the company itself is unable to benefit from this type of advantage mainly on account of the lack of a legal framework or because the spin-offs cannot be attributed individually. In that instance the firm generates positive *external effects*, which are not counted in the commercial calculations and are not expressed in the price, but are important in the government's estimate of welfare.

Another example might occur when an infant industry is just taking shape so that there are still only a few general facilities. At such a time the government's view on costs and benefits is likely to differ substantially from that of the business community. In the cases mentioned, the cost–benefit analyses of individual firms differ from a calculation that takes account of all welfare effects – and this can be regarded as a form of market failure.

External effects can also be negative: think in terms, for example, of environmental pollution, noise, and so on. In such cases a firm might consider the investment to be profitable, whereas the government considers it to be socially undesirable – unless there is compensation for the external effects.

Where market failures do occur, a government can, in principle, eliminate the effects quite easily – either by subsidizing the company (in the case of positive external effects) or by imposing taxes on it (in the case of negative external effects). The advantage of such a policy is that there is no longer any additional loss of efficiency as the result of distortions in consumption or production decisions, such as would happen if the effects of the market failure were tackled by a tariff or export subsidy (because in that case one is always left with triangles b and d in Figure 5.1 or triangles c and e in Figure 5.2).

In the case of domestic market failures, it is therefore more efficient to eliminate them through the adoption of appropriate domestic policy instruments than to use an international trade instrument to deal with the symptoms. This is why the 'solution' of domestic market failures by means of changes in trade policy is seen to be 'second best'.

In nineteenth-century Europe, and in more recent times especially in developing countries, however, the attempt to use subsidies to help launch infant industries with positive external effects often encountered the practical obstacle of an inadequate or incomplete domestic tax base. In Europe in this period, and in many developing countries from the 1930s onwards, industrialization – which was expected to produce clearly positive external effects – was stimulated principally by import restrictions at the border rather than by a system of domestic subsidies (for a discussion of this situation in relation to Latin American countries see Boulet and Boulet, 2002). It is much easier (and cheaper) for tax authorities if a country's industry is protected against foreign competition rather than being subsidized through the use of its own hard-won tax revenue.

In fact, protection is frequently an attempt to make other countries pay the bill for industrial development (and/or, if that fails, to make the domestic consumer pay by driving up the level of prices). Since this practice usually concerns building up young industries, the literature refers to it as the *infant industry argument* for protection. However, in recent decades protectionist measures have also been used increasingly to delay or halt the decline of obsolete industries.

The use of trade protection as an instrument to build up an industry is often central to an *import substitution policy*, something which has been pursued in the past by many developing countries. These measures involve a systematic attempt to replace imports by domestic production. History has taught us that such a policy often backfires in the long term (in relation to this, see Case study 5.1).

This can be explained using the theory discussed above according to which import tariffs can only increase a country's welfare if two conditions are met: first, if the country can exert substantial influence over world market prices and, secondly, if other countries do not retaliate. In that case, the negative effects of a tariff – that is, the production and consumption costs – can be eliminated through an improvement in the terms of trade. Since in the case of developing countries neither of these conditions was met in normal circumstances, the tariffs in the framework of the import substitution policy reduced welfare to such an extent that the additional, positive external effects were overshadowed. Moreover, the substantial level of import protection destroyed the dynamic effect of international competition on domestic industry, with the result that companies became increasingly bureaucratic and inefficient. Such a policy was often associated with foreign-exchange rationing, so that the allocation of foreign currency took place through inefficient (and corrupt) bureaucratic channels instead of through the market.

Over time, increasing numbers of developing countries began to realize that in the end protective measures at the border were not the correct policies to adopt in eliminating domestic market failures and establishing a healthy, competitive industry. As a result, in recent decades import substitution policies have generally been abandoned.

Although trade policy can neutralize certain effects of domestic market failures, and although import and export levies are able to improve the terms of trade, it must be stressed that these advantages can be destroyed by retaliatory activities by other countries. In more general terms, it is also true that the support given to certain sectors through protection is almost always accompanied by a negative effect on the unsupported sectors because it is rarely possible to pass on the entire cost of protection to other countries; as a result, those sectors that are unsupported automatically pay part of the cost. In that sense, protection almost always means giving an advantage to one at the expense of another – even within countries.

5.7 Summary

1. This chapter has developed the traditional trade theories discussed in Chapter 2 which, on the basis of perfectly efficient markets, concluded that free trade has a beneficial effect on the levels of national welfare. The levying of a tariff or the granting of a subsidy always distorts the decisions made by consumers and producers. In principle, traditional trade theories state two exceptional situations for which the above conclusion is false, at least in theory.
2. First, if a country is large enough to influence the situation on the world market, and as a result its terms of trade, national welfare can be increased by means of certain import or export tariffs (but not by export subsidies). In such a situation it is usually possible, at least in theory, to determine an optimum tariff. This gives the maximum positive balance of the producers' gain, the consumers' loss and the improvement in the terms of trade.
3. Secondly, trade policy intervention is sometimes regarded as defensible in the case of domestic market failures. In terms of the infant industry argument and, more generally, in the case of the external effects of production, trade policy can at least partly eliminate the effects of market failures. From a welfare point of view such a solution is regarded as 'second best' because domestic taxes and subsidies are considered the optimum – hence 'first best' – policy for eliminating the distortion. Of course, in both of these cases it is assumed that other countries will not retaliate in the face of such trade policy, because this could ultimately reverse the effects of a country's own trade protection measures.

Questions

1. What do you think are the most common reasons for governments to adopt protectionist measures?
2. Imagine India decided to introduce considerable reductions in its anti-dumping measures. What do you think would be the effects on the Indian economy?
3. Can you think of positive effects that protectionist measures might have on the general welfare of a country in both the short run and the long run?
4. Discuss why the introduction of export subsidies in order to secure domestic jobs is usually relatively ineffective.

CHAPTER 6

Modern Arguments Relating to Protection

6.1 Introduction

Chapter 5 discussed why governments influence international trade, assessing this in the traditional terms of the effects on national welfare. However, modern trade theories offer insights that may influence the present-day application of trade measures.

In the 1980s, in particular, there were a number of innovations that influenced trade policies. The common feature of these measures was that they took into account the reactions of actors from other countries. Thus, the question focused less on whether, in a static environment, trade policy is favourable or unfavourable from a welfare point of view, than on the process of action and reaction, which is brought about among the various parties concerned when politicians intervene in international trade.

These theory revisions highlighted two particular developments:

1. People were increasingly aware of the importance of the presence of certain (strategic) sectors for the rest of the economy and for their position in terms of international competitiveness. Strategic sectors are those seen as vital to a country on grounds such as employment, value added, advanced technology, defence, expected future growth potential or positive external effects. It can therefore be important to encourage certain activities because of their catalytic effect in terms of stimulating the rest of the economy. This view, based very much on the concept of internal and external economies of scale, is discussed in Section 6.2.
2. There was a growing awareness that, in its increasingly international context, trade policy can be regarded as a 'game of negotiation' which in principle involves both the enterprises and governments of different countries. Various tactics or strategies can be used in this 'game', ranging from threatened action to the formation of coalitions. The description of this type of process demands a dynamic approach that is in stark contrast to the comparative-static approach used in classical trade theory. We shall consider this approach in section 6.3.

6.2 External economies of scale and the competitive position

The development of modern trade theories sheds new light on the traditional argument for protecting industries with important positive external effects, because, as we saw in

Chapter 3, there was a growing conviction that comparative advantages were determined largely by random factors and also that patterns of specialization could very much depend on the existence of external economies of scale.

On that basis, people noticed that, in respect of industrialization, once a certain 'critical mass' is reached at a particular location, economic development becomes self-sustaining. The combination of sufficient production capacity, a sufficiently large local sales market, a well-developed network of businesses supplying one another and a healthy competitive climate (for example, a combination such as that given in the Porter diamond) can ensure that an 'endogenous' development process takes place, aided by a sound international competitive position.

If we introduce the concept of positive external effects into modern trade policy theory, then this means, for example, that the protection of certain industries, especially if there are mutually beneficial influences owing to a combination of positive external effects and external economies of scale, can sometimes be extremely effective in improving the overall levels of welfare within a country.

In practice, this combination of external economies of scale and positive external effects generated by a cluster of enterprises occurs typically in technologically advanced industries. Here, research and development (R&D) investment costs are relatively high. In general, the companies concerned cannot benefit from the whole of the return on that investment themselves, so that positive external effects also accrue for other businesses in the surrounding area. Moreover, the success of technologically advanced business is often heavily dependent upon a dynamic environment – for example, because of the possibility of attracting trained staff or the proximity of service companies as suppliers or customers.

In the above case, trade policy can help to prime the development of the advanced technology industry in the home country, leading ultimately to the creation of a comparative advantage. Here we can once again use the example given in Chapter 3 in which the production of calculators is accompanied by (external) economies of scale because enterprises in that sector have a positive influence on one another. This causes production to concentrate in one location.

In the example below, we assume that Japan is the first country to produce calculators. This means that it is almost impossible to initiate production in Thailand, even though it is actually a cheaper location. However, in relation to the previous case the difference now is that demand from Thailand represents a large proportion of international demand, as we can see from the final column of Table 6.1.

Let us also make the following two assumptions:

1. Companies in Thailand believe that, because Japan was the first to begin the production of calculators, they themselves will never be able to produce calculators, despite the fact that calculator production in Thailand would potentially be cheaper than in Japan.
2. Thailand then uses trade policy measures to prohibit the imports of calculators from Japan.

In this case, equilibrium will initially be established on the home market in Thailand, which is now self-sufficient, so that domestic demand equals domestic supply. According to Table 6.1, this occurs at a volume of 175,000 and a price of 250. The remaining world demand at this price is 875,000–175,000 = 700,000, so that there is insufficient demand left for Japan to produce at a competitive price: the Japanese price will be 1000 at a supply of 700,000. As a result, the whole of world demand will now switch to Thailand. This will cause a further decline in production costs. In a possible new equilibrium, the traded volume will be 1,000,000 at a price of 100.

Table 6.1 Calculators: supply, costs and demand

Japan			Thailand			
Supply (× 1000)	Average cost (=price)	Global demand (× 1000)	Supply (× 1000)	Average cost (=price)	Global demand (× 1000)	Domestic demand (× 1000)
1	10,000	1.5	1	5000	4	1
2	5000	4	2	1000	700	3
400	1000	700	175	250	875	175
875	250	875	1000	100	1000	700

Thus, in our example, thanks to its own adoption of protectionist policies, Thailand has become the world's sole supplier of calculators. Paradoxically, once the industry is operational it no longer requires protection. A *temporary* import ban is sufficient to bring about the switch in the location of production: it is not necessary to introduce an aggressive export promotion policy. Moreover, on balance the consumer is also better off worldwide, seeing the price of calculators ultimately drop from 250 to 100.

The figures given in Table 6.1 relate to price/sales combinations over a given period. Although not stated explicitly in the table, the demand figures could be applied to a one-year period. In other words, at a price of 250, total annual worldwide sales would total 875,000. However, this is a static picture, which assumes that the production costs will remain at this specific annual volume of sales.

In practice, however, a learning process often takes place, meaning that unit production costs are gradually reduced through improved efficiency. In this situation the average costs decline not only through the higher annual volume of sales, but also in relation to cumulative production over the years. This effect can be shown in a graph by a 'learning curve'. In terms of Table 6.1, this learning process would mean that production costs in the country where production takes place could decline still further over time. Clearly, learning effects can further increase the effectiveness of protection as an instrument for shifting the location of production.

6.3 | Strategic trade policy

Under certain circumstances, a situation can arise in which the governments of different countries become opponents, each wanting to protect the same strategic domestic sector.

This means that protection can be understood as the move in a negotiating game in which, through trade policy measures or simply the threat of such measures, a country tries to influence either foreign suppliers or their governments. The use of this *strategic trade policy* attempts to take account of the expected reactions of the other party and also aims to influence the behaviour of foreign suppliers.

One classic example of the use of strategic trade policy is the conflict between the aircraft manufacturers Boeing (in the United States) and Airbus (in Europe). In this market there are very high fixed costs because of the start-up costs of developing a prototype. This means that the break-even point (that is, the sales volume at which the overall returns match the overall costs) is not reached until there is a substantial volume of sales.

Let us assume that it is essential to be able to achieve sales in both the domestic and the overseas markets. Clearly, if this condition is true for both producers, there is a good chance that one cannot reach a situation in which both businesses are viable.

In this case the government has a number of reasons to attempt to ensure that its own enterprise emerges as victorious.

1. Because of the high fixed costs, we can expect business profits to increase very rapidly once the break-even point has been passed. As a result, the government will be able to secure tax revenues.
2. If the foreign company is driven out of the market, the national company will be able to supply the whole of the world market, so that it in fact gains a world monopoly. As a result, the profit can be further increased through monopoly pricing. In such circumstances we refer to the opportunity for the company to acquire an excess profit or 'rent'. This can create further opportunities for the government to secure tax revenue.
3. Once the monopoly has been achieved, learning effects can be expected so that future profits may increase again, further reducing the chances of a foreign rival penetrating the market.
4. Finally, arguments in favour of the government offering trade policy support can be based on considerations relating to issues such as employment, national prestige, military/strategic interests, national security or other similar arguments.

In the above case relating to Airbus and Boeing there are features that are analogous to the duopoly situation – that is, an oligopolistic market form in which two suppliers on a market each develop a strategy based on how they expect the other party to behave (see also Chapter 7).

In such circumstances tactics may emerge which attempt to influence the behaviour of the other party. However, the difference is that here, under conditions of free trade, there can be no market equilibrium in which there is room for both suppliers: if the national monopolies are maintained, only one can survive. This means that there is a strong argument in favour of strategic trade policy intervention because the survival of the domestic monopolist is at stake. This is illustrated in Box 6.1 using an example taken from Krugman (1989, pp. 12 and 13).

Box 6.1   Strategic trade policy

Let us assume that only two aircraft producers operate on the world market: Airbus in Europe and Boeing in the USA.

Let us further assume that, under conditions of free trade, there is only room for one profitable producer: if both Airbus and Boeing produce aircraft, the profit for both will be negative. This is illustrated in Table 6.2.

In Table 6.2 (as in Tables 6.3–6.5), four situations are distinguished, with different combinations of Airbus and Boeing producing or not; for each situation the Airbus profit is shown at the top right and that of Boeing at the bottom left. The top left-hand cell shows the situation in which both manufacturers produce. This yields a loss of 5 for both Boeing and Airbus. The bottom right-hand cell shows the situation in which no one produces and so no one makes a profit or a loss. The top right-hand cell shows the situation in which Airbus does not produce but Boeing does. In this case, Airbus makes a profit of zero and Boeing makes a profit of 100. The bottom left-hand cell shows the opposite situation.

It is not possible to state in advance which of the two aircraft producers will enter the market first and make the profit of 100. Let us assume that we are in a situation where

Table 6.2 Profit in the case of competition

Boeing	Airbus producing	Airbus not producing
producing	**−5**	**0**
	−5	100
not producing	**100**	**0**
	0	0

both companies are considering making the necessary investments to produce for the world market. Both know that the profit will be considerable if they ultimately gain the monopoly position, but also that they will suffer losses if they have to share the market with the other supplier.

In these circumstances they will try, in one way or another, to discourage the other party from making the investment. We are assuming that the option of concluding a cartel agreement to apportion the market does not exist (see Section 7.10 for more on this subject). Whatever techniques are used to discourage the other party, the action will always be rather unconvincing, because both know that the positions are symmetrical.

Thus, in this case there is little chance that the prospect of one supplier entering the market will definitely discourage another from doing so. This may change if one of the governments becomes involved. For example, let us assume that Airbus wins the support of the European Union (EU), which promises Airbus a subsidy of 10 units if it goes into production. The effect of this subsidy on the profits of both companies is shown in Table 6.3. Say the subsidy offer to Airbus was totally credible and Boeing does not succeed in extracting a corresponding subsidy offer from its own government.

Table 6.3 Profit in the case of a subsidy to Airbus

Boeing	Airbus producing	Airbus not producing
producing	**+5**	**0**
	−5	100
not producing	**110**	**0**
	0	0

We now have a fundamental change in the situation, because Boeing now understands that, even if it is the first to enter the market, it will still also be profitable for Airbus to produce. However, this means that Boeing can be certain of producing at a loss. The expected effect of the subsidy of 10 to Airbus is therefore that, as a result of the 'game', Airbus will produce and Boeing will not.

Part of the eventual profit for Airbus consists of the government subsidy, totalling 10 units. However, in our example this small subsidy yields a profit of 110 for Airbus, because

Boeing is forced to stop production. Thus, the subsidy has generated much higher profits than the amount of the subsidy itself. This means that the EU can easily recoup the original subsidy out of a tax levy on the profits of Airbus. For example, if the tax on profits is 30 per cent, the EU will be left with a net positive balance of 33–10 = 23.

The rest of the Airbus profit will also contribute, in one way or another, to European welfare. This means that Europe increases its welfare as a result of adopting a protectionist stance. It should also be clear that part of the profit is obtained at the expense of the USA. Thus, strategic trade policy is an example of 'beggar-thy-neighbour' policies. This means that the risk of retaliation by the other country's government is therefore normally very high.

The case described in Box 6.1 indicates that, under certain conditions, a strategic subsidy by a government to a national company can increase the level of welfare in a country. However, in practice these conditions are rarely satisfied.

First, neither a government nor a company can be entirely certain about the business profits to be generated in various production situations. In practice, they will have to make an estimate, based on the available level of information. Of course, the business may have a considerable interest in presenting the government with a distorted situation, in order to advance its own particular case. This can be illustrated by the example in Box 6.2.

Box 6.2   A strategic subsidy with inaccurate information

In this case (see Table 6.4), the initial situation of Boeing and Airbus differs somewhat from that in Table 6.3, due to the government's perception of available information.

Table 6.4 Profit in the actual situation

Boeing	Airbus producing	not producing
producing	**−5** 5	**0** 105
not producing	**100** 0	**0** 0

In this instance the difference arises because Boeing's position is actually more favourable than the European government thinks on the basis of whatever information it might possess. As a result, even if Airbus is the first to start producing aircraft, Boeing will actually still be able to produce and make a profit. Since the European government is still working on the basis of the profit figures in Box 6.1, it decides to promote production at Airbus with a subsidy of 10.

Table 6.5 shows the situation that would arise as a result of the subsidy. In this case, the European subsidy proves to be ineffective in trying to force Boeing out of the market. The result is that both Airbus and Boeing produce and each make a profit of only 5. Europe now suffers a net loss, since the Airbus producer's profit of 5 is more than offset by the European government's costs of 10.

It is conceivable that positive international external effects could occur for the producing country in the case of production. It is quite possible that certain technical innovations that form the basis of aircraft production can easily be adopted abroad. In that case some of the positive external effects make themselves felt in other countries. If it is also true that any negative external effects arising from aircraft production – such as environmental pollution or excessive noise – are only experienced at home, the judgement about aircraft production may be affected unfavourably.

Table 6.5 Profit given inaccurate information in the case of a subsidy to Airbus

	Airbus	
Boeing	producing	not producing
producing	**5**	**0**
	5	110
not producing	**110**	**0**
	0	0

Thirdly, the government offering subsidies will often be unsure about the reaction of the other government: if it is so easy to recover the subsidy and increase the level of national welfare, then, given a symmetrical case, it is logical that both governments will see sufficient reason to grant the strategic subsidy. This means that any government that begins by granting a subsidy is liable to become entangled in an international subsidy race.

A situation could arise in which, having once granted a subsidy, there is no going back and the circumstances necessitate the granting of higher and higher subsidies in order to avoid losing face because of the failure of previous subsidies.

6.4 │ Summary

1. Modern trade theories are not based on the assumption of perfectly efficient markets or the absence of economies of scale and/or learning effects during production, nor do they assume that there is always a situation of perfect competition.

   With the above considerations in mind, the possibility that the location of a given economic activity that competes successfully is often determined much more by chance than by comparative cost advantages that can be ascertained in advance. The primary factors relate to where certain activities are first started and to the existence of a right combination of circumstances to produce a dynamic process resulting in a permanently strong competitive position. Since these circumstances are determined by chance and by external effects, a situation may arise in which emerging new production locations do not develop, even though production conditions are potentially very favourable.

In that situation (temporary) protection may be a way of successfully breaking the traditional location patterns. This is essentially a restatement of the infant industry argument. It is applicable in the case of industries that produce positive external effects for the national economy.

2. Another aspect referred to in modern theories is the case in which an international market is shared among a few large producers. Large companies are often faced with the strategic question of whether or not to invest heavily in a world market with few suppliers, thus conquering a significant segment of the international market.

   The main difficulty in making such decisions lies in predicting the reaction of rival suppliers. Their response often determines the eventual profitability of the investment. If it is impossible to conclude mutual market agreements in those circumstances, a game situation occurs, with a range of possible outcomes.

3. A small trade policy measure on the part of one company's government can sometimes cause the various foreign market operators to make a fundamental change to their own investment behaviour that would benefit the domestic producer's market position, in such a way that the increase in revenue of the latter exceeds the costs of the initial trade measure. This would offer an example of strategic trade policy.

Questions

1. Can you think of an existing cluster of enterprises that are located in your country on the basis of chance rather than as a result of 'comparative advantage'?
2. In the case described in Box 6.1, how could a third aircraft manufacturer hope to penetrate the market?
3. Can you think of an example in which two or more governments engaged in a trade dispute increasingly used protectionist instruments? How did the conflict end?
4. Can you give examples of trade policy measures that were defended 'on good domestic' grounds but yet effectively reduced competing imports?

CHAPTER 7

Trade Policy and Market Forms: A Microeconomic Analysis

7.1 Introduction

Earlier chapters dealt with the welfare effects of government trade policy measures. The analysis focused primarily on the country as a whole; the aggregated effects on individual market players determined whether or not trade policy was justifiable in that country. In practice, such an approach is unusual because international trade takes place between or within individual companies that have their own objectives, such as profits, market share and continuity of supply.

For this reason there is a growing interest in the study of how businesses deal with trade policy, and in their objectives and market behaviour. The first part of this chapter considers questions such as:

o How do businesses react when confronted with foreign restrictions on their exports?
o How do businesses secure their market share?
o How will businesses try to protect certain sub-markets?

The second part of the chapter analyses the role played by governments – through trade policy measures – in setting out the rules of conduct for competing international firms.

Both history and experience show that the use of trade policy measures can easily escalate into a tariff or subsidy 'war' as governments 'attack' one another through their support for domestic businesses. The second part of this chapter assesses the implications of this for business and for welfare. Finally, we consider how firms can restrict competition through cartel agreements, and why most cartels are generally short-lived.

Another option for businesses is to try to persuade a government to take measures favourable to themselves – for example, by lobbying the government for protection or subsidies. These forms of business behaviour and their consequences are the subjects of Chapters 8 and 9.

7.2 The video recorder market: a case study

Case study 7.1 illustrates the effectiveness of trade policy pursued by the government to protect its own domestic suppliers against foreign competition and how it can be influenced by different interests. In this instance the most important factors influencing the developments are:

○ the existing form of the home market;
○ the form of the exporting country's market;
○ the competitive strategy of the foreign supplier; and
○ the trade policy of both governments.

Case study 7.1 focuses on agreements made in the early 1980s between the European Commission (EC) and the Japanese Ministry of Trade and Industry (MITI) on reducing the exports of Japanese video recorders to the EC. An interesting aspect of this case is how a creative approach to trade restrictions can shift the initiative from the domestic to the foreign supplier.

Case study 7.1   The battle for the video recorder (VCR) market

In its efforts to become the market leader in the international VCR market, it was important for the Japanese conglomerate Matsushita to establish its own VHS system as the industry standard. This meant that Matsushita adopted a twofold strategy to compete against Philips and Sony, developers of the V2000 and Betamax systems respectively.

First, through its subsidiary JVC, the conglomerate sought cooperation with the British video hire group Thorn EMI, which introduced the VHS system into the UK in return for technological support from Matsushita. The result of this agreement was that by 1982 VHS system recorders had a 90 per cent share of the UK market, which was at that time by far the largest VCR market in the EC.

Secondly, Matsushita supplied VHS video recorders at very low prices on the American and European markets, using the brand names and distribution networks of American and European electronics producers. This was done on the basis of the 'original equipment manufacturing' (OEM) concept whereby Matsushita supplied video recorders to a US or European producer who then sold it onto the market under its own name. The low prices of Japanese recorders (mostly made by Matsushita or JVC) prevented US and European companies from competing by underselling their own recorders.

In 1982, the fact that Matsushita was supplying video recorders on the EC market at very low prices led to allegations of *dumping* – that is, supplying the product on the export market at prices below those on the home market. Estimates made for 1982, by van Marion (1993, p. 189), suggested dumping rates of more than 35 per cent.

Following complaints from European producers, in February 1983 an unofficial agreement was signed by the EC and the MITI. This included the provision that Japan was to set a minimum price for video recorders exported to the EC and that the maximum number of Japanese VCRs exported to the EC should be 4.55 million in 1983 and 4.95 million in 1984. Perhaps the most significant development in this 'agreement' was the inclusion of a quota for Japanese video recorders assembled in Europe.

In spite of this 'agreement', the suspicion persisted that some Japanese suppliers were continuing their dumping policies. Since the agreement on the minimum price related to the 'free on board' price (the price of the product before delivery to the export market), Japanese producers had the opportunity to keep transport and distribution costs at a low level on the books, between DM 123 and DM 170 lower than the EC had intended in the 'agreement'.

The way in which MITI implemented the 'agreement' with the EC in its domestic economy led to suspicions that Japan aimed to gain a monopoly position in the international market for VCRs. In addition to this, MITI was allocating export licences on the basis of a company's recent export performance (thus on existing market shares). Hence, it comes as no surprise that this manner of licence allocation, coupled with the possibility of recording a low accountancy figure for transport and distribution costs, allowed Matsushita to acquire a dominant market position in the American and EC market, and to eliminate the competition from the Betamax and V2000 systems. By the late 1980s this format war was effectively at an end.

The final stand-alone JVC VHS unit was produced in 2008, bringing to an end yet another video format war that had begun in 1996 with the introduction of the DVD format. This time VHS had to give way to the superior DVD format and its high definition successors, HD DVD and Blu-ray.

Case study 7.1 shows that in pursuing a trade policy to protect domestic firms against competition from foreign firms, it is very important to understand the competitive position of the foreign suppliers on both the domestic and their own market. It is also important to understand how the government in the foreign supplier's country will react to domestic trade policy. The example showed that the EC's measure imposing trade restrictions on Japanese VCR producers – in this case via a voluntary export restraint (VER) – prompted the Japanese trade ministry to grant preferential treatment to the largest Japanese electronics group, as a deliberate attempt to enable this group to secure a stronger position in the West European market.

Case study 7.1 prompts the following questions:

1. What are the criteria that determine the market form and how can enterprises take advantage of the existence of various sub-markets – for example, by adopting different pricing policies for each sub-market?
2. What determines the way in which suppliers behave when entering the market – and how does this behaviour change if a market expands, as in the case of access to an international market?
3. How do producers react to one another's behaviour in a market with few suppliers – and what determines this reaction?
4. To what extent can national governments influence the competitive position of their national suppliers in the domestic or international market?
5. How can cooperation between producers influence the market and the competitive position of producers on that market?

Discussion of these questions will be carried out principally in the light of microeconomic theory.

7.3 | Market forms

As is clear from Case study 7.1, the market form is an important consideration for business managers and implies various questions, such as to what extent there is competition from other suppliers? What competitive strategies and instruments are used by others? And to what extent can competitive pressure be mitigated by product differentiation or other means? The case study also revealed that the overall degree of openness in the trade system is another important factor, since this largely determines the market conditions faced by the entrepreneur when selling on the international market. The degree of openness will often also have an effect on selling conditions in the national market. Thus, government policy on trade has direct consequences for all businesses, but also indirect consequences because of its impact on the form of the market. In the case of serious national or international trade policy developments, the implications for the market form can often lead companies to reconsider their market strategies.

In classification of the various market forms, consideration is generally given to the following:

(i) the number of suppliers on the market and their mutual degree of organization; and
(ii) the degree of uniformity in the goods (or services) supplied.

By combining these two criteria, we arrive at a typology of market forms, ranging from perfect competition to monopoly. Among the aspects that need to be considered in developing a more detailed definition of the various market forms are:

(iii) the extent to which suppliers can screen off sub-markets in terms of design and marketing;
(iv) the freedom suppliers have to enter the market; and
(v) the level of uncertainty facing suppliers as regards rival suppliers' behaviour.

In the case of the perfect competition markets, the situation is clear: there are many, non-organized suppliers who cannot screen off any sub-markets, who are able to enter or leave at will, and for whom the supply conditions are dictated by the market.

The position is equally clear in the case of a monopoly: the microeconomic analysis of the effects of a trade policy measure is given in this case in Box 7.1 (for a foreign monopolist selling on our market). Under such conditions there is only one supplier who can use his position on the market, or on the various sub-markets, to maximize its own profit. However, in the real world of international business, it is rare to come across either of these extreme market forms. In most cases, one encounters some intermediate form of organization. In the rest of this chapter we will devote more attention to these market forms, and try to ascertain the advantages and disadvantages of trade policy.

Box 7.1   Confronting a foreign monopolist with import protection

Figure 7.1 shows the price–sales curve or the average revenue curve (AR), the marginal revenue curve (MR) and the marginal cost curve (MC) faced by a foreign entrepreneur. As an exporter, this entrepreneur holds a monopoly position in exporting to our market. Thus, the price–sales curve corresponds to the domestic demand curve for imports; the MC curve corresponds to the average cost curve (AC curve) because it is horizontal.

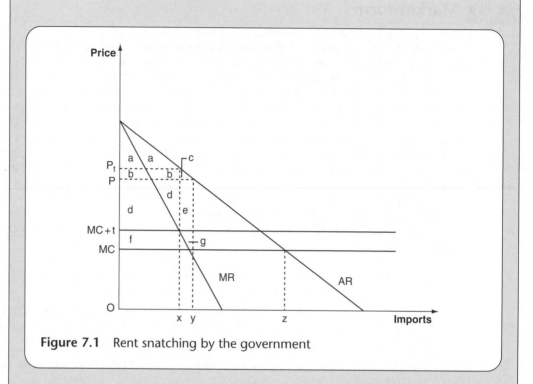

Figure 7.1   Rent snatching by the government

According to common assumptions, the monopolist follows the management rule: MR = MC. This optimum condition guarantees his maximum profit. On that basis, under the conditions of free international trade he will set his price at P and will export volume O_y.

Our country now imposes an import tariff of T in order to cream off part of the profit due to the foreign monopolist. The imposition of the tariff can be shown in the figure through an upward shift of the MC curve. Since he aims to make a profit, the monopolist will now supply less, namely O_x; the market price rises to P_t. Before the tariff was put in place, the monopolist's profit consisted of $d+e+f+g$ (the difference between total revenue and total costs), and afterwards it was $b+d$. For simplicity, let us assume that e and b are equal. (This is a simplification, which is true only if the AR curve is at 135 degrees to the horizontal axis.) On the basis of this assumption, the monopolist's profit falls by $f+g$ as a result of the tariff. Of this, f goes to our government and g represents the efficiency loss.

What has our country achieved? First, our government now receives the said tariff revenue, f; on the other hand, the tariff has driven up the domestic price to P_t, so that the consumer surplus falls by $b+c$. Our country makes a net gain from imposing the tariff on the foreign monopolist's imports if f is greater than $b+c$. If, for simplicity, we ignore the relatively small triangles c and g, this means that the gain in welfare for our country depends on whether f is greater than b.

Geometry tells us that this is in fact the case, since the MR curve, which is a median of the AR curve, is always steeper than the AR curve. Since area f results from a projection of xy on the MR curve and b from a projection of xy on the AR curve, it follows that f must always be greater than b. Thus, our country will always increase its welfare.

Paradoxically, it is thus relatively easy for our government to take trade policy measures against the foreign monopolist and also to achieve a net gain in welfare. Since the government creams off part of the monopolist's excess profit (rent), this special form of strategic trade policy is known as rent snatching. If there had been foreign supply under perfect competition, it would not have been possible for our country to increase its welfare by protection. Finally, it should be noted that the Airbus subsidy discussed in Box 6.1 was in fact the opposite of rent snatching.

With regard to these intermediate forms, the following characteristics of market forms mentioned earlier at (iii)–(v) will now be discussed:

(iii) the degree to which a supplier can take advantage of the existence of different national sub-markets (Section 7.4);
(iv)   behaviour when entering international markets (Section 7.5);
 (v)   market behaviour in relation to a small number of competing suppliers (Sections 7.6 and 7.7).

7.4   Taking advantage of different national sub-markets

Let us assume that a firm has a monopoly on the national sales market, but that it faces virtually perfect competition on the export market. This can occur, for example, if the national government in the firm's home country uses protection to safeguard the home market from foreign competition, but foreign governments cannot (or will not) apply a similar policy in their respective national markets.

For such an entrepreneur, there are two separate sub-markets: on the home market, demand is presumably relatively price-inelastic (that is, relatively insensitive to price) because consumers have no alternative; in contrast, as the result of increased competition, entrepreneurs face a more elastic demand on the international market. Obviously, to some extent entrepreneurs will often seek to create the situation described above themselves because, as we shall see, it offers good opportunities for profit making. An example of how this can happen in practice is described in Case study 7.2.

Case study 7.2   Price differences on the European car market

The European car market before the introduction of an effective policy to create greater transparency illustrates how producers were able to set different prices for their products in a number of sub-markets. Figure 7.2 shows that, in the past, car manufacturers made extensive use of differential pricing for each car type in the different sections of the EU car market.

Carmakers are able to practise such price differentiation because of the system of selective distribution that is common throughout the European car industry. Under this system the manufacturer sells his cars through a single dealer in each separate country; the dealer in turn confines his sales area to that region. This means that car manufacturers have a network of dealers who only sell his cars in a specific part of the market.

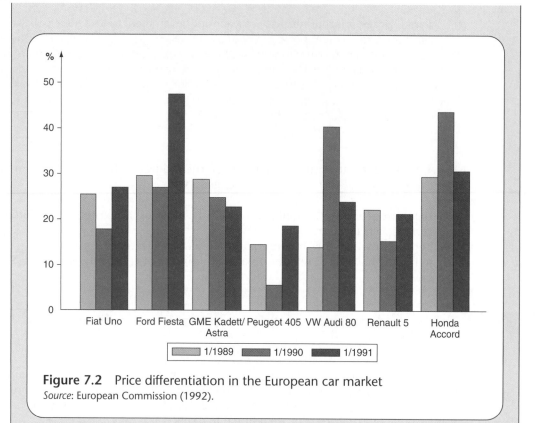

Figure 7.2   Price differentiation in the European car market
Source: European Commission (1992).

Depending upon the actual price–sales curve and the price elasticity of demand for cars in each sales region, the car manufacturer then sets the best price for each region. This creates brand monopolies in each sales region, so that a particular car is available from only one dealer; thus, the only competition in the sales region is between the different brands.

In principle, at that time such a form of artificial partitioning of geographical sub-markets was already prohibited under EU law. Nevertheless, in 1985 the EC decided to permit an exception for the application of selective distribution by the motor vehicle sector (Regulation 123/85) on condition that the price differences between the sub-markets did not exceed 12 per cent over a certain period – or 18 per cent at any one time.

This led to immediate protests from consumer organizations about the scale of the price differentiation that was permitted, and in 1990 the European Consumers' Organisation, BEUC, submitted a complaint to the EC concerning the large price differentials between various EU countries. According to the BEUC, these were due mainly to the selective distribution policy. Figure 7.2 shows that the price differences for the seven brands discussed often (greatly) exceeded the 18 per cent maximum set by the EC.

The EC did not decide to intervene immediately. They stated that the price differences were largely the result of either exchange-rate fluctuations or differences between EU member states with regard to protectionist measures against cars from countries outside the EU, such as Japan. However, from 2004 the EC took measures to make car pricing in the EU more transparent, by declaring exclusive car dealership agreements illegal. Research in that same year also revealed a convergence trend in Euro Zone car prices. However, despite continuous improvements in the price gaps there are still factors holding car prices at a considerable differential. One of the main points of contention in the EU is the substantial variation in the prosperity of its member states. In other words, some of the newer member states still have relatively less developed economies compared with the more established members, and in consequence car manufacturers will lower their prices in order to accommodate the less fortunate consumers in these markets. One good example illustrating the price gap between old and new member states can be seen in the case of Volkswagen: the price in Greece for a 2007 Passat is 40 per cent lower than the price for the same model in Germany. It is clear that some time still needs to pass before the situation in the EU car market approaches free competition.

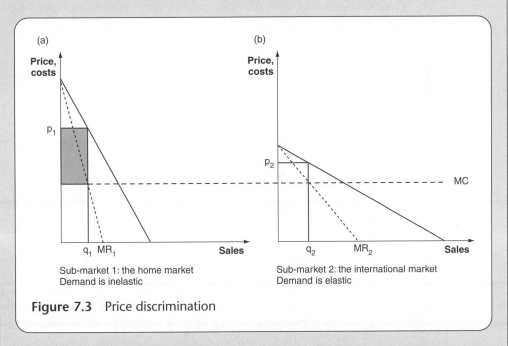

Figure 7.3   Price discrimination

The existence of different, separate sub-markets can be shown by the respective steepness and flatness of the two price–sales curves. The marginal revenues (MR curves) derived from these on the two markets will therefore show comparable differences in gradient (see Figure 7.3). For the sake of simplicity, it is assumed that marginal costs are constant (see the horizontal dotted line of the MC curve in Figure 7.3).

To maximize his profit, the entrepreneur will now apply the combination p1, q1 and p2, q2 on the home market and the international market respectively. Theory tells us that it is in the entrepreneur's interests to restrict the quantities supplied on the two sub-markets in such a way that marginal costs and marginal revenues are equal: for that is the point at which he makes the maximum profit.

In other words, if he is faced with different price sales curves on the different, separate sub-markets, he adopts a position in which the marginal revenues on all sub-markets are the same (and thus also equal to the marginal costs). If he did not do this, he could increase his net revenues – and thus his profit – by switching from a market with lower marginal revenues to one with higher marginal revenues.

In practice, this might mean that, in order to achieve maximum profit, he operates far more aggressively on one sub-market than on another, and also applies price discrimination. In practice, a firm will generally offer lower prices and better terms of supply for a sub-market on which he faces tough competition, whereas on a sub-market in which he holds, to some extent, a position of monopoly, the supplier will practise higher prices and generally offer worse terms.

If we return to the situation shown in Figure 7.3, we see that the entrepreneur does indeed adjust his pricing behaviour to fit the market situation; his domestic price is higher than the price he charges in the other country. If he knew the price elasticity of demand on the two sub-markets, e_1 and e_2, it would be easy for him to determine the optimum relationship between the prices he should charge, namely according to the formula derived in Box 7.2:

$$p1/p2 = \left(1 + \frac{1}{e_2}\right) / \left(1 + \frac{1}{e_1}\right).$$

Box 7.2   Pricing on separate sub-markets

The attempt to maximize profits by a firm that can sell on two separate sub-markets is based on the idea that the firm is confronted by a single cost function and two revenue functions. It can therefore maximize its profit if $MC = MR_1 = MR_2$. Provided that the marginal revenue on the two sub-markets is not equal to the marginal costs, the entrepreneur can still increase his profit by transferring sales from one market to the other.

Let us first recall that marginal revenue in the general sense can be redefined as $MR = p + q \times dp/dq$ (on the basis of differentiating $p \times q$ ($= TR$) according to q by the product rule). Using this we can rewrite the equilibrium condition $MC = MR_1 = MR_2$ as $MC = p_1 + q_1 \times dp_1/dq_1 = p_2 + q_2 \times dp_2/dq_2$.

Since the price elasticity of demand in general can be stated as $dp/dq \times p/q$, $q_1 \times dp_1/dq_1$ and $q_2 \times dp_2/dq_2$ can be restated as p_1/e_1 and p_2/e_2 respectively. Thus: $MC = p_1 (1 + 1/e_1) = p_2 (1 + 1/e_2)$. Therefore, in equilibrium

$$p_1/p_2 = \left(1 + \frac{1}{e_2}\right) / \left(1 + \frac{1}{e_1}\right).$$

This can be illustrated through the use of an example. If the elasticity of demand on the home market, market 1, is, for instance, -2 (meaning that a 5 per cent higher price causes demand to fall by 10 per cent) and -8 on the international market (meaning that a 10 per cent higher price causes an 80 per cent decline in volume), then it should be true that $p_1 : p_2 = 7 : 4$. (Check this for yourself.)

The question arises: under the international trade policy regime is it always permissible to cream off profits using price discrimination? The answer is negative: according to the definition used by the General Agreement on Tariffs and Trade (GATT) (see Chapter 7), and adopted by the World Trade Organization (WTO), this process constitutes dumping (that is, the sale of products abroad at a price below that in the country of origin and/or below the cost price), and the WTO allows foreign competitors to take formal action against dumping.

A more pernicious form of dumping would occur if the supplier in our example were to use the profit made on the home market (the shaded area in Figure 7.3a) in order to try to destroy the competition on the foreign market in the long term. This could be achieved by supplying the product at below its actual cost price and/or by less than the competitors' cost price on the foreign market. This can be sustained by using the profit buffer built up at home. If the foreign suppliers do not have a comparable buffer, they will inevitably lose the battle. This is known as *predatory dumping*, because its intention is to drive the foreign competitor from the market.

In the literature, part of the discussion on dumping has focused on the position on the world market of countries such as Japan. A number of anti-dumping procedures have also concerned supplies from that country. In the past some people have claimed that Japan's internal structure, in which producers cooperate in 'keiretsus' (a set of companies with interlocking business relationships and shareholdings), in fact resulted in quite effective protection against rival supplies from abroad.

Box 7.3   The *keiretsu* as a specific market form

In a *keiretsu* the companies have a stake in one another's equity and exchange their top managers on a regular basis. At the centre of a *keiretsu* is a bank around which entrepreneurs are grouped in clusters. Such an arrangement is known as a *kinyu keiretsu* – a financially united group; if, instead, a large company forms the centre, one can speak of a *sangyo keiretsu* – an industrially united group.

The *keiretsu* assigns a key function not just to the bank but also to the trading company, which supplies raw materials to companies and sells their end products. A *keiretsu* in fact excludes certain markets; the capital market is replaced by an internal financing system, and the various commodity and intermediate markets are replaced by the trading company. In this way the trading company and the bank take over much of the market mechanism coordination.

These institutional structures make it extremely difficult for foreign competitors to penetrate the market, break into domestic sales channels or secure any suppliers. Thus, from the perspective of a Japanese businessman, the situation would look roughly like that shown in Figure 7.3. These cases are sometimes labelled systematic dumping.

However, the extent to which this concept applies in certain sectors has been the subject of much debate. Although systematic dumping is seen as an unfair trade practice, and as such is covered by the trade regulations of most industrial countries, there are also good economic reasons why dumping should not be considered as damaging (except for predatory dumping) – one reason being that the consumer benefits from the lower price of the foreign supply.

7.5 Behaviour on entering international markets under monopolistic competition

In practice, the size of a market limits the number of suppliers. There are almost always entry costs, and these are particularly important where there is some form of internal economies of scale, so that the average unit costs fall as production rises. In such a situation, there are two opposing effects, which apply because there is an increase in the number of suppliers on a market of a given size.

On the one hand, it becomes increasingly difficult to benefit from economies of scale because the average size of business declines and therefore there is an increase in average production costs; on the other hand, the increase in the number of suppliers will stimulate competitive pressures and depress market prices. These opposing trends mean that the level of profit per product is reduced because the number of suppliers increases, to the point where the last supplier to enter the market just fails to make a profit. According to the theory, once that point is reached no more new suppliers will enter the market.

In such a case, if there is a sudden opportunity to expand the level of total sales on this market – as a result of the liberalization of international trade – then not only will there be new chances of achieving economies of scale, but the sales prospects will also increase so that there will be more scope for suppliers to make a profit on the market. Since there is free access (or low barriers to entry), the result of such a market expansion is that more suppliers will arrive and if each new entrant offers his own variety, type or brand of product, there will also be increased consumer choice.

As we saw in Chapter 3, this form of market situation is known as monopolistic competition; in principle, there is free access, and there are many suppliers. No single supplier is powerful enough to influence overall market conditions, but each supplier does offer his own variety of product, so that his own sub-market has some degree of protection. Thus, each entrepreneur feels that he has a monopoly in his own field, but still experiences competition as a result of the existence of many variants of his product.

Such examples of entrepreneurial behaviour patterns in an expanding market were seen in the EC in the 1960s. The creation of the common market in the EC suddenly offered scope for businesses to benefit from the economies of scale provided by the enlarged EC market. From the consumers' point of view, this meant that there was now far more opportunity than before to buy hitherto unfamiliar European products. The expansion of the market – what might be termed the liberalization of trade – increased competition, provided more scope for economies of scale and offered greater variety. In Case study 7.3 we see how the establishment of the EC in 1958 encouraged Italian manufacturers of refrigerators and washing machines to take advantage of the resulting economies of scale, and how – as a result of the enlargement of the market – there was an increase in the variety of cars on the European market.

Case study 7.3   The market in domestic electrical appliances and the car market

Domestic electrical appliances

In the 1950s Italian manufacturers of refrigerators and washing machines (in particular, Zanussi and Ignis) expanded their production on a large scale, hoping to take advantage of the potential economies of scale of an expanding European market. There were, of course, certain risks in this strategy because it was not certain to what extent the proposed trade liberalization in the EC would actually lead to a rapid improvement in access to the markets of other member states.

Fortunately, the strategy adopted by the Italian producers was a success. Since refrigerators and washing machines developed into more or less standard products, the Italians – thanks to their large-scale production – were able to offer their products in other European countries at low prices. This enabled them to take the maximum advantage of economic growth in the 1960s and the ensuing wave of mass consumption.

In 1970 Italian producers supplied a quarter of the refrigerators and almost a fifth of the washing machines sold in Germany. In France at around the same time, the Italians secured almost half the market in refrigerators and about one-fifth of the market in washing machines. In response to the Italian success, producers in other member states showed a strong tendency towards concentration, through a process of mergers and acquisitions.

By 2007, following repeated enlargement and continuous integration, the European Union's champion accomplishment, the Single Market, numbered over 500 million people – providing unprecedented opportunities for economies of scale. As a consequence, there was a considerable fall in the prices of most consumer goods. Whereas in the late 1930s an affordable refrigerator would cost about $300 (approximately $3200 in today's prices), consumers today pay around $1000 for a medium-priced model.

The car market

The European car market is a market in which it is not easy to achieve economies of scale; rather, the emphasis is more on competition by product differentiation. The establishment of the EC did lead to an increase in trade in cars within the EC, but this was on a much smaller scale than that experienced on the domestic appliance market.

Before the establishment of the EC, cars made in the various member states had been destined for the home market, with the type of car depending very much on the population's per capita incomes and tastes. The main opportunities to achieve economies of scale lay in the production of parts.

The establishment of the EC led to a sharp increase in the trade in cars between member states, with a wider range of models being made available across the continent. Simple as it was for refrigerator and washing machine manufacturers to produce on a larger scale, this appeared to be much more difficult in the car industry owing to product differentiation. Although cooperation between car producers started to increase in the 1970s it did so at an agonizingly slow pace.

Following the creation of the EC and later the Single Market, traditional product differentiation in the car industry did lead to a greater variety of cars on the market. However, it also placed restrictions on the rapid development of larger-scale production. While competition in domestic electrical appliances takes place mainly in terms of price, the 'problem' with the car industry is that it is mainly non-price instruments that are used – such as the diversity of car types, after-sales service, the reliability of servicing, durability (mainly the second-hand market price), style and design.

7.6 | Oligopoly: analysis based on reaction curves

One market form often encountered in international markets is the *oligopoly* (see also Chapter 3), which means that only a few firms are active in one market and are in competition with one another over the distribution of market shares. In most cases, the separate firms have developed their own brand or type of product, so that the products are competing, but not identical. The special situation in which there are only two competing producers on the market is referred to as a *duopoly* (see Section 7.7).

This section will consider how firms in an oligopolistic market will behave in relation to one another. If the home market enjoys a substantial level of protection against foreign competition, it seems obvious that the firms' strategy will be geared primarily to fighting off domestic rival suppliers in the home market; only then will they turn their attention to the export market. In the following analysis we initially adopt this assumption; later in the chapter we will turn our attention to an international oligopoly.

If we consider the market behaviour of an oligopolist in the case of a closed economy, we can start to make assumptions about the other supplier's behaviour in the home market. In other words, the supplier will base his strategy on his assessment of how the other suppliers will respond to his market operations.

Using this concept, the behaviour of home market suppliers can be shown in stylized form using so-called *reaction curves*. These are curves that show the market strategy that a firm believes will yield the maximum profit, assuming certain behaviour on the part of other (in this case domestic) suppliers on the market.

In order to understand reaction curves it is best to assume that, for whatever reason, the firm is a monopolist on its own market. In that case it supplies the quantity at which its own marginal revenue is equal to its marginal costs. The corresponding optimum sales are shown in Figure 7.4 by point M on the reaction curve MC*.

Now let us assume that potential competitors see interesting profit opportunities and decide to enter the same market. Taking account of the sales of our original monopolist and his expected reaction to the newcomers, they will determine, perhaps by trial and error, how much they should sell on the market.

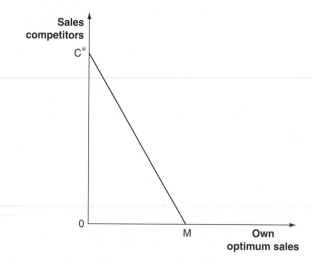

Figure 7.4   Reaction curve for a domestic entrepreneur

Let us further assume that the original monopolist continues to produce the same quantity OM, ignoring the newcomers' supply. In this case, the total supply on the home market increases by an amount equal to the quantity sold by the competitors. This causes the price to fall, according to the elasticity of demand, with a proportionate decline in profit for our entrepreneur.

If, on the other hand, our entrepreneur were to cut back his own sales by precisely the same quantity as the volume of the new supplies from competitors, the original market price could be maintained (since the total supply remains the same), but our entrepreneur's profit again falls, this time in proportion to the decline in the volume of supply.

Thus, our entrepreneur now faces a classic dilemma: if he maintains his supply, the market price will fall and so will his profit; on the other hand, if he tries to maintain the market price at the old level, he will have to cut back his supply so that his profit also falls.

We now assume that our entrepreneur can minimize the decline in his profit by adopting an intermediate position. This means that he does reduce his supply, but by less than the quantity which the others are expected to offer. Although this will still cause a fall in market price – as there is an increase in the total market supply – the slump will be lower than if our entrepreneur had maintained supplies at the original level. In fact, we now assume that the market situation is such that the combination of a small decline in sales and a small fall in price is more favourable for our supplier than the two extreme positions mentioned above.

As far as the reaction curve is concerned, this means that the greater the expected increase in the competitors' sales, the more our entrepreneur will withdraw from supplying the market, though not in the same proportion (shift from M to O projected at MC* in Figure 7.4). Finally, if the competitors end up supplying quantity OC*, then according to the graph our entrepreneur will cease supplying altogether. It is obvious that at point C* our entrepreneur is no longer able to make any profit on this market. Since this is theoretically the case under perfect competition, the total quantity sold by the other suppliers at C* corresponds to that for a market in which there is perfect competition. The less than proportionate reduction in supplies by our entrepreneur, and the fact that, under normal conditions, supplies are lower under monopoly than under perfect competition, make it easy to see that in Figure 7.4 it must be true that: OM < OC*.

7.7 Duopoly: competitive behaviour in the international market

In the previous section we discussed the reaction curve for an entrepreneur in a closed economy. We saw that its pattern is in fact based on the entrepreneur's attempts to maximize his profits if he is certain about his own cost function and price–sales opportunities but does not know how his competitors will behave.

In this section we develop this analysis by considering the particular instance of a duopoly. A duopoly is a special kind of oligopoly with two suppliers who are almost identical and challenge one another's sales on a particular market. In an international context, we assume that the competition consists of a single foreign entrepreneur.

Since this foreign entrepreneur's situation is almost identical to that of our entrepreneur, he also acts, thinks and responds in the same manner. This means that the reaction curve for the foreign entrepreneur is essentially the same reaction curve as for our own entrepreneur above – the only difference being that the coordinates are the mirror image of the position in the other reaction curve.

So, in this case, we actually have a duopoly with two broadly equal opponents. (This model is based on a classic concept developed in 1838 by the French economist Augustin Cournot.) The model assumes that a duopolist seeking to maximize his profit thinks that his competitor will not respond to his decisions when determining the optimum sales volume. The duopolist is also deemed not to learn from his mistakes. Clearly, these assumptions do not normally hold true in the real world.

Figure 7.5 shows two reaction curves relating to the sales of the two duopolists on a particular market, say our own domestic market. Thus, both suppliers are active in this market and our country also operates as an importer. The steep reaction curve, C*AM, relates to the market behaviour of the national producer on the market and shows how much the national producer sells, given the assumed sales by the foreign competitor. The flat reaction curve M*AC shows the market behaviour of the foreign supplier on the same market, given the assumed sales by our national entrepreneur.

It is interesting to note that, since we assume the two suppliers to have an identical pattern of behaviour, the graph will be the same for the sales of both of them on the foreign market. In that situation the other country thus acts as an importer and our country as an exporter.

Owing to the identical behaviour we are, in principle, faced with simultaneous imports and exports of the product supplied and thus intra-industry trade (see also Chapter 4). However, since oligopolists from different countries in practice do not produce completely identical variants of the same product, that conclusion should come as no surprise. Consider, for example, the market in passenger cars, cigarettes, computers or other markets controlled by oligopolies in which each country engages simultaneously in both the import and export of products.

Let us assume, on the basis of the situation in Figure 7.5, that the home market is initially protected against foreign competition. The national entrepreneur then sees himself as a monopolist and sells OM. Later, the market is opened up and a foreign producer enters.

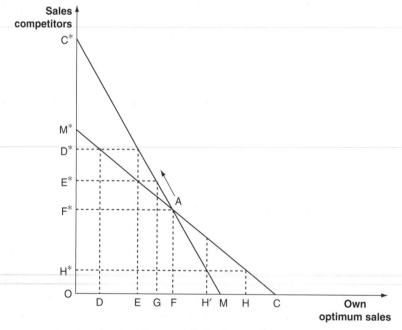

Figure 7.5   Reaction curves in a duopoly

Let us assume that he starts by selling OH*. If the domestic firm cuts its sales by OH*, then this will maintain the price. If the domestic entrepreneur maintains his sales, then there is a fall in the price. Here we recognize the dilemma outlined above and again assume that the reaction will lie between these two extremes. According to the reaction curve in Figure 7.5, the optimum reaction for the domestic entrepreneur is to supply OH′.

Market equilibrium will now occur at the intersection of the two reaction curves. This is point A in Figure 7.5, also known as Cournot's equilibrium, because if we move from point A to any point on one of the two reaction curves, then in the given situation one of the duopolists has maximized his profit but the other has not.

For example, let us assume that the national producer sells the quantity OD. In this case, the optimum quantity sold by the foreign entrepreneur is OD*. If the quantity of imports is OD*, on the other hand, the optimum sales for the domestic producer will be OE. The foreign producer then supplies quantity OE*, the national producer OG, and so on. Given the same market shares, only point A can represent the maximum profit for both operators.

We can deduce that the total volume of supply (OF + OF* in Figure 7.5) lies between the total supply in the case of a single monopolistic supplier, OM (= OM*, given perfect symmetry), and the supply that would be available in perfect competition, OC (= OC* in perfect symmetry). Since it is clear from the graph that the quantity OF + OF* is between OM and OC, the volume of goods supplied has risen and the price has therefore fallen in relation to that in the assumed monopoly situation. (However, the opposite applies when assuming perfect competition.) So, if a foreign supplier is granted access to the originally monopolistic national market, then competition increases and so does the total volume of supply, and perhaps also the number of varieties, while the price comes under pressure. Thus, our national welfare has presumably increased.

One real-world example of how an initial monopoly can, in practice, turn into a situation in which an industry suddenly faces foreign competition was the abolition of the *Reinheitsgebot* (purity law) on the German beer market. Case study 7.4 gives a brief outline of the abolition of the *Reinheitsgebot*. Although this example does not include any analysis of competition, it does indicate the context in which the reaction curve analysis described above might take place.

Case study 7.4   The *Reinheitsgebot*

One classic example of a government succeeding in pursuing a protectionist policy on the basis of health requirements is the centuries-old *Reinheitsgebot* in Germany. This law enabled the German government to stipulate rules about the composition of both home-produced and imported beer. The law specified that a drink could be sold as beer in Germany only if it contained the following four ingredients alone: hops, malted barley, yeast and pure water. This meant that the German market could be effectively protected against competition from foreign types of beer, because in practice they did not comply with the *Reinheitsgebot*.

In 1987 the European Court of Justice ruled that the *Reinheitsgebot* was contrary to the principle of the mutual recognition of EC products and services. In general terms, this principle means that differences in national legislation cannot be used for the purpose of intra-European protection. This principle was first explicitly formulated by the European Court of Justice in the case commonly known as the Cassis de Dijon case, in which the Court condemned the German government for prohibiting a French liqueur, Cassis de

Dijon, from being imported into Germany on the grounds that the alcohol percentage was too low under German law.

In its ruling the Court of Justice decided that the ban was contrary to EC rules and thus established a very important precedent for the functioning of the internal market, preventing the abuse of health regulations and the like for protectionist purposes. Similarly, the Court ruled that the *Reinheitsgebot* did not provide any grounds on which the German government could obstruct the importing of beer from the rest of the EC.

To this day, many German breweries continue to proclaim their compliance with the *Reinheitsgebot* despite striking inconsistencies (for instance, the production of wheat beer was prohibited by the *Reinheitsgebot*). This compliance is used by brewers as an invaluable marketing tool in an industry where tradition is considered priceless.

7.8   Trade policy and international duopoly

In principle, the situation described above using reaction curves for the market behaviour of oligopolists in the home market applies in a similar way if sales take place in the international market. In that case one can also depict the competitive situation between suppliers from different countries in stylized form, using two reaction curves and assuming that the competitors' behaviour can be represented by a single reaction curve.

However, there are also differences between an oligopoly consisting of a few national firms and an oligopoly in which the competition is mainly between national and foreign suppliers.

1. First, in the latter case it is more likely that governments will try to influence the market outcome by intervention on the basis of national considerations. Such intervention usually aims to improve the competitive position of the national firm. Possibilities include specifically targeted domestic subsidies and levies, but also trade policy measures (in connection to this see also the earlier comments on this subject in Chapters 5 and 6).
2. Secondly, a situation may arise in which the battle between the firms actually shifts to their governments. This can cause protection to escalate and all kinds of transfer mechanisms to emerge, depending on the changes in the volumes and prices of international trade (Section 7.9).
3. Thirdly, there will be a greater likelihood of (international) cartel agreements in relation to sales in the home market. Since the various suppliers have the greatest knowledge of their own home market, it is logical to come to an arrangement with the foreign competitors whereby each supplier has the chance to protect his own national market for the benefit of his own sales. This can lead to less rather than more competition, in spite of trade being apparently free (Section 7.10).

Can governments influence the outcome of the market process, as shown in Figure 7.5? The short answer is 'yes'. This can be shown easily if we remember that the position of the reaction curves is determined by the producers' assessment of profit and, thus, on costs and revenues. If there is a change in a producer's costs or revenues, then the profit position and, thus, the pattern of the reaction curve and the market equilibrium will change.

Let us assume that there are two companies operating in the home market (which we can regard as an independent market), a foreign firm and a national firm, both of which are making a substantial profit. The government wants to cream off part of the foreign firm's profit and therefore decides to introduce an import tariff. All else being equal, this causes an increase in the foreign supplier's marginal costs.

Under normal conditions, this firm will reduce its supplies since it aims to maximize its profit, because the entrepreneur's profits are maximized when MR = MC. (For an explanation of this, see Figure 7.6. Here we see that an increase in the level of marginal costs from MC to MC_2, such as might be caused by the entrepreneur being forced to bear the costs of an import tariff himself, given the negative trend in the MR curve normal for oligopolists, leads to a decline in the volume supplied. In the graph, the new point for maximized profits is MR = MC_2 causing the supply to shift from q_1 to q_2.)

Thus, for the reaction curve of the entrepreneur affected by the import tariff, this means a shift to the left (Figure 7.7). In the new equilibrium the volume supplied by our national supplier increases by FG, at the expense of the competitor's market supply, which declines by F*G*. Since, in the new equilibrium situation, A', the total supply has fallen (as G*A' + A'G < F*A + AF, because FG < F*G*), the price has risen. Thus, the tariff has caused an increase in both the price and the sales of the domestic supplier. This situation is, of course, disadvantageous to the consumer.

If competition takes place on the foreign market, the government can also try to influence the outcome through the use of an export subsidy. If the marginal cost curve in Figure 7.6 relates to the domestic entrepreneur, then it now shifts to a position to the right of MC_1. If we translate this trend into the reaction curves, we can derive Figure 7.8, which shows the situation on the foreign market instead of that on the home market. The reaction curve of our national supplier shifts to the right on this market as a result of the export subsidy. The new equilibrium is now A".

In this situation, too, our national entrepreneur's market share has risen at the expense of the foreign supplier. The difference from the previous situation is that in this instance there has been an increase in the total supply, as G*A' + A'G is larger than F*A + AF. Thus, the price will fall. For the foreign supplier this means a drop in profits. The impact on the domestic entrepreneur's profit is less clear and depends on whether the positive volume effect is stronger than the negative price effect or vice versa. If we move along the foreign supplier's reaction curve (from M* to C), then initially the domestic entrepreneur's profit

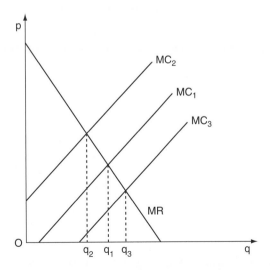

Figure 7.6 Effect on marginal costs of an export subsidy and a tariff

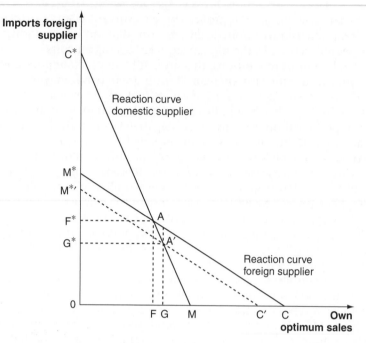

Figure 7.7   A duopoly in the case of an import tariff on goods supplied to the domestic market by a foreign supplier

Figure 7.8   A duopoly in the case of an export subsidy by the national government (situation on the foreign market)

will increase before it decreases. At M* he still exports nothing. As soon as the domestic entrepreneur enters the market, the total volume of goods sold increases, as well as the profit for the domestic entrepreneur. At C his profit will be zero again.

As a final note with respect to the former, it should be made clear that it makes no difference to the international competitive position of an exporting company if the government subsidizes its production or if it subsidizes other company activities, such as R&D. In both cases, their market share can be increased. This conclusion has important implications for policy. Thus, for example, in the Uruguay Round negotiations, it was stated that there should, of course, be no intention of replacing the EC export subsidies on agricultural products (which were to be abolished) by a system of income supplements and production-related subsidies with the same effect on the international competitive position.

7.9 Escalating protection and transfer mechanisms

Now that we have analysed two cases of trade policy effects under duopoly, it is possible to draw a complete picture. The four basic cases of trade policy – import and export levies and import and export subsidies – and their effects on the market equilibrium are shown below in stylized form. For simplicity, we assume that the duopoly is totally symmetrical (this means that the slopes of the reaction curves are reciprocal to one another, so that they intersect on an imaginary 45-degree line). The points are selected in such a way as to provide maximum comparability.

It is easy to deduce from Figure 7.9 that the total volume supplied to the market at points A and E is the same and also at points B and D, except that the supply at B and D is less than that at A and E. If we also take account of the total volume supplied before protection (corresponding to point C), then we can also deduce that $B = D < C < A = E$ for the corresponding total volumes of trade.

The conclusion is that subsidies on goods that are traded internationally cause the supply to be greater than if no subsidies were granted; the consumer will benefit because of a lower price, at the expense of the suppliers. Import and export levies both have precisely the opposite effect: the volume supplied falls, driving up the price, so that we can expect the reverse transfer from the consumer to the producer. That the effects of an import and export tariff (subsidy) are symmetrical is called the Lerner symmetry theorem, as we have noted already in Section 4.4.1 (see in this respect also Boxes 4.2 and 4.3).

The effects of import and export subsidies and import and export levies are summarized in Table 7.1.

We have already pointed out how easily trade policy measures can escalate. If one government uses instruments to enlarge the market share of the national company, what will prevent other governments from doing the same? This applies particularly where protection is the result of decisions of the public administration – for example, where it is a question of interpreting provisions, the actual implementation of trade policy, or of dealing with complaint procedures. In fact, most of this type of so-called administrative protection is beyond political control (see also Chapter 9).

Let us assume that a subsidy war breaks out between the two parties in a duopoly. The likely consequences are shown as simply as possible in Figure 7.10.

As a result of escalating subsidies, the reaction curves of the two suppliers constantly move further outwards, as we have already seen, in the direction $C \rightarrow C'$, and so on. Both suppliers constantly expand the quantity offered so that the market becomes increasingly oversupplied, prices fall and a transfer from producers to consumers is initiated.

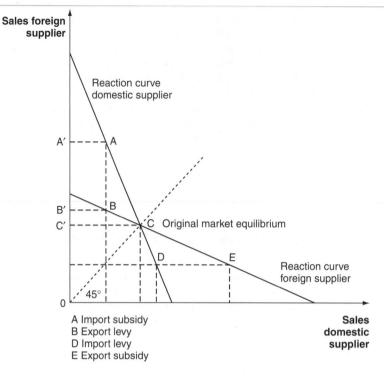

Figure 7.9 An international duopoly: equilibrium situations under various forms of national government trade policy

Table 7.1 Effects of trade instruments in a duopoly

	Foreign reaction curve	Domestic reaction curve	Volume traded	Prices
Import levy	inwards	–	falls	rise
Export subsidy	–	outwards	rises	fall
Export levy	–	inwards	falls	rise
Import subsidy	outwards	–	rises	fall

Thus, the government subsidies are in fact passed on by the producers to the consumers (who have indirectly paid for these subsidies through taxation); it is even conceivable that the fall in price might be so great that it is not offset by the subsidies, so that, paradoxically, the producers end up worse off than in the original situation C.

Similarly, we can deduce that an international escalation of import (or export) levies leads to a movement as shown by the arrow from C to the origin: international trade dries up; prices on the international market increase and a transfer takes place from consumers to producers (at least in this comparative-static context).

With respect to world welfare, assuming that free trade is the most favourable regime and bearing in mind what has been said in previous chapters about the impact of trade policy on welfare, the analysis illustrated with the aid of Figure 7.10 means that the level of world welfare will be reduced by either a tariff war or a subsidy war. Thus, in both cases there is no zero-sum game in relation to the case without protection.

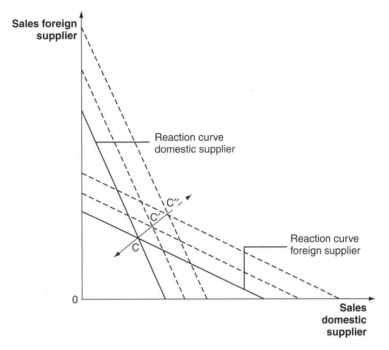

Figure 7.10 An international duopoly: a subsidy or tariff war between two countries

7.10   International cartels

The previous section illustrates that entrepreneurs in a duopoly situation face a dilemma: they can only increase their market share at the expense of their competitor, which will result in a battle.

If they try to make it easier to increase their market share by expanding sales as a whole (by, for example, calling for export subsidies), they undermine the market price and also run the risk that the process of granting subsidies will escalate, so that prices fall still further.

If, on the other hand, the government introduces trade restrictions, there is a risk of international trade drying up altogether. Thus there is a delicate interplay between suppliers, governments and customers/consumers, with the suppliers in a vulnerable position. It is therefore logical for suppliers to seek other options. Here we shall concentrate on the conclusion of cartel agreements.

Let us assume that the producers actually face a scenario in which international competition and the actions and reactions of suppliers and governments eventually lead to a 'war' between suppliers from different countries. In this situation they can either oversupply the market in an attempt to secure their own market share, or they can attack one another through price competition, causing profit margins to dwindle. The option taken may make a major difference to the entrepreneur's level of profit – an important argument for entrepreneurs always to think carefully about their choice of marketing strategy.

However, suppose that international competition is so fierce that the various suppliers end up in a situation where they are all losing but that none of them is prepared to be the first to leave the market. What is the most obvious course of action in that case?

In such a case they could try to reach a *cartel agreement* – for example, by acting as a group when setting the optimum, joint volume of supply and agree on a mutual apportionment formula – that is, the partitioning of sub-markets.

Similarly, they can also conclude mutual agreements in respect of minimum prices, in order to prevent price competition; one could also think of many other forms of formal and informal agreements aimed at reducing mutual competition. In fact, all sorts of cartel agreements like this are used in an attempt to form groups which collectively behave like a monopolist.

The advantage of such a system of agreements is not only an increase in the levels of profits for each supplier, but also greater independence from government support, which is not always totally predictable, and less need to fear unpredictable behaviour on the part of other suppliers.

As in the case of a monopolist, the power of a cartel depends on elasticity of demand. If demand is elastic, then every price increase by the cartel is punished by a relatively large fall in demand. If demand is relatively inelastic, then a cartel can increase profits by raising prices because the fall in volume remains small. Figure 7.11 shows the difference between the excess profit under perfect competition (no excess profit) and under a cartel.

If the producers decide to form a cartel, then the group's marginal cost curve will act as the supply curve (comparable to a monopolist's supply curve). The demand curve obviously remains the same. The cartel now produces quantity q_k where MR = MC. The corresponding price is p_k. The quantity supplied under the cartel has declined, but it is

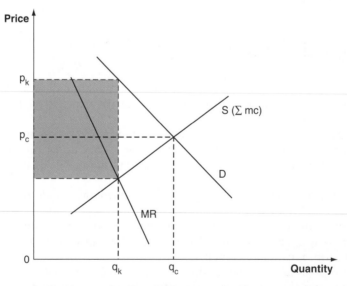

S = Supply curve for all competitors together. This is obtained by adding
    together the producers' individual marginal cost curves

D = Demand curve

p_c = Equilibrium price under perfect competition

q_c = Equilibrium supply under perfect competition

Figure 7.11 Excess profit for a cartel compared with perfect competition

sold at a higher price. Each cartel member now produces a proportionate part of quantity q_k at the higher price p_k. The resulting joint profits are indicated by the shaded area of Figure 7.11.

The question therefore is why, in the case of market forms normally regarded as imperfect competition – but where, in contrast to what the terminology suggests, one may in practice encounter the fiercest form of competition – the variant of the international cartels is generally seldom seen. The answer is twofold.

First, the establishment of a cartel among suppliers from different countries requires a high degree of organization and – especially in the case of informal agreements – trust. It often proves impossible to make all of the arrangements, simply because the transaction costs are prohibitive or in any case too high. The cartel frequently takes the form of non-explicit, informal agreements in which people's actual behaviour indicates that they are prepared to conform to the agreements.

Secondly, every cartel agreement carries the seeds of its own destruction. This is because, in a cartel, each member can benefit from cheating the group, and it is also relatively easy to do so because of the difficulty of exercising control – particularly in the case of international cartels.

Once again, the scope for evasion is presumably greater in an international context than in a purely national cartel. In other words, if a cartel is successful then there is a restriction on the collective volume of supply, thereby driving up the price level. By secretly offending against the volume agreement, it is possible to gain a relatively large additional profit by selling a little extra, on account of the high price. However, once a cartel begins to disintegrate, it ceases to be attractive to those suppliers who do adhere to the agreements. The whole system then collapses and there is an automatic tendency to return to a market form with greater mutual competition.

A historical example of how a cartel could lose its cohesion and hence its effect at a given moment is the Organization of the Petroleum Exporting Countries (OPEC) cartel during the 1970s and 1980s (see Case study 7.5).

Case study 7.5   The OPEC cartel

In the 1970s a number of oil-producing countries, united in the OPEC cartel, succeeded in increasing the price of crude oil almost tenfold in two stages (1973–74 and 1978–79) by specific mutual agreements on production volumes. This increased the OPEC countries' oil revenues in real terms from about $50 billion in 1970 to close to a projected $440 billion in 2009 and $598 billion in 2010 (Figure 7.12). So far, the highest revenue peak was in 1980 at a level of $556 billion.

However, the spectacular success of this OPEC cartel simultaneously paved the way for its collapse. The high energy prices prompted energy-saving measures in industrialized countries, and new sources of energy were tapped, causing a decline in the tensions on the energy market.

At the same time, the cartel's cohesion came under pressure because some countries tried, openly or otherwise, to secure a greater share in deliveries in order to take advantage of high market prices. As a result, OPEC production declined during the 1980s, but the fall in prices caused an even greater decline in real revenues (Figure 7.12).

Such developments meant that it was no longer possible to avoid the decline of the formerly powerful OPEC cartel. However, since the last oil price collapse of 1998–99, OPEC oil revenues have been increasing steadily, which could indicate either a revival of the cartel or a decline of the world's oil reserves.

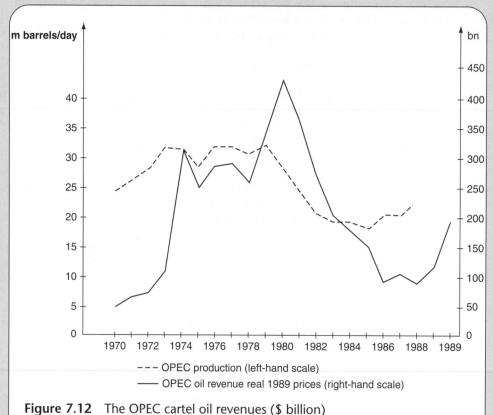

Figure 7.12   The OPEC cartel oil revenues ($ billion)
Source: Cambridge Energy Research Associates (revenues adjusted by US consumer prices).

7.11 Summary

1. This chapter has discussed the competitive behaviour of producers on international markets, using microeconomic analysis. It examined:

   - the degree to which producers can screen off sub-markets;
   - the costs involved in entering a market;
   - producers' uncertainty regarding the behaviour of their competitors;
   - how and to what extent governments adopt protective measures; and the degree to which competitors are mutually organized.

Producers active in different sub-markets will fix their price within each sub-market on the basis of the price elasticities of demand applicable to each one. In consequence, the same producer will charge a higher price on a sub-market where he holds a monopoly than on a market where he faces perfect competition. However, the higher prices charged by a foreign monopolist on the home market can be creamed off by the national government in the form of an import levy. In that case, there will be an increase in overall national welfare.

2. In the case of an oligopoly market, we analysed how, in the development of their trade strategies, competitors on the international market take account of the presumed behaviour of their competitors. We stated that if such a situation is analysed for two suppliers (duopolistic competition), the analysis can be made using reaction curves; by comparing the reaction curves of the two suppliers we can then ascertain the market equilibrium.

3. A national government can influence the competitive position of a domestic producer through the introduction of either a subsidy or a tariff policy. We have seen that if the government grants an (import or export) subsidy, the total volume supplied to the international market normally increases to a level that is higher than the original market equilibrium; in the case of an (import or export) levy, the market supply will normally fall to below the level of the original market equilibrium. Here it is assumed that the producers respond to one another's presumed behaviour by a volume policy; in this case the market price adapts to the volumes supplied.

4. If government intervention leads to counter measures on the part of foreign governments, there can easily be a tariff or a subsidy 'war'. In the first case, there will be a sharp decline in the volume of trade, followed by a price rise. In the case of an escalating subsidy war, the volume of trade increases constantly, causing the price to fall, and income to be transferred from producers to consumers. This implies that international welfare can be deemed to decline as a result of either an import levy war or a trade subsidy war.

5. If international competition is so fierce that a large group of producers makes a loss, they can form a cartel. In this form of market, producers can jointly determine the optimum price/sales combination and divide the profit amongst themselves. If operative and efficient, a cartel can actually secure a monopoly position on the market. In practice, cartels are relatively uncommon because they require a high degree of organization and therefore transaction costs, while there is also the constant internal threat of participants not adhering to the agreements. Case study 7.5, dealing with OPEC, showed that a cartel can also be threatened from outside, either if substitutes for the product are supplied or if alternatives are sought.

6. The microeconomic analysis applied in this chapter demonstrated how a producer's competitive position is determined by:

   • the market form in which the producer is operating;
   • the government's policy on market competition; and
   • the behaviour of competing firms (in an uncertain world).

It is evident from case histories that, in practice, many of the factors mentioned in this chapter come together in international trade. For some decades, the GATT/WTO has been endeavouring to foster transparency in international trade and to eliminate the present forms of protection in international free trade. The workings of the GATT/WTO will be discussed in the next chapter. Following this, Chapter 9 will examine the way in which lobbying by businesses can cause an increase in protection.

Questions

1. Why are dumping rates not always bad for the targeted market?
2. Can you think of any examples of successful predatory dumping?
3. Can you give examples of industries where economies of scale were the main driver for the increasing concentration in a limited number of companies?
4. Theory suggests that cartels are inherently unstable. Can you give real-life examples corroborating that theory?

CHAPTER 8

The Practice of Protection

8.1 | Introduction

The earlier chapters of this book discussed arguments both for and against free trade. The conclusion was that, in general, international free trade brings benefits to all, but also that protectionism can increase rapidly, especially in the absence of well-designed international policy coordination.

This chapter focuses on how protectionism and the removal of protectionist measures come about in the real world. It explains how the effective degree of protection can be assessed. At present, the only multilateral organization dealing with the rules of trade between nations is the World Trade Organization (WTO), the successor to the General Agreement on Tariffs and Trade (GATT), which has two principal functions:

o to ensure that trade flows as smoothly, predictably and freely as possible;
o to take into account the negative effects of free trade for some specific cases or for specific countries such as the developing countries (see Box 8.2).

This chapter therefore offers an extensive discussion of how the GATT/WTO framework works in practice. We end the section on trade matters by trying to explain protectionism by using the political economy approach (and in particular the theory of interest groups).

Many critics of the patterns of world trade – including some politicians from developing countries, anti-globalists and non-governmental organizations (NGOs) – claim that global trade rules are biased in favour of industrialized countries. One often-quoted example is WTO's Agreement on Trade-Related Aspects of Intellectual Property Rights (TRIPS), and in particular its meaning for the accessibility of drugs for developing countries (see Case study 8.1 for an illustration of one such international dispute).

Case study 8.1 shows just how difficult it is to formulate global trade rules. The WTO has to reconcile the conflicting interests of a wide range of global actors, including industrialized countries, developing countries, the industry and NGOs. It also shows that WTO rules are not always easy to interpret and may leave room for 'protectionism'. Brazil's patent law was used to provide cheaper, locally produced drugs and was a cornerstone of Brazil's widely praised national AIDS policy. However, the law's final effect was that Brazil's national pharmaceutical industry received an advantage in relation to the foreign industry, so that one could claim that it acted as a trade policy instrument.

Case study 8.1   Patent dispute between the USA and Brazil

The TRIPS Agreement was one of the outcomes of the Uruguay Round, which came into force in January 1995. As part of the WTO agreement, it sets minimum standards for the protection of intellectual property rights: under its provisions member countries cannot confer a lower level of protection than that provided under the agreement.

One of the agreed minimum standards was that patent protection must be available for inventions for at least 20 years. In Doha, Qatar, in November 2001, WTO members discussed the issues and the agenda for a new WTO Round of multilateral negotiations. The EU, the USA, and Japan placed TRIPS high on the agenda. These regions hold most of the world's patents, and therefore had the most to gain from protection via TRIPS. To give an example, in about the year 2000 the American pharmaceutical industry estimated its losses due to poor patent protection at $500 million per annum for its potential sales on the Indian market alone. In 2007 it was estimated that global pharmaceutical companies invest an average of up to $800 million in developing and introducing an innovative drug onto the market. Therefore a generic-drug producing company that circumvents research and development (R&D) costs can afford to offer similar treatments for only a fraction of the price of brand-name drugs.

This concerted action was one reason why some groups claimed that TRIPS works in the interests of industrialized countries but tends to discriminate against developing countries. According to the 2001 UNDP report (p. 105) 'a single set of minimum rules may seem to create a level playing field, since one set of rules applies to all. But the game is hardly fair when the players are of such unequal strength, economically and institutionally.'

TRIPS was criticized particularly strongly in the field of drugs because as long as more than two-thirds of the world production of pharmaceutical products takes place in western industrialized countries, TRIPS would deny access to essential pharmaceutical products for half the population in the poorer regions of Africa and Asia.

Why TRIPS?

The argument in favour of an agreement such as TRIPS is that patents are necessary to secure the funding of the extensive R&D that is usually required for the development of new medicines. The exclusive marketing rights provided by patents therefore represent a legitimate reward for the high levels of investment and risks that are associated with developing new drugs.

Since the agreement came into force it has become clear that it will have important implications for the availability of pharmaceuticals in developing countries, because many of the most effective drugs to treat typical tropical diseases such as HIV and malaria were covered by patents. In order to try to deal with that kind of issue, two additional clauses were included in the TRIPS Agreement, Article 31 and Article 6:

o Article 31 allows so-called compulsory licensing and governmental use of a patent without the patent holder's consent under a number of special conditions. So, while under normal circumstances the person or company must attempt to obtain a voluntary licence from the patent holder under reasonable commercial terms, Article 31 states that under circumstances such as 'national emergencies', 'other circumstances of extreme urgency', or 'public non-commercial use', licensing becomes compulsory.

However, in these circumstances the applicant must first prove that it has attempted to obtain a voluntary licence. If a compulsory licence is issued, adequate remuneration must, however, still be paid to the patent holder.

o Article 6 states that parallel imports are always allowed, meaning that products made and marketed by the patent owner in one country can be imported in another country, by a different company, without the consent of the patent owner. This provision allows countries to seek cheaper sources of a patented drug from abroad.

A drug dispute between Brazil and the USA

In February 2001, the USA filed a complaint with the WTO Dispute Settlement Body over a narrow provision of Article 68 of Brazil's industrial property law. The case was submitted by two US companies, Merck and Pfizer. Under Article 68, the holder of a patent in Brazil was obliged to ensure that the subject matter of a patent is 'worked' in Brazil, either by producing the patented good in the country or by allowing the patented process to be used in Brazil.

If this requirement is not met within three years of the patent being issued the government can issue a compulsory licence that allows others to utilize the patent without the patent holder's consent. Article 68 also states that if patent owners choose to utilize the patent through importation, then other companies will also be allowed to import the patented product or products obtained from the patented process. Under this provision Brazil permitted the local manufacture of patented drugs, including those aimed at combating HIV/AIDS.

The US government alleged that Article 68 violated the international rules enshrined in the WTO's TRIPS, and that therefore it was an illegal protectionist measure. In its turn, Brazil accused the Bush administration of launching an unwarranted attack on its successful AIDS treatment programme. To ensure the provision of a combination of drugs to some 100,000 HIV/AIDS patients, Brazil produced 7 of the 12 drugs involved. Thus, Brazilian authorities argue that the industrial property law provision allowing the production of generic drugs was an 'important instrument' in battling HIV/AIDS: since 1995 the free distribution of Brazilian-produced AIDS drugs has decreased the number of annual disease-related deaths by 50 per cent.

On 25 June 2001 the US government withdrew its complaint. Instead of seeking a resolution from the WTO, the United States and Brazil commonly agreed to appeal to the newly created USA–Brazil Consultative Mechanism for what Robert Zoellick, the then US trade representative, described as 'creative solutions'. Significant political pressure was put on the United States by several anti-AIDS organizations and leftist groups. The numerous supporters of the Brazilian approach portrayed the Bush administration as seeking to undermine Brazil's free AIDS treatment programme. Celso Amorim, Brazil's ambassador to the WTO, depicted US opposition to Article 68 as being 'unfounded and possibly politically disastrous'.

The Brazilian Foreign Ministry's Assistant Secretary of Economic, Trade and Integration Affairs, José Alfredo Graça Lima, described the agreement as 'a victory for both sides and a victory for the international community'. However, in spite of this statement, tensions still persist. In July 2003 the Brazilian Health Ministry initiated proceedings to issue compulsory licences for the production of three antiretroviral medications patented by Roche, Merck and Abbott. Furthermore, in December 2004 the chief of the Brazilian AIDS programme, Pedro Chequer, announced that on account of the high costs of drug treatments, Brazil would have to break patents in the coming year in order to bring down prices. As a consequence, on 14 March 2005 the Brazilian government asked three foreign research-based companies, Gilead, Merck and Abbott, to grant them voluntary licences for specific drugs.

Five months later, in July 2005, Abbott reported that it had reached an agreement with the Brazilian authorities only to see it invalidated by the new health minister, José Saraiva Felipe, who took office shortly after the signing of the accord. At the end of November 2005, both parties confirmed that a new agreement had been reached: the CEO of Abbott declared to the *Financial Times* that constant attacks on patents would eventually discourage the research and development of future treatments. On the other side, Pedro Chequer described the current drug pricing as being 'absolutely abusive', thus fuelling the ongoing trade conflict.

Among the questions that arise from this case study are:

1. What role did WTO rules play in this dispute?
2. What was the aim of the Uruguay Round?
3. Which government instruments can be regarded as trade policy instruments?
4. How effective are these trade policy instruments?
5. How are these instruments constructed and employed?
6. Why do governments wish to protect the pharmaceutical industry? What is the relationship between industry and government?
7. What is the position of the developing countries in the international trade system?

Questions 1–4 and 7 will be discussed in this chapter. Questions 5 and 6 will be considered in Chapter 9.

8.2   The effectiveness of protection

In some of the preceding chapters the *effects of protection at the national level* were analysed in terms of welfare theory – an analysis that takes into account the national costs and benefits of protection. Such an analysis was made in Chapters 4 and 5, which, from a general perspective on trade policy, discussed import tariffs, export taxes and subsidies (elimination of the effects of) market failures, the infant industry argument, and strategic trade policy in particular. Yet protection eventually has an effect at the level of individual businesses. For example, if the American government secures an import restriction on Japanese cars, or if Japan reduces its restrictions on the imports of textiles, those carmakers or textile manufacturers will be very interested in knowing the likely effect on their profits and jobs. They are less concerned with the overall impact on national welfare, let alone on global welfare.

Similarly, the pharmaceutical industry mentioned in Case study 8.1 will presumably have little concern about the extent to which the costs of the patent protection they receive are passed on to health insurance companies or any other group of end users.

For this reason the theory pays particular attention to the *effects of protection at the micro level*. From the perspective of the so-called theory of effective protection, this measures the extent to which a company's added value, turnover, profit, employment or market share increase when the state introduces protectionist measures. This theory usually analyses the effect a country's whole tariff structure has on a particular industry. It calculates the additional value added by an industry when a particular tariff structure is in place and compares it against the added value of the same industry when the tariff structure is removed. One can then analyse the effect that the tariff structure has on factors like investments and employment and, ultimately, how effective the protection measures are in safeguarding particular interests.

Let us assume that a domestic car industry making cars that sold for €25,000 is threatened by competition from imports. Since this industry's domestic market share declines in the face of strong competition from foreign carmakers, assume that the industry successfully lobbies the government to introduce protectionist measures. This results in a set of measures that amount, say, to a 10 per cent import duty. If we assume that the country is small, foreign suppliers will not adjust the prices of their cars that, let us assume, sell for €25,000 as well. Thus, import prices at the border do not change.

However, inside the country the imported cars have become €2500 more expensive: the import tariff is added to the import price so that the price of imported cars is now €27,500. If the domestic car manufacturer is satisfied with a similar competitive position relative to the foreign suppliers as before, he can raise the price to €27,500. Assuming that his costs remain unchanged, his profit will increase by €2500 per car. The increase in revenue translates into additional value added in the domestic production process that will be used primarily to cover the costs of production factors (such as wages for labour, rent for land and interest for capital) and pay for profits.

What we need to establish is to what extent the value added increased after the introduction of the import duty. Let us assume that the €25,000 car contained several components worth €15,000, which the company had to buy from a third party. Thus, the value added by the company available to pay for the factors of production and profits was then €10,000. Protection by a nominal 10 per cent tariff can yield a 25 per cent increase in value added, as the new selling price can go up to €27,500. The parts still cost €15,000. Thus, the value added has risen from €10,000 to €12,500. This 25 per cent rise in added value is called the 'effective import tariff'.

If, for example, the purchased parts had represented €20,000 of the cost price, then the value added would actually have increased by 50 per cent – from €5000 to €7500. Clearly, the proportion of the purchased parts (and thus any tariffs on them: see discussion below) in the value of the final product acts as a lever. This is why the percentage increase in the value added may far exceed that of the increase in the product's price resulting from the tariff.

Obviously, if tariffs had also been imposed on the imported parts, this would have reduced the increase in value added because these inputs would then have become more expensive. For this reason most western governments arrange their protection structure to protect end products but keep protection to a minimum on imported parts, semi-manufactures, and raw materials. As a result, protection on many goods is graduated, which means that protection increases at higher stages in product processing. This is also known as *tariff escalation*.

It is not easy to determine precisely the investment and employment effects, because these depend upon a wide range of factors that influence the entrepreneurial decision. However, it is evidently more important to understand the effect of protection on value added rather than to know the actual level of each nominal tariff.

By implication, it is therefore clear that under certain conditions a small degree of protection can still have substantial domestic effects, since the effective rate of protection is already substantial. An understanding of this is naturally important for those who engage in international negotiations on the abolition of protection.

8.3 | The GATT/WTO

In 1947 some 23 leading trading nations reached an agreement on rules to reduce tariff levels. With the Second World War having ended only recently, they wanted to give an early boost to trade liberalization, and to begin to correct the considerable legacy of protectionist measures which had remained in place from the time of the Depression in the early 1930s. This General Agreement on Tariffs and Trade (GATT) became the main organization arranging and advising on international trade.

The following important functions were assigned to the GATT:

○ **The settlement of trade disputes between countries**. Only governments have the legal standing to bring cases before the dispute settlement procedures.
○ **Defining the conditions concerning the trade policy of the contracting parties**. For example, these conditions include the most-favourite-nation (MFN) clause which tries to prevent discrimination between trade partners in any application of trade policy, and the ban on the imposition of quotas. The GATT does permit exceptions to these conditions: for example, regional economic integration is permitted on a limited scale (the 'preferential trading blocs'), provided that the mutual trade barriers are demolished for virtually all trade and there is no overall increase in external protection for the region as a result of the integration, or a quota may be imposed if a country has serious balance of payments problems.
○ **Promoting tariff reductions**. These often take place via multilateral rounds of negotiations, also known as tariff rounds (see Box 8.3). When a country agrees to bind a tariff on a product at a certain level, it commits itself not to increase the tariff above that level.

In 1995 the GATT was replaced by the World Trade Organization (WTO), which had a rather broader mandate and a somewhat stronger structure, including a stronger dispute settlement procedure (see Box 8.1).

Box 8.1   GATT and the WTO: the main differences

The GATT was a legal text setting out the arrangement of international trade in goods between its contracting parties. It was not ratified in the national parliaments of any of its members, and it contained no provisions for the creation of an organization. To discuss trade issues and have trade negotiations, meetings had to be arranged and secretarial support provided. This led to the temporary creation of an ad hoc organization.

In recent decades, the trade in services became much more important, as did the trade in ideas – inventions and designs, and goods and services incorporating this 'intellectual property'. This is why a new General Agreement on Trade in Services (GATS) and an Agreement on Trade-Related Aspects of Intellectual Property Rights (TRIPS) were needed (see also the Uruguay Round discussed in Box 8.3).

Together with the updated GATT, these three agreements became incorporated into the WTO along with a single dispute settlement system. The WTO dispute settlement system is faster and more automatic than the old GATT system. Its rulings cannot be blocked. Moreover, the WTO is an international organization with a sound legal basis because members have ratified agreements, and because the agreements themselves carefully describe how the WTO is to function. In July 2008 the WTO had 153 member countries.

In Chapter 5 we discussed how, in theory, there are sometimes arguments for the unilateral abolition of tariffs (which then require no negotiation), but in practice we almost always assume reciprocity – in other words, the abolition of protection by a country is regarded as a concession and other countries are expected to offer something in return. The GATT also assumed *reciprocity* in relation to its regulations negotiations. In practice, however, this system of reciprocity does not apply to those situations where little can reasonably be expected in return, such as in the case of some developing countries.

The GATT/WTO system of reciprocity can be problematic because of the common negotiating technique. This largely implies that the principal exporters try to arrange a trade policy deal with the leading customer countries, which is then declared to be applicable to all participating countries. In practice, under such a negotiating technique one cannot always secure reciprocal concessions equivalent to the amount gained by other countries from the original trade concessions. Thus, one has to accept that in this instance there is a high risk of *free riding* in such circumstances (see also below).

The fact that one participating country's trade concession is then declared applicable to all participating countries is due to another GATT/WTO principle, namely that of *non-discrimination*. This principle is contained both in the MFN clause included in trade agreements and in the rules based on a system of national treatment.

The MFN clause is a provision of an agreement between two countries which states that, if the countries reduce their mutual tariffs, the tariffs which they impose on third countries belonging to the GATT/WTO must not be set any higher. This means that if a country reduces its tariffs in relation to a particular country, that tariff reduction also applies to all other countries enjoying MFN status.

As a consequence, *bilateral* agreements have *multilateral* effects and countries that are too small or too unimportant to take part in the real GATT/WTO negotiations, such as a number of developing countries with an emerging competitive industrial production, will also benefit from any trade concessions that the large countries have extracted from one another. Furthermore, they need offer little or nothing in return. This is referred to as the GATT/WTO free rider problem.

An increasing number of calls for reciprocal concessions came also from newly industrializing economies. (It must be pointed out that developing countries sometimes actually receive preferential tariff treatment, that is, products originating from developing countries are subject to a lower tariff than imports from non-developing countries. For an illustration, see Box 8.2.)

The *national treatment* principle means that imported products must be treated in the same way as comparable domestic products on the home market of the importing country. For example, if environmental requirements are imposed upon packaging material or technical requirements on products, these must be applied in the same way to both domestic and comparable foreign products.

One may wonder just how effective the MFN clause really is for the majority of members to which it applies. Let us consider an example.

Say Japan and Europe conclude mutual agreements for a 50 per cent reduction in import tariffs on video recorders and automatic transmission systems. In this case, under the GATT system these concessions apply to each GATT contracting party with MFN status that wishes to export these goods. However, countries that do not – or cannot – supply this type of goods gain nothing from this type of concession. In more general terms, since the postwar abolition of tariffs under the GATT/WTO concentrated mainly on industrial products, many developing countries complained that in practice the non-discrimination system still discriminated against them because of the list of export products to which it refers. If the tariffs on industrial products fell while those on developing country exports had no or little share in this reduction, there would have been a relative deterioration in market access for exports from developing countries.

One important development opposing the GATT/WTO principle of non-discrimination is the emergence of international agreements of regional economic integration, whether or not these are accepted by the GATT/WTO. The period between the 1950s and 1970s saw the establishment of the EU and EFTA (European Free Trade Association), but also LAFTA (the Latin American Free Trade Association) in Latin America and ASEAN (the Association of South East Asian Nations) in South-East Asia. More recent years have also seen the establishment of NAFTA (the North American Free Trade Agreement), bringing together the USA, Canada and Mexico, COMESA (the Common Market for Eastern and Southern Africa), including 19 African states and Mercosur (Mercado Común del Sur) between the countries of South America.

Although, as has been argued already, the principle of non-discrimination is one of the leading principles of the GATT/WTO, it has nevertheless been acknowledged that even if mutual trade barriers are eliminated on a limited regional scale, this must be seen as a step towards the establishment of a system of free trade, even if the principle of non-discrimination is not satisfied from a global perspective. For this reason bona fide forms of regional economic integration, such as a customs union or free trade zone, were actually accepted into the system, albeit under certain conditions such as there being no overall increase in the levels of *external* protection (Article 24 of the GATT Agreement).

There are other exceptions to the GATT/WTO principle of trying to promote global free trade. Among the most important are umbrella clauses, such as GATT Article 20, which allow countries to take (trade policy) actions to protect human, animal or plant life or health, and to conserve exhaustible natural resources. It is important to note, however, that in practice governments and businesses often try to abuse the exceptions granted by interpreting such measures in very broad terms. This can then readily escalate into a growing protectionism. This is one of the reasons why, when GATT became the WTO, there was a reinforcement of the dispute settlement procedure. When a dispute is brought to the WTO, leading to a ruling by the Dispute Settlement Body (which consists of all of its members), the member governments have to respond accordingly.

Box 8.2   The position of the developing countries

During the 1960s, the developing countries, unified in the United Nations Conference on Trade and Development (UNCTAD) which was established in 1964, made a joint attempt to secure a special position in the GATT. This group argued that, before they could engage fully in free trade, they needed to use protective measures to build up their industries without being sanctioned for this under the GATT system. (See Chapter 5 for a discussion of the infant industry argument for protectionism and the import substitution policy adopted by many developing countries in the 1950s.) To a large extent, the developing countries did actually secure this special position in the GATT:

o they could withdraw or amend concessions on customs duties if this was thought to be necessary to build up a new industry which was likely to bring an increase in production and a higher standard of living;
o import restrictions were permitted in order to restore a severe disequilibrium of the balance of payments and secure the foreign exchange to buy the goods necessary for implementing development plans; and

o government aid was permitted where necessary to promote the establishment of businesses which could improve the population's standard of living.

From the 1960s, in particular, a number of developing countries began to expand their exports of manufactured products. These countries also exerted pressure for freer access to the industrial countries' markets and permission to subsidize their exports. As a result, in 1965 the GATT added an additional part (Part IV) to the text of the General Agreement, which was aimed specifically at improving the trading position of developing countries. Its main aim was that the non-discrimination principle did not apply to developing countries, so that they could be given preferential treatment on the import of their products into industrial countries. Further, the developing countries were not obliged to offer reciprocal trade concessions to the industrial countries.

The addition of this new part to the text of the General Agreement enabled the EU to apply the Generalized System of Preferences (GSP) in 1971. The GSP offers a ten-year exemption from the MFN clause for developing countries. This exemption meant that industrial countries could grant the developing countries unilateral trade advantages by either reducing or abolishing tariffs on their manufactured goods.

Canada began using the GSP in 1974 and, following an initial period of opposition, so did the USA in 1976. Other industrial countries also introduced a GSP. It was not until the end of the Tokyo Round in 1979 (one of GATT's multilateral negotiation rounds) that the GSP was legally incorporated in the GATT. In practice, however, the GSP offered only very marginal advantages for developing countries.

1. First, the system imposed many different restrictions on product categories: as a result, those sectors in which developing countries were traditionally competitive were often excluded from the GSP. For example, textile exports from developing countries were largely excluded from the GSP.

More specifically, in 1957 the USA tried to restrict imports of textiles by persuading Japan to apply 'voluntary' export restraint. As a result other countries, particularly Hong Kong, then took over from Japan. The USA responded by pressing for an international agreement on the trade in cotton. After a basic agreement on textile trade, in 1974, a system of agreements covering all types of textiles came into existence: the Multi-Fibre Arrangement (MFA). The MFA serves as an umbrella under which importing countries negotiate 'orderly marketing agreements' with exporting countries. In 1981 the MFA was extended and, since 1995, the WTO's Agreement on Textiles and Clothing (ATC) has taken over from the MFA. The ATC was terminated on 1 January 2005, meaning that trade in textiles is now governed by the general rules of the multilateral trading system.

2. Secondly, the GSP was not very effective because, in practice, it favoured developing countries that were already involved in a process of rapid industrialization. This was due partly to the import quota system commonly applied, consisting of rules whereby preferential treatment in any one year applies only to a small, predetermined volume of imports. This means 'first come, first served' (that is, the first to offer imports gains the benefit of the lenient trade rules). The best-organized supplier, and especially the one best able to handle the required bureaucratic processes involved in trade, will gain the greatest advantage from this system. These suppliers often came from the most advanced developing countries that were already eligible for the GSP scheme.

One of the main achievements of the GATT/WTO regime has been the conclusion of eight multilateral negotiation rounds that have succeeded in reducing the levels of protectionism and the freeing up of international trade. The result of this has been that while the global trade to global output ratio amounted to only 6 per cent when the GATT started in 1948, it had risen to more than 25 per cent by 2007. In addition, the number of issues discussed during those negotiation rounds has expanded gradually to also include the trade in agricultural products, in services (now accounting for about 24 per cent of global trade), and issues relating to the international protection of intellectual property rights.

The gradual expansion of the number of issues being tackled under the GATT/WTO regime, and therefore covered during the negotiation rounds, also posed a series of problems. During the preparatory stage of a possible ninth multilateral negotiation round under the WTO, it became clear that it was going to be difficult to reach an agreement over what topics should be placed on the negotiations agenda.

Groups of countries clearly had interests to move specific issues forward to the negotiating stage, or, instead, to try to keep them out. The most heated debates referred to whether or not, and how, to deal with production and process methods (PPMs) that could distort international competition, especially with regard to highly sensitive aspects such as human rights and the environment.

During the first meeting to try to set an agenda for a ninth negotiation round in Seattle, USA, in 1999, negotiators failed to reach agreement, possibly in part as the result of the turmoil produced by NGOs in the negotiating area, while criticizing the open trade system for increasing poverty levels, degrading the environment and violating human rights in some regions. At the subsequent meeting in Qatar in 2001, a final compromise was reached, so that the next multilateral negotiation round could start.

The meetings that followed will be discussed below. Box 8.3 offers a brief review of the progress made and the results achieved (and not achieved) during the postwar negotiations conducted under the GATT.

Box 8.3   The rounds of negotiations

To date there have been eight rounds of negotiations. Table 8.1 details for the different rounds what the main subjects were for discussion, and the number of countries involved in each round:

Table 8.1 GATT trade rounds

Year	Place/name	Subjects covered	Countries
1947	Geneva	Tariffs	23
1949	Annecy	Tariffs	13
1951	Torquay	Tariffs	38
1956	Geneva	Tariffs	26
1960–61	Dillon Round	Tariffs	26
1964–67	Kennedy Round	Tariffs and anti-dumping measures	62

1973–79	Tokyo Round	Tariffs, non-tariff measures, 'framework' agreements	102
1986–94	Uruguay Round	Tariffs, non-tariff measures, rules, services, intellectual property, dispute settlement, textiles, agriculture, creation of WTO, etc	123
2001–11	Doha Round	Agriculture, services, TRIPS (public health related issues), dispute settlements, environment, position of developing countries	142

Source: WTO (2011).

It is clear that in the early years, the GATT trade rounds focused on securing further reductions in tariffs. In this respect the first two rounds, held between 1947 and 1949, achieved considerable success (see Figure 8.1). At this time the GATT's achievements related mainly to industrial goods produced in industrial countries. The next three rounds were far less successful, as the result of a rise in protectionist measures in the 1950s.

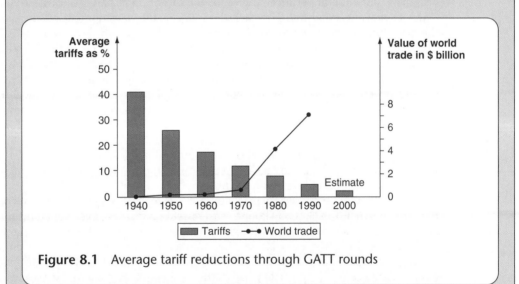

Figure 8.1 Average tariff reductions through GATT rounds

The sixth round, which lasted from 1964 to 1967 and was called the Kennedy Round, must be seen in the context of a rising European Community and of the US trade policy developments at that time. In the USA, the Trade Agreements Act (TAA) applied until 1961; its principles dated back to the protectionist era of President Roosevelt (1934).

In 1961 the Kennedy administration announced its intention to liberalize trade and asked Congress for a new trade law – a move that led to the passage of the Trade Expansion Act in 1962. The most important changes that took place under this Act were that negotiations on tariff reductions need no longer be conducted for each product but could relate to several products simultaneously; and the concept of injury in the various escape clauses (see Section 8.4) was given a stricter interpretation.

This meant that an increase in imports after a tariff reduction was no longer automatically considered to cause injury to the domestic producer. Instead it was necessary to undertake an investigation to prove that tariff reduction and the resulting increase in imports actually caused injury to a producer. Furthermore, if an actual injury could be demonstrated, withdrawing the tariff reductions to support the businesses and employees affected via 'trade adjustment assistance' was no longer a solution. This was a significant step in developing trade policy that led to a GATT anti-dumping agreement.

The Kennedy Round achieved substantial reductions in the import tariffs on manufactured goods; this meant that the round focused principally on the trading interests of industrial countries. Two-thirds of their tariffs were reduced by 50 per cent; on average, the tariffs on manufactures were cut by 33 per cent.

In 1971 the Nixon administration called for a new GATT round in which the emphasis would be on unfair trade practices against the USA and special attention would be paid to the interests of US farmers. The president hoped that this would prevent Congressional calls for protectionist measures to be introduced. At an initial ministerial meeting in 1973 the agenda for the preparation of this round (originally called the Nixon Round, but later renamed the Tokyo Round) included the following points: tariff reductions, the expansion of trade in agricultural products, the reduction of non-tariff barriers, the development of codes to prevent unfair trade practices and, finally, the development of special rules for the export products of developing countries.

The Tokyo Round lasted until 1979 and achieved a further average tariff reduction of about one-third on most manufactured goods. This GATT round was particularly successful in tackling non-tariff barriers. Codes of conduct were developed in relation to areas such as government procurement, border formalities, technical rules on health, safety, national security, environment, government subsidies, import licences, and dumping (the revision of the existing GATT code). These codes specified in detail what the appropriate government procedures and measures needed to be. In addition, each code provides for a GATT committee to settle international disputes in particular areas. However, the Tokyo Round made little progress in tackling problems relating to trade in agricultural products and the position of the developing countries.

The eighth GATT round began in Punta del Este, Uruguay, in 1986 and has since become known as the Uruguay Round. As a result of difficulties in negotiations this round lasted for seven and a half years – almost twice the length of the proposed schedule. The final ministerial conference could not be arranged for the end of 1990 as planned. The members disagreed about how to reform agricultural trade and decided to extend the talks. It lasted until 15 April 1994, when the deal was signed by ministers from most of the 125 participating governments at a meeting in Marrakech, Morocco.

This round focused on the following issues:

o *Agriculture.* The European agricultural policy was a particularly sensitive subject. There was no breakthrough until mutual agreements between the EU and the USA were adopted under a deal agreed in November 1992 and known informally as the 'Blair House accord'. The aims of the agreement were that the volume of subsidized agricultural exports should be reduced by 21 per cent in six years. Over the same period the level of total export subsidies was to be cut by 36 per cent. The industrial countries were also to reduce import tariffs on agricultural products by an average of 36 per cent and developing countries by 24 per cent. Countries with a ban on the imports of a particular agricultural product were to open at least 3 per cent of their market to foreign goods. After its signing, the agreement was rejected by France, which claimed it conflicted with commitments to the CAP and, despite the refusal of the USA to renegotiate, Germany was able to effect an agreement. The 'Blair House accord' was an important step in the signing of the 1996 Uruguay Round.

o *The services sector.* International trade in commercial services (tourism, transport, banking, insurance, telecommunication services, and related areas) amounted to more than $1435 billion in 2000. This figure was 23 per cent of the value of international trade in goods, which stood at around $6364 billion in 2000. This ratio had been growing by around 2 per cent per annum. While the world exports of goods grew at a rate of 5.8 per cent annually throughout the 1980s, the world exports in services grew by around 8.2 per cent annually during the same period. In the past, the multilateral negotiating rounds disregarded this sector because trade in goods was considered to be more important. As a result, there are still many national barriers in the services sector, but a framework agreement has now been concluded, namely the General Agreement on Trade in Services (GATS), which stipulates that, in principle, the general obligations and disciplines of the GATT, including the MFN principle and that of national treatment, are also applicable to the services sector. The GATS can be regarded as a sister agreement to the GATT. The principal services sectors on which agreements have been made are tourism and professional services, such as accountancy and consultancy activities. A first round of negotiations on the GATS regime began in early 2000, independent of the timing of new GATT/WTO negotiation rounds.

o *Intellectual property.* Over the course of the past decade there has been a sharp increase in trade in imitation products, including fake Rolex watches, pirated software, copies of books and CDs, and counterfeit drugs. Sometimes these fake goods are meant to be passed off as the branded product that they imitate. In other cases the original product is supplied without the payment of the due royalties or licence fees. These practices are causing increasing annoyance in the industrial countries, where the owners of most of the original goods are based. The USA has introduced legislation on that account penalizing countries that tolerate the imitation of brands and products. It was therefore decided, during the Uruguay Round, to set up a 'Trade-Related aspects of Intellectual Property rights' (TRIPS) agreement, which came into force in 1995. As argued in Case study 7.1, its main aim was to ensure that patented products, especially those that require significant R&D investment, would not come to suffer from unfair competition by unpatented substitutes and fakes. The GATT/WTO gave developing countries, which have no intellectual property protection laws, until 2005/2006 to introduce them. However, heated disputes over intellectual property persist to this day, the most significant example being China, which is estimated by specialists to be responsible for almost two-thirds of all the counterfeit and pirated goods in the world. One particular drawback of TRIPS, which also led to significant NGO opposition in 2000–01, applies to the distribution of western drugs to developing countries in order to combat illnesses such as AIDS and malaria. It was claimed that prices had been driven upwards, leading to a reduction in the availability of drugs. This issue received considerable attention during the WTO meetings at Seattle (1999) and Qatar (2001).

o *A ban on 'grey area' measures.* Article 11 of the Uruguay Round Agreement on Safeguards prohibited so-called 'grey area' measures – that is, bilateral negotiations that lay outside GATT's auspices such as 'voluntary export restraints' (VERs), orderly marketing arrangements, and other similar bilateral measures on both the export and import sides. All such measures either had to be modified so that they were in compliance with the agreement, or else they had to be abolished by the end of 1998. Each country could maintain such restrictions in only one specific area until the end of 1999. The only case in which this happened was in respect of the EU's restrictions on imports of cars from Japan that were introduced in 1993 to place a ceiling on the growing market segment on cars imported from Japan and abolished again six years later.

The Uruguay Round again stipulated exceptions for developing countries. Thus, the poorest countries are not subject to the subsidy disciplines and are under no obligation to reduce agricultural tariffs, whereas the industrialized countries, as mentioned earlier, are expected to reduce import tariffs on agricultural products by an average of 36 per cent. Many emerging industrial countries also regarded the Uruguay Round negotiations on the services sectors and intellectual property as a direct threat to their sovereignty. As a concession to developing countries, the industrial countries were prepared to undertake a radical review of the safeguard rules and to abolish the MFA/ATC. In 2005 the sector was fully liberalized (see also Box 8.2).

The Doha Round covers a wide variety of topics, including agriculture, services, and the position of the developing countries. The discussions in relation to TRIPS (in pharmaceutical products) and the Dispute Settlement Understanding proved the most important. The Doha Development Agenda (DDA) set out a timetable for all subjects to be negotiated, with the deadline for most subjects set at the beginning of 2005. In the interim there was a Ministerial meeting in Cancun, Mexico to discuss the progress that had been made.

Table 8.2 Percentages of tariffs bound before and after the Uruguay Round (percentages are not weighted according to trade volume or value)

	Before	After
Developed countries	78	99
Developing countries	21	73
Transition economies	73	98

Source: WTO (2001).

However, by the end of this meeting no consensus had been achieved and there was a deadlock over several core issues. Reforms in agricultural policy appeared to be one of the most difficult issues, especially in relation to the developed countries (see also Case study 5.5). In 2004, the EU announced its willingness to eliminate agricultural export subsidies, which was seen as an important step for developing countries. Some developing countries have been amongst the most heavily affected by the 'artificially' low world market prices for agricultural products, which are the result of the extensive protectionist policies in the developed countries. To the present day, important steps have since been taken to ameliorate this situation (see Case study 5.5 on EU's Common Agricultural Policy).

8.4 Non-tariff barriers

In the postwar period there was a clear reduction in the level of import tariffs imposed by industrial countries, and many import quotas (quantitative or value restrictions on imports) were abolished; nevertheless, they were replaced simultaneously by many new, often disguised forms of protectionism. From the mid-1970s onwards, in particular, traditional protectionism in the form of tariffs was largely replaced by all kinds of *non-tariff barriers* (NTBs). Given that hundreds of these NTBs have been identified, and that these measures differ significantly in respect of the restrictions they place on trade, a distinction is often made between core NTBs – considered to have clearly protective effects – and other NTBs.

The ban on 'grey area' measures of the Uruguay Round was intended to bring an end to NTBs. Table 8.3 shows the pervasiveness of core NTBs in the agricultural and industrial sectors for a number of countries. It indicates a decline in the use of core NTBs in most countries since the early 1990s and until the years following the entry of the agreements of the Uruguay Round. It also shows that developing countries are making progress in abolishing NTBs, but that they generally make more use of NTBs than do industrial countries.

NTBs are protectionist measures that can occur in any form except in terms of actual import tariffs. Sometimes, protectionist measures are introduced on the basis of explicit political decisions. These include an extension of the Multi-Fibre Arrangement or trade policy directives issued by the European Commission.

In many other cases, however, protectionist practices are based on the decisions of bureaucracies and executive agencies. There is not necessarily any explicit political decision with regard to the new resolutions that implement increased protection.

Table 8.3 Frequency of core non-tariff barriers for selected countries (as % of tariff lines affected)

a Developed countries	1993	1996	b Developing countries	1989–94	1995–98
Australia	0.7	0.7	Argentina	3.1	2.1
Canada	8.3	7.3	Brazil	16.5	21.6
EU	22.1	13.0	Chile	5.2	5.2
Iceland	3.0	0.5	Colombia	55.2	10.3
Japan	11.4	9.9	Hong Kong	2.1	2.1
Mexico	2.0	14.1	India	99	93.8
New Zealand	0.4	0.8	Indonesia	53.6	31.3
Norway	5.9	2.6	Korea, Rep. of	50.0	25.0
Switzerland	3.6	0.2	Malaysia	56.3	19.6
Turkey	0.4	0.6	Morocco	58.3	13.4
USA	23.0	16.7	Nigeria	14.4	11.5
			Singapore	1.0	2.1
			South Africa	36.5	8.3
			Thailand	36.5	17.5
			Uruguay	32.3	0.0

Sources: OECD (1997) and Michalopolous (1999).

Protectionism that comes about in this manner is referred to as *administered protection* (AP). In other words, defining the framework within which protectionist measures may be applied is normally subject to political control; the implementation of such a framework often rests with the public authorities which thus, in practice, have some degree of freedom in determining policy; and in some cases that scope is quite considerable.

Among the forms of AP permitted under the GATT/WTO rules are the following measures that national governments may take in order to protect their industries against 'injury'.

1. The adoption of *safeguard measures*. Many countries, including the USA, have incorporated escape clauses into their trade laws. These are based on Article 19 of the GATT/WTO, known as the safeguard clause, under which temporary import restrictions may be imposed or previous trade concessions withdrawn if imports are causing, or threatening to cause, serious injury to domestic industries. According to the GATT/WTO, the conditions of a safeguard clause are that such a trade law clause may only be applied without discrimination (that is, it must apply equally to all trading partners); there must be proof of the injury and the causative link between the increased imports and the injury; and countries that suffer as a result of the safeguard rules are entitled to mutually agreed compensation. If they receive nothing, then they may take their own counter measures. To date, the use of the safeguard provision has been limited. The reason is that other techniques, such as anti-dumping or countervailing duties, are preferred because they can be targeted much more accurately (on specific trading partners) and the burden of proof is not so onerous. For example, only 209 safeguard investigations were initiated from January 1995 to December 2010, compared with 245 countervailing duty investigations and 3,675 anti-dumping initiations.

Figure 8.2 shows the number of initiations of anti-dumping and countervailing investigations over the period 1995–2009.

Since the WTO agreement the safeguard rules have been accentuated; they now provide for consultations on compensation and procedures for enforcing its payment. According to a so-called 'sunset clause' in the WTO Agreement, safeguard measures are not allowed to remain in force for more than four years.

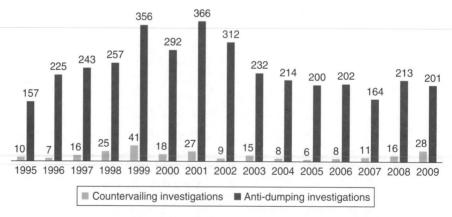

Figure 8.2 Initiations of anti-dumping and countervailing investigations, 1995–2009
Source: WTO Secretariat (2010).

2. The application of anti-dumping duties. Dumping is the sale of products at a price below that in the country of origin and/or below cost. The GATT/WTO permits countries to impose tariffs, under certain conditions, on products dumped on the home market. For example, the EU has set out its anti-dumping policy in a regulation whereby:

- a dumping margin must be established (the difference between the export price and the 'normal value');
- 'material injury' to EU industries must be established;
- there must be a causative link between dumping and injury;
- even if dumping is confirmed, it is necessary to ascertain whether intervention is in the Community interest.

Obviously, it is a complicated procedure to investigate whether, and to what extent, these four requirements are met. Thus, this kind of rule often leads to lengthy and expensive court actions based on judgements imposed by the complainant country itself. For this reason there may be variations from one country to another (and certainly not always to the detriment of the complainant, as illustrated by Case study 8.2). This could explain the growing popularity of anti-dumping actions and, in particular, the implementation of provisional measures, pending possible, permanent anti-dumping duties in the late 1990s.

However, after the 2001 peak there was a steady decline in the number of initiations. In the period from 1995 to the first half of 2008 records maintained by the WTO indicated more than 3300 initiations of anti-dumping investigations worldwide. Figure 8.3 shows that initiations of investigations on whether an anti-dumping duty could be introduced have increased steadily and significantly since 1995, reaching an all-time high of around 366 in 2001. By 2002 a significant downward trend had begun, which could imply a 'small' victory for free trade and the WTO. In the first half of 2008 the number of anti-dumping investigations fell to 85. Until the early 1990s the developed countries (Australia, Canada, the EU, Israel, South Korea and the USA) were the main initiators of anti-dumping investigations. In 2007, India was the main user, with 47 initiations. However, in the 1990s an increasing share of initiations came from 'new users', the developing countries. In 2009,

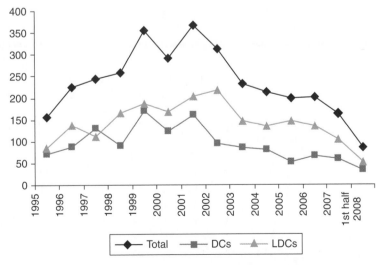

Figure 8.3 Initiation of anti-dumping investigations, 1995–2008
Source: WTO Secretariat, Rules Division Anti-dumping Measures Database, March 2009.

for example, the five heaviest anti-dumping users included four developing countries. As stated, India topped the list (31 initiations), followed by Argentina (28), Pakistan (26), the USA (20) and China (17).

Table 8.4 shows the amount of anti-dumping investigations for the most targeted countries during the period 1995 to the end of 2009. On average, China has been the most heavily targeted country. Over this period, about 40 per cent of the initiations were targeted at developed countries. Clearly, the other 60 per cent of the initiations were targeted at developing countries.

On average, around one-half of the initiated anti-dumping investigations are terminated without measures being imposed and the rest end with a definitive anti-dumping measure in the form of a duty or, much less frequently, a price undertaking by the exporter. In spite of their large number, anti-dumping practices concern only a limited import value: we know that only about 1 per cent of all EU imports are actually affected by the anti-dumping policy.

3. The introduction of countervailing duties (CVDs). If the exporting country subsidizes imports, tariffs may be imposed on those imports to offset the value of the subsidies in order to protect the national industry competing with the imports. As Figure 8.2 has shown, the use of CVD procedures is much less than for anti-dumping. The use of

Table 8.4 The number of anti-dumping investigations for the most targeted countries, 1995–2009

Exporting Country	Anti-dumping initiatives: by exporting country 1 January 1995–31 December 2009															
	1995	1996	1997	1998	1999	2000	2001	2002	2003	2004	2005	2006	2007	2008	2009	Total
Argentina	1			1	4	2	5	3	1	3	4	3	1	2	1	31
Belgium	1	2	3	3	1		5	1	3	2					3	24
Brazil	8	10	5	6	13	9	13	4	3	10	4	7	2	3	11	108
China	20	43	33	28	42	44	55	51	53	49	56	72	62	76	77	761
European Union		1	2	4	7	9	9	10	10	3	5	3	2	4	3	72
France		4	4	10	7	2	3	2	3	1	1	1	1	1	1	41
Germany	7	9	13	8	11	6	9	7	3	2	2	2	4	1	3	87
Hong Kong, China	1	4	2	3	2	1	3	3			2	1	3	2	1	28
India	3	11	8	13	13	10	12	16	14	8	14	6	4	6	7	145
Indonesia	7	7	9	5	20	13	18	12	8	8	14	9	5	11	10	156
Italy	6	5	5	5	2	5	8	3	4	1	1			2	1	48
Japan	5	6	14	14	22	12	14	13	16	9	7	11	4	3	5	155
Korea, Republic of	14	11	15	27	35	23	23	23	17	24	12	11	13	9	7	264
Malaysia	2	3	5	4	7	9	6	4	8	6	14	6	7	10	6	97
Mexico	3	5	2	9	4	1	4	2	4	3	1	2	2		5	47
Netherlands	6	1	5	3	2	3	4	1		2					1	28
Poland	2	3	3	5	3	5	1	4	1	2						29
Romania	1	2	1	5	4	4	5	8	2		2			2		36
Russian Federation	2	7	7	13	18	12	9	20	2	8	4	5	6	2	4	119

Singapore	2		4		5		12	9	1	1	1	7	2		1	45
South Africa	2	6	4	5	4	6	9	10	4		2	2	1	3		58
Spain	2	4	7	7	5	6	4	2	4	1			1	1		44
Taipei, Chinese	4	9	16	11	22	15	19	16	13	21	13	12	6	10	11	198
Thailand	8	9	5	2	19	12	16	12	7	9	13	8	9	13	8	150
Turkey	2	3	1	2	6	7	5	4	4	1		2	3	4	1	45
Ukraine	2	3	4	9	9	7	6	8	3	1	3	4		2	2	63
UK	6	4	6	4	2	9	6	2		1	1			3		44
USA	12	21	15	16	14	13	15	12	21	14	12	11	7	8	14	205
Total	157	226	246	266	358	298	371	315	234	220	202	203	165	213	201	3675

Source: WTO Secretariat, Rules Division Anti-dumping Measures Database, March 2010.

CVD initiations reached a peak in 1999 (41), but slowed down in the following years (there were only 11 in 2007). In the period between 1995 and the first half of 2008, the USA made relatively extensive use of this type of measure (85), followed by the EU (47). Before 1996 the EU had made hardly any use of this instrument.

4. The prevention of unfair trade. This can be illustrated by an example. Section 301 of the US Trade Act 1974 provides for the possibility of counter measures on the part of the USA if countries impose unfair restrictions in order to protect their markets against products from the USA. This provision was tightened in 1988, when the USA assumed the right to retaliate against unfair trade by others who damaged US exports, under the Super 301 clause. The eight countries concerned in 1989 were placed on a 'watch list' as a warning, which meant that sanctions could follow. In practice, the USA aims to use this instrument to force other countries to open their borders, which can lead to what the literature terms voluntary import expansion (VIE). Since these US measures are not based on internationally accepted political decision-making processes, but rather have to be seen as the application of existing national or international laws and regulations by the US administration, they belong to the category of AP, just as the other ones discussed above.

The overall picture that emerges from this discussion is one of a multiplicity of trade disputes. Between its introduction and the middle of 2001, 234 complaints were filed under the WTO's Dispute Settlement Understanding, with two-thirds being filed by developed countries. However, three-quarters of the complaints do not progress beyond the consultations in the panel stage. This reflects, to some extent, the frequency with which trade defence instruments among WTO members are used and the enormous activity in the sphere of international consultation, negotiating situations and lobbying. One can therefore get the impression that in a number of cases the procedures set in motion are aimed not so much at pursuing the introduction of a duty as attempting to force the foreign supplier and/or foreign government to negotiate.

This conclusion is also illustrated by the fact that a number of cases which resulted in a 'voluntary' export restraint were preceded by a large number of legal proceedings against the suppliers: this applied in the case of the restrictions on imports of Japanese cars into the USA, for example, the restrictions on imports of steel into the same country and the international agreements on trade in semiconductors. Despite the ban on VERs since 1995, governments still seem to use initiations of anti-dumping and CVD investigations in order to resolve trade disputes by VERs. Some examples may illustrate the issues involved: in 1998 the US steel industry filed an anti-dumping and CVD case against Russia. This was followed by a VER introduced by Russia against the USA. In March 1999 Brazil proposed a voluntary limit on its exports if the US anti-dumping cases were suspended (Finger and Schuknecht, 2001, p. 266). More recently, from June 2007 the USA has decided to impose limitations on civilian high-tech exports to China on the grounds that they might be of benefit to the Chinese military. In contrast to the previously described examples, in the Sino-American case, the self-imposed restrictions were indeed voluntary; moreover their introduction led to protests from the Chinese authorities, whose officials threatened to restrict other US exports to China, thereby putting additional pressure on the USA's widening trade deficit.

Although there are clear rules indicating when a national body can decide whether there is 'fair trade', or whether dumping in an anti-dumping case is in accordance with the GATT/WTO rules, it is still relatively easy to abuse the procedure in favour of the interests of national producers:

1. The abuse of procedures of complaint is hardly ever punished, and the costs of the action are often (much) higher for the accused than for the applicant;
2. The examination criteria are rather vague;
3. The complainants and the judging authority have the same nationality; and,
4. The interests of consumers – which are often best served by minimizing protection, including protection against dumping – are quite often not taken into account in passing judgement.

It has even been claimed that, before applying for the injury test, some companies actually go so far as to make deliberate cutbacks in production and fire employees in order to demonstrate that the unfair competition is actually causing injury to the industry, while hoping, of course, that the CVD imposed on the foreign competitor can more than compensate for the short-term loss resulting from lower levels of production. Action aimed at a CVD is often particularly effective for the reasons just given; sometimes simply the very threat of a CVD can prevent the foreign competitor from adopting an aggressive marketing strategy.

In the USA it is the Ministry of Trade (Commerce Department) that decides whether, and to what extent, dumping has taken place. The International Trade Commission (ITC, a commission set up by the US Congress to assess allegedly unfair cases of competing imports in the USA) judges whether substantial injury has been caused. If it is concluded that there has been some injury, the ministry will move to introduce provisional or permanent anti-dumping duties. The whole procedure must take no longer than 390 days. Once this deadline expires, the decision is taken on the basis of the information available at the time. This information has to be delivered by the defendant foreign firm. Case study 8.2 shows how the principle of the 'best possible information' often works to the advantage of the American applicant.

Case study 8.2   Protectionism through paperwork

Throughout the 1990s there was a substantial increase in the USA's use of procedural protectionism. Anti-dumping cases in the USA are particularly notorious for the amount of paperwork involved. If foreign companies become the defendants in an anti-dumping case in the USA, they have to hand over all their books.

Containers full of papers with all transactions, sales figures, prices, analyses and computer tapes are collected. Any company who, in the opinion of the authorities, supplies too little information immediately loses the case. The Best Information Possible principle applies in these circumstances. If there is just one minor error in some of the defendant's files, the Commerce Department can decide to consider only the facts presented by the accuser.

The procedure can be illustrated by one example from the early 1990s. The German firm Preussag Stahl AG supplied substantial quantities of data on sales in Germany and America. But the American ministry also wanted information on the types of steel sold only in Germany. On 7 January 1993 Preussag was informed of the deadline for supplying this information: 21 December 1992. Since Preussag was unable to meet this retrospective deadline, the ministry considered only the information supplied by the American competitor in deciding whether or not to impose a duty on Preussag. Unsurprisingly, the information presented by the American competitor was unfavourable to Preussag and the dispute resulted in a duty being imposed on imports from the German company.

Since foreign firms are subject to stricter rules in anti-dumping cases than US firms which report them to the Commerce Department, it is the US firms that usually win. For example, in January 1993 the Ministry imposed heavy import tariffs on foreign steel producers – up to 109 per cent. This kept East European producers out of the American market once and for all. Some other foreign producers had already given up the fight in advance, daunted by the enormous amount of administrative work. In 1993, a Washington lawyer working for the Dutch company Hoogovens (now British/Dutch Corus) estimated that foreign steel companies had already spent around $100 million on anti-dumping procedures! In 2002 the Bush administration decided to impose additional temporary tariffs on steel imports of between 8 and 30 per cent. Planned to stay in effect through 2005, these temporary tariffs were withdrawn two years early, under pressure from the EU and after having been declared illegal by the WTO. In December 2006 the USA lifted most of its import barriers on high-grade steel from 16 countries; however, steel imports from Germany and Korea will continue to be subject to duties imposed in 1993.

In conclusion, it is clear that there are a number of shortcomings in the application of anti-dumping duties:

1. The procedure disregards consumers' interests.
2. The anti-dumping duty makes no provision for the economically legitimate case in which a company sells its products at less than cost so that it can at least recoup the fixed costs. In an international economy where products have short life cycles, where product quality is difficult to ascertain, and where initial spending on research and development is required, sale at less than cost is a logical element in the process of competition, when marketing a new product.
3. The anti-dumping rules are implemented as if goods were uniform, standardized and not subject to change, and as if foreign competitors are always aimed at forcing domestic firms out of the market so that they can then secure a huge increase in prices.
4. The impression that a firm is dumping its products abroad may be due to the structure of the home market of the firm that is being accused of dumping. If the foreign firm is protected in its home market, through tariff or non-tariff barriers, it can generate high profits, which can be used to finance dumping.

Thus, the procedures that are allowed by the GATT/WTO rules can, in practice, be abused in order to produce arrangements that are not in line with those same rules. In this process, national legal bodies play a significant role.

8.5 Summary

1. The original economic theories discussed in the earlier chapters of the book predicted that international free trade could lead to the optimum situation for all parties concerned. One practical embodiment of this conclusion is the GATT/WTO, which aims to promote free trade.
2. The GATT/WTO operates on the basis of the principle of reciprocity and non-discrimination, and this has led to the abolition or reduction of tariffs on industrial products and, more recently, also to reduced protection of agricultural products and services.
3. On the whole, there is a relatively broad consensus that GATT/WTO has been successful in reducing protectionism and in opening up the system of international trade.
4. In assessing the effective degree of protection, one must also take account of the effect of a tariff structure on the value added of the whole industry. During the postwar period, and particularly from the 1970s onwards, all kinds of new protectionist measures were substituted for tariffs.
5. To a certain extent the reason for this lies within the GATT/WTO structure itself, because it leaves considerable scope for the protection of markets. One example of this is the way in which economic associations between countries and regions are permitted.
6. In addition, the GATT/WTO allows trade policy protection in the case of unfair trade, or in those cases where free trade is said to cause serious injury to certain industries. However, as we have shown, these rules can easily be abused by national authorities.

Questions

1. Tariff escalation can be explained with the help of the theory of effective protection. Can you provide an example that would illustrate this?
2. How can TRIPS support the ongoing research activity in, for instance, the pharmaceutical industry?
3. How do you think the WTO will respond if countries consider using trade policy to try to enforce other countries trying to free ride to join a future international climate policy regime?
4. How do you think the WTO could be reformed to better fit the current global trading paradigm?

Business, Government and Lobbying

9.1 Introduction

International management journals often feature articles about gaining access to the bureaucratic apparatus in Brussels: Case study 9.1 offers one such example. This analysis can be valuable for businesses, because various firms often lobby the European Union (EU) or their national government for trade protection against foreign imports or export subsidies in order to strengthen their competitive position. The analysis up to Chapter 7 has principally adopted the viewpoint of national or international welfare, with business interests being subordinated to national interests. However, it should be clear that the interests of particular businesses need not always coincide with the general interest.

Chapter 8 highlighted that one of the reasons for the continuing protection, which is increasingly in the form of non-tariff barriers (NTBs), lies in the pressure exerted by the business world on officials and politicians to use the scope provided for protection by the World Trade Organization (WTO) legal framework. This pressure may be so great that, on the one hand, officials defend themselves altogether against lobbyists by claiming that their hands are tied by existing rules. On the other hand, government agencies often seem to be not only willing but also resourceful in inventing all kinds of new forms of trade restrictions in order to satisfy protectionist pressures from the business community.

This chapter considers why governments yield to pressure from certain interest groups – a process in which the objectives of both politicians and officials often play a part. This seems at odds with the assumption of an omniscient government whose objective is to maximize national welfare. What is proposed here is a political-economy model in which the government consists of various individuals such as politicians, bureaucrats, and officials, who are all interested in pursuing their own objectives in policy-making. This idea recently encouraged the development of new perspectives regarding trade policy theories, by including the behaviour of the government as an explanatory factor in trade models.

9.2 The practice of lobbying: a case study

Case study 9.1 offers an example of some of the problems that can arise in lobbying an international organization such as the EU.

Case study 9.1 'Getting through to Brussels'

Over the last two decades, and particularly since the introduction of the internal market in the EU, the lobbying of EU institutions has become a rapidly growing industry. At the time of writing there are some 15,000 lobbyists in Brussels who seek to sway the legislative procedure of the EU in favour of different interest groups. Thus a great deal of time is spent on influencing new legislation, antitrust measures, and merger enquiries. However, according to a senior official at the Commission, 90 per cent of lobbying is ineffective.

What makes a lobby successful? Etienne Davignon, a former EU Commissioner, states that lobbying in Brussels cannot be compared with what happens at the national level. However, EU officials are often concerned about losing contact with the outside world, so they are much more open to outside contact than most national officials and administrators.

It is important for lobbyists to understand how to exploit this openness. The first thing is to 'get through' to the European authorities – by being received and heard. Once inside, lobbyists can make the long journey to Brussels productive by following some of the ground rules outlined below.

Choose the right objective

This is probably the most important rule, and the most frequently violated. Successful lobbying means knowing the right person to talk to about a particular issue. Newcomers to Brussels acknowledge that there is no point in sending technical experts to deal with political problems. However, few realize that the reverse is also true.

French firms, in particular, have been known to make a mess of their lobbying activity by focusing their strategy on approaching political decision-makers and overlooking the powerful bureaucratic machinery. Politicians are certainly not always receptive to lobbying. For example, one reason why special administrative agencies have been established in various countries in order to deal with trade disputes is to avoid politicians being overwhelmed with requests for trade policy protection.

In the USA, for instance, Congress established the International Trade Commission (ITC), which was to use an 'injury test' to evaluate requests for import protection. These requests were based on the idea of 'unfair injury' that is the result of competing imports, or deciding how to punish the foreign supplier for dumping. In practice, such agencies have a certain amount of freedom in their policy of judging the various cases submitted to them.

Know the process

The most common reason for failure is unfamiliarity with the complexity of the administration apparatus in Brussels. The Commission's decision-making process can be influenced at various stages, at both technical and political levels – through the Commission, the European Parliament, the EU embassies of member states, and the national ministries. However, a distinct approach is needed in dealing with each different type of agency.

Act early

Lobbying in the right place begins with junior EU officials, who are the staff responsible for writing the draft regulations on which discussions are based. The battle can be largely won if you gain the support of these officials. It is much more effective if the officials are convinced from the start, rather than having the same officials trying to reverse a decision already taken elsewhere.

Be honest

One reason why EU Commission officials are relatively communicative is their reliance on outside sources for their supply of background information. The price of this openness is accuracy. According to one senior representative of the Internal Market, Commission, officials will not go back to sources who have supplied them with incorrect information.

Avoid overkill

Exaggerated lobbying can be counterproductive. For example, in December 2008 bio-fuel lobbyists in Brussels were awarded the 'Worst EU Lobbying 2008' at the yearly satire awards ceremony organized by transparency campaigners. The Brazilian biofuels group UCICA, along with MPOC of Malaysia and Abengoa Bioenergy, an energy company from Spain, were awarded the 'Golden Raspberry' for campaigning in Brussels. Through exhaustive lobbying, the three companies tried to counter the overwhelming reports coming from academia, non-governmental organizations (NGOs), the UN, and the World Bank that depict biofuels as unsustainable and potentially hazardous for the environment. However, their campaigns were proven to be misleading and are now regarded with very little sympathy in Brussels.

Beware of playing the nationality card

It cannot be denied that nationalism plays some part in the Commission's decision-making process, but it appears that waving your passport is one of the least effective lobbying instruments. According to an official of the Brussels office of Daimler Benz, the reason is simple: 'Even if you've got a commissioner in your pocket, he's got to convince his colleagues.' To convince them requires the use of reasoned arguments and does not respond to emotional appeals that will not be shared by other nationalities.

    None of these rules will *guarantee* success. The work of the Commission often means resolving two equally strong conflicting interests. But to know how Brussels functions at least gives lobbyists a chance against competitors who have not bothered to research the European decision-making process. On the subject of lobbying, the chief of the Belmont European Policy Centre, a veteran lobbyist, asserts: 'Bad lobbying is commonplace, we see it daily. But when lobbying is effective, chances are you'll never hear about it.'

    Case study 9.1 shows that it may be worthwhile for businesses to invest in lobbying for government protection. However, it also raises the following questions:

1. Why does government give in to pressure from businesses?
2. Why do consumers not conduct a counter-campaign?

After all, free trade maximizes national welfare. If free trade produces winners and losers, in theory the government can compensate the losers through redistributive policies. The case study has lifted one small corner of the veil. Fear of losing contact with the outside world makes EU officials accessible to lobbying activities. However, it is unclear why, in the case of European agricultural policy, policy-makers sometimes give in to the interests of certain groups when this clearly implies a loss of welfare and is violently at odds with the interests of other groups, such as the consumers. Political economy can offer a better insight into these problems.

9.3   Political economy: demand for and supply of protection

The world of international trade is not as straightforward as is suggested by the trade theories discussed in earlier chapters. Even in a democracy where consumers make up the majority of the electorate, the outcome of free trade is not as obvious as one might expect. The interests of voters, when they are classed as consumers, generally lie in the abolition of trade restrictions. The reason why this interest is, in practice, often subordinate to the interests of the protected industries can be explained by *political economy*. According to political economy, protectionism is the outcome of an interaction between various players – officials, politicians, businesses, and voters. Acting rationally, these players strive to achieve their own interests.

Voters organize themselves into groups whenever they wish to promote a common interest with politicians, and they do this through a process of lobbying. Since this is a common interest, the *free rider* factor is important. The organization of a lobby group involves certain 'investments'. If the group achieves its objective, other people who did not participate in the lobbying may also benefit from the advantages that it secures. For example, each individual worker and textiles manufacturer benefits from an import tariff on textiles, regardless of whether or not he contributed to the lobbying for the tariff.

As a result, individuals have no incentive to contribute to the costs of organizing a lobby group. The larger the size of the group, the more significant role free riding can take – and the harder it is to control. Organizing an effective lobby group therefore has a greater chance of success if:

- there are only a small number of interested parties;
- the group was already formed for another objective; and
- there is a demonstrable advantage in participating in the lobby group (for example, in the form of particular information or facilities).

In political economy, it is common to assume that interests are promoted and structured according to branch or sector. Within this branch or sector, the various sub-groups – such as employees, employers and financers – work harmoniously in the interests of the group as a whole.

The basic assumption in trade theories mentioned earlier is essentially different, because one of the questions at this time was who would benefit from free trade and who would not, the interest groups being defined on the basis of the different factors of production. In the Hecksher-Ohlin-Samuelson model (HOS) (see Chapter 3), for example, the factor of labour is opposed to that of capital, regardless of the sector in which these factors are located. What is the most plausible standpoint when it comes to drawing lines between interests? On one hand we have the political economic model, which distinguishes between sectors and, on the other hand, we have the HOS model, which distinguishes between owners of factors of production.

Empirical research is required to answer this question. Magee (1980) was one of the first to try to find the answer by analysing the position of employees and management as regards acceptance of the trade law by the US president in 1973. There were 21 industries pressing for the adoption of this law and in the case of each industry the position of the employees and the representatives of capital were identified. It emerged that in only two of the 21 industries did 'labour' adopt the opposite position from 'capital'. Thus, this research supported the political economic idea that interest groups are organized mainly according to industrial branches or sectors.

Protectionism may take many forms. For the sake of simplicity, the remainder of this chapter will focus on tariffs, but other protectionist instruments could also be included. As we have noticed already in our analysis of export taxes and subsidies, as well as in the case of the voluntary export restraints (VER) of Japanese cars imported by the USA, different forms of protection can have quite different implications for welfare. In this chapter, the form of protection is not discussed; rather, we concentrate on the issue of how the emergence of protection – in whatever form – can be explained in terms of the political and administrative decision-making process.

In order to distinguish between lobby groups, we divide the interest groups roughly into two broad camps: those in favour of tariffs and those opposed to them.

9.3.1 Pro-tariff interest groups

These groups

o include national firms that are in competition with foreign firms, often supported by trade associations;
o often have a considerable political interest in protection since the direct advantages of protection (an increase in output and employment) can be clearly demonstrated. (In relation to this, see also the theory of effective protection discussed in Section 8.2.);
o will often appeal to national sentiments.

9.3.2 Anti-tariff interest groups

In any discussion of anti-protectionist interests, consumers are the first group to spring to mind. For them, protectionism means both a smaller range of products and higher prices. However, at the same time many consumers are employed in import-competing industries and may therefore have some interest in the promotion of protectionist policies.

Exporting companies also benefit from free trade. Their interests lie in a free trade climate in which they have unimpeded access to foreign markets. Multinationals may also generally be in favour of free trade: they can operate efficiently on the international market and protectionism will often be a hindrance to them. Finally, there are companies that have to import raw materials and semi-manufactures. In the first instance they, too, will gain from free trade. However, these firms are often also in the sector which competes with imports, so that their position is ambiguous.

The pro-tariff lobby group is generally more uniform in character than the anti-tariff lobby, so that the first group can clearly define its common objective: increased profits. In addition, this group is usually relatively small in size, and the free rider factor is less important. In contrast, the anti-tariff group is heterogeneous. Consumers in themselves constitute a heterogeneous group, with the result that free riding is very difficult to control.

Furthermore, this group includes multinationals and exporters, all of whom aim to protect their own trading interests. Although exporters are opposed to tariffs, they may still lobby the government for subsidies in the form of cheap export credits or export credit guarantees. Multinationals will seek to consolidate their market position towards a monopoly situation.

If we apply the interest group theory to these characteristics, we can predict that the pro-tariff interest group contains the elements of a successful lobby group:

o it is small in size,
o it has clear objectives,
o it has comparatively low organizational costs (since it is possible to operate from existing organizational structures such as employers' and employees' organizations).

By contrast, the anti-tariff interests will find it more difficult to form a successful lobby group.

The 'political' market of protectionism determines the conditions under which pro-tariff groups will conduct their lobbying and also their chances of success. We shall illustrate this on the basis of the demand for and supply of protectionism.

9.3.3 Demand for protectionism

Figure 9.1 shows the costs and benefits of lobbying for protection. The horizontal axis indicates the achieved increase in the tariff; the origin indicates the original level of the tariff. The vertical axis measures the costs and benefits of an increase in nominal protection. (The reader will remember from Chapter 8 that the effective degree of protection may deviate from this; for the sake of convenience, owing to the complications in translating from nominal to effective protection, we shall work on the basis of nominal protection.)

The OA curve indicates the costs of lobbying. In this case, we assume rising marginal costs: it becomes increasingly difficult to secure a higher tariff. The OA curve also reflects the willingness of politicians to agree to the request for protection. Thus, the curve

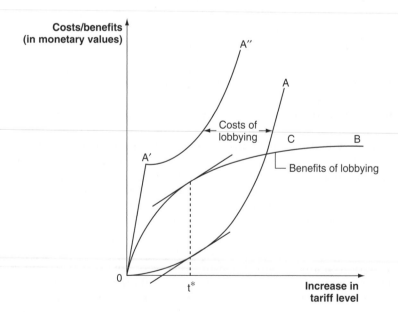

Figure 9.1 Costs and gains of lobbying

indicates the expenditure that is required for a successful lobby and this curve will be higher:

1. the less well organized the group;
2. the more inefficient the lobbying; and
3. the more other groups in society disagree with the imposition of the tariff.

Curve OB indicates the additional revenue obtained by the lobby group. The greater the increase in the tariff, the higher the lobby group's revenue until point C is reached. This is the tariff level at which nothing further is imported: the gradient of the curve is horizontal from C onwards. For the OB curve we assume that the marginal gains (the additional gain due to one extra unit of tariff protection) decline the higher the tariff. The segment OC shows this. However, the curve could have been drawn differently, namely with rising instead of falling marginal gains. Lobbying is optimal at tariff level t*, namely the level at which the marginal gains (represented by the gradient of the tangent to the 'gains curve') are equal to the marginal costs (represented by the gradient of the tangent to the 'costs curve'). For at tariff level t* the gradients of curves OB and OA are the same so that the distance between the two curves, indicating the net advantage for the lobbyists, is at its maximum. If one were to aim for higher protection than t*, then the net gains from lobbying decline until reaching the intersection point from curves OB and OA. To the right of the intersection point the net gains actually become negative.

Nonetheless, lobbying can sometimes be associated with high initial costs, represented by curve OA'; the costs curve OA'A'' lies above the lobby revenue curve. This situation can occur when the costs of organizing the lobby are very high; in this case, lobbying cannot yield net gains. Thus, Figure 9.1 illustrates what has been said before, namely that a lobbying policy can be profitable mainly if it is based on an already existing organization, for example, as in the case of curve OA.

9.3.4 Supply of protectionism

In the end, it is the government that decides whether or not to increase tariffs. As we have seen already, this may be the result of a combination of executive and legislative power. Of course, the government may be either in favour of free trade (liberal attitude) or against it (nationalist attitude) on ideological grounds.

However, a government's ideology is constrained by a number of factors, the most important being elections. The power of the lobby groups in favour of protection may be so great that a government that is strongly in favour of free trade loses the elections. In such circumstances, a liberal government that is afraid of losing elections and wants to govern at all costs will present itself as a supporter of protectionist trade policy.

Furthermore, the policy will often also depend upon the government's budget and the balance of payments. A country with a trade or budget deficit will be more inclined to pursue a protectionist policy. In both cases the government is normally subject to criticism and will have to conduct a campaign to show that it is taking action to reduce the deficit. Moreover, the reduction of a government deficit through the imposition of tariffs often provokes less political resistance than domestic cutbacks or tax increases.

When making a decision about trade policy, the government will not be faced by great objections on the part of consumers. Many voters regard protectionism or free trade as being less important than internal policy and economic election issues. People are generally better informed about the level of supermarket prices and the quality of cars, for example, than about various more 'abstract' political topics. Furthermore, it is irrational for voters to invest a large amount of energy in gathering political information on trade policy since voters know that they can exert very little influence over the election outcome.

Protectionism also depends upon the executive agencies that prepare, formulate and implement a country's trade laws. The officials of these agencies value their prestige and the influence they can exercise over their clientele, who are frequently from specific business sectors. As an example, officials responsible for the agricultural policy will often have interest groups in the agricultural sector as clientele. Their functions will generally include promoting the interests of their clientele, which often results in the introduction of protectionist measures. For this purpose, officials use the instruments which they can control themselves, and which thus are brought together under the heading of 'administered protection'. This means that they frequently prefer NTBs and subsidies to tariffs (see Box 9.1).

Box 9.1   The optimal obfuscation hypothesis

Let us assume a democratic country in which several political parties and lobby groups are active. Furthermore, suppose these lobby groups support the political party that best protects their interests, and they will also support that party in the elections.

One political party – called the industry party – promotes the interests of workers in the textiles industry. In return for doing so, this party receives financial support from the textiles union. As the result of competition from low-wage countries, wages in the textiles industry are fairly low and there is pressure on profits. If wages become too low, it will become increasingly difficult for employers to attract workers; on the other hand, higher wages will damage profit levels. In order to retain the support of the textiles union, the industry party advocates an import tariff on textiles in order to secure higher wages in the textiles industry.

As was argued in Chapters 6 and 7, trade policy is never more than a 'second-best' solution to domestic problems. The most efficient solution in terms of national welfare is a policy that encourages both labour and capital to leave the sector – that is, by retraining workers. The most efficient approach in terms of the sector's welfare is to subsidize the textiles workers directly through wage subsidies. If this is not possible, then the government could grant a production subsidy on textiles as a second-best solution, or it could impose an import tariff on textiles as another solution. Hereafter, one might consider an import quota on textiles. The most inefficient 'protective' solutions involve non-tariff barriers – for example, through the Multi-Fibre Arrangement.

In practice, people seem to ignore this ranking based on the efficiency criterion, as indicated by the increase in all kinds of non-tariff barriers such as quotas and VERs (see Chapter 8).

To make this clear, consider the *optimal obfuscation hypothesis* (see Magee et al., 1989). According to this hypothesis, politicians try to conceal the process of income redistribution through the use of indirect measures. This makes it very difficult for voters (and economists) to ascertain the cost of these measures. Trade policy is also income policy.

The protection of certain industries results in the redistribution of incomes within an economy. In the example, income is redistributed from the taxpayers to the textiles industry. However, textiles industry workers do not form the majority of the electorate. It is therefore in the interests of the industry party and the politicians in power to try to conceal the fact that they wish to transfer income. The price paid for this is the efficiency costs in terms of distortions in consumption and production decisions. The introduction of a tariff is therefore defended by referring to, for instance, employment, 'unfair competition' from low-wage countries, national support base, regional interests, the environment or health, and so on. Such a veiled presentation thus enables the industry party to secure votes and funds from the textiles industry, while at the same time limiting the number of votes that are lost.

However, at a given moment any greater 'obfuscation' on the adoption of measures will nevertheless alienate voters, since there will be increasing amounts of economic waste. Moreover, excessive 'obfuscation' can cause the lobby group itself to no longer recognize the positive effects, thus diminishing its political support. The better informed the voters are, the more serious will be the effect of the loss of votes through increasing levels of economic inefficiency. There is then a risk of what is called a *voter information paradox*: if the voters' knowledge of policy on incomes and trade increases, then politicians react with increasingly subtle forms of protection, but these are associated with greater distortions.

The switch from tariffs to NTBs in recent decades illustrates this paradox. Over the years, voters have become increasingly well informed about trade restrictions so that they have come to oppose them. Initially, this led to a decline in tariffs. However, the end result was that these lower tariffs were offset by NTBs such as VERs. These trade instruments are less transparent to the voter, but are probably more costly in terms of overall welfare.

In general, executive agencies have a certain degree of freedom since parliament and government are to a certain extent dependent on them – for example, in terms of obtaining information. Moreover, officials in executive agencies have access to far more specialist information, which may also give them a position of some power. As a result of the factors presented above, a protectionist policy may still be pursued even under a liberal government.

9.4 Competition between lobby groups

Our analysis so far has assumed that protectionism is determined by the power which one interest group exercises over officials and politicians – namely that of businesses threatened by foreign competition. In reality, the outcome is not always easy to predict, as various lobby groups can have different interests and may therefore start a process of competition to try to get the attention of the policy-makers and administration, and persuade the policy-makers to serve their interests rather than those of other competing lobby groups. The process of the lobbying activities and the way of reaching a final compromise may therefore be rather complicated, as Case study 9.2 aims to illustrate. This case is also an illustration of the optimal obfuscation.

Case study 9.2   The European banana war

In July 1993 the EU imposed a ban on the import of cheap 'dollar bananas' from Latin America. This encouraged the banana lobby in the former colonies in that region to increase their pressure on EU officials. The free trade lobbies raised concerns about the undesirable increases in banana prices for the consumer, which would occur because the new ban implied that the overall imports of bananas in the EU member states could not exceed 2 million tonnes per annum. Moreover, the market share of dollar banana importers and traders had to be cut by 33 per cent in favour of dealers/importers importing bananas from European overseas territories and former European colonies.

Traders in 'dollar bananas' warned that the measure was liable to make bananas twice as expensive in countries such as the Netherlands and Germany. Thus, there was interaction between those groups which were in favour of and those groups which were opposed to the free imports of 'dollar bananas'. The groups that had lobbied for the EU measure were supported in their campaign by environment and development groups, which appealed to sentiments such as the poor working conditions on 'dollar banana' plantations and the fact that the poor, small farmers in other countries could not compete with these plantations. In this case, the protectionist lobby won the day. The German government unsuccessfully submitted a complaint to the European Court of Justice in Luxembourg.

The effects of the victory for the protectionist lobby were felt for some eight years. The main beneficiary of the import ban was Fyffes, an Irish multinational importer of fruits and vegetables. Some international merchant houses also benefited significantly from the quota system. They received half of the price increase of the bananas in the EU. Less than 10 per cent of the price increase went to the poorest banana farmers. Specialists estimated that the transfer of $1 to a poor banana farmer in the formal colonies cost the European consumer of bananas $13.25.

Since 1993, the two American fruit multinationals Chiquita and Dole had successfully put pressure on the US administration to submit the case to the GATT/WTO under the dispute settlement understanding. In 1999, the WTO body ruled that the USA had suffered damage of $191 million from the EU banana regime, which it was allowed to counteract by introducing penalty charges on its imports of EU products. After the EU announced that it had agreed to give up its former complicated preferential banana regime favouring its former colonies by April 2001 (a transition period that lasted until 2006), the USA also indicated its intention to cancel its trade sanctions as of 1 July 2001.

True to its commitment, from 2006 the EU imposed a single tariff of $225 per tonne of imported bananas, regardless of their origins. However, additional protection was still provided for the former colonies in Africa and the Caribbean, which allowed producers from these regions 775,000 tonnes of annual duty-free imports. In consequence, Ecuador complained to the WTO who issued a further ruling against the EU's banana regime (making this the longest ongoing dispute in the WTO's history). If the verdict is enforced, Ecuador will be allowed to impose trade sanctions on the EU.

9.5　Summary

1. This chapter has shown that politically efficient decision-making processes do not always produce the results that might be expected on the basis of economic efficiency criteria. With the help of insights from political economy, we can explain how interest groups arise, under what circumstances they can operate successfully, and why governments are amenable to lobbies by such groups.

2. For trade theory this meant that the government was no longer regarded as an omniscient, exogenous factor, striving to maximize national welfare. Thus, political economy theory could be applied to trade policy. Important assumptions in this theory are that

all those concerned aim to satisfy their own interests. In the process, interest groups can be formed who put tremendous pressure on decision-makers, persuading them to favour the interests of the minority pressure group over those of the general public.

3. In this instance the rational ignorance of large groups of persons concerned is a major factor. In spite of rational ignorance, consumers are gradually becoming increasingly aware of the negative welfare effects of trade instruments. According to the optimal obfuscation hypothesis, in order to disguise the income redistribution effects governments will switch to using more complex NTBs, which are less efficient in economic terms.

4. In the Appendix we examine the fact that interest groups may have mutually opposing interests and may therefore fight one another; this interaction can be analysed through use of a reaction curve model. According to this model, both interest groups invest in lobbying until a certain equilibrium is reached. Investment in lobbying is wasteful from the point of view of national welfare.

9.6 Appendix: Competition between lobby groups

If we set aside the specific interests of politicians and officials and follow the ideas of political economy, the level of protection is determined by the interaction between interest groups. The following model shows how the interaction between lobby groups determines the level of protection. Here we assume that one factor of production, capital, can only be used in a particular sector; it is no use outside that sector, for technical reasons, for example. An example might be capital in the form of a highly specific machine. We assume that the other factor of production, labour, is mobile. This means that labour can easily move from one sector to another if more can be earned elsewhere. The point is that if we apply these assumptions, it will be obvious that international trade will yield winners and losers, because international trade can cause one sector to grow while another will have to decline. The workers' interests are not much affected because in this model labour can easily transfer to other sectors. However, owners of non-mobile capital goods are in a risky position. If the sector expands, the return on their capital investment in that sector will increase, but if their sector contracts then they will lose. Thus, in this example there are always two opposing parties as soon as there is any debate on whether or not one should give in to pressure for more free trade (or more protectionism): those who own the capital in the export sector, which expands under free trade, versus those with capital invested in the shrinking sector, which is competing with imports. For instance, we are in an economy with the following two sectors: sector 1 producing goods which are also produced efficiently abroad, the import-competing sector; sector 2 where goods are made for export. In this situation, the owners of the capital in sector 1 will therefore lobby for the imposition of a tariff; in contrast, those who own the capital in the export sector will lobby the government to ensure free trade. It is assumed that workers have no clear incentive to lobby.

The owners of the capital in both sectors are bound to incur costs if they intend to lobby. These costs consist of both the organization and use of the lobby group as well as the costs of preventing free riders. The level of 'investment in lobbying' of the two lobby groups together determines the eventual net level of protection. We can assume a priori that if the amount invested in lobbying by the capital owner in the export sector exceeds the amount invested by the capital owner in the import-competing sector, protection will probably decline.

Let us assume a situation in which the two groups compete with one another (in theory they can also cooperate with each other). This can be demonstrated by a simple model based on reaction curves such as those used in Chapter 8. In such a model the two groups (players) use the same strategy to try to maximize their profits. Each player regards the action of the other party as an established fact and takes it into account in his decisions. In terms of our model, each lobby group decides for itself how much to invest in political campaigning, always assuming a particular level of investment by the other group. Figure 9.2 shows the investment reaction curves of the two lobby groups; since we assume that the two groups are identical, both curves are symmetrical about a 45-degree line, PP. Each reaction curve in Figure 9.2 shows how much a lobby group will invest in lobbying as a reaction to the other lobby group's investments. The reaction curves therefore determine the optimum level of investment for one lobby group as a function of the (assumed) action by the other lobby group. Curves 11 and 22 are the reaction curves of the import-competing sector and the export sector respectively; the curves present a positive trend because the more one group invests in lobbying, the more the other will also invest. Curve 11 is flatter (and 22 is thus steeper) than the 45-degree line because we assume that if the opponent invests more, there will be a response, albeit that the additional investment will not be so great.

At point A the two reaction curves intersect, indicating a situation of equilibrium. It is at this point and this point only that a stable equilibrium is reached where both groups decide to keep constant the level of their investment. Let us assume that the owners of the capital in the export sector (sector 2) invest the sum OB in lobbying. On the basis of the export sector's investment level OB, the optimum investment for owners of the capital in the import-competing sector (sector 1) is now OC. The optimum level of investment for owners of the capital in sector 2 has therefore changed; if sector 1 invests OC, the optimum investment for sector 2 is OD. Sector 1 reacts once again and changes its level of

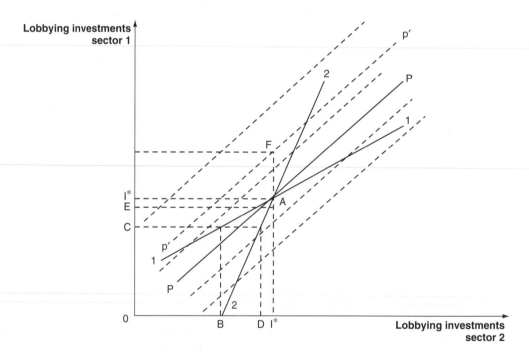

Figure 9.2 Lobbying reaction curves

investment to OE, and so on. Once sector 1 and sector 2 are investing OI*, neither sector will make any further change in its investment decision and equilibrium will have been restored.

The 45-degree curve PP, drawn through the equilibrium point, is also an iso-protection curve that indicates all combinations of investment levels for the two groups at which the level of protection – the result of lobbying; – is the same. Thus, if we move up the curve, we will find both groups investing more in lobbying; however, because they are neutralizing each other's actions, the level of protection remains constant. Thus, it is really in their interests to reach agreement on not investing anything (because the result is the same). But as they do not really trust one another, that does not happen.

Such a curve can describe very different situations (that need no longer pass through the origin). Additional examples of iso-protection curves are shown in Figure 9.2 (the dashed lines). The dotted curves left of line PP indicate a higher level of protection than the curves to the right of PP. This can be deduced as follows on the basis of the graph.

Say we are at point A on the iso-protection curve PP. This protection curve gives level of protection x. Technological developments abroad then cause the price of imports to decline while at the same time the profits of foreign producers increase as a result of higher volumes of sales and lower costs. For the sector that competes with imports, this means a decline in sales on the home market. This generates greater interest in lobbying for protection (at a given level of investment in lobbying by the other party): curve OB in Figure 9.1 moves up, and so does curve 11 in Figure 9.2. However, rising incomes abroad bring an increase in sales by the export sector on the foreign market. The export sector will make rather less effort to lobby for free trade (given the efforts of the other party); curve 22 therefore shifts slightly to the left. Let us assume that the shift in the two curves is such that the new equilibrium is at point F. The equilibrium is then on a higher iso-protection curve than A, so that protection has increased: sector 1 is investing more in lobbying, while sector 2's investment in lobbying has remained the same. Thus, lobbying by businesses and hence the level of protection depends partly on miscellaneous international developments which they themselves cannot influence.

Questions

1. Can you provide arguments in favour of lobbying?
2. Can you think of a substitute for lobbying that would allow companies to express their commercial interests but would restrict them from exercising pressure on administrative or governing bodies?
3. Can you give examples of competing pro- and anti-protection lobby groups in the same country?
4. Do you believe lobbying behaviour should be subject to an internationally agreed code of conduct?

CHAPTER 10

Economic Integration

10.1 | Introduction

In recent decades, due to the removal of barriers and rapid developments in information technology, the world economy has experienced a substantial rise in levels of economic integration. As discussed in earlier chapters, this has affected the markets for goods and services, but also – and increasingly – those for capital and labour.

In addition to this general trend towards globalization, there has been economic integration on a more limited regional scale, as shown in the development of regional trade agreements (RTAs), such as the European Union (EU), North America Free Trade Agreement (NAFTA), Mercado Común del Sur (MERCOSUR), Association of Southeast Asian Nations (ASEAN) and Common Market for East and South Africa (COMESA). Following the creation of the World Trade Organization (WTO) in 1995 more than 130 RTAs have been closed, whereas in the pre-WTO (the General Agreement on Tariffs and Trade, GATT) period, from 1948 onwards, 124 RTAs had been concluded. Since the beginning of the 1990s some 462 RTAs have been reported to the GATT/WTO up to February 2010.

In this chapter we will provide a background to economic integration and examine the main factors influencing economic integration and the forms that integration took. Globalization, for most people embodied by the WTO and the United Nations (UN) financial institutions, is seen as the main driver of economic integration and will be the subject of the first section of the chapter. The second part involves some theory of the forms of economic integration and will address the main issues by using the European Union (EU) as an example.

10.2 | Globalization

Globalization can be defined as the increase in international transactions in markets for goods, services, capital, and labour, combined with the growth and expanding scope of activities of many market players from all over the world and institutions that overlap national borders.

Surprisingly for some, the current wave of globalization can be viewed as a *second* great wave of globalization. The so-called 'first era of globalization' came about in the period of the Gold Standard and was accompanied by the industrialization process of that time. This era started in about the 1880s.

During this first era, the levels of trade and foreign direct investment (FDI) were astonishing, especially taking into account the rather limited transport and communication capabilities/technologies at this time. A comparison of the two eras shows that some countries still have not reached the same relative level of merchandise exports that they experienced in the first era (for example, Argentina and South Africa). The first wave of globalization abruptly stalled with the outbreak of the First World War and the collapse of the Gold Standard system in the late 1920s and early 1930s.

In 2003, the total value of world merchandise exports was more than $7 trillion, which, if compared with world gross domestic product (GDP) ($36 trillion), is illustrative for the second wave of globalization we are currently experiencing in 2011, especially if one realizes that the same ratio amounted to some $60 billion by 1948. This raises the question of whether the volume of international trade can continue to grow faster than the volume of production as it has been doing for the last decades, leading, of course, to ever more integrated markets.

Trade theory tries to explain the volumes and patterns of (international) trade. As was argued in Chapter 3, the Heckscher–Ohlin–Samuelson (HOS) model can be a useful tool in explaining international trade. However, subsequent empirical research – on the basis of HOS and similar models – predicted still larger volumes of international trade, particularly between regions with different factor endowments, than was observed in reality. The 'other part' of the predicted trade flows has since then become known as the mystery of missing trade (Trefler, 1995). Several attempts to explain this phenomenon have been made. In particular, the underlying assumptions of the HOS model have been questioned in order to explain missing trade; this has been focused on assumptions such as the disregard of human capital, the similarity of demand patterns across countries, or free access to technological knowledge.

Trefler showed, for instance, that the full benefits of international trade, as envisaged by the HOS model, will not be reached because of remaining productivity differences across inputs and countries which mean that the stage of factor price equalization cannot be attained. Earlier research, by Bowen et al. (1987), tried to explain the missing trade by examining international trade flows and trade flows within several Japanese regions. They found that the wage differences between developed and developing countries are persistent and generally large in comparison with wage differences between developed countries, and argued that the main reason why trade growth has been more subdued than might be expected from the traditional trade theory can probably be attributed to the fact that production technologies vary from country to country. One important underlying factor is that technology is not always freely available on the one hand, and on the other hand, that it is not always accessible to the poor or the badly educated.

A new research challenge is to analyse if the present worldwide ICT revolution may serve to reduce the international differences in technological knowledge and therefore wage levels, or rather extend international inequalities. The rapid growth of ICT services across the globe, through the Internet and otherwise, combined with the various other aspects of globalization led many people to believe that the concept of factor price equalization could be activated again, which would have a profound further impact on the worldwide level of wages. The intuition behind this reasoning is that increased labour mobility and further market integration through almost costless and unlimited international information exchange will mean that the existing relative scarcity of labour in the developed countries will disappear gradually. This could happen either directly through the net influx of migrant workers or indirectly via the generally labour-intensive imports and imports from newly emerging high-tech sectors from developing countries. This belief may also explain why some labour unions and sheltered industries in the developed countries are sceptical about the merits of globalization and lobby for limitations on international competition.

The flipside of this belief is the expected impact of globalization on labour in the low-wage countries, because the same reasoning would suggest that such labour would stand to gain in wage/employment terms from free trade. These gains are thought to include increased wage opportunities through migration to developed countries, increased job opportunities in foreign subsidiaries in their countries, and, most importantly, new jobs in their successful export industries. In China and India, for instance, each year literally tens of millions of people move from rural areas – with generally low levels of productivity – to cities to start new jobs in manufacturing and services – often for exports – at higher levels of wages and productivity. Of course, such development does not rule out the possibility that under the pressure of international competition there is no improvement in labour conditions other than those relating to wage levels and rates of employment.

The worldwide trade policy regime is obviously an important element in the globalization process and its impact on international trade. As was illustrated in some of the previous chapters, since the Second World War there has been a long tradition of multilateral negotiations to try to liberalize the international trade in goods. Only with the start of the first General Agreement on Trade in Services (GATS)(see Box 10.1) multilateral negotiations rounds by 2000, has the globalization of services been put explicitly on the agenda. Accompanied by the increased outsourcing opportunities offered by ICT, even more international wage convergence could be expected from a further liberalization of the international trade in services. One can think of health services provided in developing countries, tourism, or the newly emerging call centre and programming industry in Asia, to which a lot of multinationals have outsourced activities.

Box 10.1   What is the GATS and what is all the fuss about?

What is the GATS?

The General Agreement on Trade in Services (GATS), like the GATT for goods, contains the general rules and disciplines for conducting trade in services. Moreover, the agreement requires member countries to set up national 'schedules' listing the countries' commitments to the liberalization of trade in the service area and to the removal of market distortions. GATS identifies four modes of services supply. The first one, called 'cross-border supply', involves the services supplied from one country to another. The second mode is labelled 'consumption abroad', and includes the use of consumers of one country making use of services in another country (for example, going on holiday). 'Commercial presence', the third mode, encompasses companies from one country setting up subsidiaries providing services in another. Mode four, the 'movement of natural persons', comprises individuals who temporarily go to another country to supply services. The expected advantages that are to be expected with a reduction of government interference in the services trade area are a reduction of global poverty, increased economic growth, and an increase in the quality and diversity of services. Nevertheless, there are organizations that believe that liberalization in services will eventually jeopardize some of their universal and essential services supply, such as water supply, health care, and education. People tend to take a rather reserved position when debating these more or less 'basic rights' as a form of international competition.

What is all the fuss about?

The GATS agreement covers all services traded internationally, except for services provided to the public in the process of the exercise of government authority, and the air transport sector, traffic rights, and all directly related services to the exercise of such rights. The provision of GATS to strive for liberalizing most of the services sectors is by many interpreted as threatening for a number of traditional 'basic' services that used to operate without the pressure of international competition. However, the popular belief of some that the round of service negotiations that started in January 2000 gives the WTO the power to enforce free trade within the member countries to their services sectors is wrong: national governments will only make commitments in their national 'schedules' to the WTO in the services sectors that they see fit. Neither does the WTO demand free trade in all services sectors; nor is it possible for the WTO to enforce the services liberalization process within countries. Under GATS it is even possible for a national authority to allow for or maintain monopoly positions in any services sectors they require, such as water supply, which remains under state control in many countries. Moreover, the commitments made by member countries in GATS are to a certain extent reversible, which contributes to the flexibility of the agreement and gives countries the opportunity to slow down a too rapid liberalization process, for example.

With regard to the free movement of natural persons, GATS is also said to have adverse effects in the form of 'brain drain'. In particular, for developing countries the losses are considered to be potentially substantial. India's economy is said to lose around $2 billion per year on innovations, due to the migration of 80 per cent of their computer programmers to the USA. Every year one-third of the developing countries' research and development experts migrate to industrialized countries. While the direct effects of 'brain drain' do pose serious threats to developing countries' economies, the long-term result could just as well be beneficial for them. Due to technological advancements, it has become easier to transfer and redistribute resources, such as knowledge and investments, to remote places. Workers' remittances (see also Chapter 4) are just one of these resources. In addition, it has become clear that migrated workers do not forget where they have come from. With the help of their remittances and knowledge, businesses can be set up in developing countries, which may cause the 'brain drain' to gradually turn in to a 'brain gain'. In sum, the effects can be positive but whether this is the case depends on case-specific circumstances and related externalities.

With the ongoing economic integration and the resulting increases in migration, initiatives to facilitate the mobility of natural persons are emerging slowly. Although the net benefits for all participants involved seem obvious, the increase in terrorist attacks since the late 1990s may pose a new dilemma for governments and the WTO.

With regard to the basic provisions of health care and education, some people still fear that GATS poses a threat to the future supply of these services. As stated in Article 1:3 of the agreement, services supplied in the exercise of governmental authority are excluded from GATS under the provision that these services are provided, neither on a commercial basis, nor in competition with one or more service suppliers. However, in many countries, governments do not control the service sectors, like health care and education, entirely. These sectors are also partly run by private service suppliers, which of course provide their services on a commercial basis. The rules of the GATS agreement leave room for interpretation in this regard: these services are supplied in exercise of government authority, but they are also provided in competition with other service providers.

The essential aim of the WTO is to set rules for free trade and to identify the circumstances in which a certain degree of protection is permissible; moreover, it tries to create a 'level playing field' for all its members, who can then compete on equal terms. From this starting point, the most important questions to answer are when and under what conditions does the WTO allow protectionist measures. It is important to note in this regard that the GATT/WTO's prime goal has always been to establish a free world trade system based on competition. Other aspects, such as environmental concerns or issues of human rights and labour conditions, were, instead, seen as beyond the GATT/WTO's competence. Due to this focus, however, anti-globalist movements have increasingly perceived the WTO as an institution whose decision-making may have a destructive impact on (global) targets other than increasing welfare through free trade. This critical appraisal culminated in December 1999, when at a WTO ministerial meeting in Seattle, many anti-globalist groups demonstrated for their cause. Non-governmental organizations (NGOs) dealing with Third World issues, human rights advocates, labour rights activists, and environmental groups all had their reasons to contest the effects of international market liberalization and globalization, and one of their symbols, the WTO, and succeeded in having the meeting postponed. In the meantime the WTO has shown signs that it may gradually take on board certain concerns about the externalities of international free trade. One example where this may have happened in a dispute settlement procedure is the so-called shrimp–turtle case (see Box 10.2).

Box 10.2 The shrimp–turtle case

In 1997, the WTO dispute settlement body received a joint complaint from Pakistan, India, Malaysia, and Thailand, demanding that the USA should remove its import ban on the respective countries' shrimp and shrimp products. The USA had instated this ban under the US Endangered Species Act of 1973, which protects the five sea turtle species, amongst other endangered species, that inhabit US waters. This specific Act requires the use of so-called turtle excluder devices (TEDs), for shrimp trawlers. The methods used to catch shrimp appeared to be particularly harmful for the endangered turtle populations: turtles caught in the nets mostly drowned. The TEDs provided an effective way to minimize the amount of turtle casualties. With these environmental issues in mind, the ban on countries that did not use the TEDs seems justified. Surprisingly enough, the WTO ruled against the US import ban. This unexpected result was perceived as an intrusion of US sovereignty; naturally environmentalists were not happy with this ruling and were more or less confirmed in their belief of WTO's ignorance, or at least unwillingness, to act on policy issues other than trade.

However, many commentators failed to recognize the full significance of this ruling. The reason for the US defeat did not lie primarily in the fact that the WTO does not allow protection based on justified environmental issues; rather, it was rejected because the USA had applied the import ban in a discriminatory manner. It appeared to be that shrimp fishermen in the Caribbean were allowed a longer transitional period to start using the TEDs than the four Asian countries that filed the complaint.

More recently, the Kyoto Protocol (2005) came into effect; this protocol is an international initiative to reduce CO_2 carbon emissions, which allocates certain emission rights (quotas) to the participant countries. Its purpose is for 'polluters' to reduce their CO_2 emissions and to do so cost-effectively by allowing trade between those surpassing their quota, and those staying below the quota limits. The global impact of the envisaged reduction in CO_2 emissions of the industrialized world is, however, hampered by the fact that the world's largest polluter, the USA (being responsible for about 25 per cent of global CO_2 emissions in 2000), does not take part in this protocol. In fact, the WTO ruling suggested that – unlike earlier instances – one would no longer categorically reject the option that problems with particular production processes would be used as an accepted argument for protecting against the product at the border. This has raised the question as to whether or not the Kyoto Parties would – according to the WTO – be legally entitled to instate protectionist measures against products from the USA.

Many observers see globalization and economic integration as drivers of economic growth that are both irreversible and unstoppable. Nevertheless, as history has shown, globalization can be halted and indeed reversed. New waves of protectionism can arise, due to unforeseen events or as the result of new insights. Countries are in fact now building up strategies that may reduce the harmful consequences that could be brought about by the reverse of globalization; by means of RTAs, regions are also trying to ensure sustainable economic growth in smaller areas. Developments in regional economic integration will be the subject of the next section.

10.3 Regional economic integration

Since the creation of the WTO the world has seen a substantial rise in the number of regional trade agreements, often based on a mix of economic, cultural, and political initiatives. Because regional economic integration conflicts with the WTO non-discrimination principle, the only accepted forms of regional economic integration are free trade areas (FTAs) and customs unions (CUs), which aim for the complete removal of tariffs and trade restrictions between their members. However, most present-day FTAs cover not only goods and services, but also often other areas, such as protection, government procurement, investment, and competition policy, together with more practical issues, such as the mutual recognition of (technical) standards, customs cooperation, subsidy and anti-dumping policies, so-called e-policies and intellectual property rights. Box 10.3 gives an illustration of the complexity of the mutual recognition of diplomas.

Box 10.3   The mutual recognition of diplomas

The Bologna Declaration of 1999 on European higher education tries to achieve greater transparency and facilitate the mobility of persons through:

- a pan-European move to a Bachelor/Master (and Doctoral) system by the year 2009, with the Bachelor's degree providing access to the labour market.
- the use of the European Credit Transfer System (ECTS), a credit point system in which points are ascribed to a degree.

– the Diploma Supplement, which includes information on the holder, the qualification, the level, the result, the potential functions, and its position within the national
education system.

Essential to the free movement of natural persons within the EU is the mutual recognition of diplomas and professional qualifications; without these, the EU labour market
cannot be fully integrated. Several mechanisms have been implemented to facilitate the
process of recognition, especially in the sphere of obtaining information about foreign
papers; nevertheless, major practical issues still have to be dealt with. The topic of mutual
diploma recognition has a low profile, which means that government officials usually pay
little attention to policy relating to this issue. In addition, little or no feedback is given on
the quality of the information received, meaning that informational needs are not opti-
mally fulfilled. Another issue is the question of how people can prove their professional
experience abroad. Additionally, terminology presents important problems; for example,
the content of diplomas that appear on the surface to be more or less identical may be
totally different.

Classical theory on economic integration has materialized as a result of the contributions of Viner (1950), Tinbergen (1954) and Balassa (1961). Tinbergen distinguishes
between negative integration, which represents the removal of discrimination in national
economic rules and policies under joint surveillance, and positive integration, which refers
to the transfer to common institutions, or the joint exercise of at least some powers. Balassa
subsequently discerned five levels of integration from the shallowest level (Free Trade
Area, FTA) to the deepest level (total economic integration). His classification distinguished
between:

1. Free Trade Area – tariffs and quotas are eliminated between members of the integration initiative; however, they do retain the right to set tariffs and quotas in relation
   to third countries (no positive integration).
2. Customs Union – there is no discrimination among members in products markets and the union applies a common external tariff structure against third parties
   (no positive integration).
3. Common Market – the same as a Customs Union, but with the extra provision that
   the movement of production factors (free movement of capital, labour) is allowed
   for (no positive integration).
4. Economic Union – a Common Market that implements some degree of harmonization of the participating countries' policies, with the aim to reduce discrimination
   based on disparities in the several national policies (positive integration starts).
5. Total Economic Integration – implies the amalgamation of monetary, fiscal, social,
   and counter-cyclical policies. Decisions are made within a supranational authority,
   and a centralist and unitary state is envisaged (high positive integration).

Another author, Lawrence (1996), approaches integration in terms of 'deep' and 'shal-
low'; deeper integration is not necessarily more efficient, but it does implement potentially
efficiency-enhancing elements, such as a common competition and environmental policy.
There are also numerous RTAs between only developed or developing countries, which
appear to be more or less a logical result of the respective country groups' trade, institutional, and monetary characteristics. It is likely that similar countries can integrate

more easily, and with lower transitional costs, than non-similar countries. There are few RTAs between developed and developing countries, but some empirical research in the multidisciplinary area of trade theory, development theory, and political economy suggests that if integration between developed and developing countries is to take place, the parties involved are likely to be better off when a deeper integration scheme is pursued than with a less developed integration process.

How regional economic integration affects the overall welfare of the participants has been a topic of debate, especially since the beginning of the massive economic integration process in western Europe. Although the general belief was that economic integration would create a new dynamism (among other reasons because countries would be exposed to a greater degree of international competition), some theorists pointed out that through the process of economic integration the possibly even more competitive supplier from outside the regional group would be put at a competitive disadvantage, thereby lowering, rather than enhancing competition within the region. This led to the notion that although additional intra-regional trade for some products may be created within the region, in the case of other products supply may shift away from inherently cheaper producers outside the region to be simply replaced by supply from less efficient producers from within the region. This might occur because once the economic integration is a fact, in contrast to products imported from partner countries, products originating from outsider countries can be affected by import duties or equivalent measures. While trade creation on the whole improves welfare for the countries involved, trade diversion essentially involves a welfare loss based on a deterioration of the terms of trade. It is therefore difficult to predict the net result of these two factors.

A large number of empirical studies investigating the effects on welfare of the implementation of regional integration initiatives indicate clearly that the implications discussed above, in terms of a shift in the origin of imports and the destination of exports, have proved in practice to be just a minor factor in determining the overall impact of economic integration. Far more weight could be attached to typically dynamic factors of economic integration, such as increasing economies of scale, business integration through mergers and takeovers, and faster cross-border exchange of information and dissemination of technology.

10.4   European economic integration

To address the implications of regional economic integration in more detail, from now on we will focus on the EU. Specifically, we want to deal with subjects such as the internal market, competition policy, and some other issues on the EU agenda. Box 10.4 offers some background on the EU.

Box 10.4   The EU in a nutshell

One unique feature of the European integration process is that the member states have surrendered some of their sovereign rights and have delegated them to a number of supranational (EU) entities, who take decisions on matters of joint interest. The objectives of the EU are, amongst other things: to ensure economic and financial stability and the free movement of factors of production; to remove barriers to trade;

to promote competition and economic growth; to prevent anti-competitive collusion, and to harmonize fiscal and monetary regimes.

The Treaty of Rome (1957) established the European Economic Community (EEC), which consisted of six members: Belgium, France, Germany, Italy, Luxembourg, and the Netherlands. The main goal of the treaty was to establish a common market, which was formally finalized by the Single European Act (SEA, 1987). The SEA approved legislation to eliminate remaining non-tariff barriers and the promotion of liberalization in the sphere of capital movements. In addition, rules about government procurement, technical standards, physical barriers to trade and fiscal barriers were agreed upon. The European monetary integration process started in 1950 with the European Payment Union, which facilitated the clearing of multilateral payment imbalances. From 1959 to 1972, the European Monetary Agreement enabled the convertibility of many European currencies. The creation of the European Monetary System deepened the process of monetary integration, and created the European Currency Unit (forerunner of the euro). From here on the European System of Central Banks (ESCB), headed by the European Central Bank (ECB), took over and set the path to the introduction of a single currency, the euro, which came into effect in January 1999. Currently, the ECB is in charge of the European Monetary Policy, whose main tasks are to ensure exchange rate and price stability, interest rate convergence and monitoring national governments' budget discipline.

One essential treaty in this respect is the Maastricht Treaty, in which four 'convergence criteria' are formulated. The criteria hold that: (i) the government budget deficit has to be below 3 per cent of GDP; (ii) the total government debt is not allowed to exceed 60 per cent of GDP; (iii) inflation rates should not be more than 1.5 per cent higher than the average of the three countries with the lowest inflation; and (iv) the long-term interest rate must be within 2 per cent of the three countries' average with the lowest interest rates in the EU. The Maastricht Treaty paved the road to an economical, political, and monetary union. The most important European institutions are:

European Parliament (elected by the voters of member states)
Council of the European Union (represents member states' governments)
European Commission (the driving force and executive body)
European Court of Justice (ensures compliance with the EU law)
Court of Auditors (controls the soundness/lawfulness of the management of the EU budget)

In 2004, ten (mainly Eastern European) countries joined the EU 15 and in 2007, two more countries, Romania and Bulgaria, joined. Initially, the EU tried to establish cooperation in areas such as trade and economy; today, freedom, security, justice, job creation, regional development, and environmental protection are prominent issues on the political agenda.

It is clear that the creation of a common internal market is a daunting and extremely complex process: the various original national rules and policies of the individual EU member states have evolved in their own specific context and direction, which will generally vary from country to country. It will often be difficult therefore to find a politically acceptable common denominator. Moreover, integration has progressed differently in the various markets. For goods, the single market functions reasonably well, whereas the single market for services within the EU still lags behind. The main reasons for this are that various services are non-tradable, that on a global level little has been achieved thus far in terms of liberalizing international trade in services, and that services trade is typically characterized by large differences in national rules and regulations. In 2004 the European Commission launched a proposal for a Directive on Services in the Internal Market, with the intention of encouraging the EU's internal services by reducing impediments based on regulation in relation to service trade and investment. Since national service markets have long functioned under the supervision and control of national governments, there are externalities to be expected for third-party service providers. National requirements concerning environmental, safety, and quality standards for services are all potentially trade distorting. All these 'unique' requirements are in place, due to the fact that, before the acquisition, it is hard to assess the quality of a service product. This uncertainty flows from a relatively high degree of information asymmetry in relation to services, especially when considering complex professional services, for example those relating to the areas of medicine or finance, which often require specialist knowledge. National authorities, in reaction to this structural information asymmetry, each instated their own quality safeguards for the protection of their domestic consumers (see Box 10.5) or for other purposes, such as environmental or building requirements.

Box 10.5   Legio-Lease

In 2002, an investigation carried out by the Dutch Financial Market Authority (AFM) uncovered a series of offences committed by the Dexia Bank, concerning the selling of stock lease services. The stock lease service, available under the name Legio-Lease, concerned the investment in stocks with borrowed money. The proposed idea behind this service was to make the stock market accessible for the small investor; provided that the stock market would go up, people would be able to repay the money they had borrowed and retain the resulting profits. In reality, the structure of this service appeared to be so complex that many of the people who used it were not even aware of the fact that they were investing in stocks with money that was not their own. As stock prices fell, thousands of people were confronted with large personal debts, which they could not repay. Of course, the AFM and a number of other authorities announced measures; juridical procedures against Dexia Bank were only partly successful.

This system will probably function well in a situation of autarky, however; since the EU is trying to complete the process to create a single market, one can imagine the implications for services trade. The additional transaction costs that arise from the country-specific requirements, which are sunk costs, are borne more than once by service providers that try to do business in the EU. These costs involve the adaptation of their services to comply with the national rules and requirements, and they have to be absorbed for every new EU country that is being targeted, which reduces the effect of intra-EU economies of scale. As a result, it is practically impossible to separate the production and consumption of services in place and time, which makes it very hard to standardize services. So the EU regulation heterogeneity and intensity can be regarded as substantial barriers to services trade.

In order to reduce this trade-inhibiting effect the European Commission proposed the application of the 'country of origin' principle, meaning that a service that meets the requirements of the country of origin may not be subject to hindrance caused by additional requirements in the targeted country. This, in fact, implies that member states mutually recognize each other's domestic regulation systems. The directive proposes measures promoting the exchange of information between all national governments, measures that aim to create a solid base for mutual recognition. Another proposal, arising from the 'time and place' problem, tries to remove the barriers for intra-EU services FDI, for FDI is the general mode of expansion in services. The Commission hereby hopes to facilitate the set-up of foreign service subsidiaries and cross-border mergers and acquisitions.

With the sharp increases in the numbers of intra-EU mergers and acquisition and the rise in foreign-owned subsidiaries the internal market of the EU is also subject to potential anti-competitive forces. Large Trans-National Companies (TNCs) could obtain substantial shares of a market and could exercise their market power and exploit consumers or businesses. A strong and efficiently functioning competition policy does not guarantee anything, but it does create the environment necessary for European firms to remain competitive in a rapidly changing world. At the Lisbon Summit in March 2000 EU governments signed an agreement that intended to make the EU 'the world's most competitive and dynamic economy by 2010'. This objective has yet to be achieved, however. An important role was envisaged for competition policy. The rationale behind this agreement was that the EU simply could not compete in the world market on the basis of low-cost and low-skilled production; therefore, the goal was set to turn the EU into a knowledge-based economy. As companies started crossing borders, competition policy needed to do the same. Many anti-capitalists object to the power these TNCs possess, condemning them for taking no commitments on other than economical/profitable grounds, and object that TNCs act as they please when 'shopping' for the best places to locate their subsidiaries. Moreover, national politicians and businessmen try to remain on friendly terms with the TNCs, because of their potential for securing job and investment opportunities. EU competition policy has many challenges ahead, including:

o protection of consumers against anti-competitive practices;
o promoting the operation of the single market;
o encouraging competitiveness and innovation within the EU businesses;
o developing rules to deal with the increasing globalized nature of businesses.

There are approximately three main directions of EU competition law – namely antitrust/cartel policy, merger control and state aid.

10.4.1 Antitrust/cartel policy

Companies in the EU are not allowed to make agreements that harm the interest of consumers by creating distortions in competition and trade between member states. The Commission's powers allow them to enter company buildings without advance notice in order to look at company documents; the maximum fine the Commission can impose is 10 per cent of the convicted company's global turnover. Another property is that the Commission can grant block-exemptions for certain industries in special cases. Article 82 of the Antitrust Law prohibits the abuse of dominant market positions by companies; predatory pricing, exclusive distribution, and supply arrangement that prevent the entrance of competitors are examples of market position abuse. Sometimes, in the case of technological innovations, when a newly introduced technology becomes the industry standard, competitors are blocked out of the market; here the reason could be that the dominant company, namely Microsoft, has used its market power – although this is extremely difficult to prove.

10.4.2 Merger control

Dominant market positions can also sometimes be obtained through mergers and acquisitions (M&As). The usual case is that M&As are conducted not to abuse market power, but to generate economies of scale and efficiency gains. Nevertheless, the European Commission investigates all major M&As (those above a certain level of turnover) taking place on EU soil and has the right to block them. Moreover, M&As that fall into this category are required to report their intentions to the Commission (see Case study 1.1), which will then order an investigation which lasts one month in order to assess the competitive impact of the merger. If the merger has an expected competitive impact further investigations (four months) will result in a 'statement of objections', which will be used as a guiding line to find possible solutions. Advanced economic methods and models are used to assess the impact of a merger on the respective market; however, to some extent these assessments will always be speculative since one cannot predict the future behaviour of companies and consumers. The best predictions that can be made possess a certain amount of likelihood, which makes the formulation of law in this field particularly difficult.

10.4.3 State aid

One of the consequences of the process of European economic integration for member states is that they have renounced a considerable amount of their sovereign rights – for instance, their monetary autonomy. This leaves national governments with few options to stimulate their own economy through cases of 'bad weather'. One of the few aspects over which governments still exercise a certain degree of control is their own house-keeping book. It is generally tempting for politicians to promote policies that stimulate employment. Encouraging certain economic parties in order to retain employment can happen in many ways – for example, by means of grants, soft loans, and tax benefits; all of which fall under the provision of state aid. The potential effect of state aid on competition is a cause for concern to the European Commission, which can go as far as to enforce the repayment of the aid. Exemptions may be granted here too, generally favouring the regional development of Europe's poorer areas. In some cases, state aid given to encourage research and development (R&D) activities is permitted. In the aftermath of the September 11 attacks, which were particularly damaging to the aviation industry, aid was granted by governments to European airline companies, some of which were on the brink of bankruptcy. The exceptional situation in which the industry found itself was interpreted by many as a justification for state aid; the Commission, however, restricted the aid to the extent that 'exceptional losses' were incurred and prohibited further subsidies. Transatlantic routes, which were shut down after the terrorist attacks, counted as 'exceptional' and the losses sustained by the lower passenger quantities were excluded from aid. As a result, several national (EU) airline carriers had to undergo drastic restructuring in order to avoid bankruptcy. The US authorities were less strict in the application of their laws and granted about $15 billion of support funds to their airline carriers. The USA's leniency towards its carriers was used as an argument to justify more European state aid, but was countered by the Commission for the reason that subsidy competition with the USA is a futile exercise and creates inefficiencies. Moreover, it was apparent at this time that the most price-competitive airlines, such as Ryan Air and Easy Jet, had been unaffected by the crisis.

10.5 Summary

1. There is a general trend towards globalization. The increasing level of economic integration affects the goods and services markets but also the capital and labour markets. In addition to the general globalization trend, economic integration has seen acceleration also on regional levels through organizations such as the EU, NAFTA, and so on.

2. Globalization has meant an increase in international transactions, with the two world wars dividing the globalization process into two great waves, in which international trade has been growing more than production. A special part of the trade flows dubbed 'missing trade' is discussed alongside the issue of production technologies, which vary from country to country. Multilateral negotiations rounds organized by the GATT and later the WTO have been working towards the liberalization of international trade in goods and services.

3. With the creation of the WTO, a substantial rise in regional trade agreements has been registered in the forms of free trade areas (FTA) and customs unions (CU). Apart from covering goods and services, modern-day FTAs also address areas linked to protection, government procurement, investment, competency policy and other more practical issues. There are several classifications of economic integration. Balassa makes a distinction between free trade area, customs union, common market, economic union and total economic integration. Most of the time the numerous regional trade agreements are, in effect, between only developed or developing countries.

4. The EU is a good example of regional economic integration. The creation of a common internal market is a complex process; in the case of the EU, so far the single market has been working better for the goods than for services. This is mainly a consequence of service trade being characterized by significant variations in national rules and regulations. To reduce these trade-inhibiting effects, the European Commission (EC) has proposed the application of the 'country of origin' principal, implying that member states recognized each other's national regulation systems. In addition the EC is trying to remove barriers for intra-EU FDI. To counteract the rise of potential anti-competitive forces the EU competency law focuses on antitrust/cartel policy, merger control and state aid.

Questions

1. In what ways is globalization having an impact on climate change?
2. Why do you think that the economic integration of the EU has to date been more successful than its political integration?
3. Some specialists argue in favour of a EU-wide energy, climate, and foreign policy instead of the pursuit of national policies. Give theoretical arguments either in favour or against such arguments.

The Balance of Payments and the Foreign-Exchange Market

11.1 Introduction

A country's balance of payments is a summary of the economic transactions between that country and the rest of the world over a particular period of time – usually a month, a quarter, or a year. These transactions are classified into homogeneous groups.

The main classification of the balance of payments is into two accounts:

(i) the *current account*, which records the transactions associated with the international trade in goods and services, and

(ii) the *financial account*, which shows all international capital transactions. The main subdivision of the financial account is that between long-term and short-term capital flows, which reflects the underlying idea that long-term flows are much more stable over time than short-term flows.

One of the most notorious of all short-term flows is speculative capital, so-called 'hot' money, the enormous funds that can flow in and out of economies almost instantaneously. The growth in these flows is believed to have had a destabilizing effect on national economies and has been the subject of much criticism during the currency crises since 1990.

Although the balance of payments is drawn up for a single country, it is of course possible – and may be useful – to consolidate balances of payments for a group of countries. One important recent example is the combined balance of payments for the Euro area – those European countries that have adopted a common currency, the euro.

For the purpose of statistical processing it is necessary to have a detailed knowledge of how transactions are recorded on the balance of payments. Of course, this knowledge is also required, if in less detail, for a proper analysis of a country's balance of payments or an international comparison of balance-of-payments positions. The analysis of a country's balance of payments provides very useful information about its economic relations with other countries and delivers important information about the general economic situation in the country.

This chapter considers:

o the balance-of-payments classification system;
o the definitions of the different types of international transactions; and
o the economic insights provided by the balance of payments.

Case study 11.1 discusses trends in Japan's balance of payments over the period 1980–2006. It shows that the balance of payments is more than simply a list of figures: it can also provide important economic information. A number of the concepts introduced in the case study will then be discussed later in the chapter.

Case study 11.1   Trends in Japan's balance of payments, 1980–2006

Figure 11.1 shows the annual balances of the current account (in white) and net inflows of long-term capital from abroad (in grey) for Japan over the period 1980–2006. The addition 'net' indicates that it is the difference between (gross) inflows and (gross) out-flows. The figure also depicts the aggregate of these two balances, through the dashed line. It is called the *basic balance*.

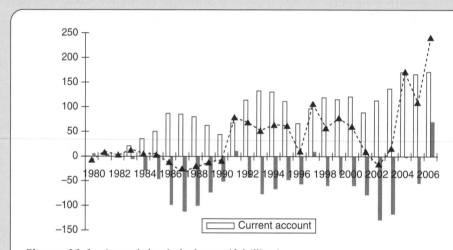

Figure 11.1   Japan's basic balance ($ billion)
Source: IMF, *International Financial Statistics,* various issues.

What does Figure 11.1 reveal about Japan's balance of payments?

First, it shows that between 1981 and 1986 Japan produced a rapidly increasing *current account surplus*. In the later part of the 1980s this surplus declined substantially, but its rise resumed in the early 1990s. Does this suggest a growing imbalance?

Second, this systematic current account surplus attracted criticism, particularly from other countries with lasting current account deficits – such as the USA. Japan was accused, rightly or wrongly, of aggressive export competition and placing restrictions on imports that competed with its domestic industries. But was the Japanese current account surplus bad for the country and/or the world – that is, was the accusation justified?

Third, the figure shows that Japan's current account surplus was associated with a net capital outflow, the result of Japan's extensive acquisition of long-term foreign assets. Over the period 1981–91, the net outflow of Japanese long-term capital amounted to $550 billion.

Fourth, the figure shows that in the late 1980s and the early 1990s a substantial change took place in Japanese international long-term capital flows: in 1991 the net outflow of capital turned into a net inflow. This was affected by a rapid rise in Japanese interest rates, following a tightening of monetary policy in 1987. The rise in interest rates meant that borrowing in Japan in order to finance investment became more expensive and therefore less attractive. The aim of this change in monetary policy was to achieve a gradual deflation of the financial bubble that had been caused by the previously low interest rates and also to bring about a reduction in Japanese investment abroad in an attempt to strengthen domestic investment.

The effects were dramatic. By the end of 1992 Japanese share prices had fallen by more than 70 per cent, and similar falls in prices had been observed in the property market. There was a real bursting of the bubble rather than a gradual reduction.

Naturally, this bursting of the bubble also affected the level of Japan's foreign investments. They declined because Japanese banks and businesses needed to strengthen their liquidity position, which had been impaired by the crises in shares and property. Japanese banks also had to prepare for the new international regulations on solvency standards. As a result of all these developments, Japan ceased to be a net long-term capital exporter.

At the end of the 1980s economic growth also stagnated in Japan as a consequence of the bursting bubbles and the higher domestic interest rates. This limited the expansion of domestic demand – a contraction that led many commentators to see the 1990s as a 'lost' decade for the Japanese economy. The stagnation of demand growth, combined with the more moderate acquisitions of foreign long-term assets after 1990, led to a reversal in Japan's basic balance, which started to show a substantial surplus from 1991. This pattern was to continue over the next few years.

The basic balance has a considerable influence on a country's exchange rate: if the basic balance is negative, the long-term forces in the economy involved (those that influence *both* the current account transactions *and* the long-term capital flows) generate a net purchase of foreign currency in exchange for the domestic currency. On the foreign-exchange market this places a downward pressure on the value of the own currency relative to foreign currencies. Of course, there may be short-term counteracting capital forces. When the Japanese basic balance reversed in 1991 from a deficit into a surplus, various experts expected this to lead to a higher value of the yen. And they proved to be right.

Case study 11.1 highlights a number of economic relationships:

o A country's international transactions have repercussions for the international economy: a Japanese current account surplus implies a current account deficit for the rest of the world, while a fall in the value of the yen on the foreign-exchange market leads automatically to a rise in the value of other currencies.

o The state of the domestic economy and the country's international transactions are inextricably linked. For instance, an interest rate increase affects both economic growth and international capital flows and, as a result, the balance of payments and the exchange rate.

o There seems to be a relationship between different types of international transactions. It appeared, for example, that Japan's current account surplus was usually accompanied by Japanese long-term capital outflow.

The case study, and the interrelationships that it highlights, prompts the following questions that will be addressed by this chapter:

1. Why and how are the various economic activities leading to transactions with other countries recorded and arranged in different accounts of the balance of payments?
2. Is there a systematic link between a current account imbalance and a simultaneous imbalance in international capital flows?
3. What is the relationship between a country's balance of payments and the country's exchange rate?
4. When can we say that the balance of payments is in equilibrium? Is a surplus on the current account or a positive basic balance worth pursuing for a country?
5. If a country has a current account surplus, are complaints of other countries about unfairness always justified?
6. Does an increase in the value of a currency on the foreign-exchange (forex) market improve the country's international competitive position?
7. How does the forex market work?

11.2 | Balance of payments: the classification system

The classification of balance of payments can be achieved by using a system like that presented in the International Monetary Fund (IMF)'s publication the *Balance of Payments Manual*, which recommends some concepts, definitions, and rules in respect of the member countries' balance-of-payments statistics. This classification has been used by almost every single country. The main subdivision in the IMF classification is between the current account, the capital account, and the financial account.

The entries in the balance-of-payments statistics can be made in one of two ways: on a cash basis (with transactions recorded at the time of payment) and on a transaction basis (with transactions recorded when the product in question is transferred to the buyer abroad; in the case of a service, this means at the time that the service is performed). In practice, the most commonly used system is recording on a transaction basis.

11.2.1 The current account

For the exporting country international trade in goods and services is an income-generating activity; this also applies to the production factors (labour and capital) that a country deploys overseas. Through such foreign activities a country's inhabitants acquire income through production. The resulting international transactions are recorded on the *current account* of the balance of payments. In addition to international trade and international factor movements, unilateral income transfers are the third category of international transactions recorded on the current account. This could include workers living abroad permanently who remit part of their income to relatives in their countries of origin. As the inflows of these transfers also generate income in the receiving country, they raise the level of national income, but, in contrast to the two former categories, not national production.

On the balance of payments, transactions are generally subdivided further into categories according to the nature of what is being supplied. The main distinction in the current account is that between trade in goods and trade in services. In terms of economics, there is no essential difference between goods and services, but in practice it is harder to keep a proper record of international services than trade in goods. One reason is that, in contrast to goods – which are by definition tangible and therefore physical – services are intangible and for that reason cannot be recorded crossing the frontier.

In 1990 the value of goods exported worldwide was $3.5 trillion and the value of services was $0.8 trillion. In 2008 the values of these export flows were, respectively, $16.1 trillion and US$3.8 trillion (WTO, 2010). The worldwide credit crisis in 2008–09 led to strong falls to, respectively, $12.1 and 3.3 trillion. Over this period until 2008, remarkably, the share of services in international trade remained almost constant, at around 23 per cent, although production in the developed countries underwent a gradual shift from goods to services. The crisis had a more damaging effect on goods trade than on services trade. Relative to world production the world exports of goods and services also increased steadily. In value terms the ratio of world exports to world gross domestic product rose between 1985 and 2008 by almost 90 per cent. The credit crisis harmed trade more than growth: in 2009 the ratio declined by some 16 per cent.

In balance-of-payments accounting, services are subdivided into the following categories: transportation, travel, communication services, construction services, insurance services, financial services, computer and information services, royalties and licence fees, other business services (such as legal, accounting, management consulting, public relations, advertising, research and development, architectural, engineering, and agricultural services), and government services.

In addition to the *goods* and *services accounts*, the current account also includes an *income account*, which has a further subdivision into the compensation of employees working abroad and income on foreign financial investments, such as dividends and interest earned abroad. These are considered to be payments for the services of financial capital that is 'working' abroad. (It is important to distinguish these payments from the original investments themselves, which appear in the financial account [see Section 11.2.2].)

The final sub-account of the current account is the *current transfer account*, which contains international transfers of money that are not connected specifically to any direct, identifiable activity. The principal examples are grants, contributions to international organizations, and workers' remittances. This covers income transfers in the form of development aid, gifts and transfers by foreign workers to the family in their original country, and so on.

Occasionally, the difference between goods and the other current account items is described as the difference between visible (goods) and invisible transactions. Thus, the latter covers not only services but also international transfers of factor and investment income as well as transferred income.

11.2.2 Capital and financial accounts

Until the last IMF revision of the system of balance-of-payments accounting in 1994, in addition to the current account there was only one other account of the balance of payments – the capital account. Now the *capital account* is restricted to only a small part of this category, solely reflecting capital transfers, such as debt forgiveness, the transfer of wealth of migrants as a result of their changes of residency, and exceptional financial transfers, such as cross-border compensation for war damage and natural disasters.

Since the IMF revision of the balance-of-payments classification, the *financial account* has become quantitatively much more important. The financial account covers all international transactions in financial assets, such as stocks, bonds, and the holdings of bank deposits. These transactions concern the cross-border payments that are associated with international capital flows. If a country's inhabitant buys a foreign stock, the payment for this stock inflow is a capital outflow for that country.

One long-standing and important distinction between the entries on the financial account is that between long-term and short-term international investments.

Long-term international investments include international transactions in financial assets with an original maturity of more than one year. The main categories are foreign direct investment (FDI) and portfolio investment and, to a lesser extent, a part of the category 'other investment'.

o *Foreign direct investment* is the international capital flows needed to set up a new foreign branch or to realize a substantial participation in a foreign enterprise (see Section 4.6). In terms of classifying the foreign acquisition as a foreign direct investment the most important point is whether or not the purpose of the investment is to secure a significant degree of influence in and control over the foreign enterprise.
o *Portfolio investment* is also investment in securities (stocks or bonds), but the investor is interested only in the expected financial return on the investment. Sometimes even substantial blocks of stocks in foreign companies are bought for portfolio investment reasons, without the investor having any ambition to become involved in management of the business.
o *'Other investment'* can also contain long-term international investments. They can be found under the headings *trade credits* (see also Section 12.2) and *loans*.

Short-term international investments are investments in securities with an original maturity of less than one year. They can be found in the financial account under the headings 'financial derivatives' and 'other investments'. Under the general heading of 'financial derivatives' the main subcategories are: forward contracts, options and futures (for explanations of these, see Section 15.4.2). The category of 'other investment' consists mainly of trade credits, loans (such as Treasury bills and commercial paper) and currencies and deposits. In this category international interbank positions are the most important because of the intermediary role played by banks in the settlement of international transactions.

Every banking transaction that affects the banks' foreign-exchange holdings is recorded by banks as a short-term capital transaction. Foreign exchange consists of:

1. foreign banknotes;
2. demand deposits with foreign banks; and
3. other claims on foreign countries that can be converted readily into foreign bank deposits.

The banks will always keep minimum holdings of such liquid assets so that they can conduct the international transactions that their customers desire at any time. The net foreign-exchange position of commercial banks (or the banks that are able to create money) is known as *net foreign assets*.

Since the banks are businesses just like any other enterprise, their security transactions, including direct investments, are shown on the balance of payments, in accordance with IMF rules.

In balance-of-payments accounting the liquid assets of a country's monetary authorities that are available for international payments are referred to as the (*official*) *reserve assets*. Usually, the central bank holds the official reserve assets and intervenes with them in the foreign-exchange (forex) market, if this is considered necessary. These official reserve assets comprise gold in the hands of the central bank, the central bank's position in the IMF accounts, and liquid claims on non-residents, both in convertible foreign currency. The term 'liquid' means available at short notice and 'convertible' means that the currency involved is generally accepted for exchange into other currencies.

The central bank is able to transform these assets into a form that can be sold in the forex market. The principal aim of such a sale is to add to the existing supply of foreign currency in the foreign-exchange market. This will put some downward pressure on the price of foreign currency in terms of the domestic currency in that market, meaning that the central bank can prevent a decline of the value of the domestic currency in the forex market.

11.3   Balance of payments: the accounting practice

In contrast to the balance sheet the balance-of-payments measures *flows*, rather than stocks. It is a record of the international flows of trade in goods and services provided and international capital movements during a particular period of time.

Not every transaction on the balance of payments involves the actual payment of money. In fact, it could well be argued that today immediate payment is the exception to the rule. Importers will usually receive a credit from the exporter. The credit period starts with the delivery of goods or services and ends when the actual international payment is made. Even if an immediate payment is required, there is often no transaction on the foreign-exchange market. For instance, the payment could be made through a transfer from a bank deposit of the importer in a bank in the country of the exporter. The result of these two finance options (trade credit and payment through a foreign bank account) is that one international transaction (the import of goods) spontaneously creates a second one (either an increase in the foreign financial assets of the exporter or a reduction in foreign financial assets of the importer). The two linked transactions are set off against one another in the balance-of-payments accounting, resulting in the absence of both a cross-border international flow of money and a foreign-exchange market transaction. This offsetting feature is characteristic of the double-bookkeeping practice of balance-of-payments accounting. Box 11.1 shows four such examples.

Box 11.1   Four illustrative cases of the double-bookkeeping nature of the balance of payments

1. If a farmer in the USA sells wheat to Russia financed by a credit from a US bank to the Russian importer, the combined transaction is included twice in the US balance of payments: as a US export of goods and as a US import of foreign assets (because there is an increase in the claim of a US bank on foreigners).
2. A Dutch company purchases computer parts from a company in the USA; the Dutch importer receives an export credit in dollars from the US exporter.
   The import of a good on the current account is compensated fully by an export of a financial asset (an export of a promissory note or an IOU) that is included in the financial account of the balance of payments.
   In these first two cases there is no forex market transaction.

3. A German citizen buys bonds in the UK and pays through its account (in pounds sterling) with a bank in London. The bond purchase is shown on the German balance of payments as an increase in foreign assets owned by a resident. The German pays for the bonds by reducing the pound deposit with the UK bank. Both of these activities lead to items on the financial account and, while they offset one another, there will be no immediate forex market transaction.

4. An Argentine importer of cars produced in the USA wants to pay the bill by selling part of its Argentine peso deposit with an Argentine bank for US dollars. This sale is a transaction on the forex market and will, ceteris paribus, lower the level of the peso against the dollar.

   The decline of the peso – and the associated rise of the dollar – will necessarily have the size that is necessary to ease off a new supply of dollars in the forex market elsewhere in the economy – generated by the higher price of the dollar against the peso. An example is a rise of Argentine exports to the USA due to the cheaper peso. This is one way to create the offsetting entry on the balance of payments.

   If, however, the Argentine monetary authorities refuse to let the peso value fall against the dollar (because they are trying to achieve a fixed dollar exchange rate for the peso), the Argentine central bank has the opportunity to satisfy the net demand for dollars out of its own international monetary reserves. The offsetting entry on the balance of payments is now a sale of official reserve assets – an item on the financial account.

   In each of these two ways the Argentine car importer induces with its demand for dollars the required additional supply thereof. Both additional supplies, due to either the cheaper peso or the forex market intervention of the central bank, are booked on the balance of payments. In doing so, they complete the double-bookkeeping practice.

This final case differs from the previous ones in that there is no spontaneous, or so-called autonomous, financial account transaction that finances the international transaction undertaken first.

All four examples given in Box 11.1 show the so-called rule of double bookkeeping with respect to the balance of payments, meaning that a single international transaction generates an equal counter-transaction. A balance-of-payments equilibrium coincides with the absence of a net international payment as well as with equilibrium on the forex market. This is always the case: *ex post* – after the transactions have taken place – the balance of payments is in equilibrium. But note that it is essential to understand that this situation may only be realized after some forex market strains were dissolved, possibly resulting in a change in the international price – or the exchange rate – of the domestic currency. Consequently, this permanent *ex post* balance-of-payments equilibrium may well coincide with a lot of equilibrating activity on the forex market front.

In the balance-of-payments accounting system all the entries are positioned according to the effect of the international transaction on the forex market and, particularly, on the price in this market – that is, the exchange rate. If a transaction generates an additional *supply* of foreign currency on the forex market, it is booked on the *credit* side of the balance of payments and provided with a '+' sign in the balance-of-payments statistics. Such a transaction can occur, for instance, either:

o if a foreigner makes a payment to the home country; or
o the domestic central bank sells foreign currencies in the foreign-exchange market.

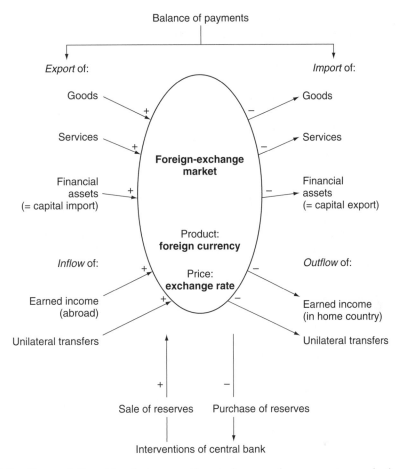

Figure 11.2 The relationship between the balance of payments and the foreign-exchange market

A transaction appears on the *debit* side of the balance of payments and is given a minus sign in the balance-of-payments statistics, if it creates an additional *demand* for foreign currency in the forex market. Figure 11.2 illustrates these features.

Ex ante it holds true that the total of *private* demand for foreign currencies (that is, the sum of the desired right-hand side or '−' transactions) differs from the *private* supply of foreign exchange (that is, the sum of the desired left-hand side or '+' transactions). Only coincidentally will these two amounts be spontaneously equal. As argued above, the restoration of the equilibrium on both the balance of payments and the forex market can occur through an appropriate:

o change of the exchange rate, and/or
o forex market interventions by the central bank.

In the next chapters it will be seen that there are yet other opportunities. The outcome is an *ex post* equilibrium of the balance of payments and an *ex post* equality of supply and demand on the forex market. This holds true under all circumstances.

This leads to the first of three essential identities in international monetary economics – that is, the balance-of-payments identity: $CA + CFA - \Delta R \equiv 0$ or

$$CA + CFA \equiv \Delta R, \tag{11.1}$$

where CA is the current-account balance, CFA the combined capital- and financial-account balance excluding the official reserve assets account, and ΔR is the increase in international monetary reserves holdings.

It is misleading to assume that both the parties involved in an international transaction have to conduct a corresponding foreign-exchange transaction. In principle, only one of the two parties needs to do this. The decision as to which of the parties to a contract takes charge of the foreign-exchange transaction is naturally a matter for mutual agreement. For example, in the second case outlined in Box 11.1 the Dutch firm might have succeeded in including in the import contract of computer parts the clause that it should settle the bill in euros; this means it is the US exporter that has to exchange the euros it receives in payment into dollars. Alternatively, the parties can agree that the Dutch firm will pay in US dollars, in which case the Dutch firm has to conduct the foreign-exchange transaction.

Either of these currency conversions will have the same effect on the foreign-exchange market for the exchange of euros against dollars, because the foreign-exchange market is a genuine world market. It is therefore irrelevant for the exchange rate whether the exchange of currencies is carried out in Amsterdam or New York (see Section 12.3 for more on this worldwide exchange rate equalization mechanism).

Table 11.1 exhibits recent balance-of-payments data (2005) for each of the G3: the USA, the Euro area, and Japan, the world's three largest industrialized countries (or institutionalized country groupings). As there is a lack of information about a number

Table 11.1 The balance of payments of the G3, 2005 ($ billion)

	USA	Euro area	Germany	Japan
Current account	−791.51	−28.06	116.03	165.78
Goods	−778.94	67.95	189.27	93.96
General merchandise	−782.74	. . .	182.30	105.27
Goods for processing	. . .	. . .	9.83	−4.19
Repairs on goods	3.85	. . .	2.07	−0.30
Goods procured in ports by carriers	. . .	. . .	−4.43	−7.12
Non-monetary gold	. . .	. . .	−0.51	−0.30
Services	62.21	42.84	−47.92	−24.05
Transportation services	−24.99	. . .	−5.58	−4.63
Travel	28.45	. . .	−43.34	−25.13
Communication services	−0.26	. . .	−1.53	−0.23
Construction services	3.10	. . .	1.02	2.45
Insurance services	−21.65	. . .	−2.70	−1.02
Financial services	22.73	. . .	2.03	2.35
Computer and information services	3.57	. . .	−0.34	−1.30
Royalties and licence fees	32.91	. . .	0.24	15.23

Other business services	22.85	...	−0.10	0.78
Personal, cultural and recreational services	6.14	...	−2.11	−1.01
Government services	−10.64	...	4.49	0.67
Income	*11.29*	*−53.97*	*10.68*	*103.44*
Compensation of employees	−6.31	7.67	−1.95	−0.13
Investment income	17.60	−61.64	12.64	103.57
From: Direct investment	134.42	0.03	6.79	20.89
Portfolio investment	116.95	−49.60	−3.61	78.38
Other investment	0.13	−12.07	9.45	4.32
Current transfers	*−86.07*	*−84.88*	*−35.99*	*−7.57*
Government transfers	−37.67	...	−22.25	−4.00
Workers' remittances	−31.84	...	−3.65	−0.12
Other current transfers	−16.57	...	−10.09	−3.45
Capital account	**−4.35**	**15.37**	**−1.69**	**−4.88**
Debt forgiveness	...	...	−3.30	−2.55
Migrants' transfers	...	...	−0.37	0.05
Other	...	...	1.98	−2.28
Financial account	**785.45**	**101.69**	**−128.39**	**−145.01**
Direct investment	*100.68*	*−192.79*	*−15.05*	*−42.22*
Equity capital and reinvested earnings	88.18	...	−10.07	−36.67
Other capital	12.50	...	−4.98	−5.56
Portfolio investment	*728.42*	*195.95*	*−15.06*	*−13.27*
Equity securities	−55.53	169.47	−25.71	108.35
Debt securities	783.96	26.49	10.64	−121.62
Financial derivatives	...	*−18.96*	*−6.08*	*−6.53*
Other investment	*−57.75*	*93.59*	*−94.80*	*−60.66*
Trade credits	4.69	1.25	−1.71	2.17
Loans	3.35	107.26	−66.24	−69.27
Currency and deposits	12.71	...	−21.93	−2.37
Other assets and liabilities	−78.50	−14.92	−4.91	8.81
Reserve assets	*14.10*	*23.89*	*2.60*	*−22.33*
Monetary gold	...	4.81	...	...
SDRs and reserve position in the IMF	14.71	11.02	2.91	3.47
Foreign-exchange and other assets	−0.62	8.06	−0.31	−25.80
Net errors and omissions	**10.41**	**−89.00**	**14.05**	**−15.90**

Note: '...' indicates lack of information.
Source: IMF, *Balance of Payments Statistics, Yearbook 2006*.

of the entries for the Euro area, we have added the balance-of-payments data for Germany, the largest country in that region. The scheme also illustrates the precise build-up of the balance of payments, as has already been described in general terms in the previous section. (The meaning of several entries will be clarified in later chapters. For example, the reserve assets Special Drawing Rights (SDRs) and reserve position in the International Monetary Fund (IMF) will be explained extensively in Section 16.4.)

The figures in Table 11.1 highlight several interesting findings in relation to international payments. The USA appears to have recorded a current account deficit of $792 billion in 2005. This is much larger than the combined current account surpluses of Germany and Japan, while the Euro area has a small deficit of $28 billion, so that the combined current account deficit of the G3 in 2002 amounted to $654 billion. This implies that the rest of the world should have had a combined current account *surplus* of the same value.

The size of the US current account deficit is roughly equivalent to the country's deficit in goods trade. The reason is that, coincidentally, the USA's surpluses in services and income and its deficit in current transfers almost fully balance one another. If we break down international trade in services into a variety of sectors, the USA seems to be strongly competitive in the areas of travel, financial services, royalties and licence fees and 'other business services', each of which has generated substantial surpluses of between $22 and $32 billion.

In contrast, from an analysis of Japanese services only the sub-balances of travel and royalties and fees recorded significant figures: there was a large deficit for travel ($25 billion) and a sizeable surplus for royalties and fees ($15 billion). Germans surpass the Japanese only in foreign travel – with an impressive deficit of $43 billion. With regard to the rest of the services the sub-balances for Germany are quite low.

The Euro area has a substantial deficit on the income account, principally as the result of the deficit of $50 billion in the income on portfolio investments, whereas Japan shows a substantial surplus in investment income ($103 billion). These disequilibria suggest that the Euro area is an international debtor region, while Japan is a creditor country. One needs to be cautious in drawing such conclusions, since, for example, the USA, which is the largest debtor country in the world, has an income account that is almost in equilibrium. The reason appears to be that for the USA the average rate of return on its foreign assets is substantially higher than that rate on its foreign liabilities.

By far the most noticeable figure of the financial accounts of the G3 is the enormous surplus of $785 billion recorded by the USA. Foreign direct investments 'only' contribute a surplus of $101 billion. The overwhelming contribution comes from the foreign purchase of US debt securities of $784 billion. Apparently, the large US current account deficit could be 'financed' through the preference of non-Americans to invest in these US securities. Germany and Japan have deficits on the financial account of over $100 billion, which partly offset their current account surpluses.

In the case of Japan the financial account deficit is principally the result of the purchase of foreign debt securities and the provision of foreign loans. In the Euro area the main source of financial imports is foreign loans. It is noteworthy that the outflow of foreign direct investments and the inflow of portfolio investments in the form of shares largely compensate each other.

Of the G3 group in 2005 only Japan showed any substantial net intervention in the foreign-exchange market. The minus sign indicates that it concerns a net purchase of foreign exchange – apparently an official attempt to weaken the yen in the forex market.

The final entry in Table 11.1 is 'net errors and omissions' – the difference between all remaining credit and debit entries. One reason for the existence of 'errors and omissions' is the various sources for the underlying figures and the difficulties in acquiring all of the relevant information. In addition, people sometimes succeed in preventing certain transactions from being recorded; think of the smuggling of goods and the underreporting of investment income.

The main source of 'omissions' appears to be international capital transactions and the ensuing flow of revenue from such investments (for example, for the purposes of tax evasion). These statistical problems explain why the bookkeeping system – which the balance of payments in fact constitutes – has to be corrected with the help of the entry 'net errors and omissions'. Its value is of limited size for the USA, Germany, and Japan, but the value of −$89 billion for the Euro area is substantial. The negative value indicates that its balances of the current, capital, and financial accounts taken together result in a net *surplus* of $89 billion instead of the expected outcome: zero dollars. Somewhere in the balance of payments an amount of −$89 billion is missing. Perhaps the current account deficit is even larger than the stated $28 billion or the inflow of portfolio investments in the country is not as large as the $196 billion indicate. Case study 11.2 presents more about the expected sources of 'net errors and omissions' on the global level.

Case study 11.2   Mystery of the worldwide current account discrepancy

One country's export is another country's import. This means that the current account balances across the world should add up to zero. The same should hold for the other sub-balances of the balance of payments – those of the capital and financial accounts. However, according to the available data this seems not to be the case, as for many years the world as a whole has been running both a current account deficit and a financial account surplus.

In a one-off attempt by the IMF to establish the size of the discrepancy, by 2001 the global current account deficit was estimated to stand at around 2 per cent of global imports, and this deficit seems to be growing (see IMF, 2002, p. 70). These missing amounts, of course, make the national imbalances uncertain, leading to a complication of the conduct of national economic policy.

Several causes are advanced to try and explain global balance of payments discrepancies. With respect to the current account the following economic factors are considered to be important (IMF, 2002, p. 70):

Transportation lags. End-of-year exports are recorded in that year, whereas the corresponding imports may only be recorded in the following year. Growing international trade over time (as it does) can lead to a lasting global current account *surplus*.

Asymmetric valuation. Exports and imports of the same good may be valued at different prices. A usual problem is whether transportation and insurance costs are included in the price. In the import value these costs, insurance, and freight (c.i.f.) are usually included.

Weak quality of data. This is thought to be a particular problem in terms of transportation services and workers' remittances from abroad.

Underreporting of investment income. Partly as a result of tax evasion capital export is underreported, while the presence of offshore centres disrupts the reporting of international capital flows and its income flows in general.

11.4   Balance-of-payments analysis

The use of the double-entry bookkeeping system means that the balance of payments as a whole is always in formal equilibrium, in bookkeeping terms: the total of the credit items is always equal to the total of debit items. This also means that the balance for a sub-part of all transactions should be equal to the reverse of the balance of all other transactions booked on the balance of payments. If, for instance, a country has a current account *deficit* of $2 billion, there will be a corresponding combined financial- and capital-account surplus of $2 billion for the country in the reporting period.

The most important sub-balance is the *current account balance*, a figure that shows the net income that a country obtains from its international transactions. As we will see in Chapter 14, a country may have a level of domestic spending that is lower than its level of national production, thereby creating a surplus on its current account. For less developed countries, such restrictions of domestic spending may be regarded as undesirable. This explains why poor countries will often have current account deficits.

Such current account deficits are financed by a net inflow of foreign capital (associated with a net sale of financial assets abroad). In other words, the country borrows from other countries or spends its foreign asset holdings. (Unless it is the capital account that offsets the current account deficit.) As a result, there will be a decline in the country's financial wealth.

By contrast, a current account surplus means that in the reporting period the country involved has provided other countries with credit. The first country's financial wealth, in terms of the claims on other countries, has therefore increased in the reporting period. A policy directed to creating a current account surplus therefore has a close resemblance with a policy of a country to save and thus postpone its expenditure.

Another sub-balance already mentioned in Section 11.1 is the *basic balance*, which combines the current account balance with the balance of long-term capital (mainly foreign direct investments and portfolio investments combined). Long-term capital is thought to be much less volatile than short-term capital flows, because it is supposed to be affected only by longer-term explanatory variables that change only gradually over time. The same is thought to be true of current account items. As a result, the basic balance is considered to show longer-term trends in the balance of payments. Therefore, it is an indicator of longer-term demand for and supply of the country's currency on the forex market and thus of the longer-term equilibrium forces that underlie the exchange rate.

There is no clear association in the movements over time of the two sub-balances of the basic balance. Under certain economic conditions, the sub-balances may produce parallel trends, so that the basic balance may vary relatively sharply – despite its inherent stability.

One typical case was the trend in Japan in the early 1990s, as illustrated in Case study 11.1. The rise in Japanese interest rates after 1987, and the consequent halving of stock market prices and reduction of solvency in the Japanese banking sector, brought an end to net Japanese capital outflows. Since the current account also improved at the same time (possibly also stimulated by the rise in interest rates, as this rise reduces expenditures and therefore also import demand), the basic balance improved from −$28.3 billion in 1987 to +$78.5 billion in 1991. It was therefore unsurprising that the yen increased in value during this period.

The *reserve assets balance* is the outcome of official forex market interventions (usually by the central bank) and thus of conscious policy choices. It offers a clue to the monetary authorities' desired exchange rate change: a purchase of reserve asset holdings (against a payment in domestic currency) points at a preferred weakening of the own currency in the forex market and vice versa. Japan's reserve assets balance of $46 billion in 2002 (see Table 11.1) shows that in that particular year the Japanese central bank has bought that amount of foreign currency (chiefly US dollars). This suggests that the authorities considered the Japanese yen to be too expensive on the forex market or that the rise in the yen's value on that market had to be slowed down. By contrast, the central banks of the other countries in the table made only negligible net interventions on the foreign-exchange market.

The discussion above might lead to the following question: are there ideal values in general for the various sub-balances of the balance of payments? The answer is an unconditional 'no'. Because countries usually experience economic growth, on average, it is unsurprising that the sub-balances of the balance of payments – which are net outcomes of inflows and outflows of similar transactions – also increase over time. But there is no ideal value. Even the desired sign of the current account balance is uncertain, but it is affected by the country's stage of economic development, the state of its economy, and the policy stance adopted by its government. Here are two examples, for the purpose of illustration, of the influence of stage and state in question. Chapter 13 will elaborate on these interdependencies.

1. For a developing country with highly profitable investment opportunities, it is preferable to maintain a current account deficit. This gives room for the import of capital goods financed by foreign financial sources. The financial account will therefore show a surplus, which offsets the current account deficit. These disequilibria are sustainable as long as the profitability of the domestic investment projects is such that the profits allow the periodic payment of interest and dividends to the foreign creditors and also the gradual repayment of the principal of the foreign loans. This view says nothing about the maximum sustainable current account deficit. Of course, this sustainability will be affected by the cause of the current account deficit. Investments in profitable production give much more room for viable deficits than a deficit that is the result of private or government consumption.
2. In a country with an ageing population it would appear to be attractive to have a high level of investment income from abroad (reported on the current account), combined with offsetting high net imports of goods and services. To arrive at such a situation, such a country should secure high levels of foreign long-term investments. Room for the associated financial account deficit must be made through operating sizeable surpluses on the current account – for example, through large net exports of goods. The latter features are visible in Japan's balance of payments in Table 11.1.

11.5   The functioning of foreign-exchange markets

This chapter examines three closely interconnected concepts: the balance of payments, the foreign-exchange market, and the exchange rate (as illustrated in Figure 11.2). We now turn to the foreign-exchange market (in this section) and the exchange rate (in the next section).

In the *customer* or *retail* part of the forex market, individuals and business can either acquire or sell foreign currencies. However, it remains the case that perhaps 90 per cent of trading takes place between banks in the *interbank* part of the foreign-exchange market.

In the customer part, banks buy and sell coins and banknotes of foreign currencies, but also trade foreign currencies through transactions booked on the demand deposit (or checking) accounts. The counterparty of the bank is its non-bank customer. For the trade in banknotes, banks use a large buying–selling spread of several percentage points.

Several features determine the size of the buying–selling spread that banks charge their customers:

o In order to carry out these buying and selling activities banks need to hold a working stock of foreign currencies, which can be affected by exchange rate risk.

○ Furthermore, the banks receive no interest on these holdings, while the transportation of these cash holdings also delivers costs.
○ Banks also attempt to minimize their imbalances in their buying and selling of foreign currencies with customers. A deep market for a foreign currency – a market with a high daily turnover – makes it easier and less costly to supplement low holdings and will therefore have a spread-reducing effect.
○ Moreover, there are personnel costs for the transactions and, of course, a certain profit margin is also required – which is relatively high in view of the small size of average transactions.

In view of the features listed above, it is not surprising that for trade in foreign currencies through demand deposits, instead of banknotes, banks can have a smaller buying–selling spread.

Interbank trading allows a bank to readjust its own position quickly and at a relatively low cost. Some interbank trading is conducted directly between the traders at different banks. The use of foreign-exchange brokers as intermediaries provides anonymity for bank traders, until an exchange rate is agreed on for a trade. The use of brokers can also reduce the costs of searching for the best available exchange rates, as the broker's business is to know the rates at which various banks are willing to trade. Brokers earn commissions for their services.

Skilled traders work at desks in their separate banks, dealing with each other and with brokers by computer and by phone. Major banks quote the exchange rates at which each is willing to trade currencies with other banks. A quotation of a bank consists of the combination of the bid and ask (or offer) rate for a specific foreign currency. The bid rate is the price (in units of the domestic currency) that a bank is prepared to pay for a unit of a foreign currency, whereas the ask rate – which is slightly higher – is the price at which the bank is willing to sell a unit of the same foreign currency. Trade in banknotes has by far the largest spread, followed by foreign-exchange trade with bank customers through their demand deposits. The spread for interbank foreign-exchange transactions is by far the smallest, say only 0.001 euro per dollar – but, as the average transaction size is quite large, profit can be substantial.

Information relating to the level of exchange rates is published on a daily basis in the financial sections of many daily newspapers. Closing rates (rates at the end of the working day) can usually be found for the last couple of working days in New York or London for trading among banks in amounts of $1 million and more. These exchange rates are published in dollars (and possibly also euros and pounds) per foreign currency and also the reverse of this rate: that is, the amount of the specified currencies per dollar (euro and pound).

There is an enormous daily turnover on the forex markets. Every three years the Bank for International Settlements (BIS) in Basel produces a survey that contains estimates of the average daily global turnover on the world's forex markets, with the most recent estimate being for April 2010. Between 1989 and 1998 the turnover on the spot market (that is, the market for the immediate deliveries of currencies – though in practice the process still takes two working days) grew rapidly, reaching a figure of $568 billion in 1998. In 2001, this turnover fell to $386 billion, before rising to a value of 621 billion in 2004, 1,005 billion in 2007, and reaching 1490 billion in 2010 (BIS, 2010).

In an increasingly globalized world it is perhaps the fall in the foreign-exchange market turnover between 1998 and 2001 that requires some explanation. The major factor seems to have been the introduction of the euro on 1 January 1999. This consolidated the

11 national currencies of the then participating countries in the Euro area so that trade in these national currencies was replaced by trade in the euro with there no longer being any need for a currency exchange. Consequently, foreign-exchange transactions between these 11 countries disappeared.

The forex market is not one single trading site. Most countries have forex markets, consisting of several sub-markets each for a specific couple of currencies (supplemented with sub-markets for foreign-exchange derivatives, as explained in Section 15.4.2). In each of these national forex markets, the sub-market where the home currency is exchanged for the US dollar is by far the largest.

BIS (2010) also contains a currency distribution of reported foreign-exchange turnover. It shows that in 84.9 per cent of the global turnover (spot plus currency derivatives) in 2010 the US dollar was one of the two transaction currencies; the dollar share peaked in 2001 with a share of 89.9 per cent, compared with a share of 'only' 82 per cent in 1992. The share for the euro amounted in 2001 and 2010 to 37.9 and 39.1 per cent, respectively. At first glance, this is a surprisingly high level for such a brand-new currency. But it should be noted that the combined share of the EMS currencies in the 1998 review was almost 53 per cent. The shares of yen and pound are third and fourth in the ranking of 2010, with percentages of 19.0 and 12.9 respectively.

The trend over time is for the shares of the four major currencies to fall slightly, in turn benefiting the currencies of emerging economies, such as the Hong Kong dollar, the Singapore dollar, the Mexican peso, and the Korean won, but in particular the Australian dollar, the Canadian dollar, and the New Zealand dollar. The currencies of those EU countries that stayed outside the Euro area (Swedish krona, Norwegian krone, and Danish krone) all saw a rise in their shares.

In 2010 the most intensively traded currency pair was the dollar/euro, with a share in all forex transactions of 28 per cent, followed by dollar/yen (14 per cent) and dollar/pound (11 per cent). At this time the euro/yen pairing had a share of only 3 per cent.

11.6 The exchange rate: concepts and presentation

The exchange rate is the price on the foreign-exchange market – that is, the price of foreign exchange (or foreign currency) expressed in terms of units of the domestic currency. So, for instance, if a US importer needs to pay $2 for every £1, we can say that the dollar/pound exchange rate is $2/£1. In this section we will consider some other definitions of the exchange rate, each with its own function, and the way in which daily newspapers inform us about exchange rate values.

The exchange rate that we have usually been talking about so far is the *nominal* and, simultaneously, *bilateral exchange rate*:

o it is 'nominal', because the value of the foreign currency is expressed in terms of money, that is, the domestic currency, while
o the rate is 'bilateral', because it concerns the value of one currency against a specific other currency.

However, the nominal bilateral exchange rate is less appropriate for other purposes such as assessing the position of one currency among many other currencies in the world. For example, after its introduction did the euro fall only against the US dollar, or was its weakness a worldwide phenomenon? Changes in the nominal exchange rate affect the international competitiveness of the countries involved in that exchange rate, but despite that the nominal exchange rate itself offers only limited information in relation to these countries' competitive positions. For that reason, different measures of the strength of a currency have been developed for these purposes: *effective* (as opposed to bilateral) and *real* (as opposed to nominal) exchange rates.

The *nominal effective exchange rate* of a currency is a weighted average of several nominal bilateral exchange rates of that currency against several other currencies, reflecting the relative importance of specific international economic relations. For example, the exchange rate between the yen and the dollar is likely to be a very important factor given the volume of trade between these two economies. Different measures are defensible in calculating the weighted average of several nominal bilateral rates: the value of exports to trading partners, the value of imports, and the sum of import plus export values are possible alternatives for weighting. This means that different effective exchange rates may be produced for the same currency. It is clear from the above analysis that the weighting procedure helps to make the effective rates less volatile than the bilateral rates of which it is composed.

The nominal exchange rate is of only limited value as an indicator of the competitiveness of the firms in the country in question. Of course, the devaluation of a currency makes the goods and services produced by a country cheaper in relation to those produced in the rest of the world. However, if this reduction in the currency's value is a response to the high inflation rate in that country, the change in the nominal exchange rate serves only to compensate for that earlier worsening of its competitive position. This already shows that the exchange rate tells us far more about the country's competitiveness when considered in conjunction with price developments at home and abroad. Real exchange rates, which combine the nominal exchange rate with these prices, are therefore constructed to indicate this competitive position.

In practice, the *real exchange rate* is calculated as the nominal exchange rate (being the price of a foreign currency in terms of the domestic currency) multiplied by the price level in the foreign country and divided by the price level in the home country. These three variables are expressed as index numbers. The real exchange rate itself is then also an index number. An increase of this real exchange rate implies an improvement of international competitiveness of the home country, through either a more expensive foreign currency or more expensive foreign goods in foreign currency prices relative to domestic goods in domestic currency prices.

In the case of the real exchange rate of the yen against the pound, for example, with Japan being the home country, the nominal bilateral exchange rate in terms of the number of yen per pound is multiplied by the price level in the UK and divided by the price level in Japan. The numerator then comprises the product of the nominal rate and the price level in the UK, or the UK price level converted to yen. The denominator consists purely of the Japanese price level in yen. Thus, the numerator and the denominator provide a direct comparison (in the same currency) of the price levels in the two countries and, hence, their relative attractiveness as suppliers of goods and services for the consumers worldwide. If this real exchange rate increases then the competitiveness of Japan improves in comparison with Britain, and vice versa.

Like the nominal exchange rate, the real exchange rate can be employed in both a bilateral and an effective version. The real bilateral rate is a useful indicator of the tendency of a country's competitiveness relative to one other specific country. As regards a country's competitive position in general, the real effective exchange rate is the best indicator. Chapter 16 will offer the opportunity to look at the nominal and real exchange rates for the major currencies in the world over a considerable length of time.

11.7 Summary

1. In this chapter we saw that the balance of payments is closely related to both the foreign-exchange market and the exchange rate. Each international transaction is entered into the balance of payments and is also mirrored on the foreign-exchange market, thereby affecting the price on this market: the exchange rate. In practice, an international transaction often evokes spontaneously another international transaction of the same size. This second transaction, which is also booked on the balance of payments, offsets the effect of the first transaction on the foreign-exchange market, and in so doing cancels out the exchange rate effect of the first transaction. A well-known example of such a 'spontaneous' offsetting transaction is the provision of an export credit.

2. We discovered that a country's balance of payments is of interest because it provides useful information about the country's international economic position and its economic relationships with the rest of the world. Diagnosis of the balance-of-payments imbalances may give indications of whether the country's external position is in a healthy state or if some kind of corrective action is necessary. As economies tend to grow, figures on balance-of-payments imbalances are much more informative for economic analysis if they are related to a scale variable indicating the country's economic size, such as the value of its domestic gross production (GDP).

3. It is the sub-accounts of the balance of payments that provide useful information for economic policy-making. A current account imbalance results in a change in the country's net international wealth position. This is because a current account surplus is, by definition, associated with a deficit on the capital and/or financial account. A financial account deficit means that there has been a net inflow of foreign financial assets (associated with a net outflow of payments for these assets) and, therefore, an increase in the country's financial wealth to the same amount. A current account surplus also means that the country exports more than it imports. So, it produces more than it consumes, investing the lower than possible expenditures in financial wealth: a nest egg. A surplus on the current account is therefore not an unqualified advantage.

4. The basic balance is the combination of the current account balance and the balance of long-term international capital flows. These comprise the country's most stable international activities. In contrast, short-term international capital flows and changes in reserve assets holdings are usually much more volatile. The basic balance provides useful knowledge about the longer-term equilibrium value of the exchange rate. A basic balance surplus points to an undervalued currency, but it does not constitute solid proof.

5. The balance of the (official) reserve assets account is usually considered to be the balance of a country's international transactions. It is here that we can discover possible tensions in the country's exchange rate system, because that balance is usually the residual of the combined imbalance of the current, capital, and financial accounts. The use of official reserve assets shows that the monetary authorities are not satisfied with the exchange rate level that would be necessary to counter that combined imbalance.

6. From the viewpoint of the policy-maker, equilibrium on the official reserve assets account is, therefore, an indication of balance of payments equilibrium. If, however, at the same time the current account balance or the basic balance is unsustainably large, this is a violation of the equilibrium. The critical values for these imbalances are country-specific and depend upon the stage of development, the state of the economy, and the structure of the population pyramid: in particular, a rich country where high

productivity investments have been used in the past, that is in the low of a business cycle, and with an ageing population, is expected to have a substantial current account surplus.

7. This means that if a country has a surplus on the current account, the complaints of other countries about unfair competition are certainly not always justified.
8. The foreign-exchange market consists of a customer part and a much larger interbank part. In recent decades, the daily turnover in the foreign-exchange market has grown enormously, despite its decline at the beginning of the present millennium following the introduction of the euro.
9. There are different exchange rates in the foreign-exchange market for a buyer or seller of a foreign currency as a result of the presence of the bid ask spread. Trade in banknotes has by far the largest spread, followed by foreign-exchange trade with bank customers through their demand deposits. By contrast, the spread for interbank foreign-exchange transactions is quite small.
10. An increase in the value of a currency on the foreign-exchange market is neither sufficient nor necessary for an improvement of the country's international competitiveness. This value is a nominal exchange rate. But an increase in the real exchange rate – that is, the price ratio of foreign and domestic goods expressed in one and the same currency, using the nominal exchange rate – does improve the competitive position of the home country.

Questions

1. Indicate how each of the following two international transactions is entered into the UK balance of payments with double-entry bookkeeping:

   (a) A Zimbabwean importer imports £10,000 worth of food from the UK and pays through her deposit in a bank in London.
   (b) The UK government gives £10,000 worth of food aid to Zimbabwe.

2. Explain how world exports can have a larger value than world production.
3. The currency shares for the four major currencies in the reported foreign-exchange turnover for 2010 (in section 11.5) add up to much more than 100 per cent. Explain this phenomenon.
4. For three subsequent years the following information is available about the two neighbour countries A and B. Over time the nominal exchange rate values are 1.00, 1.10, and 1.20, being the price of B's currency in units of A's currency. For the price level of country A the respective index numbers are 100, 108 and 117, while for country B they are 100, 102 and 105.

   (a) Determine the value of the real exchange rate between the two countries for the three years.
   (b) For which country did competitiveness in terms of the real exchange rate worsen in this period of three years?

CHAPTER 12

International Capital Flows

12.1   Introduction

The earlier chapters of this book dealt with the international flows of goods and services, as well as the cross-border movement of factors of production. However, the key global economic data presented in Chapter 2 and the extent of the daily turnover in the forex market, detailed in the previous chapter, demonstrate that the international trade in goods, services, and production factors is only a small part of the total value of international transactions.

In April 2007, for example, the average daily volume of trading on all foreign-exchange (or forex) markets in the world was some $3210 billion, of which only $64 billion (or about 2 per cent) was for the payment of international trade in goods and services. This meant that more than 98 per cent of forex market turnover were related to international capital movements and not strictly to international trade in goods and services.

This may seem surprising, in view of the predominance usually given to international trade in goods. This attention is observable not only in the media reporting on imports and exports, and the political interest in national competitiveness in international trade; it is also apparent in the emphasis on trade in goods in the theory of international economics. This is undoubtedly due in part to the importance of the export of goods and services for the achievement of essential economic objectives, such as economic growth and employment, and the fact that, historically, trade in goods was of far greater quantitative significance in the recent past. Another reason is that more thorough, theoretical explanations of international trade, relative to international capital flows, are available.

At first sight, it might appear that the value of international capital flows is a relatively insignificant aspect of balance-of-payments accounting, as presented in the previous chapter. This is because, in contrast to the trade in goods and services, the balance-of-payments statistics normally show *net* flows of capital – that is, the difference between capital outflows and inflows. International capital flows are in fact the other side, the payment side, of international trade in financial assets, such as bank accounts, bonds, and stocks.

One important distinction in the case of cross-border capital flows is that between *short-term* and *long-term* capital flows. The dividing line between the short and the long term is usually drawn at a maturity of one year, measured at the time of the issue of the asset. For example, the acquisition of a time deposit in a foreign bank for three months is a short-term international capital transaction (a capital outflow), whereas the sale of a five-year bond issued by a foreign government, with a residual maturity of less than one year, is classed as a long-term international capital transaction (a capital inflow), as is the sale of shares of a foreign firm. Here, the acquisition and sales are assumed to be carried out by a home country's resident.

Another important distinction in respect of international capital flows relates to the *motives* underlying the flows. Where an international goods transaction is financed through the use of credit, there is a clear incentive to conclude the goods transaction in question. The provision of such credit tends to increase the chance of the transaction coming to fruition. Both the importer and the exporter may decide to offer credit. Outstanding credit implies a claim. Any change in the state of a country's international claims, or in other words in its position as an international creditor, is, by definition, accompanied by an international capital transaction on the balance of payments.

In addition to the international capital movements connected with the financing of international transactions relating to goods, there are also international capital movements for the purpose of profitable (usually short-term) arbitrage and speculation and (usually long-term) international portfolio investment and foreign direct investment (FDI).

The source of an international arbitrage capital flow is a difference in prices or rates of return of similar financial assets in two countries when the prices and rates of return are known. By contrast, in the case of an international speculative capital flow one of the prices is unknown, but the investor has an expectation of its value.

We speak of an international portfolio investment if a country's resident acquires time deposits in a bank, bonds or stocks of another country. Portfolio investment in foreign shares is similar to FDI, but there is an essential difference, as has already been noted (see p. 198). In the case of a portfolio investment the return on the stocks is paramount, while in the case of direct investment the primary consideration is the active participation in the decision-making process conferred by the ownership of stocks. So the aim through the newly acquired stocks is to (partly) control the firm, to act as an entrepreneur. In the case of FDI, the entrepreneur's motive is clearly to internationalize production. The reasons why such an entrepreneur might wish to operate internationally through foreign direct investments have already been outlined in Section 4.6.

This chapter will discuss international capital flows in more detail, and will focus in particular on the following questions:

o How is trade credit provided?
o What are the various motives for other international investments and, more specifically, for the different types of international investments that we identify?
o What are the motives and incentives that a country's government can use to influence the direction and/or level of international capital flows? In practice, governments appear both to curb and to foster capital inflows into their countries, as well as sometimes to curb capital outflows.
o How are international capital markets – the intermediaries of international capital flows – organized?

The significance of these questions is made clear in Box 12.1.

Box 12.1   Gasunie's credits and cash balances

Gasunie is a Dutch company with its head offices in Groningen, the Netherlands. Its shareholders consist of the Dutch government and two multinational oil companies, Shell and Esso.

Gasunie has a monopoly over the sale of Dutch natural gas to customers in the Netherlands, and also in countries such as Germany, Belgium, France, and Italy.

In the context of international capital movements, the first choice facing Gasunie is whether or not it will provide export credit for its customers in other countries. The objective is to promote its natural gas sales by permitting its customers to postpone payments for any gas they have received. If Gasunie decides to do so, the Netherlands will have a temporary capital outflow alongside each gas export transaction, both of the same value. The former gives rise to a capital account entry on the debit side and, simultaneously, increases the claims of Gasunie, and thus the Dutch economy, on other countries.

Gasunie must then decide what to do with the receipts when the payments come in after the expiry of the export credits. Of course, the company incurs production costs, and has to cover these through use of part of the incoming payments. That is why in the past a proportion of the foreign receipts was immediately converted into Dutch guilders. Since the beginning of 1999, when the Netherlands, as a member state of the Economic and Monetary Union (EMU) in Europe adopted the euro as its legal currency, this conversion is still hardly necessary, as almost all Gasunie customers are located in countries that have also adopted the euro.

However, Gasunie makes substantial profits, much of which eventually goes to its shareholders. In the meantime, however, Gasunie has a substantial cash balance, which should, of course, be invested as efficiently as possible.

The question now is whether or not there is any advantage in investing at least part of the cash abroad. If the answer is yes, the next question is what form of investment and in what country (and currency) will secure the best return. Gasunie has first to decide on the length of the period for which to invest the cash balance. The choice ranges between keeping the foreign currency safe in a foreign bank account for several days and buying shares in another company, with a very uncertain future value.

Several factors need to be taken into account in any assessment of short-term investments:

1. Interest rates can differ significantly from one country to another.
2. An asset denominated in a foreign currency entails the risk of that currency depreciating against the euro, but also the benefit of an appreciation.
3. The nominal value of the asset involved may change, expressed in the local currency, even if the investment period is short – unless it is a foreign bank deposit.

For an assessment of longer-term investments the same factors hold, but with a different stress. The currency risk and price risk, respectively factors 2 and 3, are then more important. Regarding factor 1 – the expected rate of return – for longer-term investments, the dividend (on stocks) will play a much more important role.

In other words, when looking to invest its cash balance Gasunie faces a wide range of choices. It is therefore extremely useful to have sufficient insights and information about the determining factors of the expected rates of return associated with the different choices.

This chapter is structured as follows. As stated in Box 12.1, the motive for granting trade credit is to facilitate exports. In view of the practical importance of trade credit, it is useful to consider its technique (Section 12.2). Following this, there will be a discussion of the motives for arbitrage, speculation, and portfolio investment internationally. In contrast to the two other forms of international capital transaction – trade credit and the financing of foreign direct investment – these are purely financial transactions. These are discussed, successively, in Sections 12.3, 12.4 and 12.5. Section 12.6 focuses on government interference in international capital movements. Finally, Section 12.7 describes the truly international money and capital markets and international financial centres which have developed, partly as a response to this government interference.

12.2 Trade credit

The most common form of trade credit is an *export credit*, which is the international equivalent of supplier credit. In this situation the exporter arranges credits in favour of the importer to accompany the export transaction. In practice, this means that the importer need not pay for goods and services until a certain period after they have been delivered. Instead of the payment, the exporter receives a claim on the importer, which is made concrete through a *bill of exchange* drawn by the exporter on the importer.

The bill of exchange is a written payment order, accepted by the importer and held by the exporter. Under such an arrangement, the importer implicitly meets the costs of finance, as the total amount of the bill of exchange is equal to the price of the goods or services bought plus the interest costs chargeable until the due date of the bill of exchange.

The function of the bill of exchange is to make the credit negotiable:

1. Exporters sells the bill of exchange to their bank, which then discounts the bill. In this way the exporters receive their money immediately. This is the face value of the bill, but minus the discount (the interest component of the bill).
2. The bank keeps the bill in its portfolio until the due date, the date on which the importer has to redeem the credit. This payment of the importer is, of course, made to the holder of the bill of exchange at the moment of payment – in our case the exporter's bank – in return for the bill of exchange.

In the case of export credit we have a remarkable phenomenon: an international capital transaction, namely the provision of export credit, that does not actually lead to an international flow of money or, indeed, a transaction on the forex market. Yet the capital transaction is recorded on the balance of payments. So is this an exception to the rule that, in principle, each balance-of-payments entry must be accompanied by a transaction on the forex market? The answer is 'no'. In this case two international transactions take place simultaneously, in opposite directions and between the two same parties (exporter and importer). Both of these transactions are recorded on the balance of payments, but they cancel one another out exactly on the forex market. It is as if the payment for the export transaction is channelled back directly in the form of a payment for the claim (or the financial asset). There is no net payment at the moment of delivery of the goods, and therefore no transaction on the forex market. In fact, this case is similar to the second case illustrated in the previous chapter in Case study 11.2. Naturally, there are new consequences for both the balance of payments and the forex market once the export credit is redeemed.

It is not always the exporter who provides the importer with a trade credit; the reverse is also possible, and in this instance this is termed an import credit. In this instance the exporter obtains what is known as a buyer's or customer's credit from the importer. This transaction occurs frequently in the case of goods that take a long time to produce – such as aircraft or ships. After the conclusion of the sales contract, the exporter commences production, with financial support from the importer in the form of credit.

One very common form of short-term buyer's credit is known as documentary credit. In this sense 'short term' means a maximum of two years until maturity. A foreign bank often supplies this credit by order of the importer. It takes the form of a bill of exchange drawn by the exporter on the bank opening the credit. This bank is prepared to accept the bill of exchange against the assignment of the documents that stand for the goods (such as bills of lading, insurance certificates, and invoices). Such a bill of exchange accepted by a bank (known as a bank acceptance) can be discounted easily.

In the case of a *confirmed* credit there is agreement between a foreign bank *and* a bank in the exporter's country, whereby the latter bank will pay the exporter as soon as it receives the documents. For the exporter, the advantage of this arrangement is the elimination of the risk that payment might not be possible – for example, if the importer's country introduces restrictions on international capital outflows. The exporter's bank charges the exporter a confirmation commission for its payment guarantee.

For the medium term (two to five years) and the long term (more than five years) one interesting and useful variant of export financing is cross-border leasing. Under such an arrangement the exporter remains the legal owner of the export good until the end of the lease period – that is, until the final payment. This is particularly useful for goods with a long economic lifetime and if the importer is financially weak. In effect, the periodic payments are obtained from the use of the good.

12.3   Arbitrage and the forward exchange rate

At first glance, arbitrage and speculation behaviour appear very similar, since the object of each activity is to make a profit from the price difference of similar assets. Specifically, an arbitrager acts on the basis of a price difference that is *certain* at a particular moment in time. In contrast, a speculator operates on the basis of a price difference that is expected, and thus is *un*certain, because one of the prices is a future one. This section will explore arbitrage through the forex market, while the next section will describe speculation through the same market.

Let us begin with a simple example of *foreign-exchange* (or *forex*) *arbitrage*. In this instance a profit is made on the basis of a simultaneous currency price differential on two forex markets. Say, the euro costs 1.4 US dollars on the forex market in Frankfurt and at the same time 1.407 on the forex market in New York. This means that the euro is $(1.407 - 1.4)/1.4*100\% = 0.5\%$ more expensive in New York. In such circumstances it is profitable to spend 1.4 dollar to buy one euro in Frankfurt and sell that euro immediately in New York for 1.407. This double transaction yields the 0.5 per cent rate of return.

This example of forex arbitrage prompts two questions:

o How do we get the euros so quickly from Frankfurt to New York?
o Do we not need to take account of the costs of the two transactions (in Frankfurt and New York)?

Today, speed is no longer a problem. This type of transaction is usually conducted almost instantaneously via telephone and through banks' interlinked computer screens. Thus, the transactions can be completed within a very short time (at most a few minutes).

The transaction costs are banking costs; and they are in fact an important cost item for non-bank private individuals. By contrast, banking departments have only negligible transaction costs, and so they are able to exploit arbitrage opportunities to the full.

As a result of the actions of forex arbitragers, there will be only one worldwide euro–dollar exchange rate. This is because in our example those banks conducting arbitrage operations will buy large amounts of euros in Frankfurt. They will then immediately sell the whole of that amount in New York. These traded amounts will have their effect on prices: in response to this arbitrage activity, the price of the euro will rise in Frankfurt and fall in New York through the process of demand and supply. These price movements will not come to an end until the euro prices (expressed in dollars) are the same on both forex markets. Until that happens, there is still scope for a profit and the banks will enlarge their foreign-exchange arbitrage.

Since the banks have negligible arbitrage costs, prices are actually identical down to several figures after the decimal point. As soon as a larger price differential is imminent, the banks go back into action to restore equal prices via the prospect of an arbitrage profit followed by an actual arbitrage transaction. Of course, this analysis assumes that there is a free and unrestricted forex market between the two countries involved – that the two currencies are fully *convertible*. Foreign-exchange restrictions, on the other hand, hinder the movement of the two currencies across national borders and, thus, cause international differences in one and the same exchange rate.

One variant of forex arbitrage is *cross-currency arbitrage*, also known as inter-market *triangular arbitrage*. This occurs in a situation involving three currencies if the direct exchange rate between two currencies differs from the indirect exchange rate between these currencies that exists in terms of their individual exchange rates with the third currency. A so-called 'round-trip' of currency exchanges, starting and finishing with the same currency, then gives a positive return. This arbitrage can even be executed in one forex market. Illustration 12.2 gives an example of this form of forex arbitrage.

Box 12.2   Triangular arbitrage

Assume the following exchange rates in the forex market of London at the same moment:

1 US dollar = 1 euro
1 pound sterling = 1.5 euro
1 pound sterling = 1.6 US dollar

These values have been chosen in order to simplify the calculation and improve the insight that can be obtained. The two exchange rates of the pound imply an indirect exchange rate value of 1 US dollar = 1.5/1.6 euro – that is, less than the 1 euro of the direct exchange rate. It is evident that the dollar is relatively expensive to the euro in their direct exchange rate. This explains why the profit-making triangular arbitrage starts with a dollar *sale* in the dollar-euro market.

The arbitrager substitutes the euro for the dollar in the dollar-euro market and, subsequently, goes from the euro to the pound and, finally, from the pound back to the dollar. Starting with the sale of, say, 1.5 dollar, the profit of one round-trip (1.5 dollar → 1.5 euro → 1 pound → 1.6 dollar) is 0.1 dollar (or 0.1 dollar per 1.5 dollar, that is 6.66 per cent).

> The three transactions that complete the round-trip have an effect on all three exchange rates. Through these changes in supply and demand, the right-hand sides of the three exchange rates presented above will change: the first value will go down, the second value will rise, and the third value will fall. All the changes contribute to an equality of the direct and indirect exchange rates between the dollar and the euro.

Interest arbitrage is another variant of forex arbitrage. It is based on a difference between the rates of return on similar interest-bearing investments available at the same moment on different markets. These rates of return are known; that makes it an arbitrage transaction.

Assume, for example, that the interest rate on a one-year investment in pounds in London is 3 per cent and at the same moment the interest rate on a similar one-year investment in dollars in New York is 5 per cent. Leaving aside transaction costs, at first glance it appears advantageous to convert all intended UK investments into investments in New York. However, the actual situation is not as clear as this since at the start of the period it is necessary to buy dollars in exchange for pounds and at the end of the period it is necessary to convert the dollars that will be released back into pounds. If we knew that there would be no change in the dollar/pound exchange rate during this period then it would indeed be advantageous to shift the investments to New York.

The outcome of the interest arbitrage would be very different if it were known in advance that the value of the dollar in pounds would fall by 2 per cent over the course of the investment period. This would exactly offset the initial profitability of the arbitrage. The arbitrager will then be indifferent about the choice of the investment location. She will even prefer the investment in London as soon as the decline in the pound value of the dollar exceeds the interest differential of 2 per cent. The interest rate advantage in New York is then insufficient to offset the exchange rate loss on the dollar. The opposite is true if the decline in the value of the dollar is less than 2 per cent.

The above review of the points considered in interest arbitrage means that the arbitrager compares the interest rate in London with the interest rate on a comparable investment in New York plus the percentage change in the dollar against the pound during the investment period. One important point needs to be clarified at this point: the exchange rate of the dollar against the pound at the end of the investment period is, of course, not known at the start of the intended investment. The arbitrager can only guess; she will probably have expectations about what will happen. However, such expectations cannot form part of the arbitragers deliberations because an arbitrager works – by definition – on the basis of known prices.

The arbitrager, however, is able to avoid this undesirable exchange rate uncertainty by using the forward foreign-exchange market. In general, the forward market is a market in which a product is traded but not delivered until a future date, although the price of the product is already fixed at the time that the contract is concluded. So, at the start of the investment, the investor already knows the exchange rate that the forward investment currency sold will fetch. There is a forward forex market for various periods. For instance, in the case of the trade in US dollars there are forward markets with delivery of the currency after 1, 2, 3, 6, 12, and 24 months. The exchange rate on these markets is named the forward exchange rate. If the forward dollar is more expensive than the spot dollar (the dollar delivered immediately, so on the spot market – although, in practice, delivery takes two working days), then the dollar is being traded at a *premium* in the forward market. In the opposite case the forward dollar is at a *discount*.

Thus, in calculating the return on the investment in New York in the above example, the arbitrager now has the opportunity to replace the percentage change in the dollar relative to the pound by the percentage at which the forward dollar is at either a premium or a discount. In this manner the interest arbitrager can secure complete certainty about the total returns on investments.

The previous investment example implies that the equilibrium condition for the interest arbitrager is that the interest rate in one country (say, the home country) is equal to the interest rate in another country (say, the foreign country) plus the forward premium on the currency of the latter country, its exchange rate being expressed in units of the currency of the former country. The type and maturity of the investment in the two countries must, of course, be identical in principle. This equilibrium condition is known as the *covered interest parity*, with the term 'covered' expressing the fact that the use of the forward market insures (or 'covers') the transaction against the exchange rate risk. Expressed as a formula, the covered interest parity is:

$$i = i^* + (F - E)/E. \ 100, \tag{12.1}$$

where i and i^* represent the domestic and foreign interest rates (in percentages) and F and E the exchange rates on the forward and spot exchange markets, respectively, in terms of the domestic currency price of the foreign currency. The multiplication by 100 makes that all the three terms in the equality are percentages. The two investments and the forward transaction relate to the same time span.[1]

If the markets concerned are free, any deviation from the covered interest parity appears to prompt such activities of arbitragers that the deviation disappears. It will be illustrated by means of our previous numerical example. Let us assume that with the interest rates of 3 and 5 per cent in London and New York, respectively, the forward rate of the dollar is the same as the present spot rate. In this example let the UK be the home country and the USA the foreign country. In this situation it is profitable for the arbitrager to transfer the investment to New York. This shift creates additional demand for dollars on the spot market, and hence an increase in the value of the dollar and thus in E, the spot rate in terms of units of pounds per dollar. At the same time, the investment in the USA causes an additional supply of dollars on the forward market, and hence a fall in the forward value of the dollar and thus in F, the forward rate in terms of units of pounds per dollar. As a result of these two price movements, the forward dollar starts to be at a discount; in other words, $(F - E)$ becomes negative.

These developments make investment in the USA a less attractive proposition: in equation (12.1) the right-hand side, which records the interest rate plus exchange rate gain on a dollar investment, decreases. The arbitrager, however, only ceases to transfer additional investments from Frankfurt to New York if the covered interest parity again applies. That is, as soon as the discount on the forward dollar has increased to 2 per cent. Only at this point will the interest rate advantage that made investment in the USA more attractive disappear. Until this situation occurs, the exchange rate changes continue. (In this example, effects of the investment flow on interest rates are neglected, but these effects would also contribute to the attainment of interest parity.)

It should be emphasized that the covered interest parity only applies as an equilibrium condition if the transaction costs for the arbitragers are negligibly small. Again, it is only banks that can satisfy this condition approximately, so it is banks that operate as interest arbitragers. Figures show that the covered interest parity does actually apply in practice for convertible currencies.

---

[1] In equation (12.1) the equality is an approximation of the covered interest parity, as a small term on the right hand sight is neglected, namely the exchange rate gain on the interest yield earned during the investment period.

12.4 | Speculation

As with arbitrage, the motive for speculation is a price differential on different markets for the same product. But in the event of speculation – in contrast to arbitrage – the two prices relate to different moments in time, with at least one future (and therefore expected) and, thus, uncertain price. The essential characteristic of a speculator is that she adopts an open or uncovered position, meaning that she runs the risk of an adverse change in the price of her object of speculation.

Let us take an example: a foreign-exchange speculator buys euros at $1.4 in the expectation that the euro will appreciate to $1.407 in one month's time. If her euro assets are now larger than her euro liabilities, the speculator has an *open position* – or *exposure* – in euros.

This exposure may result in an exchange rate gain, but also a loss.

o If the exchange rate after one month comes up to the speculator's expectation, her profit will be 0.007 dollar, or 0.5 per cent.
o If, on the other hand, one month later the euro appears to be worth only 1.393 dollars, then the foreign-exchange speculator can only sell the euro at a loss of 0.007 dollars per euro or 0.5 per cent.

The above calculation of speculation profit is incomplete. In this example, the foreign-exchange speculator will, as in the case of the interest arbitrager, also take account of the interest rate differential during the exposure period in determining the anticipated profit. Obviously, the euros purchased will be invested in order to earn interest over the next month. Equally, a decision to continue holding dollars would have meant that these would be invested at the interest rate applicable to a one-month dollar investment. This means that the economic variables considered by the forex speculator can be much the same as those for the interest arbitrager. The only difference is that where the arbitrager looks at the forward exchange rate, the speculator focuses on her expectation about the exchange rate on the spot market at the end of the investment period.

It is, therefore, unsurprising that the equilibrium condition for the forex speculator is also expressed as an interest parity, but it is now the *uncovered interest parity* rather than the covered interest parity. The premium on the foreign currency is thus replaced by the expected percentage change in the value of that currency. Expressed as a formula, the uncovered interest parity is:

$$i = i^* + (E^e - E)/E. \ 100, \tag{12.2}$$

where E^e is the expected exchange rate, while the other symbols have the same meaning as in equation (12.1). (Note 1 also applies to this equation.)

One phenomenon that has become increasingly prevalent since 2000 is *carry trade*. This is speculation based on borrowing funds in a country with a low interest rate, and investing the funds in a country with a higher interest rate. As long as the exchange rate for the two currencies involved in carry trade is not fixed irrevocably, the carry trader bears exchange rate risk, fully according to equation (12.2). In the event of carry trade, the left-hand side expresses the borrowing costs, while the right-hand side shows the return on lending, including the expected exchange rate profit (which can, of course, be negative). One of the most popular channels for carry trade in the past few years has been: borrowing in Japan (with quite low interest rates) and lending in Australia (with relatively high interest rates). In the summer of 2007, when Japan increased its interest rates, part of this carry trade was stopped. Apparently, the convergence of the interest rates made it too risky to stay in Australian dollar positions. Traders returned to the yen, repaying their Japanese loans, and, in response, the yen rose in value on the forex market.

In our discussion to date we have assumed that the forex speculator buys on the present spot market and reverses this transaction on a spot market in the future, which means that the speculator must have access to the necessary financial resources. This limitation on the scale of the speculator's activities is much less relevant if the speculator conducts his activities via the forward exchange market, instead of the current spot market.

This can be made clear by an example: Let us assume that the euro rate on the forward exchange market for delivery in one month is $1.4 – equal to the present spot rate in our earlier example. If the foreign-exchange speculator expects the euro exchange rate on the spot market to be $1.407 in one month's time, it is profitable for her to buy euros on the forward exchange market now for the purpose of selling them again immediately on the spot market at maturity. Her expected profit is $\{(1.407-1.400)/1.4\}.100 = 0.5$ per cent.

The advantage of this kind of foreign-exchange speculation through the forward market is that the speculator does not need to hold substantial cash balances. The two transactions are so close together (in one month's time) that the dollars obtained by selling the euros on the spot market can be used to pay the dollar price of the euros on the forward exchange market.

In practice, however, the financial market – in this case the bank that carries out the forward transaction for the speculator – usually requires the speculator to pay a certain amount by way of security. But this will be much less than 100 per cent of the value of the forward transaction. This means that speculators can use the money holdings at their disposal in order to speculate for many times that amount through the forward market. This implies that they increase their leverage substantially. If we assume that the bank requires a deposit of 20 per cent of the size of the forward transaction as collateral, then the speculator is able to speculate to a maximum amount of five times of her money holdings – in this case her leverage is five.

Banks are not meant to engage in foreign-exchange speculation. That is an essential difference compared to interest and forex arbitrage, which are conducted almost exclusively by banks. The reason is that arbitrage is based on certainties; in the case of speculation, that is uncertainty: the profits can be huge, but so can the losses. A central bank, which exercises supervision over the commercial banks, does not therefore permit banks to pursue conscious forex speculation. Of course, this does not mean that, at the end of a working day, a commercial bank has normally covered its foreign-exchange position in full. In practice, full coverage is almost a technical impossibility, although commercial banks are required to keep their uncovered position at relatively low levels. Forex exposure should, in fact, only result from the bank's day-to-day activities on behalf of customers.

12.5 Portfolio diversification

If one has financial resources which one does not wish to use for immediate expenditure, investment of these resources is an attractive opportunity because of the expected rate of return. This investment can be made either in interest-bearing assets or in stocks. The safest variant is through a bank account on which interest is paid, offering complete certainty about the return, while the value of the investment (the principal) is not liable to change. In the international context a bank account may still bear uncertainty if its unit of account is a foreign currency. This uncertainty increases when bonds or shares are used as investment opportunities. The values of these assets may vary substantially, because they are determined daily by the interaction of supply and demand on the stock exchange. Moreover, in the case of shares the annual remittance, the dividend, is also uncertain.

The investors' uncertainty in respect of the rate of return on financial assets is what we term *risk*. This return consists of both the interest or dividend payment and the change in the market value of the asset in which investment has been made (including the change in the investment currency). Given some degree of risk aversion on the part of investors, they require compensation for these uncertainties. On average, risk-averse investors want to receive a higher rate of return on risky financial assets than on investments with a certain rate of return. That such differences are, indeed, perceivable in a comparison of the long-term rates of return on stocks, bonds, and bank deposits underscores the idea that investors tend to be risk-averse.

One of the most commonly used techniques for the reduction of risk is the diversification of the investment portfolio. The aim of this is to invest in such a combination of financial assets that the risks of the individual assets offset one another to a certain extent, something that may happen without impairing the rate of return on the investment. The diversification effect may arise if, for example, two business sectors tend to have opposite cyclical trends: if one shows an increasing growth, then the other is probably decreasing in growth. In this circumstance it can be attractive to include stocks from those two sectors in one investment portfolio. This will moderate fluctuations over time in the return of the portfolio relative to those of the individual assets.

In order to examine the size of the gains of portfolio diversification in practice one needs to choose quantitative indicators for risk and risk-offsetting. Under the influence of the pathbreaking, seminal work of Markowitz (1959) and Tobin (1958), the risk of an asset or portfolio is usually approached by the variance of the rate of return over time and the risk-offsetting power of two assets by the correlation coefficient of their rates of return over time. In statistics the variance of a random variable provides a measure of the spread, or dispersion, of observations around their mean value. The higher the variance, the more risky the asset is supposed to be. It is common in statistics to denote the variance σ^2 and the mean value μ. These symbols explain the alternative name of portfolio diversification: a mean-variance or (μ, σ)-analysis.

In statistics, the correlation coefficient is a measure of the extent of similarity of the movements over time of two variables. The way of construction of the correlation coefficient implies that its value will always lie between $+1$ and -1. A positive correlation between the rates of return of two assets indicates that the two rates of return have a tendency to move in the same direction. In that case risk reduction by means of building a portfolio of the two assets is limited. A negative correlation implies that the two rates of return move in opposite directions, providing opportunities for risk reduction. Portfolio diversification is therefore in the first place a search for financial assets with low or negative correlation between their rates of return as well as, of course, attractively high return levels. Box 12.3 gives a graphic demonstration of the practical advantage of following the mean-variance analysis.

Box 12.3   The influence of the correlation coefficient on portfolio risk

In Figure 12.1 the consequence of changes in the correlation coefficient of rates of return for the opportunity to choose diversified portfolios is illustrated for two assets. The symbol μ_p denotes the average rate of return on the portfolio P that is composed of the two assets A and B. The symbol σ_p is the standard deviation of the rate of return on this portfolio, and r represents the correlation coefficient of the rates of return of the assets A and B. (The standard deviation is the square root of the variance.) The y- and x-coordinates of point A give, respectively, the mean value and the standard deviation of the rate of return of asset A. For point B and asset B the same holds.

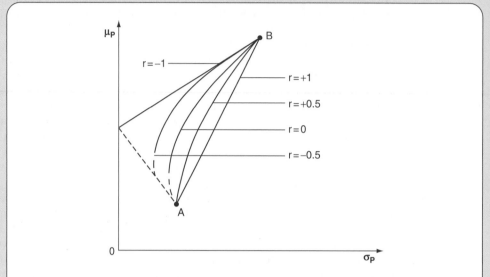

Figure 12.1   Correlation coefficient and portfolio opportunities: an example

This figure shows that if the value of the correlation coefficient is one, all of the portfolios that can be composed of the two investments A and B, through changing shares of the composing assets, are on a straight line between the points A and B.

This is unsurprising. If $r = 1$, the movements of the rates of return of A and B are exactly equal over time. This implies that, in effect, A and B are equal and, thus, perfectly substitutable. If we gradually reduce the proportion of A in the portfolio in favour of B, we follow the straight line from A to B. The investor is able to choose her preferred combination of mean and variance – measured along the vertical and horizontal axes, respectively – somewhere on this line. This preferred combination determines the optimal composition of her investment portfolio as long as $r = 1$.

For a lower value of the correlation coefficient, the line combining the portfolio compositions that are then achievable appears to be to the left of the straight line AB. This shift of the line is actually favourable to the investor, because she can then again realize her preferred mean value of the portfolio, but at a lower portfolio variance, compared with the possible portfolios on the straight line between A and B. The lower the correlation coefficient, the more the line of portfolio compositions that are achievable is bent to the left. This makes the achievable portfolios increasingly attractive, since for a preferred mean value ever-lower variances can be realized. The dashed lines represent inefficient portfolios: the points straight above them are more attractive. The most attractive portfolios are found when the correlation coefficient is -1. This means that the returns on investments A and B show exactly opposite movements: if one return rises, the other falls. The result is maximum stability of the portfolio's rate of return over time. We can see this in the figure at the furthest left position of the line that is indicated by $r = -1$. The point where this line crosses the vertical axis is a very special one: at this point the portions of the investments are in inverse proportion to the standard deviations of their returns, as can be deduced mathematically. All uncertainty regarding the return has then been eliminated.

It is clear from both theoretical and empirical research on investments that the greater the scope for composing a portfolio of more individual investments, the more there can be a reduction of the uncertainty over the return. At this point in the reasoning, it is relevant to introduce *international* portfolio investments. The creation of scope for international portfolio investments increases the number of potential investments and thus promotes a more favourable relationship between the mean value and the variance of the rate of return on the investment portfolio.

But this is not the only point: foreign financial assets quite often behave significantly differently from national investment opportunities in terms of their rates of return. Among the reasons for this are that the business cycle abroad may be in a different phase and production sectors may differ, often substantially, from those present in the investor's home country. These reasons hold in particular for foreign countries that are at different levels of economic development.

This explains why investments in, for instance, emerging countries can be such attractive additions to the investment opportunities of investors in developed countries. The correlations between the rates of return of these investments and those issued in developed countries are usually rather low. As a consequence, these foreign investments can make a strong contribution to portfolio diversification.

It is more difficult to assess the *size* of the positive influence of the option of investments abroad on portfolio diversification. Lessard (1983) carried out one of the first attempts. His starting point was an American investor and her investment in a representative American stock. In a first round of portfolio diversification Lessard allowed the American investor to amass a well-diversified portfolio of only domestic investments. For a given average portfolio return, the standard deviation of the portfolio decreased the larger the number of different stocks in the portfolio. The standard deviation of the rate of return of the portfolio appeared to converge to roughly 50 per cent of the standard deviation of the rate of return of the single, representative American stock. This result was achieved in the case of a well-diversified portfolio containing about 30 or more different American stocks.

In a second round of portfolio diversification Lessard also permitted foreign, so non-American, stocks in the portfolio of the American investor. This resulted in a further potential advantage of portfolio diversification, measured by the effect on the standard deviation of the portfolio return – at the given value of the average value of the rate of return. The standard deviation of the portfolio relative to that of the representative American stock showed a further decline. For a well-diversified portfolio of 30 or more stocks the ratio between the standard deviation of the portfolio's rate of return to the standard deviation of the rate of return of the single, representative American stock converged to around 25 per cent. So, each of the two rounds of portfolio diversification had the effect of about halving the standard deviation of the portfolio, at a given average value of the portfolio's rate of return. This outcome illustrates the substantial gain that can realized by portfolio diversification in general and international diversification in particular.

12.6 | Motives for exchange controls

The previous section describes techniques and motives for international capital flows. The implicit assumption in this description is that these capital flows are free from governmental regulations. However, for long periods of time this was the exception rather than the rule. History is full of examples of countries that have felt it necessary to impose a system of rules on international payments, meaning that the government of such a country regulates the switch over from domestic to foreign currencies (or foreign exchange) and vice versa. The implementation of such *foreign-exchange regulation*, also known as *exchange control*, is usually assigned to the central bank. The home currency of any country that applies foreign-exchange controls is called an *inconvertible currency*.

In practice, such exchange control is a foreign-exchange *restriction*. For those wishing to buy foreign currencies, the effect is that they can buy them only under certain conditions (a quantitative restriction) or at a price that differs from the equilibrium value (a price control). In order to apply stringent forms of exchange controls, the central bank can assume a foreign-exchange monopoly in which private individuals are prevented from holding any foreign exchange. All foreign currencies have then to be handed over to the central bank, which in turn issues exchange permits or announces the rate at which it sells foreign currencies – often for only a particular type of international transaction. In addition to differentiating between different types of transactions, the exchange control may also differentiate between the actions of a country's inhabitants and foreigners. Case study 12.1 gives an example of such an exchange control – in the twilight of the Bretton Woods fixed exchange-rate system (see Section 16.4 for details) – in which the room for foreigners to buy home currencies was temporarily restricted.

Case study 12.1   Bond market reopened to foreigners

'The bond guilder is to go. Last night the finance ministry announced that the government has authorized the Dutch central bank to abolish the 'bond circuit' with effect from tomorrow, 1 February. From now on foreigners will be able to buy Dutch bonds in the normal way.

The idea of the bond guilder dates from September 1971. The intention was to prevent too much foreign capital and money from flowing into the Netherlands when the dollar was weak. Thenceforth, non-residents could only buy Dutch bonds if they could lay their hands on guilders that had resulted from sales of Dutch bonds by other non-residents.

The guilders required for this were known as bond guilders and were more expensive than normal guilders, sometimes by as much as 7 per cent.'

Source: cited in *NRC Handelsblad*, 31 January 1974 (author's translation).

The reason for the exchange controls outlined in Case study 12.1 was the inflow of too many US dollars into the Netherlands at the then fixed exchange rate of the Dutch guilder against the dollar. This inflow disrupted the Dutch government's anti-inflationary monetary policy (see Section 14.6). Exchange controls are more often required because the free convertibility of the national currency into foreign currencies gives rise to the opposite situation: *net* private domestic demand for foreign currencies at the fixed exchange rate. In such circumstances the central bank has to satisfy the net demand by supplying the required currencies from its international monetary reserves. However, these reserves are finite, so that this process cannot continue indefinitely. If nothing changes in the meantime, the country's monetary authorities (usually comprising the finance ministry or treasury and the central bank) have to adjust their economic policy. They then have a choice of three 'evils': devaluation of the national currency, a more restrictive monetary policy or the introduction of exchange controls.

In specifying the exchange control, the central bank can take account of the transaction's priority in the national interest both in issuing exchange permits and in setting a gamut of exchange rates – known as a system of multiple exchange rates. The underlying idea is that foreign currencies are scarce and, thus, these currencies have to be used as effectively as possible. We might imagine that in the case of the import of basic essentials and medicines, an exchange permit will be issued almost automatically, but that a permit will be practically ruled out for the import of a luxury car. If the central bank operates a system of multiple exchange rates, then the foreign currency needed to import essential goods can be obtained cheaply, but that for the importation of the luxury car may be much more expensive (in terms of the national currency).

Clearly, such a form of market intervention will be open to corruption. It is easy for the central bank to favour certain people (this phenomenon is dubbed 'cronyism'), as each forex transaction requires an official decision and the system of foreign currency allocation soon becomes opaque to outsiders.

What are the considerations underlying the introduction of, more specifically, exchange controls on only international capital flows or, in other words, *capital controls*? In defence of the use of capital controls one can point to the protection of the desired combination of a fixed exchange rate with a monetary policy fully directed to national economic policy objectives, as argued above. In addition, a domestic financial system that is still in its infancy asks for capital controls to prevent too severe competition from full-grown foreign financial firms. Capital controls can even be seen as indispensable when the domestic economy is unstable or has insufficiently liberalized markets. In such circumstances an economy may be susceptible to surges in capital inflow but with the threat of later disruptive capital flight or give the wrong economic signals to foreign capital, so that inefficient international capital in- or outflows occur. In Section 18.5 we will explain this problem of the optimal order of stabilization and liberalization of an economy of which liberalization of international capital flows will appear to be the tail.

On top of the previous rationales for capital controls, there is the rationale of prevention of the problem of Dutch disease. This occurs if a country has to deal with a large additional supply of foreign currency on the foreign-exchange market. The cause can be diverse, but should come about to a large extent: a price rise of or foreign demand increase for the main export good(s), the discovery of and subsequent export of a new commodity, an increase of the receipt of foreign financial aid or ... an inflow of private foreign capital. The problem that then arises is dubbed Dutch disease, as it was described for the first time after the Netherlands had discovered a large stock of natural gas in the 1960s and started to export the main part of the gas production.

Though the direct cause of the Dutch disease problem is positive for the country in which it happens (namely a large increase of export values or capital inflows), the further developments are not. The problem is that the large additional supply of foreign currency initiates either an appreciation of the domestic currency or, under fixed exchange rates, an increase of the domestic money supply. The ensuing price rise of the latter will, just like the appreciation, worsen the international competitiveness of domestically produced internationally tradable goods and services. This will hurt domestic production and, thus, employment. This harm will be significant if the earlier changes are large – a typical feature of the Dutch disease problem. These large economic costs are the core of the Dutch disease problem. Now we arrive at the last rationale for capital controls: capital controls may prevent – or at least hinder – the occurrence of the Dutch disease problem if it would be caused by the capital inflow channel.

Capital controls are not cost-free either. Several types of costs are attributed to capital controls:

1. They hinder the optimum allocation of global capital. As we saw in Chapter 4, under certain conditions the thwarting of the optimum worldwide allocation of the production factor capital is at the expense of economic welfare, both for the world as a whole and for the capital exporting and importing countries individually.
2. Capital controls obstruct the risk-diversification process of investors, a desirable behaviour according to Section 12.5.
3. Capital controls prevent foreign competition on domestic financial markets. This can have a particularly negative effect on markets that lack perfect competition. In the absence of perfect competition, the possibility of free international capital inflows will result in lower domestic capital cost, including higher stock prices.
4. Capital controls will – perhaps surprisingly – impede international trade, as capital controls have a negative effect on the provision of trade credits. Even if this kind of credit is consciously excluded from the control measures, in practice it appears difficult to apply a strict watershed between controls on trade credit and other sorts of capital.
5. Capital controls tend to undermine discipline in national economic policy, including the maintenance of the exchange rate at an unsteady low level (an overvaluation of the home currency). Under free international capital flows, a worsening of domestic economic policy or an unbalanced exchange rate policy is immediately 'punished' through capital flight from the country. This danger will make policy-makers cautious in carrying out risky policy.
6. In a regime of capital controls it is tempting to please investors selectively – that is, to conduct cronyism. This undermines national welfare because permits for international capital flows are then led by incentives that do not foster economic efficiency.
7. Finally, capital controls create rent-seeking behaviour among investors: investors tend to spend a lot of time with lobbying activities in favour of import licenses for foreign currency, activities that are not productive at all from a national point of view.

The feasibility of exchange controls is undermined by the likelihood that it will be rather ineffectual if it is used over a longer time span. Today, the financial world in particular stresses the ease with which exchange restrictions can be sidestepped. This would hold especially for capital transactions that are not linked to any real transaction consisting of tangible goods.

12.7   International capital markets and financial centres

Case study 12.2   The birth of eurodollars

The Second World War led to a total disruption in the flow of international payments. Immediately after the war there could therefore be no question of restoring currency convertibility in Europe. In contrast to the position in the USA, the war had put many factories in Europe out of action. It is therefore unsurprising that European demand for products focused heavily on the USA and that Europe was threatened by chronic, substantial deficits on the trade balance. This led to the introduction of exchange restrictions in all West European countries immediately after the war. It was not until 1958, by which time a sufficient balance had been restored in international trade transactions, that many of these countries decided to make their currency convertible for current account transactions. Since the Second World War there have been some notable restrictions on currency convertibility as a result of international capital movements. In the second half of the 1950s the UK still had large trade balance deficits, which threatened the fixed exchange rate of the pound sterling against the US dollar. Although London was the leading international financial centre, with a great deal of international financing still using the pound, the UK government felt that it had to restrict capital exports by London banks, in order to relieve the downward pressure on its currency.

As a result, UK banks were liable to lose a substantial part of their international business. In addition, there were signs in those years that a significant number of non-American investors in the USA would like to convert the dollars that they held in American banks into dollar holdings outside the USA. These were principally East Europeans who were concerned that in the adverse climate of the Cold War their bank deposits in the USA might well be frozen or – worse still – confiscated. This led UK banks and non-American holders of dollars to develop a financial innovation: bank deposits in UK banks, denominated not in the currency of the country in which the bank was located but in US dollars; these deposits were named eurodollars.

The origins of the eurodollar market outlined in Case study 12.2 show that national rules concerning the financial sector, and particularly actual and expected foreign-exchange restrictions, ironically appeared to be major factors in the creation and subsequent growth of this truly unrestricted, international financial market. The innovation was a resounding success. Eurodollars were soon broadened to include dollar deposits held at banks in Europe, since the activities started by the London banks were taken up by banks elsewhere in Europe. In addition, this term quickly became too narrow, because it was only in the initial phase that the banks outside the USA were confined to banks in Europe. Banks elsewhere in the world followed rapidly. And soon it was not just banking deposits in US dollars, as similar activities were quickly developed for other currencies. That is why we talk about the eurocurrency market or even offshore market, rather than the eurodollar market. Claims on banks in foreign currencies ('foreign' from the viewpoint of the bank involved) do not have to be owned by foreigners, as was originally the case with the London banks and the East European account holders. Claims on banks in currencies foreign to the bank and held by residents of the country in which the bank is located, are also deposits in the offshore market.

It is tempting to equate the eurocurrency market with a foreign-exchange market, but there is one significant difference. On a foreign-exchange market currencies are sold for one another. In contrast, in a eurocurrency market each transaction involves only one currency and it is a bank deposit.

Today the offshore positions of banks are part of what the Bank for International Settlements (BIS) calls the *international* positions of banks. They represent bank activities with both foreign customers (in a cross-border transaction) and foreign currencies (a foreign currency from the bank's point of view), and of course a combination of these two. Providing domestic-currency loans to foreign customers is the traditional appearance of international banking activity – as has already been applied for centuries.

The BIS reporting system collects quarterly data on the gross international financial claims and liabilities of banks resident in a given country. At present, they receive reports from 41 countries. The main purpose of the statistics is to provide information on the role of banks and financial centres in the intermediation of international capital flows. According to the BIS, in September 2008 total liabilities in international banking positions amounted to $35,828 billion – almost double the amount at the end of 2003. Of the total liabilities only $10,297 billion were banking liabilities to non-banks, so the lion's share were banking liabilities to other banks. Bank liabilities in foreign currency to residents constituted a relatively small part of total liabilities, namely $4859 billion.

The UK government has long since lifted the restriction on the activities of London banks, which prompted the launch of the eurodollar market. At first sight it is therefore surprising that the eurocurrency market still exists today – and that its volume is so great. Apparently, there were other factors that also stimulated this market. Furthermore, those factors remained when the restrictions on the London banks were lifted. These factors all contributed to attractive levels of the interest rates on the eurocurrency market.

A first factor is that from the start it was not only the *type* of currency that distinguished the eurocurrency market from the domestic money and capital markets. It was also a market for only larger market parties, because transactions were subject to a minimum size of about $1 million. A second factor is that, because of their size, the firms in this market were usually known to the banks, so that there was no need to conduct an extensive check of their creditworthiness. These two features kept the transaction costs for the banks low, as a percentage of the loans. That could be reflected in attractive interest rates on the eurocurrency market for both debtors and creditors. The interest rate at which the banks attracted capital (the deposit rate) could be higher and the rate at which the banks provided credit (the loan rate) could be lower than on the national market for the currency concerned.

A third factor requires a short explanation. In principle, eurodollar trading in London involved two central banks: the Bank of England and the Federal Reserve Board, the system of American central banks. However, the Bank of England's task is to protect the stability of sterling – the dollar is not its concern, nor are the dollar liabilities of UK commercial banks. Conversely, the American central bank has no legal authority to issue instructions to UK commercial banks. This lack of any regulation gave banks greater freedom of action and lower costs regarding their eurodollar activities – but, of course, also added risk to the Eurodollar positions to a certain extent. This is the third reason why interest rates in this market could be so attractive. Finally, a fourth factor is that the banks are not tied to any specific location for their activities on this market, or only to a very minor degree. This enabled them to take account of tax advantages in choosing that location, such as in the famous – and low-tax – offshore centres. The banks were able to pass on these advantages (in part) to customers in the form of more advantageous interest rates.

The previous description concerns the money market segment of the eurocurrency market. Where longer-term interest-bearing securities are concerned, there has been a development comparable to that for bank borrowing and lending activities. The regulations of the national bond markets led to the development of *international bonds*, which are bonds issued outside the country of the issuer. In contrast, the usual domestic bonds are issued in the country of residence of the issuer. International bonds are divided into:

- *foreign bonds*, which are issued in one country only and denominated in that country's currency; and
- *eurobonds*, which are issued in several national markets simultaneously.

The currency in which eurobonds are denominated is a foreign currency for all these countries. The motive behind the choice to issue international bonds, instead of domestic bonds, is essentially the same as those underlying the uncovered interest parity in equation 12.2, except that the interest rates and exchange rate expectations in case of bond issues are long-term variables.

Foreign bonds are not a recent financial innovation: international bond loans have been issued in this form for centuries. For example, the financing of US railways with European money was carried out in this manner.

While the issue of foreign bonds is still subject to some rules imposed by the country in which they are issued, that is no longer the case for eurobonds. This illustrates the similarity between eurobonds and positions on the eurocurrency market. In principle, of course, there is still the difference in the way the interest rate is fixed and in the repayment obligation, a difference that also applies to domestic bonds vis-à-vis domestic bank loans. A bond has a fixed rate of interest, while repayment does not take place until the end of the bond's life. In contrast, a loan usually has a variable rate of interest and is repaid in installments over a predetermined period.

In practice, the gap between eurobonds and eurocurrencies is filled by the introduction of *floating rate notes* (FRNs), which are also known as medium-term notes, or euronotes. These are medium-term eurobonds with a variable rate of interest, based on a reference interest value such as LIBOR (the London Interbank Offered Rate), plus a certain mark-up, the spread. This spread serves to cover the bank's costs and risk. The amount of international bonds and notes outstanding was $22,715 billion in December 2008. Issued by residents in the developed countries, it amounted to $19,789 billion, leaving only a very small amount for residents in developing countries.

There are also marked differences between bank loans and bond issues from the point of view of the commercial banks. In the case of bank loans, the bank continues to be involved even after the arrangement of the loan. That is not the case with bonds, although a group of banks is usually active in the issuing of bonds. Through a process of underwriting the bank also sometimes guarantees the sale of a proportion of the bonds, but the involvement remains temporary in the case of a bond loan.

The development of the offshore markets has made a considerable contribution to the liberalization of domestic financial markets. Fierce competition of bank subsidiaries in off-shore centres, such as the tax havens of the Cayman Islands, Barbados, and Curacao, meant that governments in developed countries reacted by improving the competitiveness of their domestic banking sector. This happened through a relaxation of the rules and some-times even by supplying reductions in taxes if the banks fulfilled certain requirements. Through this process, at present the differences between onshore and offshore banking have been reduced substantially.

Since 2000 there has been a rapid increase in the use of electronic bank trading. At first sight, this development appears to make the banks' location irrelevant. However, external economies of scale, through the availability the financial know-how, are very important in the financial sector and encourage the concentration or clustering of banking activities and the growth of financial markets in particular centres (in this connection, compare the Porter diamond discussed in Chapter 3). That is why we can see a tendency towards the establishment of financial centres across the world.

The location of these international financial centres is not simply a matter of chance; a significant role is also played by tradition or, in other words, the first-mover advantage. Such centres often developed in locations which had a high volume of international trade in goods. Once the financial knowledge is established, there is an internal force – separate from the trade in goods – which favours continuation, although without guaranteeing it. Another important point is the economic policy pursued in the country of location. Aspects such as tax policy, the liberalization of international capital movements, the presence of an independent central bank, and exchange rate stability can all play an important role. It is an attractive proposition for a country to have an international financial centre within its territory since it guarantees:

o   high-grade jobs;
o   corporate tax on bank profits; and
o   additional tax revenue via taxes on interest and dividends paid to the accountholders and shareholders.

The part of activities of financial centres that is perhaps most closely connected to international relations is their turnovers in the foreign-exchange market. Table 12.1 shows the change over time of the shares of those centres which had, in April 2010, a share of at least one per cent of global turnover.

The UK and the USA have by far the largest forex markets. The UK's market accounts for more than one-third of global turnover and its share appears to be growing; the US market is about half the UK's present size. The share of, particularly, Germany is remarkable low and, moreover, it is in decline. Another notable finding is the high ranking of both Switzerland and Denmark, two small European countries that decided to stay outside the Euro area and retain their own currencies. Apparently, this has paid off in terms of a growing share of the forex markets since 1998 – the year before the start of the euro.

Of course, a high turnover on the foreign-exchange market is not the only clue for international financial centres. Several other indicators could be used. In line with the quantitative information in this chapter, Table 12.2 contains the country distribution of both the liabilities side of international positions of banks and the amounts outstanding in respect of the issues of international bonds and notes by residents. The table only presents figures for countries with amounts over $1 billion. These indicators do not, of course, constitute a complete delineation of international financial centres. What is also significant is the depth and liquidity of the stock market.

Table 12.1 Shares of the global forex market (countries with shares over 1% in April 2010)

Country	1995	1998	2001	2004	2007	2010
UK	29.3	32.6	32.0	32.0	34.6	36.7
USA	16.3	18.3	16.1	19.1	17.4	17.9
Japan	10.3	7.0	9.0	8.0	5.8	6.2
Singapore	6.6	6.9	6.1	5.1	5.6	5.3
Switzerland	5.4	4.4	4.5	3.3	5.9	5.2
Hong Kong SAR	5.6	3.8	4.0	4.1	4.2	4.7
Australia	2.5	2.3	3.2	4.1	4.1	3.8
France	3.8	3.7	2.9	2.6	3.0	3.0
Denmark	1.9	1.3	1.4	1.6	2.1	2.4
Germany	4.8	4.7	5.4	4.6	2.4	2.1
Canada	1.9	1.8	2.6	2.3	1.5	1.2

Source: BIS (2010).

Table 12.2 Country distribution of international bank liabilities and international bonds and notes (amounts outstanding December 2008; in $ billion)

Country	International bank liabilities	International bonds and notes
UK	6982	3134
USA	3402	5195
France	2792	1414
Germany	2107	2024
Cayman Islands	1733	1114
The Netherlands	1322	1576
Switzerland	1171	—
Ireland	1151	1090
Spain	—	1230
Italy	—	1004

Note: Bonds and notes issued by residents. In both columns: only amounts larger than $1000 billion.
Source: BIS (2009).

Only four countries are to be found in all three entries in Tables 12.1 and 12.2: the UK (London), the USA (New York), France (Paris), and Germany (Frankfurt). These are all undoubtedly international financial centres, with London and New York being by far the largest. Three countries – the Cayman Islands, the Netherlands, and Ireland – are present only twice (both in Table 12.2): They are at best on the threshold of becoming international financial centres, but are a long way behind the four true global centres.

12.8 Summary

1. In terms of shares of the foreign-exchange (forex) market turnover, international flows of capital are much greater than international flows in goods and services, although it should be noted that forex market transactions are predominantly interbank transactions.
2. Classified on the basis of motives, international capital flows can usefully be divided into five categories: international trade credit, foreign direct investment, international arbitrage capital, international speculative capital, and international portfolio capital movements connected with the need for risk diversification. In so far as capital transactions are linked to trade and investment, they are prompted by incentives in the real economy. The other three categories are principally the result of financial considerations.
3. Of the motives derived from the real economy, direct investment motives have already been discussed in Chapter 4. The same applies even more so in the case of international trade: many of the previous chapters have covered this subject. Insofar as trade is concerned, this chapter has therefore only outlined the nature of trade credits. These consist of export and import credits, often in the form of trade bills of exchange, which makes these credits negotiable. Consequently, an exporter, for example, need not wait

for her money until the end of the term of her export credit. Documentary credit is a common form of import credit.

4. The most common forms of international arbitrage capital are foreign-exchange arbitrage and interest arbitrage. In both cases, the focus is on the advantage gained from price differentials that become apparent on different markets at one and the same time. This is the motive underlying all forms of arbitrage. Foreign-exchange arbitrage concerns the difference in values of an exchange rate on two foreign-exchange markets; interest rate arbitrage regards the difference in the rates of return on a similar financial investment in two countries. These rates of return comprise not only interest rates, but also the premium on one of the two currencies in terms of the other one on the forward exchange market. On this market, foreign currencies are traded and the price is determined at the time of conclusion of the contract, but delivery and payment do not take place until the elapsing of a predetermined period. The covered interest parity is the equilibrium condition in the behaviour of interest arbitragers.

5. The uncovered interest rate parity is the equilibrium condition for currency speculators in so far as they operate on the spot market, where the foreign currency is delivered and paid for immediately. In the uncovered interest rate parity the premium on the forward currency is replaced by the expected relative change in the value of foreign currency in terms of the home currency.

6. International capital movements for the purposes of risk reduction aim to achieve a more favourable ratio between the expected rate of return (assessed as positive) and the uncertainty about the rate of return (assessed as negative). Empirical findings show that the opportunity to extend capital movements beyond national borders greatly improves the scope for risk reduction through the diversification of investment portfolios.

7. This risk reduction and international optimization of capital allocation are important reasons why governments should minimize foreign-exchange regulations on international capital movements. If all regulations have been abolished for a currency on the forex market, it is called a convertible (freely exchangeable) currency.

8. One important drawback of a convertible currency for international capital movements is that a country aiming at to achieve a stable exchange rate is subject to considerable restrictions on its macroeconomic policy for domestic economic goals, as we shall see in Chapter 14. Another important disadvantage for a country of free international capital flows is the danger of a sudden halting of capital inflows, followed by a surge in outflows and a currency crisis.

9. The international capital markets have expanded enormously since the 1950s – this applies to both the diversity of financial instruments and the volume of business. As far as the instruments are concerned, these developments began with the launch of the eurodollar market, where bank liabilities in currencies that are foreign to the bank concerned made bank credits in the same foreign currencies available. Various financial innovations were added subsequently, such as international bonds, to be subdivided into foreign bonds and eurobonds.

10. International financial centres have surprisingly survived the electronic revolution in the financial world. Centripetal forces, such as the advantage of clustering financial know-how, have apparently offset the centrifugal forces of easy electronic access to clients at a distance. London and New York are by far the largest international financial centres in the world assessed in terms of the sizes of their forex market, international bank positions, and the outstanding amounts of international bonds and notes. London has by far the largest forex market in the world, with some one-third of

global turnover taking place there, and also the largest amount of international bank liabilities outstanding. New York is largest in terms of the amount of international bonds and notes outstanding. Although Paris and Frankfurt are also international financial centres, they are both much smaller than the two leading markets.

Questions

1. The Japanese yen is selling spot for ¥85 per. The 180-day interest rate on yen is 2 percent and on the dollar 6 percent (at annual rates).

   (a) What is the 180-day forward yen–dollar exchange rate assuming free international capital flows and negligible transaction costs between the two countries?
   (b) What is the size of the forward premium or discount on the yen (at an annual rate)?

2. How can equation (12.1) be adapted to include the exchange rate gain on the foreign interest yield earned – which is mentioned in note 1?

3. Assume that in question 1 the uncovered interest parity holds. Then determine the exchange rate that the market expects after 180 days.

4. The covered interest parity is presumed to hold permanently, with a very quick adjustment back to the parity as soon as there is any disruption of this parity. That is different for the uncovered interest parity. Hence one tends to speak of the risk premium, defined as $(F - E^e)/E = $ risk premium. Which of the following risk types does this risk premium express: country risk, asset risk or exchange-rate risk?

CHAPTER 13

Exchange-Rate Explanation and Prediction

13.1 Introduction

As we saw in Chapter 11, each balance-of-payments entry and, therefore, each international transaction, results in a foreign-exchange market transaction, which has a consequent effect upon the price on that market, the exchange rate. This demonstrates that the exchange rate is the result of the interaction of a very large number of determinants: each variable that influences an international transaction, however small, has an effect on the exchange rate. As will be shown in the next chapter, at the same time many of these determinants are, in turn, also affected by the exchange rate. Particularly in this area of economics there is a strong reciprocity between the variable to be explained and its determining variables.

This chapter will provide detailed explanation of the determination and – in line with this – the prediction of the exchange rate. It is, for instance, not enough to know that international capital movements influence the level of the exchange rate. It is also necessary to have information about the particular forces underlying international capital transactions and their precise effects on the exchange rate.

Our examination of the exchange-rate explanation will draw upon a number of well-known exchange-rate theories, each of which offers a coherent pattern of the particular factors that determine the exchange rate.

Every business involved in international economic transactions would benefit from the best possible information on which to base forecasts of the future values of the exchange rate. It is therefore very important to know which factors determine the exchange rate. This applies not only to a company involved in international trade in goods, but also to an international investor or a government that has to decide on its economic policy. Box 13.1 demonstrates the various ways in which a business firm nowadays encounters the uncertainty of the future exchange rate.

The present chapter deals with the factors that can have a potential effect on the determination of exchange rates. Exchange-rate theories highlight these determining factors and can usefully be divided into long- and short-term explanations of the exchange rate. The following questions will be the subject of this chapter:

○ What are the explanatory variables of the exchange rate in the long run?
○ What are the explanatory variables of the exchange rate in the short run?
○ What is the basic difference between the long- and short-run explanatory variables?
○ Do we see the influence of international competitiveness on the exchange rate in one of the two categories of explanatory variables?
○ How can we predict the exchange-rate value?

This chapter is arranged as follows. First we examine long-term explanations of the exchange rate (Section 13.2). The key element of such explanations will lie in the equality of a currency's internal and external purchasing power. Then Section 13.3 adds the short-term explanations, where the focus principally appears to be on international investments. These short- and long-term explanations will be brought together by looking at the position of exchange-rate theories in exchange-rate predictions (Section 13.4). Section 13.5 provides a summary of the findings.

In this chapter we disregard an important co-determining factor of the exchange rate – namely, how exchange rates are influenced by agreements within the international monetary system. The very existence of such an agreement can influence the level of the exchange rate, through both economic policy tuned to the agreement and the pure effect of the agreement's existence on exchange-rate expectations in the private sector. Chapter 16 will consider the history and possibilities of such international agreements.

13.2 | Exchange-rate theory: the long term

13.2.1 Purchasing power parity

The earliest attempt to explain the level of an exchange rate is the purchasing power parity (PPP) theory, which is based on the so-called law of one price. This says that, disregarding international trade barriers and transport costs for simplicity, there will be a tendency for a specific type of good due to cross-border competition to have the same price in different countries.

This price equality will come about as follows: if the prices of the same item are different in two countries, it is profitable to buy the good in the country where it is cheaper and sell it in the country where it is dearer. This combined buying and selling activity will cause the price to rise in the cheap country and to fall in the expensive one. This arbitrage activity ceases only once the prices are the same in both countries.

A change in the exchange rate may contribute to this tendency towards price equalization and even actually be entirely responsible for realizing internationally one and the same price. This adjustment process works in the following way: prices in two countries are only genuinely comparable if they are expressed in the same currency. If we multiply the foreign price (expressed in the foreign currency) by the exchange rate (expressed in number of units of the home currency per unit of the foreign currency), we obtain the price of the good in the foreign country, but now expressed in the home currency. If the home country is the cheap country for the good involved, then the good's price in the home country is lower than its price in the foreign country expressed in units of the home country.

The subsequent arbitrage activity not only has a potential effect on the good's prices in the two countries, but also influences the exchange rate. As an intermediate step the arbitrage activity has a purchase of the home currency (in order to buy the good in the cheap home country) and a sale of the foreign currency (after the sale of the good in the more expensive foreign country). Consequently, the exchange rate falls and, therefore, the foreign good price in the home currency also falls. This is an adaptation in the direction of

Box 13.1   Exchange-rate uncertainty and the business world

In our globalized world almost every businessman has to contend with a range of exchange-rate uncertainties. To reduce these uncertainties the business world would welcome either a soundly based forecast of future exchange-rate values or adequate and cheap coverage methods to counter these uncertainties.

Every contract with an overseas customer presents a firm with the problem of exchange-rate uncertainty. The invoice can be drawn up in a foreign currency, often the currency of the counterpart, but invoices in a third currency – often the US dollar – are also quite common. Even if the invoice is drawn up in the home currency, the firm will indirectly experience the consequences of exchange-rate uncertainty because of the conduct of its trading partner, who now bears the risk.

The contract may relate to the import of intermediate goods, which are inputs in the firm's production process, but also the export of the firm's final goods. Because it is usual for a certain period to pass between the signing and the settlement of the contract, the firm will suffer from exchange-rate uncertainty during this period.

It is usual for a large proportion of the firm's production costs to be in the domestic currency – this will be especially true in the case of labour costs. It is therefore likely that the cost and income sides of the firm's business will have different experiences of future exchange-rate changes.

As we shall see in Chapter 15, there are financial instruments that a firm can use to eliminate exchange-rate uncertainty for, say, the first two years of a contract. However, international contracts often run for a much longer period. In the case of capital goods, and complicated technological equipment such as ships and aeroplanes it is not unusual to have a period of more than two years between the signing of a contract and the payment of the amount due. In practice, it is impossible to hedge exchange-rate uncertainty for such a long period.

In such circumstances it is a matter of making the most accurate possible prediction of the value of the foreign currency expressed in units of the home currency in order to determine whether or not a contract will prove to be sufficiently profitable. But this raises the question as to what such a prediction should be based on. Perhaps it should be related to anticipated, future interest rates in the countries involved, because the exchange rate is so greatly influenced by international capital flows. Or should we instead pay more attention to real world factors, such as the expected competitiveness of the two countries over the period involved?

A business firm is also subject to exchange-rate risks on its foreign currency investments, including its cash holdings of foreign currencies. The nature of these investments was outlined in Case study 12.1. There are ways of 'hedging' this risk if it is short term in nature, but investors do not always make use of them. One reason is that there are costs associated with hedging facilities. Another reason is that investors can also have clearly defined exchange-rate expectations which, if they come to pass, prove more advantageous to the investor than hedging this risk.

In both international trade and international investments the relevant period of exchange-rate uncertainty may differ substantially. Instinctively, it might be thought that the forces affecting exchange-rate changes and, thus, expectations in the short term may be different from those having an effect in the long term. But what are those differences?

international price equalization of the good involved. If the good's prices in the countries' own currency are completely rigid in the short term, this price equalization process will actually have to come about entirely through this exchange-rate change. In the world discussed above, in which only one good is being traded, the rigid prices in the two countries determine the equilibrium level of the exchange rate. The good's arbitrage activity takes care of the adjustment process towards that equilibrium value.

However, we live in a multi-good world, in which there are many comparable arbitrage processes for all internationally tradable goods. This means that in the ultimate equilibrium situation many purchasing power parities will have been realized – one for each good. If the initial international price differences for the products have different sizes, it is of course impossible that only an appropriate exchange-rate change realizes all parities. Product prices also have to move to a certain extent. What does this multi-good PPP mean for the relation between the exchange rate and the (average) price level in the two countries whose currencies are involved in the exchange rate? The national price index is a weighted average of the prices of specific goods. It is tempting to state that the law of one price also applies to countries' national price indices through the concept of price aggregation. The idea here is that if the prices of *individual* goods are the same between two countries, a *composite* set of prices will also be equal between them. This is expressed in the following equation:

$$P = E.P^*, \tag{13.1}$$

where $P(P^*)$ denotes the price level in the home (foreign) country, while E is the nominal bilateral exchange rate of the currencies of the countries involved. This equation expresses PPP between two countries or the international equality of national prices expressed in the same currency.

The same arbitrage process as described above for a one-good world also applies in this multi-goods case: If the price level abroad expressed in terms of the home currency rises and becomes higher than at home, demand will switch to domestic goods. This is associated with a decline in demand for foreign currency and an increased demand for domestic currency. As a result, the domestic currency rises in value: E falls in value. This leads to the restoration of PPP. Interpreted in this manner, the PPP of equation (13.1) is an equilibrium condition for the exchange rate where the two price levels determine the exchange rate:

$$E = P/P^*. \tag{13.1'}$$

There are three weaknesses in the PPP as described above:

1. The national price indices contain different baskets of goods. If one takes for the P's consumer price levels, we know that the consumer patterns vary from country to country. The composite set of prices mentioned above, therefore contains goods and weights of the goods that are country specific and thus different for P and P^*. That weakens the deduction of the parity on the basis of the law of one price for individual goods.
2. The arbitrage process, as described above, will be disturbed to a certain extent through the existence of transport costs and trade barriers, such as import tariffs.
3. For many goods the process of international goods arbitrage does not work, as they cannot easily be traded internationally or even not at all. These internationally non-tradable goods include many services, such as medical services, property rental, and services such as hairdressing, as well as goods that have high transportation costs.

To mitigate some of the weak points of the PPP given in equation (13.1'), there are two approaches to reformulating the PPP theory. The first is to transform the parity into a *relative version* of PPP. The formula of the so-called *absolute version*, viz. equation (13.1′), then becomes:[1]

$$\Delta E/E = \Delta P/P - \Delta P^*/P^*, \tag{13.2}$$

where Δ expresses the first difference of the variable that follows. The practical advantage of this relative version over the absolute version is that the distortion of the PPP relation through the introduction of transport costs and trade barriers plays hardly any part. The reason is that they usually do not alter significantly over a period of several years. In equation (13.1′) they then have approximately the position of a constant added to the right-hand side. But the relative change over time of a constant is zero, so that they obtain the value zero in equation (13.2). Another important advantage of the relative version of PPP is that the baskets of goods on which the price indices are based need not be exactly the same. For the relative version it is sufficient that the price increases of a good in the two countries involved – included in P and P^* – rather accurately reflect the country's inflation.

The other way of reformulating the absolute version of PPP theory stresses that the law of one price and thus goods arbitrage is only possible for goods that can, in principle, be traded internationally. For that reason PPP can arise only for goods that can be traded internationally. This means that the exchange-rate theory of PPP changes into:

$$E = P_t/P_t^*, \tag{13.3}$$

where P_t stands for the price of tradables – that is, goods that can be traded internationally. As before, the asterisk indicates the foreign variable.

Case study 13.1   The Big Mac index

Since 1986 the British weekly journal *The Economist* has published a Big Mac index. The underlying idea of this index is the concept of purchasing power parity (PPP), since it compares the prices of Big Macs in many countries where they are produced and sold.

By comparing these hamburger prices we can get a very rough impression of the domestic purchasing power of the countries' currencies. Through this exercise *The Economist* relates all currencies to the US dollar. If PPP applied in this instance, the local prices of Big Macs expressed in terms of dollars, through the use of 'the actual dollar exchange rate' presented in the fifth column of Table 13.1, would be identical. This would mean that all of the 'Big Mac prices in dollars' in the third column of Table 13.1 would be equal. But they are far from that. According to equation (13.1′), the Big Mac local-price ratio between a specified country and the US is equal to (the equilibrium value of) the exchange rate or the 'implied PPP of the dollar' presented in the fourth column. If the actual dollar exchange rate in the forex market, presented in the fifth column, is higher (lower), so there are more (less) domestic currencies per dollar in the actual exchange rate than in the 'implied PPP of the dollar', then the domestic

---

[1] This formula follows from equation (13.1′) by taking the natural logarithms of its left- and right-hand sides ($\ln E = \ln P - \ln P^*$) and differentiating the result: $d\ln E = d\ln P - d\ln P^*$. This is equal to: $dE/E = dP/P - dP^*/P^*$. By approximating the differentials (dE etc.) by the first differences (ΔE etc.), we arrive at equation (13.2).

currency is undervalued (overvalued) in the forex market (relative to its equilibrium rate based on PPP).

According to the Big Mac index for 13 July 2009, shown in Table 13.1, the euro was overvalued by 29 per cent against the dollar, while the yen and pound were near to PPP vis-à-vis the dollar.

Table 13.1 The hamburger standard

	Big Mac prices		Implied PPP of the dollar†	Actual dollar exchange rate 13 July 2009	Under (−)/ over (+) valuation against the dollar, %
	In local currency	In dollars*			
United States‡	$ 3.57	3.57			
Argentina	Peso 11.5	3.02	3.22	3.81	−15
Australia	A$ 4.34	3.37	1.22	1.29	−6
Brazil	Real 8.03	4.02	2.25	2.00	+13
Britain	£2.29	3.69	1.56§	1.61§	+3
Canada	C$ 3.89	3.35	1.09	1.16	−6
Chile	Peso 1750	3.19	490	549	−11
China	Yuan 12.5	1.83	3.50	6.83	−49
Czech Republic	Koruna 67.92	3.64	19.0	18.7	+2
Denmark	DK 29.5	5.53	8.26	5.34	+55
Egypt	Pound 13	2.33	3.64	5.58	−35
Euro Area**	€3.31	4.62	1.08††	1.39††	+29
Hong Kong	HK$ 13.3	1.72	3.73	7.75	−52
Hungary	Forint 720	3.62	202	199	+1
Indonesia	Rupiah 20,900	2.05	5,854	10,200	−43
Israel	Shekel 15	3.77	4.20	3.97	+6
Japan	Yen 320	3.46	89.6	92.6	−3
Malaysia	Ringgit 6.77	1.88	1.90	3.60	−47
Mexico	Peso 33	2.39	9.24	13.8	−33
New Zealand	NZ$ 4.9	3.08	1.37	1.59	−14
Norway	Kroner 40	6.15	11.2	6.51	+72
Peru	New Sol 8.056	2.66	2.26	3.03	−25
Philippines	Peso 99.39	2.05	27.8	48.4	−42
Poland	Zloty 7.6	2.41	2.13	3.16	−33
Russia	Ruble 67	2.04	18.8	32.8	−43

Table 13.1 Continued

	Big Mac prices		Implied PPP of the dollar†	Actual dollar exchange rate 13 July 2009	Under (−)/ over (+) valuation against the dollar, %
	In local currency	In dollars*			
Saudi Arabia	Riyal 11	2.93	3.08	3.75	−18
Singapore	S$ 4.22	2.88	1.18	1.46	−19
S. Africa	Rand 17.95	2.17	5.03	8.28	−39
South Korea	Won 3400	2.59	952	1.315	−28
Sweden	SKR 39	4.93	10.9	7.90	+38
Switzerland	CHF 6.5	5.98	1.82	1.09	+68
Taiwan	Taiwan $ 75	2.26	21.0	33.2	−37
Thailand	Baht 64.49	1.89	18.1	34.2	−47
Turkey	Lira 5.65	3.65	2.45	1.55	+2
UAE	Dirhams 10	2.72	2.80	3.67	−24
Colombia	Peso 7000	3.34	1961	2096	−6
Costa Rica	Colones 2000	3.43	560	583	−4
Estonia	Kroon 32	2.85	8.96	11.2	−20
Iceland	Kronur 640	4.99	179	128	+40
Latvia	Lats 1.55	3.09	0.43	0.50	−13
Lithuania	Litas 7.1	2.87	1.99	2.48	−20
Pakistan	Rupee 190	2.30	53.2	82.6	−36
Philippines	Peso 99.39	2.05	27.8	48.4	−42
Sri Lanka	Rupee 210	1.83	58.8	115	−49
Ukraine	Hryvnia 14	1.83	3.92	7.66	−49
Uruguay	Peso 61	2.63	17.1	23.2	−26

* At current exchange rates †Purchasing-power parity; local price divided by price in United States ‡ Average of New York, Chicago, Atlanta and San Francisco §Dollars per pound **Weighted average of prices in the Euro area ††Dollars per euro.
Sources: *The Economist* (2009), p. 66.

The dearest Big Mac in dollars in this list were consumed in Norway, Switzerland, and Denmark with currency overvaluations against the dollar to the amount of, respectively, 72, 68, and 55 per cent. The cheapest Big Mac in dollars was sold in China through a 49 per cent undervaluation of the yuan. Obviously, the current notion of an under-valued Chinese yuan gets support from the Big Mac measure. Many Southeast Asian countries are in line with China, with currency undervaluations ranging from a high of 52 per cent for Hong Kong and a low of 37 per cent for Taiwan. In between these two are Thailand, Malaysia, Indonesia, and the Philippines. The Big Mac index is a creative and light-hearted way to approach empirically both the law of one price and the 'correct' level of exchange rates. Its strength as a tool for comparison is that it concerns a homogeneous good: the Big Mac recipe is the same throughout the world. Nevertheless, the index does have some shortcomings as an analysis of PPP.

The purchasing power parity theory applies only to tradables. However, the Big Mac is not traded internationally by the most obvious potential arbitrager: McDonald's itself. The company applies a policy of strict market sharing, so that different competition in the local markets can reflect in price differences – as can differences in local tax rates. The production of Big Macs requires local inputs. They can differ in price because several inputs, such as rent and labour, are not easily traded internationally – and tend to be cheaper in poorer countries. Because of all of these shortcomings, the Big Mac index gives only a quite rough indication of the equilibrium exchange rate of currencies against the US dollar.

Empirical research offers only limited support for the PPP theory of the exchange rate, using the relative version and national price indices. The theory does not offer very satisfactory explanations of short-term exchange rates. However, for changes in exchange rate and prices when observed over a longer period a tendency towards purchasing power parity is clearly perceivable. The theory is therefore usually regarded as an essential part of exchange-rate explanations in the longer term. Although the beginnings of the purchasing power parity theory date back several hundred years, it was not until the 1920s that the Swede Cassel perfected the theory and gave it this interpretation.

Of course, one question that can be raised immediately is whether or not it is possible to improve the long-term explanation of the exchange rate by conducting a further adaptation of the purchasing power parity. Despite the long-term tendency towards this parity indeed, apparently in this parity one factor is missing: occasional changes in the relation between nominal exchange rate and the price ratio. Adaptation of equation (13.1′) in the following way closes this gap with reality:

$$E = RE.P/P^*. \tag{13.4}$$

Introduction of the variable RE weakens the link between the exchange rate and the price ratio. This variable RE is referred to as the real exchange rate. The reason is clear if we rewrite the equation as follows:

$$RE = E.P^*/P. \tag{13.4′}$$

Now RE expresses the ratio of the prices in the two countries, with the domestic currency as the common denominator for both prices, as $E.P^*$ is the price level in the foreign country expressed in the home currency. Looking at the dimensions of the ratio, it becomes clear that the dimension of the numerator of RE is domestic currency per foreign consumption basket, while the dimension of the denominator of the ratio is domestic currency per domestic consumption basket. Combined, RE has the dimension domestic consumption basket per foreign consumption basket. In other words, RE expresses the real price (in units of the domestic consumption basket) of the foreign consumption basket, so: number of domestic goods per unit of foreign goods. The absence of money in this expression explains RE's name: the real exchange rate.

By means of this economic content of the real exchange rate,we are able to indicate the economic interpretation of its addition to equation (13.4). Suppose that there is a shift in demand from domestic to foreign goods, while there is no change in production and in the two national money markets. The latter means that the two price levels will not change, as we will see in the next Section 13.2.2 of this chapter. The demand shift nevertheless affects the mutual price of the two consumption baskets. It will make the foreign basket dearer. This implies an increase in RE and, according to (13.4), an increase in the nominal exchange rate E. It is in this way, due to a more expensive foreign currency rather than through a higher price level P^*, that the more expensive foreign goods basket manifests itself. This means that through an explanation of movements in the real exchange rate we are able to explain the absence of purchasing power parity.

One remaining weak point of the PPP theory in terms of explaining the exchange rate is its defective causality. According to the underlying arbitrage process, it is not clear that prices determine the exchange rate, as in equation (13.1'). Both prices and the exchange rate are able to bridge the gap between prices in different countries. Furthermore, in equation (13.4) it is not at all clear that the real exchange rate is the result of the remaining variables in that equation, as equation (13.4') supposes. Equation (13.4) has in effect the character of a definition equation, expressing the mutual relation, but not the causality, between the variables in that equation.

13.2.2 The monetary approach

In the latter half of the 1970s the PPP theory was developed further into the monetary approach to the exchange rate. According to this theory, the longer-term exchange rate is again explained by the ratio of the price levels in the two countries, but this approach offers a deeper analysis. Rather than settling on the level of prices as an explanation for the exchange rate, it means that the prices themselves need to be explained. In order to do this the monetary approach uses the equilibrium conditions for the money markets in the two countries involved in the exchange rate.

The form of domestic money market equilibrium is generally accepted to be:

$$M = P.L(Y, i), \tag{13.5}$$

where the variable M stands for money supply and L is the real demand for money.

Multiplication of this real money demand by the price level makes the real variable nominal, so that the right-hand side of (13.5), $P.L$, represents the nominal demand for money. A widespread assumption is that real money demand depends upon real national income, Y, and the nominal interest rate, i. If Y increases, the demand for money is believed to increase, because the country's inhabitants need larger money holdings in order to be able to pay for the increased amount of transactions.

Money supply consists of cash holdings and sight deposits at a bank, which do not yield interest. The second explanatory variable, the interest rate, is therefore the opportunity cost of holding money – the loss in yield due to holding money. As the interest rate increases, it becomes more expensive to hold money, meaning that people will tend to reduce the amount of money in stock. This means that an interest rate increase reduces the demand for money.

The assumption is that the money market is in a constant state of equilibrium. This is part of the idea that after a disruption, financial markets in general find a new equilibrium immediately (within a few minutes!) by means of appropriate price changes. Here the price is the opportunity cost of money – the interest rate. If, for example, the central bank increases money supply, there is an incipient excess supply in the money market. But this will lead to an immediate fall in the interest rate, making it cheaper to hold money. The immediate response is an increase in the demand for real money. The fall in the interest rate continues until this demand increase restores money market equilibrium.

The widely accepted assumption is that the interplay of money supply and real money demand determines the *longer-term* price level. The underlying idea is that the prices of goods tend to be rigid in the short term, so that money market equilibrium cannot be achieved by appropriate price adjustments in the short run. At first the interest rate therefore does the job, but in the longer run, goods prices are flexible enough to restore the money market equilibrium. Thus, in the longer run it is P, rather than i, that is the outcome of the values of M and L, or rewriting equation (13.5):

$$P = M/L(Y, i). \tag{13.5'}$$

Equation (13.5′) implies that if there is a permanent increase in money supply, the price level will ultimately rise if the real demand for money remains the same. Conversely, if there is only a permanent increase in real money demand (for example, because of a rise in national income), the price level will ultimately fall.

In the foreign country – or, generalizing, internationally – there is a similar relationship as in (13.5′) between price level, money supply and real money demand, including the latter's explanatory variables. If we now substitute the right-hand sides of equation (13.5′) and its foreign complement for P and P* in equation (13.1′), we arrive – after some re-ordering – at the following behavioural equation for the exchange rate in the longer term:

$$E = M/M^* \times L^*/L, \text{ in which } L = L(Y, i) \text{ and } L^* = L^*(Y^*, i^*). \tag{13.6}$$

This equation shows that if the domestic money supply increases by, say, 10 per cent, the exchange rate will also eventually rise by 10 per cent. It is an 'eventual' rise, because the equation only holds for the longer run. In view of the background to equation (13.6) – and particularly equation (13.5′) – the connecting link between M and E is here the domestic price level, which eventually also rises by these 10 per cent.

13.3 Exchange-rate theory: additional short-term explanation

13.3.1 The uncovered interest rate parity

What can be stated about the short-term changes in the level of the exchange rate? It seems clear that another theoretical explanation is required. The overriding explanation of the short-term exchange rate is the uncovered interest parity, already introduced in Section 12.4, and expressed in equation (12.2). For our convenience, it will be repeated here:

$$i = i^* + (E^e - E)/E. \, 100. \tag{13.7}$$

It shows the equilibrium condition that arises from the behaviour of the foreign-exchange speculator. Equation (13.7) is her equilibrium condition. The left-hand side shows the domestic rate of return, consisting of only the domestic interest rate, i, measured as a percentage. The right-hand side expresses the rate of return on an investment abroad. This rate of return has two components: the foreign interest rate, i^*, and the expected exchange-rate gain on a investment abroad that is similar to the domestic investment. These two components are also expressed as percentages.

Equation (13.7) can be seen as the short-run equilibrium condition for the exchange rate. It relates the exchange rate to three explanatory variables – namely, the domestic and foreign interest rates, and the expected value of the exchange rate.

A change in any one of these variables will affect the equilibrium value of the exchange rate. If, for example, the foreign interest rate rises, investment abroad immediately becomes more attractive. This leads to a tendency to exchange the domestic currency for foreign currency. Once this trend is felt in the foreign-exchange market, there is an increase in the value of the foreign currency and therefore in the value of E. Given the value of the expected exchange rate, this means that there is a decline in the expected exchange gain on an investment in the foreign currency. This compensates for the more attractive foreign interest rate. A new equilibrium is reached almost immediately at an appropriately higher value for E. In other words, the domestic currency has depreciated.

Equation (13.7) also includes the feature of self-fulfilling prophecy in the forex market. If, for whatever reason, speculators start to expect a rise in the value of the foreign currency, there is a rise in the variable E^e. This raises the right-hand side value, so that investments in the foreign country become more attractive, the demand for foreign currency increases and as a result the foreign currency, and therefore E, soars following the changed expectation.

13.3.2 The overshooting model

This explanation of the exchange rate in the short term in equation (13.7) can easily be combined with the long-term exchange-rate model, expressed in equation (13.6). However, there are still two loose ends: national income and the expected exchange rate. In order to complete the model, it is assumed that national income is exogenously determined – at the level of full employment – and that the expectation of the foreign-exchange speculator about the exchange rate is rational. This means that the speculator is assumed to know the model and uses it to determine the expected exchange rate, E^e.

This combined short-term and long-term model is able to explain the remarkable practical phenomenon of overshooting (or overreaction) of the exchange rate, in which a currency value seems to overreact to a change in one or more of the variables that determine its level. Figure 13.1 displays exchange rate overshooting. We see that the

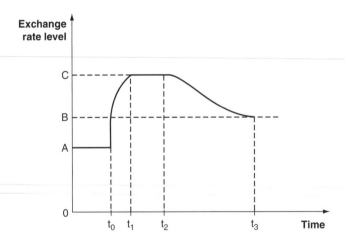

Figure 13.1   Exchange-rate overshooting

exchange-rate level moves from A to C before stabilizing at the lower level B. This portrays the volatility of the exchange rate, something that has been characteristic of exchange rates in recent decades.

We shall explain overshooting in this model on the basis of the example of a monetary 'disturbance' in the form of an unexpected, permanent 10 per cent increase in money supply. This policy change affects the model in two distinct ways.

1. This increase in money supply disturbs the equilibrium in the money market. Since the price level is sticky in the short term, there is only one variable in equation (13.6) that can restore money market equilibrium – the interest rate, which will fall to the point where equilibrium is restored via a 10 per cent increase in the real demand for money.
2. The expected value of the exchange rate will also increase in response to the increased money supply, because the rational speculator knows that, according to equation (13.6), the lasting 10 per cent increase in the money supply will lead eventually to a 10 per cent increase in the exchange rate. The speculator adjusts her exchange-rate expectations accordingly, but notices that her investment equilibrium for interest-bearing assets has currently been upset in two ways: in equation (13.7) the left-hand side has fallen as a result of the lower domestic interest rate, while the right-hand side has increased because of the 10 per cent rise in the expected exchange rate.

Speculators will respond to this two-sided disturbance of the equilibrium with a mass shift from domestic to foreign investments. This causes a huge increase in the demand for foreign currency, so that the exchange rate, E, rises quickly. A 10 per cent increase in the actual value of the exchange rate appears to be insufficient to alter the speculators' behaviour: although such an increase does restore the right-hand side of equation (13.7) to its original value before the disturbance (because both the expected and the actual exchange rate have now risen by 10 percent), there is still no reason for the domestic interest rate to rise again. This means that the left-hand side of equation (13.7) remains below the original level, so that speculators still have reason to transfer more of their investments abroad. Only if the actual exchange rate has risen so far that in equation (13.7) the right-hand side is just as far below its original value as the left-hand side will speculators again be indifferent regarding the country in which to invest. At that point the excess demand for foreign currency disappears and the actual exchange rate stabilizes for the time being at the new, much higher level.

The development in the actual and expected exchange rates over time is shown in Figure 13.1. Before the monetary disturbance both the actual and expected exchange rates were at level A. At the present stage of our analysis, after the initial adjustment resulting from the monetary disturbance, the actual rate is at level C, while the expected exchange rate is at the lower level B.

This situation may persist for some time, with the length of this period depending upon the rigidity duration of the domestic price level. As stated earlier, this exchange-rate model is based on the fact that goods prices are, to some extent, rigid. After a certain period, once the domestic price level begins to rise gradually in response to the earlier increase in the money supply, the temporary equilibrium of the exchange rate at level C is disturbed. According to equation (13.5), which underlies equation (13.6), the price increase disrupts the money market equilibrium again: there is now excess demand in the money market, which causes the domestic interest rate to rise.

According to equation (13.7), this now prompts an *in*flow of speculative capital, which goes along with a rising demand of speculators for the domestic currency. As a result, the value of the domestic currency rises or the exchange rate E begins to fall, keeping pace with the rise in the interest rate – in accordance with equation (13.7). Eventually, the price level reaches its long-term equilibrium level in accordance with equation (13.5′), which brings the changes to an end. At this point the exchange rate has reached level B in Figure 13.1, the level that the expected exchange rate had already reached immediately after the monetary disturbance.

The notion of exchange-rate overshooting is associated in particular with the economist Rüdiger Dornbusch. He was the first to present a model (in essence the model just described) to explain this phenomenon, which so obviously and often occurred in practice (see Dornbusch, 1976).

13.3.3 The currency substitution model and the portfolio balance model

In the 1980s there were two further main developments in the exchange-rate theory. In the monetary approach of the exchange rate – as described in Section 13.2.2 – domestic investors have room to hold foreign interest-bearing assets, but not foreign money. In the first, least sweeping, further theory development, the constraint that foreign money cannot be held in domestic hands was abandoned. This led to the *currency substitution model* of the exchange rate. The deciding factor for substitution between domestic and foreign money is uncertainty about the future value of the exchange rate and, more specifically, the direction in which the rate is expected to move. If people anticipate that there will be a depreciation of one currency, they will put their money into other currencies to avoid the expected exchange-rate loss.

In this currency substitution model, the differential between the domestic and foreign interest rates, which played such an important role in the monetary approach, naturally plays no role because money – that is, cash holdings and sight deposits at banks – yield no interest. This expansion of the theory produced no important new explanations for practical phenomena, but the theory is especially applicable to countries experiencing hyperinflation, where the national currency is at a large risk of being displaced – partly or fully – by a stronger and more stable foreign currency, often the US dollar.

A much more interesting and comprehensive expansion of the exchange-rate theory in the 1980s was the *portfolio balance approach* to the exchange rate. This development explicitly incorporated equilibrium conditions for a country's domestic and foreign bond markets. In the monetary approach, such interest-bearing investments are already an implicit alternative to holding money. This is hinted at by the interest rate in the money demand function, which expresses the opportunity costs of holding money. The monetary approach neglects foreign interest-bearing assets.

The essence of the portfolio balance approach is the desired allocation of financial wealth of a country's private sector over the financial assets distinguished. The assets involved are domestic money, domestic bonds, and foreign bonds. (The bundle of assets could easily be extended.) Changes in the desired allocation occur on the basis of the (expected) rates of return on the different financial assets. In this approach, domestic and foreign bonds are incomplete substitutes. (Here the term 'substitutes' means that if the foreign interest rate rises, the desired proportion of foreign bonds in the private assets portfolio will increase at the expense of money and domestic bonds. However the feature 'incomplete substitutes' implies that domestic bonds then do not disappear fully in the portfolio; they remain desirable in the portfolio, although in a smaller proportion.)

The portfolio balance approach has two other significant features:

o If there is only an increase in financial wealth – and therefore in private asset holdings – there is no change in the proportions of the individual financial assets in the desired portfolios. Demand for – and hence ownership of – each of the individual assets will then increase in proportion to the previous individual asset holdings.

o On the supply side, the supply of both money and domestic bonds is assumed to be exogenous as they are supposed to be determined by the home country's central bank and government, respectively. In contrast, the supply of foreign bonds is endogenous and changes as a result of any current account surplus or deficit, as shown by the balance-of-payments identity of Chapter 11.

Thus, a current account surplus is associated with an increase in the home country's foreign claims. Because of the simplicity of the model used in the portfolio approach, this can only be in the form of an inflow of foreign bonds. However, this is not the only channel for the supply of foreign bonds in the home country to increase; it can also rise as the result of an increase in the value of the foreign currency – the unit of account of the foreign bonds. If the exchange rate rises (so that the foreign currency becomes dearer), then the value – and, in fact, also the supply – in terms of domestic currency of foreign bonds in the domestic portfolios will also rise.

Case study 13.2   Portfolio adjustment due to financial liberalization in Japan in the 1980s

In the period following the Second World War, Japan's financial system was initially largely closed. The 1973 oil price shock led to a temporary current account deficit for Japan. In response, Japan eased restrictions on capital imports to help finance the increased account of oil imports.

In subsequent years Japan gradually increased its liberalization of international capital movements. As the US dollar rose in value throughout the first half of the 1980s (see Section 16.5), President Reagan brought considerable pressure to bear on the Japanese government to open its borders still further to financial transactions.

This pressure led to the intended Japanese measures, but not to the intended behaviour: the main result was a sharp increase in Japanese capital *exports* (Figure 11.1, p. 194). Japanese net long-term capital exports started in 1984 and reached a high in 1987. Since most of these flows went to the USA, the dollar received a further upward boost – the opposite of Reagan's intentions.

However, Japanese capital imports from the USA also increased. The portfolio approach, in particular, can explain such an increase in mutual capital inflows between two countries following cross-border capital liberalization. In both countries, people are adjusting their investment portfolios to the new possibilities that have been opened up. Contrary to what one might expect at first glance, these adjustments do not lead to a situation in which both countries only invest in the country with the highest rate of return.

In order to develop a proper understanding of the portfolio balance approach to the exchange rate, we shall describe the adjustment process that occurs following a disturbance of the equilibrium.

Say, again, the disturbance is that the domestic central bank increases the domestic money supply. In this model that means more than just an increase in money supply, because in practice the central bank usually brings additional money into circulation by buying domestic bonds. An alternative way, also often practised, is an exchange of money for foreign bonds. This is in fact a foreign-exchange market intervention in which the central banks buys and sells foreign currency in the form of foreign bonds for domestic currency. This transaction does not alter the level of private asset holdings, but it does change their composition.

If all domestic financial markets are in equilibrium, a central bank's purchase of foreign bonds against domestic money results domestically in an excess demand in the market for foreign bonds and an excess supply in the money market. The excess demand of foreign bonds also entails excess demand for foreign currency, which leads to an appreciation of that currency. As a result, there is an increase in the *value* of the supply of foreign bonds, caused not by a larger volume of foreign bonds in the home country but solely by an increase in their value expressed in terms of domestic currency. This increase in value of foreign bonds domestically reduces the excess demand for them.

This rise in the value of foreign bond supply also means an increase in the value of the sum of all financial assets in the private sector, or private financial wealth, in the home country. This in turn leads to an increased demand for all assets, depressing the excess supply of money that has just arisen, but creating excess demand for domestic bonds, and again enlarging net demand for foreign bonds.

The resulting excess demand for domestic bonds lowers their rate of return – that is, the domestic interest rate. This in turn generates higher demands for money and foreign bonds and a lower demand for domestic bonds. Thus, the markets for money and domestic bonds tend towards a new equilibrium. In the foreign bond market the increased demand leads to a further rise in the value of foreign currency, instigating another round of changes, until the three financial markets have regained equilibrium. This is a short-run equilibrium in the portfolio balance model.

Another line of disturbance of the financial equilibrium resulting from central bank action works along a current account improvement with the lapse of time through the appreciation of the foreign currency, as just argued. It does not occur immediately, since in practice an improvement of a country's competiveness has a delayed effect on the country's imports and exports. The current account surplus that arises will result in net capital inflow, due to the balance-of-payments identity, which materializes through an increase in the number of foreign bonds in the hands of the domestic private sector. This line of disturbance of the financial equilibrium implies a surplus of foreign bonds with the lapse of time, causing a gradual decline over time in the value of the foreign currency. The earlier short-term financial equilibrium was apparently characterized by an overshooting of the exchange rate.

Under certain realistic assumptions a new definite equilibrium is eventually reached in all three domestic financial markets. The final result is that the central bank's initial action causes an increase in the stock of reserves held by the central bank, a fall in the domestic interest rate, a net decline in the value of the domestic currency on the foreign-exchange market, and also a new current account equilibrium.

The current account is indeed in equilibrium again, but with changed sub-balances. As the country experienced a net inflow of foreign financial assets during the adjustment period, the inflow of foreign capital *earnings* is now higher than it was in the initial equilibrium. In the new equilibrium the goods and services balance must, therefore, have necessarily been worsened compared to the initial situation. The new equilibrium with this feature requires a worsening of the home country's competitiveness relative to the starting situation. This occurs because of higher domestic prices, whereby, relative to the initial equilibrium, the percentage rise of these prices exceeds that of the exchange rate. This price increase is a response to the higher foreign and domestic demand for domestic goods. The initial cause of the higher foreign demand is the depreciation of the home currency. The lasting cause in this model of higher domestic demand for domestic goods is the increase in the real value of private holdings of financial assets, in response to the temporary current account surplus.

13.4 Exchange-rate predictions

A business firm has much to gain if it can minimize the exchange-rate uncertainty associated with its international transactions. This holds true even for a foreign-exchange speculator: the more certainty she can obtain about the future exchange rate, the more certain the calculated expected profit.

There exist several so-called hedging instruments to cover exchange-rate risk. These will be described in Section 15.4. As an alternative to the use of such a hedging instrument, a firm and any other investor can employ a prediction of the future exchange rate to counter exchange-rate uncertainty. In making exchange-rate predictions, there are two approaches, which can also be used simultaneously.

The first approach is to dispose of predictions on the basis of a qualitative or quantitative study of exchange-rate fundamentals. To do this one can conclude a contract with an agency specialised in predicting exchange rates. However, this is a rather expensive proposition.

The alternative way is for the firm to have its own staff to produce these predictions. The basis of the prediction will be a macroeconometric analysis of the two countries involved in the specific exchange rate. It is an econometric (or quantified model) study with an emphasis upon exchange-rate determination. If, subsequently, actual values or predictions for the main determining variables, or fundamentals, of the exchange rate are fed into the model, it is possible to produce a prediction of the exchange rate. This method is dubbed a *fundamental analysis*.

The exchange-rate theories discussed in the previous sections of this chapter form the foundation for the choice of the fundamentals in such a model. The quality of the exchange-rate predictions produced in this way appears to be mixed at best. One interesting recent explanation of this mediocre quality is that, in contrast to present practices in the explanation of exchange rates, expectations of future values of fundamentals have a much greater weight than their current values in determining the exchange rate in standard models (Engel et al., 2007).

The second approach to arrive at useful exchange-rate predictions is to determine predictions on the basis of so-called *chart reading*. The only input for this method is a long-term time series of the actual exchange rate concerned: economic theory is not involved. It is a purely technical analysis focused on the detection of specific patterns in the graphical representation (so a chart) of the exchange rate's time series. The prediction evolves out of the patterns that the exchange rate exhibits over time. These patterns naturally concern events in the recent past. Therefore, the underlying assumption of chart reading is that history repeats itself to a certain extent – this applies, incidentally, to all statistical and econometric research.

The continuation of trends, for instance in the form of a moving average, forms the simplest pattern for the calculation of predictions by chartists through chart reading. Other important concepts that they use are support levels and resistance levels. The first is seen as a lower limit of an ongoing downward trend in the exchange rate, whereas a resistance level is an upper limit that the market does not expect a rising rate to exceed. If, nevertheless, the assumed barriers are crossed by the exchange rate, then the market normally interprets this as a breakthrough, after which the trend in the rate will probably be intensified towards new support and resistance levels. These notions are based on market sentiments, which are strongly influenced by psychological elements.

Chart reading is principally successful in making short-term predictions, which is understood by users. Surveys of the use of technical analysis and chart reading by foreign-exchange dealers in the world's leading centre – London – appears to confirm this knowledge. Where longer prediction periods than one month ahead are desired, analysts tend to focus more on market fundamentals.

The forex market is often regarded as the clearest example of an efficient market. One of the features of an efficient market is that all the relevant and publicly available information on the market at any given time has already been reflected in the current market price. If we take that view, publicly available historical information cannot offer an opportunity to make an extra profit out of trading, since if it is relevant the historical information in question will already have found its way into the process of price determination. Chart reading and technical analyses, therefore, are at odds with the assumption of an efficient foreign-exchange market. Then such information cannot help to improve the market price prediction.

The widespread practice of chart reading and fundamental exchange rate analysis counters the notion that everybody believes in the efficient market character of the forex market. These analysts expect, apparently, that knowledge about exchange rate determination still leaves considerable room for improvement.

13.5 | Summary

1. Exchange-rate theories aim to explain the nominal exchange rate. They give an indication of the relevant factors that determine the exchange rate. These theories can offer support to attempts to predict the value of the exchange rate. Sound exchange rate predictions are very useful for both the international trade in goods and international investments. The government also finds exchange-rate theories helpful in its exchange-rate policy, where clues relating to the equilibrium level of the exchange rate are of importance.
2. In this chapter, exchange-rate theories have been divided into two broad categories. The first category of theories focuses on an explanation of the exchange rate in the long term – that is, over a number of years. The second category explains shorter-term exchange-rate values.
3. The earliest long-term theory is the purchasing power parity (PPP) theory. This assumes a close link between the exchange rate and the ratio of domestic and foreign price levels. In addition to this absolute version, there is also a relative version of the theory. Here, the relative change of the exchange rate is equal to the difference between the domestic and foreign inflation rates. The PPP only holds in the (very) long run. This gives ample room for a changing real exchange rate – the rate that expresses the rate of exchange of a unit of the foreign goods basket in terms of units of the domestic goods basket.
4. The absolute version of the purchasing power parity theory is also part of the monetary approach to the exchange rate, in which the exchange rate is linked – via the price ratio and permanent money market equilibrium – to the ratio between the domestic money supply and demand relative to that ratio abroad.
5. In short-term exchange-rate theories the emphasis shifts from an explanation based on goods prices to one based on rates of return of financial assets. The basic assumption in these theories is that imbalances in the financial sector are rectified immediately, whereas a longer or shorter adjustment period is necessary where goods imbalances are concerned.
6. The uncovered interest rate parity, introduced in Chapter 12, with its interaction between the exchange rate, its expected value and the domestic and foreign interest rates, is one of the starting points for the monetary approach to the exchange rate with

the feature that goods prices are assumed to be rigid during a certain time span. This model is usually dubbed the Dornbusch model. Its second building block is money market equilibrium, but with the interest rate as a short-term restorer of the equilibrium. This model explains the phenomenon of overshooting, so characteristic of the short-term behaviour of exchange rates.

7. The uncovered interest rate parity is characterized by the complete substitutability of domestic and foreign interest-bearing financial assets. As soon as the substitutability between domestic and foreign interest-bearing assets is incomplete these assets are considered to be different with a concomitant difference in perceived risk. This is the essence of the portfolio balance approach to the exchange rate. In addition to markets for domestic money and domestic interest-bearing assets, this approach also distinguishes a market for foreign interest-bearing assets. In addition, the allocation of financial wealth over the investment assets distinguished is important in this instance.

8. The portfolio approach is also capable of explaining exchange-rate overshooting. But in deviatiation from the Dornbusch model it occurs through an explicit consideration of current account imbalances in the adjustment process – and not sticky goods prices.

9. In a spirit of generosity we can consider the technique of chart reading to be a third theoretical line of exchange-rate explanation. Here, the exchange rate is determined fully through autoregressive patterns that arise from charts displaying the historical pattern of the time series of the relevant exchange rate.

Questions

1. In high-inflation countries the relative price changes between individual goods are overwhelmed by the general price level movement. Argue whether PPP holds better for high-or low-inflation countries.

2. Labour-intensive services (medical care, domestic servants, haircuts, etc.) that are, in principle, non-tradables are, expressed in the same currency, usually cheaper in poorer countries than in wealthy countries. What does this reveal about the applicability of the PPP theory to approach the equilibrium exchange rate for different types of countries, wealthy versus poor?

3. Using the monetary approach with flexible prices to the exchange rate, explain how (direction and channel of change) the following events will affect the exchange rate:

   (a) a foreign increase of national production;
   (b) an increase of the domestic interest rate.

      These channels of influence are not unique and quantitatively possibly even not the most important ones.

   (c) Mention for both (a) and (b) one competing channel of influence and indicate the direction of the influence on the exchange rate.

4. In the case of exchange-rate overshooting as displayed in Figure 13.1, prices start to increase only at time t_2. But price rigidity can have another form, for example, prices that start to move without any delay, but to a much smaller extent than its cause, the money supply shock, and again spread over time. In what direction(s) would in that case the solid line in the figure change?

CHAPTER 14

Exchange-Rate Systems and Effects

14.1 Introduction

In Chapter 13 we discussed the influence of various factors *on* the exchange rate. These influences are incorporated into theories that attempt to explain the exchange rate. In this chapter our interest shifts towards the influence *of* the exchange rate – in other words, there is a move from a consideration of the exchange rate as outcome to an examination of the exchange rate as cause.

The chapter will show that a change in the exchange rate may produce a range of consequences. In order to give an orderly analysis of these consequences, it is useful to distinguish between the influence of the exchange rate on (i) the objectives and (ii) the instruments of economic policy.

The size and frequency of changes in the exchange rate will appear to be important for the influence generated by the exchange rate. These characteristics of exchange-rate changes are not only the outcome of the determining variables of the exchange rates, as discussed in the previous chapter, but also connected with the particular exchange-rate system used by the monetary authorities of individual countries. Section 14.2 will consider the various exchange-rate systems that are available. This section also reviews the consequences for exchange-rate stability of these systems and describes the instruments which a central bank can use to influence the exchange rate.

The principal economic variables influenced directly by the exchange rate are international trade and international capital flows. These, in turn, affect other economic variables, including economic policy objectives. This is true not only in the case of the most obvious objective variable – the balance of payments – but the international flows can also have an effect on other economic variables, such as wage rates and business profits, and, in doing so, ultimately, on economic policy objectives such as inflation, economic growth, and employment. These potential influences of the exchange rate are discussed in Sections 14.3–14.5.

The main dividing line in the instruments of macroeconomic policy is that between monetary policy and fiscal policy. In Sections 14.6 and 14.7 it will appear that the topical exchange-rate system, including the opportunity of exchange-rate changes, is relevant for the effectiveness of these economic policies.

14.2 Exchange-rate systems and policy

In the global economy, there are a wide variety of exchange-rate systems (or regimes). In terms of the overall classification, the two most extreme – and opposed – systems:

floating and *fixed* exchange rates. A system of floating exchange rates is also often termed a flexible exchange-rate system. In practice, people are often inclined to talk about floating versus fixed exchange rates although in doing so they generally also mean modified, more intermediate systems.

In a fixed exchange-rate system a country's monetary authorities maintain a chosen value for the exchange rate of the domestic currency in relation to a chosen foreign currency. This task is usually carried out through the actions of the central bank, which defends the chosen exchange rate through interventions in the foreign-exchange market by means of buying and selling foreign currencies for domestic currency. By increasing its demand for foreign currency, it can bring about a fall in the value of its domestic currency. Similarly, an increased demand for its own currency drives up its price relative to that of other currencies. The official reserve asset holdings are the buffer stock for these foreign currencies. The bulk of these are usually made up of gold and freely convertible currencies held by the central bank.

Today, gold is the odd man out. Its position in international monetary reserves dates back to the days of the gold standard (see Section 16.3), when gold was central to the operation of the international monetary system. It has now lost this position altogether.

The system that was applied internationally in the first two decades after the Second World War is a more flexible variant of the fixed exchange-rate system, the so-called *adjustable peg* system, which is often referred to as a fixed exchange-rate system. In the adjustable peg system the exchange rate is only allowed to fluctuate within a small band around a central rate – known as the peg value. The central rate is the officially fixed value of a major foreign currency in terms of the domestic currency. The use of a fluctuation band reflects the fact that it is technically difficult to keep the exchange rate at an entirely fixed value. It is impractical for a central bank to react to every single small change in the exchange rate by making interventions. The band usually has a width of just a few percentage points on either side of the central rate. The adjustable-peg feature of this system is the permission of a one-off adjustment in the central rate from time to time.

By contrast, in a flexible exchange-rate system the monetary authorities abstain from any interventions on the forex market in order to attempt to influence the level of their currency's exchange rate. Moreover, they also refrain from the so-called accommodating adjustments of other economic policy instruments, which could be carried out with the explicit intention of affecting the exchange rate. Of course, this does not rule out changes in these instruments in the pursuit of other economic goals. But such changes are regarded as autonomous from the viewpoint of the exchange-rate system. The way in which this system and a fixed exchange-rate system with a fluctuation band work can be clarified by the example discussed in Box 14.1.

Box 14.1   A graphical presentation of the foreign-exchange market

In Figure 14.1 the straight lines abe and fac are the supply and demand lines of the private sector for the foreign currency on the foreign-exchange market. They have the characteristic directions of a supply and demand line, as the vertical axis shows the exchange rate, *E*, or the price of foreign currency – in terms of units of the domestic currency. If the horizontal lines bd and cg were not present, the figure would represent a system of flexible exchange rates, in which the central bank abstains from intervening on

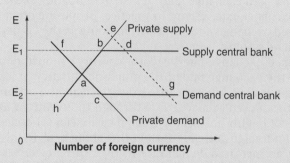

Figure 14.1 Supply and demand on the foreign-exchange market

the foreign-exchange market. In this circumstance there would be no supply and demand of the central bank in this market. Only private supply and demand would determine the exchange-rate value, namely a.

Under a system of flexible exchange rates the consequence of, say, an exogenous increase in the level of private demand for foreign currency is that the (private) demand curve shifts to the right – for example, to the position of the dashed line eg. This causes a rise of the exchange rate – from level a to level e. As a result the value of the foreign currency increases, the currency appreciates. Its counterpart is that the domestic currency value on the forex market falls or the domestic currency depreciates.

Under a fixed exchange-rate system that has E_1 and E_2 as its upper and lower limits, the initial equilibrium value a of the exchange rate is within the fluctuation band. The horizontal supply and demand curves of the central bank at the level of these two exchange rate limits restrict the width of the fluctuation band of the exchange rate accordingly.

In this fixed exchange-rate system the total supply and demand curves of the foreign-exchange market are obtained through the horizontal aggregation of, on the one hand, the two supply curves and, on the other, the two demand curves. These total curves are the two hooked lines in bold: the supply curve hbd and the demand curve fcg.

The result of an exogenous increase in private demand for foreign currencies (or a shift of the private demand curve to the dashed line eg) is now, under a fixed exchange-rate system, a rise of the exchange rate from the level of the initial intersection point a to the level E_1: the exchange rate reaches the upper limit of its fluctuation band. This is a more moderate increase of the exchange rate compared with the flexible exchange-rate situation and could only come about with the help of periodic central bank interventions in the form of a sale of foreign currency out of the official reserves holdings to the amount of bd. This intervention is carried out at the level of the upper intervention point E_1.

For the period after the Second World War a fixed exchange-rate system with only a small fluctuation band was considered to be too rigid for a country's monetary authorities. Hence, the introduction of the adjustable peg system. Between the end of the Second World War and 1973 the adjustable peg system was applied throughout the world (for details, see Section 16.4). After that time it held a prominent position in the European Monetary System (EMS) until the transition to the euro in 1999. Figure 14.2 illustrates a typical time path of the exchange rate and its fluctuation band under an adjustable peg and allows a discussion of its weak points.

In this figure, *E* again denotes the exchange rate and the horizontal dashed lines represent the central rate at a certain moment in time. The horizontal solid lines on both

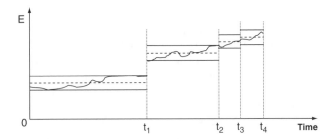

Figure 14.2 The adjustable peg system over time

sides of and at equal distances from the central rate are the limits of the fluctuation band. The erratic line that moves within the fluctuation band represents the exchange rate itself over time.

At time t_1 the monetary authorities of the home country raise the central rate, leading to a devaluation of the home currency. (Of course, it is simultaneously a revaluation of the foreign currency.) In the case of a flexible exchange rate we tend to use the term depreciation rather than devaluation and appreciation rather than revaluation.

In the final period before t_1 the exchange rate has already been pushed against the upper limit of the band. This pattern suggests central bank interventions in the foreign-exchange market in order to support the home currency.

If the bank had not conducted these interventions the exchange-rate line would have crossed the upper limit in the upward direction. This has been prevented by a sale of the foreign currency from the official reserve asset holdings. Of course, these reserves are limited and there will come a time when the central bank decides to stop further support-ing interventions – for example, because remaining holdings are too small to be effective for future interventions. Such a withdrawal from the forex market implies that the pri-vate market forces regain their control of the exchange rate and that the central rate has to be adjusted upwards. This happens at t_1. Of course, the fluctuation band shifts at the same time.

The central bank's holdings of reserve assets are available in published statistics. If for-eign currency speculators discover the low level of remaining reserves before t_1, they may start to speculate against the home currency. This will lead to a further shift of the private demand curve to the right (as shown in Figure 14.1) and, thus, the need for even more intensive official interventions to defend the actual central rate. These interventions will be impossible under the then ruling low reserves level and will accelerate the adjustment in the central rate. At this point one frequently chosen way out of this situation is to let the exchange-rate float (temporarily) rather than to bring about an adequate adjustment of the central rate. One reason might be that in uncertain times it is often difficult to make a good estimate of the adequate adjustment of the central rate.

The usual pattern of the exchange rate immediately after the adjustment of the central rate is that it is pushed against the lower limit of the new fluctuation band. The rea-son is that currency speculators unwind their currency positions immediately after the adjustment: the large amounts of the home currency that they sold before time t_1 are repurchased. They return to their initial investments or repay their initial loans in the now cheaper home currency. This action will make the home currency temporarily more expensive, which explains the low value of the exchange rate during the short period immediately after t_1. Incidentally, an exchange-rate adjustment at t_1 is also then profitable for the speculators as they repurchase the home currency at a lower price in terms of the foreign currency than the price they received for the sale of the home currency before t_1.

Under an adjustable peg system, the exchange rate can move freely within the fluctuation band. In this circumstance there is no formal need for any intervention in the foreign-exchange market, although intra-marginal interventions (interventions while the exchange rate is not at one of the limits of the fluctuation band) may actually make sense: a central bank can thereby avoid being cornered as the limits of the fluctuation band are approached and it prevents a one-way bet for speculators.

On the other hand, when a broad fluctuation band is used there can be advantages for the central bank to allowing the rate to move to the limits of the band because the foreign-exchange speculator who is gambling on devaluation is exposed to a substantial exchange-rate risk. If a currency that is under pressure eventually recovers, it can quickly gain several percentage points in value within the band, as the exchange rate can go down over a great distance. This danger will moderate the level of speculation.

In an adjustable peg system the central bank is still likely to stick to the fixed exchange rate when the central rate has gone out of balance. It is not immediately apparent whether or not the imbalance is only a transitory or permanent disruption of the equilibrium – and only in the latter case should a central rate adjustment be considered. Another reason for this possible rigidity is the fear that devaluation will cause a loss of prestige on the part of the country. The imbalance in the value of the exchange rate can then be aggravated, and in that case more severe tensions will have to be released later – with more disruptive effects.

Interventions on the forex market are not the only – nor even the most powerful – instrument that the central bank has at its disposal in order to defend a fixed exchange rate. In general, changes in interest rates are more effective. Furthermore, the advantage of interest rate adjustments over forex market interventions is that there is almost no limit to the use of the interest rate instrument to defend a flagging currency. Each of these statements requires some explanation.

The holdings of international monetary reserves are, of course, limited. At the end of April 2007, and based on calculations from statistics supplied by the International Monetary Fund (IMF), the global value of these holdings was estimated to be some $6118 billion. On the other hand, in the same month the average daily turnover on the world's forex spot markets amounted to just over $1000 billion. In the event of a substantial speculative attack this turnover is likely to grow substantially. The reserve holdings are, therefore, equal to only a few days' turnover on the forex market. In terms of size the reserves are, for that reason, an instrument with only limited power to resist a surge of speculation against particular currencies. Of course, once the reserves have been used up, a creditworthy country can borrow additional funds from other central banks or from the international capital markets, but that does not alter the fact that there is little scope for forex market intervention to counter strong sentiments of exchange-rate changes.

With changes in the interest rate the situation is somewhat different. A country can, in principle, raise the interest rate to a very high level – and in practice this does occur now and then. In the industrial countries, a central bank occasionally actually raises the short-term rate to several hundred per cent in order to defend the exchange rate. This happened, for example, in both Sweden and France in the 1980s. Of course, such actions are usually taken for a limited period of, say, several days, because the aim is to discourage foreign-exchange speculators, who mostly work on a time scale of no more than a few weeks.

The theoretical basis for using the interest rate instrument is the uncovered interest rate parity, shown in equation (12.2). Here we see that if foreign-exchange speculators start to believe that the home currency will depreciate, there is a rise in the term 'expected relative exchange-rate change' on the right-hand side of the equation. According to the uncovered interest parity, the central bank in charge of the home currency will have to set the short-term interest rate differential with the other country at the same level as the value of the expected relative exchange-rate change to create a compensating, opposing force. Only then will the central bank be successful in counteracting speculative capital outflows. Under such circumstances, it may be necessary to introduce a very high interest rate, as Box 14.2 demonstrates.

Box 14.2 The interest rate weapon against capital flight

Capital flight out of a currency (the home currency) is encouraged by the expectation that its value is likely to fall at some point in the near future.

For example, let us assume that forex speculators estimate that the currency is overvalued by around 10 per cent and they believe that there is an 80 per cent chance of the fixed rate falling by that percentage in the next week. The flight out of the threatened currency, with the intention of returning as soon as the devaluation has taken place, provides the speculator – according to her own expectations – with an expected value of the speculation gain of 0.8×10 per cent $+ 0.2 \times 0$ per cent $= 8$ per cent in one week's time. Converted to an annual basis, a profit of 8 per cent in one week is equal to an annual profit of 52 (weeks) $\times 8$ per cent $= 416$ per cent!

If the domestic central bank is to resist capital flight successfully, then we must think in terms of the creation of a short-term interest rate advantage for domestic investments of the same size. Interest rates are published on an annual basis. Only as the result of an interest rate hike of more than 400 per cent can a foreign-exchange speculator become indifferent between a one-week investment abroad or at home.

Obviously, because of the potentially very disruptive effects of such high interest rates for the rest of the domestic economy, a policy such as this can only be maintained over a short period of time. The speculator is aware of this fact, so that it may become a battle of wills as to who can and will hold out longer: the monetary authorities or the speculators?

The interest rate parity in equation (12.2) reveals that if the fixed exchange-rate policy is credible, interest rates in the two countries involved in the exchange rate will have to be almost identical because the term 'expected relative change in the exchange rate' in the parity is then very close to zero. In such circumstances, a small variation between the two interest rates will suffice to prompt an immediate and large capital flow to the country with the higher interest rate. The interest rate weapon, therefore, is very effective in supporting a weakening currency as long as its central rate is credible.

In their intervention policy the monetary authorities also keep an eye on the 'expected relative exchange-rate change' – in the uncovered interest parity. For their part, foreign-exchange speculators do not know everything.

If these speculators are hesitant in certain situations, then they are likely to be susceptible to signals from the central bank. This means that if the bank in such an occasion takes firm and convincing action to support the currency through market interventions, these will have a stabilizing effect on the expectation of the speculators about a change in the exchange rate.

This signalling effect may cause foreign-exchange speculators to back off. They then use the central bank's (presumably) good insight into the future exchange rate to justify the revision of their own behaviour. The tendency to follow central banks will be greatly increased if several central banks decide upon joint, coordinated intervention in the forex market in order to support a currency that is under pressure. This brings in the psychological effect of intervention, and underlines the relevance of the art of good timing.

If, on the other hand, the market intervention appears unfounded, the signalling function of intervention lacks this psychological effect – and may even work in the opposite direction. If the central bank loses its 'game' with the speculators and the value of the currency falls in spite of the (coordinated) support operation, then the central bank has lost some of its credibility in the eyes of the forex speculators. This may mean that a future intervention in the foreign-exchange market will lack its signalling effect.

In addition to the adjustable peg system and floating exchange rates, there are a number of other exchange-rate systems that allow for an adjustment of the exchange rate: the target zone, the crawling peg, and the managed floating exchange rate.

In recent years the *target zone* has attracted considerable attention in relation to plans to establish a new adjustable peg system throughout the world. The idea is a cautious form of the adjustable peg system with wider fluctuation margins of, say, 10 per cent on either side of the central rate for the world's leading currencies. The *weak* target zone is a variant that even allows that the exchange rate crosses the limits of the fluctuation band. It is distinguished from a floating exchange-rate system because if the exchange rate is outside the band in a weak target zone, a change in the country's economic policy involved has to give support to a return of the exchange rate to the band.

A *crawling peg* is an adjustable peg which has the additional feature that central rate adjustments are made regularly and in small steps. This system became notorious during the 1960s and 1970s when it was applied by various developing countries in Latin America during periods of very high domestic inflation. The large inflation differential with countries such as the United States forced these countries to make a great many adjustments to their central rates.

However, under more moderate economic conditions such a system can certainly have some attractions. If the exchange-rate changes are small, it is possible that the subsequent fluctuation bands partly overlap as a result of the frequent parity adjustments. That is the case in Figure 14.2 with the adjustments at times t_2 and t_3. Such situations generate additional uncertainty among speculators because even if the central rate adjustment that they expect is actually made, they can still suffer a foreign-exchange loss. This is, in fact, what happens in Figure 14.2 at t_2, because immediately following the adjustment – when the speculative pressure is over – the weak currency recovers so that, in spite of the new and higher central rate, the actual exchange rate is below the old level of the upper intervention bound for some time.

A *managed floating* exchange-rate system exists if the central bank occasionally enters the foreign-exchange market, using interventions to steer the exchange rate. The bank resists, for example, looming (further) changes in the exchange rate. This is particularly useful if a change is expected to be temporary. If the domestic currency is weakening, it is supported by selling foreign currencies, while conversely a strengthening currency is countered by the purchase of foreign currencies. This kind of intervention policy is known as 'leaning against the wind', a variant of managed floating.

From 1990, exchange-rate systems with *irrevocably fixed* exchange rates have become increasingly popular. They manifest themselves as a monetary union (or currency area), a currency board, and so-called dollarization. In a monetary union the co-operating countries choose to introduce a common currency. A country that applies a currency board fixes the exchange rate of its currency irrevocably to another currency, often the US dollar, and follows some specific rules to give support to this exchange rate. In the event of (full) dollarization, a country abolishes its currency, whereupon another currency – again usually the US dollar – is accepted officially as money for domestic payments. In Chapter 19 we will discuss recent applications of each of them.

14.3 The current account and international trade

In any discussion of the effects of exchange rates on international trade, a distinction should be made between a one-off change in the exchange rate and an exchange rate that shows a pattern of volatility over time. The influence of a one-off change of the exchange rate on the value of a country's international trade flows and hence on its trade balance (i.e., the balance of the goods and services accounts of the balance of payments) will be analysed in Sections 14.3.1 and 14.3.2. The subject of Section 14.3.3 is the effect of exchange-rate volatility.

14.3.1 The absorption approach

The exchange rate is a macroeconomic variable par excellence. The starting point for a macroeconomic review of the exchange-rate effect on the trade balance is the income identity, which indicates that a country's domestic production is made up of various components. Expressed as a formula, this identity is:

$$Y \equiv C + I + G + X - IM, \tag{14.1}$$

where Y is domestic production, C is consumption by residents, I is investment by residents, G is the country's government spending, and X and IM denote the country's exports and imports, respectively. All these economic variables are nominal, expressed in terms of domestic currency.

The sum of the first three variables on the right-hand side of this identity ($C + I + G$) is also known as total spending by residents or domestic spending; it is also labelled absorption, denoted A. By deducting imports we arrive at residents' spending on domestic products. If we next add exports – that is, foreign purchases of domestic products – we obtain a figure for the total spending on goods produced in the country. In the statistics for a particular period in the past, this total expenditure on domestic goods will always be equal to domestic production – which explains the identity character of equation (14.1). If there is an incipient production surplus, then domestic producers are obliged to stockpile their unsold products. However, these stocks are, by definition and thus in the statistics, included in investments – voluntary or enforced – so that equation (14.1) also holds true in that surplus situation.

By substituting A for ($C + I + G$) in equation (14.1) and after a minor rearrangement of the other variables, we arrive at the following identity:

$$X - IM \equiv Y - A \tag{14.2}$$

This shows that the trade surplus ($X - IM$) is always equal in value to the difference between domestic production Y and absorption A.

Equation (14.2) is an identity. In contrast to behavioural equations, it presents no causal relationships. It merely expresses the feature that a balance of payments problem in the form of an import surplus is necessarily associated with surplus spending of the country's residents to the same amount. This relation has become known as the absorption approach to the balance of payments and it became known mainly through the work of Alexander (1952). The equation also shows us that if a country succeeds in increasing domestic production and/or reducing spending by residents, this is bound to be associated with an improvement in the trade balance of the country in question.

Equation (14.2) can be developed somewhat further to include the whole current account balance. Its left-hand side does not comprise the complete current account balance. Net income earned abroad by production factors (or the international transactions on the income account of the balance of payments) misses, as does net inflow of unilateral transfers (or the current transfers account). (See Chapter 11 for the the insertion of the accounts between brackets in the balance of payments system.) If we add in equation (14.2) the combined balance of these two missing accounts, denoted N, to both the left-hand side and the right-hand side, the outcome, equation (14.3), remains an identity:

$$CA \equiv (Y + N) - A \tag{14.3}$$

Once again this represents the absorption approach, but in a slightly different form. Now the current account balance, CA, is identical to national income, $(Y + N)$, minus domestic spending or absorption A.

Another interesting relationship is obtained from equation (14.3) if we add government income from taxes, T, twice to the right-hand side: once with a plus sign and once with a minus sign. This change does not alter the identity character of equation (14.3). Replacing absorption by its component parts, we arrive at the following identity:

$$CA \equiv Y + N - C - T - I + T - G.$$

Private savings are defined as the part of national income not spent on either consumption or the tax bill. On the right-hand side of this identity the combination $(Y + N - C - T)$ is therefore equal to private savings, S. If we replace them by S, the result is:

$$CA \equiv (S - I) + (T - G) \tag{14.4}$$

The left-hand side represents the current account balance. The first term on the right-hand side gives the difference between private savings and private investments. The second term is the difference between the government's tax revenue and government spending. This difference is the fiscal surplus or the government's savings. Equation (14.4) shows that the current account balance is fully linked to private savings surplus and the government's fiscal surplus. Once again, there is no causal relationship as equation (14.4) is an identity. We can only state that any current account deficit must imply a simultaneous private savings deficit and/or government deficit. In order to reduce a current account deficit it is necessary either to reduce the private savings deficit or the government deficit (or both).

Identities (14.2)–(14.4) contain important information about the influence of the exchange rate on the trade balance and the current account balance. Equations (14.2) and (14.3) state that currency devaluation will only improve these two balances if it increases domestic production and national income and/or decreases absorption. This can be seen as a boundary condition for this effect. According to identity (14.4), an alternative boundary condition for an effective devaluation is that the devaluation improves the level of private net savings and/or the government budgetary position. In Section 16.4 we will see that these boundary conditions influenced the IMF in formulating its policy conditions for member countries that want to receive an IMF credit.

Note that these macroeconomic relations for the exchange-rate effect on the balance of payments are not derived from any specific economic theory. They are identities obtained without the use of any behavioural equations. (Behavioural equations describe the behaviour of economic subjects – the private sector and government. It is in the specific assumptions regarding this behaviour that economic theories differ from one another.) The attention paid to the identities (14.2)–(14.4) in practical policy-making dates mainly from the 1980s. A well-known application regards the debate since 1985 on the reduction of the American trade deficit, which was then considered to be worryingly large. The ruling conviction was that the so-called twin deficit of a current account deficit and a fiscal deficit was linked irrevocably, so that the current account deficit could only be reduced through a reduction of the fiscal deficit. This idea obviously relies heavily on equation 14.4, but this equation also proves that the link is not irrevocable: the potentially disturbing factor is private net savings.

14.3.2 The Marshall–Lerner condition

In the equation below the left-hand side defines the balance of the (value of the) trade account with, as in the previous sub-section, X (IM) being the value of exports (imports).

$$X - IM \equiv P_x.x - P_{im}.im \equiv E.P_x^*.x - E.P_{im}^*.im \tag{14.5}$$

This formula expresses that, by definition, the export (import) value in domestic currency is equal to price of exports (imports) in domestic currency multiplied by the export (import) volume. Here, P_x is the export price level and P_m the import price level, both expressed in domestic currency, and the small letters x and im represent the volume of exports and imports, respectively.

On the right-hand side of equation (14.5) the prices in domestic currency have been rewritten by subdividing these prices into the exchange-rate component and the price of the same goods expressed in terms of the foreign currency. The addition of an asterisk (*) to a variable indicates that it is denominated in foreign currency. The symbol E expresses the nominal exchange rate as usual, as the number of domestic currency units per unit of foreign currency.

Because equation (14.5) is a definition equation, on the right-hand side it shows the variables through which an exchange-rate change affects the trade balance. However, in order to itemize that, we need to introduce behavioural assumptions for these variables. A simple assumption is that *supply* prices are constant. This implies that the country in question is merely a price taker for its (demand for) import goods and is evidently a small consumer in comparison with the world economy. In contrast, on its export side the country is able to fully determine its (supply) price in domestic currency. Here it is the price in foreign currency that is derived from that domestic price. The underlying assumption is that in the export sector domestic supply is so elastic that demand changes do not influence the domestic price of export goods.

Let us consider the influence of a depreciation of the domestic currency – so an increase of E – by 1 per cent, assuming constant supply prices. Then, in equation (14.5), depreciation does not affect the export price in domestic currency, whereas it increases the import price in domestic currency by the same 1 per cent. This implies that the term of the import value on the right-hand side of equation (14.5) also increases by 1 per cent. Consequently, as the export value remains constant, the trade balance will deteriorate through the depreciation effect on prices. This is opposite to the desired – and also usually expected – improvement of the trade balance in the case of depreciation. This improvement will therefore have to come from positive changes in trade volumes. The depreciation causes a decrease in the foreign currency price of the country's exports. This will foster foreign demand for these export goods and, thus, expectations are that it fosters the export volume, x. On the import side the depreciation causes an increase in the domestic price. The usual assumption is that this will hamper domestic demand for import goods, im. These two volume effects of depreciation cause, in equation (14.5), a rise in the export volume and a fall in the import volume, both contributing to an improvement of the trade balance.

Clearly, these two volume effects will only more than offset the negative import price effect of the depreciation on the trade balance if they are sufficiently large. Only then will the depreciation lead to a net improvement in the trade balance. The so-called Marshall–Lerner condition describes this requirement. It confronts the price elasticities of the demand volumes of exports and imports with the devaluation percentage (also being the size of the price effect). In its simple form the Marshall–Lerner condition requires that the sum of the (absolute) values of the price elasticities of both export demand (abroad) and import demand (at home) exceeds the value one (being the assumed depreciation percentage). Then the combined sizes of the (positive) demand effects of depreciation are larger than the (negative) price effect. Only in this circumstance will depreciation improve the trade balance.

In deriving the simple form, it is assumed that there is a trade balance equilibrium in the starting situation and, moreover, that the supply elasticities are infinitely large. There are more general forms of the Marshall–Lerner condition. They depend upon weakened assumptions regarding the initial trade balance and the size of supply elasticities, and thus the degree to which depreciation pushes up import and export prices.

The absorption approach described in the previous sub-section is in its simple form – equation (14.2) – also a condition for a positive effect of depreciation upon the trade balance. Does it obstruct the Marshall–Lerner condition? Not at all: it simply stresses its relevance. If the domestic demand for imports is to be reduced by depreciation, then absorption must fall. If that does not happen, then the import value in domestic currency cannot decrease either. Moreover, there is only room for the export value in domestic currency to increase if the export volume increases and, thus, domestic production increases and/or absorption decreases. The latter two are precisely the two terms on the right-hand side of the absorption approach equation (14.2). Increase of domestic production requires unemployment and spare production capacity in the starting situation, whereas decrease of absorption necessitates a domestic expenditure-reducing policy.

To this point the Marshall–Lerner condition has been interpreted as the requirement for an improvement in the trade balance as a result of depreciation of the domestic currency. The significance of the Marshall–Lerner condition goes beyond this finding. The question that the Marshall–Lerner condition answers is essentially this: Under what exchange market conditions will a depreciation have the effect of reducing a trade deficit or, more generally, will a higher price of the foreign currency bring about a net demand reduction for that foreign currency? In other words, under what condition is the exchange market stable? If the equilibrium on a market is disrupted, then a *stable* market implies that the disruption leads to a price change that, in its turn, rectifies the disruption.

Let us assume that there is a trade deficit. This implies excess demand for foreign currency and the spontaneous market reaction is a higher price of the foreign currency – and thus a depreciation of the domestic currency. If the latter reduces that excess demand, the market will be stable. If it does not, then we have an unstable market with growing imbalances and a price that diverges increasingly from its equilibrium value as soon as the market equilibrium is upset. In the case of an unstable exchange market, the forces of demand and supply push the exchange rate further away from its equilibrium value.

In practice, even just from the point of view of the trade balance, the foreign-exchange market certainly need not be stable. Absence of stability occurs if the Marshall–Lerner condition is not fulfilled. This phenomenon has even been given a name if it only comes about in the short term: the J-curve effect. It ties in with our previous analysis of the price and volume effects of depreciation.

In the J-curve effect the price effect in the Marshall–Lerner condition takes place immediately after depreciation, but the volume effects take some time to appear. This means that the deterioration of the trade balance as the result of the price effect occurs immediately

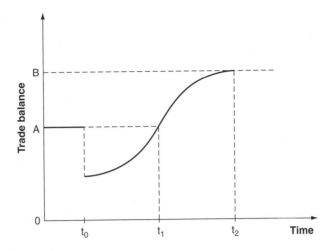

Figure 14.3   The J-curve

after the depreciation at time t_0, as observable in Figure 14.3. The positive volume effects on the trade balance arise only gradually over time. This response is observable in the pattern in the trade balance after t_0 in Figure 14.3. From time t_1 onwards, the volume effects gain the upper hand, after which it is not until time t_2 before the effect of the depreciation wears off. Eventually the trade balance has improved to the extent of AB. (The name of the curve is easy to understand if Figure 14.3 is turned slightly in an anticlockwise direction.) In the figure in the short term the forex market is unstable, because the depreciation of the domestic currency – and, thus, the higher value of the foreign currency – initially *increases* the net demand for foreign currency on the forex market. But in the end it is stable after all, since in the longer term this exchange-rate change reduces the net demand for foreign currency.

14.3.3 The effect of exchange-rate volatility

As has been stated earlier, exchange-rate volatility adds an element of uncertainty to international trade transactions that is absent in domestic trade. This uncertainty arises because an international trade contract always includes an invoice currency that is foreign for at least one of the two contracting parties.

The currency in which the international transaction is denominated is called the *invoice currency*, because that is the one in which the invoice is made out. Normal practice in an international market may determine the invoice currency. For example, in the international oil market it is common to use the US dollar as invoice currency. The market position of each contracting party may also affect the choice of invoice currency. A goods trader usually prefers invoicing in her own currency, and if she has a strong negotiation position she will make that choice – in order to avoid the uncertainty that a foreign invoice currency creates. On the other hand, if, for example, a Dutch exporter is very keen to clinch a deal with an Australian importer, then she might be willing to make a concession by offering the option of the Australian dollar as the invoice currency. If both contracting parties have a preference for their own currency, then a compromise is to invoice in a third currency – often the US dollar.

It is unusual for a trade contract to be executed immediately. Once the contract has been signed it is usual for some time to lapse before the delivery of the goods. It will often be several more months before payment is made. In the period between the signing of the contract and the eventual payment the exchange rate may change, sometimes by a considerable amount.

Since an international goods trader normally wishes to avoid risk, this uncertainty has a negative value for the trader concerned. By contrast, a transaction within national borders does not entail this foreign-exchange uncertainty. That is why we expect increasing exchange-rate variations, and the greater uncertainty that is directly associated with them, to bring about a shift from international to national trade. From a welfare point of view this implies a failure to make full use of the advantages of international specialization of production. As we also saw in Chapter 3, this is detrimental to the welfare of the world as a whole and the countries involved in the afflicted international trade transaction in particular.

In practice, the adverse effect of short-term exchange-rate fluctuation and uncertainty on the volume of international trade is far less than expected, because goods traders have the option of hedging their exchange-rate risk – something which will be discussed further in Chapter 15. Normally, a hedge transaction involves additional costs, which an exporter will pass on in the sales price. This means that the export cost is likely to be somewhat higher than the price of a purely domestic transaction. This effect may, to some extent, also undermine the optimum allocation of production in the world.

In the medium and the long term, possible exchange-rate movements can cause other problems. In practice, we are talking here about fluctuations in the rate over a period of more than one year. Over such long periods it is much more difficult to hedge exchange-rate risks.

In addition, the international trader faces a different problem: international trade is seldom confined to a single, independent transaction. In most cases it will be part of a long series of transactions generated by the opening up of a trade channel. This usually entails substantial initial investment (so-called sunk costs) by the exporter in the country to which goods are to be sold. The nature of this investment may vary from one product to another. Sometimes it is only a matter of finding a suitable importer; in another case it is a question of opening up retail sales channels. Another future investment often necessary to 'breaking open' a market is to establish a service network to provide after-sales service and also advertising campaigns.

It can take many years for a business to recoup the cost of these initial investments, so that one must be reasonably certain that the export being launched will continue for a number of years. However, one problem is that a profitable competitive position can be turned into loss-making exports simply as the result of exchange-rate fluctuations. A permanent increase in the value of the exporter's currency in the future has a serious and lasting negative impact on its international competitiveness. There is no way of covering this effect of this exchange-rate uncertainty. This is therefore the source of the real danger of future exchange-rate changes for the exporter.

The consequence may be that – afraid of the possibility of undesirable long-term changes in the exchange rate – goods traders refrain from launching exports, even if they are sufficiently competitive on the international market. For large companies, in particular, this may mean that direct investment in the target country is the preferred option (see Chapter 4). In this way they create production costs in the foreign currency against the foreign currency income. This will substantially diminish their exchange-rate risk.

In addition to exchange-rate uncertainty, there is another link between exchange-rate volatility and international trade: the link via protectionism. The central idea is that an increase in the value of the domestic currency makes it harder for domestic producers to sell in export markets and also for the domestic sector to compete with imports. It appears that in the case of a substantial currency appreciation domestic producers may make calls for protectionist measures, in the form of arguments in favour of temporary import levies and export subsidies. All too often a government gives in to these demands.

As soon as the value of the domestic currency reverts to its former level the reason for protection will have disappeared. However, the political economy of protection indicates that once preferential rights have been granted it is difficult for the government to withdraw them. Once rights have been acquired, they often prove to be structural. (For a more detailed discussion of the political economy of protectionism, see Chapter 9.) If the value of the domestic currency subsequently rises again, there are renewed calls for protection, which is often granted once again, so that in the end it, too, becomes permanent. The final result of this gradual accumulation of protection over time is that, with no net increase in the value of the domestic currency, the level of international trade will lag further and further behind the level that it would have attained in the absence of these exchange-rate fluctuations.

As described above, the negative influence of exchange-rate uncertainty on the volume of international trade flows affects the trade balance. Since, however, similar effects are at work in other countries, even the direction of the net effect on a country's trade balance is uncertain.

14.4 | Inflation

There are four channels along which flexible exchange rates can fuel inflation in a country and hence in the world as a whole. Little need be said about the first channel, the price-increasing cost of covering exchange-rate risk. As far as possible, the exporter will pass on these hedging costs to the customer. Insofar as this can be done, the prices of import and export goods give an upward boost to the general price level.

The second channel through which flexible exchange rates can stimulate inflation is the result of the lack of discipline in government behaviour that such rates may engender. Under flexible exchange rates a lax macroeconomic policy that boosts inflation will also undermine the level of international competitiveness. The latter development will be countered by a spontaneous depreciation of the domestic currency. This depreciation gives a boost to inflation through an increase in the domestic prices of internationally tradable goods. Permanently fixed exchange rates make such a lax policy much more dangerous and will, therefore, promote discipline in macroeconomic policy.

The system of fixed exchange rates requires a country's inflation to be kept in line with that in the other countries that participate in the fixed exchange-rate system. This assumed advantage of fixed exchange rates for high-inflation countries is dubbed *borrowing credibility* from an acknowledged low-inflation country. The argument became fashionable in the first years of the existence of the European Monetary System (EMS), an adjustable peg system that functioned between 1979 and 1999, in which most member countries of the European Union took part. It was expected that EMS member countries could borrow credibility from the German central bank, the Deutsche Bundesbank, for their anti-inflationary policies (see Section 19.5 for a more detailed description). After a false start with frequent adjustments of the central rate, during which the EMS displayed some of the features of a crawling peg system, the Netherlands was the first member country that the policy of borrowing credibility energetically put into practice, as is elaborated in Case study 14.1.

Case study 14.1   Dutch exchange-rate policy

In March 1983 the Netherlands devalued the Dutch guilder by 2 per cent against the Deutsche mark (DM) as part of a general realignment of exchange rates within the EMS. It is clear that there was a division of opinion among Dutch policy-makers about this decision. The finance ministry was in favour of the devaluation, but the central bank was opposed. The ministry hoped that, by improving the competitive position in relation to its principal trading partner, Germany, the devaluation would help to reduce the level of unemployment in the Netherlands. According to the central bank, devaluation would have at best only a temporary effect on employment, whereas a constant guilder/DM rate would have a permanent, positive effect on employment. The Dutch central bank got its way with a delay in that the finance minister promised shortly afterwards that this devaluation would be the last. That promise remained unbroken.

The Dutch central bank's position can be defended using the following argument: At this time wages in the Netherlands were totally indexed for price rises. Devaluation would produce a general price rise through an increase in the prices of imports. In a situation of full wage indexation this would initiate a wage-price spiral with a price rise eventually equal to the initial devaluation. Therefore the resulting price increase soon destroys any initial competitive advantage gained from devaluation. In that respect nothing is gained in comparison with a situation without devaluation, except during the price adjustment period.

However, there is a great advantage in refraining from devaluation. In these circumstances the financial markets notice that the guilder is a strong currency, in that it can keep pace with the DM. As a result, like the DM, the guilder acquires the aura of a currency with a tendency to revalue against the other EMS currencies. In the context of the uncovered interest rate parity, this gives the Netherlands scope to cut the interest rate. As the result of lower interest rates, domestic demand for investment and consumer goods receives a permanent boost and that, in turn, promotes employment, or so the argument goes. The irrevocable link to the revaluing DM makes that, moreover, via lower import prices domestic inflation falls.

One objection to the discipline effect on inflation is that it also works in the opposite direction: its effect is symmetrical. This is because countries that, on account of a tight labour market, wish to pursue a restrictive macroeconomic policy that will foster lower inflation are prevented from doing so as this policy is ineffective if exchange rates are fixed. The reason is that lower inflation is likely to improve the country's international competitiveness, stimulate the domestic production of tradable goods, and therefore increase the demand for labour. This encourages the existing labour shortage and thus produces a new stimulation of inflation.

Under flexible exchange rates, a country advocating lower inflation would not be discouraged from achieving its labour market objective in the case described above. The improvement in its international competitiveness due to the restrictive macroeconomic policy can then generate a currency appreciation, which in turn leads to even lower prices for its tradables and therefore to still lower inflation.

If the discipline effect of fixed exchange rates works in both directions and is thus symmetrical, higher average world inflation will not occur a priori with flexible exchange rates. On the one hand, there are countries that use the scope under flexible exchange rates to attain a higher inflation situation. But, conversely, there will also be countries that use it to reduce their inflation rates. This means that it is only to be expected that the spread of national inflation rates in the world will be greater than under a system of fixed exchange rates.

The third channel from variable exchange rates to inflation is related in some ways to the previous one. It is not only a country's policy-makers who lack a disciplinary effect under flexible exchange rates. This applies equally to the private sector. If the exchange rate is flexible, it is, for instance, far less expensive in terms of unemployment for the labour unions to submit high wage claims. If competitiveness is impaired at all, a compensating depreciation of the country's currency will follow promptly so that employment is not at risk. In the case of depreciation, however, the point of such wage demands is dubious: improvements in real income through the realized wage increase are removed by the combination of higher prices of domestically produced goods prompted by higher wage costs and the more expensive imports resulting from the depreciation.

The fourth channel to inflation that may come from flexible exchange rates arises due to a *ratchet effect* in inflation variations. An exchange rate alters because one of the two countries involved has an impending balance of payments surplus and/or the other a looming deficit.

In the deficit country with the depreciating currency, import prices increase because the depreciation makes them higher in terms of the domestic currency. This has an upward effect on the other prices in the country so that the result is an overall price rise. If wages are either partly or totally index-linked for rising prices, then this results in a wage–price spiral. Conversely, however, import prices in the surplus country can and should fall as its currency appreciates, but in practice this often does not happen, or only to a limited extent. Exporters in the depreciating country and/or importers in the appreciating country often prefer to raise their profit margins instead. Thus, prices evidently rise in the country with the depreciating currency, but decline to a much lesser extent, if at all, in the country with the appreciating currency. Prices are upwardly flexible, but it is assumed that there is a great deal of resistance to price reductions, as if there were a ratchet to prevent them. Hence the use of the term 'ratchet effect'. The end result is that price rises in one country are accompanied by a smaller or zero price reduction in the other country, so that worldwide there is a net increase in prices as a result of the exchange-rate change.

However, there is some dispute over the evidence of this boost to inflation resulting from exchange-rate changes. People have questioned this asymmetric ratchet effect. In practice, the import price of the depreciating country often does not actually increase. One reason is that in the case of an appreciation of their currency, export companies are often afraid that a complete pass-through of the appreciation on the domestic prices of the import country will impair their export market shares. In order to prevent this, they reduce their export prices in terms of their own currency.

Up to this point we have compared flexible exchange rates with a situation in which exchange rates are fixed permanently. This may offer a useful basis for comparison, but it is not realistic. In practice, as we saw in Section 14.2, often even fixed exchange rates can be adjusted. Of course, they are kept fixed as far as possible, but if a fundamental disequilibrium develops – often only gradually – in the economy concerned, then a one-off adjustment is made in the exchange rate. The adjustable peg system is a clear example of this practice.

Following the adjustment, every effort is made to keep the rate fixed at that new level. But such attempts are not always successful. It is these occasional exchange-rate adjustments that can equally well stimulate inflation in the manner described above. A counter-argument here is that, in practice, the cumulative exchange-rate changes are normally far smaller in an adjustable peg system than under flexible exchange rates.

14.5 | Growth and unemployment

The influence of exchange-rate variations on both trade and inflation are also felt in terms of a country's level of economic growth and unemployment. Exchange-rate variability, as a result of the associated uncertainty and the introduction of protectionist measures, reduces the volume of world trade, and this has a direct negative effect on world production and employment. If exchange-rate variations stimulate world inflation, they may also stimulate employment in the short term. However, in the longer term, inflation could well have the reverse effect on employment, reflecting the present-day view from economic theory that a negative relation exists between the inflation *level* and production and employment levels, particularly in the event of high inflation.

In addition to the indirect links described above, there are also two direct connections between variable exchange rates and unemployment. Let us confine ourselves to the case of a flexible exchange rate showing just swings, but no upward or downward trend. These swings will generate similar swings in the mutual competitive position of the two countries concerned. As a result there will be swings in production and labour input between the tradable and non-tradable sectors of these countries. The usual rigidities and lack of transparency in the labour market generate a permanent increase in the level of frictional unemployment and thus in welfare costs associated with these labour movements.

Worse is the unemployment that arises because some of the firms producing internationally tradable goods are forced to stop production completely due to a merely temporary currency appreciation and the associated temporarily increased international competitive pressure. Subsequently, in better times, they are unable to return as producers if the required initial investments (or sunk costs) for restarting production are too expensive in comparison with the expected profitability. In this way exchange-rate swings may contribute to permanent or structural unemployment.

A final, indirect link between flexible exchange rates and unemployment regards the implication of exchange-rate uncertainty for foreign direct investment. An exporting firm may respond to exchange-rate uncertainty by deciding to switch part of its production to the country in which it is sold. This will mean that, henceforth, revenues in a foreign currency (assuming that that currency was the invoice currency of the former export contracts) can be set against production costs in the same currency. The attraction of this foreign direct investment is that it reduces – or even eliminates – the influence of exchange-rate changes on the profitability of foreign sales. This foreign direct investment reduces employment in the home country, but increases it in the host country. Economic welfare effects of the foreign direct investment for the countries involved are nonetheless not so clear as they also depend on the possible transfer of profits to the home country, the (loss of the) learning-by-doing effect of production, and so on.

14.6 | Monetary policy

When we refer to the effectiveness of macroeconomic policy, what we are considering is the sensitivity of domestic policy objectives to a particular change in the intensity of that policy. The level of domestic production is normally at the forefront of domestic policy objectives and therefore also in this and the next section.

The effectiveness of monetary policy is supported by a *flexible* exchange rate, as may be seen from the following example. The monetary authorities of a country believe that its economy needs a temporary stimulus. Therefore they decide to bring about a temporary increase in the money supply. This monetary expansion leads to a decline in the interest rate. In the absence of free international capital movements, we can assume that this will stimulate the country's investment and consumer expenditures, prompting an increase in the level of domestic demand. This is an incentive for producers to increase their output, and in so doing boosting domestic production.

However, in the case of free international capital movements, the picture is different. In that situation, by virtue of the uncovered interest rate parity, the earlier cut in the domestic interest rate will result in massive capital outflows. Under flexible exchange rates, this development causes an immediate and substantial depreciation of the domestic currency. The depreciation is encouraged further by a gradual deterioration of the current account: it is the result of the increase in domestic production and the concomitant increase in national income and hence also in the domestic demand for tradable goods and services.

The domestic currency depreciation implies that the price of home-produced goods and services becomes more attractive relative to foreign products. This stimulates demand for exports while also causing part of the demand for imports to be switched to domestic production. Over time, increases in demand for home-produced goods give a second boost to domestic production. Overall, it is clear that this room for currency depreciation enlarges the effectiveness of the expansionary monetary policy.

In practice, monetary policy is seen in general as being only temporary effective in countering the economic effects of cyclical economic fluctuations. Over time, a one-off monetary expansion raises the price level. This is because prices are rigid in the short term, but in the longer term they are considered to be much more flexible.

In the medium term, therefore, monetary expansion is followed by a price increase. The immediate effects of monetary expansion mentioned earlier – the decline in interest rates followed by the currency depreciation – which initially stimulated domestic production, thus appear eventually to become totally negated. This is because the eventual price increase will lead to a greater demand for money, so that the initial fall in interest rates is reversed. When this happens the depreciation advantage of large capital outflows is also lost.

Furthermore, the price increase destroys the improvements in competitiveness: the depreciation of the domestic currency is followed with a delay by a domestic price increase, which offsets the improvement in competitiveness. Thus, in the longer term, domestic production gains no real effect at all from the expansionary monetary policy. Breaking this relationship with the price level is the only way for an expansionary monetary policy to have a permanent, positive effect on domestic production.

If the exchange rate is *fixed* and capital movements are free, expansionary monetary policy with the intention of boosting domestic production has little hope of being effective. This is already true in the short term. Under a fixed exchange rate the fall in interest rates as a result of monetary expansion threatens to lead to a devaluation of the domestic currency through both a current account deterioration and huge capital outflows, as under a flexible exchange rate. But in a system of fixed exchange-rates devaluation is not permitted, so the central bank has to avoid it. The primary instrument for that purpose is central bank intervention in the foreign-exchange markets. By selling official monetary reserves in exchange for domestic currency the central bank increases the supply of foreign currency while at the same time reducing the supply of its own currency – two changes which support the value of the domestic currency against foreign currencies and which, if they are sufficiently large, will prevent the devaluation. However, in doing so the central bank takes domestic money out of circulation, thus counteracting – or even totally offsetting – the initial monetary expansion. The monetary stimulus is cancelled out immediately by the rules of the fixed exchange-rate system and domestic production will not even leave its initial level. So, in a system of fixed exchange rates the monetary boost will not even produce a temporary expansionary production effect.

And if a country – despite this knowledge – stubbornly conducts an expansionary monetary policy, the only policy effect it will experience will be a large loss of the reserve asset holdings of the central bank.

The previous policy restriction proves, in effect, the famous *incompatible* or *impossible trinity* in international economics. This states that it is impossible for a country to simultaneously realize three desirable economic policy features: fixed exchange rates, free international capital flows, and national autonomy of monetary policy. There are several serious theoretical arguments in favour of each of these three desirable features, but a country is only able to achieve two of them at the same time. In the description in the two previous paragraphs, monetary policy autonomy was sacrificed in order to secure fixed exchange rates and free capital flows. In the modern world the USA is the example par excellence of a country that prefers autonomy for its monetary policy and free capital flows, but sacrifices fixed exchange rates for that purpose. By contrast, in the present Euro area the member countries have a common currency – the euro – meaning an extreme form of fixed exchange rates. As there is also free capital mobility in this area, the countries had to sacrifice their independent national monetary policy. This explains the centralization of monetary policy at the European Central Bank.

14.7 | Fiscal policy

As in the case of monetary policy, we shall analyse the effectiveness of an expansionary fiscal policy under conditions of first flexible and then fixed exchange rates. An expansionary fiscal policy is reflected in an increased positive difference between government spending and tax revenue. This policy may take the form of higher public spending and/or a cut in taxes. In the latter case, the growth in demand for goods comes not from the government but from an increase in spending of the private sector, where lower taxes imply a higher disposable income.

Let us, as an illustration, consider the increase in public spending. (A lower tax revenue has similar effects.) In a situation where the production factors are not utilized fully, this will stimulate domestic production. However, it will also increase the demand for money, since the public prefers to have larger cash holdings for transactions purposes. At a given level of money supply, this will drive up the interest rate. In response, there is a reduction in private spending, partly offsetting the effect of the initial public spending increase on production.

The increased demand for goods will be aimed partly at foreign goods. The resulting higher level of imports will cause a deterioration of the trade balance. However, in the case of free international capital movements, this effect on the balance of payments via the demand for imports is much lower than the influence of the higher interest rate on the financial account. By virtue of the uncovered interest rate parity, a slight increase in the interest rate immediately draws in huge amounts of foreign capital.

Under a *flexible* exchange rate, this huge capital inflow causes an immediate increase in the value of the domestic currency, in turn causing a deterioration of competitiveness. This prompts a shift in demand both at home and abroad in favour of foreign goods at the expense of domestic products, thereby cancelling out the initial increase in demand.

As a result, there is a depression in the level of domestic production. The resulting fall in money demand for transaction purposes leads to a fall in the level of domestic interest rates. This adjustment process continues until the increase in the value of the domestic currency has brought about a sufficient reduction in the demand for and production of home-produced goods to totally offset the upward movement of money demand and thus interest rates. In order for this to happen, the decline in demand must be equal to the original increase in demand brought about by higher public spending. As a result, demand for and production of domestic goods returns to its original level. Overall, the expansionary fiscal policy has therefore forfeited all influence over the level of production. In other words, fiscal policy is ineffective under a system of flexible exchange rates.

In a *fixed* exchange-rate system the adjustment process following an expansionary fiscal policy will differ from the process described above as soon as the interest rate rises, producing an increase of domestic output, as under a flexible exchange rate, and an incipient revaluation. Under fixed exchange rates, however, the revaluation is not allowed; the threatened rise in the level of the domestic currency has to be resisted. To this end, the central bank has to counterbalance the huge private supply of foreign currency in the foreign-exchange market. For the central bank, this means buying foreign currencies – adding them to the official reserve assets – in return for supplying domestic currency, an activity that increases the amount of money in the hands of the private (non-bank) sector or domestic money supply.

The effect is a reduction in the initially increased level of the domestic interest rate. This gives a second boost to domestic demand, now in the private sector. As under a system of floating exchange rates, this adjustment process continues until the domestic interest rate has returned to its original level. Only then is there an end to the inflow of capital, necessitating foreign-exchange market intervention. We can therefore conclude that, in a system of fixed exchange rates, an expansionary fiscal policy is effective. Not only does this fiscal expansion in itself stimulate domestic production: the increase in the money supply resulting from the obligatory foreign-exchange market intervention is another contributory factor through its incentive for additional private spending.

14.8 Summary

1. Exchange-rate systems vary substantially, with purely flexible and irrevocably fixed exchange rates at the two extremes. In the case of fixed exchange rates the central bank is responsible for the value of its currency, and is obliged to defend its fixed exchange rate. In order to do this, it has three main weapons: international monetary reserves, which it can use to intervene in the foreign-exchange market; the interest rate to affect international capital in- and outflows; and foreign-exchange restrictions.

2. Forex market intervention has not only a direct effect on the exchange rate through effects on the demand and supply of currencies, but may also have a signalling effect on the private users of the forex market. Through its interventions a central bank expresses its view of the equilibrium value of the exchange rate. If foreign-exchange speculators and other market operators have confidence in the central bank's view, they will be guided by the rate advocated by that bank. This holds true particularly when the private speculators are themselves uncertain about the future movements in exchange rates. In following the central bank's view, speculators in fact support unintentionally the bank's intervention actions.

3. Other exchange-rate systems that are blends of the two extreme systems, and are applied in practice more or less frequently, include (in order of increasing exchange-rate freedom) the adjustable peg, the crawling peg, and the managed floating exchange rate. The adjustable peg was used across the world from the end of the Second World War until its collapse in 1973. Subsequently, it was the underlying structure of the

EMS, until most of the participating countries switched over to the euro as their common currency in 1999.

4. A decrease in the value of a currency in the foreign-exchange market (devaluation under fixed exchange rates and depreciation under flexible exchange rates) will:

    (a) promote the country's export volume and diminish its import volume;
    (b) improve the trade and current account balances under specific conditions. These conditions are that the lower currency value:

    - stimulates domestic production and/or reduces domestic expenditure (or absorption), according to the absorption approach;
    - increases the volume of foreign demand for the country's export goods and lowers the volume of domestic demand for import goods sufficiently in order to compensate for the decline in the currency's value – that in itself worsens the trade balance. This is the well-known Marshall–Lerner condition.

5. There are strong indications that exchange-rate fluctuations (or swings):

    (a) cause a permanent slowdown in international trade,
    (b) promote domestic inflation, and
    (c) lower domestic production and also aggravate unemployment.

6. The negative influence of a fluctuating exchange rate on international trade is exerted through greater exchange-rate uncertainty and stronger requests for protection in the appreciating phase on the part of domestic producers. The resulting protectionism seems to exhibit a downward ratchet effect, so that there is the danger of a structural increase for more protection in spite of symmetrical exchange-rate fluctuations – without any upward trend in the exchange-rate movements.

7. A flexible exchange rate stimulates domestic inflation via the cost of hedging of exchange-rate uncertainty and the absence of the disciplinary effect produced by a fixed exchange rate. It is not only the policy makers who lack discipline, but also the private sector, including the trade unions and their periodic wage demands. The disciplinary effect on policy makers under fixed rates is characterized as borrowing credibility for the national anti-inflationary policy from the central bank of the low-inflation country that is the counterpart in the fixed exchange rate. Another factor stimulating domestic inflation is the ratchet effect, whereby the depreciation of the currency generates an increase in inflation but appreciation produces a much smaller decrease of inflation.

8. A flexible exchange rate causes more unemployment not only through its effects on international trade and inflation, but also via an increase in frictional unemployment and the asymmetrical reaction to devaluations and revaluations on account of the initial investment (sunk costs) that a company usually makes in order to launch new exports.

9. A flexible exchange rate also has an influence on foreign direct investment through the associated exchange-rate uncertainty. To hedge this uncertainty, companies consider the opportunity to shift production to the outlet country. Such a shift causes a direct shift in employment from the home country to the host country of the then multinational enterprise. In a worldwide context there is probably almost no employment effect.

10. Under fixed exchange rates and free international capital movements – the latter being relatively common nowadays – monetary policy cannot affect domestic production in either the short or the long term; in other words, monetary policy has no effect.

This outcome is part of the so-called incompatible trinity for a country: the impossibility to apply simultaneously a fixed exchange rate, capital mobility, and national autonomy (and effectiveness) of monetary policy. It implies that, in contrast, under flexible exchange rates monetary policy can be effective, at least in the short run. In the longer run this effectiveness may be lost if wages and prices respond to the change in monetary policy.

11. In the case of fiscal policy, the effectiveness on domestic production is precisely the opposite: with free international capital movements this policy is effective under fixed exchange rates, but not under flexible rates.

Questions

1. Explain how the crawling-peg system of exchange rates might promote overvaluation of the domestic currency in a period of domestic hyperinflation.
2. Since 2002 the USA contends with a large and non-declining trade deficit, varying between 3 and 6 per cent of its GDP, despite a declining tendency of the US dollar value in the foreign exchange markets. What are possible causes in the light of the absorption approach and the Marshall–Lerner condition? Use for the answer your knowledge about disequilibria in the economy of the USA after 2000.
3. For the Netherlands and Switzerland the following information about the price elasticities of demand for import and export is available. One distinguishes the elasticities in the short run, the intermediate run and the long run after a currency devaluation. For the Netherlands for the long run the value is 0.89 for the export elasticity and 1.22 for the import elasticity. For Switzerland they are, respectively, 0.73 and 0.25. Do these values fulfil the Marshall–Lerner condition and is a currency depreciation the recipe for a trade balance improvement in both countries?
4. We also know the corresponding elasticities for the short run. For the Netherlands they are 0.24 for the export elasticity and 0.71 for the import elasticity. For Switzerland they are, respectively, 0.28 and 0.25. Do these values point at the existence of the J-curve effect in one of the countries or both?

CHAPTER 15

International Risk: Types and Hedges

15.1 Introduction

Business activities are associated with uncertainty and with the handling of risk. Even if the entrepreneur operates exclusively in her own country, she is subject to a variety of business risks. Prices may change, consumer tastes will vary, debtors may default, and laws can be altered.

However, there are grounds for arguing that the internationalization of business transactions increases both the level and the variety of business risks. One reason is that risk that also exists for domestic business increases in the case of foreign business transactions. For example, since some customers are now located overseas, there is perhaps a greater risk of being caught out by defaulting debtors – in most cases a supplier has less information on foreign than on domestic customers. A second reason is that international transactions introduce new sources of risk – for example, exchange-rate risk, due to international trade, foreign production or international credit and loans.

This chapter evaluates the effects on a company's risk profile that arise as a result of the internationalization of its activities and addresses the following questions:

o What does internationalization add to existing risk types of a company?
o What typical types of risk do entrepreneurs have to consider when they go abroad?
o What instruments are available to reduce or eliminate these risks?

In this chapter we shall use the term 'company' in its broadest sense: it can be applied to an industrial company, a financial business such as a commercial bank or an investment company.

Section 15.2 reviews a large range of risks, such as credit or debtor risk and market risk in the case of purely domestic transactions, as well as country risk, political risk or sovereign risk, policy risk, transfer risk, exchange-rate risk, transaction risk, economic risk, and translation risk in the case of typical international business activities. It will show that in order to acquire a good understanding of these types of risks it is important to set them in a clear framework so that the mutual connections and differences will become apparent.

Having established our framework, Sections 15.3 and 15.4 introduce the instruments that entrepreneurs may use in seeking to reduce these risks – or possibly to eliminate them altogether. The financial industry provides many solutions, ranging from a careful set-up of business in order to avoid risk to different forms of insurances to cover risk once they are unavoidable. Section 15.5 provides a summary of our findings.

15.2 | Types of international risk

15.2.1 Country risk

The most obvious financial risk for a company in national transactions is the possibility that interest on and the redemption of an outstanding claim will not be paid in accordance with the original agreements. This is the so-called credit risk (or debtor risk). The agreed annual sum of redemption and interest payments is known as the debt service. Breach of the original agreements may relate only to the interest payment or the redemption of the principal, but it may also concern both debt service components at once.

In one sense, the international dimension of the credit risk is merely an extension to foreign debtors. However, there are additional complications. Different practices and customs, and different views of business ethics abroad compared with domestic ones, can more easily cause the creditworthiness of foreign contracting parties to be misjudged.

In addition, a typical international transaction involves additional credit risks resulting from particular legal, social, and political differences in the debtor's country. These risks, which are obviously country-specific, are collectively known as *country risk* (also dubbed *sovereign risk*).

Country risk can be broken down into three separate kinds of risk:

1. *Political risk*: the risks of war, revolution, the expropriation of foreign property (with compensation), and the confiscation of foreign property (seizure, without compensation).
2. *Policy risk*: the risk of all foreign government interventions that may have the side effect of having a negative influence on the value or payment of the foreign debt service. For example, a highly restrictive government policy will have a serious impact on the level of economic growth in the debtor's country. As a result, a private debtor's business may get into such great difficulty that the debtor defaults, becoming unable to service her debt to other countries. One specific form of policy risk is *transfer risk*, which occurs if government restrictions on the use of foreign currency prevent the foreign debtor from converting her domestic-currency funds available for the debt service into a payment in foreign currency to another country. A transfer restriction will lower the market value in foreign currency of debt paper of the restricting currency. This is what we saw in the 1980s with debt paper of the Latin American countries during the debt crisis (see Chapter 17 for an analysis of this crisis). Another form of policy risk, the introduction of restrictions on international capital flows, will also have an effect on the prices of financial assets, as shown in Case study 12.1 on the Dutch bond circuit at the beginning of the 1970s.
3. *Legal risk*: the risk that overseas legal rules may be less favourable for the position of a creditor than those in her own country. In several countries, the legal system is biased against the interests of foreign creditors. For example, experience may show that court rulings tend to be unfavourable to foreigners. The principal difference between national and international claims is that the first implies a legal obligation to repay which can be enforced through the courts. That does not hold true for an international claim. The creditor can only force a foreign debtor to meet her financial obligation work indirectly,

for instance, by using her influence to exclude the unwilling debtor from any new international (export) credits.

15.2.2 Exchange-rate risk

A creditor, being the holder of financial assets, is subject not only to a credit risk on its claims, and thus on these assets, but also a market risk. Market risk applies in the event of possible changes in the prices of financial assets. In such circumstances, the amount of wealth tied up in the financial assets is liable to alteration.

We are familiar with this market risk in the case of equities and bonds: their market prices on the stock and bond markets are changing constantly. By contrast, only in exceptional cases are financial assets such as bank deposits subject to market risk. Of course, a bank may go bankrupt, so that the deposits become worthless (if, moreover, a government's guarantee is absent), or a government may prohibit banks from paying out the value of bank accounts so that the accounts are valued at a discount – as occurred in Argentina after the breakdown of its currency board system at the end of 2001 (see Section 19.4). But these price changes of bank deposits are rather exceptional.

The holder of foreign financial assets faces an international extension of market risk, namely exchange-rate risk, or currency risk. In the case of a foreign asset, a change in the price of the asset expressed in terms of the foreign currency is only one possible market-risk component. For the creditor or asset holder the asset price will also change if there is a change in the exchange rate between the foreign currency concerned and the currency of the asset holder's country of residence. As a result of the exchange-rate risk, a foreign bank deposit in a sound bank in a sound country is also subject to serious market risk. In this case it is only the exchange rate that causes uncertainty over the value of the bank account (in terms of the asset holder's currency).

Exchange-rate risk occurs in three forms: transaction risk, economic risk, and translation risk, which are discussed in the following sub-sections. For simplicity, the exchange-rate risk will be considered from the point of view of a firm exporting goods or services. However, the exchange-rate risk – in all three forms – applies equally to other international economic activities.

15.2.2.1 Transaction risk

For an exporter the most obvious variant of exchange-rate risk is *transaction risk*. This relates to the possibility that the financial outcome of a specific international transaction will differ from the initial expectation as the result of an unexpected exchange-rate change in the period between the beginning and the end of the transaction.

Both the exporter and the importer would prefer the contract price to be expressed in their own currency, because that would entirely avoid this transaction risk. Thus at the start of the transaction they will know exactly how much of their own currency they will receive or will have to pay. However, it is clear that either the exporter or the importer will be unable to realize her preference: the price on the invoice can only be stated in one currency at a time – the invoice currency. The party for which this currency is a foreign one is then burdened with a transaction risk. The choice of the invoice currency mainly depends upon the market position of the exporter and the importer: if an entrepreneur has market power, it will be relatively easy for her to impose the own currency preference.

In general terms, around one-third of international goods and services transactions are invoiced in the exporter's currency and one-third in the importer's currency. The final third of transactions are in a third currency – often the US dollar. The dollar is chosen because of the enormous daily volume of trading in the US dollar on the foreign exchange markets. Expressed in technical terms, the dollar market is deep and, therefore, liquid. As a result this currency can easily be bought or sold in large amounts without there being any perceivable effect on its price, the exchange rate.

Another advantage of the dollar is that this currency has an exceedingly well-developed system of derivative financial markets, such as forward, option and futures markets. (See Sub-section 15.4 for a discussion of how these derivatives work.) It is, therefore, straightforward and relatively cheap for non-Americans to hedge the exchange-rate risk on the dollar in comparison with that on other foreign currencies.

Consequently, in the case of an international transaction, transaction risk arises for one or both of the parties involved. This risk may exist for some time, as there is often a considerable period between the start of the transaction (when the contract is signed) and the end of the transaction (when the payment is made). Usually, it takes some time before an order (or the signing of the contract) is executed by the delivery of the goods. Not only does it take time to transport the goods; a firm often also produces to order, so that the production time also has to be taken into account. In addition, it is customary for the seller to tempt the buyer with a supplier's credit. In the case of an international transaction this is an export credit. The credit period begins with the delivery of the goods and ends with the actual payment. From the date of the signing of the contract to the date of payment a contracting party is exposed to a transaction risk, at least in so far as the contract price is expressed in a foreign currency.

In the case of large transactions such as the sale of capital goods (for example, ships and aircraft) and the execution of infrastructure works (such as the construction of airfields and ports), it is common for the signing of the contract to be preceded by a period in which the transaction risk already exists.

These transactions begin when the intended exporter submits a tender, including a price offer. If this price is expressed in terms of foreign currency, then as soon as the tender has been submitted this exporter is subject to transaction risk. Already in the period up to the importer's decision about the tender the exchange rate may change to the disadvantage of the potential exporter. One factor that complicates tendering is that the exporter is not certain that this risk will actually arise, because she is unsure that the importer will accept the bid. As we shall see in Sub-section 15.4.2, this kind of uncertainty makes it more challenging, but not impossible, to hedge the transaction risk attached to tendering.

15.2.2.2 Economic risk

A second variant of exchange-rate risk is economic risk. Whereas transaction risk concerns the effect of a future exchange-rate change on one specific international transaction that is already underway, economic risk concerns the effect on all future international transactions yet to be arranged. Future exchange-rate changes may actually impair the future competitiveness of a domestic exporter and thus its export revenues and, subsequently, its future profitability. We call this the *economic risk*. Note that this risk applies not only to an exporter. It may even apply to a domestic company producing solely for the home market, which has to contend constantly with the threat of foreign competition in the home market. In fact, economic risk holds true for producers of all goods that can be traded internationally (see Case study 15.1).

The relation between a future change in the exchange rate and future profitability is as follows. A future appreciation of the domestic currency will result in a deterioration of the competitiveness of domestic companies as soon as the appreciation materializes. In response, they will lower prices in terms of the domestic currency and/or will suffer from lower market shares. Since production costs expressed in terms of the domestic currency are often rather rigid, the appreciation of the domestic currency then damages the future profitability of the domestic companies.

Case study 15.1   Economic risk of the Corus group

On 12 June 1999 *The Economist* published an article about the worsening competitive position of UK exporters, which was the result of the persistent strength of the pound against the currencies of continental Europe (at that time these currencies were irrevocably fixed against the euro, which was a little over five months old).

The article described how British export volumes declined during 1998 and 1999, but concluded on an optimistic note: most economists predicted the tide would turn as soon as the German economy recovered, and the first signs of this were already present.

However, the exchange rate of the pound did not behave as predicted. It strengthened still further against the euro and there was a further worsening of the competitive position of British producers of internationally tradable goods.

One of the most badly affected companies was the steelmaker Corus. Formed in October 1999 following the merger of British Steel and Hoogovens, a Dutch steel and aluminium producer, Corus is active in three markets: carbon steel, stainless steel, and aluminium.

Of these, the production of carbon steel was its core activity. For the most part, this was produced in the UK and sold in Europe: during 2000, 83 per cent of Corus's total carbon steel production was sold in Europe, of which 37 per cent was in the UK. It is clear from these figures that Corus's sales are extremely sensitive to movements in the exchange rate between the pound and the euro.

On the other hand, Corus also imports large amounts of coal and iron ore, both traded in world markets, where prices and trades are traditionally denominated in US dollars. The exchange rates between the pound and the dollar and the euro and the dollar are therefore also important to the results of Corus.

In its annual report for 2000, Corus described how the strength of the pound had had an adverse impact on its results: the exports of steel have fallen, foreign competition has both gained market share in the UK and has caused steel prices in the UK to fall and, finally, the exports of the UK customers of Corus have dropped, so that these customers have cut back their production and therefore bought less steel. These are, of course, the textbook consequences of adverse exchange-rate developments. It should be noted, however, that in addition to the strong pound, Corus also faced more expensive inputs as the result of a rising dollar and a worldwide oversupply of carbon steel in the second half of 2000. In total, during 2000 Corus lost approximately £1 million a day on its carbon steel activities.

In order to improve the performance of its UK activities, Corus announced 4700 job losses during 2000. At the end of the year, however, it became clear that this measure had not fully addressed its problems. Two members of the executive committee were fired and the chief executive, Sir Brian Moffat, announced that new reorganization plans were under way.

These plans were revealed in February 2001 and involved a further 6000 job cuts. Of course, both labour unions and politicians reacted furiously and even the then UK prime minister, Tony Blair, opposed these radical measures.

The real problem with the exchange-rate risk lies in this economic risk, because it cannot be hedged. The future period to which it relates is almost unlimited and the size of the turnover at risk is entirely unclear. The problems in attempting to quantify economic risk seem to be insoluble, as may be seen from the following questions that an exporter needs to answer in order to quantify the risk:

○ *How is the exchange rate going to move in future?* This requires an accurate prediction not only of the exchange rate against the currency of the country to which goods are being exported, but also of the rate against the currencies of competing suppliers in this market.
○ *How sensitive is foreign demand to an increase in the price of our products compared with those of our competitors?*
○ *How sensitive is the cost side of our business to an appreciation of the domestic currency?* Each component of the production costs (wages, financing costs, raw materials, semi-manufactures) then has to be considered.
○ *How quickly and to what degree can the cost side be restructured in the case of a lasting appreciation of the domestic currency?* The restructuring must then be such as to reduce the production costs in terms of the domestic currency.

In the event of an appreciation, the necessary reduction of production costs can be brought about in one of two ways: (1) cutting the domestic cost components and increasing the use of foreign inputs in the production process; or (2) extending foreign subsidiaries which provide for part of the production process. That such a restructuring of production can be realized successfully, even if massive adjustments are required, is illustrated in Case study 15.2.

Case study 15.2   Japanese restructuring in response to the high value of the yen

Since the peak in the value of the US dollar in February 1985, the currency has shown a steep fall against the world's other major currencies. Figure 15.1 displays the fall in the value of the dollar against the Japanese yen between 1986 and 1995. The vertical axis shows the yen (¥) price of the dollar. The most remarkable aspect of the figure is the rapid fall in Japanese production costs, which keep pace with the waning dollar. This implies that the fall in Japanese production costs expressed in yen remained roughly equal to the fall in the value of the dollar (in percentage terms). Japanese firms managed to achieve this through a combination of downward pressure on domestic production costs, the contracting-out of parts of production to foreigners (located specifically in East and South-East Asia), and setting up new firms abroad.

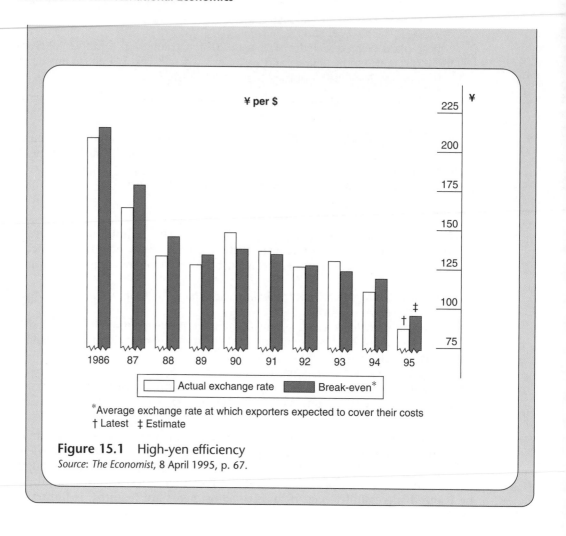

Figure 15.1   High-yen efficiency
Source: The Economist, 8 April 1995, p. 67.

15.2.2.3   Translation risk

The third and final type of exchange-rate risk is *translation risk*, which is related to the influence of exchange-rate changes on a company's annual balance sheet. More specifically, it is the threat to a company that the values of its assets and liabilities denominated in a foreign currency have changed to the detriment of the company's equity when they are translated into the reporting currency (usually the domestic currency) as the result of exchange-rate changes during the reporting year. A company operating internationally often has a range of assets and liabilities, most commonly claims and debts, denominated in foreign currencies. Other familiar forms of assets and liabilities in foreign currencies are foreign branches and foreign subsidiaries.

The volume and composition of a company's assets and liabilities in foreign currencies are changing constantly. Even if their volume and currency breakdown remain the same as on the previous balance sheet date, the company still incurs a translation risk. That risk is present as soon as the company has a net investment position – a so-called open position – in a specific foreign currency. This is the difference between the values of assets and liabilities in one and the same foreign currency. At any one moment in time, a company may of course have an open position in more than one currency. The overall extent to which a company is exposed to exchange-rate risk, that is the open positions for all foreign currencies taken together, is known as exposure. In this specific case concerning the consequences for the balance sheet it is called translation exposure.

One particular characteristic of translation risk is that its possible influence on the balance sheet has no connection with the operating result in the period between the balance sheet dates. Nevertheless, an interim exchange-rate change influences the company's equity as well as its profit and loss account.

Another characteristic is that there are a number of methods for handling the valuation of the exchange rate, which often have widely varying effects on the extent to which the company is exposed to translation risk. The valuation methods permitted are linked to the principles underlying the valuation of a company's assets and liabilities. Two separate accounting standards are available for the non-monetary assets and liabilities (such as fixed assets, participations, and stocks of goods):

o the closing rate method; and
o the historical (or temporal) method.

Under the first method, the items are valued against current cost (in fact, replacement costs); in the latter method valuation is against historical cost. For the monetary assets (claims and debts), there is only a current cost evaluation. It is usual for the same method to be adopted in successive balance sheets, but the chosen accounting method may nevertheless substantially influence the size of the reported profit.

In accordance with the historical cost method of valuation, for the purposes of preparing the balance sheet a company could decide to use the historical exchange rate for its non-monetary assets and liabilities that are expressed in foreign currencies. The choice of this method means that, for example, a Japanese firm with its business premises located in the USA and bought at a time when the exchange rate was slightly above 200 yen per dollar (roughly the position in 1986 – see Figure 15.1) were in 1994 still valued at this exchange rate for the purpose of preparing the balance sheet (although the exchange rate had declined in the meantime to around 100 yen per dollar). Thus, the effect of choosing the historical exchange rate-method is that the company does not in fact incur any translation risk on its foreign assets: there is no annual uncertainty over the exchange rate to be applied.

However, uncertainty over the exchange rate does exist if the company, by analogy with the current cost method of valuation, uses the closing exchange rate when preparing its balance sheet. The closing rate method means taking the actual exchange rate at the end of the reporting period. On the balance sheet date, 1 January 1995, the premises of the Japanese company in the USA would then have dropped in value by some 50 per cent, in terms of yen, against the purchase price (in 1986).

This example makes it clear how enormously the effects on the balance sheet can vary according to the choice of the exchange-rate valuation method. At first sight, it is an attractive proposition for a company to select the most advantageous exchange-rate translation method in order to show the balance sheet in the most favourable light. However, under initial accounting rules such an approach is not allowed. A company has to choose a method at a given moment and is, in principle, obliged to adhere to this in subsequent periods. Countries have guidelines about the method to be used, which are closely related to International Financial Reporting Standards (IFRS) on this point. These standards are described in Box 15.1.

> ## Box 15.1   Foreign currency treatment in financial statements
>
> IFRS is a set of internationally agreed standards for annual reports. The International Accounting Standards Board (IASB) manages these standards as IAS norms. IAS 21 prescribes how to include foreign currency transactions and foreign operations in the financial statements of an entity and how to translate financial statements into a presentation currency (the currency in which the financial statements is presented). The principal issues are which exchange rate(s) to use and how to report the effects of changes in exchange rates in the financial statements. Here are the main lines of IAS 21.
>
> A stand-alone entity, an entity with foreign operations (such as a parent with foreign subsidiaries), or a foreign operation (such as a foreign subsidiary or branch) that reports starts to determine its functional currency; this is the currency of the primary economic environment in which the entity operates. If the functional currency is equal to the presentation currency, then the following rules apply.
>
> A foreign currency transaction should be recorded initially at the rate of exchange on the date of the transaction (use of averages is permitted if they are a reasonable approximation of the actual). On each subsequent balance sheet date:
>
> o foreign currency monetary amounts should be reported using the closing rate;
> o non-monetary items carried at historical cost should be reported using the exchange rate on the date of the transaction;
> o non-monetary items carried at fair value should be reported at the rate that existed when the fair values were determined.
>
> Exchange differences arising when monetary items are settled or when monetary items are translated at rates different from those at which they were translated when initially recognized or in previous financial statements are reported in profit or loss in the period, with one exception. This exception regards exchange differences arising on monetary items that form part of the reporting entity's net investment in a foreign operation.
>
> As regards a monetary item that forms part of an entity's investment in a foreign operation, the accounting treatment in consolidated financial statements should not be dependent on the currency of the monetary item. Also, the accounting should not depend on which entity within the group conducts a transaction with the foreign operation. If a gain or loss on a non-monetary item is recognized in other comprehensive income (for example, a property revaluation), any foreign exchange component of that gain or loss is also recognized in other comprehensive income.

15.3   Hedging country risk

Country risk does not really seem to be capable of measurement – although attempts are made to adopt a criterion for it. Not only is country risk multifaceted, as seen in Sub-section 15.2.1, but it is also very difficult to quantify its components. Despite this lack of information, experts do agree that this type of risk is often very large. It is therefore unsurprising that governments in industrialized countries play an important role in insuring this risk for their exporters. Box 15.2 underlines this practice.

Box 15.2   Export credit insurance

While importers usually wish to receive an export credit, they present exporters with various risks. Exporters can, however, insure themselves against most of these risks. In many developed countries export credit guarantee agencies (ECGAs) provide insurance against both the commercial risk (for example, the bankruptcy of a buyer) and the country risk involved in international trade.

Although commercial insurance companies also provide export credit insurance, the major parties in this market have traditionally been official institutions. These include the Ex-Im Bank (USA), Hermes (Germany), COFACE (France), ECGD (UK) and the Export–Import Insurance Department of the Ministry of International Trade and Industry (EID/MITI, Japan). Traditionally, the main reason for government involvement in export credit insurance has been to encourage exports.

It is not hard to see how a government could stimulate exports by providing financial support to an ECGA. Exporters who can insure export credits against subsidized premiums are able to provide their counterparts these credits at lower interest rates than exporters who lack such subsidized insurance. Therefore, the former exporters have a competitive advantage, based on an indirect export subsidy.

In the 1970s, those industrialized nations participating in the Organisation for Economic Co-operation and Development (OECD) agreed on a series of guidelines for officially supported export credits. The aim of the agreement was to encourage competition based on the quality and the price of exports, rather than on the most favourable officially supported terms. Initially, this arrangement only set out the most favourable repayment terms which exporters were allowed to impose on their customers if their export credit had a repayment term of more than two years and was the result of government support (for example, by credit insurance with an official ECGA). These guidelines still apply:

o Exports that are accompanied by credit (with a repayment period of over two years) require a minimum cash payment of 15 per cent of the total contract value at or before the starting point of the credit.
o Repayment is bound to be finished within five or ten years, depending upon the status of the import country.
o Repayment has to proceed in regular instalments: at least one instalment per six months and the first instalment within six months of the starting point of the credit.

From April 1999 this arrangement was extended following the implementation of the so-called Knaepen Package. According to this package, the insurance of export credits comes at no less than a minimum benchmark premium. This minimum premium is based on the country risk involved and should be adequate to cover operating costs and losses in the long run.

The Knaepen Package also introduced a model to assess the credit risk involved for a certain import country and to classify countries into one of seven risk categories. For each of these categories a minimum premium benchmark is determined. The ultimate goal of this extension of the 'Arrangement on Guidelines for Officially Supported Export Credits' is, of course, to achieve a level playing field for the exports of OECD members.

Despite the detailed guidelines laid out in the OECD arrangement, ECGAs have considerable freedom to offer different packages of export credit insurance to their customers.

The Ex-Im Bank in the USA, for example, offers insurance packages that provide cover against commercial and political risk, but also exchange-rate risk.

In the US case variation is possible in the percentage of coverage, where short-term export credits can be insured for the total gross invoice value and medium- and long-term credits can only be covered for the financed portion, which amounts to a maximum of 85 per cent of the gross invoice value (because a 15 per cent cash payment by the importer is required by the OECD arrangements, as described above). In addition to different levels of coverage, the exporter can also choose between different policy packages. A 'multi-buyer policy' requires the exporter to insure several export credit sales in different countries at once, while a 'single buyer policy' covers a single or repetitive sale to a single foreign customer. Of these two policies, the multi-buyer policy is relatively cheaper because it provides the Eximbank with a spread of risks.

One interesting question is how the OECD arrangements have influenced the amount of support provided by ECGAs. Research into the effects of the Knaepen Package is not yet available. From earlier research we know that during the 1980s large differences existed in terms of the amount of support (subsidies) which was provided to exporters in different industrialized countries. Haniotis and Schich (1995) compute the intentional losses (effective subsidies) of several ECGAs. These intentional losses are expressed as subsidy-equivalent rates. During the period from 1984 to 1990 modest or even negative subsidy-equivalent rates are found for the official ECGAs from Australia, Austria, Canada, New Zealand, and the USA. The calculated rates for these countries range from -0.5 per cent to 0.7 per cent, indicating that the part of the insurance premium that is covered by government support on average does not exceed 0.7 per cent of the insured value. The highest rates are found in Italy, Norway, Spain, Switzerland and, although less pronounced, Germany. Rates for these countries vary between approximately 3.9 per cent for Hermes (Germany) and 9.6 per cent for SAGE (Italy). Belgium, Finland, France, the Netherlands, Sweden and the UK are all ranked among the middle group of countries: The ECGAs in these countries provide insurance with a subsidy-equivalent rate between 1 and 3 per cent.

To estimate the country risk, a business can make its own attempt to determine the creditworthiness of a country to which it plans to grant credit. Alternatively, of course, a business can simply use the credit-rating agencies that conduct the constant monitoring of countries. An agency gives each country a particular credit rating.

Any estimate of the size of the country risk can only be a rough approximation. What are the determining factors of country risk? For a specific country that has defaulted on only a few occasions – if at all – in the past, there are too few cases of default to establish a statistically reliable relation between country risk and measurable variables that might explain it. Moreover, the method implicitly assumes that 'history repeats itself', although in practice every situation is different. That is why this method is unreliable, although it can form one useful additional instrument of a country risk study. But it is impossible to develop hard criteria that can subsequently be applied automatically. For that reason a country-risk assessment is not only a rough approximation, but also a labour-intensive process. Any such assessment involves a great deal of information.

Standard assessment forms may be another instrument for the purpose. Box 15.3 offers an example. Although the source of the table is old, the items included in this assessment still reflect current concerns.

Box 15.3   Assessing country risk

Table 15.1 illustrates the considerations that are deemed important in the determination of country risk. The weightings assigned to them are necessarily rather subjective.

Table 15.1 A country risk assessment form

	Approximate weighting (%)
A Legal considerations	10
B Political considerations	25
C Economic considerations	
– Power of the government (e.g. a minority government which finds it difficult to introduce unpopular measures compared with a government in a two-party system)	6
– Assessment of current plans for the economy. Feasibility of development plans, main bottlenecks, etc. Resource base: natural and human resource, etc.	15
– Recent events and present state of the economy	
GNP growth	0.3
rate of inflation	0.6
government budget position	0.6
money supply growth	0.3
current account balance of payments	0.3
unemployment	0.6
level of external debt	1.2
debt service ratio	1.2
latest date of published statistics	0.9
	6
– Future prospects for the economy if present trends and policies continue	
GNP growth	0.7
rate of inflation	1.3
government budget position	2.0
money supply growth	0.7
current account balance of payments	2.0
unemployment	1.3
level of external debt	2.5
debt service ratio	2.5
	13

Table 15.1 Continued

	Approximate weighting (%)
– Ability of the country to correct adverse implications of present binds and to withstand unforeseen shocks (vulnerability)	
imports as a proportion of GDP	0.7
exports as a proportion of GDP	0.7
diversification of imports by category and by geographical area	4.6
diversification of exports by category and by geographical area	4.6
compressibility of imports (i.e. the extent to which imports consist of non-essentials)	6.4
vulnerability of the economy to changing prices of main exports and imports. Energy dependence	8.0
	25
	100

Source: *The Banker*, January 1981, p. 74.

This information in fact consists of a series of isolated data and ratios. Non-economic data (categories A and B) account for roughly one-third of the assessment. As one would expect, the actual situation and the economic outlook (in category C) are viewed mainly in the light of the current account position and the country's debt position.

Among the possible causes for a current account deficit are the growth in GNP, inflation, the government's budget deficit and excessive money creation. These are all incorporated in the form. Of course, the latter economic variables are also relevant as economic goals and instruments, respectively, indicating the country's economic stability. Low unemployment provides an indication of the government's freedom of action for reducing the current account deficit through a restrictive fiscal policy.

The seriousness of the country's international financial problems can be seen most directly in the level of debt and the debt–service ratio (that is, debt service in relation to the value of the country's exports, both on an annual basis). This ratio expresses the percentage of the annual export revenue of the debtor country that has to be set aside to pay the financial charges associated with the foreign debt. The country cannot use that proportion of the foreign-exchange revenue for the often desperately needed imports. In practice, we find that the greater a country's financial problems, the less statistical information is made available – either deliberately or as the result of circumstances beyond the country's control. This explains the presence of that item on the assessment form.

In a country assessment, the two most important economic factors appear to be the options available to a country for: (i) correcting an existing, undesirable balance of payments position; and (ii) confronting unexpected adverse influences. These options account for 25 per cent of the assessment items. They are assessed using information on aspects such as the country's degree of economic openness, the degree of diversification of its imports and exports, and the country's adaptability to adverse foreign economic developments.

One essential question, however, concerning the reason for the current account deficit is missing from the assessment form. If the deficit is due to excess spending on productive investment goods, the funding of the deficit certainly need not be regarded as loss financing. South Korea offers an example of this type of growth financing in recent decades. It can also be worth granting credit to a country that is either confronted by only a cyclical current account deficit or is pursuing a credible adjustment policy. However, in the case of structural excess consumer spending and non-productive investments, we can say that foreign credit finances only losses. The assessment form is an inadequate tool for differentiating between these situations.

Determining the creditworthiness of a country on the basis of an assessment form as in Box 15.3 simply means forming an opinion on the basis of largely unrelated, but relevant information.

Leading credit-rating institutions, such as Moody's and S&P, bring country risk determination per country together into a single framework, so that a country ranking for country risk is established. Case study 15.3 gives an example obtained from the financial magazine *Euromoney*.

The country risk assessment plays a crucial part in setting interest rates of international credits at the right levels. Interest rates are not only set as a reward for lagged consumption of the lender and a compensation for the expected rates of inflation until maturity. They also reflect the risk of the investment. As stated earlier, country risk is part of the complete risk assessment. So in addition to the insurance of credits, lenders also hedge credit risk (and thus country risk) through the size of the spread included in the interest rate of specific credit.

A hedge against country risk is, of course, to spread credits across countries employing assessments of individual countries' risk. In any case in theory, by doing this creditors could diversify away their risk – as in the case of investment diversification. In practice, the similarities are limited because it is difficult to find countries that have such divergent risk profiles. These profiles tend to be correlated, partly as the result of worldwide economic downturns and contagion between poorly performing countries. Additionally, in contrast to international investments in stocks, one cannot expect that the value of credits to strongly performing countries will rise, compensating for the losses on credits to the worst-performing countries.

Case study 15.3   Euromoney's country-risk rating

The monthly journal *Euromoney* compiles for, in principle, all countries a country-risk score, ranging from 0 (worst) to 100 (best), with frequent revisions. To determine these country scores, the journal uses for six country-risk factors the input from three sources: (i) Assessments of experts around the world, rating each country for which they have knowledge. They rate a country's: economic performance; political risk; structural risk; and its accessibility to international capital markets. (ii) The sovereign ratings of the three credit rating agencies Moody's, Standard and Poor's, and Fitch IBCA to consolidate them into one credit rating for a country. (iii) The Word Bank's Global Development Finance figures to combine them into one debt indicator for a country. Table 15.2 gives all these scores for a sub-set of countries for March 2011. The scores for the six country-risk factors

Table 15.2 Country-risk rating, March 2011

Rank	Country	Total country score	Economic	Political	Structural	Credit rating	Debt indicators	Access to capital markets
1	Norway	93	90	93	84	10.0	10.0	10.0
2	Luxembourg	91	81	94	86	10.0	10.0	10.0
3	Switzerland	90	83	87	87	10.0	10.0	10.0
4	Denmark	89	78	92	83	10.0	10.0	9.8
5	Sweden	89	78	91	83	10.0	10.0	9.8
6	Singapore	87	78	86	84	10.0	10.0	9.8
7	Finland	87	74	89	80	10.0	10.0	10.0
8	Netherlands	87	76	87	78	10.0	10.0	10.0
9	Canada	86	74	89	77	10.0	10.0	9.8
10	Australia	85	75	86	78	9.8	10.0	9.8
11	Hong Kong	85	82	83	83	9.2	10.0	8.0
12	Germany	85	71	85	78	10.0	10.0	10.0
15	USA	82	61	85	78	10.0	10.0	10.0
16	UK	80	60	83	75	10.0	10.0	9.8
18	France	80	63	79	73	10.0	10.0	10.0
25	Japan	75	54	77	71	8.5	10.0	9.9
30	Italy	71	58	66	70	8.1	10.0	9.0
40	China	64	67	48	52	7.7	8.7	7.3
41	Brazil	63	68	65	61	4.4	8.6	4.5
56	India	57	57	50	52	4.4	8.4	7.0
57	Russia	57	62	44	49	5.2	8.5	6.5

Note: The total country score ranges from 0 (worst or highest risk) to 100 (best or lowest risk). The scores for economic performance, political risk and structural risk are in percentages; for the last three factors the scores are out of 10. For all factors holds: the higher the better. The scores are rounded off compared with the presentation in the source publication.

Source: http://www.euromoney.com/Article/2773235/Country-risk-March-2011

are weighted in determining the total country-risk score. The weights are 0.3 for both the economic and political factors and 0.1 for each of the four other factors. The country selection in this table is: the twelve countries with the highest country-risk scores, supplemented with the (other) countries of the G8 and the BRIC countries (the large emerging economies: Brazil, Russia, India, and China).

Each of the six factors consists of some sub-factors; their scores are not published. Economic performance has been built upon: bank stability, GNP outlook, unemployment rate, government finance, and monetary policy and currency stability. Political risk consists of: corruption, government stability, transparency, and the institutional and regulatory environment. Structural risk elements are: demographics, infrastructure, and labour market and industrial relations. Debt indicators are assessed by means of three ratios: total debt stock to GNP, debt service to exports (or debt-service ratio), and the current account balance to GNP.

In Table 15.2 the high position of the four Scandinavian countries is noticeable. The same holds for the three mini areas: Luxembourg, Singapore, and Hong Kong. In the country top ten the three financial indicators cause no differentiation: for almost all countries they have the maximum value. Remarkable is the mediocre scores for economic performance in the USA, UK, France, Japan and Italy, ranging from 54 to 63. The bottom of the ranking (not shown) consists of the three countries Somalia, Mauritania and, last, Laos, Each has a total score of around 10. The countries that are focal points in the sovereign debt crisis of 2010–11 in the Euro Zone, Greece, Portugal, and Ireland, displayed substantial falls in the ranking between September 2010 and March 2011. Greece fell from position 56 to 65, Portugal from 33 to 44, and Ireland from 26 to 43. However, two other countries that suffer from a moderate threat of the crisis, Spain and Italy, even saw an improvement of their ranking in this six-month period.

It is unsurprising that the overall risk and credit of a country is assessed: there is an obvious need for that information for international traders and investors. But these assessments also create a risk, the risk of a self-fulfilling prophesy. If for whatever reason a country's situation worsens, a concomitant deterioration of the country's risk score will make financial markets more reticent in providing that country credits. And if they continue this lending, it will be at higher costs. This will further worsen the country's economic situation, creating a downward spiral movement – or a vicious circle.

15.4 Reducing exchange-rate risk

In practice, exchange-rate risk exists as long as money is in circulation. The existence of two independent monetary systems is enough to ensure this. It is therefore unsurprising that there is a long tradition of attempts to reduce these risks. Although a risk can end either in an advantage or a disadvantage, there is still a prevalent need in business for the level of risk to be reduced. In general, people are risk-averse in that uncertainty has a negative value.

This section will discuss the various instruments available to reduce exchange-rate risk. We will do this through examining a particular business example: a Japanese carmaker who is selling some of its cars in the USA. As a result, it is a net receiver of US dollars, but its profits are measured in Japanese yen, meaning that profits are sensitive to changes in the yen–dollar exchange rate.

We identify two types of instruments to overcome this exposure to exchange risk:

o natural instruments that avoid exchange-rate exposure by reorganizing the way business is financed; and
o artificial (financial) instruments that are designed to counter exchange-rate risk once it exists.

Both types of instruments are designed to reduce uncertainty and are named hedges in the finance literature and hereafter.

15.4.1 Natural hedges

Natural hedges alter the way in which a company is financed. In our case they are designed to minimize the number of dollars the Japanese carmaker has to convert into yen. Among the instruments that reduce the exchange-rate risk in this way are:

o netting;
o leading and lagging;
o the borrow-deposit technique; and
o the parallel loan.

Netting is a useful instrument that is principally available to multinationals or companies with financially autonomous divisions. If various subsidiaries of the same multinational have a network of mutual claims and debts in foreign currencies in relation to other subsidiaries and other companies, multilateral clearing at the level of the multinational's central treasury has financial advantages for all parties concerned. Through a policy of netting, the multinational achieves a lower exchange-rate exposure and is thus able to reduce the hedging cost of exchange-rate risk for each subsidiary. Netting decreases the frequency with which the multinational and its subsidiaries should use the foreign-exchange market, the amounts of foreign currency they must trade there, and thus the costs of currency exchange.

For example, say our Japanese carmaker owns two subsidiaries in the USA. Subsidiary A has a claim worth $1 million on an American company, while subsidiary B owes $2 million to a Brazilian company, both with a maturity of three months. By agreeing that in three months' time B will take $1 million from A to pay off one half of B's debt at the exchange rate valid now, A eliminates and B reduces the exchange-rate risk. In addition, they reduce the use of the foreign-exchange market and therefore lower transaction costs on that market.

Leading is the disbursement of claims or payment of debts both in foreign currencies at a date prior to the initial intentions; and *lagging* is its opposite – namely delayed disbursement or payment. A contract often permits the adoption of either option. Say, our Japanese carmaker has delivered an export credit in yen to a US importer. If the importer expects the yen to appreciate against the dollar, it may be advantageous for the US importer to pay off the credit early – that is, before the appreciation. Conversely, if the US importer expects a depreciation of the yen, she will try to postpone paying off the loan until after the depreciation.

A traditional instrument also used by multinationals and investment firms for operations abroad is the *borrow-deposit technique*. In order to limit the exchange-rate risk, under this technique foreign assets (valued in foreign currencies) are financed (or associated) as far as possible by creating debts in the same foreign currencies. This approach is particularly effective in reducing the level of translation risk.

If, for example, our Japanese carmaker starts to produce cars locally in the USA, she needs money to buy or build US factories. This money could be raised in either of two ways: by means of either a loan in the Japanese market in yen or a loan in the US capital market in US dollars. A yen loan raises the financing costs as the loan proceeds should be converted from yen to dollars. Now the Japanese carmaker possesses an additional dollar asset and an additional yen liability – thus, an additional translation risk. It also means that the US factory has to pay off a yen loan from a dollar income flow, which adds to the transaction risk. The alternative of attracting a US dollar loan prevents the two exchange-rate exposures – and avoids forex market costs.

A *parallel loan* is an attractive instrument for a parent company wishing to lend money to a foreign subsidiary in the currency of the country where the subsidiary is located. Until the maturity of this loan the parent company would be exposed to an exchange-rate risk. This can be avoided if there is another parent company with a subsidiary and the countries of origin of parent and subsidiary are reversed. The two parent companies then have the opportunity to grant a loan to one another's subsidiaries. This basic idea is illustrated in Figure 15.2, in which there are now two companies: our own Japanese firm with a subsidiary in the USA, and a US-based firm with a Japanese subsidiary.

Both these parent companies need to finance their subsidiaries, but are worried about their exchange-rate exposure. If they use the parallel loan construction, they will give a loan not to their own subsidiary, but to the subsidiary of the other parent located in their own country. This means that the Japanese firm finances the US subsidiary in Japan and the US firm finances the Japanese subsidiary in the USA.

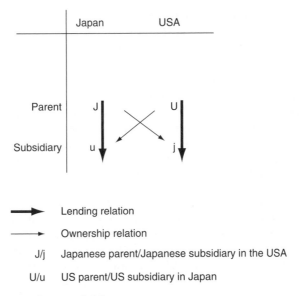

Figure 15.2 Structure of a parallel loan

The advantage of this instrument is that the parent companies make the loan in their own currency, which means that there is no longer any exchange-rate risk attached to the loan. At the maturity of the loans the principal is simply paid off in the same currency in which the loan was made. Another advantage is that in this way the parent companies can sidestep any restrictions on capital exports and imports: they are not exporting any capital, they are simply granting a domestic loan. The drawback of such an arrangement is its legal complexity because of the involvement of four parties. This problem can be crystallized as follows: what happens if one of the subsidiaries is declared bankrupt before the maturity of the loans?

15.4.2 Artificial hedges

Artificial hedges consist of financial contracts that have been purposely developed to reduce the level of exchange-rate risk. The best-known artificial hedge is the *forward exchange* contract or outright forward, which has already been in use for a considerable time. The forward exchange contract has the following features:

o This is an agreement on the delivery of a specific amount of foreign currency at a particular date in the future (more than two business days later) at a price that is already fixed on the day of the agreement.
o It is an agreement between a bank and its customer or between banks. The price in the contract is called the forward exchange rate.
o Banks indicate on request their forward rates for the delivery and purchase of foreign currency for different maturities.
o Firms can cover the exchange-rate risk on both their claims and their debts by such a forward. If a firm, for example, knows that a claim it possesses in a foreign currency will be repaid at a specific moment in the future, say in three months' time, that firm can sell that foreign currency now on the three months' forward market. Then the recipient firm already knows how much domestic currency it is going to receive for the foreign currency claim.

o The covered interest parity is the main tool for the setting of the forward rates. (See Section 12.3 for the background of this parity.)

The advantage of a forward exchange transaction is flexibility in the size of contracts. It is possible to do a deal for any desired amount, making it possible to cover the exchange-rate risk in full, even in the case of unusual amounts.

However, one disadvantage of forwards is the lack of flexibility in respect of maturities. The usually available maturities are half a month, one, two, three, and six months and one year. Forward transactions for periods in excess of two years are uncommon, so that these markets are thin and therefore relatively illiquid. Because forwards are tailor-made, they cannot be traded on exchanges. In order to counteract the problem of the restricted number of maturities for forward transactions, national credit insurance companies often offer companies facilities for concluding long-term exchange risk insurances.

As an example of the usage of forwards, say that at present our Japanese firm knows that it will receive $2.5 million in three months as a payment for a car sale to the USA. It is now in a position to sign a forward contract with a bank in which they agree that the firm will sell the bank those $2.5 million for yen in three months at a specified exchange rate – the forward exchange rate. The huge advantage for the Japanese firm is that from this time onwards it is certain how many yen it will receive for its present dollar claim. Its revenues are no longer dependent upon the yen–dollar exchange rate at the moment of disbursement of the claim. This means that there is no longer any exchange-rate risk.

Currency futures are another artificial hedge. A currency future has some similarity to a forward exchange contract. It can be regarded as a standardized version of a forward. This standardization makes futures trading much more straightforward and allows public trading on exchanges; for that reason a future is readily negotiable. Its standardization emerges from: the futures' denomination in round sums, the availability for only a limited number of currencies and, like a forward contract, a very limited set of maturities. Standardization means that futures contracts are relatively cheap.

Currency futures are less useful for a goods exporter, such as our Japanese carmaker, because of the fixed amounts of currency futures, since a contract in commodities will seldom come to such a round figure. On the other hand, the foreign exchange speculator will appreciate a futures contract particularly for its good negotiability, as that greatly increases the speculator's room for manoeuvre.

The activities of currency arbitragers ensure that a close link is maintained between the prices of the two related financial instruments: currency futures and forward exchange contracts. In the case of futures contracts, the principle of 'marking to market' applies (for an explanation, see Box 15.4). Currency futures were introduced in 1972 on the Chicago Mercantile Exchange, a logical place for such an innovation since by this time Chicago had more than a century's experience with futures for cereals and other commodities.

Box 15.4 Marking to market

At the end of each day's futures trading the holder of a futures contract has to take his profit or loss. That is one reason why the holder is obliged to keep an initial amount of cash, a margin, with a clearing house. The latter acts as an intermediary for futures contracts.

Let us give an example. Say, a holder has one futures contract to buy euros at a specified future date for a specified price in US dollars. Assume that price equals the spot exchange rate at the contract date. A usual minimum contract size is 125,000 euros. If the euro rises by $0.01 on the first day's trading on the futures market, then $1250 ($125,000 \times \$0.01$) is added to the holder's account at the end of the day. This amount compensates the worsened price if the holder would have bought the euros at the end of this first day at the spot market.

Moreover, the original futures contract lapses and is replaced by a new contract stating the futures price of the euro at the end of that day's trading. Using this technique, the risk of serious consequences resulting from a holder's insolvency is very small on a futures contract, as the holder's losses are written down immediately. If the margin has become too small because of previous losses, then the holder has to top it up again. This process is known as marking to market. If he cannot, then the clearing house and the other party still do not suffer financially since the holder's losses up to that time have already been paid for.

Two market parties can enter into a *foreign exchange swap* contract. This is, in effect, an agreement for the temporary exchange of currencies and the reason for such an operation can be clarified by means of a simple example.

Say, party A is our Japanese firm, which has a good track record on its (existing) yen debt, but would now like to take out a loan leading to periodic payments of interest and repayments of principal (or debt service) in dollars. Party B is an established and creditworthy American firm. It also wants a loan, but with a periodic debt service payment in yen.

Firm A could borrow directly in dollars and B in yen; then they would not need each other. However, it is probable that A can borrow on more advantageous terms than B on its domestic market in yen and, conversely, that B can borrow in the American financial market on better terms in dollars. On their home markets they are well known and respected market parties and they can, therefore, obtain advantageous interest rates. It is also possible that capital restrictions prevent A and/or B from borrowing in foreign currencies.

In either of these two situations it is mutually advantageous if A takes out a loan in yen and B a loan in dollars. Subsequently, the two parties swap the two loans, including the financial obligations bound to the currency loan received. At the end of the contract period the exchange of currencies is reversed. This structure of the currency swap prevents exchange-rate uncertainty for the two contract parties, although they receive a foreign currency loan.

Obviously, it is quite unlikely that parties A and B prefer to carry out a swap of the two same currencies, over the same term, and with the same underlying amounts. Moreover, a swap contract remains risky because of the risk of default on the part of the counterparty. For these two reasons, banks usually have an intermediary role in currency swaps. In their other dealings with customers banks will quite commonly also be facing temporary foreign currency exposures. A compensating currency swap is then an adequate financial instrument. It will, therefore, come as no surprise that the swap market consists mainly of interbank transactions. Currency swaps date from the mid-1970s.

A *currency option* is a financial instrument that entitles – and expressly does not oblige – the holder to buy or sell a stated amount of foreign currency at an agreed price. The right to sell is called a *put* option; the right to buy is a *call* option. A currency option is a useful instrument for companies operating in a sector where tendering for contracts is the norm, such as contracting civil projects and the production of large capital goods.

If the Japanese firm submits a tender in dollars to an American company, the Japanese firm is exposed to a particular type of exchange-rate risk during the period for which the tender applies. The tender may be accepted and the Japanese firm will receive dollars after the expiry of a period stated in the tender. However, the outcome is uncertain because the tender may also be rejected. For the Japanese entrepreneur a forward exchange contract is then in fact too risky: it would oblige her to supply the dollars on expiry of the term – dollars that she will not receive if the tender is not accepted. A currency option is the appropriate instrument in that case, because a put option for dollars offers the option holder the right, but not the obligation, to supply the dollars at a future date.

There is one distinction between an American and a European option. An American option can be exercised at any time up to a specified date whereas a European option confers this right only on the specified date. (Note that this American and European style has nothing to do with the area of trading, but simply indicates a specific type of option.)

Like futures contracts, currency options are in standard sizes, which may vary from one stock exchange to another; they are often similar in size to currency futures. The buyer of an option has to pay an option premium to the other party (the option writer). The size of the premium depends upon various aspects, not least the difference between the spot exchange rate at the moment of arranging the contract, and the strike price or exercise price of the option, stated in the contract (see Box 15.5 for more details). Where the buyer of the option has a right, the option writer has an obligation to fulfil. The first currency options were traded on the European Options Exchange (EOE) in Amsterdam at the end of 1982, followed by their introduction on the Philadelphia Stock Exchange early in 1983.

Box 15.5   Return profile of a currency option

If in the case of a call option for dollars, the strike price (the price at which dollars can be bought with the option) is €0.80 and the spot rate at that moment is €1.00, then the option is said to be 'in the money'. If the option holder were willing and able to use (or 'exercise') the option at that moment, then she could buy the dollars from the option writer for €0.80 and sell them immediately for €1.00 on the spot market. This would be a profitable deal. This profitability potential is reflected in the high level of the premium (the price) of the option if such a call option would be bought at that time.

A strike price of €0.80 for the option is riskier for the writer than a strike price of, say, €1.00 or even more extreme: €1.20 (then the option would be 'at the money' or 'out of the money', respectively). However, in almost all the cases the premium is at least a few per cent. This makes currency options more expensive than currency futures.

Options do have an attractive return profile for speculators, because one can hardly make a loss by holding an option. The worst conceivable situation for the holder of a call option is that she does not exercise the option because it is not profitable: she has then 'only' lost the premium paid on purchasing the option. On the other hand, the potential profit associated with holding an option is unlimited. The higher the spot rate above the strike price on the strike date, the greater the profit is for the holder of the call option.

The artificial hedges for exchange-rate risk, described above, belong to the group of financial derivatives. These are contracts that give one party a claim on an underlying asset at a specified future time, with the other party having a corresponding obligation. In the cases described in this section the underlying asset is, of course, foreign currency.

The explosive growth of derivatives in recent years has caused great concern to the central banks, as there is limited scope for the supervision of this trade. Moreover, derivatives cannot reduce the overall risk in the international financial system – although they can be used effectively to reduce the risks for an individual. Derivatives merely transform and reallocate the risk. There is even some concern that the risk is being concentrated in the leading commercial banks via the trade in derivatives (cf., for example, IMF Capital Market Division, 1994, p. 49). These banks are very active in some derivative markets. This makes it possible that the total risk for the financial system (the so-called systemic risk) will ultimately have increased.

The Bank for International Settlements (BIS) (2010) gives an idea of the growth of the turnover in some of these forex market derivative instruments. In April 2010 foreign exchange swaps had a daily turnover of $1,765 billion – compared with just $324 billion in April 1992. Over the same period the daily turnover of outright forwards rose from $58 billion to $475 billion. In April 2010 foreign exchange options reached a daily turnover of $207 billion; the comparable figure for April 1998 had been $87 billion. Although these are huge amounts, the trade in foreign exchange derivatives pales into insignificance compared to the similar interest rate instruments. The former have a turnover that only is between 10 and 20 per cent of the latter.

15.5 Summary

1. Financial risks for the business world can be divided into two broad categories: the *credit or debtor risk* and the *market risk*. Not only do companies that operate internationally face these two types of risk to a greater degree than at home but the risks also appear in new forms.

2. The specifically international form of credit risk is the *country risk*. This concerns uncertainty as the result of the specific country of the debtor, and may impede the payment of outstanding claims. The country risk can be further divided into *political risk* (which includes transfer risk), *policy risk*, and *legal risk*.

3. The specifically international form of market risk is the *exchange-rate risk* (or the currency risk). Again, there are three variants: *transaction risk*, *economic risk*, and *translation risk*. The main problem is the economic risk.

4. The government often plays an important role in insuring the country risk. In practice, it is very difficult to ascertain the level of country risk because the circumstances in which a country gets into payment difficulties are not systematic. Nevertheless, quantitative and qualitative analyses of the country risk are used widely.

5. The exchange-rate risk has long been countered by the use of instruments that hedge this risk – either in whole or in part. The natural hedges include: *netting, leading and lagging*, the *borrow-deposit technique*, and *parallel loans*.

6. Artificial hedges of exchange-rate risk, often more recently developed hedge instruments, include *forward exchange contracts, currency futures, foreign exchange swaps*, and *currency options*. In spite of their dynamic growth, trading in this type of derivative in the foreign exchange market still accounts for less than 20 per cent of the total volume of trading in this type of instrument on the financial markets.

7. Exchange-rate predictions – described in Section 13.4 – are also used widely in an attempt to counteract the exchange-rate risk. The point of such predictions is contrary to the idea that the foreign exchange market is a particularly efficient market. If that were the case, historical information could add no useful knowledge for predicting the rate: all information is deemed to be already discounted in the current price.

Questions

1. A Brazilian producer of man-made fibre garden furniture concentrates its sale totally on the domestic market. This producer obtains the raw materials and intermediate products from Brazilian suppliers. Even this producer of garden furniture incurs an exchange rate risk and even along two channels. Explain.

2. An Australian firm possibly receives $1 million after 6 months. The present exchange rate is one Australian dollar for one US dollar. The Australian firm wishes to cover the risk that the US dollar will become cheaper in the meantime and decides to take an option on the amount of US dollars that is possibly received. The strike price of the option is 0.98 Australian dollars per US dollar.

   (a) Is this a call or put option?
   (b) One month later the spot exchange rate appears to be 0.97. Is the option then in, at or out of the money?

3. Formulate in your own words the differences between forward exchange contracts and currency futures.

4. Look on the Internet for a recent country risk rating.

CHAPTER 16

International Monetary Cooperation

16.1 Introduction

The existence of international economic transactions, discussed in previous chapters, implies that countries have a mutual impact on one another's economies. Whether this occurs through international trade or international capital flows, a serious change in the economic behaviour of a country will, to a greater or lesser extent, influence the economies of other countries. These mutual influences – termed economic spillovers – prompt countries to consider international economic cooperation.

Such economic spillovers are usually an unintentional side effect of economic behaviour – they are not a consideration in the establishment of this behaviour. Take as an example a change in a country's economic policy. As the result of the presence of cross-border external effects of this policy change, from the viewpoint of total world welfare the country adjusting its economic policy does not apply the optimal dosage of adjustment. This is because the country is concerned only with its own economic costs and benefits that are associated with that adjustment in policy and ignores the effects that the policy adjustment has on other countries.

The aim of international economic cooperation is, first, to ensure that such national economic policy decisions take account of the unintentional spillover effects on the economies of other countries. It is, of course, possible that a country does have an open eye for the spillover. This is even commonly in cases that it wants to influence other countries' economy to the benefit of its own economy. An example is an increase in protectionism in bad economic times. But countries protecting themselves at the cost of other countries can expect retaliation from these countries. This can easily turn into a process of increasing levels of protection on both sides that has a negative impact on all economies. A second aim of international economic cooperation is to prevent such 'beggar-thy-neighbour' policies.

International economic cooperation usually needs to be organized, and this process of organization is the subject of this chapter. Dealing with both the possibilities and the facts as they have unfolded in the past, this chapter focuses only on international cooperation in the monetary sphere, although we shall see that in general it is not sensible to draw too strict a division between monetary policy and economic policy. For this reason the chapter will also touch on fiscal policy and trade policy insofar as this helps to achieve a better understanding of international monetary cooperation.

The chapter is structured as follows. Section 16.2 surveys the various appearances of international economic cooperation in practice and examines in greater depth the theoretical concepts just touched on. This section also deals with the practical problems facing international economic cooperation. Section 16.3 examines international monetary cooperation up to the end of the Second World War. This is followed by Section 16.4 on international monetary cooperation between 1945 and 1973, when there were two violent shocks in the world economy. The section also includes an account of the International Monetary Fund (IMF), the main postwar organization that is active in the area of international monetary cooperation. The IMF started its activities in 1947. Finally, Section 16.5 considers international monetary cooperation after 1973.

The chapter will address the following questions:

o What different appearances of international economic cooperation can be identified?
o How does harmonization differ from coordination as a method of international economic cooperation?
o Is international monetary cooperation a postwar phenomenon?
o What is the function of the widespread phenomenon of groups of cooperating countries, such as the G3, G5, G7, G20 and G24?
o Can we draw useful lessons through studying the behaviour of the exchange-rate systems that have been put in place in recent decades?
o Why did the worldwide system of fixed exchange-rates collapse in 1973?
o Why is intervention in the foreign-exchange market sometimes internationally coordinated?
o What time paths have the major currencies, in both nominal and real terms, followed since 1973 and do they exhibit purchasing power parity (PPP)?
o Why did the IMF introduce Special Drawing Rights (SDRs) in 1970 and what are their principal characteristics and perspectives? Are they a possible successor of the US dollar as international money?
o Is there any role left for the IMF in the present international monetary non-system?

16.2 Types of international economic cooperation

Long before the twentieth century, countries have engaged in international economic cooperation. However, this involved little more than an international *exchange of information* on the state of the countries' economies and the governments' plans for national economic policy. It was not until well into the twentieth century that international economic cooperation deepened and became more permanent in character.

At the end of the Second World War the Organization for Economic Co-operation and Development (OECD), headquartered in Paris, assumed the role of exchanging and publishing information about the economic policies of developed countries. It offers an environment for government representatives to hold regular meetings at which they can exchange ideas about the current economic situation and the forthcoming economic policies in their countries. The OECD also supplies its members with periodical economic advice that helps them to formulate future policies.

For example, if it is apparent that Germany is preparing to introduce an expansive economic policy, the governments of countries such as Belgium and the Netherlands – which have traditionally exported a substantial percentage of their output to Germany – can react by moderating any plans that they have for economic expansion. They can anticipate that increased German expenditure will stimulate German demand for imports and that therefore Germany's new policy will in turn stimulate their own economies.

A more intensive type of international cooperation is *policy coordination*, with the aim of encouraging countries involved in the coordination attempt to adjust their policy instruments in the best interests of the whole set of economic objectives of all countries.

Since the mid-1970s, international economic policy coordination has taken place mainly in the G7, which consists of the seven leading industrialized countries: the USA, Japan, Germany, the UK, France, Canada, and Italy. The G7 members hold annual meetings of their heads of state or government leaders. The Group of 8 (G8), also known as the Political 8, was conceived when Russia first participated in the part of international political affairs of the 1994 Naples Summit of the G7. At the 1998 Birmingham Summit, Russia joined as a full participant, marking the establishment of the G8. However, the G8 did not replace the G7, which continues to function as a forum for discussion of economic and financial issues among the major industrial countries.

These summits produce general statements. What has changed over time, however, is the range of topics covered by the G7. The summits of the 1970s and 1980s aimed to pursue broad economic goals to the benefit of the world economy, including issues such as macroeconomic policy and the alignment of exchange rates. The goals set in those years were, for instance, to reduce the American fiscal deficit, to cut taxes in Japan, and to pursue a more expansive economic policy in Germany, but also the general aim of exchange-rate stabilization. Today the scope of the G8 is much wider, ranging from combating terrorism to AIDS prevention and from nuclear proliferation to global warming.

G7 and G8 summits are important events. They set the stage for other high-level international meetings by providing a forum for the meetings of national leaders to discuss matters of global importance. These meetings serve two goals: (i) the coordination of national policies in international affairs; and (ii) the improvement of the reputation of the politicians present at the summit. Associating with other international leaders enhances the domestic reputation of a politician: 'our leader is respected by other important politicians and helps solving international problems'. In practice, these two goals can be in conflict: if national leaders speak only to enhance their own national reputation, this may damage the outcome in terms of international cooperation.

Case study 16.1, which focuses on a specific G7 meeting, illustrates the nature of summit results. There has been no general retrospective monitoring or evaluation of these events, but Case study 16.2 describes one of the few attempts at assessment. One complicating factor for assessments is that it is not unusual for an agreed measure to remain unimplemented because, according to the country that was designated to carry out this measure, new developments after the summit necessitated revision of the agreed policy intentions.

Case study 16.1   The G7 summit in Halifax, 1995

On 15–18 June 1995 the leaders of the seven principal industrial countries held their annual meeting in the Canadian town of Halifax, Nova Scotia. The usual final economic and political declarations contained a number of specific recommendations. The main reason for this was that earlier that year the world had been surprised by a serious financial crisis in Mexico, which once again shook the foundations of the international financial system. (For more on this crisis, see Section 18.3.)

The Mexican crisis was the reason for recommending that the IMF be enabled to develop an early-warning system for such crises. This required a tightening of IMF monitoring of its then 179 member countries, and an effort had to be made to supply more open, better, and faster information. If a financial crisis were nevertheless to break out in a country, then the IMF had to be able to provide a large amount of support more quickly than hitherto through an Emergency Financing Mechanism.

It was proposed to create such a mechanism by increasing the amounts that are available under the General Arrangements to Borrow (GAB). (For an explanation of the GAB, see Sub-section 16.4.1.) Under these arrangements, the G10 countries and Saudi Arabia could provide the IMF with a maximum of $27 billion. The summit conference recommended a doubling of this figure and also asked other countries – such as the developing Asian countries and the Scandinavian countries – to join the GAB.

The final declarations also referred to the topic of multilateral aid to developing countries. It was stated that the global institutions working in that field should direct their policy to the poorest countries and to the combating of poverty. Another recommendation was that the World Bank and the IMF should develop new mechanisms for reducing countries' debts to these institutions. The G7 countries also expressed their support for the new World Trade Organization (WTO), and undertook to guarantee an efficient and well-respected mechanism for settling trade disputes.

In addition to the G7 and G8 there have also been other groupings of the larger, richer countries. These have also engaged in coordination, but generally with regard to a specific aspect of economic policy. There have been periods in which a G5 (the G7 minus Italy and Canada) appeared likely to develop as a permanent consultation agency. However, the G5 now seems to have had its day. Instead, there was a tendency to establish a G3 consisting of the USA, Japan and, initially, Germany (later replaced by the European Union (EU)). The G7 coordination meetings might then become a matter for the G3, but China's recent economic rise undermines Japan's position in international consultations.

The G10 has been in existence since 1962. Initially, it consisted of the G7 countries plus the Netherlands, Belgium, and Sweden, with Switzerland being added in 1964. Japan, a member of the G7, joined in 1964. Although the group in fact has 11 members, the name G10 has never been changed. On the initiative of the USA this group became involved in the IMF's liquidity position; Section 16.4 will examine this activity in more detail.

The growth of emerging market economies was the incentive for the formal establishment of the Group of 20 (G20) at the G7 finance ministers' meeting on 26 September 1999. The inaugural meeting of this organization took place on 15–16 December 1999 in Berlin. The G20 was formed as a new forum for cooperation and consultation on matters relating to the international financial system. It studies, reviews, and promotes discussion among key industrial and emerging market countries of policy issues pertaining to the promotion of international financial stability, and seeks to address issues that go beyond the responsibilities of any one organization. The membership of the G20 comprises the finance ministers and central bank governors of the G7, 12 other key countries, and the country that has the presidency of the European Union (provided it is not a G7 member). The 12 'other key countries' are Argentina, Australia, Brazil, China, India, Indonesia, Korea, Mexico, Russia, Saudi Arabia, South Africa and Turkey.

Case study 16.2   The effectiveness of G8 summits

The University of Toronto has established a G8 research group that attempts to evaluate the outcomes of each meeting through the measurement of the level of compliance by each member state to the final declaration of each summit. This, of course, does not address the question of the significance of any particular declaration. Surprisingly, the level of compliance does not vary greatly over time: it scores roughly 40 per cent for the period 1975–2001 on a scale where minus 100 per cent means no compliance and plus 100 per cent means full compliance. What does seem to influence the compliance rate is the hosting nation. The G7 meetings are hosted by each of the members in turn and some states tend to invest much more money, time, and credibility in preparing the summit. For example, the 2001 Okinawa summit, hosted by Japan, was a good example of a summit where the Japanese successfully invested in, resulting in a compliance rate that reached an all-time high of +80 per cent.

Source: *The G8 Compliance Report* (G8 research group, University of Toronto), various issues (http://www.g8.utoronto.ca/).

In 1971 the Group of 24 (G24) was established in an attempt to coordinate the positions of developing countries on international monetary and development finance issues and to ensure that their interests received adequate representation in IMF and World Bank meetings. The group, whose official title is the Intergovernmental Group of Twenty-Four on International Monetary Affairs and Development, is not an official organ of the IMF, although the IMF provides it with secretarial services in order to permit developing country members to discuss agenda items beforehand. Although membership in the G24 is strictly limited to 24 countries, in reality any developing country member of the IMF can join its discussions. The latter countries are formally dubbed the G77, although the present number of countries involved is much greater than 77.

A third form of international economic cooperation, in addition to the exchange of information and policy coordination, is international *policy harmonization*. This occurs if the object of cooperation is to achieve a degree of convergence in policy intervention in the various countries. Thus, harmonization does not so much concern intervention in macroeconomic policy in a broad sense, but rather policies that influence the international competitive position of business firms. These include the setting of tax rates – such as indirect taxes and corporate taxes – and government regulations aimed at protecting the health and safety of consumers.

In recent years the European Union has probably been the most active promoter of policy harmonization. In respect of indirect taxes, for example, so much progress has been made that all EU member countries impose their indirect taxation on the basis of the system of value added taxation (VAT), while a minimum level has been set for both the low and high rates of VAT. This system combats price advantages that are not based on low production costs but on something other than comparative advantages, such as favourable national tax rates.

Finally, the fourth and most radical form of international economic cooperation is the *total integration* or *unification* of economic policy in the cooperating countries. Obviously, such an economic policy is supranational in practice. This means that the implementation of economic control is at a higher level than the national level. It is through a policy body mapping out and implementing economic policy for the countries involved in the unification. Another form of supranational decision-making is majority decisions by participating countries.

The EU contains important examples of economic policy unification. Since the start of the Economic and Monetary Union (EMU) in 1999 (see Section 19.5), the monetary policy of the EU countries participating in the EMU is carried out by the supranational European Central Bank (ECB). By contrast, the Common Agricultural Policy (CAP) in the

EU (see Sections 8.3 and 10.4) operates on the basis of qualified majority decisions among member states.

In conclusion, we can identify four types of international economic cooperation. In ascending order of intensity, these are: exchange of information, coordination, harmonization, and unification. For each of these types a further distinction can be made according to the scope of the cooperation, which ranges from strictly sector policies (for example, international cooperation on trade policy for the textile sector only, in the form of the Multi-Fibre Arrangement, described in Section 8.3) to fully integrated economic policy. There is also a geographical differentiation in scope: from small-scale, regional cooperation (for example, by Belgium, the Netherlands, and Luxembourg in the so-called Benelux area) to truly global cooperation (as in the IMF).

As stated in Section 16.1, the advantage of international economic cooperation is undeniably that the effects on other countries' economic developments are taken into account in determining a country's national economic policy. It is self-evident that this also has a drawback and a complication: the sacrifice of national autonomy in policy-making. Furthermore, there are three other complicating factors in the conduct of international cooperation. They arise through (i) the complexity of implementation of international cooperation; (ii) the risk of cheating; and (iii) the possible presence of free riders (Frankel, 1988). These four problems will now be explained in more detail.

Loss of national autonomy in the implementation of economic policy is often, in itself, a psychological disadvantage for a national government. Independence and autonomy are both regarded as positive attributes of an independent country. The optimum level of international economic cooperation leads to a maximizing of economic welfare for the whole of the cooperating region. However, one cannot rule out the possibility that part of the region, for instance, one of the cooperating countries, will nevertheless suffer a welfare loss or hardly gain anything at all.

Large countries have little interest in cooperation since their economies are relatively closed and are, therefore, relatively little influenced by other countries. For small countries the exact opposite applies. As a result, the largest countries will be able to impose the greatest demands in the cooperating activities – and they will do so.

International economic cooperation in the form of *policy coordination* is *difficult to implement* because it is difficult to quantify the different elements involved. One is the combined welfare function for those countries taking part in the coordination. Another is the choice of national econometric models that are considered to give a good quantitative description of the participating economies. At the national level, this information is already so hard to come by that people continue to disagree about the best model. Where several countries together are concerned, the level of disagreement can clearly increase significantly. One complication here is that the simulation results of econometric models for policy coordination indicate that use of a model which, on closer examination, proves to be incorrect or unsatisfactory as a reflection of the economy involved, can easily more than negate the positive result of coordination (Frankel, 1988).

A third problem of policy coordination is that participants can make a unilateral decision not to carry out a cooperation agreement. This is because once the form in which the coordinated economic policy is to be implemented has been decided upon by mutual consultation, it can be to the advantage of a single participating country to decide not to carry out its own part of the agreement.

The coordinated policy of other countries will, in itself, make a positive contribution to the desired economic development of the country in question. The country's own agreed contribution to the implementation of the coordinated policy might entail net costs for that country – for example, through a coordinated expansionary fiscal policy that stretches the country's fiscal deficit.

Such *cheating behaviour* cannot be avoided altogether; at best, the risk of cheating can only be reduced to a certain extent. In this connection, retrospective legal action serves no practical purpose, because there are no legal rules for this type of international agreement. A country's decision not to comply with agreements will be less attractive if such policy coordination is not an isolated event, but recurs on a periodic basis. Cheating in one year then entails costs for the country concerned, in that it is bound to be excluded from the policy coordination in subsequent years – and hence also from the important phase of devising the coordination policy. The risk of cheating may be reduced further if the policy for countries taking part in the cooperation is laid down in a formal agreement and if an organization is set up to supervise compliance with the rules.

A fourth problem attached to policy cooperation is that a number of countries that benefit from such coordination decide to behave as *free riders*. These countries withdraw not only from implementing the cooperation policy, but also from devising it. They make a deliberate decision to remain outside a system of international economic cooperation. They will have no cooperation costs, but may benefit from the outcome of the cooperation policy undertaken by the participating countries.

One very clear example of free riding is the global oil market. Countries that are members of the Organization of the Petroleum Exporting Countries (OPEC) apply successful upward pressure on oil prices, through the operation of production quotas. Oil-exporting countries that are not members of OPEC, such as Norway, Russia, and the UK, benefit from this upward pressure on world oil prices without having OPEC restrictions placed on their own oil production. Nothing can be done about this problem, apart from bringing political pressure to bear on the free rider.

16.3 International monetary cooperation prior to 1945

Modern international monetary history can be said to have begun around 1870 when most of the leading economic powers of the day adopted a monetary system based on the value of gold: the gold standard. Under a gold standard it is not necessary to have gold coins in circulation with a gold content that determines the value of the coins through its price on the gold market. Although, initially, gold coins circulated, over the course of time the gold exchange standard gradually came into use. Its characteristic is that all monetary gold in a country is stored at the country's central bank, which instead of solid gold coins circulates fiduciary money – that is, money with a value based on the users' trust in it. This essentially means trusting that the central bank will at all times be prepared to fulfil its obligation to exchange the fiduciary money at a fixed price for gold. The essence of a gold exchange standard is the central bank's exchange obligation into and out of gold if the private sector wishes to do so. If such an obligation no longer exists, we speak of a paper standard. This standard rests on the faith that the central bank will not undermine the purchasing power of the fiduciary currency by issuing too much of it.

If two countries use the gold standard for their monetary systems, then it follows that their currencies are linked by a fixed exchange rate. The value of the exchange rate corresponds to the relationship between the gold values of each of the central currencies of the two countries. If at a certain moment in time the value of a certain volume of fine gold expressed in British pound sterling was 4.8666 times higher than the value expressed in the US dollar – gold values guaranteed by the respective central banks – then $4.8666 were equal in value to £1. In fact, this was the official exchange-rate value between these two currencies in the period 1837–1931 when both countries applied the gold standard (*cf.* Officer, 1996, p. 55).

If the actual exchange rate of these two currencies diverged excessively from this gold parity, a gold arbitrage would result, in which case arbitragers bought gold from the central bank of the undervalued currency and sold it to the central bank of the overvalued currency. The arbitragers thus received substantial volumes of the overvalued currency, which it subsequently sold on the foreign-exchange market against the undervalued currency.[1] This so-called 'round trip' contributed to a reduction of the over- and undervaluation of the two currencies.

The global adoption of the gold standard around 1870 led indirectly to the acceptance of a near-universal regime of fixed exchange rates. This system was therefore associated with the known advantages and disadvantages of fixed exchange rates: the advantage of certainty for international trade and investment, but the disadvantage that a situation such as a permanent deficit on the balance of payments combined with high domestic unemployment cannot be rectified through devaluing the currency. Although devaluation remained formally possible through a reduction in the gold content of the national currency or the compulsory exchange of fiduciary currency for a smaller quantity of gold by the central bank, this possibility was hardly ever used in practice.

The gold standard worked extremely well in the period between 1880 and 1914. However, at the start of the First World War countries abandoned the gold standard en masse, not returning to it until the early 1920s. This restoration of the gold standard appeared to be short-lived.

In 1929 a financial crisis on the New York stock market led to a downturn in the world economy, with rapid increases in unemployment. In 1931 the UK decided to abandon the gold standard: this entailed the end of the fixed exchange rate for the UK in favour of a depreciating pound. The pursuit of an internal macroeconomic objective, namely a low level of unemployment, was accorded precedence over the external objective of a fixed exchange rate. Other countries followed suit.

As a result, the 1930s saw a series of competitive devaluations between countries that were attempting to pursue their own objectives. Countries also introduced foreign-exchange restrictions and additional barriers for imports in order to provide additional support for domestic producers to protect employment. These measures were undertaken at the expense of employment in those countries that did not devalue, or which devalued their currencies by less than their trading partners. The countries that rapidly devalued their currencies thus 'exported' their unemployment to their trading partners, often neighbouring countries, which is why such a process of competitive devaluations is called a 'beggar-thy-neighbour' policy.

A period of intense disunity and hardship tends to provide favourable conditions for the establishment of international cooperation, and the final days of the Second World War were no exception. In the 1930s the world witnessed the disintegration of the global economy and the emergence of inward-looking countries; and between 1939 and 1945 this trend was worsened by the ravages of war. With the end of the war in sight, in July 1944 the leading countries met at Bretton Woods in the USA to lay the foundations for a restored world economy once the conflict had ended.

The Bretton Woods meeting decided to set up a number of international economic organizations that would control world economic cooperation in the postwar years. These

---

[1] As a numerical illustration, assume that the market exchange rate at some time in the period 1837–1934 was \$5/£. Buying gold in the USA to the amount of \$4.8666 against the official gold price and, subsequently, selling that gold in the UK against the official gold price of £1, resulted in a profit of \$0.1334 as soon as the arbitrager sold the pound on the foreign-exchange market against \$5. This sale reduced the value of the pound against that of the dollar on the foreign-exchange market and thus let the market exchange rate converge to the gold parity of the two currencies.

were the International Monetary Fund (IMF), the World Bank (officially known as the International Bank for Reconstruction and Development, or IBRD) and an International Trade Organization (ITO), which was later to function, in truncated form, as the General Agreement on Tariffs and Trade (GATT). Eventually, this trade agreement was incorporated into an international trade organization: the World Trade Organization, or WTO, which came into operation on 1 January 1995.

The central aim of this attempt to restore international economic cooperation in the postwar world was to avoid a repetition of the economic chaos of the 1930s and to promote international trade and, hence, world economic growth through certainty and freedom. It was believed that this would undoubtedly be accompanied by a substantial increase in economic welfare and high levels of employment. For this purpose, people thought that the primary requirement was stable – and therefore predictable – exchange rates (see Chapter 14). Fixed exchange rates would make clear the pattern of the countries' comparative advantages and therefore contribute to the optimum allocation of production in the world. Apart from stable exchange rates, maximum efficiency in production naturally also required the absence of both foreign-exchange controls and trade barriers.

In the light of this approach, the new international economic institutions were assigned specific tasks. The aim of the IMF was to promote exchange-rate stability without countries retreating into foreign-exchange restrictions. For this purpose the Fund was permitted to provide member countries with short-term credits as balance-of-payments support. This allowed those countries to protect the fixed value of their currency against market disruption by intervening in the foreign-exchange market. Where a balance-of-payments problem required a structural rather than a temporary solution, the IMF credits at least gave the country the flexibility to spread the required structural adjustment of the domestic economy over a number of years.

The World Bank was given the task of supporting the postwar process of economic reconstruction and growth. In contrast to the IMF, it was given the freedom to raise capital on the international financial markets on the basis of guarantees from its more creditworthy member countries. This capital could then be lent to member countries which need it for the purpose of stimulating their economic development. Since the World Bank has an excellent credit rating because of the guarantees from all its member countries, it can raise capital at a relatively low interest rate – a benefit it can pass on to its less creditworthy developing country members in the form of low interest loans.

In recent years the functions of the IMF and the World Bank have increasingly overlapped. The problems afflicting the countries to which the IMF grants credit require such a long adjustment period that the IMF has increasingly tended to extend the maturity of some of its credits. On the other hand, since the mid-1980s the World Bank has shifted its lending activities in the direction of support for solving macroeconomic problems rather than project aid. This interweaving of spheres of activity is acknowledged, as witnessed in the passage in the final communiqué of the summit conference of heads of state and government in Halifax (see Case study 16.1) in June 1995: 'the IMF and the World Bank should concentrate on their respective core functions (broadly speaking, macro-economic policy for the IMF and structural and sector policy for the World Bank)'.

The IMF and the World Bank were established at the Bretton Woods conference. However, this was not the case for the third institutional cornerstone of the postwar world economy: the GATT. As we have seen already, the aim of the GATT – which came into force in 1947 – was to help reduce restrictions on trade. The agreement proved extremely successful in this respect. Of these three institutional cornerstones of the postwar international economic system, only the IMF plays a substantial role in international monetary cooperation. Therefore, this institution will now be examined in more detail.

16.4 International monetary cooperation between 1945 and 1973

16.4.1 The IMF

The IMF, headquartered in Washington, DC, was able to start work at the end of 1945 when 29 countries had signed its Articles of Agreement. By March 2010 the Fund had 186 member countries – a number that has expanded in fits and starts. For example, in the 1990s the number of members increased greatly as a result of the accession of many former planned economies, including those countries that emerged from the collapse of the Soviet Union and Yugoslavia.

The organizational structure of the Fund is headed by a Board of Governors and a Board of Executive Directors, the latter being chaired by the managing director. The managing director is also the head of the IMF staff. The Board of Governors is the highest decision-making body of the IMF and consists of one governor and one alternate governor from each of the IMF's member countries. This board normally meets once a year at the IMF/World Bank Annual Meeting in September/October. A country's governor is usually either the minister of finance or president of the central bank.

The 24 governors have a seat on the IMF's International Monetary and Financial Committee (IMFC) which meets twice a year and guides the work of the Board of Executive Directors. That board handles the day-to-day management of the IMF. There are 24 executive directors. Eight of the member countries have their own representatives on the Board of Executive Directors: the G5 countries plus Saudi Arabia, China, and Russia. The other 16 executive directors represent voting groups of countries. The German Horst Köhler resigned as managing director in March 2004, and was replaced by Rodrigo de Rato from Spain, who succeeded him in June 2004. In turn, de Rato stepped down in November 2007, and was replaced by the Frenchman Dominique Strauss-Kahn followed by his country woman Christine Lagarde in June 2011.

Every country that joins the IMF pays a subscription, which gives it an equal amount of quota in the Fund and a closely related number of votes on the Board of Executive Directors. In principle, the size of the subscription of a member country depends upon a quota formula based on a few economic characteristics of that country, particularly its gross domestic production (weight 50 per cent), economic openness, economic variability, and holdings of international monetary reserves. The Fund uses the subscriptions to provide loans to its members to finance balance-of-payments deficits. Since international payments – and therefore balance-of-payments deficits – tend to grow over time, the IMF considers that it should also be able to increase the sizes of its loans by the same degree. This means that from time to time subscriptions have to be adjusted upwards. For that reason, every five years the IMF conducts general reviews to assess the adequacy of its resource base and, in line with this process, to adjust the quotas. The Fund also uses this opportunity to adjust the quota of an individual member in order to reflect a change in its relative position in the world economy. The Board of Executive Directors completed the 12th and 13th General Review of Quotas in 2003 and 2008 without proposing any adjustments. This left the value of the sum of the quotas unchanged. Under the influence of the worldwide credit crisis, in November 2010 the Board of Executive Directors approved proposals to conclude the 14th General Review of Quotas. Once implemented, it will result in an unprecedentedly large, 100 per cent, increase in total quotas to about $755 billion. Due to a major realignment of quota shares, China will become the third-largest member country.

A country has to pay 25 per cent of its subscription in the form of reserve currencies, from its international monetary reserves holding, and the remaining 75 per cent in the form of its own currency. This rule also applies to payments of the periodic quota increases.

For a country the payment is in fact no burden, because in return for the payment in reserve currency it is entitled to draw on the IMF for the same amount in the form of withdrawals in convertible currencies as soon as the country runs into balance-of-payments problems. Thus, in essence, the payment of 25 per cent of the quota by means of reserve currencies means that a country is exchanging two components of its international monetary reserves: the loss of reserve currencies is offset by a corresponding increase in the country's (unconditional) general drawing rights on the IMF. Likewise, the payment of the 75 per cent in its own currency is not a burden at all for a country. If need be, the payment can be met simply by printing the money.

Access to IMF credits is an unmitigated benefit of IMF membership. Over the years these credits have developed into an ever-larger, multifaceted system. Through the miscellaneous IMF credit facilities, a member country with serious balance-of-payments problems can obtain IMF loans to the amount of more than six times the value of its quota. Apart from the first 25 per cent, mentioned above, the loans are subject to economic policy conditions to be formulated by the staff of the Fund and adopted by the Board of Executive Directors. Section 17.3 will give an outline of the different credit facilities and the part they play in IMF credits.

On a number of occasions, the IMF's own resources – that is, members' subscriptions – have proved insufficient for lending purposes. The periodic increases in quotas were sometimes too late or simply too small to cope with the world's balance-of-payments finance requirements. In such cases the IMF sometimes successfully called on members to make money available in the form of a loan to the Fund. Some of the IMF's credit facilities are financed in this way – as we shall see in Section 17.3.

An important special form of financing IMF credits is the lending arrangement organized by the IMF with ten industrial countries in 1962. The countries concerned subsequently formed the G10 (see Section 16.2), and the loan agreements were known as the General Arrangements to Borrow (GAB). These arrangements form a network of bilateral credit facilities between the participating countries. They were introduced when it was anticipated that the UK would make heavy demands on the IMF as the result of serious balance-of-payments problems, and the IMF's resources at the time would have been insufficient for the purpose.

The G10 countries then agreed that in such cases they would, in future, make substantial amounts available to one another on a temporary basis. The GAB still exists, and the maximum amounts of the arrangements have been periodically increased: since 1982 they are available to the IMF for other difficult situations. The facility has also been extended to situations that involve countries who are not members of the G10. The borrowing country is then also subject to IMF conditionality (see Chapter 17). This development was a response to the world debt crisis that broke out during that year (see Chapter 17) and which imposed a huge strain on the international financial system. Since that time an associated arrangement of the GAB has been in operation with Saudi Arabia, which, as a rich OPEC country, was also prepared to make credit available to other countries.

Following the Mexican financial crisis in 1994, there was concern that substantially more resources might be needed to respond to future financial crises. As we saw in Case study 16.1, the result was that the 1995 G7 summit conference called on members of the GAB and other financially strong countries to double the resources available under the GAB. With a delay, the IMF's Executive Board was able to establish the New Arrangements to Borrow (NAB), a set of credit arrangements between the IMF and 26 member countries, which came into effect from November 1998. In 2009 the maximum amount of resources available to the IMF under the NAB and GAB was some $50 billion.

The aim of IMF's financial support to member countries discussed above is to give financial markets additional confidence in the supported countries. The general resources of the

Fund are temporarily available to them under adequate safeguards, thus providing them with financial means to smooth adjustments of their balance-of-payments disequilibria without the need to resort to measures that are destructive of national or international prosperity (see IMF, 1978, p. 2).

The task of providing finance has been one of the IMF's purposes from its foundation. This also holds for the more general tasks of the IMF: the promotion of international monetary cooperation and the facilitation of a balanced growth of international trade.

The IMF task relating to exchange rates, updated in the 1970s, is to promote exchange-rate stability, to maintain orderly exchange arrangements among members, and to avoid competitive exchange-rate depreciation (IMF, 1978, p. 2). This IMF task is the topic of the next sub-section.

16.4.2 The Bretton Woods exchange-rate system

The shape of the postwar international monetary system was outlined at Bretton Woods. For the first time in history, this led to the creation of a deliberately constructed international monetary system. Previously, arrangements had always been spontaneous, resulting from countries' individual decisions about their national monetary system.

The postwar system re-assigned an important monetary role to gold. Gold was again given a fixed official price, but only in terms of US dollars. The other participating currencies were assigned a fixed price in terms of this dollar. This system meant that all other currencies were tied to gold once again, but, in contrast to the previous gold standard, the tie was now only indirect, via their links with the dollar. Essentially, the fixed gold price meant that one could still speak of a gold standard. This price was maintained by the American central bank (the Federal Reserve System), which was obliged to honour requests to exchange dollars for gold at the agreed fixed gold price of $35 per troy ounce (equal to 31.103 grams). At Bretton Woods it was the American negotiators, in particular, who wanted to preserve this central element of the gold standard.

As mentioned in Section 14.2, it is nearly impossible to keep the exchange rate to one exact value, the peg value. The official exchange rate against the dollar was, therefore, assigned a fluctuation band within which the exchange rate was allowed to move. In the Bretton Woods system, the upper and lower interventions points of this band were set 1 per cent above and below the peg value, resulting in a fluctuation bandwidth of 2 per cent.

In addition, from time to time the IMF could permit the adjustment of a currency's peg value. This scope was a clear departure from the traditional gold standard. In the case of a peg adjustment, the fluctuation band naturally moved too. This gives us the adjustable peg system already explained in Section 14.2 and shown in Figures 14.1 and 14.2. The IMF allowed a member country to adjust its peg if the country faced a so-called fundamental balance-of-payments disequilibrium. This vague concept only gradually acquired the more specific meaning whereby a fundamental disequilibrium is present if a balance-of-payments disequilibrium could only be rectified by a domestic policy adjustment advancing an even greater domestic economic imbalance. In most of these cases, it concerned a situation of a balance-of-payments deficit alongside a high level of unemployment. This room for adjusting the peg value satisfied the UK preference at the time of the Bretton Woods negotiations that there should be no return to the rigidity of the gold standard – an understandable view given the fact that in the 1930s the UK had been the first to leave that standard.

The exchange-rate system designed in Bretton Woods has never worked in an entirely satisfactory manner. Initially, up to the end of the 1950s, the European central banks did not permit their currencies to be converted freely into US dollars – not even for current account transactions. The economic reconstruction of Europe following the devastation of the Second World War caused a chronic shortage of dollars, because the USA became the main area of the world where production facilities had not been destroyed, and hence this country was the focus of the European demand for goods. It was not until the second half of the 1950s that the European economies recovered sufficiently to have any hope of balancing the current account at the set exchange rates. For current account transactions the convertibility of the European currencies was restored in 1958. For capital account transactions this situation came about (often much) later.

It was not long after 1958 that the exchange-rate system of Bretton Woods again came under considerable pressure. The American balance of payments began to move into deficit. Revaluations of the German currency, the Deutsche mark (DM), and restrictions on American capital exports in the first half of the 1960s did not, in the end, provide a structural solution. In addition, in the early 1970s capital began to flee the USA because the owners considered the dollar to be overvalued and feared a devaluation of the currency. In May 1971, West Germany and some other countries ceased to intervene in the foreign-exchange market to support the dollar. In fact, in so doing they abandoned the adjustable peg system of exchange rates in favour of a floating rate.

The guarantee of a fixed gold price for private individuals had been abolished as early as 1968, because the central banks were no longer able to defend the gold price in dollars on the free gold market at the level set at the time of the Bretton Woods agreement. The dollar might have been allowed to fall in value in relation to gold. However, the Americans felt that this would have damaged the essence of the Bretton Woods system, and therefore found an alternative: a dual gold market – one for official gold and the other for private gold transactions. The unaltered gold price of $35 per troy ounce was maintained for official gold only. On the private market the price of gold was left to float freely, and it rose substantially.

In August 1971 it was necessary to take another step backwards: the USA actually had to suspend the convertibility of official gold against dollars. The suspension subsequently proved to be a final abolition of the dollar convertibility into gold. The dollar value of all currencies was left free for a time. Although this was a significant breach of the agreement reached at Bretton Woods, it would be going too far to say – as has often been asserted – that this marked the end of the Bretton Woods agreement. That agreement consisted of more than just an exchange-rate system based on gold.

In December 1971 the main industrial countries approved a general realignment of exchange rates, including a devaluation of the dollar against gold to $38 per troy ounce. However, there was no restoration of the convertibility of dollars into gold. The agreement only restored the adjustable peg system with new dollar peg values. In order to add flexibility to the exchange-rate system, the margins of the fluctuation band were increased to 2.25 per cent on either side of the peg value. This set of decisions became known as the Smithsonian Agreement, but it proved to be only a temporary reprieve: in February/March 1973 these new parities also proved indefensible. Following this, in March 1973 the industrial countries allowed their currencies to float against the dollar anew – and as yet forever.

The collapse of the Bretton Woods exchange-rate system was the result of a combination of factors:

1. The American government was never prepared to place more emphasis on external objectives (the system of fixed exchange rates and balance-of-payments equilibrium) than on internal economic policy objectives (inflation, growth, and employment). It was too attached to its economic-political autonomy. As a result, the European countries, in particular, had to contend with the importation of higher American

inflation via their fixed exchange-rate obligations – through their obliged interventions in the foreign-exchange markets. However, European flexibility as regards violations of their economic-political autonomy also had its limits.

2. In the 1960s international capital movements expanded more rapidly than the international flows of goods and services. The causes for capital movements are quite different from those for international trade. As we know from Chapter 12, one of the important factors determining international capital movements is the expected change in the exchange rate. When, at a given moment, the devaluation of the dollar looked imminent, there was a massive capital flight from the USA to Europe. This was the final blow for the exchange-rate parities of the time.

3. Timely parity adjustments might have been a solution, but the IMF members were repeatedly far too cautious in this respect. It was not the exchange-rate system itself that proved unsound, but the way in which it was implemented. In the final phase of the system the stumbling block proved to be whether the devaluation of the dollar should take the form of a lower gold value for the dollar or higher gold values for the other currencies – a political question, which is totally irrelevant from the point of view of economic theory. The significance of the debate was purely psychological: arranging for the USA to change the gold parity was an attempt to demonstrate publicly that they were (also) responsible for the imbalance – and therefore to blame for the necessary exchange-rate adjustment.

16.4.3 The liquidity issue

In the postwar monetary system, gold was not only given a leading role by linking its value to that of the dollar. Gold was also a reserve asset, which central banks used to pay one another. However, the great drawback of gold in this respect is that its supply is unpredictable and subject to fluctuations. Moreover, gold is also used for non-monetary purposes in the private sector, for industrial ends and making jewellery, as well as for speculative purposes.

As a result, the supply of gold for monetary purposes can fluctuate sharply. If speculators, for example, rush into gold, this causes strong upward pressure on its price, and vice versa. In such events, under the postwar exchange-rate system that was in place until 1968 (the start of the dual gold market), the central banks had to defend the fixed gold price in dollars.

Another important source of international monetary reserves was – and is – the US dollar, because this currency played a central role, alongside gold, in the postwar international monetary system. In the 1960s the US balance of payments displayed substantial deficits. The USA could simply finance these deficits by paying foreign claims with its own currency, if necessary by creating new money. In this respect, the country was in a unique position. Other countries first had to earn monetary reserves, through surpluses in their international transactions, after which they could use them to finance later balance-of-payments deficits. By financing their deficits with dollars, the American monetary authorities let increasing quantities of their currency flow into the international financial system. A proportion of these dollars ended up with foreign monetary authorities and thus were added to their international monetary reserves. The remainder of the dollars was absorbed by the private sector.

There was, however, an upper limit to the USA's provision of new dollars to the world economy. So long as the net world demand for dollars persisted, there was no problem. But that demand was not self-sustaining and was fuelled in part by worldwide confidence in the dollar. Ultimately, this confidence in the value of the dollar was determined by its backing in gold, which the USA had to provide on demand – under the IMF Articles of

Agreement – for dollars in circulation. However, the US balance-of-payments deficits in the 1960s caused a gradual reduction in the percentage of cover of dollars in foreign hands by USA's official gold holding. Initially, it stood at over 100 per cent, but in the 1960s it dropped well below that level. The prolonged US balance-of-payments deficits gradually undermined confidence in the dollar. People therefore realized that the US government would have to rectify these deficits in the foreseeable future, even though this would reduce an important source of supply for the world's international monetary reserves.

Thus, in the end, both gold and the US dollar, by far the major reserve assets, proved problematic. The international monetary system was in need of an alternative to gold as a reserve asset, because the supply was too volatile. A supplement to the creation of reserve assets was also desirable since it was foreseen that through US adjustment policy there would have been a drying up of the supply of American dollars. This justified a serious search for an alternative and explains why the IMF came up with a new reserve asset: the Special Drawing Right (SDR).

The IMF introduced the SDR in 1969, with the explicit, impressive aim of becoming the major reserve asset in the world. The SDR has the character of a composite reserve currency: its value is defined as the value of a basket of, at present, the four major currencies in the world For the period 2006–10 the composition of the SDR basket was $0.6320; euro 0.410; yen 18.4000; £0.0903. The advantage of the SDR is that the IMF is able to create it (out of nothing) as the need arises for more international monetary reserves in the world. In 1970 the IMF allocated the first SDRs to its member countries.

The method of creating SDRs as a reserve asset is as curious as it is simple: once the IMF Board of Governors believes that there is a worldwide need for new SDRs, to supplement the existing official reserves of member countries, and to ensure satisfactory growth of the world's monetary reserves, all member countries taking part in the SDR Department are allocated an additional quantity of SDRs on their SDR accounts. This allocation is in proportion to the countries' IMF quotas and is free of charge.

At first glance, this costless receipt of SDRs seems odd, but on closer examination it is not. These SDRs can merely be held in the official sphere. A country can only use the SDRs indirectly, rather than directly, to finance balance-of-payments deficits. If it needs to use its holding of SDRs for this purpose, it has to ask the IMF to designate another member country that has a sufficiently strong external position. According to the rules of the SDR account, after this designation the latter country is obliged to accept the former country's SDRs in exchange for foreign currency reserves. Today, the IMF uses this designation mechanism only if the country that wants to exchange its SDRs is not able to realize this exchange through voluntary trading arrangements with other IMF member countries.

The country that has used SDRs in this way now disposes of an additional stock of foreign currency reserves, and is able to intervene with them directly in the foreign-exchange market. As soon as a country has sold its assigned SDRs in this way, it has to pay interest on them. On the other hand, the country that has received these SDRs starts to receive interest on them. Thus, the allocated SDRs have, in essence, a close similarity to an unconditional right to borrow to the value of the SDR allocation reserve currencies from other member countries. That resemblance makes it easier to understand why the allocation of SDRs is in itself free of charge.

According to the IMF, the SDR is neither a currency nor a claim on the IMF. It is a potential claim on the freely usable currencies of IMF members. In addition to being a reserve asset, the SDR also became a unit of account: the IMF itself uses it in this function, while in the past some countries, for example Latvia and Libya, used the SDR as the anchor currency for the fixed exchange-rate arrangement of their currencies.

The SDR was initially given the same value as the US dollar. But that formula was soon dropped, with the SDR being given a value based upon a combination of national currencies. At first, the 16 most important currencies in the world were used, but soon a simpler formula was adopted in which the value of the SDR was set equal to a basket of the world's five leading currencies: the US dollar, the Japanese yen, the German Deutsche mark, the British pound sterling and the French franc. In 2000, after the introduction of the European common currency, the DM and franc were replaced by the euro. Every five years the amounts of the different currencies in the basket are reviewed and readjusted on the basis of the exports of goods and services and the amount of reserves denominated in the currencies held by other members of the IMF. As the mutual exchange rates of these currencies change on a daily basis, the SDR value and the shares of the composing currencies in this basket value also change over time. On 13 May 2010 the value of one SDR was $1.48, while the currency shares in this basket value were: 43 per cent dollars, 35 per cent euros, 13 per cent yen, and 9 per cent pounds. The weekly SDR interest rate is calculated as a weighted average of the short-term (mostly three-month) market interest rates for the currencies that make up the SDR valuation basket. The weights of the national rates are the currency shares in the basket.

On the face of it, the SDR formula should be attractive. Giving the SDR a value and an interest rate corresponding to a portfolio of the world's five leading currencies makes that value and interest rate relatively stable. As uncertainty is always an undesirable feature, this stability is clearly an attractive characteristic of the SDR. However, the SDR was created under adverse conditions. When the first SDRs were allocated in 1970, there was no shortage of international monetary reserves – contrary to earlier expectations. Quite the reverse was true: the US balance-of-payments deficits had persisted and were even increasing. In 1981 there was a new round of SDR allocation, but again there was no real need. SDRs were also introduced in the private sphere, although they were kept strictly separate from those circulating in the official sphere. Despite its theoretically attractive characteristics, the SDR has only a marginal existence in both spheres. This is the more surprising because such a stable basket currency would expected to flourish in a post-1973 world characterized by floating exchange rates and, therefore, volatile major currencies.

One of the responses to the global credit crisis of 2008–09 was a decision of the G20 in April 2010 to permit the IMF to issue new SDRs. The IMF carried out a new general SDR allocation to the amount of $283 billion in August–September 2010. This does mean a near tenfold increase in allocated SDRs, but, as is seen in Table 16.1 (p. 318), even then the SDR remains quantitatively far away from the initial aim of principal reserve asset.

16.5 | International monetary cooperation after 1973

As we observed in the preceding section, postwar international monetary cooperation increasingly had to contend with:

○ an adjustment problem (a reluctance to adjust exchange rates);
○ a confidence problem (the position of the central currency, the dollar, was increasingly undermined); and
○ a liquidity problem (the supply of international monetary reserves became more uncertain with a real chance of shortage).

To a large extent, these problems were settled by the switch to worldwide floating exchange rates in March 1973. The phenomena persisted in part, but no longer represented a problem, though related problems arose, as we shall see in this section.

16.5.1 The adjustment problem

Post-1973 policy relating to the exchange rates between the dollar, the yen, and the major European currencies can best be defined as a system of managed floating exchange rates. In this context the term 'managed' refers to the occasional need in Europe and Japan to comply with the wish to adjust tendencies in the exchange rates to some extent by foreign-exchange market intervention through the central bank. Demands for intervention arose in particular if exchange-rate changes were large and were felt to be totally out of line with the trend in the exchange-rate fundamentals – that is, the fundamental forces that determine the equilibrium value of the exchange rate (see Chapter 13). The first complaints of an alleged imbalance in the exchange rate often emerge in the private sector, especially from internationally oriented businesses in countries where the currencies have appreciated strongly.

Opposition to forex market intervention comes generally from advocates of free markets. In the 1970s, in particular, they argued that pure intervention in the forex market (or sterilized intervention) was pointless. Sterilized foreign-exchange market intervention is neutral in terms of its effect on the domestic money supply in the intervening country. In other words, the intervention effect on domestic money supply is sterilized.

In theory, indeed, intervention will not affect the exchange-rate movement unless it changes the domestic money supply (either by reducing or increasing it). The monetary approach to the exchange rate, discussed in Section 13.2, clearly portrays this decisive influence of money supply on the exchange rate, whereas sterilized indeed, intervention is absent among the determining factors. Sterilized intervention does not affect the exchange rate in that theory, unless this intervention has a signalling effect. In this event, it is able to influence the expected exchange-rate change and, thus also, through equation (12.2) of the uncovered interest parity, capital flows between home and foreign country and therefore, eventually, the actual exchange rate itself.

The worldwide abandonment of fixed exchange rates in March 1973 removed one of the IMF's most essential tasks: the implementation and continuous support of the adjustable peg system. This abandonment was formally confirmed when the IMF's Articles of Agreement were revised in 1978. Member countries were permitted to operate any desired exchange-rate arrangement, although the IMF did take on the role of surveillance over members' exchange-rate policy. Since this time the Fund has endeavoured to give this role some practical significance, but to date the IMF's activities (in the form of annual consultation with each member country) with respect to exchange-rate policy do not appear to have been particularly relevant.

It was only in 1985 that clear signs emerged of a revival in international monetary cooperation. In the preceding years the adjustment problem dating from the period prior to March 1973 seemed to have turned into a surfeit of exchange-rate changes. Figure 16.1 illustrates this point for the leading exchange rates. After a gradual decline in the initial phase of floating exchange rates, the dollar reached a low in the period from 1978 to 1980. In the first half of the 1980s the dollar recovered strongly – even rising above the level it had held against the European currencies at the time of the Bretton Woods exchange-rate system.

The reason for this rise in the value of the dollar was the change of course in American macroeconomic policy that occurred around 1980. In 1978 and 1979 the world economy was suffering from the effects of a second oil price shock (after having experienced the first shock in the last quarter of 1973). This gave a new impetus to inflation, which had already been high in the preceding years of that decade.

The US monetary authorities saw the new inflationary stimulus as a decisive reason for introducing a compelling change in economic policy. At the end of 1979 they introduced a highly restrictive monetary policy. After an initial bedding-in period, interest rates in the USA soared, making investment in that country highly lucrative. As a result, a large volume of capital flowed into the country. This was an unintentional effect, the result of a lack of international policy coordination. This inflow of capital caused a sharp rise in the value of the dollar.

The increase in interest rates was reinforced further by the effect of the expansive US fiscal policy as the unintentional result of tax cuts introduced by President Reagan in the early 1980s. Reagan believed that tax cuts would lead automatically to higher levels of economic growth and consequently higher tax yields. This latter effect proved incorrect, so that the American fiscal deficit expanded rapidly, and so did the bond financing of this deficit. This gave a further boost to US interest rates, meaning that in practice US macroeconomic policy had driven up the value of the dollar.

There was yet another force at work that strengthened the dollar. In the first half of the 1980s, in an attempt to curb the rise of the dollar, Reagan successfully brought pressure to bear on the Japanese government to liberalize their financial markets. He hoped – and expected – that improved market access would encourage Americans to start investing in Japan, which would weaken the value of the dollar. However, the result was the exact reverse: international financial liberalization in Japan gave the Japanese the opportunity to diversify their investment through a policy of foreign investments. They rushed en masse into investments, particularly in the United States, with the result that this simply reinforced the upward trend in the value of dollar. (See also Case study 13.2, p. 249, on this subject.)

This placed American exporters in an extremely uncompetitive position, and also meant that American producers on the domestic markets had to compete against cheap imports. In response, there were concerted calls in the USA for the introduction of protectionist measures. Although President Reagan was attached to free market principles, in the end he could not avoid government intervention in the forex market. In making a choice between these two evils for a free market adherent – raising trade barriers and official forex market intervention – Reagan opted for the latter to reduce the value of the dollar.

This explains the at first sight surprisingly positive attitude of the US government to coordinated exchange market intervention in September 1985. In that month the G5 countries decided on this approach in the Plaza Agreement (named after the decisive meeting in the Plaza Hotel in New York). Their object was to reduce the value of the dollar by intervening, in an internationally coordinated manner, in the foreign-exchange markets. It was believed that by coordinating the interventions of the G5, and thus always intervening jointly at the same time and in the same direction, policy makers could be much more convincing with regard to the forex markets. Possibly the expected dollar value could (also) be reduced by the psychology of intervention, and thus dollar investments could be discouraged, according to the uncovered interest rate parity. In practice, this idea proved correct. The dollar had already peaked at the end of February 1985 and by September of that year it had fallen (slightly), but after the Plaza Agreement the fall of the dollar continued steadily (see Figure 16.1).

A second agreement, the Louvre Accord, followed in February 1987. This set out the principles of coordinated intervention, but now aimed to keep the dollar at the much lower value that it had reached by this time. The Louvre Accord was an agreement concluded by consultation in the G7. Rumours said that it was decided secretly to apply a weak target zone for their currencies against the dollar with a wide fluctuation band. (See Section 14.2 for a short description of this arrangement.) It should be noted that the IMF was not involved in these coordination agreements.

In the years following 1987 coordinated intervention to counter exchange-rate fluctuations seems to have weakened. In those years in the leading industrial countries the aim

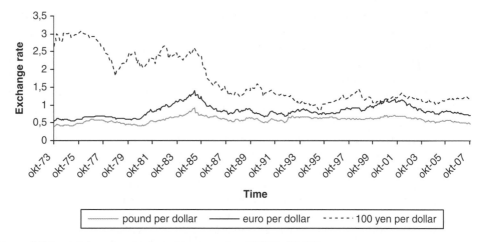

Figure 16.1   Major nominal exchange rates (1973–2007)

Note: Before 1999 the euro changes are set equal to the exchange-rate changes of the Deutsche mark.

Source: IMF, *International Financial Statistics*, various years.

of stabilizing the exchange rate at an equilibrium value in any case proved subordinate to interest rate policy for domestic economic purposes.

The most striking development in Figure 16.1 is the trebling of the value of the yen in the years 1975–95 – from 300 to 100 yen per dollar. After 1995, the pattern of the yen against the dollar follows much more closely the time paths of euro and pound against the dollar. In those years the long-term movements of the euro/dollar rate are strongest.

It is interesting to observe the consequences of nominal bilateral exchange-rate volatility for the real effective exchange rates or countries' competitiveness. Figure 16.2 depicts these rates for the same four major currencies. The value of the yen displays the greatest extremes. In the 20 years that its nominal value trebled against the dollar, its real exchange rate also almost trebled. However, in the case of the latter it is quite remarkable to see that this movement was largely reversed in later years. For the three other currencies, the values

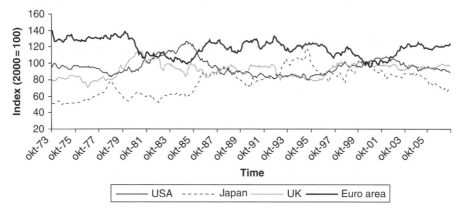

Figure 16.2   Major real effective exchange rates (1973–2007)

Note: An increase of the real exchange rate in this figure means a real appreciation or a worsening of competitiveness. This construction of the real exchange rate is the reversal of the way the real exchange rate is defined in Chapters 11 and 13.

Source: IMF, *International Financial Statistics*, various years.

of their real exchange rates at the end of Figure 16.2 are surprisingly close to those at the beginning, despite large movements in between. These patterns give empirical support to the long-run relevance of the PPP theory for exchange rates.

The hotly debated current adjustment problem is focused on the exchange rate between the Chinese currency, the renminbi, and the US dollar. One criticism of the stance of US policy-makers is that China resists a higher value of the renminbi against the dollar, despite an enduring large Chinese surplus and large US deficit on the balance of payments. The impressive size of Chinese reserve holdings – the largest of all countries – is telling. In response to this criticism in 2007 the Chinese government abandoned the policy of a fixed exchange rate against the dollar. Since then the yuan has appreciated by 20 per cent.

In the second half of 2008 there was a shrinking of the two balance-of-payments imbalances. It remains a questionable point to what extent this is a response to the exchange-rate change. The reason is that the worldwide economic slowdown as a result of the onset of the global credit crisis that began in the USA in 2008 has also affected these imbalances in the same direction. The contagion of this crisis to China worked through a fall in US (import) demand and, subsequently, a fall in Chinese exports. To minimize this contagion channel China stopped the gradual appreciation of the yuan against the dollar. Since then, or at least up to the beginning of 2011, China, and some other Asian countries, track the dollar.

16.5.2 The confidence and liquidity problems

During the period of floating exchange rates there was a persistence of the confidence problem regarding the dollar, in principle. But it no longer imposed a strain on the monetary system, because after March 1973 it was no longer necessary to defend the dollar rate.

As we have just seen, there were renewed periods of dollar weakness, characterized by the dominant expectation of a lower dollar in the near future. But these alternated with periods of the reverse movements. One such period was the first half of the 1980s, when the dollar was in strong demand as a private investment currency. As we saw earlier, the reasons for this were: the high American interest rates, the tendency for the dollar to appreciate that positively affected the expected dollar value, and the need for international diversification that was able to manifest itself in Japan. After a gradual weakening of the dollar against the continental European currencies from 1985 to 1990, the dollar strengthened again between 1995 and 2002. After this it fell gradually but unmistakably until autumn 2009, notably against the euro. The concomitant lack of confidence in the dollar in the latter period stems from the impressively large US current account deficit – not only in value but also as a percentage of the country's GDP – and the huge and increasing US foreign debt. This debt is by far the largest national debt in the world, but much less impressively large in terms of the US GDP.

At first glance, strains on the international monetary system belonged to the past as the dollar floated – and still floats – against the other major currencies. But the wide fluctuations and often the trend in the dollar exchange rate produce a lot of uncertainty for international traders and investors. Hence, it is unsurprising that there is occasionally demand for reform of the exchange-rate system towards more stability among the major currencies in the world (for example, McKinnon, 1982 and 1984, and Williamson, 1983). It is not to be expected that such a reform will become reality in the foreseeable future.

Table 16.1 displays the growth of worldwide international monetary reserves over time and also of their constituent reserve assets. The bottom two lines of the table illustrate a huge growth in the value of international monetary reserves. Between 1994 and 2008 its growth was even stronger than that of global trade. There is no convincing measure for

Table 16.1 The composition of the world's international monetary reserves (end of year, %)

Type of reserve asset	1978	1982	1986	1990	1994	1998	2002	2006	2008
Reserve position in IMF	3.5	3.5	4.9	2.7	3.0	4.2	3.2	0.5	0.5
SDRs	1.9	2.5	2.7	2.3	1.5	1.4	0.9	0.5	0.4
Foreign currencies	52.5	39.5	50.4	66.6	72.8	80.7	84.7	89.3	89.3
Gold*	42.1	54.5	42.0	28.5	22.7	13.7	11.2	9.8	9.8
Total	100.0	100.0	100.0	100.1	100.0	100.0	100.0	100.1	100.0
(in bn SDRs)	(427)	(721)	(722)	(892)	(1,052)	(1,446)	(2,092)	(3,751)	(4,880)
(in % of world exports)					(29.2)	(29.8)	(35.6)	(38.2)	(39.2)

*Gold reserves have been valued at London market prices.
Source: IMF, *Annual Report*, various issues.

reserve adequacy at the country level. Sometimes three months of import financing is used as a rough gauge. Transplanted to the world level, reserve adequacy would imply total reserves being at least 25 per cent of annual world trade. The last line of the table therefore indicates that, based on that criterion there is no need for additional reserves since 1994.

From time to time the IMF has made an attempt to give 'its' currency, the SDR, a more prominent place in the international monetary system through proposals of new allocations of SDRs. One constant motive was the original official aim that the SDR should develop into the world's principal reserve asset. According to Table 16.1, quite the opposite happened: by 2008 the SDR share in world reserves had faded away to a negligible 0.4 per cent. The near tenfold increase in allocated SDRs in August–September 2009 will hardly bring this aim nearby. The shares in the international monetary reserves of gold since 1982 and the reserve position in the IMF since 1998 have also declined rapidly. By far the largest reserve asset is now the 'foreign currencies' component – with 89.3 per cent in 2008 – and, moreover, the trend for this component still seems to be upward.

Table 16.2 shows the individual currency components of the 'foreign currencies' line in Table 16.1. Between 1978 and 1990 the proportion of the US dollar in foreign currencies fell from 78 to 58 per cent. Against this, shares for the DM, yen, French franc, and pound sterling, as well as the category 'other currencies' all showed increases. In the 1990s the dollar share rallied, but in the 2000s it gradually declined again. In the 2000s the euro and the pound sterling show a gradually rising proportion. The euro is well on its way to becoming a major international currency.

It seems obvious to consider changes in the currency share in international monetary reserves in Table 16.2 as an indicator of the attractiveness of or confidence in that currency. For this role movements in the currency share are only of limited value, for two principal reasons.

First, central banks' objectives go beyond obtaining a good return on their holdings of monetary reserves. In particular, when a reserve currency is weakening the central banks of the currencies anchored to that reserve currency will tend to give it support through central bank purchases. Consequently, central banks hold an increasing proportion of that depreciation-prone currency in their reserves. If a reserve currency is strengthening, the opposite tendency may apply. For example, the rising dollar in the first half of the 1980s contributed to a dollar sale by central banks and thus to the falling dollar share between 1978 and 1986.

Table 16.2 The composition of foreign currency reserves (end of year, %)

Currency	1978	1982	1986	1990	1994	1998	2002	2006	2008
US dollar	78	70	67	58	58	63	67	66	64
Deutsche mark/euro	11	12	15	18	16	14	24	25	27
Yen	3	5	8	8	8	5	4	3	3
Pound sterling	2	3	3	3	3	4	3	4	4
French franc	1	1	1	3	3	2	–	–	–
Swiss franc	2	3	2	1	1	1	0	0	0
Other currencies	3	6	4	9	11	11	2	2	2

Notes: The figures are based on about 63.5% of total reserves, namely all industrial country reserves and just over 50% of developing country reserves.
The euro was introduced in 1999 and replaced 12 European currencies, including the DM and the French franc. The share for the DM/euro since 2002 is the euro share. For all previous years it is the DM share.
'Other currencies' also includes foreign currency reserves for which no information on currency composition is available.
Source: IMF, Annual Report, various issues.

Second, a currency share in Table 16.2 is also driven by value changes of this currency – even if its number of units in the reserves does not alter. This is shown by the fact that the decline in the dollar share since 2002 largely reflects the depreciation of the dollar over the same period, which offset robust official purchases of dollars (IMF, 2008, Appendix I).

Private investment behaviour gives a better clue about the attractiveness of and confidence in a currency as international money. The currency distribution of forex market turnover is one such expression of private preferences. As we already saw in Section 11.5, between April 2001 and April 2010 the dollar share in the average daily turnover on the forex market declined from 89.9 to 84.9 per cent (BIS, 2010). The second-largest share, for the euro, rose slightly from 37.9 to 39.1 per cent. But the yen shares fell too – from 23.5 to 19.0 per cent. Interestingly, the pound sterling share remained stable, at around 13 per cent. All other currencies have shares of less than 10 per cent.

The liquidity problem, which was still such an important factor at the time of the exchange-rate system of Bretton Woods, lessened under the later system of (managed) floating exchange rates. One essential point was that the transition in March 1973 to (managed) floating exchange rates totally eliminated the obligation to intervene in the foreign-exchange market in order to keep the national currency within the fluctuation band.

In essence, in the case of pure floating exchange rates, there is no need at all for international monetary reserves. The current widespread practice of managed floating only requires reserves for ad hoc intervention. Since there is then no obligation to intervene, there cannot really be a reserve shortage. In spite of this, all monetary authorities prefer to hold reserves, if only to enable them through such a war chest to give an impression of some market power. This may be necessary to give some force to their public pronouncements on the correct level for the exchange rate and forex market intervention, because even a compelling view or action is powerless without the support of a solid instrument. In line with this reason, since the Asian financial crisis of 1997 emerging economies such as Taiwan, China, India, and several South-East Asian countries have built up huge reserve holdings to prevent speculative currency attacks, particularly in the event that their exchange-rate fundamentals are not bad.

It should be borne in mind that, although after 1973 the dollar, the DM (later the euro) and the yen have been floating against one another, many of the less important currencies have kept a fixed exchange rate in relation to one of these three currencies. For these exchange-rate arrangements monetary reserves remain relevant. It is noteworthy that through international financial integration and the associated huge growth of international capital movements since the 1980s, it is today comparatively easy for creditworthy countries to borrow on the international capital markets to make up for a shortage of reserves. This feature, in combination with the rapid growth of international monetary reserves worldwide, means that there are at present no signs at all that the world is short of reserves.

16.6 Summary

1. International economic cooperation makes sense if national economic policy has external effects on the economies of other countries – as it usually has. Such cooperation can then take account of these effects in shaping national policy.
2. The following forms of international economic cooperation can be identified, in ascending order of intensity: (i) exchange of information; (ii) policy coordination; (iii) policy harmonization; and (iv) total integration or unification of economic policy. The ultimate aim of international policy coordination is that countries adjust their policy instruments individually in the best interest of all economic objectives of the cooperating countries. In the case of international policy harmonization, the countries concerned try to achieve convergence of their national policy measures in the economic process.
3. The grouping of countries for the purpose of international cooperation often combines the exchange of information on and coordination of economic policy. The group of the seven leading developed countries, the G7, was the major example. Groups are also often used for the purpose of speaking with a single voice at international conferences, in order to be heard well. This is the central aim of the G24, a large group of developing countries.
4. In practice, there are four drawbacks to international policy coordination. One of these is a certain *loss of national political autonomy*; psychologically, that is a problem in itself. Owing to a severe *shortage of information*, it is difficult to determine the right form of coordinated policy, and that makes the policy difficult to implement. By *cheating*, participating countries can undermine the jointly devised policy. Finally, coordinated policy suffers a serious loss of power and continuity in the case of *free riders*: countries that have an interest in – and hence often an effect on – the attempt at coordination, but do not wish to take part in the devised policy.
5. Substantial international monetary cooperation began after the Second World War in the form of the introduction of the postwar monetary system mapped out at the Bretton Woods conference in 1944. The central feature was the IMF and the adjustable peg system of exchange rates. This differed from the fixed exchange-rate system in that the fixed peg value could be changed from time to time, with the consent of the IMF, in the case of a so-called fundamental disequilibrium in a country's economy.
6. The Bretton Woods exchange-rate system collapsed in 1973. One central reason was that the USA considered exchange-rate stability to be less important than internal economic objectives. Another reason was the vastly increased international mobility of capital, which implies that economic divergences between countries have an immediate impact on exchange rates as the result of a strong effect upon international capital movements. This postwar experience was an important, rather discouraging, lesson for other attempts at implementing an adjustable peg system of exchange rates.

7. In the present 'non-system' of floating and sometimes managed floating exchange rates among the world's leading currencies, the IMF has a very limited function in relation to the exchange-rate system. According to its Articles of Agreement, the IMF has a surveillance function, but this remains rather vague. Its role as an international lender is important and much more concrete, as we will see in the next chapter.

8. In 1970 the IMF introduced the first SDRs, which were allocated to those member countries who wished to take part in the SDR scheme. The IMF believed that this would allow the world's actual international monetary reserves holdings to be better matched with the needs. As there was an unexpected excess supply of reserves in the world at the time of the first allocation of SDRs, the aim of making SDRs a reserve asset came to nothing. As an accounting unit, the SDR has a reasonably stable value and interest rate because its value is determined by a basket of currencies. Nevertheless, this function of the SDR has never been fully used outside the IMF.

9. As a result of large fluctuations in value around a declining trend, the dollar became less important as an international currency until the mid-1990s. The rallying of the US dollar since 1995 seems to have contributed substantially to its attractiveness as a currency to hold. In both international monetary reserves and the foreign-exchange markets the dollar share has recovered since this time. Although far behind the dollar, the euro is well on its way to becoming a major international currency. In the shadow of both currencies, the pound is surprisingly resilient in this respect, but the yen is disappointingly weak – despite its impressive trebling in value against the US dollar in the years between 1975 and 1995.

10. This increase in the value of the yen was associated with a similar rise of the real effective exchange rate of the yen. In the years after 1995, this was largely offset. As a result of that the tendency to PPP seems to be a leading principle for the yen. This also holds for the dollar, the euro, and the pound over the past 30 years.

Questions

1. In 1989 the Asia-Pacific Economic Cooperation (APEC) was founded. Today it includes 21 member states from both sides of the Pacific Ocean. Among them are large countries such as Canada, China, Indonesia, Japan, Russia, and the USA. Have a look at its website (www.apec.org) and assess the intensity of economic cooperation in the APEC using the four types distinguished in Section 16.2.

2. Go to the website of the IMF (www.imf.org) and find the name and nationality of the executive director who represents your country in the Board of the IMF. Moreover, how many votes does your country have in the IMF and what is the amount (in million SDRs) and percentage of its IMF quota in the total of IMF quota?

3. In what ways did the exchange-rate system of Bretton Woods differ from the gold exchange standard?

4. There is no convincing measure for reserve adequacy at the country level. Sometimes three months of import financing is used as a rough gauge. For which period after the Second World War would this measure yet be defensible? In what direction relating to economic variables would you search for an improvement of the measure today?

CHAPTER 17

A Financial Obstacle to Economic Development: The World Debt Crisis

17.1 Introduction

On 12 August 1982 Mexico announced to the world that it could no longer meet the financial obligations arising from its international debt of over $80 billion; it thereby became the first in a long line of defaulting countries. These events endangered the stability of the entire global financial system, even though – or perhaps precisely because – the large banks in the richest countries then became extremely reluctant to extend further credit to the largest debtor countries. This in turn forced the heavily indebted countries to implement stringent austerity programmes. Thus, one important feature of the 1980s was a combination of an extremely fragile international financial system and declining economic welfare, mainly among heavily indebted developing countries.

During the 1990s the economic situation of developing countries substantially improved. Economic growth returned, partly because these countries gained the advantages of market liberalization. On the other hand, tensions easily arose between internal and external equilibrium in countries that were going through a liberalization process. From time to time this tension resulted in currency crises. The most significant currency crises during that period are the Mexican crisis (end of 1994/beginning of 1995), the Asian crisis (mid-1997), and the Argentine crisis (end of 2001).

This chapter discusses the main economic events in developing countries in the 1980s, offering a series of case studies that consider how, in principle, positive developments can have negative consequences. The currency crises are the theme of the next chapter.

The focus of the present chapter is on the economic policies of growth, stabilization, and liberalization pursued by many of the developing countries during the 1980s and the role played by the international monetary institutions – particularly the International Monetary Fund (IMF) – in avoiding global financial collapse and in shaping and implementing the necessary adjustment policy in the member countries. We shall discuss the lessons that can be drawn from this experience. These will answer, among others, the question of whether the international monetary system is making an optimal contribution 'to the promotion and maintenance of high levels of employment and real income and to the development of the productive resources of all members' – an objective given prominence in Article 1 of the IMF's Articles of Agreement.

In Section 17.2 we will first review the causes behind the outbreak of the world debt crisis in the early 1980s. These fall into two main categories:

○ *external causes*, or causes outside the influence of the countries that suffered from that outbreak; and
○ *internal causes*, which can be attributed to these countries themselves.

Section 17.3 then examines the set of instruments that the IMF possesses both to provide financial support and to extricate countries from a debt crisis. Next, we consider the way in which these instruments were used during the 1980s. Section 17.4 focuses on the development of the world debt crisis in the decade involved and the progress achieved over these years. Section 17.5 concludes.

17.2   The causes of the world debt crisis of the 1980s

Economic problems are usually caused by the interaction between a number of factors. This was certainly the case for the debt crisis that began in Mexico in August 1982 and, subsequently, contaminated other Latin American and several other developing countries. We can make a distinction between the internal and external causes of the increase of country debt beyond manageable proportions.

External causes are the result of adverse developments that are exogenous to the debtor country: these are causes over which the country has no influence. Usually, heavily indebted countries appear to have causes in common, such as adverse developments in the world economy – though the intensity of the impact varies across the debtor countries.

By contrast, internal causes of the debt crisis arise in the debtor country itself. In effect, the country could have avoided them: from the viewpoint of the country they are endogenous causes. This section will first examine the external causes of the world debt crisis of the 1980s and will then deal with its most familiar internal causes in the crisis countries.

17.2.1 External causes

17.2.1.1 *The oil price shocks of the 1970s*

At the beginning of the 1970s there was a remarkable shift of power within the global oil-producing sector. Until then power had been in the hands of the seven large oil companies – the so-called 'Seven Sisters' – which were able to fix the price of crude oil, although this was formally achieved during periodic talks with the oil-producing countries.

In October 1973 the oil-producing countries broke off such a round of talks and found themselves capable of imposing their will on the oil companies. The prices proposed by the oil-producing countries, united in the Organization of the Petroleum Exporting Countries (OPEC), were supported by an OPEC boycott of the USA, the Netherlands, South Africa, and then Rhodesia. The boycott was used as a means of coercion in the brief war between Israel and its neighbours in October 1973. The boycott caused a dramatic increase in the speculative demand for oil – something that usually happens in times of market instability and leads to a rapid growth of oil stocks. The main result of the ensuing rise in the free market price of oil was that oil importers were forced to accept price increases with OPEC. As a result, the price of crude oil increased fivefold between October 1973 and January 1974.

Table 17.1 Current account balances, 1973–88 ($ billion)

	1973	1974	1975	1976	1977	1978	1979	1980
Industrial countries	18.1	−13.2	16.2	−2.1	−5.1	30.8	−23.3	−62.0
Developing countries*	−11.3	−36.9	−45.8	−32.1	−28.0	−36.2	−62.0	−86.2

	1981	1982	1983	1984	1985	1986	1987	1988
Industrial countries	−20.0	−22.1	−22.0	−61.7	−54.7	−9.3	−17.9	−25.0
Developing countries*	−111.9	−90.7	−56.3	−40.9	−43.9	−34.5	−41.6	−34.9

*Non-oil exporting developing countries.
Source: IMF, *World Economic Outlook*, several issues.

The industrial countries reacted to the oil price surge by reducing expenditures, in a successful attempt to offset the negative effect of the higher oil import value on their balance of payments. Table 17.1 shows the success of this policy: after a decline in 1974, by 1975 the industrial countries' combined current account balance had returned to its 1973 level. In contrast, the non oil-exporting developing countries gave precedence to continuing economic growth as their objective, leading to a lasting deterioration in their current account. These countries also succeeded rather well in their plan, according to Figure 17.1. During the 1970s they maintained their annual economic growth at a level of around 5 per cent, in stark contrast to the rich countries with their much lower – and also much more erratic – growth. In fact, the developing countries were the driving force, the locomotive, of world economic growth in the 1970s.

Once the OPEC balance-of-payments surplus had disappeared in 1978, the OPEC countries were able to successfully repeat their price trick in 1978–79. On this occasion they exploited the global uncertainty about the world oil market caused by the revolution in Iran, which brought a temporary halt to the export of Iranian oil. Since Iran supplied

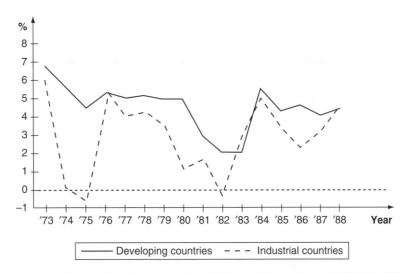

Figure 17.1   Annual growth of gross national/domestic product, 1973–88 (%)
Source: IMF, *World Economic Outlook*, several issues.

around 10 per cent of the world's oil exports at the time, this pushed up the oil price. Once again, this influence was greatly enhanced by speculative oil purchases. The effects for the oil-importing countries of this second oil price shock were comparable to those witnessed in 1973–74. The developing countries' current account deteriorated sharply in 1979–80, while their level of economic growth was initially maintained. In industrial countries, economic growth again declined, although less sharply than after the first oil shock. On the other hand, the current account of these countries taken together did not recover as in 1975.

Current account deficits on the balance of payments have to be financed. The oil-importing developing countries achieved this by borrowing abroad. The corollary is, of course, the associated rise of the burden of these countries' debt service (the sum of annual repayments and annual interest rate charges on the debt). Although an annual increase in the debt was accompanied by an annual increase in the cost of servicing that debt, this was not an immediate concern to the oil-importing developing countries. The value of their exports also grew in the 1970s, so that during this period the debt service ratio (the ratio of the debt service and the country's annual export value) increased hardly at all.

The debt service ratio is in fact the most important indicator of a country's creditworthiness. Table 17.2 displays this ratio for groups of developing countries for the years 1973–86 – prior to and during the world debt crisis. Until 1981 the increase in the debt service ratio for all developing countries taken as a whole still appeared to be small: from 15.9 to 17.3 per cent. However, Table 17.2 also shows that this aggregate figure conceals large regional variations. For Africa, and to a lesser extent the developing countries of Central and South America, the ratio already increased sharply during that period, but at the time hardly anyone knew about it, as there was a chronic lack of data on international debt.

17.2.1.2   The world's financial markets were a borrowers' market in 1974–79

The large increase in oil revenues also surprised the oil-exporting countries. It took some years after 1973 for them to adapt their spending to their greatly increased financial resources. In the meantime they invested their earned oil dollars in the global financial markets – mainly short term. So, the huge current account surpluses of oil-exporting countries were a first source of supply on the world's financial markets in the 1970s.

A second source of supply consisted of the USA's annual current account deficits. At first sight, it is surprising that such deficits can also contribute to the supply on international financial markets, but in the case of the USA this holds true. The USA can finance its deficit

Table 17.2 Debt service ratio of developing countries, 1973–86 (%)

	1973	1974	1975	1976	1977	1978	1979	1980	1981	1982	1983	1984	1985	1986
All developing countries	15.9	14.4	16.1	15.3	15.1	18.7	18.9	17.3	20.9	24.6	22.2	22.5	23.1	22.0
Interest payments only	6.1	6.1	6.7	6.0	5.8	7.2	8.2	8.9	11.9	14.3	13.5	13.5	12.7	11.4
Africa	8.8	6.7	8.0	8.5	11.9	15.6	15.0	14.4	16.7	20.9	23.7	28.3	30.0	27.7
Asia	9.6	7.8	8.5	7.7	7.9	9.8	8.9	8.1	9.6	11.3	10.7	10.9	11.2	11.0
America	29.3	27.9	32.2	31.4	28.7	37.8	38.9	33.5	41.5	51.6	41.1	39.4	40.5	40.0

Source: IMF, *World Economic Outlook*, several issues.

through its own currency because of the international demand for dollars. This means that the USA does not require external finance, so long as the international financial markets are able to take the dollars offered by the USA and channel them to those who want them. The recession conditions that prevailed in the industrial countries after 1973 (see Figure 17.1) kept the demand for dollar loans low.

These three developments of credit supply and demand explain the excess supply on the international financial markets after 1973. In markets with a prolonged excess supply, the borrowers have market power. The international banks tried – successfully – to avoid the imminent surplus of credit by offering a low interest rate and adopting a less critical attitude towards borrowers.

As a result of keen competition between the banks, the lending conditions became too relaxed: this is reflected in the fact that the real interest rate (that is, the interest rate minus the expected rate of inflation) was actually negative in the period 1973–78 and the banks charged their customers at a rate that was too low for the banks to build up substantial reserves to cover their loan risks. This is attractive for the debtor. The interest that a country has to pay on an international loan consists of a basic rate that is the same for all loans plus a surcharge that is specific to the debtor country. The basis rate is equal to the interest rate that well-known banks in major financial centres charge to one another; in London it is the London Interbank Offered Rate (LIBOR). A surcharge, called the spread, is added. This includes a risk premium as well as a number of cost components. The risk premium is specific to the borrowing country in question, and depends upon that country's creditworthiness, in practice quantified by its credit rating through renowned credit rating agencies such as Moody's and Standard & Poor's. (See also Section 15.3.)

The excessively low basic interest rate and spread in the 1970s were important factors in the vulnerability of the international financial system. The oil-importing developing countries had ready access to loans, even for projects that were scarcely viable. This was a major contributor to the high and stable levels of growth in these countries during those years. Initially, given the prevailing negative real interest rate, this was not a problem, but over time such a negative rate is an exception to the rule.

In addition, the banks did not do enough to build up their defences against future bad debts. Their levels of reserves were too small. Where the banks had good, quantitative information about the creditworthiness of debtor countries, they often took country risk too lightly. It was believed that countries could not go bankrupt because their assets, such as mineral resources, were still several times their levels of foreign debts. In other words, countries would almost always remain solvent. But a lack of assets that are capable of being converted quickly into cash – in other words, a lack of liquidity –can be enough to render a country incapable of meeting its international financial obligations at a given time. For that, country insolvency is not a necessary condition.

17.2.1.3 Extensive use of rollover credits

In the mid-1960s American banks introduced a form of credit on the eurocurrency market that became known as rollover credit. In the 1970s this form of credit was commonly used for loans to oil-importing developing countries. In essence, it is *long-term* credit, but with a rather *variable* interest rate. The interest rate on these long-term loans is adjusted, for example, every six months in line with the prevailing short-term rate (for instance, LIBOR).

The reason for the use of rollovers was that banks were developing the practice of financing long-term credit – to finance balance-of-payments deficits – through money offered to them on a short-term basis by the oil-exporting countries. This practice of financing long-term lending through short-term borrowing enabled the banking system to balance out shortages and surpluses for differing maturities on financial sub-markets.

The banks had to pay mainly the short-term interest rate on the funds they raised, but they ran the risk that at the very time they needed to refinance their mainly long-term lending, there might be a higher rate of interest on short-term borrowing. The banks overcame this risk by charging the long-term borrower the short-term interest rate (plus a mark-up) and regularly adjusting this rate according to the funding rate *during* the term of the loan. The result of this was that the risks of such interim interest rate increases were passed on to the debtor countries. In turn, these countries had the advantage that the short-term interest rate was normally lower than the long-term rate giving them cheaper access to long-term credit.

17.2.1.4 The use of syndicated loans

As a result of the enormous size of the loans required by oil-importing developing countries, the banks began arranging loans collaboratively. Such a loan in which several banks participate is called a *syndicated loan*. One bank acts as lead manager, and forms a group of interested banks with which agreements are made on each bank's share in the loan. The advantage of such a loan is that the risk is spread across many banks. By participating in various syndicated loans, a bank shares – and therefore reduces – the risk, which enables it to expand its total level of lending.

However, this practice creates the very real danger of over-lending, particularly because it does not protect the bank against systemic risk. This occurs if many debtors simultaneously fail to service their debts, a possibility that becomes genuine in the event of a large disruption of the world economy.

Furthermore, the banks that participated in syndicated loans were not keen observers of borrowers' creditworthiness. This was left to the lead manager. However, the fact that the latter had only a small share in the loan tended to make it rather careless. The risk was aggravated by the fact that considerations of fashionable (or herd) behaviour and honourable invitations of renowned lead banks to participate affected the banks' decision to take part in a syndicated loan. Such feelings can easily distort one's view of the true credit risks.

17.2.1.5 US adoption of a stringent anti-inflationary monetary policy

According to Table 17.3, in the decade up to 1973 inflation in the industrial countries remained at just under 4 per cent. The first oil shock caused their inflation to peak at over 13 per cent in 1974. It subsequently fell back, though about it remained in the range of 7–9 per cent over the next few years. At the end of the decade the second oil shock, in 1978–79, caused a new surge in inflation, which reached 9 per cent in 1979 and almost 12 per cent in 1980.

The prevailing belief among the monetary authorities of the rich countries had become that inflation was subject to a downward ratchet effect: while inflation could easily rise, reductions were difficult to achieve. According to this view, inflation encountered downward resistance, as if it experienced a ratchet in a downward direction. The monetary authorities considered that a stringent anti-inflation policy was needed to overcome this ratchet. For that reason, the strong rise in inflation due to the second oil shock resulted in a U-turn in monetary policy, chiefly in the USA. From October 1979, it became strongly anti-inflationary. To a certain extent other industrial countries followed.

This change in policy stance resulted in a sharp rise in interest rates around the world, but particularly in the USA. The concomitant increase in interest rate differentials between the industrial countries also led to a strong appreciation of the dollar as capital flowed

Table 17.3 Inflation, 1963–88 (%)

	Average 1963–72	1973	1974	1975	1976	1977	1978	1979		
Industrial countries	3.9	7.7	13.1	11.1	8.3	8.4	7.2	9.0		
Developing countries	9.1	20.4	27.1	27.9	24.2	27.1	23.6	24.7		

	1980	1981	1982	1983	1984	1985	1986	1987	1988
Industrial countries	11.8	9.9	7.5	5.0	4.8	4.1	2.4	3.0	3.3
Developing countries	31.6	30.6	30.9	43.2	50.5	54.7	36.1	37.1	36.2

Note: Inflation is measured by the weighted average of the countries' consumer prices.
Developing countries are the non-oil exporting developing countries.
Source: IMF, *World Economic Outlook*, several issues.

towards the highest interest rate. The higher interest rates worldwide caused a sharp decline in economic growth in the developed countries, and hence a plunge in their import growth. Traditionally, it is the exports of developing counties, with their strong emphasis on commodities, which suffer most from such a negative development.

These three effects of the developed countries' anti-inflation policy – higher interest rates, a higher dollar and a decline in import growth, especially from developing countries – caused considerable damage to the financial position of the world's debtor countries. In particular, their debt service ratios deteriorated in the following ways. The appreciation of the dollar increased the repayment burden expressed in terms of the debtor country's own currency, since most loans were denominated in dollars. Interest rates – and therefore interest payments – rose sharply due to variable interest rates. In this way there was an increase in both terms in the numerator of the debt service ratio. Slower growth in developed countries' imports tends to affect the exports of developing countries in two ways: by leading to slower growth in the volume of exports and through a fall in the price of exports. In the two-year period 1980–81 the import volume of developed countries even fell, by almost 4 per cent. Due to the consequential decrease in both volume and price of the developing countries' exports, there was a fall in the denominator of these countries' debt service ratios.

This increase in the two terms in the numerator and simultaneous fall in the denominator of the debt service ratio even appeared to have a disastrous effect upon the value of the ratio. Table 17.2 shows that for the developing countries as a whole it indeed rose steeply, from 17.3 to 24.6 per cent between 1980 and 1982. The latter percentage means that in 1982 the developing countries had to spend almost one-quarter of their export revenues on servicing their debt. Naturally, within the group of developing countries there was substantial variation in this ratio, not only from one continent to another but also between individual countries of one continent. In 1982 the figure for Asia was 'only' 11.3 per cent, whereas for Central and South America it was a startling 51.6 per cent. The increase in interest payments among the components of the debt service ratio was particularly impressive: between 1978 and 1982 this component (expressed as a ratio to exports) doubled in value.

17.2.2 Internal causes

In addition to these external causes, several internal causes, present in the 1970s, also contributed to the outbreak of the 1982 world debt crisis.

17.2.2.1 Large fiscal deficits

Governments in developing countries were more inclined than those in developed countries to run up substantial fiscal deficits. The former governments were usually weaker and, in order to remain in power, more willing to give in to demands from pressure groups, demands that lead to an increase in levels of government spending.

17.2.2.2 The monetary financing of fiscal deficits

Because of the limited scope for employing the (usually badly developed) domestic capital market, governments of developing countries often resorted to fiscal deficit financing through printing more money or taking on additional foreign debts in the 1970s. In many developing countries the first option, the monetary financing of government deficits, was the main source of domestic inflation. This can easily lead to wage–price spirals, particularly in countries with official wage indexations for price increases. Compliance produced a rigid economy in which wage flexibility and the relative price adjustments had almost disappeared. As a result, therefore, wages and prices cease to reflect the underlying relative scarcities, at the expense of efficiency in the economy.

17.2.2.3 An overvalued currency

Many developing countries also suffered from overvalued currencies. A first important reason why governments may wish to maintain an overvalued currency is to combat inflation. An overvalued currency suppresses the price of both imports and exports in terms of domestic currency, and this helps to curb domestic inflation.

A second reason is that, in some cases, the government deliberately encouraged the overvaluation of its currency in an effort to favour certain groups in the population. A government would often assist town-dwellers with an overvalued currency, because overvaluation means that imports are relatively cheap. In developing countries, imports include many products (luxury consumer goods and food) that are bought by consumers in the towns. However, the disadvantage of an overvalued currency is that a country's exports (with prices in foreign currency often determined on the world market) bring in relatively small amounts of domestic currency. This is part of the loss of competitiveness resulting from currency overvaluation. The downward effect also applies to domestic production that competes with imports. In many cases, these hurt exports and domestic production competing with imports consist largely of minerals and agricultural products produced in the countryside. So, a country having an overvalued currency may work out positively for the urban population while having a negative impact on the rural population in the country.

A third reason for currency overvaluation is that it was an unintentional effect of the application of the chosen exchange-rate system. The crawling peg system had been used frequently in developing countries. As outlined in Section 14.2, when applied correctly, this entails frequent, small devaluations of the domestic currency. With such a degree of flexibility, it is usually straightforward for the exchange rate to return to its equilibrium value. However, in the case of a high rate of inflation – say a double-digit rate per month – the parity adjustments have to be very frequent in order to offer adequate compensation for the domestic inflation. Moreover, the government also often underestimates the necessary frequency of parity adjustments, because in a highly inflationary environment the current inflation used to be an underestimation of future inflation. In that case, the country in question also had to contend with an exchange rate that is constantly lagging behind the inflation reality, which leads to a permanently overvalued domestic currency.

A variant of the previous reason for overvaluation is that many developing countries used a fixed exchange rate against one of the leading currencies – often the US dollar. The movements of the latter currency, however, may be entirely counter to the trend in the equilibrium value of the currency of the developing country concerned. Moreover, as the developing country usually had a larger inflation relative to the country of the anchor currency, over time it caused a worsening of competitiveness and thus growing current account deficits. This adverse effect was, for example, seen after 1985 in the many African countries whose currencies were then linked collectively to the French franc – as we will see in Section 19.3. As a result of the increasing overvaluation, those African currencies had to be devalued by 50 per cent at the beginning of 1994.

Clearly, an overvalued currency is bad for a country's competitiveness, prompting current account deficits and hence rising foreign debts. In such circumstances, economic growth is also put at risk. For example, the fact that the emerging economies of Asia produced much stronger growth than the countries of Latin America is often attributed in large part to the exchange rates. In the first group the currencies were considered to be roughly at their equilibrium value, whereas in the second they were grossly overvalued.

Among the familiar side effects of an overvalued domestic currency are capital flight to other countries and a domestic black market in foreign currencies. An overvalued currency means that the actual price of a foreign currency, expressed in terms of units of the domestic currency, is below its equilibrium value. Speculators believe that such a difference cannot be maintained permanently, because economic forces will ultimately level out the difference. For foreign currency speculators the expected appreciation of the foreign currency is an attractive source of profits: by buying the foreign currency now, with relatively little domestic money, and expecting to sell it again in the near future, for a larger amount of domestic currency, the speculator expects to make an exchange-rate gain. If the central bank of the overvalued currency cannot cope with such demand for foreign currencies, it faces a choice: either to decide on an immediate devaluation of the domestic currency or to cease to honour the demand for foreign currencies through imposing foreign currency restrictions.

One frequent reaction to restrictions on foreign currency is the establishment of a black market. On the black market there will be an interplay of demand and supply, which results in an unregulated price. In our instance of an overvalued domestic currency, the black market price of the foreign currency will be higher than the official market price. People offering foreign currency on the black market include exporters who are able and willing to sell their foreign currency earnings at the lucrative, higher black market price. Their willingness to do so will naturally depend to a large extent upon the punishment that the government inflicts on black market traders.

17.2.2.4 The presence of high trade barriers

In the 1970s developing countries generally had high trade barriers. Import tariffs and quotas for industrial products were often set deliberately high in order to stimulate domestic production and promote industrialization through a policy of import substitution.

It was also fairly common for governments of a developing country to generate tax revenues by imposing an export levy on both agricultural products and commodities for export. These taxes are comparatively easy to collect. Other forms of taxation necessitate well-developed administrative machinery, which was often lacking in these countries. The export levy also depressed the domestic price of agricultural products, thereby lowering the cost of living. In this way, it helped to reduce inflation and also assisted domestic industrialization through lower wage demands and thus cheaper labour. The principal objection to this and other forms of protectionist policy is, of course, that it frustrates the optimum allocation of production and consumption, and brings about a reduction in the level of economic welfare.

17.2.2.5 Regulated financial markets

In the 1970s and 1980s the developing countries had poorly developed and strictly regulated financial markets. Regulation often meant financial repression in the sense that the government kept interest rates artificially low with the aim of promoting domestic investment, while also gaining cheap government access to loans. Naturally, the low level of interest rates discouraged domestic savings. The problem with such a regulated market is that it does not clear spontaneously: the demand for loans always exceeds the supply of credits. Inevitably, then, the government has to allocate credit via a system of credit rationing. This way of market clearing is welfare distorting and, moreover, open to corruption and cronyism.

17.3 The IMF and the debt problem

17.3.1 IMF lending

The IMF seemed the appropriate body to help finance the balance-of-payments deficits resulting from the first oil price shock. As we saw in Section 16.4, from its very beginning the IMF was assigned an essential function in relation to balance-of-payments financing, but in practice, what happened in the 1970s was very different. Between 1974 and 1978 less than 4 per cent of the current account deficits in oil-importing developing countries were covered by IMF credits.

In the 1970s we saw a spontaneous division of functions between the IMF and the private banks, the latter providing loans for the most creditworthy countries, while the other oil-importing developing countries had to apply to the IMF as a last resort. Moreover, the IMF had the thankless task of offering a helping hand to countries in the first group if their balance-of-payments difficulties became so pressing and acute that at that point the banks promptly dropped out altogether. In short, this meant that the problem cases were left to the IMF.

Paradoxically, the reason for the countries' preference for using bank finance lay in the required policy conditions that were attached to IMF credits. Countries have a great reluctance to allow foreign intervention in their policy, since it impairs their political autonomy.

The process of IMF lending starts with a request by a member country for financial support. An IMF loan is usually provided under an arrangement, which stipulates specific policies and measures a country has agreed to implement to resolve its balance-of-payments problem (the well-known policy conditions). Box 17.1 describes IMF's loan facilities. The economic programme underlying an arrangement is formulated by the country in consultation with the IMF and is presented to the Fund's Board of Directors in the country's letter of intent. Once an arrangement is approved by this Board, the loan is usually released in phased instalments as the programme is implemented.

Box 17.1   The nature of IMF loan facilities

Over the years, the IMF has developed various loan instruments, or facilities, that are tailored to address the specific circumstances of its diverse membership. Low-income countries may borrow on concessional terms (or lower cost). Non-concessional loans are provided mainly through Stand-By Arrangements (SBA), the Flexible Credit Line (FCL), and the Extended Fund Facility. The IMF also provides emergency assistance to support recovery from natural disasters and conflicts. The Fund keeps its facilities under review to ensure that they remain responsive to the changing global environment and the evolving needs of members. In the years after the oil price shocks of the 1970s the Fund introduced, for example, two successive temporary Oil Facilities to increase the room to lend to member countries.

All non-concessional facilities are subject to the IMF's market-related interest rate, known as the rate of charge, and large loans (above certain limits) carry a surcharge. The rate of charge is based on the SDR interest rate. The amount that a country can borrow from the Fund, known as its access limit, varies depending on the type of loan, but is typically a multiple of the country's IMF quota. This limit may be exceeded in exceptional circumstances. The Flexible Credit Line has no pre-set cap on access.

It would take too long to describe each facility, because every one has its own policy conditions, phasing, monitoring, interest rate charges, and repayment terms. We shall therefore confine ourselves to the regular credit facilities providing non-concessional financial assistance.

The bulk of Fund assistance is provided through Stand-By Arrangements (SBAs), chronologically the first IMF facility, introduced in 1952. The SBA is designed to help countries address short-term balance-of-payments problems. Programme targets are designed to address these problems and Fund disbursements are made conditional on achieving these targets ('conditionality'). The length of a SBA is typically 12–24 months, and repayment is due within 3¼–5 years of disbursement. SBAs may be provided on a precautionary basis – where countries choose not to draw upon approved amounts but retain the option to do so if conditions deteriorate – both within the normal access limits and in cases of exceptional access. The SBA provides for flexibility with respect to phasing, with front-loaded access where appropriate.

The Extended Fund Facility (EFF) was established in 1974 to help countries address longer-term balance-of-payments problems requiring fundamental economic reforms. Arrangements under the EFF are thus longer than SBAs – usually three years. Repayment is due within 4½–10 years from the date of disbursement

The Flexible Credit Line (FCL) is for countries with very strong fundamentals, policies, and track records of policy implementation and is particularly useful for crisis prevention purposes. FCL arrangements are approved for countries meeting pre-set qualification criteria. This facility was introduced in 2009 during the global economic crisis of 2008/09. The length of the FCL is six months or one year (with a mid-term review) and the repayment period the same as for the SBA. Access is determined on a case-by-case basis, is not subject to the normal access limits, and is available in a single up-front disbursement rather than phased. Disbursements under the FCL are not conditioned on implementation of specific policy understandings as is the case under the SBA. There is flexibility to draw on the credit line at the time it is approved, or it may be treated as precautionary.

Also in 2009, fostered by the global economic crisis, non-concessional loan access limits for countries were doubled, with the new annual and cumulative access limits for Fund resources being 200 and 600 per cent of quota, respectively. These higher limits aim to give confidence to countries that adequate resources would be accessible to them to meet their financing needs. Access above these limits will continue to be provided on a case-by-case basis.

Source: http://www.imf.org/external/np/exr/facts/howlend.htm.

The IMF has demonstrated a great deal of flexibility in adjusting the nature of the credit facilities to fit circumstances. For example, immediately after the first oil shock the Oil Facility was introduced. This was followed a few years later by two facilities funded by individual member countries so that the IMF's regular resources were unaffected. When, in the 1980s, it became clear that the restoration of the balance-of-payments equilibrium would require more long-term solutions, the Fund developed two funds offering loans on easy terms to low-income countries with permanent balance-of-payments problems. Under the scheme the drawing period was extended to three years and the repayment period to ten years. In 1993 the IMF introduced a facility targeted specifically at Russia and the other economies that were in transition from a centrally planned economy to a market economy.

In 1999 the Fund started Contingent Credit Lines (CCL) in response to the Asian financial crisis that began in mid-1997 (see Section 18.4). The aim was to provide a precautionary line of defence for members with first-class policies that might nevertheless be vulnerable to contagion. However, at the end of 2003 the IMF allowed the CCL to expire since they had remained unused. The two funds that the IMF developed in the 1980s – mentioned above – came close to development aid. As a result, the IMF became more of a competitor for the World Bank.

A link with development aid was even explicitly proposed in the discussion in the 1970s about the way of allocation of SDRs. Under its Articles of Agreement, the IMF is entitled to create additional SDRs 'to meet the need, as and when it arises, for a supplement to existing reserve assets'. As we have already seen in Section 16.4, the IMF allocates new SDRs to member countries that joined the IMF Special Drawing Rights department, according to their IMF quotas. Allocated SDRs are in fact also a form of available IMF loans, albeit an indirect one. The holder of SDRs can use them to acquire unconditionally freely usable foreign currency, SDR allocation according to the IMF quotas implies that the overwhelming majority of SDRs came in the hands of the rich countries. It was therefore no surprise that soon after the first allocation of SDRs a link was proposed between the allocation of SDRs and the granting of development assistance. The underlying idea was that if additional international monetary reserves have to be created for the benefit of the world economy, it is highly effective to serve a second objective at the same time – namely development aid. It was proposed that this could be done by allocating new SDRs only to poor countries. However, this link between the issue of SDRs and the provision of development aid never arose. Following lengthy discussion in the 1970s, the subject was dropped from the agenda.

The main objections put forward by opponents of this so-called link proposal were:

1. 'the need for a supplement to existing reserve assets' concerns the need for additional SDRs on a *worldwide* scale, not the needs of just one group of countries;
2. in the 1970s, inflation increased dramatically, particularly in the developing countries (see Table 17.3). A supplementary allocation of SDRs could – through the room they provided for additional expenditures – easily reinforce increasing inflationary tendencies in the developing countries;

3. international monetary reserves are resources to hold for possible *temporary* use for balance-of-payments and exchange-rate purposes. As time goes by, a country will top up its reserves again after use. Thus, in essence it is about 'reserves to hold' rather than 'reserves to spend'. If SDRs were to be used for development purposes, then they would undoubtedly fall into the second category. The developing countries would use them up once and for all. It was thought that this would seriously impair the character of the SDR as a reserve asset, and would almost certainly undermine its prestige.

In practice, many developing countries did in fact use up their SDR allocation almost immediately and were hardly ever in a position to buy back the SDRs they had used earlier. When the world debt crisis unfolded in the 1980s, therefore the SDRs were unable to play a role in financing the balance-of-payments deficits of the oil-importing developing countries.

17.3.2 IMF conditionality

The IMF provides temporary credits for members who are experiencing balance-of-payments deficits. These credits are meant to prevent a country from being forced to reduce a balance-of-payments deficit very rapidly as the result of a shortage of monetary reserves. According to the definition equation (17.1) – which is the same as equation (14.3) – current account equilibrium, or CA equalling zero, means that a country's national income, $Y + N$, must be equal to the residents' spending, or absorption A.

$$CA \equiv (Y + N) - A. \tag{17.1}$$

In the short term, it is only spending that can be changed significantly; it is much more difficult to adapt the level of production, Y, quickly. This means that a current account deficit (CA is negative) can only be rectified immediately by putting a squeeze on spending. Then residents' demand for consumption and investment has to decline sharply. This can lead to distressing situations, especially in the poorest countries.

There is therefore much to be said for giving a country the chance to spread this current account adjustment over a period of some years. This offers, moreover, the opportunity to raise domestic production in the meantime so that there can be a less severe squeeze on demand. The country can achieve this spread adjustment by raising loans abroad, including IMF loans.

IMF conditionality is intended to make use of such temporary balance-of-payments financing as a means of inducing the country in question to arrange an efficient adjustment process of its balance-of-payments deficit. A second reason for the IMF to impose conditions is to protect its resources, to have this money available for re-use for a next member country with financing problems. If a country were unable to repay the IMF credit, then the IMF would be unable to re-use the money for subsequent lending to other member countries. In other words, IMF loans need to be revolving in character. As countries are independent, it is not possible for the IMF to obtain a collateral as a coverage for the non-repayment risk. The conditions are in fact a substitute for the collateral.

Thirdly, the IMF conditions also prove successful, on occasion, in persuading member country governments to pursue policies that they would really have liked to adopt even without the IMF, but did not dare to because of opposition from domestic political forces. If the country concerned is subject to the IMF conditions, then it can use the IMF as a scapegoat for any problems that it encounters or any unpopular policies that it has to introduce. Fourthly, the IMF conditions, if accepted by the debtor country, work as an inceptive for other investors to add loans to the rather small IMF loan. Fifthly, the IMF conditions are considered to be a serious burden for the debtor country. The conditionality can therefore prevent the moral hazard problem that countries conduct too easily policies that create financial problems in the knowledge that the IMF is there as a cheap haven of refuge.

According to the IMF, its conditionality is designed on a country-by-country basis: the policy conditions are tailored to the individual country that is applying for a credit. Yet there is a clear thread running through the IMF conditions, as set out in the following five standard conditions for a country to obtain an IMF loan:

1. In the overwhelming majority of cases, the country has to carry out a *large devaluation*, often even before the IMF agrees to the policy eventually proposed by the country. Thus, the devaluation also appears to be a sign of goodwill. The object of devaluation is, of course, to rectify the initial overvaluation of the national currency. Under the Marshall–Lerner condition and the condition embodied in the absorption approach the devaluation will tackle the current account deficit. (See Section 14.3.)

   In the event of a devaluing developing country a model of tradables (consisting of importables and exportables) and non-tradables is often taken up. Its starting point is the perception that a developing country's economy is usually so insignificant to the world economy that it cannot influence the world market price (in foreign currency) of its tradables. That price is therefore set for the country, so that devaluation increases the domestic price of these goods, corresponding to the percentage devaluation.

   As a result, part of the domestic demand for these goods is transferred to non-tradables – with a price that lags behind that of tradables. This shift in demand releases goods for exports and also reduces imports, both improving the current account.

   On the supply side, the reverse shift takes place. The price rise of tradables will attract domestic producers in so far as they can transform their production at the expense of non-tradables and in favour of tradables. This transformation likewise releases more goods for export and reduces the country's net demand for imports. Devaluation therefore improves the current account via the volume effects of both the demand and the supply side of export and import goods.

2. The IMF often considers the excessive growth of the country's money supply to be at the heart of a balance-of-payments problem. Excessive money creation fuels inflation and undermines a country's competitiveness. *Money-growth ceilings* are therefore prominent among the IMF policy conditions.

3. In developing countries, the government is often the main source of money creation. As stated earlier in this chapter, the government often finances a substantial part of the fiscal deficit by new money. The IMF therefore almost always requires a *sharp reduction in the government's fiscal deficit*.

4. Developing countries are often subject to considerable price distortions. The government frequently subsidizes several basic essentials (such as energy and food), fixes artificially low prices (such as the interest rate) and intervenes via trade policy in the pricing of tradables. The IMF is fervently opposed to this and therefore demands a *reduction in protectionism* and urges *the lessening of subsidies*. The latter also helps to cut the fiscal deficit. In practice, the abolition of subsidies on basic essentials by and large causes uproar in countries that bring in the IMF.

5. The IMF allows that only part of the increase in the price of tradables can be passed on in wages and the prices of other products. This is meant to *avoid creating a vicious circle of devaluation and inflation*, in which a devaluation, through higher inflation at home – via imported inflation combined with domestic wage and domestic price indexation for inflation – leads to the need for another devaluation, and so on.

In the past the IMF's policy conditions have been the subject of much criticism. In the early 1980s, given the deregulation advocated by the Reagan administration in the USA, the IMF was accused of ignoring the supply side of the economy. The IMF defended itself by drawing more attention in its conditionality to the influence of devaluation on the supply side.

A decade later, the main criticism of the IMF was that it disregarded income distribution within countries, so that IMF policies often caused suffering to the poorest sectors of the population. The IMF responded that it had no right to interfere in domestic affairs. The IMF's mandate did not extend beyond the balance-of-payments objective, for which a rough macroeconomic framework was sufficient. Nevertheless, the Fund did accept the criticism in practice and in later years, wherever possible, its policy recommendations have placed a greater emphasis on aspects such as presence of a social safety net to spare the poor. See the next chapter, Section 18.5.5, for later developments of IMF conditionality.

17.4 The debt crisis

When the debt crisis broke out in August 1982 following Mexico's suspension of its debt servicing, the great significance of international organizations watching over the interests of the world economy became apparent. The first reaction from the global private banking sector was to call a total halt to further lending to the debtor countries, and to extricate themselves as quickly as possible from outstanding claims on those countries. If all the banks had actually carried out this policy, all the debtor countries would have been heading for default.

In 1981 and 1982 the net inflow of capital to those countries was still, respectively, $50 and $38 billion. Such an abrupt reversal as the private banks had in mind was, therefore, entirely impossible. Even if the net inflow of capital to these countries had been zero, credit would still have been necessary, in the form of a gross inflow of capital, in order to enable the debtor countries to finance the terminating principal repayments and interest charges.

If credit is cut off altogether, collective defaulting or – worse – debt repudiation, ceasing to acknowledge the debts, is an appealing alternative for heavy borrowers. However, such a reaction would have been disastrous for the international financial system. The private banks' equity would have been entirely inadequate to bear such losses.

Let us consider the situation of the nine largest US banks then operating internationally. At the end of 1982 they had outstanding claims totalling $57 billion in the 15 countries with the largest debts, while their equity (stock capital and reserves for bad debts) was $29 billion. In other words, at this time their outstanding claims on these debtor countries were almost double their equity. If an individual bank had a more favourable than average ratio, it was still so closely intertwined with the other banks by extensive interbank lending that it would undoubtedly have also been dragged down if the other banks had gone bankrupt.

Consequently, following the outbreak of the debt crisis all of the private banks were very anxious to continue to provide credit in such a way that the debtor countries would not default. However, individual banks could still cheerfully opt for the role of free rider: it would no longer grant credit itself in the hope that the majority of the other private banks would carry on doing so. This threat of inconsistency in banking behaviour was prevented in 1982 and subsequent years through the actions of international organizations.

In August 1982, on the initiative of the Bank for International Settlements (BIS), and with the support of a number of the world's central banks, Mexico was granted a short-term loan. The BIS was set up in 1930 as a clearing centre for the German reparations payments resulting from the First World War. Its headquarters is in Basel. The Bank's general objectives include promoting cooperation between central banks and providing supplementary facilities for international financial operations. The bridging loan for Mexico in 1982 ties in well with this. The resources temporarily required for the purpose came from central banks, which the BIS asked to participate in the loan. Since then this form of bridging loan has been used by the BIS on several occasions.

In this way Mexico received some breathing space until the IMF was able to reach agreement on the adoption of credit facilities. It was the only institution prepared to continue to grant credit to the debtor countries, under the usual policy conditions. However, the resources available to the IMF for that purpose were insufficient to meet the credit requirements. In the world debt crisis of the 1980s the IMF therefore adopted a tactical approach and acted as a catalyst for continued lending to debtor countries. The formula was this: first the IMF tried to reach agreement with a debtor country concerning the policy conditions under which the IMF was willing to lend money to the country. The resulting agreement was then subject to the important supplementary condition that the private banks with outstanding claims on the country in question would continue to extend credit facilities, even if only to refinance maturing credits. As a result, the banks were placed in a dilemma: the IMF policy conditions would certainly help to give them a chance of recovering the money that was already outstanding, but they would not be implemented unless the banks could provide more finance. During the 1980s this form of coercion worked extremely well.

In addition to the provision of supplementary finance, debts were often rescheduled. In practice, this always meant the postponement of principal repayments on loans by a number of years and the extension of the repayment period. The governments of developed countries were also active in rescheduling the debts of developing countries, because they were often involved in such debts. Sometimes directly in the form of outstanding official debts, and sometimes indirectly as the result of government credit guarantees to bank and business loans. The Paris Club was used for the rescheduling of multilateral official debt. This 'club' is an informal group of official creditors, mostly developed countries that seek solutions for debtor nations facing international repayment difficulties.[1] Depending on the debtor country, the club's composition of creditor countries varies.

It can be seen that the major achievement of the 1980s was that there was a maintenance of the overall level of lending to major debtor countries, so that the debt crisis was kept under control and a financial collapse of the world economy was avoided. Initially the developing countries saw a further increase in the values of their foreign debt and the associated debt service, with peaks in the period 1982–86 for these values in relation to the value of exports. In 1986 the figures for the ratios were, respectively, 178 per cent and 22 per cent (see Table 17.2); however, by 1993 these had fallen to 'only' 118 per cent and 15 per cent. Throughout this period, regional variations within the group of developing countries remained as large as ever, but the same tendency of improvement was evident for almost every regional group – although barely in Africa's case.

More importantly, the ratio between the outstanding bank claims on debtor countries and bank equity improved even more sharply. At the end of 1986 this ratio had already dropped to 121 for the nine largest US banks operating internationally, referred

---

[1] This voluntary gathering dates back to 1956, when Argentina agreed to meet its public creditors in Paris. The Paris Club and the IMF have extensive contact, since the Paris Club normally requires debtor countries to have an active IMF-supported programme.

to earlier. Since then the decline has continued, so that by 1990 the ratio was well below 100 per cent. The risk of a wave of bankruptcies in the banking system as the result of collective defaulting on the part of debtor countries then was trigger a thing of the past.

The adjustment of the debt situation described above was certainly not painless. The developing countries, in particular, suffered. The required macroeconomic adjustment policy, triggered by the IMF's policy conditions, caused a substantial and inevitable slowdown in economic growth in those countries.

By the end of the 1980s many large developing countries had a lower per capita income than at the beginning of that decade, which is why people tend to refer to the 1980s as a lost decade for the developing countries. But that is not entirely correct. Even at first sight, this picture is dubious. Figure 17.1 shows that the developing countries saw an abrupt decline in their growth rate in the period 1981–83, but that after that hiatus the growth figures in that decade were nearly as high as in the second half of the 1970s. Almost without exception, in this respect they outstripped the industrial countries year after year. Moreover, on closer examination we see efficiency improvements in the economy of many developing countries. The positive trends apparent in many of these countries after the 1980s bear that out. It is only the continent of Africa that was still ailing.

Once the banks had reduced the ratio between their outstanding claims on debtor countries and their equity to below 100 per cent – mainly through retained earnings – they were able to adopt a much more flexible approach to taking losses on outstanding loans. In this period banks started to sell debt paper of the debtor countries on the secondary market, which had recently developed for these debt instruments. The resale prices were, of course (often much) lower than the face value of the debts. This was how the banks took their losses.

The cut-price debt instruments were bought up in particular by companies wishing to invest in such a debtor country, thus acquiring a low-cost debt instrument of the country. These companies were not interested in having the debt paid out in dollars; they wanted the underlying value in the local currency to facilitate local investment. For the country concerned, supplying the local currency was naturally not a problem in itself. The local currency needed not be earned first, so for the debtor country it was not scarce in principle. In practice, such a transaction – in which a foreign company converted a debt instrument denominated in dollars into shares in local firms, hence the name: debt–equity swap – was often financially advantageous for both the company and the government concerned. Of course, someone also had to be the loser in such a debt–equity swap, but we have already considered that: it was the bank that sold the debt instrument for a reduced price. In their newly acquired financial position, the banks did not opt exclusively for the secondary market. Other, more direct methods of writing off bad debts were used.

In March 1989 the then American Treasury Secretary, Nicholas F. Brady, launched a debt alleviation plan. Named in his honour, the Brady Plan implied an official recognition that the full repayment of all outstanding debts was not possible. Brady proposed a reduction in commercial bank debts, offering the banks various options for reducing outstanding claims.

It was no coincidence that this plan was advanced at around the same time that the banks were restored to a position in which they could write off their claims, as described above. Mexico was the first country to conclude such a debt reduction agreement. Banks with claims on Mexico were obliged to exchange old claims for new ones. With respect to these new claims they had a choice of three evils: the value of the old claims at a lower interest rate, new claims with a lower face value or the old face value with the promise of supplementary loans. The attraction of the new loan was that it had a repayment guarantee via a transaction with the American government. The Brady Plan also included an IMF adjustment programme for the debtor country in question and the possibility of allowing the debtor country to use IMF and World Bank funds to buy back debts on the secondary market.

17.5 | Summary

1. The world debt crisis that began in August 1982 nearly brought financial ruin to many heavily indebted developing countries and a very large number of banks operating internationally. There were many apparent causes for this world debt crisis.

2. Among the key external causes of the world debt crisis were: the two oil-price shocks in the 1970s; the fact that during those years the international financial markets were a borrowers' market; the fact that the oil-importing developing countries had made extensive use of bank rollover credits with variable interest rates; banks' large-scale participation in syndicated lending; and the strict anti-inflationary policies adopted by industrial countries from the end of 1979.

3. For those countries with large debts, the following are regarded as internal causes of the debt crisis: tightly regulated domestic financial markets, large government deficits, high levels of domestic inflation greatly stimulated by the monetary financing of government deficits, an overvalued currency, and domestic price distortions caused by government intervention and international trade barriers.

4. Although the IMF offers a range of credit facilities to its members, the Fund played only a minor role in the period prior to the world debt crisis. Instead, recycling oil dollars through the international banking system largely financed balance-of-payments deficits of the debtor countries. The new IMF credit facilities created in response to the first oil shock and the introduction of the SDR did little to change this. However, during those years of world debt crisis the IMF's resources were very important to countries that were unable to obtain commercial bank credit.

5. The policy conditions imposed by the IMF as a requirement for the granting of its credit were decisive in dissuading many oil-importing developing countries from asking the IMF for help before the debt crisis.

6. Following the outbreak of the debt crisis, however, these developing countries had to reach agreements with the IMF because the commercial banks called an abrupt halt to international lending. It was thanks to the energetic intervention of the BIS and the IMF, in cooperation with a number of central banks, that credit for major debtor countries did not dry up altogether. Essentially, these international monetary institutions thus avoided the collapse of the international financial world.

7. The fragile balance consisting of IMF loans under policy conditions that compelled the commercial banks to provide supplementary credit eased the world debt crisis throughout the 1980s. This gave the commercial banks the time to put matters in order as regards the initial shortage of their equity relative to their outstanding claims on defaulted international debtors.

8. The IMF has exhibited considerable flexibility in adapting its financing facilities to changing international economic environments and external criticism.

9. By the end of the 1980s an acceptable financial position was restored on many bank balance sheets, which gave these banks the ability to deal realistically with their bad debts. Debt instruments for countries with heavy debts were sold at a loss by the banks on the secondary market. Debts were also rescheduled, not only by extending the period of repayment but also in the form of partial remission. This process enabled heavily indebted countries to achieve a substantial improvement in their debt service ratio.

10. This chapter on the world debt crisis of the 1980s contains several relevant, ongoing lessons for banks and governments. One such lesson is that countries can go bankrupt, even if they have extensive mineral resources. Furthermore, solvency is not a sufficient condition to prevent a country's bankruptcy: solvency combined with illiquidity is already risky for a country and may be a trigger to start speculation against the country and to usher in economic collapse.

11. Another lesson is that the risks of banks that operate internationally cannot be over-estimated. The propensity to contagion across debtor countries and the propensity across banks to herd behaviour are at the root of systemic risk. This is strengthened further by the belief that governments – if necessary, with the help of international organizations – will rescue large (or system) banks. Bank equity will hardly ever be sufficient to cope with systemic risk. In this respect the world debt crisis of the 1980s provided some useful lessons for bank behaviour prior to – and governments' reaction during – the world economic crisis of 2008–09.

Questions

1. In the decade 1973–82 there were three years with negative economic growth for the industrial countries, according to Figure 17.1. Show that the frequency is high by tracing the other years since then that this happened.

2. Not all developing countries suffer from strong increases in the debt service ratio due to the higher value of and the higher interest rate on the dollar in the beginning of the 1980s. Construct the external position of a hypothetical country, for example in Africa, that experiences a *decrease* of its debt service ratio in response to the steep increases in dollar value and interest rate.

3. Various variants of the debt–equity swaps were soon invented at the end of the 1980s: debt for child survival programmes, debt for conservation, debt for education, debt for micro-enterprises, not forgetting more exotic swaps such as debt for soccer stars. The latter swap financed the transfer of Brazilian soccer star Romario to the Dutch team PSV Eindhoven in 1988. Take one of these swap variants and explain how the financial advantage can occur.

4. This chapter presents five rationales for IMF conditionality. Summarize them.

CHAPTER 18

A Financial Obstacle to Economic Development: Currency Crises

18.1 Introduction

The world debt crisis discussed in Chapter 17 is an example of the sort of crisis that afflicts countries with restricted private international capital inflows. Until the end of the 1980s this international capital restriction was a major characteristic of the economic setting in which financial crises occurred in developing countries.

These financial crises were rooted in a cycle of domestic overspending, high inflation, and thus, if the currency had a fixed exchange rate, a real appreciation – usually against the US dollar. This real appreciation or worsening of competitiveness was followed by a deterioration of the current account. This in turn, financed by mainly official capital inflows, led to increases in the country's foreign debt.

Periodic interest payments on an increasing foreign debt contributed to a further worsening of the current account. This was a gradual process that could easily lead to a crisis. To finance the servicing of the debt from domestic production and to improve the level of competitiveness, there had to be a fall in the country's real wage level.

Such crises could eventually be prevented through a combination of devaluation with incomplete wage indexation for price rises and a restructuring of the debt. If such a policy was not adopted, the crisis was likely to lead to arrears in servicing foreign debt and the sources of new foreign loans drying up.

Dornbusch (2001) has termed this type of financial crisis an *old-style* (or *slow motion*) *crisis*, which he contrasts with a *new-style crisis*, driven by private international capital flows. These capital flows require a financially open economy, the necessary condition for new-style financial crises, usually currency crises, to occur.

A currency crisis has a significant impact upon a country's economy. One indication of the size of the negative effect of currency crises is that in the crisis year the median fall in economic growth in eight crises in the years 1994–98 amounted to some 9 per cent (IMF, 2002, pp. 128–9). It is also notable that, on average, these countries recovered quickly: in the second year following the crisis the average growth rates in these countries had already returned to pre-crisis levels. However, expressed in terms of levels of national production, even in that second year production was still, on average, 9 per cent lower than the level that would have existed without the crisis.

This chapter aims to explain the occurrence of currency crises, both theoretically and in practice. Currency crises are a long-standing phenomenon. Their theoretical foundations are to be found in Gresham's Law, formulated in the sixteenth century, which states that bad money always drives out good money. The essence of the argument is that within a country the private sector will supply overvalued (or bad) currencies in exchange for undervalued (or good) currencies. The latter will then fall out of circulation. Section 18.2 will clarify this rule and show that in essence it is also applicable to *international* monetary relations, and can generate currency crises. Although modern-day currency crises have some similarities with the domestic currency crises of the distant past, there are also considerable differences. The section will then go on to describe three different explanations for speculative attacks on currencies.

Sections 18.3 and 18.4 analyse the two most attention-grabbing currency crises in developing countries in the 1990s: these were the crisis of the Mexican peso in 1994–95 and the Asian crisis that began in Thailand in the summer of 1997. These were also the major currency crises of the 1990s in terms of their impact on the world economy. They are therefore informative case studies and thus fruitful contributions for a sound understanding of the effects of recent speculative attacks that have led to a currency crisis. In the course of the 1990s other newsworthy currency crises occurred in Turkey (1994), Russia (1998) and Brazil (1999).

These two case studies lead on to the core of the chapter: a consideration of the lessons that can be drawn from theory and the experiences of the recent past. Section 18.5 outlines a number of recommendations with respect to economic policy, including some lessons for the International Monetary Fund (IMF). Section 18.6 summarizes these findings.

18.2 Currency crises: three generations of theories

18.2.1 Gresham's Law

Several centuries ago the money system consisted of a full-fledged coinage: under a gold standard gold coins were valued entirely according to their gold content. There was no scope for currency speculation. If there was an increase in the net demand for gold in the private sector, the value of gold increased and so did the purchasing power of the gold coins. This implied that there was a fall in the prices of other goods expressed in terms of gold coins.

Currency speculation occurred as soon as a country had a so-called bi-metallic standard, usually the simultaneous existence of a gold and silver standard in the country – a situation that occurred on many occasions in the past. The (much) more expensive of the two metals – gold – was used for the minting of more valuable coins, whereas silver was employed for those coins with much less purchasing power. But in the domestic monetary system all coins were given fixed mutual value relations, which indirectly fixed the official gold and silver prices in relation to each other.

However, on the gold and silver markets there were daily changes in prices, which created a permanent danger of currency arbitrage. A situation could soon have developed in which the market price of gold in terms of silver diverged substantially from the official price, included in the fixed value relation of the gold and silver coins. If, for example, gold on the private markets had become more expensive over time, then gold coins would have become too cheap relative to silver coins. In other words, gold coins would have been undervalued or, in terms of Gresham's Law, good money. According to their intrinsic value of gold, the gold content of the gold coins was more expensive on the gold market relative to silver. If the price increase of gold on the private market was sufficiently large, it became possible to make an arbitrage profit. The profitable way to do this was to remelt gold coins, selling their gold content in the private gold market against its high price in terms of silver coins and, subsequently, exchanging the yield in the form of silver coins into gold coins at the country's money-issuing bank. Of course, the increase in the price of gold in the private market should be sufficient to cover the costs of these transactions, particularly the re-melting costs of gold. If this price divergence continued for long enough, a situation would arise in which all gold coins were melted down. In such circumstances, bad money (overvalued silver coins) would have driven out good money (gold coins). This is Gresham's Law. The consequence of its working was a disrupted domestic monetary system, as, in the case just described, all currencies with large purchasing power (gold coins) would have disappeared. This would have been a considerable drawback for the payment of large sums of money.

An *international* currency crisis occurred in the era of gold and silver standards if two countries had a bi-metallic money system, with, in the domestic market, both a gold and silver standard but with different official values of gold in terms of silver. This situation was not unusual: it occurred often that the two countries began their bi-metallic system at different times – undoubtedly with different gold prices in terms of silver in the private markets. Under these circumstances it is profitable for arbitragers to buy the gold coins in the country where gold has the lowest value in terms of silver. Here gold is undervalued or, in the terms of Gresham's Law, good money. Remelted gold specie is, subsequently, sent to the country with the high gold price. Then the earnings of silver coins in the second country are sent back to the first country in the form of remelted silver specie and there offered to the money-issuing bank for re-melting into silver coins.

This round trip would have been profitable if the price difference was large enough to cover the two melting-down operations and the transport costs of both gold and silver specie. Moreover, there was a necessity that the money-issuing banks in the two countries were prepared to accept gold and silver for minting coins at the official metal price – but their obligation to do so was one of the characteristics of a metallic standard. In addition, the export and import of specie had to be free. Through the round trip, in the first country good money (gold) was (again) driven out by bad money (silver), causing disruption to that country's monetary system. For the second country it was the other way around: there silver coins were undervalued (good money) and these were driven out by the overvalued gold (bad money).

Present-day, new-style currency crises develop in a financially open economy in which the monetary authorities strive for a fixed exchange rate, with a key role being played by the capital account and capital flight. The difference between the official value and the market price of species, of Gresham's Law, is now replaced by strong and weak currencies. A strong currency is considered by the public to be undervalued, so that it has a tendency to revalue. By contrast, a weak currency is expected to devalue in due time as it is considered to be overvalued. A currency speculator uses a weak currency to buy a strong currency in the foreign-exchange market.

To defend the fixed exchange rate of its currency against the strong currency, the central bank of the weak currency buys its currency against the strong currency by using its international monetary reserves. Currency speculators do not melt down the strong currency that they receive (of course, an impossibility with the current fiat money), but invest the strong currency provisionally in the home country of the strong currency pending the anticipated depreciation of the weak currency. Thus, in spite of the differences with the era of gold and silver standard, the outcome of this speculation is that the weak-currency country gets rid of the 'good money', in a manner similar to the outcome of Gresham's Law. The mechanism is, however, different. Under the metal standards it was specie arbitrage; in modern times it is currency speculation.

18.2.2 Speculative attack model: the first generation

Since the end of the 1970s, there have been several important contributions to the analysis of new-style currency crises. Theorizing on currency crises – and on financial crises in general – dates from a much earlier period (see Kindleberger, 1978, for a survey). The recent contributions, however, were the first to develop explanatory models of such events in mathematical terms, an important feature in present-day economic theory.

Krugman (1979) offers much theoretical evidence about wrong economic fundamentals as the cause of a speculative attack in the foreign-exchange market. This type of explanation is called the *first generation* of speculative attack models. In Krugman's case the wrong fundamental regards a fiscal policy that is money financed. This fiscal policy is too expansive to maintain the fixed exchange rate. Walters (1986) gives the initial impetus to another variant of a first-generation model, where the source of the attack is a vulnerable anti-inflation policy that undermines the fixed exchange rate.

In Krugman's model the wrong fundamental is a lasting money-financed expansionary fiscal policy that is, implicitly, also expansionary relative to the country that functions as the anchor country for the fixed exchange rate – a difference that undermines the fixed exchange rate. A good reason for this expansive policy according to the policy-makers could be a current rate of unemployment that they consider to be too high. With a stable demand for money in the country involved, the additional supply of money through money financing of the government reveals itself, according to the monetary approach to the exchange rate – or equation (13.6) – in an increase of the equilibrium exchange rate or a lower equilibrium value of the home currency. Prevention of an actual depreciation requires supporting non-sterilized forex market interventions of the central bank: a purchase of the home currency against foreign currency. So, there is a gradual loss of international monetary reserves. Observing this reserve loss and its cause, currency speculators will consider a speculative attack against the weak currency.

At first glance, one would expect a start of the speculators' sale of the home currency if the reserve holdings of the central bank are almost exhausted. If the speculators have perfect foresight expectations, however, they are conscious of the presence of many co-speculators with large speculative funds. They know that their speculation is too late to be fully profitable if they delay their actions until the reserves are almost or fully depleted. In order to avoid this, the average speculator moves the intended moment of speculation somewhat forward in time. Of course, in anticipation that other speculators will apply the same tactic, they all move the intended speculation increasingly further backward in time until the moment that the first sign of a weakening of the currency is perceivable – that is, at the start of the expansionary money-financed fiscal policy. If all speculators have the same information and expectations, there will be an immediate large-scale speculation. Normal reserve holdings will be unable to cope with such a speculative attack. Accordingly, the ultimate timing of the attack will be long before the time that the country gets rid of its reserves.

As the fixed exchange rate is only just out of equilibrium at the start of the expansionary fiscal policy, the notable outcome is that after the successful attack the freed exchange rate will have a value that is near to the original fixed value. This is in contrast to the practice of successful speculative attacks, where it is normal for the exchange rate to exhibit a large upward jump. This stylized fact of a speculative currency attack has been brought into line with Krugman's first-generation speculative attack model by, for example, adding uncertainty among speculators with respect to the knowledge of co-speculators and some heterogeneity in the behaviour of speculators (see, for example, Botman and Jager, 2002). This retards the moment of a successful attack, as a result of what in the meantime a substantial overvaluation of the weak currency could arise – with a consequent immediate substantial fall of the currency through the attack, in contrast to Krugman's model outcome.

In the 1980s and the first half of the 1990s one popular policy for achieving price stabilization in Latin America and western Europe was to peg the exchange rate to the currency of a country that had pursued a successful low-inflation policy. The underlying reasoning was as follows. When a country fixes its exchange rate decisively, while the country has a substantially higher rate of inflation than the anchor country, the high-inflation country will moderate its inflation through its imports. Instead of a large annual devaluation, which results in large rises in import prices, the exchange rate and import prices remain (almost) constant. This policy is called a convergence play (of inflation).

In the 1980s Sir Alan Walters, economic advisor to the then British Prime Minister Margaret Thatcher, criticized this policy for its inherent inconsistency (Walters, 1986). It was a warning (albeit issued in vain) to prevent the pound sterling from joining the fixed exchange-rate system of the European Monetary System (EMS) (see Section 19.5). In the same period, Edwards expressed a similar warning against the application of this anti-inflation policy in Latin American countries (Edwards, 1992).

At the beginning of this policy, or in any case in the short run, in effect a constant exchange rate can be expected. In terms of the uncovered interest parity (UIP), equation (12.2), the expected exchange-rate change is lowered from positive to zero. In order to prevent a surge of capital inflows, according to the UIP, the nominal interest rates of the two countries must be equalized. Yet this implies that the high-inflation country should lower its interest rate substantially. As its inflation is still high at the first stage, its real interest rate will then be quite low and likely even negative, whereas the inflation-shy anchor country has a much higher, positive real interest rate. Through the very low real interest rate, there will be a large demand for credit in the high-inflation country and strongly expansionary private expenditures – with inflationary impulses. This is precisely the opposite development to that which moves towards inflation convergence. So far this follows the Walters critique.

In an attempt to circumvent this development, the high-inflation country could decide to keep its nominal interest rate high – in line with the national inflation level. *Ceteris paribus*, this interest rate policy would contribute to a convergence in the rates of inflation. But the concomitant interest rate differential between the two countries combined with the expectation of an unchanged exchange rate in the near future result in the left-hand side being now much higher than the right-hand side in the UIP equation (12.2). Under free international capital flows a large capital flow is likely to begin, from the low-inflation country to the high-inflation country. In response, in order to prevent its currency from *ap*preciating, the central bank in the high-inflation country is obliged to buy the inflow of foreign currency in the forex market against issuing domestic currency. But this is a highly expansive monetary policy, whereas that country needs to pursue a restrictive monetary policy in order to allow inflation rates to converge in a downward direction with that of the anchor country. The outcome is that this alternative policy approach of a high interest rate in the high-inflation country also leads to just the opposite of the intended inflation convergence.

The persistence of high inflation in either of these two ways will, in combination with the fixed exchange rate, lead to a gradual weakening in the competitiveness of the inflation-prone country. Consequently, its current account deficit will grow over time. At a certain point in time the currency speculators will come to view this situation as unsustainable. They will begin to anticipate a significant fall in the value of the inflation-prone country's currency. This expected fall will soon surpass the interest rate advantage of the inflation-prone country and – according to the UIP equation – currency speculators give preferentiality to a capital outflow. In such circumstances it will be difficult to even achieve an orderly devaluation, because financial markets tend to overreact. It is to be expected that the country will be hit by a huge flight of speculative capital. Such a speculative attack leads to a steep fall in the value of the currency of the country that tries in vain to lower inflation through stabilizing its exchange rate.

18.2.3 Speculative attack models: later generations

In contrast to first-generation models of speculative attacks, the analysis in Obstfeld (1986) looks at a situation in which the economic fundamentals of the exchange rate are sound. This means that the economic variables, such as the money supply, the national income, and the interest rate, which are explanatory variables of the exchange rate according to exchange-rate theories, have values that justify the actual exchange-rate value. The weak point for the exchange rate in Obstfeld's analysis is that there are objectives of economic policy with current values that differ from the values that policy makers desire. For example, the rate of unemployment might be too high. Nevertheless, in their behaviour policy-makers appear to support the actual value of the fixed exchange rate.

Speculators, of course, observe this tension between the policy stance with respect to the exchange rate and the policy-makers' dissatisfaction with the high rate of unemployment. For that reason, speculators may anticipate that as soon as they launch a fierce attack on the fixed exchange rate in the forex market, there is a serious chance that the policy-makers will abandon the fixed exchange rate system and focus their policy entirely on achieving the economic goal of lower unemployment. The more so because to counter the attack could necessitate an interest-rate hike, which would be good for the exchange rate but bad for employment. So, a speculative attack could lead to a change in economic policy that justifies a new, higher equilibrium value of the exchange rate. But then in such circumstances the speculative attack is *self-fulfilling*: the successful attack yields its own justification, because the equilibrium value of the currency after the attack is lower than before due to a lowered interest rate, which would reduce unemployment.

Such a self-fulfilling model is called a *second-generation model* of speculative attacks. Compared with the previous first-generation models, the start of the speculative attack comes at an earlier point, occurring *before* the change of economic policy that both validates the attack and makes the attack successful. In first-generation models the success of the attack is a certainty, in the second-generation model success only comes if the attack is self-fulfilling – through bringing about the policy change after the attack that the speculators expect.

The experience of the Asian currency crisis in 1997 led to the emergence of what is sometimes called the *third-generation model* of speculative attacks. In fact, this model is a set of models combining (a part of) the next potential causes of a currency crisis, which were stressed in the analysis in retrospect of the origins of the Asian crisis:

1. *Moral hazard.* The crisis is due to an initial over-investment in the crisis country. The reason for this is that domestic firms, but also banks and foreign lenders, feel that the investments are, often only implicitly, insured by the government. If the insurance is real, an apparent soundness of fiscal policy prior to the crisis comes to be seen as an illusion after the onset of the crisis. This view may be sufficient to start capital flight.
2. *Financial fragility.* The crisis occurs through a liquidity squeeze, caused by panic of foreign and/or domestic lenders who cause a run on domestic financial intermediaries. The ensuing liquidity problem provokes intermediaries to liquidate assets prematurely against discount, which can make them insolvent. This cause considers a currency crisis to be a byproduct of a bank run.
3. *Balance sheet problems through mismatched exposures.* A bank and a corporation are vulnerable if liabilities are short term and/or in foreign currency, whereas assets are

longer term and/or in domestic currency. Then capital flight may start as a result of the fear that the short-term liabilities cannot be rolled over or the expectation that a devaluation blows up the domestic currency value of net foreign debt. An additional vulnerability is that in countries under pressure it is often difficult to figure out the extent of the foreign exposure. And international monetary reserves are often lower than reported (for example, a part might already be set aside for financing forward contracts).

One of the attempts to produce a mathematical model of the wide-ranging third-generation model is Krugman (1999), who combines causes (2) and (3).

18.3   The Mexican currency crisis, 1994–95

18.3.1   Previous history and growing imbalances

As we saw in Chapter 17, Mexico was always at the forefront of the debt problem, fluctuating between disaster and success. In 1994 Mexico suffered another serious setback: at the end of the year, the country faced a major currency crisis, which shook the foundations of the international financial system. A massive rescue operation, led by the USA in collaboration with the IMF, was necessary to avoid Mexico's financial collapse and to restore, to some extent, the confidence of the financial world. In essence, the situation was far less alarming than it had been in 1982. In 1993 the Mexican economy did not actually demonstrate any fundamental imbalances.

The process of adjustment to a stable economic situation following the outbreak of the debt crisis in August 1982 was not exempt from some vulnerable moments. Economic reforms started in Mexico in 1983 when a government-led policy of import substitution was renounced. Over the next few years, restrictions on international trade and capital movements were abolished, the role of the state was diminished, and the domestic financial sector was deregulated. In 1987 a new stabilization programme, the 'Pacto', was begun in an attempt to break inflation through wage and price regulations, as well as using a fixed exchange rate against the US dollar as an anchor for anti-inflationary policy. Fiscal deficits were eliminated and real interest rates became positive. Although many indicators suggested that there had been a successful transformation of the economy, others gave cause for concern. Large-scale restructuring temporarily reduced the supply potential of the Mexican economy. Employment declined and the level of real wages remained depressed. Export growth, although eventually vigorous, was initially weak, while there was a rise in the level of imports. In addition, there was a decline in the propensity to save. One underlying cause for this was the rapid growth in credit, despite the high real interest rates. This was a direct outcome of the deregulation of the financial sector.

In many respects there had been an encouraging economic situation in Mexico in the few years preceding the crisis (at the end of 1994). Between 1989 and 1994 the average level of annual economic growth was 3.1 per cent – quite high in regional terms. In 1993–94 the annual inflation rate was 5–8 per cent – the first single-digit inflation rates for around two decades. In addition, government finances were in good shape: there had been no fiscal deficits since 1991. In response, the ratio of government debt to GDP fell from 67 per cent in 1989 to just 30 per cent in 1993.

However, the Mexican economy also suffered from some hazardous imbalances.

1. Until March 1994 there was a massive capital inflow, as the result of the structural economic reforms, combined with trade and financial liberalization, and a lower level of

debt servicing. In response to this capital inflow, the current account deficit, expressed as a percentage of GDP, increased to 6.8 per cent in 1993 and 7.9 per cent in 1994, although the monetary reserves also increased during this period.

2. The domestic counterpart of this growing current account deficit were, according to the income identity – equation (14.4) – increased investments and decreased savings related to GDP. The ratio of savings to GDP dropped from 19 per cent in 1990 to only 15 per cent in 1994. The complement of the decline in the savings ratio was an increase in the ratio of consumption to GDP. This higher propensity to consume was financed largely by capital inflows. The imbalance created by increasing consumption, declining domestic savings, and the heavy reliance on capital inflows was reflected in substantial domestic price rises. These were the main channel for the real appreciation of the Mexican peso of more than 20 per cent between 1990 and 1994. A 10 per cent official devaluation of the peso against the dollar in March 1994 was helpful, but proved insufficient in limiting this peso overvaluation.

3. In this era of capital account liberalization, the Mexican banking sector was still fragile. The banking system transformed the inflow of short-term, dollar-denominated capital into longer-term peso loans for property and consumer loans in Mexico. This transformation process signifies that bank assets were generally held in longer-term peso loans, whereas the bank liabilities consisted mainly of short-term dollar deposits. This implied a maturity and currency transformation through the banking sector. Maturity transformation is a normal banking activity. But it is particularly hazardous if banks disregard significant coverage of the concomitant currency risk, as happened in Mexico.

4. Mexico endured a process of financial deepening; this is a development towards a mature domestic financial sector. The usual quantitative indicator for financial deepening is an increase of ratio of M_2 to GDP. In Mexico by the end of 1993 this ratio had been increased to some 33 per cent. In itself, financial deepening is positive, because it is an indicator of economic development: the higher the ratio, the more developed the country. But domestic money is also a potential source of speculation against the domestic currency, as the money holders can offer their money for exchange against foreign currencies.

The Mexican central bank sterilized the effect of capital inflows on the money supply by issuing short-term peso debt – the so-called Cetes. By the end of 1993 the amount of Cetes was already equal to the total amount of the central bank's international monetary reserves. And M_3 (that is, M_2 plus non-bank short-term securities, thus including Cetes) was much higher: six times the amount of these reserves. It is obvious that these financial assets available for exchange into foreign currency at short notice comprise a powerful amount of potentially speculative funds, which could prove very hazardous for the maintenance of a fixed exchange rate.

It is noteworthy that these four hazardous imbalances of the Mexican economy – massive capital inflows, currency overvaluation, the banks' currency mismatch, and financial deepening – were all the result of positive developments within the Mexican economy, such as economic-structural improvements, international liberalization, a fall in inflation, and economic development. An initial excessive surge of optimism and overblown expectations, the result not only of the structural changes in Mexico, but also of the passage of theNorth American Free Trade Agreement (NAFTA) law in the US Congress, and Mexico's admission to the Organization for Economic Co-operation and Development (OECD), had an effect on both the outbreak and the depth of the Mexican currency crisis. By themselves these need not be sufficient reasons for a currency crisis, but they can make an economy particularly susceptible to a crisis. At this point the occurrence of relatively insignificant shocks suffices. Once events that are relatively trivial in economic terms begin to undermine confidence in the country, large-scale speculation to the detriment of the country can result – as was the case for Mexico in 1994.

18.3.2 Direct causes of the Mexican currency crisis

These relatively insignificant shocks consisted in the 1994 Mexican case of some unexpected policy incidents. The first was an uprising of Indians in Chiapas province in January 1994. This was followed, two months later, by the assassination of the ruling party's presidential candidate, Colosia. These two events greatly increased the political risk premium demanded by foreign investors. Later in the same year, two other events further intensified the political risks. Following a series of political disappointments, the Deputy Attorney-General, Massieu, resigned in November. At the end of the year anti-government riots broke out again amongst the Indians in Chiapas.

The policy response to the weakened trust in investments in Mexico was inadequate.

1. Instead of the capital inflows – which stagnated – official reserves were used to finance the large current account deficit, selling US dollars against pesos.
2. Interest rates were not allowed to rise freely because of fears about bank bankruptcies. Hence, the central bank sterilized foreign-exchange market interventions, creating new pesos. But this added to speculative funds and, thus, to a prolonged need for the use of official reserves.
3. The average maturity of domestic government debt was shrunk deliberately. Reasons for this were the relative low short-run interest rate through a steeper yield curve as well as the confidence of the government that the reversal of international capital flows was only a transitory shock.
4. The government's aversion to interest rate rises and the private sector's perceived devaluation risk necessitated that the government should roll over Cetes (the short-run peso debt) into short-term dollar-indexed debt of the government, the so-called Tesobonos. At the end of September 1994 the amount of Tesobonos was already equal to the total amount of official reserves, so that, in fact, the *net* stock of official reserves became zero.

In the middle of 1994 the ratio of M_2/reserves had a value of 7, and this rose to 10 in November. In April, the foreign currency part of M_3 was already larger than the amount of official reserves. When M_3 'headed for Miami' – and so became flight capital – in late 1994, available official reserves proved unable to cover the country's liabilities and the currency crisis became a reality.

18.3.3 Type of crisis

The exchange rate as an inflation-stabilizing anchor was central to the adjustment policy pursued by Mexico from the end of the 1980s. The exchange-rate policy had the intention of devaluing the Mexican peso against the US dollar by less than the differential between the (higher) Mexican inflation and US inflation. Thus, moderating the imported inflation through moderated devaluations curbed the level of Mexican inflation.

In the first few years, this policy was successful. Inflation dropped from an annual rate of over 100 per cent at the start of the adjustment policy to 7 per cent at the beginning of 1994. High inflation is usually accompanied by a high nominal interest rate, and this was certainly the case in Mexico. Since the peso was not expected to devalue so sharply, investors could anticipate a higher return on their investments in Mexico than they received on their investments in the USA.

Through the uncovered interest rate parity (equation (12.2)), this prompted a substantial inflow of capital into Mexico, meaning that the value of the peso within the fluctuation band maintained with the dollar was consistently high. As a result, initially Mexico had no trouble in keeping to a moderate devaluation of the peso. However, this use of the exchange rate as an anchor to curb inflation has an inherent inconsistency, as is demonstrated by the Walters critique outlined in Section 18.2.2. The country's competitive position deteriorates, perhaps gradually yet unmistakably, causing a continuous worsening of the current account. This pattern was evident in Mexico in the years 1990–94. It gradually undermined confidence in the exchange-rate policy: after all, the current account balance is one of the fundamental forces behind the setting of the exchange rate. This was too much for the fragile exchange-rate anchor. Capital flight caused a shortage of Mexico's monetary reserves. In response, the fixed exchange rate for the peso was abandoned at the end of 1994.

This series of economic events made the Mexican currency crisis a prototype of the first-generation speculative attack model, supplemented with the balance sheet problem from the third-generation model. The peso went into free fall, depreciating rapidly by double-digit figures. In the Mexican stock market, shares lost on average more than half of their value.

18.4 The Asian crisis

18.4.1 The previous history of the crisis in figures

The summer of 1997 witnessed the eruption of the Asian currency crisis. The unofficial beginning of the crisis was a dramatic fall in the value of the Thai baht on 2 July. In the space of six weeks the currency crisis spread to the Philippines peso, the Malaysian ringgit and the Indonesian rupiah. In these circumstances, the objective of the IMF was clear: to do as much as possible to restrict the impact of the shocks. In the case of the Philippines an IMF programme was already in force. On 20 August an IMF-led support package of $20 billion for Thailand was approved, and this was followed, on 5 November, by the approval of an IMF-led support package of $40 billion for Indonesia. In the second half of November 1997 the Asian crisis deepened as the Korean won got into trouble – an event that led to the approval of a $57 billion support package in early December.

Since the early 1990s, the East Asian countries, Malaysia, the Philippines, and Thailand (see Table 18.1), had pursued a policy of keeping their currency values stable against the US dollar. During those years officially all of them were using basket pegs – with the value of the currency tied to a basket of other currencies – but the dollar weight in the baskets was so high that the basket peg was effectively tantamount to a dollar peg.

Table 18.1 shows that in the crisis year 1997 the East Asian currencies fell by large percentages in relation to the US dollar, but relative to other currencies (see the depreciations of the mark and the yen) the fall was more modest. At this time the currency crisis was, in effect, partly the result of a steeply rising dollar, something which was already ongoing from 1995. If we consider the combined currency depreciations over the two-year period 1996–97, the fall of the East Asian currencies relative to the mark and the yen is even smaller. The crisis then partly acquires the character of a 'catching-up' change. The total falls in the value of the ringgit and peso in the last two years are 'only' slightly more than double the depreciations of the mark and the yen.

Table 18.1 Exchange rates against the US dollar (end of year)

	1995	1996	1997	Last-year change (%)	Two-year change (%)
Indonesian rupiah	2308	2383	4650	95	101
Malaysian ringgit	2.54	2.53	3.89	54	53
Philippine peso	26.21	26.29	39.98	52	52
South Korean won	774.7	844.2	1695.0	101	119
Thai baht	25.19	25.61	47.25	84	88
Deutsche mark	1.424	1.530	1.755	15	23
Japanese yen	101.5	112.8	125.2	11	23

Note: For Germany and Japan the exchange rates are averages of the fourth quarter of the year involved.

Table 18.2 Change in the stock market index (in domestic currency, %, in 1997)

Indonesia	−37
Malaysia	−52
The Philippines	−41
South Korea	−42
Thailand	−55
The Netherlands	+40

The Asian crisis of 1997 appears to have been as much a stock market crisis as a currency crisis. Although in Table 18.2 the falls in the stock market indices of the East Asian countries appear at first glance to be somewhat smaller relative to the currency values, there is a larger drop relative to other countries. This can be explained largely by the fact that 1997 was a very good year for global stock exchanges; see, for example, the figure for the Netherlands in Table 18.2. Moreover, the composite stock price indexes of Thailand and South Korea had already experienced their end-of-year peaks in 1993 and 1994, respectively. Their total falls from these peak values to the end of 1997 amounted to more than 70 per cent.

In the mid-1990s it was still common to hear discussion of the East Asian 'economic miracle'. With the exception of the Philippines, the crisis countries had annual growth rates of more than 7 per cent (see Table 18.3). By 1996, a government-led slowdown in economic growth rates was perceivable in Korea and Thailand. Again with the exception of the Philippines, the level of inflation was moderate in the crisis countries. Moreover, the level of inflation was falling, if only slowly. Even if the level of inflation in these countries showed no alarming signs, they surpassed – sometimes substantially – the levels of inflation in the USA throughout the 1990s.

Table 18.4 shows that only South Korea had no real exchange-rate increase (or a worsening of competitiveness) as the result of a substantial nominal depreciation of the won. The Philippines experienced by far the largest deterioration in competitiveness. There the near fixed exchange rate, combined with still high inflation rates, created a large external friction. The high growth rates in the East Asian countries, and the associated high levels of import growth also contributed to the currency overvaluation. The current account deficits (see Table 18.3) were really too large in most of the crisis countries in 1996 – in view of a rough empirical rule of thumb that a deficit of more than 4.5 per cent of gross

Table 18.3 Growth, inflation, and current account deficits (%)

	Real GDP growth			Inflation			Current account deficit/GDP		
	1990–95	'96	'97	1990–95	'96	'97	1990–95	'96	'97
Indonesia	7.2	7.8	4.6	8.7	8.0	6.6	2.5	3.7	2.9
Malaysia	8.8	8.6	7.8	3.7	3.5	2.7	5.9	4.9	5.1
The Philippines	2.3	5.7	5.1	11.0	8.4	5.1	3.8	4.7	5.2
South Korea	7.8	7.1	5.5	6.6	4.9	4.4	1.2	4.8	1.9
Thailand	8.9	6.4	−0.4	5.0	5.8	5.6	6.7	8.1	2.0
USA				3.1	2.9	2.3			

Note: Annual changes. Inflation is the consumer price rise.

Table 18.4 Change in real exchange rates against the USA, 1992–96 (period total, %)

	Inflation differential	Nominal exchange rate change	Difference
Indonesia	39.0	22.2	16.8
Malaysia	7.4	−8.0	15.4
The Philippines	34.6	−4.3	38.9
South Korea[1]	14.4 (8.0)	19.2 (4.5)	−4.8 (4.5)
Thailand	11.4	0.4	11.0

Note: The formula that is used is $\Delta P/P - \Delta P^*/P^* - \Delta S/S$, with P domestic price level, P^* US price level, S the exchange rate in domestic currency price of the US dollar, and Δ is the first-difference sign. A negative nominal exchange-rate change indicates an appreciation of the domestic currency. A negative difference means an improvement of competitiveness of the country involved.
[1] The figures between brackets for South Korea relate to the years 1994–96.

domestic product (GDP) is considered to be unsustainable. Of course, it is important for that sustainability how the country uses this deficit. The imports of investment goods, for example, have better perspectives than the imports of consumer goods. Investment goods have a rate of return, which can be employed to finance the country's debt service.

In the years leading up to 1997, the current account deficits in the crisis countries seem to have been financed in full by inflows of private capital (see Table 18.5). In addition, private capital inflows were so much higher than current account deficits that there was an increase in the holdings of international reserves. Net official capital inflows were very small – a picture that was reversed in the crisis year. This led to the same pattern as we observed in previous crises: the private investors fled, and official investors felt it necessary to partly replace private flight capital.

18.4.2 Causes of the crisis

If one compares the economic fundamentals, the prelude to the Asian crisis exhibited smaller fundamental imbalances relative to those to the world debt crisis and the Mexican currency crisis. One of the serious Asian imbalances was deficits on the current account. The Thai current account deficit was much too large, but the current account

Table 18.5 Capital flows and reserves in Asia (in billion $; annual amounts)

	1990–95	1996	1997	1998
Net private inflows	33	81	−45	−69
Net official inflows	14	4	37	29
Net reserve increase	41	58	15	66

Note: Asia includes China, India, Indonesia, South Korea, Malaysia, the Philippines, Singapore, Taiwan and Thailand.

deficits in Malaysia, the Philippines, and South Korea were also too large, as seen in the previous sub-section. Moreover, the holdings of reserves in Korea were too small (with a value of only 2.3 months of imports – where three months is regarded as being an empirically critical lower limit), while for the Philippines the reserve holdings were only at the value of the critical limit. The most problematic fundamental imbalance was the size of the countries' debt service compared to their reserve holdings. Only Malaysia (69 per cent) had a manageable value for this ratio. For the other four countries the ratio was more than 100 per cent: in descending order, these were 294 per cent for Indonesia, 243 per cent for South Korea, 138 per cent for Thailand, and 137 per cent for the Philippines.

The key cause of the outbreak of the Asian currency crisis was a combination of serious current account deficits and large short-term debts plus interest payments relative to official reserves. These suggest that the region's currencies were overvalued. The East Asian overvaluation was not only in terms of the USA, but also in relation to the rest of the world. These imbalances could keep growing due to a prolonged financing opportunity. This was for two main reasons: the credible fixed exchange rate against the US dollar and a positive interest differential vis-à-vis the USA. The effectively fixed exchange rates gave borrowers a false sense of security. Throughout this period not only the attractively high interest rates in the East Asian countries, but also declining interest rates in the developed world made this financing attractive.

In the case of the Asian crisis these wrong fundamentals reflect that here the first-generation model of speculative attacks also seems to fit well. There were also some crisis-reinforcing features in the East Asian countries that suggest the relevance of the third-generation model of speculative attacks. Moral hazard based on the expectation that the government would eventually prevent domestic banks from failures furnished foreign investors with increased certainty about future repayments. Foreign capital was, to a large extent, invested over the short term, in particular in banks. They used the money to provide loans in domestic currency – an activity that increased the banks' foreign-currency exposure and exposed their balance sheet problems. From that perspective, it is unsurprising that in some of the East Asian countries stock market indices fell in the final years before the crisis.

Moreover, the domestic financial sector was fragile, as witnessed by the high percentage of non-performing bank loans (15–20 per cent as compared to around 1 per cent in, for example, the USA) and the excessive reliance on cross-border interbank funding. The actual rates of return on real-sector investments were low as the result of over-investments and an associated impending over-capacity in the industrial sector in those countries. Another consequence of this over-investment was a shift of investment towards real estate, causing speculative price bubbles in those assets.

18.4.3 Contagion

One new phenomenon that did emerge in the explanation of the Asian crisis is the idea of contagion, as the crisis spread from country to country throughout a region. This was evidenced by the speculative attacks on four currencies in the same area over the course of a few weeks. According to the current thinking about contagion, a currency crisis in one country may have a negative effect on the credibility of a fixed exchange rate in another country, through the following three main channels.

1. *Trade linkages*

   o The mutual trade flows transmit price and demand shocks from one country to another. A crisis in one country, A, has a negative effect on the level of production and imports of that country. Through that import decline there is a spillover effect, or a crisis incentive is passed on, to another country through its damaged exports.
   o The fall of the currency of country A as the result of the currency crisis reduces the relative competitiveness of country B. This results in the expectation of a larger trade deficit in B and, subsequently, an expected (competing) devaluation of the currency of country B. This is a huge stimulus for capital flight out of the country.

2. *Actual financial linkages*

   o A negative economic shock in country A will reduce its investments, including those of country A in country B. This will negatively affect the value of the currency of country B.
   o Often international investors are highly leveraged. This means that they have borrowed a substantial part of their investment funds. As the result of significant investment losses in crisis country A, highly leveraged investors are required to withdraw part of their investments from country B in order to be able to repay their loans. This withdrawal will be attended by currency depreciation in country B.

3. *Supposed financial linkages*

   o The financial world uses some developing countries as a financial risk benchmark for a group of similar countries. If country A is such a financial benchmark, then an unanticipated currency crisis in A, with the concomitant fall in currency value, will result in a higher risk premium for investments in the similar country B. This can easily lead to capital outflow from B and an ensuing fall in the value of its currency.
   o A wake-up call effect, or the presence of reputation externalities, means that a currency crisis in country A as a result of weak structural conditions and vulnerabilities (such as a fragile financial system) will cause the financial world to become aware of the fragility of country's B economy. This change in investment attitude can easily lead to a large capital outflow and a consequent currency crisis in country B.
   o The irrational behaviour of investors, such as panic and herding performance, after a crisis in country A can easily lead to the indiscriminate withdrawal of funds from similar countries, such as country B.

In practice, it is difficult to distinguish contagion from the presence of a common external shock that hits countries A and B simultaneously. One clear example of such a common shock in the Asian crisis was the worldwide increase in the value of the US dollar. It is as a consequence of this difficult distinction that empirically it is not yet plain what the size is of the contribution of contagion to the Asian crisis. (An attempt was made in Van Horen et al., 2006.) In view of the speed of contagion, the limited mutual economic relations, and the small size of these countries in the international financial system, in the Asian crisis the supposed financial linkages seem to have been the major vehicle for contagion.

18.4.4 Asian adjustment policies

As we saw in Section 18.4.1, shortly after the outbreak of the currency crises in Asia the countries involved reached agreements about an adjustment programme shored up by IMF credits. The only crisis country that preferred to follow its own course of action, without the help of the Fund, was Malaysia – however, in practice, the Malaysian adjustment programme differed little from those adopted by its neighbouring countries.

The outbreak of the crisis led to an immediate transition to floating exchange rates in the countries involved, with large depreciations of between 45 and 80 per cent. On the orders of the IMF, the programme countries at first pursued a very restrictive monetary policy with strong rises in the interest rate. The aim of this policy was to moderate exchange-rate rises – in effect, to prevent exchange-rate overshooting – in order to minimize the effect of a dearer dollar on both the additional burden of the dollar-debt service and the degree of insolvency of financial and non-financial corporations due to their net liabilities in dollars that had been built up in the years before the crisis.

The interest rate rise has its limits because a higher domestic interest rate leads to an additional danger for financial and corporate firms of non-performing on their bank debts. The higher the interest rate, the higher the debt service of the debtors – particularly in the case of rollover credits. Initially, the IMF used as another policy condition fiscal restraint – although as late as 1996, in the last pre-crisis year, all Asian crisis countries had (small) fiscal *surpluses*. The IMF saw this fiscal constraint as a useful contribution to the necessary reduction of the current account deficits (according to income identity (14.4)). Furthermore, the IMF was afraid that later government support for failing banks would absorb a lot of government income (IMF, 1998, p. 27).

But soon afterwards, in the first months of 1998, the IMF changed its stance in this respect, allowing countries to run up substantial fiscal deficits. The IMF's justification for this change in opinion was that at the start of the crisis one could not have anticipated that so many countries in the region would eventually be affected. These multifold fiscal restraints would have caused too much damage to the economic growth in the region. But it seems that an even important motivation for the IMF was that it was receptive to the criticism that it received on this policy condition.

The restructuring of the banking sector in the crisis countries also ranked high on the IMF agenda – as did structural transformations to increase efficiency, deepen the role of the private sector, and reinforce the countries' outward orientation (IMF, 1998, p. 27). The latter means the liberalization of international trade and capital flows (especially in South Korea, where it seems to have been included in the IMF conditions – as the result of US political pressure).

A year after the start of the Asian crisis Malaysia introduced, for a period of 12 months, restrictions on its capital outflow. After its unwillingness to use IMF loans (and, in so doing, to avoid the performance of IMF conditions), this was the second main disparity with the adjustment policy introduced in neighbouring countries. It is striking that it appears to be difficult to find salient differences between the recovery paths of Malaysia and its neighbours, bearing in mind the differences in the countries' economic objective values that were already in existence in the pre-crisis years.

The first positive signals of a successful adjustment were the substantial current account improvements observed in Indonesia, South Korea, and Thailand. By the end of 1997 their deficits had shrunk to less than 2.5 per cent of GDP, although this was mainly (but unsurprisingly) as the result of import reductions caused by negative economic growth. The fall in domestic production was strongest in 1998. In 1999 there was a rapid recovery of growth and the crisis belonged to the past.

18.5 Lessons from the crisis

18.5.1 Problem prevention

1. A strategy of rapid economic transformation and exchange-rate-based inflation stabilization usually creates capital inflow and, in this way, a combination of real currency appreciation and a substantial current account deficit. The latter makes the currency vulnerable to the loss of investor trust. Paradoxically, the danger of a crisis is largest just before the realization of the goal of low inflation. The explanation is, of course, that this is the point at which the deterioration of competitiveness and the concomitant current account deficit that has occurred year on year during the stabilization process will have reached their maximum values. It is common for currency speculators to become nervous about such a deficit – although well-invested current account deficits are sustainable as they are able to produce a yield that suffices to pay the debt service. But in spite of this, policy-makers should not rely on the sustainability of huge capital inflows, particularly not short-term capital.

2. In order to counteract the loss of foreign trust, the government could strive to achieve (small) fiscal surpluses or to fix to a real (rather than a nominal) exchange-rate target. In any case, policies should err on the side of caution. But this policy stance is no guarantee of preventing a currency crisis, as is demonstrated in the case of South Korea.

3. Financial fragility is a usual circumstance in emerging economies; it causes substantial vulnerability and restricts the central bank in raising interest rates, because the associated higher interest burden for bank debtors will increase the number of the banks' non-performing loans. Financial fragility is particularly threatening in combination with financial deepening. Financial deepening enlarges the holdings of private liquid assets relative to the size of domestic production. These assets can easily be exchanged for foreign currencies. In combination with a low level of official reserves and a pegged exchange rate, a bank run can therefore easily be converted into a currency crisis. A rumour of an imminent crisis is already a sufficient condition for this to happen.

4. A policy of reducing the maturity and switching to a foreign currency of denomination of government debt lowers the country's credibility in a pre-crisis situation and is, therefore, excessively risky. With a large share of short-run debt the government is largely defenceless if investors refuse to roll over their government bonds. In the case of Mexico, the government's issue of Tesobonos (de facto dollar-denominated bonds) further increased Mexico's level of vulnerability, as the government's liabilities could rise substantially in the event of devaluation.

5. A central bank should restrain forex intervention during a currency crisis. It is preferable to let the market first give indications about the new equilibrium value of the nominal exchange rate. Moreover, it is costly to replenish the holdings of official reserves, as the foreign currencies are likely to be available for repurchase after the crisis against much higher prices in domestic currency.

18.5.2 Policy lesson 1: apply the optimal order of liberalization

The liberalization policy that currency crisis countries pursued before the outbreak of the crisis has revealed a relatively new problem. Not only is the overall package of the liberalization policy components important to its success, it is also important to apply the optimal sequencing over time of applying those components. Applying them in the wrong sequence can wreck the liberalization policy. Liberalization packages include the liberalization of labour market, goods markets, and financial markets. The liberalization of the last two market types has implications for both domestic and international transactions. Liberalization policy is not only a one-sided abolition of restrictions for transactions. It may also include the adoption of rules of surveillance or a strong supervisor that imposes strict rules in respect of the role of a central bank as a supervisor of the behaviour of private banks. McKinnon (1973, 1982 and 1991) was a leading economist in this respect, but his optimal order view seems to have remained disregarded among policy-makers (including the IMF) until far into the 1990s.

The currency crises brought the optimal sequencing problem to the fore, as in both the Mexican and the Asian crises international capital flows were liberalized prior to the liberalization of domestic financial markets, including the application of good rules of governance. The fragile domestic financial system that resulted from this sequence of events proved to be a source of instability and risk under free international capital movements.

A coherent order of (market) liberalization begins with domestic economic stabilization. Only in a stabilized economy, with a moderate rate of inflation, will price incentives and a market process be able to work effectively. Economic stabilization implies the elimination of money overhang (if present), the reduction of the government's fiscal deficit – and, in particular, the reduction of money financing of this deficit – and the application of a generally restrictive monetary policy. This will bring about a substantial reduction in the level of inflation.

Preferably, the regulations in the domestic economy that prevent the realization of right prices of goods and services should be tackled before the cross-border goods and services transactions are liberalized. Right prices are a correct reflection of the production costs that lie behind them. The reverse sequence can cause international trade liberalization to foster a production specialization domestically that is adverse to the country's true comparative advantage. Once economic stabilization has been achieved, for that reason, it is time to liberalize the domestic goods and labour markets (including cuts in distorting subsidies). This means minimizing government interventions in these markets and a substantial movement towards perfect competition. There is an additional argument for this order, namely that the liberalization of the labour market and, to a lesser extent, goods markets are the longest-lasting liberalization processes, so these should be in place early in the liberalization order.

Before turning to the liberalization of the country's international transactions, it is useful to have a certain flexibility in the exchange rate, so that an overvaluation of the domestic currency can be reduced spontaneously. One serious option is a transition to a crawling peg, based on a published table of future devaluations at a slower pace than the expected increase in domestic inflation – but only if inflation is only moderate to prevent the problem included in point 1 of Section 18.5.1.

This stabilization and liberalization of the real side of the domestic economy is followed by the liberalization of the goods markets for international transactions through the elimination of trade barriers and other distorting measures, such as export subsidies. Only after these stabilization and domestic liberalization measures are in place is it possible to clearly identify the true efficient production sectors in the domestic economy, so that the domestic industries with a comparative advantage will be visible.

If the domestic financial sector is liberalized simultaneously with the country's international trade, domestic capital can flood into these efficient goods sectors – to the detriment of the obsolete sectors – resulting in the optimum allocation of domestic capital. The liberalization of the domestic financial markets means the abolition of financial repression, a development towards perfect competition, and the introduction of stringent supervision of the financial sector.

Following domestic financial liberalization, the domestic interest rate settles at its equilibrium level. Only then can international capital movements be liberalized, because from that point on it is clear how the country in question fits into the pattern of relative capital scarcity in the world. The issue of international capital liberalization should certainly not be addressed prematurely. In this optimum order of liberalization steps international capital flow liberalization should come last. Only if the domestic banking system is stable and sturdy, with an effective supervision system, can this step towards liberalization be taken with a sufficienct degree of security.

18.5.3 Policy lesson 2: apply restrictions on capital inflows only temporarily

Investors usually overreact to changes in economic circumstances. This is an important argument in reducing a country's exposure to the volatility of short-term international capital flows. Another important argument in favour of capital restriction is that it is a way out of the incompatible trinity of a fixed exchange rate, an autonomous national monetary policy, and free international capital flows. (See for a survey of costs and benefits of capital restrictions Section 12.6.) In other words, capital restriction allows the application of the first two features of this trinity.

If a country decides to use capital restrictions, a temporary restriction on capital inflows seems to be strongly preferable. It should be temporary in order to minimize leakages in the application of the restriction and thus to improve effectiveness of the restriction. Such leakage tends to increase with the duration of the restriction because investors have the time to discover ways around the restriction. Similarly it should also be imposed only on capital *in*flows in order to prevent foreign investors being deterred for a long time. If free capital exports are guaranteed, foreign investors will restart their capital inflows as soon as 'the door is open again'.

There are several potential measures, three of which will be discussed here. These have been chosen either because of the intensive attention for or the success in practice of the measure.

1. The levy of a so-called *Tobin tax*, named after the economist James Tobin. This is a low tax rate of, say, 1 per cent, that is to be imposed on each transaction on the foreign-exchange market. It has often been proposed from different sides, ranging from the French president to anti-globalist protestors. A Tobin tax would press hard on short-term capital, but would have hardly any effect on long-term capital. The explanation is that a small one-off percentage of the invested amount is only a very small share of total returns on an investment for many years. The problem with the application of a Tobin tax is that to prevent avoidance application must be, in principle, worldwide. This means that it should be accepted by the governments of every country that has a substantial foreign-exchange market. It is very likely that in practice there will be free rider countries, which refuse to apply the Tobin tax and which can easily attract the international capital flows for currency conversion to their foreign-exchange markets. An ideal working – without leakages – of the tax is desirable, but not necessary. It is

already an improvement when the tax 'throws sand in the wheels' of the efficient – but very volatile – international capital markets.

2. The use of *a dual exchange rate*. A dual foreign-exchange market consists of two foreign-exchange markets that are kept strictly separate: a commercial and a financial market, each with its own exchange rate. The commercial rate is fixed and only available for currency exchange to pay for current account transactions; the fixed rate is assumed to foster international trade as the rate is insensitive to the volatile capital flows. Only the financial rate is available for international capital flows; this rate is flexible with the aim of checking speculative capital flows, but other capital flows might also be damaged. Of course, there is a serious chance of leakages between the two markets. In order for the measure to be effective, however, it is not necessary that each leakage is banned. The dual exchange market has been successfully applied by Belgium over almost four decades until 1990.

3. *Unremunerated reserve requirement* on foreign loans. The experience of Chile in the 1990s with this restriction on capital inflows is very promising for other emerging countries with sound financial systems. In the early 1990s Chile experienced a surge in capital inflows. When it attempted to stabilize its competitiveness, these inflows hindered its tight monetary policy. In 1991, the country resolved the policy dilemma of the incompatible trinity by imposing a tax on capital inflows. This was made up of 30 per cent of non-equity capital inflows that had to be deposited without interest at the central bank for a period of one year. This unremunerated reserve requirement on foreign loans was designed to discourage Chileans from short-term borrowing abroad, without substantially affecting long-term foreign investment inflows. The reason for this outcome is that the fixed holding period implied that the financial burden diminished with the maturity of the investment. Empirical evidence seems to give some support to this intended outcome of reducing short-term external debt without reducing the total amount of capital inflows (see, for example, *The Economist* (1998a), p. 100, and IMF (1999)). Soon after the Asian crisis Chile abolished its capital controls, as they had become redundant.

18.5.4 Policy lesson 3: apply an exchange-rate anchor only temporarily

An exchange-rate anchor for a period of, say, only two years may prevent the unavoidable bad outcome that the Walters critique predicts for countries that have – at the start of the anchor period – a much higher inflation rate than the anchor country. A temporary anchoring provides an opportunity to correct the worsened competitiveness position in time, at the end of the anchor period. The problem with this solution is, of course, the internal inconsistency that arises as a result. If it is known beforehand that the anchor period is only temporary, this knowledge will add to the country's inflation rigidity through higher inflation expectations and will therefore apply additional pressure to the collapse of the anchor policy. So, from the perspective of the policy-makers, the best policy is to try to convince the private sector that the anchoring is permanent – but to cheat as soon as the domestic inflation has become reasonably low. After having stabilized the level of inflation, the country will immediately introduce a more flexible exchange rate.

A less extreme alternative is to use a wider fluctuation band for the anchored exchange rate. This feature will increase the uncertainty of profits from speculation, as the domestic currency may fall substantially over a very short time period, while staying within the band. This possible loss on the domestic currency can compensate a significant part of the interest rate advantage for inward investments in the developing country.

A currency board system and full dollarization seem to be offer interesting alternatives for inflation-stabilization policy on the opposite side of the spectrum of exchange-rate regimes. This side will be the subject of chapter 19.

18.5.5 Lessons for the IMF

Criticism of the role of the IMF during the currency crises of the 1990s, and particularly during the Asian crisis, focuses on: (1) the Fund's application of its traditional mix of restrictive fiscal policy and money tightening that were successful in the past; and (2) the Fund's insistence on fundamental changes in economic and institutional structures as a condition for receiving IMF credits (see Feldstein, 1998).

The response of the IMF to the critique regarding restrictive fiscal policy was given in Section 18.4.4. With respect to the condition of monetary tightening the IMF's reply was that the much higher interest rates produced by this policy will have prevented excessive capital flight, and thus curbed the fall in the value of the Asian currencies. Naturally, a very high interest rate is bad for the economy – particularly if the longer-term rate is affected upwardly – but so is a steep fall of the currency, because then the liabilities of government and companies, including banks, denominated in dollars will increase in value expressed in the domestic currency (Fisher, 1998, p. 23). For that reason, according to the IMF, there is a trade-off between an increase in interest rates and currency depreciation, so that some combination of the two should give an optimum.

The second point of critiques is more fundamental. Stanley Fischer, the deputy managing director of the IMF in the days of the Asian crisis, stated that financial and corporate inefficiencies were at the core of the Asian crisis, meaning that delays in economic restructuring would worsen banking problems (Fischer, 1998, p. 23). It may be countered that during the Asian 'economic miracle' period these inefficiencies were already present, apparently without any problem, and that restructuring during a crisis may be much more painful than doing so in a later, calmer period.

Apparently, the IMF accepted the critique of its conditions on economic and institutional structures, because in 2000 IMF management issued an Interim Guidance Note on Streamlining Structural Conditionality. This note states that the IMF would streamline its conditions, splitting its traditional conditions into two distinct groups: reform conditions that are critical to achieving the macroeconomic objectives that lie within the IMF's core areas of responsibility, and conditions that are not. Only the first group will be maintained in the IMF conditionality. The second group may be couched in the form of IMF advice (Khan and Sharma, 2002). Moreover, the IMF would refine its conditionality to achieve greater country ownership, reflecting a firm commitment from the programme country's government, and encouraging countries to design 'homegrown' programmes.

Among the additional features of the new conditionality are a stricter pre-selection of the countries considered eligible to borrow from the IMF – compensating in part for the streamlining of conditions; greater flexibility in the timing of measures to fulfil the conditions; and an increased stress on outcome of the adjustment policy, rather than on policy measures, as the basis of the IMF's disbursing credits.

Significantly, the intention of streamlining the conditions has been put into practice: there has been a decrease in the number of conditions per IMF country programme, while the conditions are now more focused on the core area of the IMF: macroeconomic adjustment. Nowadays outcome-based conditions are used successfully, but only for quantitative conditions, such as the fiscal deficit and the holding of international reserves, which are under strict supervision of the policy-makers.

18.6 Summary

1. In currency crisis theories two basic ideas have been advanced: (i) the wrong economic fundamentals for the equilibrium value of the exchange rate; and (ii) self-fulfilling currency crises that arise from the assessment of currency speculators of the existence of a political tension between economic objectives. In essence, the difference between the two consists of the moment of a change in economic policy that is detrimental for the exchange-rate value. In the basic idea (i) this change has already been attained; (ii) speculators expect this change in the near future, particularly, if decisively sustained by their active speculation. This view might make this speculation self-fulfilling.

2. As discussed in the literature, among the wrong economic fundamentals are: (i) a money-financed fiscal policy that is too expansive for the ruling exchange-rate value; and (ii) an anti-inflationary policy based on the rigid use of an exchange-rate anchor. The latter gave rise to the so-called Walters critique on anti-inflationary policy through pegging the exchange rate to the currency of an inflation-shy country, which predicts in that event a successful speculative attack.

3. In addition to the theoretical approaches of a speculative attack on a currency in (1) and (2), which are labelled the first- and second-generation models of speculative attacks, the vague outline of a third-generation model has been in existence since the Asian currency crisis of the late 1990s. This model stresses the relevance for the start of an attack of the incidence of a moral hazard problem, financial fragility, and balance sheet problems.

4. Three hazardous imbalances of the Mexican economy before the currency crisis of 1994 – massive capital inflows, currency overvaluation, and financial deepening – all had their origins in positive developments in the Mexican economy, including economic-structural improvements, international liberalization, falls in inflation, and a promising level of economic development. These imbalances point to the Walters critique as the explanation of the Mexican crisis of 1994. Contributions to the timing and depth of the Mexican currency crisis came from private banks' currency mismatch, the government's shortening of the maturity of government debt, the conversion of a large part of government bonds into short-term dollar-indexed government liabilities (the so-called Tesobonos), and an initial excessive surge of optimism and overblown expectations in the private sector.

5. The Asian crisis of 1997 appears to have been as much a stock market crisis as a currency crisis. The key cause of the onset of the Asian currency crisis was the combination of serious current account deficits and large short-term debts plus interest payments relative to official reserves. This suggests that the currencies were overvalued. The credible fixed exchange rate against the US dollar and a positive interest differential vis-à-vis the USA caused the continued growth of these imbalances. These features indicate that this crisis also exhibits the elements of the Walters critique. In East Asia in 1997 moral hazard, the fragility of the domestic financial sector, and balance sheet mismatches were considered to be factors that intensified the crisis.

6. One new phenomenon that emerged strongly in the explanation of the Asian crisis is contagion. As four Southeast Asian currencies were attacked by currency speculators in a time span of just a few weeks, this prominent place in the Asian crisis for contagion is unsurprising. Contagion occurs through either trade linkages or financial linkages. In the latter case one can distinguish between actual and supposed linkages.

7. It is possible to identify three economic policy lessons that can be derived from the experience of the Asian crisis: apply the optimum order of liberalization, apply only a temporary restriction on capital inflows, and apply a temporary exchange-rate anchor.

8. In the aftermath of the Asian crisis, and in response to public criticism, the IMF has streamlined the number of performance criteria to confine them to macroeconomic variables, and to allow the IMF to remain outside the political domain as much as possible.

Questions

1. As we saw in Section 18.4.4, on the orders of the IMF, the programme countries in the Asian countries at first pursued a very restrictive monetary policy with strong rises in the interest rate. Through its experience with this crisis, the IMF has streamlined its policy conditions. Do you think that the obligatory interest rate rise would not have been part of the conditions if the streamlining would have occurred before the Asian crisis?

2. International capital liberalization of capital-account liberalization could be split up in sub-categories. The Economist (1998b) proposes to distinguish openness to international capital flows and openness to international financial competition. The latter means openness to activities of foreign financial firms, such as banks. Usually, one discusses only the former. What is the advantage of the second form of financial openness and what could be the optimal position in the sequence of liberalization?

3. The sub-category openness to international capital flows could be sub-divided further, distinguishing the different types of capital lows: foreign direct investment, portfolio investment and short-term capital flows. Is there also a defence for a mutual optimal order of liberalization for these three capital flows?

4. The experience of the Belgian dual exchange market (see Section 18.5.3) shows that the difference between the two exchange rates never becomes substantial, say more than 10 per cent. In Belgium there was a commercial rate for current-account transactions and a financial rate for financial account transactions. What, do you think, was the impediment for the difference in the two exchange rates in the dual system?

CHAPTER 19

Irrevocably Fixed Exchange Rates: Recent Experiences

19.1 Introduction

In 1973 the worldwide system of adjustably pegged exchange rates ended when the exchange-rate system agreed at Bretton Woods in 1944 was shattered. The world's major currencies have been floating since this time. However, around the world there are still several 'islands' of countries where variations of fixed exchange-rate regimes have been maintained. In effect, these fixed exchange rates were intermediate regimes, such as adjustable pegs and crawling pegs. The world debt crisis of the 1980s and the currency crises of the 1990s occurred in countries with such regimes. Through these disappointing experiences it is not surprising that the so-called bipolar view, that for financially open emerging economies these intermediate regimes are prone to crises and that only extreme variants of fixed and floating exchange rates might be crisis-free, received broad support in the fallout from the Asian crisis of 1997. Weaker versions of fixed exchange rates are deemed to offer speculators a one-way bet to profit. If a currency is considered weak, monetary authorities will either succeed in defending the exchange rate (with no change in the rate) or fail (and the rate will change substantially in the expected direction). This is a bifurcation in which speculators will suffer no losses, but may achieve substantial profits.

This chapter analyses a number of attempts since 1990 to implement extreme variants of fixed exchange rates and considers the feasibility of each variation. Each scheme is closely connected to the concept of monetary integration, which can be interpreted as either a state or a process. As a state, *monetary integration* is the stage at which the countries concerned have irrevocably fixed mutual exchange rates (without fluctuation margins) for their freely convertible currencies. Generally, these countries have abolished any restrictions on mutual capital movements. If countries have tied their currencies together in this way, then they may as well opt to take the next step and achieve full monetary integration, or a monetary union, through the adoption of a common currency and the absence of mutual capital restrictions. As a process, monetary integration expresses the movement of countries in the direction of monetary integration – without necessarily wishing to achieve this final stage.

Variation in the nature of monetary integration also arises from geographical bounds. Monetary integration could be virtually worldwide, as with the exchange-rate system of Bretton Woods. Since 1973 there has been only regional monetary integration, a situation in which monetary integration is confined to a smaller group of (commonly neighbouring) countries.

By far the best-known case of regional monetary integration is the current European Economic and Monetary Union (EMU) consisting of many member countries of the European Union (EU). In this case the addition 'economic union' refers to the concomitant real integration (that is, the free cross-border movements of goods, services, and production factors) and the coordination and integration of aspects of economic policy (to the extent that is necessary for the efficient operation of the real and monetary integration). The description of that system takes up much of this chapter (Section 19.5).

Another interesting case can be found in the Franc Zone in Africa, involving a large number of former French colonies, in which the common currency had a fixed exchange rate with the French franc and then – from 1999 – with the euro. This case is of particular interest because, in contrast to the EU, it relates to a group of developing countries. This is discussed in some detail in Section 19.3. Section 19.4 then focuses on two forms of irrevocably fixed exchange rates that have been applied recently by individual countries with the conscious purpose of avoiding currency crises. Specifically, we look at the introduction of a currency board, as applied by Argentina between 1991 and 2002, and the phenomenon of dollarization, which Ecuador applies since 2000.

The question of whether or not, for a particular type of country, the maintenance of genuinely fixed exchange rates is relevant is the subject matter of the theory of optimum currency areas. This sets out criteria for examining whether it benefits the economic welfare of the set of participating countries if they have mutually irrevocably fixed exchange rates. We shall start this chapter in Section 19.2 with an explanation of this theory.

19.2 The theory of optimum currency areas

In view of the successful attempts to achieve a monetary union in Europe and Africa, it seems obvious that this form of cooperation is advantageous to the countries involved. Theoretical support for this hypothesis is not unequivocal, however. The theory of optimum currency areas provides the theoretical foundation for a monetary union. It constitutes a textbook example of a cost–benefit analysis – the underlying principle of economic science.

The benefits of participation in a monetary union are considered to be the known advantages of a fixed exchange-rate system. In the case of regional monetary integration, of course, the advantages are rather more limited in scope than in a global system, because they extend only to the geographical boundaries of the area covered by the monetary integration. The establishment of a monetary union has the following benefits for the participating countries:

o The removal of exchange-rate risk in transactions within the union.
o The elimination of currency conversion costs in transactions within the union.
o The enlargement of the geographical area with a single unit of account; the existence of such an accounting unit in an extended area will cause markets in that area to become more transparent.
o The increased liquidity of the foreign-exchange market and also of the markets in currency derivatives. A liquid market means that there is a high volume of trading. The advantage is that transactions can be concluded at all times and without affecting the

market price because of the large size of the market. Increased liquidity is brought about by the markets for the national currencies of the participating countries being combined into a single market for the common currency.

○ In the event of the alternative situation of a national anchor currency: the possibility of using the liquid financial markets of the anchor currency. This held true for the French franc as the anchor currency for the African countries in the Franc Zone. As a result of the fixed link with the French franc, the currency risk in those countries could adequately be covered on the French financial markets until 1999. Since 1999, with the establishment of the link of the Franc Zone to the euro, this coverage is even extended to the financial markets across the whole of the Euro Zone. This possibility prevents the need to develop own forward markets.

○ The removal of the possibility of speculative capital movements within the monetary union. If separate national currencies no longer exist in the union, there can no longer be any capital flight from one national currency to another.

○ A reduced need for international monetary reserves. These reserves are no longer required to finance payment imbalances within the monetary union area.

○ The institutions of the monetary union can make a substantial contribution to a member country's anti-inflation policy. This is particularly beneficial for countries that have had difficulties in achieving low inflation through their own policies, often because they are regarded as being inflation-prone. The institutions of the monetary union foster the credibility of anti-inflationary policy if the union's anchor country has an established reputation as a low-inflation country and the union's institutions include an independent central bank, which works transparently and has a policy focus on price stability.

○ For any country that joins the union, fiscal policy becomes more effective. This follows from what we learnt in Section 14.7, that national fiscal policy is ineffective under floating rates, but effective if exchange rates are fixed.

By contrast, there are only two drawbacks to membership of a monetary union, namely: (i) the loss of national control in monetary policy, because it is transferred to the central bank; and (ii) the loss of the exchange rate as a national instrument of economic adjustment. So, there are clearly more advantages than disadvantages to participating in a monetary union. However, this does not, of course, tell us anything about the eventual outcome of the process of weighing up the costs and benefits of a *particular* monetary union – a single disadvantage may be more important than numerous advantages.

The theory of optimum currency areas contains several criteria to assess whether or not it is worthwhile a country joining a geographically delimited monetary union. All of these criteria focus on the disadvantage side of membership of the union. The advantages are, implicitly, accepted as a fact. (This is not an entirely correct approach, because the *sizes* of the advantages are not fixed, but will in fact depend upon the specific size and country composition of the area of the monetary union.)

The loss of monetary policy as a national instrument is only a cost factor if the country in question faces country-specific (or idiosyncratic) economic shocks or has a business cycle that is out of step with that of the other union members. Only in such circumstances will the country need to retain national monetary policy as an instrument to redress the country-specific developments. If the business cycle is synchronized throughout the monetary union, then the nature of the centralized monetary policy required to compensate for it will probably not differ greatly from that of the desired national monetary policy.

Each of the criteria for assessing the costs of joining a monetary union constitutes a response to the loss of the exchange-rate instrument for an individual country. So long as all countries of the union suffer from the same economic disturbance, then an exchange-rate change of the common currency against currencies outside the union is sufficient for adjustment to counteract the effects of the disturbance (although even then one country may need a larger exchange-rate change than another). In that situation the absence of a country's individual exchange rate per country is not a problem. But in the case of a country-specific shock it is, as is shown by the following example. Assume that two countries A and B together constitute a monetary union and that there is full employment in both countries. There then occurs a shift of demand for goods produced by country A to goods produced by country B. This demand shift creates unemployment in country A and a labour shortage in country B. Now the countries lack the exchange rate as an adjustment instrument. Devaluation of A's currency against the currency of B – through the associated effects on competitiveness – could resolve the labour market problems in the two countries.

The absence of a mutual exchange-rate adjustment is still not a cost item so long as the wages and prices in both countries are flexible. An appropriate wage and price moderation in country A and wage and price rise in country B can also bring about the desired changes in their relative competitive positions and so restore the full employment equilibrium in both countries. However, if wages and prices are rigid, then an adjustment problem occurs.

However, if there is a high degree of labour mobility between the two countries, the damage is not too great. The demand shock will then be an incentive for labour to move from country A to country B, and full employment is thus restored through supply adjustments on the labour market. The only long-term problem allied with this adjustment may be that the population size in the two countries of the monetary union becomes an issue. An exodus from one country to another may be undesirable – for example, because of the danger of the depopulation of specific parts of a country or wider adverse effects on the economic structure.

This description of the scope for adjustment in an economy without using the exchange-rate instrument brings us to the first two criteria for joining a monetary union according to the theory of optimum currency areas. Combined, these two criteria run as follows: the greater the country's wage and price flexibility or labour mobility with the member countries of the union, the more incentive there is to join the monetary union. Clearly, the two characteristics are complementary: wage and price flexibility together with high labour mobility mitigates the objections to joining a monetary union even more.

The extent of diversification of the economy's production and export – the third criterion – also has a positive effect on minimizing the costs of joining a monetary union. The argument is that economic shocks to an economy are often either product- or sector-based. In a highly diversified economy, a disturbance of the market for one product will have relatively little impact on the entire economy, including the international trade of the country concerned. Often it will be compensated in part by simultaneous, opposite developments in the country's other products. The instrument of exchange-rate adjustment is in such a case therefore less necessary than if exports are heavily concentrated on a few products.

A fourth criterion concerns the similarities between the economic structures of the partner countries in the monetary union. The more similar the production structures in the two countries, the more similar will be the impact of an economic shock on the countries concerned. They will then all have greater need for the same adjustment to the exchange rate, which can readily and effectively be carried out on the union level.

A fifth criterion states that monetary integration is more worthwhile the more advanced the integration or centralization of public spending within the union. The reason for this is that in such circumstances countries hit by an adverse economic shock can be compensated financially by transfer payments from other union countries. Take our previous example of the shift in demand for goods of A to those of B. As a result of higher production, inhabitants of country B pay more taxes which then – through transfer payments at the level of the union – end up as unemployment benefits in country A. An exchange-rate adjustment on the national level then becomes less urgent.

A sixth criterion is that monetary integration is more attractive the more similar the inflation rates in the intended partner countries. This idea is based on the (implicit) assumption that the equilibrium value of the real exchange rate is more or less constant. The more equal the inflation rates in the individual countries, the more constant the nominal exchange rate can be – and the less relevant an exchange-rate change is for the economies concerned. In that case the exchange rate is irrelevant as an adjustment instrument.

A seventh, and final criterion – and one that is widely in use – is whether or not the country that contemplates a monetary union membership has an open economy in terms of international trade. The basic idea is that an exchange-rate adjustment in an open economy will have a greater impact on wages and prices, because devaluation leads to a lot of imported inflation. The more open the economy, the greater the impact. The wage/price spiral that follows then pushes the country's inflation rate to an even higher level. This spiral will be intense in open economies, because people there are fully aware of the decline of real wages through currency devaluation. In this way, in an open economy, much of the improvement in competitiveness gained by devaluation is lost. The exchange rate is therefore not particularly effective as an instrument of international payments adjustment in an open economy, meaning that it can be abandoned at relatively little cost.

In principle, the plans for joining a monetary union can be assessed in economic terms on the basis of the above summary of the costs and benefits of the membership of a monetary union. This theory of optimum currency areas is difficult to apply in practice, however. The seven criteria lack benchmark values of good and bad; only the right directions for a beneficial monetary union have been identified. After the 1990s, the theory was often applied to the question whether it would be advantageously for specific Central and Eastern European countries if they would join the EMU or Euro Zone.

The usefulness of forming a monetary union can also be judged retrospectively, if the monetary union is already operational. This approach also has a weakness, because it is unknown how the countries involved in the monetary integration would have developed economically if they had not joined the union. Despite that, this is the way in which we will use this theory in assessing existing monetary unions to be analysed in the following sections.

19.3 The Franc Zone

Many countries maintain fixed exchange rates as a deliberate policy. At present, the US dollar and the euro are the primary currencies against which exchange rates are fixed, although in the past the pound sterling, the French franc and the SDR (see Section 16.4) have also been used in some instances. This fixing is usually carried out unilaterally: it does not require the country of the anchor currency to play an active role. The distinctive feature of the monetary integration that has occurred in the EU is that the countries have deliberately maintained fixed exchange rates within the group. Africa is the only other place in the world where we see anything similar: the Franc Zone.

The Franc Zone, involving a system of mutually fixed exchange rates, includes 14 Sub-Saharan African countries, along with the Comoros Islands and France. Since 12 of the 14 African countries are former French colonies, it was unsurprising that the French franc became the initial peg for this exchange-rate system. Following the changeover to the euro, on 1 January 1999, the system's peg was changed to the euro. The 14 African countries are divided into two groups – one of eight and one of six countries – each with a joint central bank and a common currency, thus comprising two distinct monetary unions.

The group of eight countries comprises the West African countries: Benin, Burkina Faso, Ivory Coast, Guinea-Bissau (a former Portuguese colony), Mali, Niger, Senegal, and Togo, who have banded themselves together as the West African Economic and Monetary Union (WAEMU). The full name of their currency is 'franc de la Communauté financière d'Afrique', hereafter the CFA franc. Export from these WAEMU countries is concentrated in a few primary commodities, making them highly vulnerable to economic shocks. The share of the two main commodities in total exports, cotton and cacao, averaged 50 per cent in 1994–98.

The second group consists of six Central African countries: Cameroon, the Central African Republic, Chad, Congo, Equatorial Guinea (a former Spanish colony), and Gabon. Together, they form the Central African Economic and Monetary Community (CAEMC) and their common currency is known as the 'franc de la Coopération financière en Afrique centrale', again abbreviated to CFA franc. The CAECM is a full-fledged oil economy: five of the six members are oil-exporting countries, with oil accounting for 75 per cent of total exports within the group. Although the currencies in the two country groups have the same name and value, coins and banknotes of the one group are not accepted as unit of exchange in the other group.

The CFA franc was created just after the Second World War, in December 1945. Then CFA stood for 'Colonies françaises d'Afrique' (French colonies of Africa). This CFA franc had a fixed exchange rate versus the French franc. It was changed only once, in 1948, following a French franc devaluation against the US dollar. The integration activities within these groups began just after the independence of the former French colonies at the beginning of 1960. Since this date the CFA has stood for 'Communauté Financière Africaine' (the African Financial Community). Between the two African country groups of the Franc Zone the exchange rate has remained constant. With respect to France's currency it was only in January 1994 that the first and only adjustment took place: the exchange rate went up from 50 to 100 CFA francs to the French franc, so that the CFA francs were devalued by 50 per cent against the French franc. (The price of CFA 1 changed from 0.02 to 0.01 French franc, so that the percentage change amounted to $(0.01–0.02)/0.02 \times 100$ per cent $= -50$ per cent.)

The structure of the link between the CFA francs, the Comorian franc, and the French franc is based on a so-called operating account that each of the two African central banks and also the Central Bank of the Comoros hold with the French Treasury. These accounts are similar to overnight deposits. The three central banks keep a mandatory 65 per cent of the foreign-exchange reserves in these accounts, with interest paid on the deposits. In special circumstances, the account holders can go into the red, in which case France charges interest. Over the years a number of preventive measures have been established to avert lasting overdrafts on these accounts. In return, the French Treasury guarantees unlimited currency convertibility and international capital movements with France are free of charge.

If a central bank's balance falls below a specified amount it has to restrict its levels of lending. The coverage ratio of base money by external assets has a mandatory minimum threshold of 20 per cent. The African central banks are also subject to an upper limit on the monetary financing of budget deficits: they may finance up to a maximum of 20 per cent of the previous year's government revenue in that way. Until 2000, such a degree of financial discipline in developing countries has been particularly rare. In order to strengthen the levels of budgetary discipline, the monetary authorities of the African countries agreed in principle to the phasing-out of direct advances from central banks to governments. The implementation of this policy began in 2003.

Up to the mid-1980s, the economic effects of the Franc Zone for its African members were correspondingly good. Between 1970 and 1984 their inflation rates averaged 10 per cent and the average annual growth of the gross domestic product (GDP) was 4 per cent. By way of comparison, the corresponding figures for countries surrounding the area were 18 and 2.5 per cent. A clear benefit for the African members of the Franc Zone is the discipline of the anchor currency, which has resulted in the maintenance of relatively low inflation.

However, from the mid-1980s onwards there had been a dramatic deterioration in the economic situation within the Franc Zone. The principal reason has been a significant deterioration in the terms of trade of the African members, the result of a slump in the world market price of many of their primary exports. Between 1985 and 1992 their terms of trade deteriorated by more than 40 per cent – although the exact impact on individual countries was subject to considerable variation. Another problem was that during the last half of the 1980s the value of the dollar fell sharply against a number of other currencies, including the French franc. This caused the CFA franc to appreciate substantially against the US dollar, which contributed to a further deterioration in the terms of trade. This requires a clarification. The countries' exportables are mainly commodities with prices in US dollars set on the world markets. Their importables are much more diverse with more price differentiation for the individual trading countries. This means that due to the appreciation of the CFA franc, with the CFA franc as the denominator the countries' export goods fell in price (*viz.* equal to the appreciation) more than the fall in price of their imported goods.

The rigid exchange rate in the Franc Zone against a European currency implants for the African member countries the danger of a deteriorating competitiveness unconnected to their balance-of-payments situation and of an associated growing current account deficit. Apart from a negative price effect, resulting from a fall in the terms of trade, this appreciation also reduced the volume of exports and increased the volume of imports of African countries of the Franc Zone. All in all, three negative effects on their trade balances.

For several years, a devaluation of the CFA franc appeared increasingly likely. Under free international movements of capital, a devaluation expectation naturally led to a flight of capital, which placed even greater strains on the position of the CFA franc. The devaluation of the CFA franc against the French franc in January 1994 was therefore inevitable. Given the seriousness of the economic upheavals, the size of the devaluation (50 per cent) did not seem particularly large.

The devaluation was accompanied by ambitious stabilization and structural adjustment programmes. As a result, the newly competitive economies initially experienced strong economic expansion, a more balanced macroeconomic performance, and progress in structural economic transformation. After 1998 the strong economic momentum brought about by the devaluation was gradually dissipated, with weaker output growth and improvements in fiscal and external deficits reversed in several countries.

In more recent years, there is again clear evidence of an erosion in the level of the countries' competitiveness. Furthermore, structural policies, particularly those aiming to increase labour productivity and lower production costs, have proved disappointing (Van den Boogaerde and Tsangarides, 2005). One weak point is the large current account deficit of CAEMC.

Following the introduction of the euro on 1 January 1999, the euro was substituted for the French franc as the anchor currency for the CFA franc. Via the fixed exchange rate of 100 CFA franc per unit of French franc, the fixed exchange rate against the euro became 0.1524 euro for 100 CFA franc.

Mutual trade in the countries of the CFA Franc Zone is estimated to be less than 10 per cent of their total exports; by contrast, in the EU the figure is well above 50 per cent.

The advantages of eliminating exchange-rate risk and conversion costs are very much less significant in Africa than they are in the EU. However, if we consider that, through its link with the French franc, the African countries can also regard the EU area as part of their area of fixed exchange rates, then the balance of this argument changes dramatically. This larger area is also the focus of over half the trade of the countries in the Franc Zone. Moreover, the African countries gain an enormous advantage from monetary integration because of the resulting opportunity to cover their international risks on the French franc market and, since 1999, on the euro financial markets.

In Europe, wages and prices are rather rigid while the mobility of labour is relatively low – both phenomena are disadvantages for a monetary union. In this respect, Africa is in a better position. For example, Ivorian censuses in 1988 and 1996 estimated that at least 25 per cent of the resident population had originated in other WAEMU countries (Van den Boogaerde and Tsangarides, 2005, p. 9). On the other hand, in respect of the diversification of the national economy and the similarity of production structures, Europe again scores much higher than the WAEMU area. By contrast, the CAEMC has – because of the importance of the production and export of oil within the output of their economies – very considerable production similarities.

The analysis given above makes one thing clear, namely that the eventual decision in relation to joining a monetary union depends to a large extent on the weights that are attached to the different costs and benefits that are brought about by such a step.

19.4 The Argentine currency board

In the 1980s, in common with many Latin American countries, Argentina suffered from a high rate of inflation that appeared to be a permanent feature of the economy. The government tried several stabilization programmes, but these had all failed and at the end of the 1980s hyperinflation had reached a rate of around 10,000 per cent. For this reason in April 1991 Argentina introduced its so-called Convertibility Law, which established a currency board with the US dollar as the anchor currency.

19.4.1 A currency board

An exchange-rate system based on a currency board combines three characteristics:

1. The commitment of the currency board (which coincides with or collaborates closely with the country's central bank) to convert the domestic currency on demand at an irrevocably fixed exchange rate into a pre-specified foreign currency, the anchor currency.
2. A domestic currency that can only be issued if it is backed by foreign-exchange reserves.
3. A long-term commitment to the system, which is often institutionalized by law (so that it is more difficult to change).

Because of the second characteristic listed above it is clear that foreign-exchange reserves have to amount to at least 100 per cent of base money, M_0. Closely related to this is the requirement of an orthodox currency board that no money financing of the fiscal deficit is to be allowed.

In several countries currency boards are – or were recently – in operation. Two prominent examples are Hong Kong (since 1983) with the exchange rate of 7.8 HK dollar against 1 US dollar and Argentina (between 1991 and 2001) with 1 peso vis-à-vis 1 US dollar.

At present there are also currency boards for the following currencies against the euro: the Bosnian mark, the Bulgarian lev and the Lithuanian litas.

The main reason for countries to introduce a currency board is the pursuit of a credible anti-inflationary policy which is able to make rapid responses to changes in circumstances. This high credibility is due to the rule-based nature of the policy and the institutionalization of the commitment. A quick reduction in the rate of inflation can be expected through the strict policy discipline (both fiscal and monetary), combined with the irrevocably fixed exchange rate against a currency of an inflation-shy country and the high credibility of the policy.

For the country that applies it, the currency board policy has a number of disadvantages:

1. Loss of the exchange-rate instrument.
   Country-specific shocks to the economy must, therefore, be accommodated by changes in prices and wages. If these are downwards sticky, the adjustment to economic shocks will be sluggish and painful, associated with serious costs such as additional unemployment.
2. Often, a loss of competitiveness over time.
   Even if the period of inflation adjustment from usually sky-high (before the currency board) to low levels of inflation (during the currency board) is exceptionally short, the country's currency has the time to become substantially overvalued.
3. The loss of national monetary autonomy.
   The currency board outlaws any national discretion in monetary policy.
4. Often more volatile interest rates.
   Money supply is the automatic adjustment variable in the case of country-specific (or asymmetric) shocks. Such shocks therefore reveal themselves initially in interest rate leaps.
5. The automatic adjustment process is usually pro-cyclical.
   Strong economic growth attracts foreign investors. This requires the currency board to purchase foreign currency and thus the issuing of new domestic money. The increase in money supply stimulates additional economic growth. In times of economic stagnation, the reverse adjustment process works. Investors leave the country. Consequently, money supply and, thus, economic growth receive a further downward push.
6. Loss of the lender of last resort facility for banks.
   Supplying additional liquidity to domestic banks in an attempt to give support in case of a looming banking crisis is no longer possible, unless excess coverage of M_0 by foreign-exchange reserves is available.
7. At the start of the currency board, therefore, substantial prerequisites need to be in place:

   – official reserves holdings must be sufficient to cover the whole amount of M_0;
   – well-regulated and well-capitalized banks are a necessity, due to the loss of the lender-of-last-resort function.

19.4.2 The rise and fall of the Argentine currency board

Argentina's currency board was not an orthodox one: in respect of the full coverage of base money it was allowed that up to a maximum of one-third of the coverage could consist of dollar-denominated bonds issued by the Argentine government. This provided a certain degree of flexibility over the financing of government deficits.

In the first few years of its operation the Argentine currency board achieved a considerable level of success, which was reflected in the main economic indicators:

o In 1994 inflation fell to a level that was similar to that of the USA.
o Capital inflows resumed, growing rapidly to a level of more than 4 per cent of GDP.
o After average annual negative economic growth rates of more than 2 per cent in the period from 1988 to 1990, there was a resumption of strong economic growth, averaging around some 7 per cent per annum in the four subsequent years.

However, not all of the indicators were favourable. A negative corollary of the high levels of growth was a substantial increase of imports and an associated worsening of the current account. But this worsening was also to the result of the deterioration in the level of competitiveness. It explains why exports fell steeply (by some 3 per cent of GDP) between 1990 and 1992. The cause of the deterioration in the country's competitiveness – despite the irrevocably fixed exchange rate – was that though inflation fell quickly, it remained high relative to the USA during the first years of the currency board. Consequently, between 1990 and 1994 the Argentine current account changed from a surplus of 3.5 per cent of GDP to a deficit of 4 per cent of GDP. Nevertheless, official reserves still grew slightly in 1994, as capital imports surpassed the current account deficit to a small extent.

The year 1995 proved to be a dramatic one for the Argentinean economy, with the country experiencing a substantial contagion from the Mexican crisis at the end of 1994. Through the automatic workings of the currency board, an outflow of capital resulted in a fall in the money supply, although the central bank counteracted this development in part through its purchase of dollar-denominated government bonds. Despite that, the real interest rate rose and economic growth became negative again, with a damaging effect on the unemployment rate, which reached 17 per cent in 1995. Probably in response to the determination that Argentine policy-makers showed in maintaining – and, if necessary, defending – the currency board, the fixed rate between the Argentine peso and the US dollar was easily sustained throughout this critical period.

In 1996–97 the Argentine economy showed signs of recovery with renewed high levels of economic growth and increasing capital inflows. One important reason will have been the negligible rate of inflation, which meant that real interest rates reached substantial levels. Alongside the high real interest rates, another drawback for the Argentine economy was that the high unemployment remained relatively unchanged. This resulted in growing levels of social unrest. A third negative development for the Argentine economy was that between 1996 and mid-1999 the real exchange rate (or competitiveness) worsened by some 20 per cent. This was a consequence of the worldwide rise in the value of the US dollar and the fall of the Brazilian currency, the real, after a currency crisis in Brazil that began in 1999. (Brazil was Argentina's main trading partner.) Argentina's economy did not recover from these blows. In 1999 it again recorded negative growth. This improved the current account balance, but at the same time led to a decline in the capital account surplus.

In such uncertain times, the emergence of an additional economic weakness may be sufficient to destroy the final credibility of a country's exchange-rate policy. In the case of Argentine's currency board this was the combination of a large percentage of government debt denominated in dollars and signs of indecisiveness on the part of policy-makers. A sign of the latter was the announcement of the plan to replace, at an appropriate moment in time, the dollar by a basket consisting of the euro and the dollar as the anchor currency. With respect to the government debt weakness, although it was largely long term in nature – which was able to inspire some confidence – by late 2001 more than 80 per cent of public debt was denominated in dollars. It was part of a large spontaneous dollarization (see Box 19.1 for the features of this system). This awareness raised even a priori scepticism about the benefits of devaluation of the Argentine peso, as devaluation in any case would result in a large debt increase (in pesos) of the government, but undoubtedly also the private sector, and probably an ensuing string of bankruptcies.

The Argentine currency board, which had remained in place for more than a decade, finally broke down in the period between the end of 2001 and early 2002, when bank deposits were frozen by the government in order to prevent more massive capital outflows, the peso was devalued, and the government defaulted on its debt. Under the conditions of the currency board the public was repeatedly told that 'a peso is a dollar, and a dollar is a peso'. Following its collapse 'a peso was not even a peso', since the freeze on bank deposits did not even allow the account holders to use their own pesos. This freeze prevented the large Argentine money overhang from being resolved through yet larger upward jumps in the price level and the nominal exchange rate, as soon as the exchange rate floated. The currency crisis was followed by a massive collapse of the Argentine economy.

19.4.3 The currency board idea after Argentina

The most important lessons to be drawn from the crisis experienced by Argentina are:

1. A remaining positive inflation differential with respect to the anchor country in even a short adjustment period towards low inflation of only two or three years can easily lead to a substantial and dangerous real appreciation (cf. the Walters critique in Section 18.2.2).
2. Situations of (real) exchange rate overvaluation are very costly.
3. Through the currency board system, the peso had a fixed exchange rate with respect to the US dollar and was, therefore, completely dependent on its time path. The appreciation of the dollar since mid-1995 and the huge fall of the Brazilian real against the dollar therefore vastly eroded the competitiveness of the Argentine tradables. Argentine policy-makers could only be resigned to the outcome.
4. Argentina had to adopt the US monetary policy stance, although the ongoing unemployment rise in Argentina called for lower interest rates than those in place in the USA.
5. Even if the level of official reserves is equal to the amount of base money, total money supply is not fully covered. This creates a vulnerable situation as soon as the currency board loses some of its credibility.
6. In the presence of de facto dollarization, large devaluations wreck balance sheets and may then very easily lead to the generation of costly bankruptcies. Should emerging economies, therefore, not inhibit any foreign-currency-denominated bank deposits or, at least, any net foreign liability positions of banks?
7. The bipolar solution, according to which emerging economies should avoid intermediate exchange-rate regimes, seems to have lost one acceptable extreme fixed exchange-rate variant: the currency board.

Box 19.1   Dollarization in Ecuador

Dollarization is another example of an irrevocably fixed exchange rate. As a term it has a variety of meanings, from the widespread and illegal use of foreign currency alongside the domestic currency to official approval for the use of a foreign currency as the sole legal means of payments and unit of account. The latter variety, where a foreign currency is adopted as the only domestic legal tender, is dubbed full or official dollarization. In effect, it is a unilateral monetary union, as the anchor country is not active at all.

There were and are many cases of full dollarization in practice. Schuler (2005) lists about 100 such cases. Many of them concern microstates, which have extremely small populations and only rudimentary financial systems. Examples of full dollarization in larger countries that still exist today (with starting year), are: Ecuador (2000), El Salvador (2001), Panama (1903), Puerto Rico (1899), Kosovo (1999), and Montenegro (1999). The last two cases concern, in fact, official euroization, since the euro is the anchor currency.

Because the transition to a dollarization is unilateral, it does not require a long process of building common institutions and reaching consensus. Of course, for the dollarizing country it has the drawback that the country can no longer affect its own monetary policy (to foster its economic goals) and loses the profits for the central bank attached to the creation of domestic banknotes and coins (the seigniorage). The loss of one's own currency may also mean the loss of an important symbol of national independence. The main gain for the dollarizing country is its relief from the poor credibility of the country's monetary institutions. It even yields a higher credibility than a currency board, because a return to own currency is difficult. Dollarization lowers the cost of capital. Although it does not by itself reduce country risk, it reduces currency risk and it raises the country's credibility with respect to anti-inflationary policy. The last two effects should have a downward influence on interest rates. Two additional benefits of a common currency are: (i) the easy use of derivative markets in the (large) home country of the new currency; and (ii) the absence of any danger of currency speculation any more.

The introduction of full dollarization in Ecuador provides a clear case study for the introduction of dollarization in many countries. In the 1980s, and after Ecuador had a long history of government budget crises, hyperinflation, currency devaluations, default on its foreign debt, a banking sector collapse because of a rush on banking accounts in an attempt to put the accounts in a more stable currency, and, finally, a wave of spontaneous dollarization.

The causes of these difficulties did not only include economic mismanagement. The country also suffered from wildly fluctuating export prices, earthquakes, the eruptions of volcanoes and the destructive El Niño[1] in the period 1997–98. These had a catastrophic effect on the Ecuadorian economy: at the beginning of 1999 the rate of producer price inflation was 300 per cent. Consumer price inflation was much lower, but had an annual rate of around 50 per cent. Retailers and companies began to display prices in US dollars, while cars and houses were sold in dollars. The constant complaint of firms was that the prices of inputs and capital goods increased on a daily basis and that customers delayed payments. It became very difficult for businesses to plan ahead or to set profitable price levels. In that year the proportion of bank deposits held in dollars rose to almost 60 per cent. Such a spontaneous dollarization, driven by public action, is a common start. In January 2000 the government made the official announcement of a dollarization scheme. By the end of December 2000, the exchange of the Ecuadorian currency, the sucre, for dollars had been accomplished: full dollarization of the economy was completed; the domestic currency had disappeared from circulation.

The reduction of inflation has been undoubtedly the most important social achievement of dollarization. By 2004 Ecuador's rate of inflation had fallen to 2.7 per cent – well

---

[1] El Niño is a quasiperiodic climate pattern that occurs across the tropical Pacific Ocean with on average five year intervals. It causes extreme weather (such as floods and droughts) in many regions of the world. Developing countries dependent upon agriculture and fishing, particularly those bordering the Pacific Ocean, are the most affected.

below the average of 6.5 per cent for the western hemisphere. Following a fall in output of 6.3 per cent in 1999, economic growth picked up again in 2000, with an average annual growth in the period 2001–05 of 4.3 per cent. The western hemisphere had an average annual growth of only 2.5 per cent. Despite the successful reduction in inflation, economic growth remained vigorous. A success for official dollarization.

19.4.4 Fear of floating?

The failure of the once highly praised Argentine currency board shifted interest towards the option of floating for emerging economies' currencies. The focal point of interest became the presumed 'fear of floating' across emerging economies.

Among the cited reasons for this fear of floating are (Edwards, 2002):

o Emerging economies export commodities and/or light manufactures; the world markets in these goods are relatively volatile. Such large external shocks would lead to excessively volatile exchange rates under a system of floating.
o Emerging economies do not have a good policy framework for the conduct of monetary policy under a floating exchange regime, while the effects of monetary policy on their economy are less certain.
o In emerging economies significant exchange-rate movements have major adverse effects on inflation and debt denominated in foreign currency.
o As a result of the previous reasons, there is a lack of credibility in the countries' ability to float.

However, empirical research tends to contradict the 'fear of floating' hypothesis. Data about how exchange-rate regimes have changed since the early 1990s suggest a trend towards greater flexibility in emerging economies. Broadly speaking, this tendency is evenly distributed across every region of the world, across the past decade, and between crisis-driven and voluntary transitions (Hakura, 2004). In the event of voluntary transitions, the volatility of real and nominal exchange rates increased immediately after the transition. But thereafter there was a restoration of stability. There is even some weak evidence that countries with genuine floating exchange rates are somewhat less affected by terms of trade disturbances and tend to growth faster than those countries with rigid or semi-rigid exchange-rate regimes.

Calvo and Reinhart (2002) analysed the fear of floating from the other end of the flexibility spectrum. They examined whether countries that claim they are floating their currency are, indeed, doing so. They present systematic evidence that the official label of floating does not provide an adequate representation of actual country practice; countries usually conduct more exchange-rate rigidity than they claim. This fear of floating is widespread and cuts across regions and levels of development. Therefore, also from the floating side it appears that the middle in the spectrum of exchange-rate regimes has certainly not disappeared.

19.5 The process of European monetary integration

19.5.1 The Snake Arrangement

The process of monetary integration in the European Community (EC, the forerunner of the European Union) was launched at the European Summit in The Hague in December

1969. This meeting of European heads of state and government decided to set up the Werner Committee, which was given the task of examining the feasibility of introducing monetary integration in the EC. The committee's report was completed in October 1970 and contained a plan whereby the EC – in those days a customs union – would be further integrated into an economic and monetary union (EMU), to be achieved by about 1980.

At the time, the principal motive for monetary integration was political – it was intended to give a new impetus to the process of European integration. There was also an economic motive derived from a problem in the EC's Common Agricultural Policy (CAP). In the latter half of the 1960s that policy had suffered serious problems because of the realignments of the European currency parities – still in the Bretton Woods system at the time. Agricultural prices were fixed each year in a common accounting unit; this was done at the beginning of the crop year. If exchange rates were adjusted during the year, so that the value of the national currency was generally also realigned in relation to the common accounting unit, then agricultural prices in the national currency were adjusted at the same time.

The countries within the EC did not want this price uncertainty. They preferred their producers to receive agricultural prices that were fixed in terms of the national currency, or were at least as stable as possible. However, from time to time this would cause differences between agricultural prices in the EC expressed in the common accounting unit, bringing the risk of distortions of competition. In a system of adjustable exchange rates this necessitated the reintroduction of trade policy measures between EC countries. This protection would naturally be a major breach of the then ruling customs union in the EC, which explains the fundamentally positive attitude at that time in the EC towards a process that would lead to a system of full monetary integration – and no longer mutual exchange-rate adjustments.

A second economic motive for the pursuit of greater economic integration was, of course, the argument that increased exchange-rate stability would promote mutual trade within the EC through the reduction of uncertainty and transaction costs, making intra-EC trade increasingly like domestic trade. According to that view, goods market (or real) integration ought to be followed by monetary integration; if this does not happen, not all the fruits of a common market are reaped. A third economic motive was that goods market integration must be followed by monetary integration to prevent a policy of competing devaluation, in order to gain a competitive advantage over the partner countries. Such competing devaluations are an expression of the so-called 'beggar thy neighbour' policy.

The Werner plan for the formation of an EMU in the EC was ultimately unsuccessful for reasons unrelated to its design. A three-stage process was planned for the introduction of monetary integration in the EC, with each stage being given a detailed description. The plan might have become reality if it had not been overtaken by events. The collapse of the Bretton Woods exchange-rate system in March 1973 caused such turmoil in the foreign-exchange market that almost every exchange rate came under pressure. The first oil price shock at the end of 1973 further exacerbated this worldwide upheaval of the foreign-exchange markets. The recession of the mid-1970s in the industrial countries, which was greatly intensified by this oil shock, completed the highly adverse conditions under which the Werner plan was to be implemented.

However, before the currency crisis of early 1973, the EC did succeed in establishing its own exchange-rate system that, to some extent, withstood the collapse of the Bretton Woods adjustable peg. This EC system, known as the Snake Arrangement, came into effect in May 1972. The reasons for the introduction of the Snake Arrangement can be traced back to the Smithsonian agreement drawn up in December 1971, which had restored the Bretton Woods exchange-rate system after a brief period of floating exchange rates.

As we saw in Section 16.4, this restoration did not mean a complete return to the previous situation. What was important to Europe was the enlargement of the margins within which an exchange rate could fluctuate around the dollar parity, from 1 to 2.25 per cent on either side of this parity. In other words, the fluctuation band was increased from 2 to 4.5 per cent of the parity value. However, it should be clear that if two currencies from the EC area have such a fluctuation band against the dollar, the result for the exchange rate of the two EC currencies is a mutual fluctuation band of twice 4.5 per cent, that is, 9 per cent.

A bilateral exchange-rate alteration of 9 per cent for EC currencies was considered to be unacceptable for a customs union. It was agreed that under the Snake Arrangement these currencies should have a maximum fluctuation band of 2.25 per cent either side of a central value – a total bandwidth of 4.5 per cent. Thus, the fluctuation band against the dollar would no longer be narrower than that used against any EC currency participating in the Snake. Indirectly, this imposed a further limitation on an EC currency's freedom to move against the dollar. The upper and lower intervention points against the dollar were often no longer reached because the fluctuation band against other EC currencies was frequently more constricting. It was usual for the EC currencies as a group to move over time up and down like a snake within the wider fluctuation band against the dollar. Hence, the name 'Snake Arrangement'.

In May 1972 this Snake Arrangement came into operation for the currencies of those countries that belonged to the EC at that time, plus the currencies of the UK, Denmark and Norway (followed by Sweden's currency in March 1973). Several currencies only remained in the Snake for a short period. For example, the pound sterling dropped out after only one month, followed soon afterwards by the Italian lira. The French franc also had to leave the arrangement at one point, but it later rejoined, only to be forced out once again. This was because, given their different domestic economic objectives, the individual national central banks for these currencies proved unable to maintain the fixed exchange rate against the other Snake currencies. Over the years the Snake increasingly degenerated into a kind of Deutsche mark area that, apart from the mark as the central currency, comprised only the less important currencies of Germany's small neighbours. The Snake lasted until 1979, when the European Monetary System (EMS) began to operate.

19.5.2 The European Monetary System

In 1978 Germany and France emerged clearly as the main drivers behind the process of European unification. (They forged a power bloc which, initially very much against the will of the other EC countries, became increasingly dominant in EC affairs.) After a period of mutual consultation, the German Chancellor Helmut Schmidt and the French President Giscard d'Estaing produced a plan for closer European monetary integration. The outcome of this process was the European Monetary System (EMS), which operated from 1 March 1979, and was finally replaced by the European Economic and Monetary Union (EMU) in 1999.

The EMS had three main components:

1. An adjustable peg exchange-rate system, again with a fluctuation band of 4.5 per cent, within which participating currencies were allowed to move against one another. This differed from the Snake only in the respect that it included all of the EC currencies, with the exception of the pound. Although the UK decided to join the EMS, it was not prepared to take part in the Exchange Rate Mechanism (ERM) of the EMS because of fears that it would undermine its political autonomy.

2. A system of large credit facilities that members were both willing and obliged to provide for one another. One of the most important functions was the financing of temporary balance-of-payments deficits. In that sense, these facilities were intended specifically to discourage speculative international capital movements.

3. Introduction of the ECU (European Currency Unit) with official monetary functions. As a financial innovation the ECU has been the subject of considerable attention, although it was not a particularly novel development. The basic idea was not new: the ECU was created along the lines of the SDR and was also made up of a basket of currencies; similarly, the establishment of the ECU was not really necessary for the monetary functions that it was assigned. It concerned all three official functions of money: unit of account, store of value (or acting as a reserve asset), and a means of payments. The ECU developed 'spontaneously' in the private sector, though strongly supported by the EC institutions and without a connection with the official ECU circuit. The ECU basket consisted of 12 EMS currencies, including the pound. The major feature of the ECU was, in effect, its importance as a symbol of European monetary unification.

In the first few years of its existence the ERM was only partially effective, as is reflected by a large number of parity adjustments, or exchange-rate realignments. In the first few years of its existence, the ERM therefore shared many similarities with a crawling peg system. At first, the only real achievement of the ERM was, in effect, that none of the currencies left the system – in contrast to what had happened during the period of the Snake. The Deutsche mark (DM) proved to be the strongest currency in the EMS, in that if exchange rates were realigned the mark never devalued against any other EMS currency. The Italian lira underwent the largest accumulated devaluation among the currencies taking part in the ERM from the start.

For the ERM the year 1985 represented a clear break with the policies of the past. The frequency of realignments declined markedly after that year. Although inflation differentials between the EMS countries had still not disappeared in full, there was a decline in the level and frequency of the devaluations against the DM. Given the continuing inflation differential compared with Germany, this led to a real appreciation of currencies such as the lira, initially the French franc and later the Spanish peseta. This meant that the competitive positions of the countries with these currencies deteriorated in comparison with other ERM participants. This appears to have been the outcome of a deliberate policy. By allowing devaluation to lag behind the inflation differential, countries such as Italy and France ensured that the rise in import prices was less than the increases in domestic price levels. This enabled them to moderate their rates of inflation. So in the mid-1980s these countries discovered an additional reason for European monetary integration: a fixed exchange rate acting as an instrument of inflation stabilization. For the EMS countries the exchange-rate anchor for low inflation was a fixed exchange rate against the currency of inflation-shy Germany.

The deteriorating competitive position of these countries might have wrecked the anti-inflationary policy, since foreign-exchange speculators could have taken this deterioration as a sign of the imminent devaluation of the currencies concerned. However, there was no speculation against these currencies. The explanation for this is found in a phenomenon described as 'borrowing the credibility of the German anti-inflation policy' via membership of the ERM. Over the years, German anti-inflation policy is recognized as having been extremely successful. By opting through ERM membership for a fixed link between their currency and the DM, the other ERM countries signaled that they were also committed to a macroeconomic policy that supports this link. If the policy patently fails to offer that support, the market will be unconvinced of the stability of the prevailing exchange rates and currency speculation will readily break out. However, once the supporting policy does become apparent, it will immediately gain considerable credibility owing to ERM membership, and there may be no currency speculation.

Ironically, in the case of borrowing German credibility, market sentiment gave support to the fixed exchange rates in the short run, but in the longer run it could easily work in the other direction, creating severe tension within the ERM. This problem can actually arise along the lines of the Walters critique (see Section 18.2.2). There can then suddenly come a time when, in the eyes of currency speculators, this latent imbalance in competitiveness and current accounts crosses a certain threshold so that these fundamentals become decisive in determining market sentiments. Currency speculators then move en bloc against such a currency – often encouraged by the bandwagon effect or herd behaviour. The resulting capital flight then makes devaluation of the currency with relatively high inflation virtually inevitable. Such a situation can also easily arise without relatively high inflation – for example, if the attainment of an economic objective such as full employment becomes a political issue, as in the case of self-fulfilling speculative attack (see Section 18.2.3).

In September 1992 and again in August 1993 these dangers to the ERM became a reality. The currency crisis of September 1992 was made considerably worse by the gradually enlarged differences in the mutual competitive positions of the ERM countries. Taking 1987 as the base year, there were some countries that, according to their real effective exchange rates, faced a marked deterioration of some 20 per cent (Spain) and 10 per cent (Italy, the UK, and Sweden). It should be pointed out here that, after much hesitation, the UK eventually joined the ERM in October 1990, albeit with a much wider fluctuation band of 12 per cent. Before that, the pound had more or less shadowed the ERM for a number of years. The Swedish currency, the krona, also shadowed the ERM for years. In this instance it could not join because Sweden was not a member of the EC until 1995.

The straw that broke the camel's back came in the summer of 1992 when a Danish referendum on the acceptance of the Maastricht Treaty for participation in a future EMU (see next sub-section) had a negative outcome. This Danish 'No' vote came as a considerable shock. Subsequently, the outcome of a French referendum on that Treaty that would be held soon after seemed to turn out negative too. In addition to concerns about the loss of economic autonomy, the argument that the EMU seemed to give a relatively high priority to the achievement of low inflation was important in the electoral battle before the referendums. Through the political costs (the loss of part of the electorate), governments in several countries in Europe could be expected to adapt their economic priorities at that time. The currency speculators tested this change successfully for a number of EU countries. This part of the explanation of the currency crisis is a variant of the second-generation model of speculative attacks (see section 18.2.3).

The exchange-rate changes in September 1992 led to a recovery in the national levels of competitiveness. Compared with the 1987 values there was actually an over-adjustment, except in the case of the Spanish peseta. The September 1992 rate adjustment concerned a 5 per cent devaluation of the peseta, although the currency did remain in the ERM. In contrast, the lira and pound left the ERM at that time, with only the lira returning some years later. Troubles on the exchange-rate front also persisted: in November the peseta and the Portuguese escudo were forced to devalue by 6 per cent. In 1993 the problems continued: in February, the Irish punt was devalued by 10 per cent and in May again the peseta and the escudo, then by 7 and 3.5 per cent, respectively.

In early August 1993 tensions between EMS members on the monetary policy that should be adopted ushered in a second currency crisis. The 1990 reunification of the two German states led to a rapid increase in expenditures in the former East Germany, which led to a rise in Germany's levels of inflation. In order to counter this, the German monetary policy-makers intensified their usually restricted monetary policy (Germany is tradition-ally an inflation-shy country) with a consequential increase in German interest rates. Since the unemployment rate in Europe was high at that time, other ERM countries faced the characteristic situation of the eternally incompatible trinity – that fixed exchange rates, free international capital movements, and national autonomy of monetary policy cannot all be achieved simultaneously. In this connection we should also bear in mind that, since mid-1990, capital restrictions between the original EC member states had almost disap-peared. The other EMS countries now had a choice: either to follow the higher German interest rate or to devalue their currencies against the DM. They chose the first option, but in statements French policy-makers in particular expressed their dissatisfaction about the high interest rates.

The financial markets started to operate on the expectations that if they could break the rigidity in maintaining the fixed exchange rate in some countries, these countries might use this circumstance to change their policy priorities in the direction of plac-ing more importance on the attainment of full employment. In this period international capital flows turned against the French franc, in particular. In spite of foreign-exchange market intervention on a massive scale, in which the German central bank was also closely involved, the exchange-rate values proved unsustainable. This explanation is also an application of the second-generation model of speculative attacks outlined in Section 18.2.3.

Yet instead of a formal devaluation, the very surprising decision taken was that there should be a substantial widening of ERM fluctuation margins. At the beginning of August 1993 these were expanded to twice 15 per cent – that is, a total bandwidth of 30 per cent – for the participating currencies (with the exception of the guilder/mark rate which main-tained the old bandwidth of 4.5 per cent). We are entitled to ask whether an exchange-rate system with such a bandwidth can still be referred to as an adjustable peg system.

Although everyone expected the ERM countries to use this increased exchange-rate freedom to pursue a more independent monetary policy, what happened in practice was different: the interest rate cuts paralleled those in Germany, and there was no relaxation in monetary policy. Thus, the speculators proved to be mistaken: these countries did not change their priorities following the attack. The result was that, after dropping at first, those currencies that had been given a 30 per cent fluctuation band recovered rapidly. Within a period of just a few months both the Belgian and the French francs were back within the old bandwidth of 4.5 per cent against the DM.

Nevertheless, in mid-1995 the monetary authorities still did not feel that the time was ripe for a restoration of the old bandwidth against the DM for currencies other than the guilder. Such a conclusion was quite understandable. After a prolonged period of exchange-rate stability since 1987, foreign-exchange market tensions had built up in the ERM, and these erupted in 1992 and 1993 in the form of large-scale speculative capital movements.

This short history of the ERM of the EMS delivers a number of important lessons. It is, of course, unsurprising that there is some common ground with the lessons drawn from sections 18.3 and 18.4 on the recent currency crises in emerging countries:

1. An adjustable peg system of exchange rates is vulnerable not only to realignments that are too frequent, but also to alignments that are too sporadic. In the period between 1979 and 1985 we saw the first problem in the ERM, and in the period from 1987 to 1991 we witnessed the second. Evidently, the operation of such a system nowa-days, within a context of such massive and mobile international capital movements, demands such sophisticated management that the system has in practice become dif-ficult to apply. This European experience contributed strongly to the bipolar view of favourable exchange-rate regimes.

2. Price stabilization based on pegging the exchange rate has an inherent weakness.
3. The voice of the electorate can have a substantial effect upon both the economic priorities of the policy-makers and the behaviour of the currency speculators.
4. The occurrence of country-specific shocks, such as German unification, is not only a reason to prefer a more flexible exchange-rate regime, but may also be a source of currency speculation.
5. If a currency crisis starts, the central bank should not resist it if after a forex market intervention test it appears that the attack is serious. Prolonged resistance will only cost the central bank official international reserves and lead to a loss for the central bank (it sells its reserves cheap, and then after a period they must be bought back more expensively, in order to replenish the stock) and a profit for the speculators.
6. The UK case shows that when inflation is sufficiently low, say within single figures, it is not necessarily unwise to abandon a fixed exchange rate. In the UK economic growth has appeared to be impressive since September 1992, while the level of inflation has remained low.

19.5.3 The European Economic and Monetary Union

In June 1988 at the European summit in Hanover, Germany decided to establish a committee chaired by the then French President of the European Commission, Delors. The committee was instructed to examine practical measures and make proposals for establishing an Economic and Monetary Union (EMU) within the EC. This new monetary momentum in Europe came from the spreading mood in favour of change in the EC, which had been created by the closer integration of the goods and services market by means of the project 'Europe 1992'.

The Delors Committee produced its report in April 1989. Like the Werner Committee report 20 years earlier, the Delors Committee decided that EMU should be achieved in three distinct stages. There were a number of other striking similarities between the content of the two reports – although there were also, of course, some differences. Thus, the Delors Committee went further in the direction of a system of central banks that would be independent of the finance ministers. In its day, the Werner Committee had suggested a greater centralization of fiscal policy in the EMU. In June 1989 the European Council of Ministers accepted the proposal for the first stage in the Delors committee report. This stage began on 1 January 1990.

In December 1991 an intergovernmental conference was held in Maastricht, the Netherlands, which reached agreements over both the EMU and a European Political Union (EPU) in the EC. In the Maastricht Treaty two new pillars were added to the first, economic pillar, namely, foreign and defence policies as the second pillar and justice and internal security as the third pillar. An intergovernmental conference was necessary because these decisions required amendments to the Treaty of Rome, the treaty establishing the European Economic Community. The agreements about EPU remained bogged down in a large number of generalized principles, which are beyond the scope of this book. The EMU treaty agreed in Maastricht is entirely in line with the Delors Report, although the ideas are often developed in more detail, such as the specific timing of the launch of stages 2 and 3. Ratification of the Treaty of Maastricht was completed on 1 November 1993, so that the treaty could enter into force on that date. From then on we refer to the European Union (EU) as the successor to the EC.

As planned, stage 1 of EMU was intended to lead on to stage 2 on 1 January 1994. In stage 1 all of the participating countries had to switch to the narrow fluctuation margin that was already in operation. As we have seen, nothing came of this. As a result of the currency crisis in the EMS in 1993 for most countries the fluctuation margin had actually been increased to 30 per cent. The possibility of realignment was to be retained in the first stage and all capital restrictions had to be abolished. Denmark, France, Italy, and Belgium had already done this by 1 July 1990. They were preceded in this respect by Germany, the UK, and the Netherlands.

In stage 2, exchange-rate realignments could take place only under exceptional conditions, and there was also a prohibition on any central bank financing of the public sector. The European Monetary Institute (EMI) began its activities at the start of stage 2. The functions of the EMI concerned an examination of the conditions that had to be imposed on a European Central Bank (ECB), and making recommendations in relation to the coordination of monetary policy and economic policy in general in the participating countries.

After a considerable political struggle, Frankfurt became the headquarters of the EMI (and, thus, later of the European Central Bank). Convergence criteria were formulated during the Maastricht intergovernmental conference at the end of 1991, together with EMU reference values for each of these criteria. These reference values are the critical values that the countries should satisfy if they wish to be able to join the third stage, or the actual EMU, at the end of stage 2, then and in the event of future accessions. Box 19.2 sets out these criteria and also gives quantitative information on the critical values and the country positions, the latter in the last year before the start of stage 2 (1 January 1994) and the last full year for which data were available for making the decision about accession to stage 3 (1 January, 1999).

Box 19.2   The Maastricht convergence criteria

Table 19.1 shows the convergence criteria for measuring the countries' degree of convergence. The note relating to the table specifies the convergence criteria and the structure of the reference values.

The choice of inflation and interest rates as convergence criteria is understandable in the light of exchange-rate theory. According to exchange-rate theories based on purchasing power parity (see Section 13.2) and the uncovered interest rate parity (Section 13.3.1), an invariable exchange rate requires inflation and interest rate differentials between countries to be only quite small. Inflation convergence towards the average of the three lowest inflation rates achieved by the EU member countries illustrates the importance of low inflation among the economic goals of the EMU. The convergence requirements in the note relating to the table appear rather arbitrary, and to a certain extent they are. The critical value of 1.5 per cent could equally well have been 1 per cent or perhaps 2 per cent.

The criteria derived from public finance have a less direct connection with an invariable exchange rate and are therefore also more subject to criticism. The motive for these criteria seems to have been fear that an invariable exchange rate – and thus certainly a single currency – would intensify the use of fiscal policy. The underlying motive could be that a fixed exchange-rate regime enhances the effectiveness of fiscal policy, as we saw in Section 14.7, through the effect of mobile international capital. The greater effectiveness of fiscal policy could prompt countries to make imprudent use of it, which would naturally not be in the interests of the countries in the future EMU. An expansionary fiscal policy

Table 19.1 Convergence criteria: contents, critical values and fulfilments

EU countries	Inflation		Long-term interest rate		Budget deficit		Government debt	
	1993	1997	1993	1997	1993	1997	1993	1997
EMU reference value	3.3	2.7	9.3	8.0	−3	−3	60	60
Belgium	2.8	1.5	7.2	5.8	**−6.6**	−2.1	**139**	**122**
Denmark	1.3	1.9	7.3	6.3	**−4.4**	0.7	**80**	**65**
Germany	**4.2**	1.5	6.4	5.6	**−3.3**	−2.7	48	**61**
France	2.1	1.3	6.8	5.6	**−5.8**	−3.0	46	58
Greece	**14.4**	**5.4**	**21.2**	**9.9**	**−13.3**	**−4.0**	**115**	**109**
Ireland	2.0	1.2	7.7	6.3	−2.5	0.9	**96**	**66**
Italy	**4.5**	1.9	**11.3**	6.9	**−9.5**	−2.7	**119**	**122**
Luxembourg	**3.6**	1.4	6.9	5.6	1.1	1.7	8	7
Netherlands	2.6	1.9	6.4	5.6	**−3.3**	−1.4	**81**	**72**
Portugal	**6.5**	1.9	**12.2**	6.4	**−7.2**	−2.5	**67**	**62**
Spain	**4.6**	1.9	**10.2**	6.4	**−7.3**	−2.6	60	**69**
UK	3.0	1.8	7.4	7.1	**−7.9**	−1.9	48	53
Austria	**3.6**	1.2	6.6	5.7	**−4.1**	−2.5	**64**	**66**
Finland	2.2	1.2	8.2	6.0	**−7.2**	−0.9	**62**	56
Sweden	**4.6**	1.8	8.5	6.6	**−13.3**	−0.8	**77**	**77**

Explanatory note: The last three countries only became EU members through the fourth enlargement at 1 January 1995. The bold figures indicate compliance with the relevant convergence requirements, given a certain interpretation of the criteria. The EMU reference values (maximum values) are: for inflation (annual average, %): 1.5 per cent points above the inflation rate of 'at most' the three best performing countries in terms of price stability (interpreted here as the average inflation rate in the three best performing countries in this respect); long-term interest rates (annual average, %): 2 per cent points above the interest rate in 'at most' the three best-performing EU countries in terms of price stability (interpreted here as the average interest rate in the three best-performing countries with regard to inflation); budget deficit (total government net lending, % of GDP): 3%; government debt (gross total debt, % of GDP): not more than 60% (or showing a satisfactory decrease). Moreover, the currency must have shown a sufficient degree of exchange-rate stability by staying within the normal fluctuation margins of the EMS exchange-rate mechanism without devaluation, for two years.
Source: De Nederlandsche Bank (1995), p. 105 and (1998), p. 68.

in another member state would have the effect of driving up interest rates there and contributing to a current account deficit in the EMU area (according to the income identity or equation (14.4)). Since there will be only one integrated capital market in the EMU, interest rates on that market would rise. The other member states naturally regard this as harmful. There is also the fear that a country with large government debt will exert pressure in order to be permitted, in that 'exceptional' case, to finance the large debt by monetary means as a one-off rescue operation – despite the prohibition of money financing of fiscal deficits. This would boost inflation, very much contrary to the wishes of the other countries.

A final criterion, which is not mentioned in the table, states that a country that participates in the ERM must not have devalued its currency in the two years preceding stage 3. The criterion was undoubtedly introduced on the basis of the width of 4.5 per cent of the fluctuation band at that time. However, the widened fluctuation band of 30 per cent was accepted as the 'normal EMS fluctuation margins' in judging a country's performance in this respect – a severe weakening of this non-devaluation criterion.

Stage 3 is synonymous with a country joining the EMU. This means that a common currency then replaced the individual national currencies. At the end of 1995 the name of the common currency was changed from ECU in euro and the launch date for stage 3 was 1 January 1999.

Of the 15 EU members at that date, 11 had been accepted for EMU accession: Austria, Belgium, Finland, France, Germany, Italy, Ireland, Luxemburg, the Netherlands, Portugal, and Spain. Greece followed as an EMU member on 1 January 2001. As shown in Table 19.1, the convergence criteria values have improved considerably between 1993 and 1997. They have benefited from the stable and strong growth of the world economy in that period. The convergence criteria only eliminated Greece as a member on 1 January 1999. However, several countries were saved by the clause that the critical value for government debt to GDP of 60 per cent could be replaced by a clause that a movement of that ratio in a downward direction was also sufficient. Four EU countries were excluded. Greece was only to achieve convergence later on, joining in January 2001. The UK and Denmark preferred to use an opt-out clause that they had negotiated in the Maastricht Treaty. Accordingly, they have the right to decide when they will apply for monetary union membership. The remaining country, Sweden, did not satisfy the exchange-rate condition as it had never participated in the ERM. Here we see that monetary integration at varying speeds has actually been programmed into the Maastricht Treaty and has also become practice in the EU.

The danger loomed that after a country had joined the EMU it would consider itself free from any economic policy discipline. For the convergence criteria describe pre-accession conditions. Fed by some general remarks in the Maastricht Treaty and on the instigation of Germany, the so-called Stability and Growth Pact was accepted in June 1997. The Pact requires for participants in the EMU to commit themselves to a medium-term fiscal balance or surplus. Additionally, fiscal deficits larger than 3 per cent of GDP are regarded as excessive and should be avoided, unless the country involved has a negative growth of more than 0.75 per cent. After having failed to reach a deadline, such a country could be sanctioned.

In the first years of the EMU the Stability and Growth Pact came under pressure as a consequence of a stagnating world economy during this period, followed by only a weak recovery in the EMU area. The criticism was that the Pact substantially counteracted a vigorous economic recovery as a result of its pro-cyclical character. Ironically, it was the architect of the Pact, Germany, which came under fire due to the Pact since it had fiscal deficits that were persistently too large. Similar problems were also experienced by France, Portugal, and Italy. However, this did not result in the imposition of the sanctions that had been incorporated into the Pact. They consist, for a country, at first, of a payment of a non-remunerated deposit and, if the excess is not corrected in time, conversion of the deposit into a fine. In 2005 the rules of the Pact were, unsurprisingly, somewhat weakened. In the worldwide economic crisis of 2008–09 the rules were temporarily suspended to allow governments to help promote the global recovery.

The EU expanded in 2004 with the accession of ten new member countries: Hungary, Poland, the Slovakia, the Czech Republic, Slovenia; the three Baltic states, Estonia, Latvia, and Lithuania; and the two mini-states, Cyprus and Malta. At the beginning of 2007 Bulgaria and Romania followed as new members. They were all supposed to enter the EMU eventually, but first they were required to fulfil the convergence criteria, including the exchange-rate requirement. For the latter criterion to apply there exists an ERM-II. In the meantime five of them have gained accession to the EMU: Slovenia (2007), Cyprus (only the Greek part) and Malta (2008), Slovakia (2009) and Estonia (2011).

The Maastricht Treaty contains a 'no bailout' clause meaning that if one of the member countries of the EMU requires financial support, the other member countries are not entitled to provide it. This clause became particularly significant at the beginning of 2010. At this time Greece appeared to be incapable of financing its large fiscal deficit (more than 13 per cent of its GDP) together with that part of its large government debt that had to be re-financed in 2010. The international bond market reacted by demanding a sharply rising interest rate on Greece's government debt, imposing a burden that was too large for the country. After a long period of hesitation, the other EMU countries decided to give Greece substantial financial support in the form of the guarantee of loans with a reasonable interest rate, in cooperation with the IMF and under severe policy conditions – setting aside the 'no bailout' clause. In the EMU this event had the effect of a wake-up call (see Section 18.4.3) since soon after this Ireland, Portugal, and, to a lesser degree, Spain suffered from rapidly rising interest rates on their government debts. At the end of 2010 it appeared necessary to provide Ireland the same loan guarantee as that which Greece had received earlier that year. Portugal followed suit in 2011.

The surprising element of Greece's experience in 2010 is that, unlike the initial expectation, the financial market reacted so late to the growing financial problem in Greece. Despite that problem and the gradual worsening of the country's competitiveness, country risk surcharge in the interest rates that Greece had to pay on the loans it received remained quite low in the years before 2010. The same held true for those other member countries of the EMU that had a deteriorating economic situation. In contrast to the initial expectation of the architects of the EMU, the international financial markets do not appear to incorporate country risk smoothly into their market interest rates. In addition – as in the case of exchange-rate changes – it appears to be a matter of running to extremes or a combination of under- and overreacting. This experience has given a firm blow to the notion that markets know best.

19.6   Summary

1. Parts of both the European Union (EU) and Africa have an advanced form of regional monetary integration. The EU has carried out a long process of monetary integration. This process began in 1970 with the adoption of the Werner report and ended at the beginning of 1999 with 11 EU countries proceeding to the final stage of full monetary integration, now known as European Economic and Monetary Union (EMU). This stage features a common currency – the euro. The total liberalization of mutual capital movements is another feature of a monetary union. In 2011 the EMU counted 17 member countries.

2. In Sub-Saharan Africa, 14 countries that have the CFA franc as their currency have been in the Franc Zone in the final stage of monetary integration for decades, together with France and the Comoros Islands. In this instance more than one currency is involved, but they are in principle linked by irrevocably fixed exchange rates.

3. The optimum currency area theory is the theoretical basis for regional monetary integration and advances many points both for and against such integration. It offers various criteria for judging whether or not it is worthwhile for a country to participate in regional monetary integration. These are all related, in some manner or other, to a minimization of the costs of such participation that arises through the loss of both national monetary autonomy and the exchange rate as an adjustment instrument. These costs occur if the monetarily integrated countries endure substantial country-specific economic shocks. The benefits of participation are accepted as a fact.

4. The criteria of the optimum currency area theory show that joining a monetary union becomes less costly and thus more worthwhile: the greater labour mobility in the union area, the greater mutual economic openness, the greater similarity of economic structures between the intended union partners, and the more advanced international integration of public spending in the area. Wage and price flexibility and a diversified range of exports for the intended partners also help to minimize the costs of monetary integration. Taken together, the criteria provide a good indication of whether or not participation is worthwhile, although there is an inevitable problem if the criteria do not all point in the same direction. Consequently, policy-makers are still faced by a subjective process of weighing up the clues of the criteria when it comes to deciding whether or not to join a monetary union.

5. Full monetary integration in the form of the Franc Zone suffered a serious setback in January 1994 when, for the first time in its existence, the CFA franc had to be devalued against the French franc – by up to 50 per cent. Two external factors can be blamed for this occurrence: a strong deterioration of the terms of trade of the CFA Franc Zone and a rising French franc vis-à-vis the US dollar after 1985, causing serious economic disturbance in the area from the mid-1980s onwards. The use of the French franc – and from 1999 the euro – as anchor currency caused a very low inflation in the African members of the Franc Zone and a somewhat higher economic growth relative to the neighbouring countries.

6. In addition to the regional monetary union, the currency board and dollarization are also applications of a system of irrevocably fixed exchange rates.

7. The currency board has been applied successfully in countries such as Hong Kong and Estonia, but the best-known currency board of the recent past was that in operation in Argentina in the period 1990–2002. This proved to be a failure. Although it was very effective – eliminating hyperinflation within a few years – this success was related closely to an inherent weakness: however short the adjustment period, it brings the country in a position of sharply reduced competitiveness. This increases the country's level of fragility: if it encounters a hard headwind, such as adverse international developments, there is a very real chance of a currency crisis. For Argentina that headwind consisted of a worldwide strengthening dollar – Argentina's anchor currency – and a steep fall in the value of the Brazilian real – the currency of Argentina's largest trading partner. A highly dollarized economy adds to the country's weakness to speculative attacks, as Argentina experienced in the year before the collapse of its currency board, at the end of 2001.

8. Ecuador's short period of official dollarization, during which the US dollar was substituted for the domestic currency, gives the provisional impression that a system of full dollarization is more stable than a partial, spontaneous dollarization, as occurred

in the case of Argentina. Since the dollarization in Ecuador in 2000, the level of economic growth has been impressive, while inflation quickly fell to a level of around 2 per cent.

9. Returning to the most impressive monetary integration process, that of the EU, this process is now far advanced. It began with the introduction of the Snake Arrangement in May 1972, in which the mutual fluctuation margins for the exchange rates were halved in comparison with the rules of the Bretton Woods exchange-rate system, as revised under the Smithsonian agreement in December 1971. However, the Snake Arrangement soon foundered and in the end consisted only of the Deutsche mark (DM) and the currencies of a few small 'satellite' countries.

10. The introduction of the European Monetary System (EMS) in March 1979 again prompted greater activity among all EC countries in relation to monetary integration. All of these countries joined the EMS, but not all were prepared to take part in the EMS Exchange Rate Mechanism. This took the same form as the Snake, with additional support being given in the form of a system of mutual credit facilities. The new artificial currency – the European Currency Unit (ECU) – was also a product of the introduction of the EMS. The ECU fulfilled all three functions of money in the official sphere.

11. For various high-inflation member countries, the EMS was a means of helping to curb inflation at home, although this function of the EMS contributed to the increasingly unstable balance in this system. This was part of the reason for the system's final collapse in August 1993.

12. Nevertheless, the monetary integration process is making steady progress in Europe. The Economic and Monetary Union (EMU) was initiated on 1 January 1999. For the EMU member countries the new common currency – the euro – has replaced the domestic currencies, which have been abolished. The Maastricht Treaty of December 1991 laid the legal foundation for this European EMU. A sufficient convergence of the economies of the EMS members, according to the convergence criteria included in the Maastricht Treaty, was a necessary condition for accession. In future, only those EU countries that meet all of the convergence criteria will be entitled to join.

13. In 2010 the EMU had to cope with a substantial setback when Greece, followed by Ireland, proved unable to finance the fiscal deficit in a viable way. After much hesitation the EMU countries decided to set aside the 'no bailout' clause of the Maastricht Treaty and to guarantee government debt of EMU countries through the establishment of a large common financial fund.

Questions

1. In January 1994 the CFA franc devalued by 50 per cent against the French franc. This wiped out the overvaluation of the CFA franc.

   (a) What are the positive and negative economic effects of an overvalued currency for the home area of this currency?
   (b) Discuss the principal advantages and disadvantages of the link between the CFA franc and the French franc (and later the euro) in the Franc Zone for both the African member states of the Franc Zone and France (and later the Euro Zone).

2. Section 19.4.2. about the Argentine currency board refers to a plan to replace the dollar by a basket consisting of the euro and the dollar as the anchor currency. What do you see as the pros and cons of such a currency basket rather than one currency as the anchor currency of a currency board?
3. What seems to be the weakest and what seems to be the strongest criterion of the optimal currency area theory in the case of the dollarized Ecuador?
4. The Euro Zone left the no-bail-out clause with its decision to provide Greece with financial support in 2010. What would have been the positive and negative consequences if the Euro Zone would not have left its position relating to no-bail out – and Greece would have been obliged to find an agreement for financial support with only the IMF?

Bibliography

Aghevli, B. B., Khan, M. S. and Montiel, P. J. (1991) *Exchange Rate Policy in Developing Countries: Some Analytical Issues*, IMF Occasional Paper, no. 70. Washington, DC: IMF.

Alfaro, L., Kalemli-Ozcan, S. and Volosovych, V. (2005) *Why Doesn't Capital Flow from Rich to Poor Countries? An Empirical Investigation*, NBER Working Paper, no. 11901. Cambridge, MA: National Bureau of Economic Research.

Amity, M. and Freund, C. (2007) 'China's Export Boom', *IMF Finance and Development*, 44(3).

Associated Press (2006) 'U.S. Drops Most Import Barriers to High-Grade Steel', *The New York Times*, 15 December. Available online at: http://www.nytimes.com/2006/12/15/business/worldbusiness/15steel.html?fta=y (accessed 18 February 2009).

Alexander, S. (1952) 'The Effects of a Devaluation on a Trade Balance', *IMF Staff Papers*, 2: 263–78.

Allen, E. A. (1989) *International Capital Markets: Developments and Prospects* (World Economic and Financial Surveys series), Washington, DC: IMF.

BIS (Bank for International Settlements) (1993a) *Central Bank Survey of Foreign Exchange Market Activity in April 1992*, March. Basel: BIS.

BIS (Bank for International Settlements) (1993b) *63rd Annual Report*, 1st April 1992–31st March 1993, 14 June. Basel: BIS.

BIS (Bank for International Settlements) (1995) *65th Annual Report*. Basel: BIS.

BIS (Bank for International Settlements) (2001) *71st Annual Report*, Basel: BIS.

BIS (Bank for International Settlements) (2001) *Triennial Central Bank Survey 2001*. Available online at: www.bis.org (accessed 18 May 2003).

BIS (Bank for International Settlements) (2004) *74th Annual Report*. Basel: BIS.

BIS (Bank for International Settlements) (2007) *Triennial Central Bank Survey of Foreign Exchange and Derivatives Market Activity in April 2007*, September 2007. Available online at: www.bis.org. Basel:BIS.

BIS (Bank for International Settlements) (2009) *BIS Quarterly Review*, March. Available online at: http://www.bis.org/publ/qtrpdf/r_qt0903.htm (accessed 25 May 2009).

BIS (Bank for International Settlements) (2010) *Triennial Central Bank Survey of Foreign Exchange and Derivatives Market Activity in April 2010*, September 2010. Available online at: www.bis.org (accessed 6 December 2010).

Bakker, A. F. P. (1995) *The International Financial Institutions*. London and New York: Longman.

Balassa, B. (1961) *The Theory of Economic Integration*. Homewood, IL: R.D. Irwin.

Baldwin, R. E. (1992) 'Are Economists' Traditional Trade Policy Views Still Valid?', *Journal of Economic Literature*, 30: 804–29.

Baldwin, R. and Krugman, P. R. (1989) 'Persistent Trade Effects of Large Exchange Rate Shocks', *Quarterly Journal of Economics*, 54: 635–54.

Baldwin, R. and Wyplosz, C. (2004) *The Economics of European Integration*, London: McGraw Hill.

Baroncelli, E., Krivonos, E. and Oarreaga, M. (2004) *Trademark Protection or Protectionism?*, Policy Research Working Paper no. 3214. Washington, DC: World Bank.

Bate, R. and Tren, R. (2006) 'U.S., Brazil Dispute Patent Protection', *Health Care News*, 1 March. Available online at: http://www.heartland.org/policybot/results/18587/US_Brazil_Dispute_Patent_Protection.html (accessed 4 May 2009).

Bayoumi, T. (1990) 'Saving–Investment Correlations; Immobile Capital, Government Policy, or Endogenous Behavior?', *IMF Staff Papers*, 36: 360–87.

BBC News (2008) 'EU Suffers Defeat in Banana Sars', 7 April. Available online at: http://news.bbc.co.uk/2/hi/business/7335070.stm (accessed 15 July 2009).

Bergsten, C. F. and Williamson, J. (1983) 'Exchange Rates and Trade Policy', in W. R. Cline (ed.), *Trade Policy in the 1980s*, 99–120. Washington, DC: Institute for International Economics.

Bhagwati, J. N. (1971) 'The Generalized Theory of Distortions and Welfare', in J. N.

Bhagwati, J. N. (1988) *Protectionism*. Cambridge, MA: MIT Press.

Bhagwati, J. N. (1989) 'Is Free Trade Passé after All?', *Weltwirtschaftliches Archiv*, 125: 17–44.

Bhagwati, R. W. Jones, R. A. Mundell and J. Vanek (eds), *Trade, Balance of Payments and Growth: Papers in International Economics in Honour of Charles P. Kindleberger*, 69–90. Amsterdam: North-Holland Publishing.

Botman D. B. J. and Jager, H. (2002) 'Coordination of Speculation', *Journal of International Economics*, 58: 159–75.

Boulet, O. and Boulet, B. (2002) *Latin America and the Caribbean: Historical Geography of Latin America*. New York: John Wiley & Sons.

Bowen, H. P., Leamer, E. E. and Sveikauskas, L. (1987) 'Multicountry, Multifactor Tests of the Factor Abundance Theory', *American Economic Review*, 77: 791–809.

Brander, J. A. and Spencer, B. J. (1983) 'International R and D Rivalry and Industrial Strategy', *Review of Economic Studies*, 50: 702–22.

Brander, J. A. and Spencer, B. J. (1985) 'Export Subsidies and International Market Share Rivalry', *Journal of International Economics*, 18: 83–100.

Brulhart, M. (2008) 'An Account of Global Intra-Industry Trade, 1962–2006'. Background paper for the WDR 2009, Département d'économétrie et économie politique, HEC Lausanne, University of Lausanne.

Callen, T., Reynolds, P. and Towe, C. (2001) *India at the Crossroads: Sustaining Growth and Reducing Poverty*. Washington, DC: International Monetary Fund.

Calvo, G.A. and Reinhart, C.M. (2002) 'Fear of Floating', *Quarterly Journal of Economics*, 67: 379–408.

Campa, J. M. and Goldberg, L. S. (2002) *Exchange Rate Pass-through through Import Prices: A Macro or a Micro Phenomenon?*, NBER Working Paper, no. 8934. Cambridge, MA: National Bureau of Economic Research.

CIA (2008) *World Factbook*. Available online at: https://www.cia.gov/library/publications/the-world-factbook/index.html (accessed 15 December 2010).

Centre for International Competitiveness. 'World Knowledge Competitiveness Index 2008'. Available online at: http://www.cforic.org/downloads.php (accessed 21 September 2009).

China Daily 'China Posted High-Tech Export Value of US$71.8b in 1st Quarter'. Available online at: http://www.chinadaily.com.cn/bizchina/2007-06/08/content_890412.htm (accessed 17 November 2009).

Clément, J. A. P. (1994) 'Striving for stability: CFA Franc Realignment', *Finance and Development*, 31(2): 10–13.

Cline, W. R. and Williamson, J. (2007) *Estimates of the Equilibrium Exchange Rate of the Renminbi: Is There a Consensus and, If Not, Why Not?*, Paper presented at the Conference on China's Exchange Rate Policy, Peterson Institute for International Economics, October 12. Washington, DC: Peterson Institute for International Economics.

Cohn, T. H. (2005) *Global Political Economy: Theory and Practice*. New York: Pearson and Longman.

Committee on Banking Regulations and Supervisory Practices (1988) 'International Convergence of Capital Measurement and Capital Standards', *Kwartaalbericht*, vol. 2, 37–50. Amsterdam: De Nederlandsche Bank.

Cooper, R. N. (2001) 'Is the U.S. Current Account Deficit Sustainable? Will it be Sustained?' *Brookings Papers on Economic Activity*, 217–26.

Corden, W. M. (1972) 'Monetary Integration', *Essays in International Finance*, no. 93. Princeton, NJ: Princeton University Press.

Corden, W. M. (1994) *Economic Policy, Exchange Rates and the International System*. Oxford: Oxford University Press.

Curry, D. (1990) 'International Policy Coordination', in D. Llewellyn and C. Milner (eds), *Current Issues in International Monetary Economics*, 125–48. Basingstoke: Macmillan.

De Nederlandsche Bank (1995) *Annual Report 1994*. Amsterdam: De Nederlandsche Bank.

De Nederlandsche Bank (1998) *Annual Report 1997*. Amsterdam: De Nederlandsche Bank.

Diao, Xinshen and Burfisher, M. E. (2001) *Agricultural Policy Reform in the WTO: The Road Ahead*. Washington, DC: United States Department of Agriculture.

Dicken, P. (1986) *Global Shift, Industrial Change in a Turbulent World*. London: Harper & Row.

Dornbusch, R. (1976) 'Expectations and Exchange Rate Dynamics', *Journal of Political Economy*, 84: 1161–76.

Dornbusch, R. (1987) 'Purchasing Power Parity', in J. Eatwell, M. Milgate, and P. Newman (eds), *The New Palgrave: A Dictionary of Economics*, 1075–85. Basingstoke: Macmillan.

Dornbusch, R. (2001) *A Primer on Emerging Market Crises*, NBER Working Paper, no. 8326, June. Cambridge, MA: National Bureau of Economic Research.

Drazen, A., Limão, N. and Stratmann, T. (2004) *Political Contribution Caps and Lobby Formation: Theory and Evidence*. Cambridge, MA: National Bureau of Economic Research.

Dunning, J. H. (1993) *Multinational Enterprises and the Global Economy*. Reading, MA: Addison-Wesley.

Eaton, J., Gersovitz, M. and Stiglitz, J. E. (1987) 'The Pure Theory of Country Risk', *European Economic Review*, 30: 481–513.

ECB (European Central Bank) (2004) *The Euro Bond Market Study*, December. Frankfurt: ECB.

Economist, The (1993) 'Multinationals', 27 March, 5–28.

Economist, The (1998a) 'Of Take-offs and Tempests', 14 March, p. 100.

Economist, The (1998b) 'Two Kinds of Openness', 12 September, p. 93.

Economist, The (2008) 'Europe's Surprising Labour Flexibility', 28 November. Available online at: http://www.economist.com/node/12676787?story_id=12676787 (accessed 10 August 2011).

Economist, The (2009) 'The Big Mac Index – Cheesed Off', 18 July, p. 66.

Edwards, S. (1992) *Exchange Rates as Nominal Anchors*, NBER Working Paper, no. 4246. Cambridge, MA: National Bureau of Economic Research.

Edwards, S. (2002) 'The Great Exchange Rate Debate after Argentina', *North American Journal of Economics and Finance*, 13: 237–52.

Eiteman, D. K., Stonehill, A. I. and Moffett, M. H. (2001) *Multinational Business Finance*. Boston: Addison-Wesley Longman.

Engardio, P. (2005a) 'A New World Economy', *Business Week*, 22 October.

Engardio, P. (2005b) 'Crouching Tiger, Hidden Dragons', *Business Week*, 22 October.

Engel, C., Mark, N. C. and West, K. D. (2007) 'Exchange Rate Models are Not as Bad as You Think', Paper prepared for the *NBER Macroeconomics Annual, 2007 Conference*. Cambridge, MA: National Bureau of Economic Research.

Enoch, C. and Gulde, A.-M (1998). 'Are Currency Boards a Cure for all Monetary Problems?', *Finance and Development*, 35(4): 40–3.

European Commission (1990) 'One Market, One Money: An Evaluation of the Potential Benefits and Costs of Forming an Economic and Monetary Union', *European Economy*, 44.

European Commission Directorate-General for Agriculture and Rural Development (2007) 'The Common Agricultural Policy Explained', Brussels, Belgium. Available online at: http://ec.europa.eu/agriculture/publi/capexplained/cap_en.pdf (accessed 12 March 2011).

Ex-Im Bank 'Foreign Currency Guarantee'. Available online at: http://www.exim.gov/products/guarantee/foreign_curr.cfm (accessed May 2, 2011).

Feldstein, M. (1989) 'The Case against Trying to Stabilize the Dollar', *American Economic Review*, 79: 36–40.

Feldstein, M. (1998) 'Refocusing the IMF', *Foreign Affairs*, 77: 20–33.

Finger, J. F. and Schuknecht, L. (2001) 'Market Access Advances: the Uruguay Round', in B. Hoekman and W. Martin (eds), *Developing Countries and the WTO: A Pro-active Agenda*. Oxford: Blackwell.

Fischer, S. (1998) 'Lessons from a Crisis', *The Economist*, 3 October, pp. 23, 24, and 30.

Fischer, S. (2001). 'Exchange Rate Regimes: Is the Bipolar View Correct?', *Journal of Economic Perspectives*, 15(2): 3–24.

Frankel, J. A. (1988) 'Obstacles to International Macroeconomic Policy Coordination', *Princeton Studies in International Finance*, vol. 64. Princeton, NJ: Princeton University Press.

Frankel, J. A. (2004) 'Experience of Lessons from Exchange Rate Regimes in Emerging Economies', in Asian Development Bank, *Monetary and Financial Integration in East Asia: The Way Ahead*, vol. 2, 91–138. New York: Palgrave Macmillan.

Frankel, J. A., Dooley, M. P. and Wickham, P. (eds) (1989) *Analytical Issues in Debt*. Washington, DC: International Monetary Fund.

Frankel, J. A. and Froot, K. A. (1990) 'Chartists, Fundamentalists, and Trading in the Foreign Exchange Markets', *American Economic Review*, 80: 181–5.

Frankel, J. A. and Johnson, H. G. (eds) (1978) *The Economics of Exchange Rates: Selected Studies*. Reading, MA: Addison-Wesley.

Frankel, J. A. and MacArthur, A.T. (1988) 'Political vs Currency Premia in International Real Interest Differentials: A Study of Forward Rates for 24 Countries', *European Economic Review*, 32: 1083–121.

Frey, B. S. (1984) *International Political Economics*. Oxford: Basil Blackwell.

Froot, K. A. and Klemperer, P. D. (1989) 'Exchange Rate Pass-through When Market Share Matters', *American Economic Review*, 79: 637–54.

GATT (General Agreement on Tariffs and Trade) (1990) *International Trade 89–90*, vol. 1. Geneva: World Trade Organization.

GATT (General Agreement on Tariffs and Trade) (1991) *International Trade 90–91*, vol. 2. Geneva: World Trade Organization.

Gärtner, M. (1993), *Macroeconomics under Flexible Exchange Rates*. New York: Harvester Wheatsheaf.

Giddy, I. H. (1994) *Global Financial Markets*. Lexington, MA, and Toronto: D.C. Heath and Company.

Goldstein, M. (1984) *The Exchange Rate System: Lessons of the Past and Options for the Future*, IMF Occasional Paper, no. 30. Washington, DC: International Monetary Fund.

Goldstein, M., Isard, P., Masson, P. R. and Taylor, M. P. (1992) *Policy Issues in the Evolving International Monetary System*, IMF Occasional Paper, no. 96, June. Washington, DC: International Monetary Fund.

Goldstein, M. and Folkerts-Landau, D. (1994) *International Capital Markets: Developments, Prospects, and Policy Issues* (World Economic and Financial Surveys series). Washington, DC: International Monetary Fund.

Grauwe, P. de (1989) *International Money: Post-War Trends and Theories*. Oxford: Clarendon Press.

Grauwe, P. de (1994) *The Economics of Monetary Integration*, 2nd edn. Oxford: Oxford University Press.

Greenaway, D. and Miller, C. (1986) *The Economics of Intra-Industry Trade*. Oxford: Basil Blackwell.

Grilli, E. and Sassoon, E. (1990) *The New Protectionist Wave*. Basingstoke: Macmillan.

Gros, D. and Thygesen, N. (1998) *European Monetary Integration: From the European Monetary System to European Monetary Union*, 2nd edn. London and New York: Longman.

Guardian, The (2008), 'How Detroit Took the Wrong Road', 21 October. Available online at: http://www.guardian.co.uk/business/2008/nov/21/ford-general-motors-cars (accessed 10 August 2011).

Hakura, D. (2004) 'Learning to Float: The Experience of Emerging Market Countries since the Early 1990s', in International Monetary Fund, *World Economic Outlook*, pp. 89–103, September. Washington, DC: International Monetary Fund.

Hamm, S. (2005) 'A Brain Thrust in Bangalore', *Business Week Online*, 29 July.

Haniotis, T. and Schich, S. (1995) *Should Governments Subsidize Exports through Export Credit Insurance Agencies?*, United Nations Conference on Trade and Development Discussion Paper 103. Geneva: UNCTAD.

Hausmann, R., Panizza, U. and Stein, E. (2001) 'Why Do Countries Float the Way they Float?', *Journal of Development Economics*, 66: 387–414.

Helpman, E. and Krugman, P.R. (1985) *Market Structure and Foreign Trade*. Cambridge, MA: MIT Press.

Hermes, C. L. M. (1992) *De Internationale Schuldencrisis* [*The International Debt Crisis*]. Groningen: Wolters-Noordhoff.

Hoekman, B. M. (1988) *Agriculture and the Uruguay Round*, IPPS Discussion Paper, no. 292, University of Michigan.

Horen, N. van, Jager, H. and Klaassen, F. (2006) 'Foreign Exchange Market Contagion in the Asian Crisis: A regression-based Approach', *Review of World Economics (Weltwirtschaftliches Archiv)*, 142: 374–401.

Indian Ministry of Commerce and Industry (2006) *Annual Report 2006*. New Delhi: Indian Ministry of Commerce and Industry.

IMF (International Monetary Fund) (1978) *Articles of Agreement of the International Monetary Fund*. Washington, DC: IMF.

IMF (International Monetary Fund) (1990) *Direction of Trade Statistics Yearbook*. Washington, DC: IMF.

IMF (International Monetary Fund) (1991) *Determinants and Systemic Consequences of International Capital Flows: A Study by the Research Department of the International Monetary Fund*, IMF Occasional Paper, no. 77, March. Washington, DC: IMF.

IMF (International Monetary Fund) (1993) *World Economic Outlook*. Washington, DC: IMF.

IMF (International Monetary Fund) (1993) *International Capital Markets*, Part I. Washington, DC: IMF.

IMF (International Monetary Fund) (1994a) *Annual Report 1994*. Washington, DC: IMF.

IMF (International Monetary Fund) (1994b) *IMF Survey: Supplement on the IMF*, 23. Washington, DC: IMF.

IMF (International Monetary Fund) (1995) 'G-7 Offers Proposals to Strengthen Bretton Woods Institutions', *IMF Survey*, 24: 201–5.

IMF (International Monetary Fund) (1998) 'Emerging Markets in the New International Financial System: Implications of the Asian Crisis', *International Capital Markets: World Economic and Financial Surveys*, pp. 59–81. Washington, DC: IMF.

IMF (International Monetary Fund) (1999) *Balance of Payment Statistics Yearbook*, Part 1. Washington, DC: IMF.

IMF (International Monetary Fund) (1999) 'Chile's Experience with Capital Controls', *International Capital Markets*, 176–9. Washington, DC: IMF.

IMF (International Monetary Fund) (2000) *World Economic Outlook*. Washington, DC: IMF.

IMF (International Monetary Fund) (2000) *India: Recent Economic Developments*, Series: IMF Staff Country Report no. 00/155. Washington, DC: IMF.

IMF (International Monetary Fund) (2000) Annex V, 'Conceptual Framework of the Balance of Payments and International Investment Position', and Annex VI, 'Classification and Standard Components of the Balance of Payments', *Balance of Payments Statistics Yearbook*, pp. xxi–xxvii. Washington, DC: IMF.

IMF (International Monetary Fund) (2001a) *The World Economic Outlook (WEO) Database*. Washington, DC: IMF.

IMF (International Monetary Fund) (2001b) *Direction of Trade Statistics*. Washington, DC: IMF.

IMF (International Monetary Fund) (2001c) *International Capital Markets*. Washington, DC: IMF.

IMF (International Monetary Fund) (2002) *World Economic Outlook*, April. Washington, DC: IMF.

IMF (International Monetary Fund) (2002), 'Essays on Trade and Finance' (Ch. 2), *World Economic Outlook*, pp. 65–80. Washington, DC: IMF.

IMF (International Monetary Fund) (2004) *Annual Report 2004*. Washington, DC: IMF.

IMF (International Monetary Fund) (2006) 'Operational Guidance to IMF Staff on the 2002 Conditionality Guidelines', Revised 9 January 2006, *IMF Memorandum*. Washington, DC: IMF.

IMF (International Monetary Fund) (2008) *Annual Report 2008*. Washington, DC: IMF.

IMF (International Monetary Fund) (2008/2010a) *World Economic Outlook 2008/2010*. Washington, DC: IMF.

IMF (International Monetary Fund) (2008/2010b) *International Financial Statistics*, June. Washington, DC: IMF.

IMF (International Monetary Fund) *International Financial Statistics*, various issues. Washington, DC: IMF.

IMF (International Monetary Fund) Capital Market Division (1994) 'Banks and Derivatives Markets: A Challenge for Financial Policy', *IMF Survey*, 23: 49–51.

Jager, H. (1991) 'The Global Exchange Rate System in Transition', *De Economist*, 139: 471–96.

Jager, H. and Pauli, R. (2001) 'Anti-Inflatoir Wisselkoersbeleid via een Currency board; de Walters-kritiek Doorbroken?' ['Anti-Inflationary Policy via a Currency Board: A Breakthrough of the Walters Critique?'], *Maandschrift Economie*, 65: 446–76.

James, H. (1998) 'From Grandmotherliness to Governance: The Evolution of IMF Conditionality', *Finance and Development*, 35 (4): 44–7.

Jeffery, S. (2003) 'The EU Common Agricultural Policy', *The Guardian*, 26 June.

Johnsen, D. G., Hemmi, K. and Lardinois, P. (1985) *Agricultural Policy and Trade: Adjusting Domestic Programs in an International Framework*, Task Force Report to the Trilateral Commission. New York: New York University Press.

Jungnickel, R. (1993), 'Recent Trends in Foreign Direct Investment', *Intereconomics* May–June: 118–25.

Jurgen, O. (2008), 'Falsche Debatte über Nokia', *Financial Times Deutschland*, 17 January.

Kee, H. L., Olarreaga, M. and Silva, P. (2004) *Market Access for Sale: Latin America's Lobbying for US Tariff Preferences*, Policy Research Working Papers 3198. Washington, DC: World Bank.

Khan, M. S. and Sharma, S. (2002), 'Reconciling Conditionality and Country Ownership', *Finance & Development*, 39(2): 28–31.

Kindleberger. C. P. (1978) *Manias, Panics, and Crashes: A History of Financial Crises*. New York: John Wiley.

Krugman, P. R. (1979) 'A Model of Balance of Payments Crises', *Journal of Money, Credit and Banking*, 11: 311–25.

Krugman, P. R. (1987) 'Is Free Trade Passé?', *Journal of Economic Perspectives*, 1(2): 131–44.

Krugman, P. R. (1989) *Rethinking International Trade*. Cambridge, MA, and London: MIT Press.

Krugman, P. R. (1999), 'Balance Sheets, the Transfer Problem, and Financial Crises', *International and Public Finance*, 6: 459–72.

Krugman, P. R. and Obstfeld, M. (1989) *International Economics: Theory and Policy*. Boston, MA: Scott, Foresman and Company.

Krugman, P. R. and Obstfeld, M. (1994) *International Economics, Theory and Policy*. 3rd edn. New York: Harper Collins.

Lawrence, R. Z. (1996) *Regionalism, Multilateralism, and Deeper Integration*. Washington, DC: Brookings Institution.

Lessard, D. (1983) 'Principles of International Portfolio Selection', in A.M. George and I. H. Giddy (eds), *International Finance Handbook*, vol. 2, pp. 8.2.3–8.2.19. New York: Wiley.

McKinnon, R. I. (1973) *Money and Capital in Economic Development*. Washington, DC: Brookings Institution.

McKinnon, R. I. (1982) 'Currency Substitution and Instability in the World Dollar Standard', *American Economic Review*, 72: 320–33.

McKinnon, R. I. (1982) 'The Order of Liberalization: Lessons from Chile and Argentina', *Carnegie-Rochester Conference Series on Public Policy*, 17: 159–86.

McKinnon, R. I. (1984) *An International Standard for Monetary Stabilization*. Washington, DC: Institute for International Economics.

McKinnon, R. I. (1991) *The Order of Economic Liberalization: Financial Control in the Transition to a Market Economy*. Baltimore and London: The John Hopkins University Press.

McKinnon, R. I. (1993) 'The Rules of the Game: International Money in Historical Perspective', *Journal of Economic Literature*, 31: 1–44.

Maddison, A. (1989) *The World Economy in the Twentieth Century*. Paris: Organisation for Economic Co-operation and Development.

Magee, S. P. (1980) *International Trade*, Perspective in Economics Series. Reading, MA: Addison-Wesley.

Magee, S. P., Brock, W. A. and Young, L. (1989) *Black Hole Tariffs and Endogenous Policy Theory: Political Economy in General Equilibrium*. Cambridge: Cambridge University Press.

Manager Magazine (2008) 'Rechnet Nokia falsch', 18 January. Available online at http://www.manager-magazin.de/unternehmen/artikel/0,2828,529481,00.html.

Markowitz, H. (1959) *Portfolio Selection: Efficient Diversification of Investments*. New York: Wiley.

Mattoo, A. and Wunsch, S. (2004) *Pre-empting Protectionism in Services: The WTO and Outsourcing*, Policy Research Working Papers 3237. Washington, DC: World Bank.

Meierjohann, W. (1984) 'Charting a Course through the Waves', *Euromoney*, July: 157–65.

Michalopoulos, C. (1999) 'Trade Policy and Market Access Issues for Developing Countries: Implication for the Millennium Round', mimeo. Washington, DC: World Bank.

Milner, H. V. (1988) *Resisting Protectionism: Global Industries and the Politics of International Trade*. Princeton, NJ: Princeton University Press.

Moran, T. H. (1998) *Managing International Political Risk*. Malden, MA, and Oxford: Blackwell.

Morgan Guaranty (1987) *World Financial Markets*, June/July. New York: Morgan Guaranty.

Mulle, V., 'Warum Nokia Richtig Handelt', *Financial Times Deutschland*, 17 January.

Nsouli, S. M., Rached, M. and Funke, N. (2002) *The Speed of Adjustment and the Sequencing of Economic Reforms: Issues and Guidelines for Policy Makers*, IMF Working Paper, no. WP/02/132. Washington, DC: IMF.

NRC Handelsblad (1974) Obligatiemarkt heropend voor buitenlanders, 31 January.

Oatley, T. (2004) *International Political Economy: Interests and Institutions in the Global Economy*. New York: Pearson and Longman.

Obstfeld, M. (1986) 'Rational and Self-Fulfilling Balance of Payments Crises', *American Economic Review*, 76: 72–81.

O'Brien, R. and Williams, M. (2004) *Global Political Economy: Evolution and Dynamics*. Basingstoke: Palgrave Macmillan.

OECD (Organisation for Economic Co-operation and Development) (1990a) *Development Co-operation, 1990 Report*, December. Paris: OECD.

OECD (Organisation for Economic Co-operation and Development (1990b) *Financing and External Debt of Developing Countries, 1989 Survey*. Paris: OECD.

OECD (Organisation for Economic Co-operation and Development (1991) *Employment Outlook*. Paris: OECD.

OECD (Organisation for Economic Co-operation and Development (1997) 'Assessing Barriers to Trade in Services: A Pilot Study on Accountancy Services', TD/TC/WP(97)26, Working Party of the Trade Committee. Paris: OECD.

OECD (Organisation for Economic Co-operation and Development (1998) *Financial Market Trends*, February. Paris: OECD.

OECD (Organisation for Economic Co-operation and Development (2000) *OECD Economic Outlook*, no. 68, pp. 183–201. Paris: OECD.

OECD (Organisation for Economic Co-operation and Development (2009) *International Migration Outlook: SOPEMI 2009*, p.44. Paris: OECD. Available online at: http://www.oecd.org/document/51/0,3746,en_2649_33931_43009971_1_1_1_1,00.html (10 August 2011).

OECD (Organisation for Economic Co-operation and Development (2010) *International Migration Outlook: SOPEMI 2010*, pp. 44, 295. Paris: OECD.

OECD (Organisation for Economic Co-operation and Development (2011) 'Arrangement on Officially Supported Export Credits', version March 2011. Available online at: http://www.oecd.org/officialdocuments/ech/act/xcred-en.htm (accessed 3 May 2011).

Officer, L. H. (1996) *Between the Dollar–Sterling Gold Points: Exchange Rates, Parity, and Market Behavior*. Cambridge: Cambridge University Press.

Owen, D. (2005) 'The Betamax vs VHS War', 1 May. Available online at: http://www.mediacollege.com/video/format/compare/betamax-vhs.html (accessed 9 April 2010).

Perkmans, J. (1984) *Market Integration in the European Community*, Studies in Industrial Organization, vol. 5, The Hague: Martinus Nijhoff.

Pilbeam, K. (2005) *International Finance*, 3rd edn. Basingstoke: Palgrave Macmillan.

Porter, M. E. (1990) *The Competitive Advantage of Nations*. New York: Free Press.

Prava (2007) 'American Automakers Lose their Leadership on US Auto Market', 2 August. Available online at: http://english.pravda.ru/business/companies/02-08-2007/95565-american_automakers-0/ (accessed 10 August 2011).

Ralph, N. (2008) 'Statement on Auto Industry Bailouts', Washington, DC, 17 September. Available online at: http://www.nader.org/index.php?/archives/2060-Statement-on-Auto-Industry-Bailouts.html (accessed 10 August 2011).

Ravenhill, J. (ed.) (2005) *Global Political Economy*. Oxford: Oxford University Press.

Sachs, J. D. (ed.) (1989) *Developing Country Debt and the World Economy*. Chicago: University of Chicago Press.

Salisbury, R. H. and Cohen, D. (2001) *Lobbying, Pluralism and Democracy*. Basingstoke: Palgrave Macmillan.

Sasseen, J. (1992) 'Getting through to Brussels', *International Management*, 92 (47/3): 62–3.

Schuler, K. (2005) 'Some Theory and History of Dollarization', *Cato Journal*, 25: 115–25.

Shurmer-Smith, P. (2000) *India, Globalization and Change*. London: Arnold; New York: Oxford University Press.

Smith, A. and Venables, A. (1991) 'Counting the Cost of Voluntary Export Restraints in the European Car Market', in E. Helpman and A. Razin (eds), *International Trade and Trade Policy*, 187–220. Cambridge, MA: MIT Press.

Stevenson, C. and Filippi, I. (2004) *The Global Trade and Protection Report 2004*. London: Mayer, Brown, Rowe & Maw.

Tavlas, G. S. (1991) *On the International Use of Currencies: The Case of the Deutsche Mark*, Princeton Essays in International Finance, no. 181. Princeton, NJ: Princeton University.

Tavlas, G. S. and Ozeki, Y. (1992) *The Internationalization of Currencies: An Appraisal of the Japanese Yen*, IMF Occasional Paper, no. 90. Washington, DC: International Monetary Fund.

Taylor, M. P. (1995) 'The Economics of Exchange Rates', *Journal of Economic Literature*, 33: 13–47.

Taylor, M. P. and Allen, H. (1992) 'The Use of Technical Analysis in the Foreign Exchange Market', *Journal of International Money and Finance*, 11: 304–14.

Tinbergen, J. (1954) *International Economic Integration*. Amsterdam: Elsevier.

Tobin, J. (1958) 'Liquidity Preference as Behavior towards Risk', *Review of Economic Studies*, 25: 65–86.

Torre, J. de la and Neckar, D.H. (1988) 'Forecasting Political Risks for International Operations', *International Journal of Forecasting*, 4: 221–41.

Trefler, D. (1995) 'The Case of the Missing Trade and Other Mysteries', *American Economic Review*, 85: 1029–46.

Turner, P. (1991) *Capital Flows in the 1980s: A Survey of Major Trends*, BIS Economic Papers, no. 30, April. Basel: BIS.

Tyers. R. and Anderson, K. (1986) 'Distortions in World Food Markets: A Quantitative Assessment'. Background paper prepared for the *World Development Report 1986*. Washington DC: World Bank.

'Two European Countries 40% Difference in Price of Volkswagen Passat', GoCurrency.com; http://www.gocurrency.com/articles/stories-car-prices.htm.

Ungerer, H., Mayer, T. H. and Hauvonen, J. J. (1990) *The European Monetary System: Developments and Perspectives*, IMF Occasional Paper, no. 73. Washington, DC: IMF.

UN (United Nations) (2001) *Population, Environment and Development*. New York: UN, Department of Economic and Social Affairs, Population Division.

United Nations Conference on Trade and Development (UNCTAD) (2000) *World Investment Report 2000*. New York: UN.

UNCTAD (United Nations Conference on Trade and Development) (2008) *UNCTAD Handbook of Statistics 2008*. Available online at: http://stats.unctad.org/Handbook/TableViewer/tableView.aspx (accessed 16 November 2009).

UNCTAD (United Nations Conference on Trade and Development) (2008a) *World Investment Report 2008*. New York: UN.

UNCTAD (United Nations Conference on Trade and Development) (2008b) *Cross-Border M&A Database*. Available online at www.unctad.org/fdistatistices (accessed 6 August 2010).

United States Mission to the European Union (2006) 'Congress Passes Bill ending WTO Export Tax Break Dispute with EU', Brussels. Available online at: http://useu.usmission.gov/Article.asp?ID= BF20671F-5ACA-41C3-9AA9-142963220D62 (accessed 12 March 2011).

Valdés, A. and Zietz, J. (1980) *Agricultural Protection in OECD Countries: Its Costs to Less Developed Countries*, Research Report no. 21. Washington, DC: International Food Policy Research Institute.

Van den Boogaerde, P. and Tsangarides, C. (2005) *Ten Years after the CFA Franc Devaluation: Progress toward regional Integration in the WAEMU*, IMF Working Paper, no. 05/145. Washington, DC: IMF.

van Marion, M. F. (1993) Liberal Trade and Japan: The Incompatibility Issue. New York: Springer-Verlag.

Vernon, R. (1966) 'International Investment and International Trade in the Product Cycle', *Quarterly Journal of Economics*, 80: 190–307.

Vernon, R. (1979) 'The Product Cycle Hypothesis in a New International Environment', *Oxford Bulletin of Economics and Statistics*, 41: 255–67.

Viner, J. (1950) *The Customs Union Issue*. New York: The Carnegie Endowment for International Peace.

Walters, A. (1986) *Britain's Economic Renaissance: Margaret Thatcher's Reforms, 1979–1984*. New York and Oxford: Oxford University Press.

Wells, L. T. (ed.) (1972) *The Product Life Cycle and International Trade*. Cambridge, MA: Harvard University Press.

Wersch, M. P. F. M. van (2003) *Balance of Payments in the Netherlands: The Road to a Modern Survey System, Statistical Bulletin*; Special Issue. Amsterdam: De Nederlandsche Bank.

Williamson, J. (1983) *The Exchange Rate System*. Washington, DC: Institute for International Economics.

Williamson, J. and Milner, C. (1991) *The World Economy*. New York: Harvester Wheatsheaf.

World Bank (1993) *East Asian Miracle*. New York: Oxford University Press.

World Bank (2001) *World Development Report 2000/2001*. Washington, DC: World Bank.

World Bank Development Prospect Groups (2008) *Migration and Remittances Factbook 2008*. Available online at: http://web.worldbank.org/WBSITE/EXTERNAL/EXTDEC/EXTDECPROSPECTS/0, menuPK:476941~pagePK:51084723~piPK:51084722~theSitePK:476883,00.html (accessed 27 Novemeber 2009).

WTO (World Trade Organization) (2001) 'Overview of Developments in the International Trading Environment', annual report by the Director-General. Available online at: http://www.wto.org (accessed 23 December 2009).

WTO (World Trade Organization) (2006) *International Trade Statistics*. Geneva: WTO.

WTO (World Trade Organization) (2008)*International Trade Statistics*. Geneva: WTO.

WTO (World Trade Organization) (2008) 'Market Access: Unfinished Business, Post-Uruguay Round Inventory and Issues', Special Studies 6. Geneva: WTO.

WTO (World Trade Organization) (2010) *International Trade Statistics 2010*, World Trade Developments in 2007. Available online at: http://www.wto.org/english/res_e/statis_e/its2008_e/its08_world_trade_dev_e.htm. (accessed 21 December 2010).

WTO (World Trade Organization) (2010) *World Trade Report 2010*, Geneva: WTO.

3G.co.uk (2006) 'Mobile Subscribers in China to Reach 595.46 Million in 2009', April. Available online at: http://www.3g.co.uk/PR/April2006/2863.htm (accessed 21 June 2009).

Index

absorption approach 261–3, 274, 336
absolute costs 31–2
adjustable peg system 255–60, 267, 269, 310–11, 315, 381
administered protection (AP) 160, 174
Agreement on Textiles and Clothing (ATC) 153
agriculture
    European Union policy 101–2, 156–7
    government policy 102
    import tariffs on agricultural products 156–7
    tariffs and subsidies 103
America, *see* USA
American International Group (AIG) 92
anti-dumping agreement 89, 127, 156
    initiations of 160
anti-dumping duties, application of 161–2, 165
Antitrust Law 190
arbitrage 217–20
Argentine currency board
    characteristics of 371–2
    currency board idea 374
    'fear of floating' hypothesis 376
    rise and fall of 372–4
Asian currency crisis (1997)
    adjustment policies 356–7
    causes of 353–5
    contagion phenomenon 355–6
    origins of 347–8
    previous history of 351–3
Association of South East Asian Nations (ASEAN) 1, 11, 152, 180
average export ratio 94
average propensity to import 17

balance of payments
    accounting practice 199–205
    analysis of 205–7
    classification system 193
        capital and financial accounts 197–9
        current account 196–7
    double-bookkeeping, rule of 199–200, 205
    essential identities in 202
    of G3 countries 202–3
    of Japan 194–5

    relationship with foreign exchange
        market 201
Balance of Payments Manual (IMF) 196
banana war, case study 175–6
Bank for International Settlements (BIS) 208–9, 229–30, 297, 337
banknotes, exchange rates 198
basket currency 314
beggar-thy-neighbour policy 115, 299, 306
Big Mac index 240–3
bilateral exchange rate 209–10, 239, 317, 378
bill of exchange
    bank acceptance 217
    functions of 216
Birmingham Summit (1998) 301
Blair House accord 156–7
Bologna Declaration (1999) 185
borrowing credibility 267
Brady Plan 339
brand name 68, 73, 119, 146
Brazil
    Article 68 of industrial property law 147
    drug dispute with USA 147–8
Bretton Woods conference 307
    exchange-rate system 310–12

capital account 197–9, 311, 344, 373
capital control 227, 228, 360
capital flows
    and emerging market economies 20
    gross 19
    international 18–21
        sources and uses of global capital 21
        volatility in 20
    levels of 20
    and reserves in Asia 354
capital-intensive goods 38
capital markets 1, 7, 49, 62, 214, 216, 292
    domestic 330
    and financial centres 228–33
    international 228–33, 258, 321
cartel
    agreement 140–1
    policy 190

case study
  Big Mac index 240–3
  birth of eurodollars 228–9
  car exports and export of car production facilities
    53–4
  Corus group, economic risk of
    280–1
  domestic electrical appliances 128–9
  Dutch exchange-rate policy 268
  emerging industrial countries 24–30
  Euromoney's country-risk rating
    289–91
  European banana war 175–6
  European car market 123–6, 129
  export policies in India 86–9
  financial liberalization in Japan 249
  Foreign Sales Corporation Act, USA 90–1
  growing role of China and India in world
    economy 24–9
  G7 summit in Halifax (1995) 301–2
  impact of Eastern Europeans on labour market 60
  Japanese restructuring in response to high value
    of yen 281–2
  Japan's balance of payments 194–5
  mobile telephone market, internationalization
    of 3
  motor vehicle sector 53–5
  Nokia's relocation of its factory from Bochum to
    Cluj in Romania 73
  OPEC cartel 141–2
  patent dispute between USA and Brazil 146–8
  practice of lobbying 167–70
  protectionism through paperwork 164–5
  Reinheitsgebot (purity law), Germany 133–4
  trade restrictions, welfare effects of 105–7
  video recorder market 119–20
  worldwide current account discrepancy 205
'Celtic Tiger' economy 60, 68
Central African Economic and Monetary
    Community (CAEMC) 369–71
Cetes 349
CFA franc 369, 370
China
  consumer markets 26
  entry to WTO 92–3
  growing role in world economy 24–9
  as industrial powerhouses 27–8
  manufacturing exports 28
  merchandise exports 26
Common Agricultural Policy (CAP), Europian
    Union 102, 157, 303, 377
common market 128, 186, 188, 377
Common Market for Eastern and Southern Africa
    (COMESA) 152, 180
company, international environment of 2–6
comparative costs
  concept of 23
  model for international trade 32–5

competing devaluation 355, 377
competition
  countervailing duties for prevention of 164
  duopoly 131–3
  excess profit for a cartel compared with 140
  imperfect 141
  between lobby groups 175, 177–9
  oligopoly 130–1
consumer markets, in China and India 26
consumer preference/demand, influence on
    international competitiveness 48
contagion 289, 318, 355–6, 373
Corn Laws 35
countervailing duties (CVDs) 86, 89–90, 160, 162–4
country risk
  assessment of 287–9
  hedging of 284–9
  rating 290–1
  types of 277–8
Cournot's equilibrium 133
covered interest parity (CIP) 220–1, 234, 294
credit crisis 197, 308
creditor countries 62, 204, 338
credit rating agencies 5
cronyism 227, 332
cross-border payments 197
cross-currency arbitrage 218
currency
  capital flight 259
  inconvertible 226
  nominal effective exchange rate of 210
  overvaluation of 330–1
  return profile of 296
currency board 260, 261, 278, 365, 371–6, 387;
    currency board in Argentina 371–4
currency crisis
  Argentine crisis (2001) 373–4
  Asian crisis (1997)
    adjustment policies 356–7
    causes of 353–4
    contagion phenomenon 355–6
    origins of 347–8
    previous history of 351–3
  EMS crisis (1992–93) 380–2
  lessons from
    direct lessons 357
    IMF 361
    policy lesson 358–61
  Mexican crisis (1994–95)
    direct causes of 350
    previous history and growing imbalances
      348–50
    type of 350–1
  three generations of theories
    Gresham's Law 343–4
    speculative attack model 345–8

current account 196–7
   balance 63–4, 206
   deficit 18
   effects of exchange rates on 261–7
   surplus 206
current transfer account 197
customs unions (CUs) 152, 185–6, 377–8

debt crisis 61, 277, 309, 324, 326, 335, 337–40, 348,
   364
debtor country 62, 204, 323–4, 327–9, 335, 337–40
Delors Committee 382
developing countries, position under GATT system
   152–3
dispute settlement system 150
Dispute Settlement Understanding 158, 163, 176
documentary credit 217, 234
Doha Development Agenda (DDA) 158
Doha Round 158
dollar 19, 20, 58, 71, 176, 202, 206–10, 217–22,
   229, 230, 248, 279, 291, 292, 294–6, 305,
   310–20, 368–70, 373
dollarization, in Ecuador 374–6
domestic earnings 8
domestic electrical appliances 128–9
drug dispute, between Brazil and USA 147–8
dual exchange rate 218, 360
dumping, concept of 86
duopoly
   in case of
      export subsidy by national government 136
      import tariff on goods supplied to domestic
         market by foreign supplier 136
   competitive behaviour, in international market
      131–3, 143
   effects of trade instruments in 138
   international, *see* international duopoly
   reaction curves in 132
   Reinheitsgebot (purity law), abolition of 133–4
   trade policy and 134–7
Dutch disease 227–8

eclectic theory, of international entrepreneurial
   behaviour 65
   for multinational enterprises (MNEs) 81–3
Economic and Monetary Union (EMU) 215, 303,
   365, 369, 377–8, 382–6
economic integration
   antitrust/cartel policy 190
   European 187–90
   merger control 191
   regional 185–7
   state aid 191
economic relationships, internationalization of 1
effective protection, theory of 148–9
elasticity of demand 79, 124, 126, 131, 140
electronic bank trading 231
E-plus (telecommunications service provider) 4–6

Euro 7, 188, 193, 202, 204, 205, 208, 209, 217–19,
   221, 222, 232, 256, 272, 274, 280, 314, 317–20,
   365, 368, 370
euro area, *see* Euro Zone
eurobonds 230–1
eurocurrencies 231
eurodollars 228–30
Euro Zone (or EMU) 21, 125, 291, 366, 368
European banana war 175–6
European car market 123–6, 129
European Communities (EC) 119, 120, 124, 125,
   128, 129, 133, 134, 137, 192, 376–82
European Credit Transfer System (ECTS) 185
European Currency Unit (ECU) 188, 379
European Economic Community (EEC) 78, 188,
   382
European economic integration 187–90
European Free Trade Association (EFTA) 152
European Monetary Agreement 188
European monetary integration, process of
   Economic and Monetary Union (EMU) 382–6
   European Monetary System (EMS) 378–82
   Snake Arrangement 376–8
European Monetary System (EMS) 188, 256, 267,
   378–82
   components of 378–9
European Payment Union 188
European Political Union (EPU) 382
European Union (EU) 1, 11, 152, 180
   agricultural policy 101–2, 156–7
   anti-dumping policy 161–2
   banana war 175–6
   Common Agricultural Policy (CAP) 102, 157, 377
   common market 186
   Directive on Services in the Internal Market 189
   economic integration 187–90
   labour market 186
   mobile markets 6
   mutual recognition of diplomas policy 185–6
   price differentiation in European car market 124
exchange control 226–8
exchange rate
   Bretton Woods system 310–12
   concepts and presentation 209–10
   Dutch policy 268
   effects on current account and international
      trade
      absorption approach 261–3
      exchange-rate volatility 265–7
      Marshall–Lerner condition 263–5
   fiscal policy 272–3
   fixed 255
   floating 255
   growth and unemployment, influence of 270
   inflation, effects of 267–9
   long-term changes
      monetary approach 244–5
      purchasing power parity (PPP) 239–44

monetary policy 270–2
predictions 251–2
ratchet effect 269
short-term changes
    currency substitution model 248–50
    overshooting model 246–8
    portfolio balance model 248–50
    uncovered interest rate parity 245–6
systems and policy 254–60
uncertainties 238
against US dollar 352
exchange-rate risk
    procedure for reducing
        artificial hedges 293–7
        natural hedges 291–3
    types of
        economic risk 279–81
        transaction risk 278–9
        translation risk 282–4
exchange rate system
    adjustable peg 255, 260, 378
    crawling peg 260, 273, 330
    fixed exchange rate 226, 227, 255 , 258–60, 271,
        272, 305–7
    flexible (or floating) exchange rate 255–7,
        267–75, 360
    irrevocably fixed exchange rate 364–84
    managed floating 260, 273, 315, 320
Exim certificates 87
export credit 216
    insurance 285–6
export credit guarantee agencies (ECGAs) 285, 286
export flows, within regional blocs 13
export levies
    effects of 97–9, 137
    international escalation of 138
export policy
    export subsidy 100–3
    export tax 97–9
export shares 16
export subsidies
    effects of 100–1, 137
    marginal costs and tariff 135
    policy of 86, 100–3
export tax 97–9
    effects on other country 99
external economies of scale
    and international trade 40, 43–4
    in Japan and Thailand 43–4

factor price equalization (FPE) 37, 57, 181
factor reversal, phenomenon of 39
fear of floating 376
financial account 193, 197–9, 204–5, 272
financial markets, internationalization
    of 21
fiscal deficits, monetary financing of 330
floating rate notes (FRNs) 231

foreign bonds 230, 231, 234, 248–50
foreign currency
    composition of reserves of 320
    treatment in financial statements 284
foreign direct investment (FDI) 8, 18, 20, 52, 64–8,
    198
    balance of long-term capital 206
    globalization factors 181
    indicators of 66–7
    in three major economic areas 64
foreign exchange 198
    arbitrage 217–20
    currency distribution of 209
    interest rate 259
    swap contract 295
foreign-exchange (forex) markets 8
    buying and selling activities, factors influencing
        207–8
    currency distribution of 320
    exchange rate, concepts and presentation 209–10
    functioning of 207–9
    graphical presentation of 255–6
    interbank trading 208
    regulation, see exchange control
    relationship with balance of payments 201
    reserve assets balance 206
    restriction 218, 226, 229, 307
    shares of 232
    supply and demand on 256
Foreign Sales Corporation Act, USA 90–1
foreign subsidiaries 2, 65, 71, 81, 182, 281–2, 292
Franc Zone 365–6, 368–71
free trade 34, 35, 38
    advantages of 85
    protective measures, use of 152
free trade areas (FTAs) 185–6

Gasunie, credits and cash balances 214–15
General Agreement on Tariffs and Trade (GATT) 1,
    53, 127, 145
    achievements of 154
    adoption of safeguard measures 160
    in agriculture sector 156–7
    anti-dumping agreement 156, 161–2
    Article 20 of 152
    average tariff reductions through 155
    ban on 'grey area' measures 157–8
    codes of conduct 156
    countervailing duties (CVDs), introduction of
        162–3
    differences with WTO 150
    functions of 150
    in intellectual property 157
    national treatment principle 151
    for prevention of unfair trade 163
    principle of non-discrimination 152
    rounds of negotiations 154–8
    in services sector 157

General Agreement on Tariffs and Trade
    (GATT) – *continued*
  system of reciprocity for abolition of tariffs 151
  in tackling non-tariff barriers 156
  Tokyo Round (1979) 153
General Agreement on Trade in Services (GATS) 1,
    150, 157
  meaning of 182
General Arrangements to Borrow (GAB)
    302, 309
Generalized System of Preferences
    (GSP) 153
globalization 180–5
  definition of 180
  foreign direct investment (FDI) 181
  General Agreement on Trade in Services (GATS)
    182
  impact on labour in low-wage
    countries 182
  worldwide trade policy 182
goods and services account 197, 261
Gresham's Law 343–4
gross domestic product (GDP) 17, 87, 181, 197,
    308, 370
Group of 8 (G8) summits 301
  effectiveness of 302–3

Halifax Summit (1995) 301–2
Heckscher–Ohlin–Samuelson (HOS) model, for
    international trade 35–8, 170, 181
  in symbols 37–8
human capital 39, 48, 55, 58, 181

import
  average propensity 17
  marginal propensity 17
  quota 104–7, 153, 159, 174
  subsidies, effects of 137
  substitution policy 108, 152
  tariffs 93–4, 99, 104–6, 108, 135, 148, 149, 159,
    331
import levies, *see* import tariff
import tariff
  anti-tariff interest groups 171–2
  effects of 137
  escalation 149
  international escalation of 138
  on agricultural products 156–7
  pro-tariff interest groups 171
  reductions through GATT rounds 155
income
  account 197, 204, 262
  elasticity 11, 80
  identity 261, 349, 356, 384
India
  anti-dumping measures 89
  consumer markets 26
  creditworthiness 87

exim certificates 87
foreign exchange crisis 87
growing role in world economy 24–9
as industrial powerhouses 27–8
macroeconomic performance, improvements in
    88
protectionism, policy of 86
structural adjustment programme 87
tariff barriers 88–9
inflation, effects on exchange rate 267–9
Information and Communications Technology
    (ICT) 5
intellectual property 150, 157–8
intellectual property rights
  international protection of 154
  Uruguay Round agreement for protection of 146
interbank trading 208
interest arbitrage 219–21, 234
interest parity
  covered 220
  uncovered 221
inter-industry trade 39
internal economies of scale
  and international trade 40–3
  production, consumption and trade with 41
International Accounting Standards Board (IASB)
    284
international bank liabilities, country distribution
    of 233
international bonds 232, 235, 386
  country distribution of 233
  development of 230
  factors influencing choice of 231
international capital flows
  arbitrage and forward exchange rate 217–20
  exchange controls, motives for 226–8
  international capital markets and financial
    centres 228–33
  portfolio diversification 222–5
  purpose of 214
  speculation 221–2
  trade credit 216–17
international capital mobility, phenomenon of 52,
    271
international cartels 134, 139–41
international competitiveness 34
  consumer preference/demand, influence of 48
  role of national location factors in determining
    level of 46
international competitive relationships, influence
    of location factors on 23–4
international duopoly
  equilibrium situations 138
  subsidy or tariff war between two countries 139
  trade policy and 134–7
international economic cooperation, types of 300–5

international factor mobility
    impact on income distribution 58–61
    similarities in international trade and 55–9
international markets
    duopoly competitive behaviour in 131–3
    under monopolistic competition 128
    oligopoly, analysis based on reaction curves
        130–1
international migration of labour, consequences
    of 56
international monetary cooperation
    after 1973
        adjustment problem 315–18
        confidence and liquidity problems 318–21
    between 1945 and 1973
        Bretton Woods exchange-rate system 310–12
        IMF 308–10
        liquidity issue 312–14
    prior to 1945 305–7
International Monetary Fund (IMF) 87, 196, 203,
    258
    Articles of Agreement 308, 312–13, 315
    conditions for temporary credits 335–7
    Interim Guidance Note on Streamlining
        Structural Conditionality 361
    international monetary cooperation 308–10
    lending issues 332–5
    lessons during currency crisis 361
international portfolio investment 18, 214, 225
international price ratio 34, 42
international relocation of production activities,
    theories for
    eclectic approach 81–3
    product life cycle theory 78–81
international risk, types of
    country risk
        assessment of 287–9
        hedging of 284–91
        rating 289–91
        types of 277–8
    exchange-rate risk
        economic risk 279–81
        procedure for reducing 291–7
        transaction risk 278–9
        translation risk 282–4
international trade
    in commercial services 157
    comparative cost theory for 32–5
    effect on factor prices 57
    effects of exchange rates on 261–7
    expansion of 9–14
    external economies of scale and 43–4
    in goods and services 16
    Heckscher–Ohlin–Samuelson (HOS) model for
        35–8
    of industrial products 15
    internal economies of scale and 40–3

international factor mobility, similarities with
    55–9
Mercantilist theories for 30–2
national significance of 14
    openness of economy 16–18
oligopoly models in 45
in principal types of goods 10
restrictions on 139
Ricardo's model for 32, 34–7
volume restrictions on 103–4
    import quota 104–7
    voluntary export restraint 104
world merchandise exports 9
world output of principal types of goods 10
International Trade Commission (ITC) 164, 168
international trade flows 9–14
    measurement of 13–14
    system for classification of 13
inter-temporal trade 52, 61–4
intra-industry trade (IIT) 11, 22, 39, 132
    classification scheme 13
    indices used to express intensity of 14
invoice currency 265, 270, 278

Japan
    balance of payments 194–5
    financial account deficit 204
    portfolio adjustment due to financial
        liberalization in 249
joint ventures 2, 71
    KPN and Qwest 4

keiretsu 127
Kennedy Round 155–6
Knaepen Package 286
KPN (Dutch telecoms company)
    consumer market, segmentation of 4
    innovation policies 3
        SMS services for pre-pay clients 4–5
    international strategic issues for 5–6
    joint venture with American company
        Qwest 4
    strategy for internationalization 4
    telecom monopolies 2
Kyoto Protocol 1, 184

labour-intensive goods 37, 39
labour market
    impact of Eastern Europeans on 60
    integration of 186
labour productivity 31–4, 46, 54, 370
Latin American Free Trade Association
    (LAFTA) 152
Legio-Lease 189
Leontief paradox 38–9
Lerner's symmetry theorem 99, 137
Libertel 3

liberalization, optimal sequencing of
  economic 358–9
Lisbon Summit (2000) 190
lobby groups, competition between 175, 177–9
lobbying
  costs and gains of 172
  optimal obfuscation hypothesis 174–5
  practice of 167–70
  reaction curves 178
London Interbank Offered Rate (LIBOR)
  231, 327
Louvre Accord (1987) 316

Maastricht Treaty (1992) 188, 380, 382, 385–6
marginal propensity to import 17
market forms, classification of 121–3
Marshall–Lerner condition, for balance of trade
  account 263–5
Mercado Común del Sur (MERCOSUR)
  152, 180
Mercantilist theories, of international trade
  30–2
merchandise trade
  growth rate of 9
  intra-regional and inter-regional 11
    share of 12
  leading exporters in 27
  by major product group 18
  share of services of industrialized countries 18
mergers and acquisitions 9, 68
  by region/economy of
    purchaser 69
    seller 69
    seller and purchaser 69
  value of 69
Mexican currency crisis (1994–95)
  direct causes of 350
  previous history and growing imbalances 348–50
  type of crisis 350–1
mobile network operators 6
mobile telephone market, internationalization of 3
monetary integration
  Argentine currency board
    characteristics of 371–2
    currency board idea 374
    'fear of floating' hypothesis 376
    rise and fall of 372–4
  European monetary integration, process of
    Economic and Monetary Union (EMU) 382–6
    European Monetary System (EMS) 378–82
    Snake Arrangement 376–8
  Franc Zone 368–71
  optimum currency areas, theory of 365–8
monopolistic competition 45
  international markets and 128
most-favourite-nation (MFN) 150, 151, 153
motor vehicle sector, case study 53–5

Multi-Fibre Arrangement (MFA) 153, 159,
  174, 304
multinational enterprises (MNEs) 52, 68
  characteristics of 72–73
  definition of 71–3
  establishment of 71
  international relocation of production activities,
    theories for 74–83
    eclectic approach 81–3
    product life cycle theory 78–81
  process of development into 71
  relative importance of 73–4
  transfer pricing 73
  Vernon model for development of 80–1

Naples Summit (1994) 301
national economic identity, concept of 1
National European Competitiveness Index
  (2006–7) 46
national income, effect of improvement in terms of
  trade 93–4
national labour productivity 33
national location factors, for determining level of
  international competitiveness 46
national sub-markets 123–8
net foreign assets 198
New Arrangements to Borrow (NAB) 309
newly industrialized countries (NICs) 37
Nixon Round, see Tokyo Round (1979)
Nomenclature Générale des Activités Économiques
  dans les Communautés Européennes
  (NACE) 13
nominal exchange rate 209–10, 243–4, 263,
  368, 376
non-tariff barriers (NTBs) 86, 159–66
  Single European Act for elimination of 188
North American Free Trade Agreement (NAFTA) 1,
  11, 37, 152, 180, 349
North–North trade 11

official reserve assets 198, 200, 202, 255,
  257, 273
Okinawa Summit (2001) 303
oligopoly models
  based on reaction curves 130–1
  in international trade 45
optimal obfuscation hypothesis 174–5, 177
optimum currency areas, theory of 365–8
optimum tariff theory
  optimum import tariff 93–7
  protection and welfare 91–2
Organisation for Economic Co-operation and
  Development (OECD) 2, 285, 300
Organization of the Petroleum Exporting Countries
  (OPEC) 94, 305, 324
  cartel 141–2
original equipment manufacturing
  (OEM) 119

Paris Club 338
patent
    compulsory licensing 146
    dispute between USA and Brazil 146–8
    governmental use of 146
Plaza Agreement (1985) 316
Political 8, *see* Group of 8 (G8) summits
political economy, demand for and supply of
        protection 170–1
    anti-tariff interest groups 171–2
    pro-tariff interest groups 171
    protectionism
        demand for 172–3
        supply of 173–5
Porter approach, for determining international
        competitiveness 24, 46–7
    application of 49–50
    availability and quality of factors of
            production 48
    business strategy, structure and competition
            48–9
    consumer preference/demand 48
    diamond as a system 49
    suppliers and related industries 48
Porter diamond 47, 49, 111, 231
portfolio diversification 222–5
portfolio investment 20, 198, 204
    in foreign shares 214
    international 225
    in three major economic areas 64
portfolio risk, influence of correlation coefficient
        on 223–5
predatory dumping 127
preferential trading blocs 150
price competition 139–40, 191
product differentiation 44–5
    monopolistic competition 45
    oligopoly models 45
production and process methods (PPMs) 154
product life cycle theory 43, 64
    MNE phenomenon of 79–81
    trade patterns in USA 80
protectionism, concept of 86–90
protectionist measures
    Best Information Possible principle 165
    case study 164–5
    concept of 86–90
    demand for 172–3
    effectiveness of 148–9
    non-tariff barriers 159–66
    supply of 173–5
purchasing power parity (PPP) 237–44, 383

ratchet effect, in inflation variations 269
reaction curves
    for analysis of international market strategy
            130–1
    for domestic entrepreneur 130

    in duopoly 132
    lobbying 178
regional economic integration 150, 152, 185–7
regional trade agreements (RTAs) 180, 185
Reinheitsgebot (purity law), Germany
    abolition of 133
    case study 133–4
rent snatching 122–3
reserve assets balance 206
rollover credits, use of 327–8
Rome, Treaty of (1957) 188, 382

safeguard measures, adoption of 160
shrimp-turtle case 184–5
Single European Act (SEA, 1987) 188
Smith, Adam 30
Snake Arrangement, for European monetary
        integration 376–8
South–South trade 11
Special Drawing Rights (SDRs) 203, 300, 313, 334
speculation 221–2
speculative attack model, for currency crisis
    first generation 345–7
    later generation 347–8
Stability and Growth Pact 385
Standard International Trade Classification (SITC) 13
stock lease services 189
subsidy, strategic 115–16
Super 301 clause (USA), for prevention of unfair
        trade practices 163
swap contract 295
syndicated loans, use of 328

telecom monopolies
    background of 3
    strategies for reducing 2
textile quotas, international 27
time preferences of countries, concept of 62
Tobin tax 359–60
Tokyo Round (1979) 153, 156
Trade Agreements Act (TAA), USA 155
trade credit 198–9, 228
    forms of 215
    importance of 215
Trade Expansion Act (1962), USA 155
trade policies
    equilibrium situations under various forms of 138
    escalating protection and transfer mechanisms
            137–9
    and international duopoly 134–7, 138
    and market failures 107–9
    optimal obfuscation hypothesis 174–5
    strategic 112–16
Trade-Related Aspects of Intellectual Property
        Rights (TRIPS) Agreement 1, 145, 150, 157–8
    Article 6 of 147
    Article 31 of 146–7
    importance of 146–7

trade restrictions, welfare effects of
  abolition of trade restrictions 105–6
  common trade restriction 106–7
  'comparable' import tariffs 106
trade sanctions 90–1, 176
trade theories
  new theory 39–40
    external economies of scale 43–4
    internal economies of scale 40–3
    national location factors and Porter analysis
      46–50
    product differentiation 44–5
  traditional theory
    comparative cost theory 32–5
    criticism 35
    factor reversal 39
    Heckscher–Ohlin–Samuelson (HOS) model
      35–8
    Leontief paradox 38–9
    mercantilism 30–2
transfer pricing, concept of 73
Trans-National Companies (TNCs) 190
  non-financial 75–7
triangular arbitrage 218–19

uncovered interest parity (UIP) 221, 231, 245,
  258–9, 315, 346
unfair trade practices 127, 156
  prevention of 163
United Nations Conference on Trade and
  Development (UNCTAD) 152
Uruguay Round 156–8
  agreement on protection of intellectual property
    rights 146, 150
  Agreement on Safeguards 157–8
  ban on 'grey area' measures of 159
  percentages of tariffs bound before and
    after 158
USA
  anti-inflationary monetary policy
    328–9
  attempts to block China's entry to
    WTO 92–3
  drug dispute with Brazil 147–8
  Endangered Species Act (1973) 184
  Foreign Sales Corporation Act (2006)
    90–1
  Super 301 clause for prevention of unfair trade
    practices 163
  Trade Agreements Act (TAA) 151, 155
  Trade Expansion Act (1962) 155

trade policy
  developments 155
  strategic 112–16
  unfair trade practices 156

value added taxation (VAT) 303
Vernon model, for development of multinational
  enterprises 80–1
voluntary export restraints (VERs) 53, 104, 120,
  153, 157, 163, 171
voluntary import expansion (VIE) 163

Walters critique 345, 350, 359, 373, 379
Werner Committee 377, 382
West African Economic and Monetary Union
  (WAEMU) 369, 371
world debt crisis of the 1980s, causes of
  external causes
    extensive use of rollover credits 327–8
    oil price shocks of the 1970s 324–6
    US adoption of stringent anti-inflationary
      monetary policy 328–9
    use of syndicated loans 328
    world's financial markets 326–7
  internal causes 329
    large fiscal deficits 330
    monetary financing of fiscal deficits 330
    overvalued currency 331
    presence of high trade barriers 331–2
    regulated financial markets 332
world export
  of goods and services 197
  of industrial products 15
  of merchandise and commercial services 17
  rate of growth 157
world intra-industry trade 12
world's international monetary reserves,
  composition of 319
world trade, see international trade
World Trade Organization (WTO) 1, 90, 127
  achievements of 154
  Agreement on Textiles and Clothing (ATC) 155
  Agreement on Trade-Related Aspects of
    Intellectual Property Rights (TRIPS) 1, 145–6,
    150, 157–8
  anti-dumping policy 161–2
  differences with GATT 150
  Dispute Settlement Body 147, 152
  dispute settlement system 150
  Dispute Settlement Understanding 158, 163
  principle of non-discrimination 152
  safeguard clause 160